Buffalo Public Library

Finding List of Books and Pamphlets in the Buffalo Public Library

Buffalo Public Library
Finding List of Books and Pamphlets in the Buffalo Public Library
ISBN/EAN: 9783337376123
Printed in Europe, USA, Canada, Australia, Japan
Cover: Foto ©Paul-Georg Meister /pixelio.de

More available books at **www.hansebooks.com**

OF BOOKS AND PAMPHLETS IN

THE BUFFALO PUBLIC LIBRARY

FICTION

POETRY, DRAMA, LITERARY HISTORY AND CRITICISM, ESSAYS, ORATORY, HUMOR, ETC.

LANGUAGE AND BIBLIOGRAPHY.

PRICE, TWENTY-FIVE CENTS.

BUFFALO, NEW YORK,
AUGUST,
1897.

INDEX OF SUBJECTS.

African languages and literature................79
American literature. See English literature.
American (aboriginal) languages and literature...79
Ancient literature...........................15-27
Anecdotes......................................14
Anglo-Saxon language..........................80
Anonyms..1
Aphorisms.....................................13
Arabian language and literature...............16
Arthur, King, Romances of.....................28
Assyrian language and literature.............15-16
Authorship.....................................1
Babylonian literature........................15-16
Ballads......................................88-92
Basque language and literature...............78-79
Bibliography: General and national............9-10
Book arts.....................................1-4
Book rarities.................................9-10
Books: Care and keeping of....................3-4
Production of.................................1-3
Books and reading............................10-12
Bornu language................................79
Buddhist literature..........................15-17
Carols, Christmas.............................13
Celtic languages and literature...............76
Chaldean literature...........................16
Charlemagne, Romances of......................29
Chinese language and literature...............18
Christmas carols..............................13
Classification.................................4
Composition...................................6-8
Copyright......................................1
Cuneiform inscriptions.......................15-16
Danish language and literature...............29-31
Debate...8
Dialects: English.............................81
Dialogues....................................97-98
Dictionaries. See Language.
Drama, English: Collections..................92-98
English: History and criticism...............82-85
English: Individual authors.................106-275
For amateur acting...........................97-98
French.......................................47-72
German.......................................32-46
Greek..19-24
Italian......................................72-74
Latin..24-27
Spanish and Portuguese........................75
Dramatic composition, Art of...................7

Dutch language and literature.................46
Eddas..29-30
Egyptian language and literature.............15-16
Elocution......................................8
Elocutionary selections......................95-99
English drama: Collections...................92-98
History and criticism........................82-85
Individual authors..........................106-275
English language.............................79-82
Dictionaries..................................82
Etymology.....................................81
Grammar.......................................80
Spelling, pronunciation, etc................80-81
English literature: Bibliography..............85
General collections..........................85-88
History and criticism........................82-85
Individual authors..........................106-275
English poetry: Collections..................88-92
Individual authors..........................106-275
Epics of the middle ages.....................27-29
Epigrams......................................14
Essays, English: Collections................99-100
Individual authors..........................106-275
Fables..14
Festival poems................................13
Fiction: Arabian..............................16
Art of.......................................7-8
Bibliography..................................15
Chinese and Japanese..........................18
Dutch and Flemish.............................16
English: Collections.......................101-106
English: History and criticism..............82-85
English: Individual authors................106-275
French.......................................47-72
General collections...........................14
German.......................................32-46
Italian......................................72-74
Mediæval.....................................27-29
Persian......................................16-17
Russian......................................77-78
Scandinavian.................................29-31
Spanish and Portuguese.......................74-76
Flemish literature............................46
French language and literature...............47-72
Gaelic language and literature................76
German language and literature...............31-46
Greek language and literature................18-24
Gypsy language and literature.................78
Hebrew language and literature................16

INDEX OF SUBJECTS.

Hindu language and literature...17
Humor...14
   English: Collections...101
   English: Individual authors...106-275
Hungarian language and literature...78-79
Icelandic language and literature...29-31
Indian (East) languages and literature...17
Indian (North American) languages and literature...79
Irish language and literature...76
Italian language and literature...72-74
Japanese language and literature...18
Jewish language and literature...16
Language: Aboriginal American...79
   African...79
   Arabian...16
   Assyrian...15-16
   Basque...78-79
   Bornu...79
   Celtic...76
   Chinese...18
   Dutch...46
   Egyptian...15-16
   English...79-82
   French...47
   Gaelic...76
   General and comparative...5-6
   German...31-32
   Greek...18-19
   Hebrew...16
   Hungarian...78-79
   Indian (East)...17
   Irish...76
   Italian...72
   Japanese...18
   Latin...24
   Malayan...18
   Persian...16-17
   Polish...76
   Polynesian...79
   Portuguese...74-75
   Roumanian...79
   Russian...76
   Scandinavian...29
   Scottish...76
   Semitic...16
   Slavonic...76
   Spanish...74-75
   Turkish...78
   Volapük...78
   Welsh...76
Latin language and literature...24-27
Letter-writing...7
Letters: Collections...13
   English: Collections...101
Libraries...3-4
Library classification...4

Library economy...3-4
Literature: General collections...12
   General history and comparative criticism...9
Malayan language and literature...18
Mediæval literature...27-29
Nibelungenlied...28-29
Norse languages and literature...29-31
Novels. See Fiction.
Oratory, Art of...8
   English: Collections...98-99
   English: Individual authors...106-275
   Greek...19-23
   Latin...24-27
Oriental languages and literature...15-18
Parody...14
Persian language and literature...16-17
Philology. See Language.
Phonography...2
Poetry: Art of...7
   Celtic...76
   Dutch and Flemish...46
   English: Collections...88-92
   English: Individual authors...106-275
   French...47-71
   General collections...12-13
   German...32-46
   Greek...19-23
   Hungarian...78-79
   Italian...72-74
   Latin...24-27
   Mediæval...27-29
   Oriental...15-18
   Portuguese...75
   Scandinavian...29-31
   Slavonic...76-78
   Spanish...75
Polish language and literature...76-78
Portuguese language and literature...74-76
Printing...2-3
Pronunciation: English...80
Prose fiction. See Fiction.
Proverbs...13
Pseudonyms...1
Publication...1
Quotations...13-14
Reading: Hints and helps...10-11
   Selections for...98-99
Reference books, General...10
Rhetoric...6-7
Romance, prose. See Fiction.
Romances of the middle ages...27-29
Roumanian language and literature...78-79
Russian language and literature...76-78
Sagas...29-30
Sanskrit language and literature...17
Satire, English: Collections...101
   Individual authors...106-275

Scandinavian languages and literature...........29-31	Stenography......... 2
Scottish language and literature..........................76	Style.. 6-7
Shakespeare: Collected works.................235-237	Swedish language and literature....................29-31
Separate plays....................................237-241	Synonyms...82
Shakespeariana..................................241-245	Syrian literature..16
Shorthand...2	Tamul literature..18
Slavonic languages and literature.................76-78	Turkish language and literature.......................78
Songs: Collections—English, Scotch, and	Volapük language..78
Irish 88-92	Welsh language and literature..........................76
Spanish language and literature.....................74-76	Wit 14
Spelling: English...80	Writing, Art of............ 1-2

THE BOOK ARTS.

PRODUCTION OF BOOKS.

AUTHORSHIP AND PUBLICATION.

Agenda-annuaire de la librairie française. 1894.................................9 5
Authors and publishers. 1883.............9 1
Authorship and publication. 1884........9 3
Besant. The Society of authors. 1893....9 Pam. 4
Curwen. History of booksellers............9 8
Derby. Fifty years among authors, books, and publishers. 1884..............928.1 111
Disraeli. The literary character. 1818......928 5
Exposition de la librairie française, Chicago, 1893.........................606 B-13
Humphreys. Piccadilly bookmen......928.2 641
Literary year-book.......................805 23
Paley. Bibliographia Græca: book-writing among the Greeks. 1881..........21 Pam. 4
Paul Book Co. Bookmaking..............9 Pam. 1
Putnam. Books and their makers during the middle ages. 1896. 2v..............9 6
Shepard, ed. Authors and authorship. '82.928 16
Sprigge. Methods of publishing. 1890....9 4
Stevens. Who spoils our new English books? 1884.........................9 2

PSEUDONYMS, ETC.

Cushing. Anonyms. 1889................14 B-8
Initials and pseudonyms. 1885-8. 2v...14 B-6
Drake. Key to assumed names, American ....in 920.1 B-1
Famous pseudonyms....................14 Pam. 1
Franklin. Dictionnaire des noms, surnoms, et pseudonyms (1100-1530). 1875........14 3
Frey. Sobriquets and nicknames. 1888....14 4
Halkett and Lang. Dictionary of anonymous and pseudonymous literature. 1882. v. 1-4........................14 B-1
Hooe. Authors of the day. 1879.....928.2 Pam. 1
Haynes. Pseudonyms of authors. 1882...14 2
Marchmont. Concise handbook of literature, anon., under pseudonyms or initials. 1896........................14 5
Moore. List of pseudonyms, etc.........in 16 9
Thomas. Handbook of fictitious names. 1868...............................14 1
Wheeler. Noted names of fiction, pseudonyms, etc........................803 1

COPYRIGHT.

Bowker. Copyright. 1886................8 5
Colonial copyright acts; ed. by Daldy. 1889..8 9
Copinger. Law of copyright. 1870........8 1
Cutler, et al. Law of musical and dramatic copyright. 1890.....................8 7
Dawson. Copyright in books. 1882.....8 Pam. 2
Drone. Law of property in intellectual productions, Gt. Britain and U. S. 1879......8 2
Great Britain. Copyright commission. '78..8 B 1
Correspondence respecting international copyright union. 1886.................8 B 2
Hedeler, comp. Gesetze über das Urheberrecht im In- und Ausland...........8 10
International copyright. Meeting of authors and publishers, N. Y. 1868....8 Pam. 1
International copyright union. Articles. '87..8 6
Jerrold. English and foreign copyright. '81...8 4
Putnam. International copyright. 1879..8 Pam. 3
The question of copyright. 1891........8 8
Same; 2d ed., rev.; with additional matter. 1896....................8 8A
Reade. On international copyright......in 174 3
Scudder. On early history of copyright in U. S..........................in 928.1 70
Solberg, ed. Catalog of books and papers relative to copyright............in Pub. wkly., v.21, no.14
United States. Copyright law in force July, 1895, etc..................8 Pam. 6
Directions for securing copyright. '91..8 Pam. 5
Van Dyke. National sin of literary piracy. 1888.............................8 Pam. 4
White. American view of copyright question. 1880........................8 3

WRITING.

Astle. Origin and progress of writing. 1876..............................651 B-1
Bore. Invention of steel pens............672 25
Frazer. Manual of the study of documents. 1894..............................652 2
Hoffman. Beginnings of writing. 1895....651 3
Hooper. Rational recreations [cipher writing].............................793 1

Keene. Mystery of handwriting. 1896......652 3
Lacouperie. Beginnings of writing. 1894...651 2
Massey. Origin and progress of letters.
   1763...411 1
Newlands *and* **Row.** ‡ Natural system of
   vertical writing. 1895........................652 4
Salamanca. Philosophy of handwriting.....652 1
Spineto. Elements of hieroglyphics...........492 1
Thompson. Greek and Latin palæography.
   1893..651 1
Wait. Key to N. Y. point system of writing.
   1893..651 Pam. 1

SHORTHAND, STENOGRAPHY, ETC.

Anderson. History of shorthand. 1882....653 7
Barker. Which system of shorthand should
   we learn? 1892.............................653 Pam. 1
Bell. Universal line-writing and steno-pho-
   nography. 1869....................................653 2
Cross. Eclectic short-hand. 1884................653 5
Davis. Short-hand simplified. 1891..........653 26
Graham. Handbook of phonography........653 4
International shorthand congress, Lon-
   don, 1887. Transactions......................653 8
Lindsley. Elements of tachygraphy. 1881....653 9
Longley. American manual of phonog-
   raphy. 1855...653 1
Munson. Art of phonography. 1896........653 24
   Complete phonographer. 1877............653 3
Osgoodby. Phonetic shorthand. 1886......653 10
Pitman, B. Manual of phonography..........653 6
Pitman, I. Manual of phonography. 1889....653 21
   Same, Phonographic reporter, etc.......653 20
   Phonographic and pronouncing diction-
   ary. 1889..653 22
Rockwell. Teaching, practice, and litera-
   ture of shorthand.................*in* 370 66 (v.5)
Slocum. Autograph list of word-signs, etc.,
   in phonography. 1884..................653 Pam. 2
Spencer. System of lucid shorthand. '94...653 23
Thornton. Modern stenographer. 1882....653 25

PRINTING.

Aldine press. 1546. De oratore, Ciceronis...23 2
Amerbach press. Basle. 1492. De refor-
   matione virium anime ; Consolatorium
   theologicum ; Tambaco ; etc...................23 1
American dictionary of printing, etc., '94...655 B-4
Arte della stampa nel rinascimento Italiano:
   Venezia. 1894...................................655 B-6
Arts and crafts...704 32
Bigelow. Preparing copy and proof-read-
   ing...655 Pam. 7

Blades. How to correct printers' proofs.
   1893...655 Pam. 6
   Pentateuch of printing. 1891.............655 B-5
Bock. Zincography.....................................655 11
Bouchat. The printed book. 1887..........655 12
British manufacturing industries. v.8........670 8
Canada. Dept. of public printing. Repts.,
   1887 —...655 Pam. 4
Caxton, first English printer ; by Knight...926.2 43
Childs. Celebration of birthday, 1888..655 Pam. 5
Clarke. Bibliographical miscellany. 1806...11 8
Figgins. Specimens of type...................655 B-2
Follett. Press of western N. Y. 1847...655 Pam. 1
Gordon. Centenary of the rotary press..*in* 670 27
Greswell. View of early Parisian Greek
   press. 1833. 2 v......................................12 1
Gutenberg. And the art of printing ; by
   Pearson..926.3 1
   Was he the inventor? by Hessels. 1882...926.3 3
Hansard. History of printing............*in* 609 8
Hart. Amateur printer. 1883.....................655 9
Hessels. Haarlem the birth-place of print-
   ing, not Mentz. 1887......................655 B-3
Hildeburn. Printers and printing in colonial
   N. Y. 1895...655 14
Humphreys. History of the art of printing.
   1868...655 R-1
Johnson. Typographia. 1824. 2v..........655 3
Kerr. History of govt. ptg. off., Washing-
   ton. 1881...655 8
Koenig, F., J. Walter, *and* **W. Clowes.**
   Sketches of ; by Smiles..................*in* 926 14
MacKellar, T. The American printer. '89..655 13
MacKellar, Smiths & Jordan foundry,
   Philadelphia. 1796-1896 : 100 years...655 R-2
Millington. Are we to read backward ?
   1884..655 10
New York. Investigation of legislative
   printing. 1886-7...........................655 Pam. 2
   Press of western N. Y........................*in* 98.8 1
Pennsylvania historical society. Celebra-
   tion of the birthday of Wm. Bradford.
   1863...655 Pam. 3
Renonard. Annals de l'imprimerie des
   Alde. 1803..24 2
Ringwalt. American encyclopædia of print-
   ing. 1871..‡655 B-1
Roberts. Printers' marks. 1893...................24 3
Salisbury. Early history of press of Erie co..98.8 1
Savage. Dictionary of printing. 1841.......655 5
Sensenschmidt press. Nuremburg. 1474.
   Thomas Aquinas : XII quodlibeta dis-
   putata..23 R-1
Stark. Printing, its history, etc. '63...*in* 824.2 180
Thomas. History of printing in America.
   1810. 2v..655 1
   Same ; rev. ed................*in* 972 B-3 (v.5-6)

‡ For reference.

THE BOOK ARTS.

Timperley, *ed.* Encyclopædia of literary and typographical anecdote. 1842......11 11
United States. House of Representatives. Rept. on govt. ptg. off..................
..................50-1, 1887-8, H. R. rept. 11

Wilson. Stereotyping and electrotyping. 1880...655 7
Typographic printing machines. 1880....655 6

BOOKBINDING.

(See Part 3 of FINDING LIST, p. 394.)

CARE AND KEEPING OF BOOKS.

LIBRARIES.—LIBRARY ECONOMY.

Aflalo, *ed.* Literary year-book. 1897.......805 23
Albany. Children's home libraries. List of books. 1895......................19.1 Pam. 11
American library association. Constitution, etc. 1889.....................19 Pam. 129
Papers and proceedings, 1879—..........19 B-3
Armour Institute, dept. of library science. Circulars............................19.2 Pam. 12
Axon. Statistical notes on the free town libraries of Gt. Britain and the continent. 1870....................310 6 (v.33)
Brett. Relations of the public library to the public schools. 1892...........371 Pam. 20
Brown. Village libraries................*in* 17 Pam. 4
Clark. Libraries, medieval and renaissance. 1894.....................................19 29
Cole. American libraries. 1895.......19 Pam. 191
Crunden. The free public library ..19.1 Pam. 10
Function of a public library. 1884...19.1 Pam. 6
Cutler. Children's home libraries....19.1 Pam. 19
Home libraries. 1896..................19.1 Pam. 18
Denver. Public library. Public library handbook; ed. by Dana. 1895..........19.2 3
Dewey. Librarianship as a profession for college-bred women. 1886........19.1 Pam. 3
Libraries as related to the educational work of the state. 1888............19.1 Pam. 1
Drexel Institute, library class..........19.2 Pam. 11
Eastman. Free traveling libraries. 1895. ....19.1 Pam. 12
Edwards. Free town libraries. 1869..........19 5
Libraries and the founders of libraries. 1865..:................................19 3
Lives of the founders of the British museum.................................62 5
Memoirs of libraries. 1859. 2v..........19 1
Statistical view of public libraries. 1848. ....310 6 (v. 11)
Fletcher. Public libraries in America. '94..19 12
Flint, W. Statistics of public libraries, U. S. and Canada. 1893...............19 28A

Foster. Public support of public libraries. 1891..............................19.1 Pam. 9
Gasquet. Notes on mediæval monastic libraries. 1897 ....*in* 220.0 268
Green, B. R. Book stack and shelving for libraries..............................19.2 R-1
Green, S. S. Library aids. 1881......19.2 Pam. 5
Public libraries and schools. 1884..19.1 Pam. 5
Greenwood's library year book. 1897.......19 35
Hedeler, *comp.* List of private libraries, U. S. and Canada. 1897...............19 32
Humphreys. The private library. 1897...10 30
Jewett. Public libraries in the U. S. 1851..*in* 40 6
Larned. Influence of a public library. 1883.........................95 2X Pam. 26
Mission and missionaries of the book. 1896..................................19.1 Pam. 20
Learned, Soule, *and* Green. Papers on library trustees. 1890.................19.1 Pam. 8
Librarians' institute, Wisconsin.......19 Pam. 178
Library association of the United Kingdom. Monthly notes. 1880-83. 4v. 19 B-4
Rept. on library appliances. 1891..19.2 Pam. 13
Rept. on public library repts. '91...19 Pam. 164
Rept. on regulations for examining assistants. 1891............................19.2 Pam. 14
Transactions and proceedings, 1878 —...19 B-2
Year-book, 1891 —..........................19 26
Library bureau. Catalog, 1876........19.2 Pam. 9
Catalogs, 1890 —...........................19.2 B-2
Library chronicle. 1884-8. 5v.............19 B-5
Library journal. 1877— v. 1—..............19 B-1
Library list: public libraries, U. S. and Canada. 1887........................19 B-6
Library notes..............................19.2 B-3
Library school (Columbia College). Circulars, registers, etc..................19.2 Pam. 7
Same (N. Y. state library). Handbook, etc....................................19.2 Pam. 7
Maire. Manuel pratique du bibliothécaire. 1896..19.2 4
Minerva: Jahrbuch der gelehrten Welt. 1893-4......................................378 106

‡ For reference.

Massachusetts. Free public library commission. Rept., 1891—..................19 25
Mullins. Free libraries and newsrooms. 1879..........................19.1 Pam. 4
New Hampshire. Board of library comrs. Repts., 1893—..................19 Pam. 174
New York. Library law. 1892....19.1 Pam. 15
University covocation, library session, 1896..........................19.1 Pam. 20
Nichols. Indexing. 1892 ....10 Pam. 3
Perkins. Free libraries and unclean books. 1885.......................*in* 19 Pam. 2
Free public libraries, especially that of San Francisco. 1885..........19.1 Pam. 2
Petzholdt. Katechismus der Bibliothekenlehre; neubearb. von Gräsel. 1890...19.2 1
Plummer. Hints to small libraries. 1894...19.2 2
Poole. Remarks on library construction. 1884..........................19 Pam. 74
Rept. on progress of library architecture. 1882..........................19 Pam. 63
University library and curriculum. 1894....10 27
Pratt Institute free library, training classes. Circulars, etc..............19.2 Pam. 1
Public libraries. 1896— v. 1—.........19 36
Rhees. Manual of public libraries, etc. 1859...19 4
Richter. Verzeichniss der Bibliotheken. 1893..........................19 27
Shinn. Concerning school libraries. 1896. ....19.1 Pam. 21
Shurtleff. Decimal system for the arrangement of libraries. 1856........19.2 B-4
Smithmeyer. Suggestions on library architecture..........................19 Pam. 70
Traveling libraries in Wisconsin. '96..19 Pam. 193
United States. Bureau of education. Public libraries in the U. S. 1876........19 10
· Statistics of public libraries in the U. S. 1886..........................19 28
Vattemare. Rept. on international literary and scientific exchanges, organized in 1849 ....N. Y. Assembly docs., 1849. v. 5

Vermont. Board of library commissioners. Rept., 1895—..................19 Pam. 179
Wilcox. Work of a public library. 1897. ....19.2 Pam. 17
Wilson. World's largest libraries. 1894....19 30
Wisconsin. State library commission. Act creating. 1895...............19.1 Pam. 23
Biennial rept., 1895 —..............19 31
Wolfenbüttel. Herzoglichen Bibliothek. Bearbeitung des alphabetischen Zettelcatalogs. 1893 ....19.2 B-1
World's library congress, Chicago, 1893; ed. by Dewey. 1896..........19.2 5

CLASSIFICATION.

American library association. Catalog of 'A. L. A.' library. 1893 ....17 48
Boston Athenæum. How to get books. 1882..........................112 Pam. 3
Buffalo charity organization society. Classification-index to card catalog of library. 1894..........................112 B-2
Cutter. Boston Athenæum: way of marking books. 1882...........*in* 112 Pam. 3
Expansive classification. 1892......112 9
Dewey. Decimal classification. 1885........112 7
Same. 1891..................112 7A
Edmands. New system of classification, etc. 1883..................112 Pam. 5
Fletcher. Library classification. 1894.....112 10
Garnett. System of classifying books, British museum. 1878..........19.2 Pam. 3
Milwaukee. Public library. Synopsis of classification. 1886..........112 B-1
Perkins. Rational classification of literature. 1881..................112 Pam. 1
Same; rev. ed. 1882..........112 Pam. 2
Rowell. Classification of books. 1894..112 Pam. 6
Schwartz. New classification and notation. 1882..................112 Pam. 4
Smith. Classification of books. 1882........112 5

LANGUAGE AND LITERATURE.

PHILOLOGY.

GENERAL AND COMPARATIVE.

Abel. Linguistic essays. 1882....................404 26
American philological association. Proceedings, 1883 ....406 Pam. 1
Transactions, 1869. v. 1-.......................406 1
American philosophical society. Supplementary rept. on an international language. 1888..............................408 Pam. 2
Apostolides, *ed.* Our Lord's prayer in 100 languages..418 1
Arnold. Teaching deaf and dumb speech, etc...362.5 B-1
Babbitt. How to use modern languages as a means of mental discipline........407 Pam. 3
Baedeker. Travellers' manual. 1873........413 1
Bell. Science of speech. 1897...................414 4
  Visible speech. 1867.........................411 B-1
Bopp. Comparative grammar. 1862. 3 v...415 1
Cust. Linguistic and oriental essays. 1880-1895. 4 v..404 29
Darmesteter. Life of words. 1886...........401 6
Delbrück. Study of language. 1882........410 13
Dictionary of abbreviations. 1886............411 7
Dwight. Modern philology. 1859.............409 1
Elliott, *et al.* Methods of studying modern languages. 1896..................................407 5
Farrar. Chapters on language. 1865.......400 5
  Families of speech. 1869...................410 10
  Language and languages. 1878.........400 12
  Origin of language. 1860....................400 4
Garner. The speech of monkeys. 1892....409 2
Gilman. Short stories from the dictionary. 1886..404 27
Gouin. L'art d'enseigner et d'étudier les langues. 1894..407 1
Art of teaching and studying languages..407 2
Hadley. Essays, philological and critical. 1873...404 3
Harrassowitz. Antiquarischer Catalog; Grammatiken, Lexica und Chrestomathien von fast allen Sprachen. 1895...410 16
Harris. Hermes. 1794...............................415 6
  Philological inquiries. 1802. 2v........810 17
Harvard University. Studies and notes in philology. 1892..............................404 32
  Contents: V. 1. Authorship of the English ' Romaunt of the rose '; by Kittredge.—Origin of English names of letters of the alphabet; by Sheldon.—Lok-Sounday ; by Manly.—Henry Scogar; by Kittredge.—Etymological notes.

Hinsdale. Teaching the language-arts: speech, reading, composition. 1896....407 3
Hovelacque. Science of language. '77...401 5
Jespersen. Progress in language. 1894...410 15
Johnes. Philological proofs of unity. '46...410 3
Johnson. Meaning of words. 1854.........401 1
Jones. Works. 1807. 13 v.
  Contents: V. 1-2. Life........................401 11
  V. 3-4. Papers before the Asiatic society.—Tales by Nizami, tr.................................404 13
  V. 5. Plants of India and spikenard of ancients.—Persian language....................404 15
  V. 6. Poescos Asiaticæ commentarii..........404 16
  V. 7-8. Charges to the grand jury.—Institutes of Hindu law.—Mahomedan law of succession to property.—Law of inheritance.—Law of bailments....401 17
  V. 9. Speeches of Isæus.—Sacontala ; by Cálidás, tr...404 19
  V. 10. Moallakat.—Poems tr. from Asiatic languages..404 20
  V. 11-12. Histoire de Nader Chah.—Traité sur la poesie orientale..............................404 21
  V. 13. Hitópadésa or Vishnusarman.—Enchanted fruit.—Hymns.—Extracts from the Vedas.....404 23
Journal of philology. 1854-59, 1868-71. 7v..405 P-1
Kavanagh. Origin of language. 1871. 2 v...400 1
Key. Philological essays. 1868................404 2
Lassalle. Origin of western nations and languages. 1883..................................410 12
Latham. Comparative philology. 1862...410 6
  Opuscula. 1860.....................................404 6
Lepsius. Standard alphabet. 1863...........411 3
Marcel. Study of languages. 1869...........407 4
Massey. Origin of letters. 1763...............411 1
Meyer. Organs of speech. 1884...............414 1
Modern language association of America.
  Proceedings. 1885.........................407 Pam. 1
  Publications. 1886-96......................406 2
Monboddo. Origin and progress of language. 1774. 6 v.................................400 6
Morris. Historical outlines of English accidence. 1872......................................415 5
Müller. Biographies of words. 1888......404 28
  Chips from a German workshop. 1869-1881. 5 v..404 7
  Languages of the seat of war (Crimean). 1855...410 4
  Science of language. 1862.................410 7
  Same. 2d series. 1865......................410 8
  Selected essays. 1881. 2 v................404 24

‡ For reference.

Murray. History of European languages.
1823. 2 v...410 1
Oldenburg. Epitome of comparative philology. 1890...410 14
Paul. Principles of history of language. '90..400 13
Peile. Philology. 1877................................402 1
Pezzi. Aryan philology. 1879....................410 11
Philological museum. 1832-33. 2 v.......405 1
Porson. Tracts, etc.; ed. by Kidd. 1815....404 1
Renan. L'avenir de la science. 1890........401 8
Sainte-Claire. Dictionary of English, French, and German idioms. Part 1. 1878...‡413 B-1
Sayce. Science of language. 1880. 2 v.....401 3
Schrader. Kulturgeschichte der Indogermanen auf sprachwissenschaftlicher Grundlage. 1887............................410 Pam. 1
Stoddart. Philosophy of language. 1849...415 4
Sweet. History of English sounds. '88.....414 2
  Primer of phonetics. 1890.........................414 3
Taylor. The alphabet. 1883. 2v................411 5
  Greeks and Goths......................................411 4
  Words and places.......................................911 3
Tooke. Diversions of Purley. 1860...........410 5
Trübner. Catalog of dictionaries and grammars...16 41
Wagner. Names and their meaning. '91...‡412 1
  Significance of names. 1893..................‡412 2
Webster. Observations on language. '39....40 18
Wedgwood. Origin of language. 1866.....400 3
Whitney. Language. 1870..........................410 9
  Life and growth of language. 1875........401 2
  Oriental and linguistic studies. 1st series. 1873..404 4
  Contents: The Veda.—The Avesta.—Science of language.
  Same. 2d series. 1874..............................404 5
  Contents: East and west.— Religion and mythology.— Othography and phonology.— Hindu astronomy.
Williams. Roman alphabet for languages of India. 1859...411 2
Wright. Growth of language. 1878...409 Pam. 1
  Philology: catalog of books. 1877..16 Pam. 38
  Words. 1876..413 Pam. 1

RHETORIC.—STYLE.—COMPOSITION.

Abbott. How to write clearly. 1887........815 26
Abbott *and* Seeley. English lessons for English people. 1872..............................815 13
Adams. Lects. on rhetoric and oratory. 1810. 2 v..815 1
Albee. Literary art. 1881............................801 6
Aristotle. Treatise on rhetoric. 1869........185 2
Bain. English composition and rhetoric. 1887. 2 v...815 27
Bainton, *ed.* Art of authorship. 1890.....815 33
Bates. Talks on writing English. 1896.....815 45

Blair. Lects. on rhetoric, etc. 1873........815 17
Brewster. Studies in structure and style. 1896...815 44
Carpenter. Metaphor and simile in the minor Elizabethan drama. 1895.......815 40
Channing. Lects., Harvard college. 1856..815 3
Cicero. On rhetorical invention................875 7
Coleridge. Principles of criticism. 1895.....814 5
Cook, *ed.* The Bible and English prose style. 1892...815 47
Coppée. Elements of rhetoric. 1860.........815 7
Courthope. Liberty and authority in matters of taste. 1896..............................801 Pam. 1
Cousin. Philosophy of the beautiful. '49.....701 7
Cox. Arts of writing, etc.............................815 9
Craik. English of Shakespeare. 1867......822.3 92
Day. Science of æsthetics. 1872..............701 21
De Mille. Elements of rhetoric. 1878......815 15
Diderot. Thoughts on art and style; sel. and tr. by Tollemache. 1893................844 54
Earle. English prose. 1890.........................815 35
Eastman. Composition. 1880..........815 Pam. 3
Genung. Outlines of rhetoric. 1893........815 38
Hart. Handbook of English composition. 1896...815 48
Harvard College. Com. on composition and rhetoric. Rept., 1895............815 Pam. 1
Haven. Rhetoric. 1870................................815 11
Higginson. Hints on writing and speechmaking. 1887.......................................815 24
Hill, A. S. Our English. 1887....................815 31
  Principles of rhetoric. 1878..................815 16
Hill, D. J. Elements of rhetoric, etc. '78..815 18
Holyoake. Public speaking and debate. 1895...815 41
Husted. Lessons in English. 1888...........815 30
Jennings. Curiosities of criticism. 1881....814 1
Kames, *Lord.* Elements of criticism. 2v......801 1
Lang. How to fail in literature. 1890.......815 34
Lewis. First book in writing English. '97..815 51
  History of the English paragraph. 1894...815 43
Longinus. On the sublime; tr. by Stebbing. 1867...815 8
Lord. Characteristics, etc., of figurative language. 1855..815 5
Luce. Writing for the press. 1889.............815 32
Marmontel. Élémens de littérature. 1787. 6 v..840 308
Monkhouse. The précis book. 1878......815 14
Nichol. English composition. 1880..........815 22
Nisbet *and* Lemon. Everybody's writingdesk book. 1892..420 9
Parker. Aids to English composition. '70.815 12
Phelps. English style in public discourse. 1883...815 25
Pittenger. Toasts, etc. 1895......................815 39
Quackenbos. Advanced course of composition, etc. 1857...815 6

‡ For reference.

LANGUAGE AND LITERATURE.

Reade. How to write English.................815 21
Saintsbury, ed. Specimens of English
   prose style. 1886............................815 50
Sherman. Analytics of literature. 1893...815 37
Skipton. The essay writer. 1889.............814 4
Spencer. Philosophy of style. 1882 ....815 23
Stead. Journalist on journalism. 50 7
Stories for composition exercises. 1888....*815 29
Townsend. Art of speech. 1880-81. 2v...815 19
Wendell. English composition 1891.......815 36
Whateley. Elements of rhetoric. 1853.....815 4
Wright, A. A. Fables, stories, and descriptions. 1895...815 49
Wright, W. B. Literary style............815 Pam. 2

MODELS FOR LETTER WRITING.

Cooke. Universal letter-writer. 1873...........816 5
Eaton. Letter-writing. 1891 ....816 10
Frost. Original letter-writer.....................816 9
   New letter-writer.....................................816 6
   New universal letter-writer........................816 7
   Parlor letter-writer...................................816 8

ART OF POETRY.

Aristotle. The poetic............................185 2
   Theory of poetry, etc.; with text and tr.
   of Poetics, by Butcher. 1895............811 101
Austin. Poetry of the period. 1870.........811 18
Bayly. Alliance of musick, poetry, and oratory. 1789 ....811 2
Bigelow. One element of poetry.......811 Pam. 2
Boileau. L'art poétique.........................840 233
Bridges. Milton's prosody. 1893..............426 4
Chamberlin. Landscape in life and in
   poetry. 1886.....................................811 Pam. 1
Coblentz. Rime-index to York mystery
   plays..in 406 2 (v.10)
Corson. Primer of English verse. 1892.....811 92
Dallas. The gay science. 1866. 2v.........801 3
Davidson. Poetry of the future. 1888.....811 88
Doyle. Lectures, Oxford, 1868................811 17
Dryden. The art of poetry..................821.2 705
   Same. 821.2 690
Everett. Poetry, comedy, and duty. 1888..811 89
Guest. Hist. of English rhythms. 1838. 2v...426 1
Hayley. Essay on epic poetry (in verse)..821.2 193
Hood and Matthews. The rhymester:
   rules of rhyme. 1882.........................811 63
Horace. Ars poetica. 1757......................874 3
   Ars poetica; verse tr. by Sibley.......874 Pam. 1
   Art of poetry; tr. by Conington. 1872..874 24
   Art of poetry; tr. by Smart......................874 1
   English paraphrase of Art of poetry; by
   Russell. 1896....................................811 116
Horace, Viada, and Boileau. Art of
   poetry; ed. by Cook. 1892...................811 33

Hunt. Imagination and fancy. 1875......811 68
Hurd. On poetical imitation. 1757......in 874 4
Lanier. Science of English verse. 1880....426 3
Palgrave. Landscape in poetry. 1897.....811 118
Raymond. Poetry as a representative art
   1886..811 82
   Rhythm and harmony in poetry and music.
   1895..426 5
Schelling. Poetic and verse criticism of the
   reign of Elizabeth. 1891.......................811 91
Scudder, V. D. Life of the spirit in the
   modern poets. 1895.............................811 100
Shairp. Aspects of poetry. 1881..............811 62
   Poetic interpretation of nature. 1878.....811 31
Shelley. Defense of poetry..................820.2 192
Sidney. Defense of poesy. 1831................811 1
Stedman. Nature and elements of poetry.
   1892...811 93
Swanwick. Poets the interpreters of their
   age. 1892...811 95
Wadham. English versification. 1869.....426 6
Wordsworth. Prefaces and essays on
   poetry. 1892..811 94

ART OF DRAMATIC COMPOSITION.

Archer. How to write a good play. 1892...812 45
Bossuet. Sur la comédie. 1870..............840 B-3
Corneille. Sur l'art dramatique................842 6
Donne. Essays on the drama. 1858..........812 7
Fitzgerald. Principles of comedy. 1870...812 5
Freytag, G. Technique of the drama. '95..812 47
Girardin. Lects. on dramatic literature.
   1849...812 1
Hennequin. Art of playwriting. 1890.....812 44
Hurd. Provinces of the drama. 1757....in 874 3
Jones. Lects. on dramatic poets, etc. 1862.
   2v..812 3
Meredith. Essay on comedy. 1897..........812 50
Polti, G. Trente-six situations dramatiques.
   1895...812 48
Schlegel. Lects. on dramatic art, etc. 1833...812 2

ART OF PROSE FICTION.—THE NOVEL.

Art of writing fiction..................................813 48
   Contents: Norris, W. E.: Style in fiction.— Parr, Mrs:
   A story to tell.— Walford, L. B.: The novel of manners —
   Gould, S. Baring-: Colour in composition.— Macquoid K.
   S.: On vision in literature.— Gray, Maxwell: On the development of character in fiction.— Author of 'Mademoiselle Ixe': The short story.— Molesworth, Mrs.: On the
   art of writing fiction for children.—Church, A. J.: The
   historical novel.—Douglas, R. K.: The ethical novel.—
   Meade, L. T.: From the editor's standpoint.
Besant. Art of fiction. 1884....................813 41
Brunetière. Le roman naturaliste. 1896..813 62
Crawford. The novel. 1893.....................813 39
Dunlop. History of fiction. 1845...............813 1
   Same. 1842. 2 v.....................................813 2

---

* Of interest to young readers.

How to write fiction. 1895.................813 58
Howells. Criticism and fiction. 1891.......813 36
Kite. Fiction in public libraries.........813 Pam. 1
Lanier. The English novel. 1897.............813 22
Moulton, R. G., ed. Four years of novel
  reading. 1895...................................813 51
  Contents: Study of fiction, by R. G. Moulton.—The Backworth classical novel-reading union, by J. U. Barrow.—Four years' work done by the union.—Representative essays: Why is Charles Dickens a more famous novelist than Charles Reade? by E. Cumpston; Character of Clara Middleton, by J. Fairney; The ideal of asceticism, by C. G. Hall; Character development in 'Romola,' by T. Dowson.
Reading diary of modern fiction. 1881......813 20
Selby. Theology of modern fiction. 1896...813 65
Stevens, ed. How men propose. 1888....813 33
Thomson. Fiction. 1894................813 Pam. 2
Townsend, ed. Great characters of fiction.
  1893...813 40
Warren. History of the novel to 17th century. 1895...................................813 49
Wheeler. Dictionary of noted names of fiction..‡803 1
Zimmern, ed. Half-hours with foreign novelists. 1880. 2v........................813 12

ELOCUTION.—ORATORY.

Ayres, A. Essentials of elocution. 1886...815.1 30
Bacon. Manual of gesture. 1875...........815.1 12
Bell, A. M. Essays on elocution. 1886....815.1 33
  Principles of elocution. 1878...........815.1 19
Bell, D. C. and A. M. Standard elocutionist. 1881................................815.1 24
Boston school of expression. Catalog. '88.
  ....815.1 Pam. 2
Bronson. Elocution. 1845.................815.1 7
Brown. Synthetic philosophy of expression.
  1886..815.1 34
Campbell, et al. Voice, speech, and gesture. 1895....................................815.1 39
Chapman. The music, or melody and rhythmus, of language. 1818............815.1 2
Comstock. Elocution.......................815.1 11
Corson. The voice and spiritual education.
  1896..815.1 41
Curry. Province of expression. 1891......815.1 38
Delaumosne. Art of oratory, system of Delsarte. 1882................................815.1 27
Delaumosne and Delsarte. Delsarte system of oratory. 1887........................815.1 28

Dwyer. Essay on elocution. 1848.........815.1 6
Fobes. Elocution simplified. 1877........815.1 16
Graham. Reasonable elocution. 1875....815.1 13
Hall. How to teach reading. '86....815.1 Pam. 1
Hamill. Science of elocution. 1876.......815.1 15
Hardwicke. History of oratory and orators. 1896..815 46
Legouve. L'art de la lecture..............815.1 37
  Reading as a fine art. 1879...............815.1 20
McIlvaine. Elocution. 1870...............815.1 9
Magill. Pantomimes, or wordless poems.
  1895..815.1 40
Mathews. Oratory and orators. 1879....815.1 17
Millard. Grammar of elocution. 1882...815.1 25
Morgan. An hour with Delsarte. 1889...815.1 35
Pittinger. Oratory. 1873..................815.1 10
Plumptre. King's college lects. on elocution. 1895....................................815.1 22
Raymond. Orator's manual. 1879.......815.1 23
Rush. Philosophy of the human voice. '33..815.1 3
Russell, F. T. Use of the voice in reading and speaking. 1883.........................815.1 31
Russell, W., comp. Orthophony. 1878....815.1 21
Sears. History of oratory. 1896............815 42
Sheppard. Before an audience. 1887....815.1 36
Sheridan. Lects. on the art of reading.
  1798...815.1 1
  Lessons on elocution. 1834..............815.1 4
Shoemaker. Practical elocution. 1883...815.1 29
Stebbins. Delsarte system of dramatic expression. 1886...............................815.1 32
Vandenhoff. Art of reading aloud. '78...815.1 14
  Plain system of elocution. 1845..........815.1 5

DEBATE.

Brookings and Ringwalt, eds. Briefs for debate. 1896................................815.3 5
Cicero. On oratory and orators; tr. by Watson. 1862.......................................875 3
McElligott, ed. American debater. '68...815.3 2
Neil. The young debater....................815.3 3
Pittenger. Debater's treasury. 1891......815.3 4
Quintilian. Institutes of oratory. 2 v......875 1
Rowton. How to conduct a debate........815.3 1
Tacitus. Dialogus de oratoribus; ed. by Gudeman. 1894.............................875 28
  Same; ed. by Peterson. 1893............875 26

HISTRIONIC ARTS.

(For books on Acting and on the Theater and the Stage, see Part 3 of FINDING LIST, p. 427.)

‡ For reference.

LITERATURE AT LARGE.

GENERAL HISTORY AND COMPARATIVE CRITICISM.

Austin. Poetry of the period. 1870..........811 18
Backhaus. Originality in literature...801 Pam. 2
Blakey. History of political literature. '54 2v...................................320 29
Bury. Philobiblon; with tr. by Thomas. 1888..810 5
Carlyle. Lects. on history of literature (1838). 1892..............................809 17
Delepierre. Supercheries littéraires. '72.....810 35
Dobson. The classic poets. 1879..........811 58
Forsyth. History of ancient manuscripts. 1872.................................21 1
Goodrich (Peter Parley). Literature. '45....809 16
Hallam. Introduction to literature of Europe, 15-17th centuries. 1867. 4v..........809 4
Herford. Literary relations of England and Germany, 16th century. 1886..........809 11
La Marche. Les manuscrits, etc. 1884......13 2
Pater. The renaissance. 1877..............709 6
Perry. From Opitz to Lessing. 1885.........809 10
Philobiblos, *pseud.*, *ed.* Book-lover's enchiridion. 1883..........................10 20
Posnett. Comparative literature. 1886.....801 7
Putnam. Authors and their public in ancient times. 1894.......................809 19
Schlegel. Lects. on the history of literature. 1868....................................809 8
Schlosser. History of 18th century. 1843. v. 1-2..................................940 83
Schopenhauer. The art of literature. '91..810 41
Contents: Authorship.—Style.—Study of Latin.—Men of learning.—Thinking for oneself.—Some forms of literature.—Criticism.—Reputation.—Genius.
Sismondi. Historical view of literature of south of Europe. 1846. 2v...............809 1
Staël, *Madame de.* De la littérature dans ses rapports avec les institutions sociales. 1820............................840 247
Influence of literature upon society; with memoir. 1813. 2v......................810 8
Taylor. Transmission of ancient books. 1875..................................13 1
Thompson. Ethics of literary art. 1893....810 46
Underhill. Literary epochs. 1887. ....809 18
Williams. Studies in folk-song and popular poetry. 1894............................811 97

BIBLIOGRAPHY.

Allen. American book-plates. 1894..........27 3
American book-prices current. 1896—......20 10
American catalog; ed. by Leypoldt. 3v... 15 B-5
Same; ed. by Bowker. 1876............15 B 7
Beloe. Anecdotes of scarce books, etc. 1807. 6v.................................10 4
Bibliographer, The. 1882-4. 6 v. in 5......10 B-1
Bickley, *ed.* Bibliographical notes (Gentleman's magazine library)..................10 25
Blades. Books in chains, etc. 1892..........20 7
Book-lore. 1885. v. 1-2......................10 B-1
Book-lovers' almanac. 1895....................26 3
Book-prices current. 1897—..................20 11
Book-seller, The. 1879. v. 2—............805 P-67
British museum. Hand-list of bibliographies, etc. 1881............................10 16
Brunet. Manuel du libraire. 1860-65. 6v.....11 14
Same, supplement. 1878. 2v............11 20
Brydges. Censura literaria. 1805. 10 v.....15 1
Burton. The book-hunter. 1863............10 10
Casper. Directory of antiquarian booksellers. 1885................................11 33
Clarke. Bibliographical dictionary. 1802. 6v..11 1
Bibliographical miscellany. 1806. 2v....11 7
Darling. Cyclop. bibliographica. '54. 2v..16 B-1
Dibdin. Bibliographical tour. 3v..........914.4 3
Bibliomania. 1809........................20 3
Library companion. 1824..................11 13
Rare and valuable eds., classics. 2v......16 1
Reminiscenses. 2v.....................928.2 150
Ditchfield. Books fatal to their authors. '95..28 2
Duff. Early printed books. 1893............23 5
English catalog, 1835—......................15 25
Farrer. Books condemned to be burnt. '92..28 1
Field. Love affairs of a bibliomaniac. '96..10 28
G., A. B., *ed.* Literary curiosities and notes. 1898..................................10 24
Grolier club. Transactions, 1884-5..........27 4
Haight. Canadian catalog of books. 1896. Part 1................................15 55
Hardy. Book-plates. 1893....................27 2
Hartshorne. Book rarities, Cambridge......11 12
Hinrich. Verzeichnitz der Bücher; Landkarten, etc. 1882—........................15 31
Horne. Introduction to bibliography. '14. 2v..11 9
Kelly, *ed.* American catalog, 1866-71......15 23
Lang. Books and bookmen. 1886............20 4
London catalog, 1814-34. 1835..............15 24
Madan. Books in manuscript. 1893..........21 7
Memoirs of literature; by M. de la Roche. 1822. v. 2-7............................11 36
New memoirs. 1825-26..................11 41
New York state. List of books, etc., by women of. 1893......................18 Pam. 14
Petzholdt. Bibliotheca bibliographica. '66..11 34
Philomneste, *jr., pseud.* Bibliomania........20 1

Publishers' trade list annual. (U. S.) '76—
....15 B-1
Publishers' weekly. 1872—. v. 3—...805 P-B-4
Rees. Pleasures of a book-worm. 1886......10 21
Roberts. The book-hunter in London. '95.....27 5
   Rare books and their prices, etc. '96........20 8
Russell. Gesammt Verlags Katalog des deutschen Buchhandels. Vollständig bis Ende. 1880. v. 1-14................15 B-10
Sabin. Bibliography of bibliography. '77....10 11
Savage. The librarian. 1808. 3v..............10 1
Scott. Book sales of 1895.......................20 9
Slater. Book collecting. 1892..................10 26
Timperley. Literary and typographical anecdote. 1842...........................11 11
Trade circular annual. (U. S.) 1871.......15 B-2
Tredwell. Privately illustrated books......20 2
Tuer. History of the horn-book. 1896. 2v...20 B-1
Westwood. Paleographia sacra pictoria..220.1 B-3
Wheatley. Dedication of books. 1887......810 36
Whitney. A modern Proteus: books under different titles. 1884..........................16 56
Whittaker, *ed.* Reference catalog. (Gt. Britain.) 1877 —.................................15 26

GENERAL REFERENCE BOOKS.

A. L. A. index to general literature. '93......‡40 32
   Same..40 33
Année littéraire, L', 1893. ....809 ƒ0
Brewer. Dictionary of phrase and fable.
   ....‡423 14
   Same; rev. and enlarged. 1895......‡423 14A
Reader's hand-book. 1880...................‡803 2
British museum. Hand-book for readers; by Nichols. 1866..................................16 40
Campbell. Theory of national and international bibliography. 1896................10 29
Chambers, *ed.* Book of days. 1863. 2v...‡394 B-2
Companion to the playhouse. 1764. 2v.....822.2 4
Edwards. Words, facts and phrases. '82..‡423 22
Griswold. Index to collections of essays. 1883..‡814 2
Hodgkins. Guide to the study of 19th century authors. 1889........................‡16 79
Hone. Every day book. 1866. 2v......‡390 1
   Year book. 1866...................................‡390 3
Hume. Learned societies and printing clubs, United Kingdom. 1853..............62 1
Killikelly. Curious questions. '94. 2v......‡803 6
Literary year-book. 1897.......................805 23
Reddall, *comp.* Fact, fancy, and fable. 1889..‡40 30
Smith, *ed.* Dictionary of terms, phrases, etc.; American ed. by Johnson. '95..‡803 B-2
   Glossary of terms, etc. 1883................‡803 B-1

Walsh. Handy book of literary curiosities. 1893..‡803 5
Wheeler, W. A. Who wrote it? 1881.....‡803 3
Wheeler, W. A. *and* **C. G.** Familiar allusions. 1882...................................‡803 4
Winsor. Most useful reference books (Harvard univ. bulletin, v.2, p.341)...16 B-17
Year-book of learned societies. 1884......‡62 2

HINTS AND HELPS TO READERS AND STUDENTS.

Abbott, *ed.* Hints for home reading........*374 10
Acland, *ed.* Guide to the choice of books. 1891..‡16 113
Adams. Plain living and high thinking. '80..374 13
Alger. The school of life. 1881................374 12
Arey. Home and school training. 1884......98.3 3
Atkinson. Right use of books. 1878.........*374 9
Azarias. Books and reading. 1890..........*374 8
Baldwin. The book-lover. 1895..............‡16 61
Balfour. Pleasures of reading. 1887......374 Pam. 3
Best reading, The. 1873..........................‡16 12
   Same; rev. and enlarged ed. 1877-87. Series 1-3..‡16 13
Besten Bücher, Die. Berlin. 1889..........16 124
Bibliothèque nationale. Dept. des imprimés. Liste alphabétique des ouvrages unis a la libre disposition des lecteurs. 1886......................................16 69
Birmingham. Free public library. Lects. on books in reference dept. 1885........‡16 71
Blackie. Self-culture. 1874.....................374 3
Boston. Public library. Catalog of Barton collection. 1888..................................16 B-23
   Contents: Part 1. Shakespeare's works and Shakespeariana.—Part 2. Miscellaneous.
   Catalog of bibliographies of special subjects. 1890...16 101
   Class lists for poetry, drama, arts, sciences, etc., (Lower hall), 1870-71......16 B-3
   Handbook for readers.............................16 20
   Index to notes about books and reading, etc. 1883...‡16 B-9
Bowdoin College library. Bibliographical contributions..16 Pam. 68
British museum. List of books of reference in the reading room. 1890........16 108
Brown, *ed.* Readers' helps. 1885.....16 Pam. 20
Buffalo Library. Books for young readers. 1881..*95.2X 7
Burt, B. C. References for students in English literature. 1887........................‡16 77
Burt, M. E. Literary landmarks. 1889.....16 98
California, University of, library. Contents-index. 1889-90. v. 1..............‡16 102

* Of interest to young readers.   ‡ For reference.

LANGUAGE AND LITERATURE.

Caller. Literary guide for home and school. 1895.................................‡16 146
Cambridge. Young men's society for home study. Repts...........................374 Pam. 1
Carlyle. On the choice of books. 1881....*374 14
Channing. Self-culture. 1838................374 16
Channing club, Boston. Catalog of books for boys. 1888..................16 Pam. 45
Chester. Chats with girls on self-culture. 1891.................................*374 20
Clarke. Self-culture. 1880.....................374 11
Cornell University. Library bulletin. 1882-5. v. 1-2..................................16 83
Corson. Aims of literary study. 1895......807 1
Eggleston. How to educate yourself. '72...*374 2
Foster. Libraries and readers. 1883........‡16 51
Monthly reference lists. 1881-4.........‡16 55
Goodrich. Fireside education. 1838........374 19
Griswold, *comp.* Descriptive list of books for the young. 1895................‡16 B-13
The reader. 1893—. no. 1—..........‡16 143
Hale. How to read. 1871................*177 8
What career? 1878........................373 4
Hamerton. The intellectual life..............374 5
Hardy. Five hundred books for the young. 1892..................................‡16 127
Harrison. The choice of books. 1886...824.2 384
Harvard University, library. Bibliographical contributions; ed. by Winsor. 1879-1882................................16 B-16
Bulletin. 1879-92........................16 B-17
Hewins, C. M. Books for the young. '82...‡16 87
Same..*16 Pam. 7
Hood. Self-formation. 1883..................374 15
Iddesleigh, *earl of,* (Stafford Northcote). Desultory reading. 1885................374 17
Indianapolis. Public library. Selection of books for young readers. 1888..........‡16 85
Johnson. Living to purpose. 1870..........*374 7
Kent. Course of English reading. 1853....16 11
Knapp. Advice in pursuits of literature. '32..810 10
Langford, *ed.* The praise of books......829.2 89
Larned. A talk about books. 1897..........374 24
Ladies' commission on Sunday school books. Catalog. 1890-94..........16 Pam. 63
Leypoldt *and* Iles. Books for girls and women and their clubs. 1895........‡16 B-37
Same..16 137
Leypoldt *and* Jones, *eds.* Books of all time. 1882..................................11 32
Loomis. Mental and social culture. 1873....374 6
Lubbock, *et al.* The best 100 books. '86..‡16 B-7
MacAlister. Study of modern literature. 1887..............................807 Pam. 1
Martineau. Household education. 1877.....372 6
Mason. Home education. 1886..............372 45
Matson. References for literary workers. 1892..................................‡16 130

Milwaukee. Public library. Catalog of books for young people. 1895........16 99
Moore. What to read and how. 1870.......*16 9
Morley. Study of literature. 1887..........374 18
New York city. Apprentices' library. Classified lists of most popular books. 1883-4...............................‡16 B-14
Northrop. The reading of our boys and girls. 1882............................‡16 88
Parsons. The world's best books. 3d ed. 1893..................................‡16 97
Philadelphia. Library company. Bulletin. 1882-92. 2v............................16 84
Mercantile library. Bulletin. v. 1....16 B-18
Porter. Books and reading. 1871............16 8
Same; with appendix. 1881................‡16 8½
Poughkeepsie. City library. Books for pupils in schools. 1887-8..........16 Pam. 30
Providence. Point street grammar school library. Catalog and notes on children's books. 1883....................*16 Pam. 10
Pryde. Highways of literature. 1882........16 46
Putnam. Best reading. 1873................16 12
Same; ed. by Perkins. 1877..............16 12A
Same; 2d series. 1882...................16 12B
Same; 3d series. 1887..................16 12C
Pycroft. Course of English reading. 1871....15 17
Quaritch. Catalogue of English literature. 1884..................................16 70
Rollin. Method of teaching and studying the belles-lettres. 1804. 3 v........810 1
Ruskin. Sesame and lilies..................374 4
St. Louis. Public library. Reference lists..‡ 16 82
Contents: Astronomy; by Pritchett.— Buddhism; by Bryant.— French history; by Snow.— Music; by Otten.— Renaissance; by Waters.— Training of children; by Mrs. Learned.— Travels; by Clements.— Wordsworth; by Crunden.
Sargant *and* Whishaw, *eds.* Guide book to books. 1891....................‡ 16 B-30
Sargent. Reading for the young. 1890...‡ 16 B-27
Supplement to same. 1896............‡ 16 B-27
Sawin. Books for young people. 1888....16 91
Same. 1890..............................16 Pam. 47
Sigourney. Letters to mothers. 1839......372 7
Smart. Books, etc., for the young. 1880...*16 27
Smiles. Self-help. 1872.................*374 1
Sonnenschein. The best books. 1887...‡ 16 B-28
Same; 2d ed. 1891....................‡ 16 B-28A
Reader's guide to contemporary literature: 1st supp. to above. 1895......‡ 16 B-29
Staël, *Madame de.* Influence of literature. 1813. 2v................................810 5
Teachers' national reading circle. Courses, etc. 1887............................374 Pam. 2
Thwing. Reading of books. 1883..........16 52
Van Dyke. Books, and how to use them. 1883..................................*16 50

* Of interest to young readers. ‡ For reference.

Van Rhyn. What and how to read. 1875"‡16 10
Warner, *et al.* Hints for home reading.
   1880..*374 10
Willmott. Pleasures of literature. 1860......801 5

GENERAL COLLECTIONS.

Aikin *and* Barbauld. Evenings at home...*42 39
Bolton, *ed.* Books for the people. 1882-4.
   Series 1-3..41 5
Botta. Hand-book of universal literature...810 20
Burt. The world's literature. 1890. v.1....809 12
Chambers's information for the people.
   1849. 2v..42 B-1
Chambers's miscellany of tracts. 20 v......42 63
Chambers's pocket miscellany. 12 v........42 24
Collet. Relics of literature. 1823...............819 8
Cooper, *ed.* Rhyme and reason of country
   life. 1855...819 11
Darlington. Book of wonders. 1846........40 14
Disraeli. Curiosities of literature. 1st
   series. 1858. 3 v.......................................810 29
   Same; 2d series. 1824. 3 v....................810 32
Fame's tribute to children. 1892...........819 B-5
Goodrich. Peter Parley's thousand and
   one stories...41 9
Hunt. Book for a corner..........................810 15
Knight. Half hours with the best authors.
   4v..810 11
Masterpieces of foreign literature........810 7
   Contents: Schiller's tragedies; tr. by Coleridge.—
   Goethe's Faust.—La Fontaine's Fables.—Picciola; by
   Saintine.
Merrick. Nugæ inutiles; specimens of
   translations. 1874..................................811 8
Morley, *ed.* A miscellany. 1888................814 3
   Contents: Richard of Bury's Philobiblon.—
   The Basilikon Doron of King James I.—Monks and giants; by John H.
   Frere.—The cypress crown; by La Motte Fouqué.—The
   library, a poem; by George Crabbe.
Morris, *ed.* Half-hours with the best foreign
   authors. 4v.
   V. 1. Greek and Roman........................810 37
   V. 2. German.......................................810 38
   V. 3. French..810 39
   V. 4. Italian, Spanish, etc...................810 40
Nisbet. Excelsior: helps to progress in
   religion, science and literature. '54. 6v..42 13
Owen. The five great skeptical dramas of
   history. 1896..812 49
   Contents: The Prometheus vinctus of Æschylus.—The
   book of Job. Goethe's Faust.—Shakespeare's Hamlet.—
   El magico prodigioso (by Calderon).
Southey. Commonplace book. 1876. 4 v..819 42
Spofford *and* Gibbon, *eds.* Library of
   choice literature. 1882. 8v......................810 21
Timbs. Knowledge for the time. 1861......42 37
   Illustrated book of wonders, events, and
   discoveries..42 38
   Things not generally known. 1867.......42 36

Touches of nature. 1867..........................810 R-1
Townsend, *ed.* Every-day book. 1870....810 16
Warner, *ed.* Library of the world's best
   literature. 1896. v.1................................810 47
World of wonders....................................42 B-4

POETICAL COLLECTIONS.

Adams, *ed.* Poets' praise. 1894................811 96
Baker, *ed.* Ballads of bravery. 1877........811 60
Bates. Wedding-day book.........................811 121
Boulton, *ed.* Songs of four nations. '92...784 B-22
Boyle. Book of the heavenly birthdays. '93..811 87
Bunce, *ed.* Fair words about fair women...811 73
Child, *ed.* Poems of sorrow, comfort, etc.
   1863..811 86
Clarke, J. F. *and* L. Exotics. 1875........811 26
Cole, *comp.* Thousand best poems..........811 98
Dana, *ed.* Household book of poetry......‡811 5
Delepierre. Macaronéana: mélanges de
   littérature macaronique. 1852................811 79
Eliot, *ed.* Poetry for children..................*811 80
Emerson, *ed.* Parnassus...........................811 6
Franklin square song collection. 1881-91.
   nos. 1-8..784 B-8
Heroic ballads; ed. by D. H. M. 1890....*811 90
Horder, *ed.* The poet's Bible. 1881........225 77
Hulme. Bards and blossoms. 1877...........716 51
In the saddle. 1882...................................811 65
Johnson, *ed.* Tears for the little ones....811 30
Longfellow, *ed.* Poems of places:
   Africa...811 37
   Asia. 3v..811 34
   Belgium and Holland............................811 25
   British America, Mexico, South America, etc...811 54
   Denmark..811 41
   England and Wales. 4v........................811 44
   France. 2v...811 48
   Germany 2v..811 42
   Greece and Turkey in Europe..............811 29
   Ireland...811 38
   Italy. 3v...811 20
   Middle states..811 56
   New England. 2v..................................811 50
   Norway and Sweden.............................811 41
   Oceanica, etc..811 55
   Russia..811 32
   Scotland. 3v..811 39
   Southern states....................................811 52
   Spain and Portugal. 2v........................811 24
   Switzerland and Austria......................811 23
   Western states.....................................811 53
   Poets and poetry of Europe. 1845. 2v...‡811 3
Mother Goose's melodies, with notes, etc..*819 35
Mother Goose's melody, The original; ed.
   by Whitmore. 1892................................819 49

* Of interest to young readers.   ‡ For reference.

LANGUAGE AND LITERATURE.

Poems and pictures. 811 66
Rabb. National epics. 1896.................811 85
  Contents: Râmâyana.—Mahâ-bhârata.—Iliad.—Odyssey.—Kalevala.—Æneid.—Beowulf.—Nibelungen Lied.—Song of Roland.—Shah-nameh.—Cid.—Divine comedy.—Orlando Furioso.—Lusiad.—Jerusalem delivered.—Paradise lost.—Paradise regained.
Ricord. English songs from foreign tongues. 1879.................811 57
Roberts, *ed.* Book-verse. 1896.................811 103
Schaff *and* Gilman, *eds.* Library of religious poetry. 1881.................‡811 B-1
  Same: 1882.................811 B-1A
Sea and shore. 1874.................811 27
Songs of eastern Europe; ed. by Kappey. 784 B-19
Sousa. National, patriotic, and typical airs of all lands. 1890.................784 B-28
Stevenson. Biography of certain hymns. *in* 922 14
Strettell, *tr.* Lullabies of many lands. 1894.................811 102
Waddington, *ed.* Sonnets of Europe. '86...811 84
Watts, *ed.* Laurel and lyre. 1867.................811 16
White. National hymns. 1861.................811 7
Whittier, *ed.* Child life. 1879.................*811 61

FESTIVAL POEMS.

Bramley *and* Stainer, *eds.* Christmas carols, with music.................784 B-24
Festival poems. 1884.................811 74
Ffoulkes. Noël: carols; with music by Ransom. 1894.................784 B-25
Husk, *ed.* Songs of the nativity.................811 77
McCaskey. Christmas in song, sketch, and story. 1891.................784 B-27
Morris, *ed.* In the yule-log glow. '92. 2v...810 44
Sandys, *ed.* Christmas carols, ancient and modern. 1833.................811 75
Christmastide; history, carols, etc.........394 44
Festive songs, 16-17th centuries........821.2 466
Sylvester, *ed.* Garland of Christmas carols, ancient and modern. 1861.................811 76
Wright, *ed.* Old Christmas carols.......821.2 447
Songs and carols, 15th century.........821.2 466

EPISTOLARY COLLECTIONS.

Holcombe, *ed.* Literature in letters. 1866.....816 1
Martel, *ed.* Love-letters of eminent persons. 1859.................816 4
Roberts. History of letter-writing. 1843....816 3
Seton. Gossip about letters and letter-writers. 1870.................816 2

QUOTATIONS.—PROVERBS.—APHORISMS.

Adams, H. G., *ed.* Sacred poetical quotations.................‡811 67
Adams, W. D., *ed.* English epigrams...829.2 46

Allibone, *ed.* Poetical quotations. 1873....‡811 28
Baer. Sprichwörter und Sinnbilder. (Catalog.) 1889.................819 Pam 1
Ballou, *ed.* Edge-tools of speech. 1886.....‡819 36
Banvard, *ed.* Wisdom, etc., of ancient philosophers. 1855.................‡819 14
Bartlett, *ed.* Familiar quotations.............819 6
  Same. 1891.................‡819 6C
Bate, *ed.* Illustrations, moral and religious..‡819 37
Belton, *ed.* Foreign quotations. 1891.....‡819 59
Bent, *ed.* Short sayings of great men. '82..‡819 53
Bigelow. Wit and wisdom of Haytians.....819 18
Bohn, *ed.* Hand-book of proverbs. 1893....‡819 16
Cheviot, A., *ed.* Proverbs, etc., of Scotland. 1896.................‡829.2 78
Christy, *ed.* Proverbs, maxims and phrases. 1888. 2 v.................‡819 56
Dalbiac. Dictionary of quotations, English. 1896.................‡819 79
Edwards, *ed.* The world's laconics. '66....‡819 12
Friswell, *ed.* Familiar words. 1880.......‡819 50
Gentleman's magazine library: dialect, proverbs, etc.................427 6
Gilbert, *ed.* Dictionary of burning words. 1895.................‡819 58
Grose, *ed.* English local proverbs...*in* 914.2 B-27
Hartford library association. How to find quotations, etc.................*in* 16 Pam. 51
Henderson, *ed.* Scottish proverbs.......‡829.2 47
Hennequin. Dictionnaire de maximes. 1828.................‡819 55
Hazlitt, *ed.* English proverbs, etc.......‡829.2 49
Herbert. Jacula prudentum.................820.2 118
Hislop, *ed.* Proverbs of Scotland........‡829.2 18
Hood, *ed.* World of proverb and parable...‡819 1
Hoyt *and* Ward, *eds.* Cyclop. of practical quotations. 1882.................‡819 B-3
J., A., *ed.* Le véritable Sancho-Panza. '56...819 32
Jermyn. Book of English epithets. '49...‡819 B-6
King. Classical and foreign quotations. 1889.................‡819 40
Langford, *ed.* The praise of books........829.2 89
Linn, *ed.* Dictionary of living thoughts. 1896.................‡819 81
Long, *ed.* Eastern proverbs and emblems...‡819 51
Michelson, *ed.* Manual of quotations.....‡819 48
Mills, *ed.* Pebbles, pearls, and gems of the Orient. 1882.................819 38
Moore, *ed.* Dictionary of quotations. 1831..‡819 2
Morley. Aphorisms. 1887.................819 39
Moulton, *ed.* Prize selections: familiar quotations.................819 83
New dictionary of quotations: Greek, Latin, etc. 1860.................‡819 3
Riley, *ed.* Dictionary of Latin quotations, proverbs, etc. 1866.................‡819 4
Rollins. Aphorisms for the year. 1895..829.1 40
Unfamiliar quotations. 1895.................819 78

* Of interest to young readers.   ‡ For reference.

Spencer. Things new and old. 1867. 2v...819 9
Trench. On the lessons in proverbs. 1853...819 17
Wallace. Popular sayings dissected. 1895...819 75
Weld, *ed.* Sacred quotations. 1851............‡249 2
West, *et al., eds.* By the way. 1887............819 82
Wood, J., *ed.* Dictionary of quotations. '93..‡819 7
Wood, K. B., *ed.* Quotations for occasions. 1896..‡819 80

WIT.—HUMOR.—PARODY.—EPIGRAM.

Adams, *ed.* Quips and quiddities. 1881.....819 52
American Joe Miller.................................818 5
Book of humour, wit, and wisdom............819 15
Book of humorous poetry...........................818 4
Brown, *ed.* Bulls and blunders. 1893......818 13
Burton, *ed.* Cyclop. of wit and humor. 1866. 2v...818 B-1
Callaway. The wit on the staircase. '90...819 84
Carey. Commonplace book of epigrams. 1872..819 20
Clouston. The book of noodles. 1888......818 14
Cox. Why we laugh. 1876.......................818 1
Dodd. The epigrammatists. 1870..............819 19
Doran. History of court fools. 1858......818 15
Enchiridion of wit. 1885.........................828.2 57
Galaxy of wit and wisdom. 1875..............818 3
Hannay. Satire and satirists. 1855.........817 1
Lear, *ed.* Here and there. 1882..............818 6
Lemon, *ed.* Jest book. 1865.....................818 2
Martin. On parody. 1896..........................817 2
Morley, *ed.* Burlesque plays and poems. 1885..818 12
Southwick. Wisps of wit and wisdom......40 31
Spofford *and* Shapley, *eds.* Library of wit and humor. 1884. 5 v................818 7
Wheatley. Literary blunders. 1893..........818 16

ANECDOTES.

Addison (*pseud.*). Interesting anecdotes, etc. 6 v..819 25
Beloe, W. Anecdotes of literature, etc. 6 v..10 4
Buck, *ed.* Anecdotes, religious, etc. '56...249 3
Encyclopædia of literary and typographical anecdote. 1842..11 11
Hazlitt, *ed.* Anecdotes; modern. 1872...819 33
Hindley, *ed.* Tavern anecdotes 1881......390 5
Hood, *ed.* The world of anecdote. 1880.....819 46
Kirkland, *ed.* Cyclop. of commercial anecdote. 2v. 1865..380 6
Miles, *ed.* One thousand and one anecdotes..819 65
Percy anecdotes; with American anecdotes..819 85
Spence. Anecdotes, etc. 1858..................819 31
Thoms, *ed.* Anecdotes of early English history and literature. 829 2 10

FABLES.

Æsop, La Fontaine, *and* Kriloff. Fables; child's version, by Stickney. 1886......*819 34
Bewick's select fables. 1871.....................819 23
Bussey, *ed.* Fables. 1842........................819 21
Treasure house of fables. 1892...........*819 60
Keidel. Manual of Æsopic fable literature. pt. 1. 1896...819 Pam. 3
My book of fables......................................*819 41
Newbigging. Fables and fabulists. 1895....819 74
Northcote, Bewick, *et. al.* Fables. 1847...819 54
Saxe. Fables and legends in rhyme........819 22

ROMANCE.

Baldwin. Fifty famous stories retold. '96...*41 7
Bates. Classics of babyland. 1891..........*819 B-4
Beeton, *ed.* Fact, fiction, etc....................*42 41
Historical romances, etc..........:............*42 42
Tales of chivalry, etc..............................*42 40
Golden fairy book. 1894............................*813 47
Goodrich. Peter Parley's merry stories........41 3
Henderson. Dunderviksborg, etc.: epitome of modern European literature. 1881..813 14
Hope. Stories of old renown. 1883..........813 21
Jacobs, J., *ed.* Book of wonder voyages. 1896..*813 60
Modern ghosts; introduction by G. W. Curtis. 1890..813 35
Contents: Introduction.— The Horla; by Maupassant.— Siesta; by Kielland.— The tall woman; by Alarcon.— On the river; by Maupassant.— Maese Perez, the organist; by Becquer.— Fioraccio; by Magherini Graziani.— The silent woman; by Kompert.
Morris, *ed.* In the yule-log glow: Christmas tales and poems. 4 v. 1892.
Contents: V. 1. Three kings of Cologne; by Morris.—Three Christmas masses; by Daudet.— Russian Christmas party; by Tolstoi.—Two Christmases; by Schuster.— Tale of a turkey; by Morris.—A still Christmas; by Repplier.— Throud; by Björnson.— Christmas in the desert; by Edwards.............810 42
V. 2. Christmas with the baron; by Lewis.—A Christmas miracle; by Morris.— Wolf tower.— The pence egg; by Ewing.— Story of Nuremberg; by Repplier.—Picture of the nativity by Fra Filippo Lippi; by Lee.—Melchior's dream; by Ewing.— Mrs. Grapewine's Christmas dinner; by Morris.....810 43
Ranking. Streams from hidden sources. 1872..813 17
Rhys, *ed.* Garden of romance. 1897.......813 64
Rolfe, *ed.* Fairy tales in prose and verse. 1889..*813 34
Scudder, H. E., *ed.* Children's book...*819 B-1
Silver fairy book. 1895.............................*813 53
Swinton *and* Cathcart, *eds.* Golden book of tales. 1882..*819 13
Underhill, *ed.* Dwarfs' tailor, etc. 1896...*813 61
World of romance. 1892..........................813 B-1
(*See, also, under* "Fairy Tales.—Folk Lore," *in part* 3 *of* FINDING LIST, pp. 519-520; *and under* Mediæval Literature *in this part, a few pages ahead.*)

* Of interest to young readers.   ‡ For reference.

BIBLIOGRAPHY OF FICTION.

Bowen. Descriptive catalog of historical novels, etc. 1882..................‡16 17
Brookline. Public library. Catalog of historical fiction. 1897...................‡16 91
Griswold. Descriptive lists of novels and tales:
  American city life. 1891..................‡16 114
  American country life. 1890............‡16 107
  Ancient history. 1895......................‡16 135
  British novels. 1891.........................‡16 115
  History of North America. 1895.....‡16 136
  International novels. 1891................‡16 116
  Life in France. 1892........................‡16 122
  Life in Germany. 1892.....................‡16 129
  Life in Italy. 1892...........................‡16 128
  Romantic novels. 1890....................‡16 112
Hartford library association. Novels, humorous works, etc. 1893..................‡17 49
  Short stories, selections and humorous works : a list. 1891..................‡16 111
Peoria. Public library. Reference list of fiction and juveniles. 1882............‡16 B-8
Philadelphia. Mercantile library. Historical novels. 1885-9..................‡16 B-25
  List of prose fiction. 1891..................16 119
Plimpton. Classified list of historical and descriptive fiction. 1892...........‡16 125
St. Louis. Mercantile library. Catalog of English prose fiction. 1892.........;16 B 31
San Francisco. Free public library. Classified English prose fiction. '91..‡17 B 36
Silas Bronson library, Waterbury, Conn. Class list, fiction. 1884..........‡16 Pam. 35

MISCELLANEOUS.

Elegant extracts. 1785......................819 62
Flower lore...................................716 54
Friend. Flowers and flower lore. 1881.
  2 v...716 52
Norton *and* **Stephens,** *eds.* Heart of oak books. 1894-5. v. 1-5.................*819 67
Porter, *ed.* About children : what men and women have said. 1896.............137 9
  About men : what women have said. 1895...819 76
  About women : what men have said. 1894...819 63
Raynor, *ed.* The spinster's scrip. 1896.....819 77
Ryder, *ed.* New every morning : a yearbook for girls. 1886...................*819 66
Southgate, *ed.* What men have said about women. 1868...........................829 1
Tegg, *ed.* One hour's reading. 1877.........390 5
Treasury of table talk. 1894................819 64
World of wonders.............................42 B-4
  Same. 1873..................................41 B-1

ORIENTAL LANGUAGES AND LITERATURE.

Alger. Poetry of the Orient. 1865............895 4
Conder. Altaic hieroglyphs and Hittite inscriptions. 1887......................499 17
Cory, *ed.* Ancient fragments, Phœnician, Chaldean, Egyptian, etc. 1832.........890 1
  Same ; rev. ed. 1876.......................890 2
Hearn. Stray leaves from strange literature. 1884...............................890 4
Herder. Blumenlese aus morgenländischen Dichtern. 1820........................830 97
Oriental Translation Fund. Miscellaneous translations. 1831-4. v. 1-2 (*in* 1 v.)....894 4
  Contents: Journey into northern Africa ; by Ebn-ed-din.—Extracts from the Sakaa Thevan Saasteram.—Mahabharat: Last days of Krishna.— Vedâla Cadai.— Indian cookery.— Genealogical catalog of kings of Armenia ; by Hubboff.— Siege of Chaitûr by Emperor Akabar ; by Abul-Fazl.— Motives of Alemdâr Mustafâ Pâshâ, march to Constantinople, 1222.— Ritual of Buddhist priesthood.— Extract from a horticultural work ; by Radhakant Deb.— Account of festival held by Amir Timûr, A. H. 803.

Palmer, E. H. Grammar of Hindustani, Persian and Arabic. 1882.............494 2
Phenix, The : fragments : by Confucius, Zoroaster, et. al. 1835..................890 3
Quackenbos. History of ancient literature..880 16
Renan. Histoire des langues sémitiques. 1858...493 10
Rule. Oriental records, monumental. '77....893 15
Sagas from the far east. 1873................299 14
(See also, Sacred Literature and Folk Lore, in Part 3 of FINDING LIST, pp. 513-521.)

ANCIENT EGYPTIAN, BABYLONIAN, AND ASSYRIAN.

Bertin. Abridged grammars of languages of the cuneiform inscriptions. 1888....493 14
Birch, *ed.* Archaic classics : Egyptian texts. 1877................................892 1

---

* Of interest to young readers.   ‡ For reference.

Boscawen, *ed.* Assyrian texts............893 Pam. 1
Evans. Essay on Assyriology. 1883.......493 13
Forster. Monuments of Assyria, Babylonia
   and Persia. 1859...........................493 3
Ishtar and Izdubar ; tr. by Hamilton. '84.
   v. 1...893 44
Jastrow. Fragment of the Babylonian
   'Dibbarra' epic. 1891.....................893 52
Maspero, *tr.* Contes populaires de
   l'Égypte. 1882.................................892 2
Petrie, *ed.* Egyptian tales. v. 1-2. 1895......892 3
Records of the past, Assyrian and Egyptian,
   tr. 1873. 12 v. 893 2
   Same ; new series ; ed. by Sayce.
     1888-93. v, 1-6..........................893 13
Sayce. Babylonian literature. 1878.........893 24
   Lects. upon Assyrian language. 1877...493 11
Schrader. Cuneiform inscriptions and the
   Old Testament. 1885-8....................893 50
Sharpe, *ed.* Decree of Canopus. 1870......492 3
   Egyptian hieroglyphics. 1861...............492 4
   Rosetta stone. 1871............................492 2
Smith, G. Phonetic values of cuneiform
   characters. 1871.........................493 B-2
   Chaldean account of Genesis. 1876.....893 16
   Same ; new ed.; rev. by Sayce. '81...893 16A
   History of Sennacherib ; ed. by Sayce.
     1878..893 B-1
Spineto. Elements of hieroglyphics. '45...492 1
Virey. Études sur le papyrus Prisse : le
   livre de Kaqimna et les leçons de
   Ptah-Hotep. 1887............................892 6

(See also, Sacred Literature and Ancient Folk Lore, in Part 3 of FINDING LIST, pp. 513, 516, and 518-521).

HEBREW AND SYRIAN.

Ephraem Syrus. Metrical hymns, etc. ;
   tr. by Burgess. 1853.......................893 14
Fuerst. Hebrew-Chaldee lexicon, Old
   Testament. 1871..........................‡493 2
Gesenius. Hebrew-English lexicon, Old
   Testament. 1850..........................‡493 1
Irish. Hebrew charts. 1872....................493 B-1
King. Moab's patriarchal stone. 1878.....493 9
Sekles. Poetry of the Talmud. 1880.......893 29
Sharpe, *ed.* Hebrew inscriptions. '75.....493 12
Stuart. Grammar of Hebrew. 1831..........493 5
Warschawski. Progressive Hebrew
   course. 1879...................................493 4
Wright. Short history of Syriac literature.
   1894..893 53

† See, Sacred Literature of the Hebrews, in Part 3 of FINDING LIST, pp. 449, 453-463, 514-515.

ARABIAN LANGUAGE AND LITERATURE.

Antar ; *tr.* by Hamilton. 1819. 4 v.........893 46
Arabian nights' entertainments................893 19
   Same..893 18
   Same ; rev. by Chapman. 1888.....*893 18A
   Same ; tr. by Forster..........................893 17
   Same ; tr. by Lane. 1877. 3 v.........893 26
   Same ; tr. by Payne. 1882-4. 9 v.....893 35
   Same ; ed. by Scott. 1883. 4 v.......893 31
   Same ; in N. Y. point, for the blind.
     1883.....................................362.4 N-Y-9
   Tales from the Arabic ; tr. by Payne.
     1884. 3 v.................................893 43A
Burckhardt. Arabic proverbs. 1875.......893 23
Caliphs and Sultans ; ed. by Hanley. '69...893 20
Carlyle, *tr.* Specimens of Arabian poetry.
   1810..893 25
Church. Stories of the magicians. 1887...*893 54
   Contents: Thalaba and the magicians of Domdaniel.—
   Rustem and the genii.— Kehama and his sorceries.
Clouston, *tr.* Arabian poetry for English
   readers. 1881................................893 30
Enchanted keys, etc.; ed. by Pardoe. '69...893 21
Green. Practical Arabic grammar. 1887.....493 6
Jones, *tr.* The Moallakat........................404 20
Kalila and Dimna ; *tr.* by Knatchbull. '19....893 1
Koran, The ; *tr.* by Sale. 1850................297 51
Lyall, *ed.* Translations of ancient Arabian
   poetry. 1885..................................893 55
Magic ring, and other Oriental fairy tales ;
   from German of Herder, et. al..........893 22

(See also, Literature of Mohammedanism, in Part 3 of FINDING LIST, p. 515.)

PERSIAN LANGUAGE AND LITERATURE.

Adventures of Hatim Tai ; tr. by Forbes ;
   ed. by Alger. 1896.......................*895 21
Avesta ; tr. by Spiegel and Bleeck. 1864....295 1
Bakhtyar nama ; tr. by Ouseley. 1883......895 10
Dabistan, The ; tr. from the Persian by
   Shea, et al. 1843. 3v....................290 B-4
Djami. See **Jami.**
Firdusi. Epic of kings ; tr. by Zimmern.
   1822..895 R-1
   Episodes from the Shah Nameh ; tr. by
     Weston. 1815.............................895 13
   Heldenbuch von Iran, aus dem Schah
     Nameh ; übersetzt v. Görres. '20. 2v..895 15
   Poems ; tr. by Champion. 1785........895 B-5
   Roostum and Zoohrab ; tr. by Anderson.
     1882.......................................895 Pam. 1
   Shah Nameh ; tr. by Atkinson. 1886....895 12
   Soohrab ; from the Shah Nameh ; tr. by
     Atkinson. 1814..............................895 14

* Of interest to young readers.   ‡ For reference.

LANGUAGE AND LITERATURE.

Hafiz. Ghazels from the divan of; tr. by
McCarthy. 1893.....................................895 19
Persian lyrics. 1800..........................895 B-3
Persian song; tr. by Jones.................404 20
Selections from poems; tr. by Bicknell.
1875...895 B-2
Haug. Language, writings, etc., of Parsis.
1878...295 2
Hussein vais Kashify. Persian fables;
ed. by Michael. 1827......................895 B-4
Jami. Baharistan, book 6: Persian wit;
tr. by Wilson. 1883..........................895 11
Yusuf and Zulaikha; tr. by Griffith. '82...895 7
Nizami. Loves of Laili and Majnun; tr.
by Atkinson. 1894...........................895 18
Tales and fables; tr. by Jones..............404 14
Omar Khayyám. Quatrains; tr. by Whinfield. 1882..895 3
Rubáiyát; English, French, and German
translations comparatively arranged
with Fitzgerald's version; ed. by Dole.
1896. 2v...895 22
Same; tr. by Fitzgerald. 1881...............895 1
Same; tr. by Fitzgerald, drawings by
Vedder. 1894..................................895 20
Same; tr. in English prose; by J. H.
McCarthy. 1889...............................895 17
Ouseley. Notices of Persian poets.........928.5 18
Saadi. Garden of fragrance; tr. by Davie.
1882...895 9
Gulistan; or rose garden; tr. by Gladwin. 895 2
Same; tr. by Eastwick. 1880...............895 8
Specimens of popular poetry of Persia;
tr. by Chodzko. 1842......................895 B-1
Tales of the genii; tr. by Morell. 1781. 2 v. 895 5
(See also, Sacred Literature and Folk Lore, in Part 3 of FINDING LIST, p. 513-514, 516, 518-521.)

INDIAN LANGUAGES AND LITERATURE.

Akber. Ayeen Akbery: institutes; tr. by
Gladwin. 1800. 2v............................894 B-2
Bana. Kadambari; continued by Bhushanabhatta; tr. by Ridding. 1896...........894 19
Bidpaï. Fables of. 1872..........................894 9
Kalila and Dimna; tr. by Knatchbull.....893 1
Calidas. Sacontala; tr. by Jones..............404 19
Chatterjee. Krishna Kanta's will............894 42
Cust. Modern languages; East Indies. '78...494 2
Gover. Folk-songs of southern India. 1872.
....894 B-5
Hitopadesa; tr. by Jones........................404 23
Same; tr. by Pincott. 1880...............894 B-1

Kalidasa. Birth of the war-god; tr. by
Griffith. 1853...................................894 28
The Megha-duta (cloud messenger); tr.
by Wilson. 1867.............................894 B-4
Sacontala; tr. by Jones.......................404 19
Sakuntala; ed. and tr. by Williams. '76..894 14
Same; tr. by Williams. 1885..............894 18
Karmawakya: ritual of Buddhist priesthood...in 894 4
Mahabharata, tr. published by Protáp
Chandra Roy. 1884-94. v. 1-13......894 29
Indian idylls from, by Arnold. 1883......894 16
Last days of Krishna, from; Persian
version ....in 894 4
Story of; by Oman. 1894..................894 21
Story of Nala, from; ed. by Williams,
with tr. by Milman. 1860..................894 15
Manning. Ancient and mediæval India.
2v...934 6
Muir. Metrical tr. from Sanskrit. 1879....894 12
Müller. History of ancient Sanskrit literature. 1859...294 39
Sanskrit grammar. 1870.......................494 1
Oldenburg. Study of Sanskrit............in 410 14
Oman. Great Indian epics: Ramayana
and Mahabharata. 1894...................894 21
Percival. Tamil proverbs with English tr.
1875...894 13
Pilpay. See **Bidpaï.**
Raju. Tales of sixty mandarins................894 22
Repentance of Nussooh; tr. by Kempson.
1884...894 17
Shakespear, J. Grammar of Hindustani
and Dakhni. 1855.............................494 B-1
Small. Hand-book of Sanskrit literature.
1866...894 7
Stone. Cradle-land of arts, etc. 1880......954 60
Válmiki. The Rámáyan; tr. by Griffith.
1870. 5 v..894 23
Same. Iliad of the East; legends
from the Ramayana, by Richardson. 1870..894 8
Story of the Ramayana; by Oman. 1894....894 21
Vikram and the vampire; adapted by Burton. 1870..894 10
Weber. History of Indian literature. '78..894 11
Wheeler. History of India. v. 1-4..........954 55
White. Classic literature. 1877...............880 8
Wilson. Essays on Sanskrit literature.
1864. 3 v..894 1
Wilson, tr. Specimens of the theatre of
the Hindus. 1871. 2 v......................894 5

SACRED LITERATURE.—MYTHOLOGY.—
FOLK TALES.

(See Part 3 of FINDING LIST, pp. 513-514, 516-517, and 513-520.)

CHINESE LANGUAGE AND LITERATURE.

Chinese classics; tr. by Legge. 1875-7. 3 v.
  V. 1. Life and teachings of Confucius.........891 9
  V. 2. Life and works of Mencius............891 10
  V. 3. The She-king......................891 11
Chuang Tsze. Divine classic of Nan-Hua;
  ed. by Balfour. 1881........................891 18
Confucius. Confucian analects; tr. and ed.
  by Jennings. 1895.......................891 29
  The great teacher; by Alexander. '90...891 25
  Life and teachings; by Legge. 1875......891 9
  Proverbial philosophy; comp. by Jennings. 1895.........................891 30
Davis. Poetry of the Chinese. 1829......891 B-1
Douglas. Language and literature of
  China. 1875...............................491 3
Edkins. China's place in philology. 1871...491 1
Giles. *tr. and ed.* Gems of Chinese literature. 1884...............................891 19
Hearn. Some Chinese ghosts. 1887........891 24
Jade chaplet; tr. by Stent. 1874............891 8
Lacouperie. Languages of China before the
  Chinese. 1887............................491 6
  Oldest book of the Chinese, Yh-king.
  1892. v. 1..................................891 27
  On a Lolo manuscript. 1882.........491 Pam. 1
Lâo-tsze. The great thinker; with tr. of
  Thoughts on nature, etc., by Alexander. 1895...............................891 32
  Speculations. 1868.........................891 1
Martin. The Chinese, their letters, etc.....915.1 57
Mencius (Meng-tsze). Life and works;
  tr. by Legge. 1875........................891 10
  Mind of; ed. and tr. by Faber. 1882.....891 16
  Works, chapters 1-3, 6-8; ed. by Tchou-hi.
  2v..891 22
Neumann. Translations from Chinese and
  Armenian. 1831..........................891 2
Sacred edict: Maxims of Kang-he; tr. by
  Milne. 1817...............................891 4
Selby. The Chinaman in his own stories.
  1895..891 31
Strange stories from a Chinese studio; tr.
  by Giles. 1880. 2 v......................891 12
Summers. Rudiments of Chinese. 1864...491 5
Tai T'ung. Six scripts; tr. by Hopkins. '81. 491 4

Tcheng-ki-Tong. Le théatre de Chinois.
  1886..891 21
(See also, Sacred Literature and Folk Lore, in Part 3 of FINDING LIST, pp. 513-514, 516-520.)

JAPANESE LANGUAGE AND LITERATURE.

Bakin. Captive of love; tr. by Greey........891 20
Chamberlain. Classical poetry of Japanese. 1880................................891 15
  Simplified grammar of Japanese. 1886...491 2
Florenz. Japanese poems...................891 35
Genji Monogatari; tr. by Kenchio. '82...891 17
Japanese fairy tale series..................*891 26
  Contents: Momotaro.— The tongue-cut sparrow. — Battle of the monkey and the crab.— Hanasaka Jiji.— Kachi-Kachi mountain.— The mouse's wedding.— The old man and the devils.—Urashima.— The serpent with eight heads.—The Matsuyama mirror.— The hare of Inaba.— The cub's triumph.— The princes Fire-flash and Fire-fade.— My lord Bag-o'-rice.
Japanese lyrical odes; tr. by Dickins. 1866...891 5
Mitford. Tales of old Japan. 1871. 2v......891 6
Riordan *and* **Takayanagi.** Sunrise stories: a glance at the literature of Japan.
  1896..891 33
Shunsui. The loyal Ronins; tr. by Saito
  and Greey. 1880..........................891 14
Tsurayuki. Log of a Japanese journey.
  1891..891 28
(See also, Sacred Literature and Folk Lore, in Part 3 of FINDING LIST, pp. 513-514, 518-521.)

OTHER ASIATIC LANGUAGES.

Hodgson. Languages, literature, etc., of
  Nepal and Tibet. 1874..................294 B-2
Morris. Simplified grammar of Telegu.
  1890..499 24
Newbold. Laws, language and literature
  of the Malays. 1839................*in* 919.1 7
Ralston, *ed.* Tibetan tales. 1882..........294.1 5
Sakaa Thevan Saasteram: extracts, from
  the Tamul............................*in* 894 4
Vedala cadai; Tamul version of Vetâla
  panchavinsati.......................*in* 894 4
(See also, Sacred Literature and Folk Lore, in Part 3 of FINDING LIST, pp. 513-514, 518-521.)

GREEK LANGUAGE AND LITERATURE.

Blackie. Horæ Hellenicæ. 1874............880 17
Felton. Greece, ancient and modern. 1867.
  2v...880 4

Mure. Language and literature of ancient
  Greece. 1850. 3v........................880 20

* Of interest to young readers.

LANGUAGE AND LITERATURE.

LANGUAGE.

Alexander. Grammatical system of Grecian language. 1796............................485 1
Autenrieth. Homeric dictionary. 1891....483 2
Curtius. Grundzüge der griechischen Etymologie. 1858..................................482 1
Donaldson. Greek grammar. 1867..........485 5
Geldart. Simplified grammar of modern Greek. 1883..489 2
Hadley. Greek grammar. 1881...............485 17
Halsey. Etymology of Latin and Greek.....472 1
Harding. Greek inflection. 1886.............485 2
Henry. Short comparative grammar of Greek and Latin. 1890 ....485 19
Jelf. Grammar of Greek language. 2v......485 3
Jones. Exercises in Greek prose. 1882....485 18
Keep. Greek lessons. 1886.....................485 15
Kuehner. Elementary Greek grammar. 1857..485 10
Lamberton. Πρός, with the accusative: note on the Antigone..........................485 14
Liddell *and* Scott. Greek-English lexicon ....‡483 B-1
Madvig. Syntax of Greek language. 1873..485 6
Robinson. Greek-English lexicon of the New Testament....................................‡483 1
Sayce. On the language of Homer. 1880...880 25
Sophocles. Catalog of Greek verbs. 1844...485 9
Stedman. Modern Greek mastery. 1896..489 3
Winchell. Greek syntax. 1886...............485 16
Wordsworth, C. Greek primer. 1886.....485 7
Wylie, Samuel B. Introduction to knowledge of Greek grammar. 1838..........485 11

MYTHOLOGY.
(See Part 3 of FINDING LIST, p. 518.)

LITERATURE.

HISTORY AND CRITICISM.

Abbott, *ed.* Hellenica. 1880.....................880 23
  Contents: Æschylus; by Myers.—Theology and ethics of Sophocles; by Nettleship.—Aristotle's conception of the state; by Bradley.— Speeches of Thucydides; by Jebb.— Xenophon; by Dakyns. — Polybius; by Strachan-Davidson. — Greek oracles; by Myers.
Anthon. Classical dictionary................‡938 64
  Manual of Greek literature. 1871.........880 24
Browne. History of Greek literature. '52...880 6
Browning, *Mrs.* Greek Christian poets..826.2 40
Butcher. Some aspects of the Greek genius. 1891.......................................880 38
Campbell. Guide to Greek tragedy. 1891..882 50
Clinton. Fasti Hellenici. 3 v..................‡938 B-2

Darley. Grecian drama. 1840.................882 1
Dickinson. Greek view of life. 1896......880 42
Donaldson. Theatre of the Greeks. '75...882 21
Eschenburg. Manual of classical literature. 1867..880 7
Francklin. Dissertation on antient tragedy. 1809..*in* 882 5
Herder. Schriften zur griechischen Literatur. 1820..830 98
Jebb. Greek literature. 1878...................880 15
  Growth and influence of classical Greek poetry. 1893......................................881 13
Jevons. History of Greek literature.........880 33
Krumbacher. Geschichte der byzantinischen Litteratur. 1897............................880 44
Lawrence. Primer of Greek literature. '77..880 28
Louage. History of Greek and Roman literature. 1873.....................................880 9
Lytton, Bulwer-. Athens. 2 v................938 53
Mahaffy. History of Greek literature. 1880. 2v.
  V. 1. The poets......................................880 25
  V. 2. Prose writers..................................880 26
Mayor. Guide to classical books. 1879......16 72
  Same; supp., 1879-96............................16 72 A
Morris. Manual of classical literature. '80..880 27
Moulton. Ancient classical drama. 1890...882 57
Müller. Greek literature to Isocrates. '47..880 3½
Müller *and* Donaldson. History of Greek literature. 3v..880 1
Murray. History of ancient Greek literature. 1897..880 45
Packard. Studies in Greek thought. 1886..880 32
Pater. Greek studies. 1895.....................880 41
  Contents: A study of Dionysus: the spiritual form of fire and dew.—Bacchanals of Euripides.—The myth of Demeter and Persephone.—Hippolytus veiled. a study from Euripides.—The beginnings of Greek sculpture.— The marbles of Ægina.—The age of athletic prizemen: a chapter in Greek art.
Quackenbos. History of ancient literature 1878..880 16
Sears, *et al.* Classical studies. 1843.........880 10
Symonds. Studies of Greek poets. 1880. 2v..881 7
  Theatre of Greeks; list of works relating to (B. P. L. bulletin, v.4, p. 336).......17 B-14
Wilkinson. Classic Greek course in English. 1892...880 39
  College Greek course in English. 1884...880 31
  Preparatory Greek course in English. 1883..880 30
White. Classic literature. 1877...............880 8

COLLECTIONS.

Appleton, *ed.* Greek poets in English verse. 1893..881 12
Arnold. Poets of Greece. 1869...............881 5
Baldwin. Story of the golden age.........*883 66

* Of interest to young readers.   ‡ For reference.

Burt. Stories from Plato, etc. 1894........*880 40
  Contents :— Plato.— Hesiod.— Homer.— Aristophanes.— Ovid.— Catullus.— Pliny.
Church, A. J. Heroes and kings. 1883...*883 50
  Stories from Greek tragedians. 1880...*882 23
  Stories from Greek comedians. 1893...*882 60
Collectanea Græca majora; ed by Dalzel. 1831.....................880 36
Collectanea Græca minora; ed. by Dalzel. 1821.....................880 34
Elton, *tr.* Specimens of classic poets. 1814. 3v.....................881 1
Felton, *ed.* Selections from modern Greek writers. 1857................489 1
Greek anthology; tr. by Burges. 1852.......884 1
Greek folk-songs; tr. by Garnett. 1885......884 21
Jacobs, *ed.* Greek reader. 1829..............880 35
Jebb. Attic orators. 1876. 2v............885 10
Jennings *and* **Johnstone,** *eds.* Half-hours with Greek and Latin authors. 1882...880 29
McPherson, *tr.* Poetry of modern Greece, specimens. 1884.................881 11
Neaves. Greek anthology. 1874..........884 12
Oratores Attici; rec. G. S. Dobson. 1827. 16 v.
  V. 1. Antiphon et Andocides...............885 16
  V. 2. Lysias............................885 17
  V. 3. Isocrates.........................885 18
  V. 4. Isæus, Dinarchus, Lycurgus, Dimades, etc. . . 885 19
  V. 5-11. Demosthenes...................885 20
  V. 12. Æschines........................885 27
  V. 13. Interpretatio Latini: Antiphon, Andocides, et Lysias............................885 28
  V. 14. Same: Isocrates, Isæus, etc..........885 29
  V. 15-16. Same: Demosthenes et Æschines... .885 30
Peter, *ed.* Specimens of poetry. 1847......881 4
Ramage. Bible echoes in ancient classics. 220.0 88
Ramage, *ed.* Beautiful thoughts from Greek authors. 1864..................‡880 11
Selections from Greek anthology; ed. by Tomson...................884 23
Thompson, *ed.* Sales Attici. 1867........‡882 55
Tozer. Ballads, etc., of modern Greece..914.12 29
Warr, G. C. W. The Greek epic. 1895....883 77
Wright, R. S., *ed.* Golden treasury of ancient Greek poetry. 1889...........881 14
Wright *and* **Shadwell,** *eds.* Golden treasury of Greek prose. 1870..........880 43

INDIVIDUAL AUTHORS.

Achilles Tatius. Clitopho and Leucippe; tr. by R. Smith. 1855..................887 1
Æschines. Opera, Greek; Dobson. '27...885 27
  Opera, interpretatio Latina; Dobson. 1827.........................885 31
Æschylus [Greek text]; rec. Paley. '60....882 43
  Agamemnon; tr. by Browning.....*in* 821.2 1076
  Same.........................*in* 821.2 1061

Agamemnon; tr. by Carnarvon. 1879....882 22
For English readers; by Copleston. '79..882 18
House of Atreus; tr. by Morshead. '81...882 29
  Contents: Agamemnon.—Libation-bearers.—Furies.
Lyrical dramas; tr. by Blackie. '50. 2 v.
  V. 1. Genius and character of Greek tragedy.— Life of Æschylus.—Agamemnon.— Choephoræ.— The Eumenides..........................882 24
  V. 2. Prometheus bound.— The suppliants.— The seven against Thebes.—The Persians.......882 25
New readings in Hermann's posthumous edition; tr. by Burges. 1853............882 9
Oresteia; tr. by Campbell. 1893..........882 52
  Contents: Agamemnon—Choëphoræ.—Eumenides.
Tragedies; tr. by Buckley. 1849..........882 7
  Contents: Prometheus chained.— The seven against Thebes.—The Persians.—Agamemnon.—The Choephori. — The furies.—The suppliants.
Tragedies; tr. by Plumptre. 1890........882 46
  Contents: Life.—The Persians.—The seven who fought against Thebes.— Prometheus bound.— The suppliants.— Agamemnon.— Coëphori, or the libation-pourers.— Eumenides.— Fragments.— Appendix of rhymed choruses.
Tragedies; tr. by Potter. 1809..........882 5
  Contents: Prometheus chained.—Suppliants.—Seven chiefs against Thebes.— Agamemnon.— The Choephoræ. —Furies.— Persians.
Tragœdiæ; ed. by Paley. 1879..........882 33
Æschylus *and* **Sophocles.** Specimens of Greek tragedy; tr. by Goldwin Smith 1893.........................882 53
  Contents: Æschylus: Prometheus bound.—The Persians.—The seven against Thebes.—Agamemnon.— The Chœphori.— The Eumenides (furies).
  Sophocles: Œdipus the king.— Œdipus at Colonus.— Antigone. — Ajax.— Electra. — The Trachiniæ.— Philoctetes.

Æsop, *et al.* Fables, as printed by Caxton, 1484; ed. by Jacobs. 1889.
  V. 1. History of the Æsopic fable..........888 27
  V. 2. Text and glossary..................888 28
Æsop. Fables; child's version; by Stickney...........................*819 34
  Fables; tr. by James....................888 26
  Fables; with applications by Croxall. 1839............................888 24
  Fabulæ; ex rec. C. Halmii. 1884........888 25
  Three hundred fables; tr. by Townsend. *888 10
Anacreon. Odes; tr. by Moore. 1820. 2v..884 17
  [Works]; ed. by Bullen, with tr. by Stanley. 1893.........................884 24
  Works; tr. by Fawkes. 1822.............884 2
Andocides. [Opera, Greek]; Dobson.....885 16
  Opera, interpretatio Latina; Dobson. 1827............................885 28
Antiphon. [Opera, Greek]; Dobson. '27..885 16
  Opera, interpretatio Latina; Dobson. 1827............................885 28
Apollonius Rhodius. Argonautics; tr. by Preston. 1822....................883 33

---

* Of interest to young readers.   ‡ For reference.

LANGUAGE AND LITERATURE.

Aristænetus. Love epistles; tr. by Kelly.
1854...874 12
Same; tr. by Sheridan and Halhed.
1854.......................................*in* 874 12
Aristophanes. The Acharnians; tr. by
Billson. 1882.........................882 31
The birds; tr. by Hodges. 1896...........882 62
Clouds; ed. by Humphreys. 1885......882 34
Comedies; tr. by Hickie. 1869. 2v.
V. 1. Acharnians.—Knights.—Clouds.—Wasps.
—Peace.—Birds..................................882 15
V. 2. Lysistrata.— The Thesmophoriazusæ.—
Frogs.— Ecclesiazusæ.—Plutus................882 16
For English readers; by Collins. '75...882 20
Plutus; ed. by Quinn. 1896............882 61
Translations from; by Frere. 1874......882 26
Contents: The Acharnians.—The knights.—The birds.
—The frogs.— The peace.
Vespæ; tr. by Plaistowe. 1893..........882 51
Wasps; tr. by Rundall. 1896........;.......882 63
Aristotle. Ethics, Greek text; ed. by
Grant. 1874. 2 v............................171 39
For English readers; by Grant. 1877......185 5
Metaphysics; tr. by M'Mahon. 1857......185 1
Nicomachean ethics; tr. by Chase. '77...171 2
Opera; rec. Bekkeri. 1837. 11 v........888 12
Organon; tr. by Owen. 1853. 2 v........185 3
Politics; tr. by Jowett. 1885. 2 v........320 39
Politics; tr. by Walford. 1866............320 33
Rhetoric and poetic; tr. by Buckley.......185 2
Synopsis of the virtues and vices; tr. by
Bridgman. 1804..............................*in* 888 23
Athenæus. The Deipnosophists; tr. by
Yonge. 1854. 3 v.............................880 12
Babrius. Fables; tr. by Lewis and Davies.
1860...888 29
Bikelas. Loukis Laras; tr. by Gennadius...887 5
Tales from the Ægean........................887 7
Bion. Idyllia, etc.; tr. by Polwhele. 1822....884 9
Idyls; tr. by Banks and Chapman. '64....884 8
Works; tr. by Lang. 1880....................884 14
Callimachus. Works; tr. by Banks, et al.
1856..884 7
Demades. [Opera, Greek]; Dobson........885 19
Opera, interpretatio Latina; Dobson.
1827...885 29
Democrates. Golden sentences; tr. by
Bridgman. 1804..........................*in* 888 23
Demophilus. Pythagoric sentences; tr. by
Taylor. 1804.................................*in* 888 23
Similitudes; tr. by Bridgman. 1804....*in* 888 23
Demosthenes. For English readers; by
Brodribb. 1877..............................885 6
Olynthiacs, etc.; tr. by Kennedy. 1869....885 5
[Opera, Greek]; Dobson. 1827. 7 v......885 20
Opera, interpretatio Latina; Dobson.
1827. 2 v..885 30
Orations; tr. by Kennedy. 1855-63. 4 v...885 1

Orations; tr. by Leland. 1831. 2 v......885 8
Political eloquence; by Brédif. 1881......885 7
[Works]; with tr. by Whiston. 1859.
v.1-2..885 12
Dinarchus. [Opera, Greek]; Dobson. '27..885 19
Opera, interpretatio Latina; Dobson.
1827..885 29
Euripides. Bacchantes; ed. by Beckwith.
1885..882 35
For English readers; by Donne. 1875...882 17
Hecuba; ed. by Major. 1830...............882 40
In English verse; by Way. 1894..........882 54
Contents: Alcestis.—Hecuba.—Medea.
Iphigenia among the Taurians; ed. by
Flagg. 1889....................................882 44
Phœnissæ; ed. by Major. 1833...........882 41
The rationalist; Verrall. 1895............882 58
Tales from; by Cooper. 1879.............882 30
Three dramas; tr. with essays, by Lawton. 1889.....................................882 45
Contents: Attic tragedy.—Alkestis.—Medea.—Hippolytos.—Epilogue.
Tragedies; tr. by Buckley. 1867-8. 2v.
V. 1. Hecuba.—Orestes.—Phœnician virgins.—
Medea.— Hippolytus.— Alcestis.— The Bacchæ.—
The Heraclidæ.—Iphigenia in Aulis.—Iphigenia
in Tauris......................................882 11
V. 2. Hercules furens.— The Troades.— Ion.—
Andromache.—Suppliants.—Helen.—Electra.—Cyclops.— Rhesus............................882 12
Tragedies; tr. by Wodhull. 1809. 3v.
V. 1. Hecuba.—Orestes.—Phœnician damsels.
—Medea.— Hippolytus.— Alcestis.— Andromache.
—Iphigenia in Tauris........................882 2
V. 2. Suppliants.— Iphigenia in Aulis.— Rhesus.— Trojan captives.— Bacchanalians.—Cyclops.
—Children of Hercules.....................882 3
V. 3. Helen.— Ion.— Hercules distracted. —
Fragments.— Index..........................882 4
Gladstone. Landmarks of Homeric study.
1890..883 67
Heliodorus. Ethiopica; tr. by R. Smith.
1855..887 1
Herodotus. Ancient empires of the east:
books 1-3; ed. by Sayce....................930 62
Books 6-7; ed. by Merriam................930 66
Boys' and girls' Herodotus; ed. by
White..930 63
For English readers; ed. by Swayn.....930 25
[Greek] text; ed. by Schweighæuser and
Long. 2 v.......................................930 74
History; tr. by Beloe. 1819. 2 v.........930 1
History; tr. by Rawlinson. 1860. 4 v...930 3
Stories from; by Church. 1881..........930 64
Stories from [in the Greek]; ed. by
Keep..930 65
Story of the Persian war; Church.......935 21
Terpsichore, Erato; ed. by Abbott......938 180
Hesiod. For English readers; by Davies.
1873..884 11

Works; tr. by Banks, et al. 1856..........884 7
[Works]; tr. by Elton. 1894............884 26
Works and days; tr. by Chapman. '58..*in* 884 6
Homer. Adventures of Ulysses; by C.
  Lamb...824.2 311
  Same...824.2 316
  Same.. ....820.2 490
  And his translators; by Prof. Wilson.. 824.2 299
  And the epic; by Lang. 1893..............883 75
  And the Homeric age; by Gladstone.
  1858. 3v...883 1
  And the Iliad; by Blackie. 1866. 4 v.
    V. 1. Homeric dissertations................883 41
    V. 2 and 3. Iliad in English verse..........883 42
    V. 4. Notes, philological and archæological...883 44
  Art and humanity in; by Lawton. '96...883 78
  Batrachomyomachia, hymns and epigrams; tr. by Chapman. 1858............884 6
  Burlesque translation. 1797. 2 v..........883 34
  Concordance to Odyssey, etc.; by
    Dunbar. 1880..................................883 B-1
  Familiar studies in; by Clerke. 1892....883 73
  Homer; by Gladstone. (Literary primer.)
    1878..883 37
  Homeric ballads; tr. by Maginn. '56....884 10
  Homeric synchronism; by Gladstone.
    1876..881 6
  Iliad; ed. by Leaf. 1886-8. 2 v...........883 58
  Same; books 1-9, 18, 22; rec. Heyne.
    1822..883 68
  Same; books 16-24; ed. by Tyler. '86..883 69
  Same; Flaxman's illustrations..........749 R-1
  Same; Græce et Latine; rec. Clarke.
    1832. 2 v..883 4
  Same; éd. par Planche. 1825.............883 76
  Same; tr. by Barter. 1854..................883 13
  Same; tr. by Bryant. 1870. 2 v..........883 23
  Same; tr. by Buckley. 1854...............883 14
  Same; tr. by Caldcleugh. 1870..........883 20
  Same; tr. by Chapman. 1865. 2 v......883 6
  Same; tr. by Collins. 1870.................883 31
  Same; tr. by Cordery. 1871. 2 v........883 21
  Same; tr. by Cowper. 1809...............883 36
  Same..821.2 204
  Same; tr. by Earl of Derby. '65. 2 v.. 883 28
  Same; tr. by Herschel. 1866..............883 12
  Same; tr. by Hobbes..........................192 32
  Same; tr. by Lang, Leaf, and Myers.
    1883..883 49
  Same; tr. by Newman. 1856.............883 48
  Same; tr. by Pope. 1891...................883 72
  Same; tr. by Simcox. 1865...............883 18
  Same; tr. by Way. 1885...................883 53
  Same; tr. by Worsley. 1865. 2 v......883 16
  Same; book 1, tr. by Dryden............821.2 702
  Iliad; companion to; by Leaf. 1892..883 74
  Same; stories of, and of Æneid; by
    Church. 1885.................................*883 65

Same; story of; by Church..............883 70
Ilios; by Schliemann....................915.6 146
Introduction to Iliad and Odyssey; by
  Jebb. 1887.......................................883 62
Introduction to language and verse of;
  by Seymour. 1885..........................883 55
Minor poems; tr. by Parnell et al. '72....884 5
Odyssey; ed. by Merry and Riddell.
  1876. v.1. Books 1-12....................883 45
Same; books 1-12; with tr. by Palmer.
  1886..883 52
Same; Flaxman's illustrations.........749 R-1
Same; for English readers; by Collins.
  1870..883 32
Same; tr. by Bryant. 1871-2. 2v......883 25
Same; tr. by Buckley. 1867.............883 19
Same; tr. by Butcher and Lang. '79...883 39
Same; tr. by Chapman. 1857. 2v......883 8
Same; tr. by Cowper. 1809.............883 30
Same..821.2 205
Same; tr. by Hobbes.......................192 32
Same; tr. by Morris. 1887. 2v........883 63
Same; tr. by Pope. 1822.................883 11
Same; tr. by Pope; ed. by Cary. '91...883 72
Same; tr. by Worsley. 1877. 2v......883 56
Same; story of; by Church. 1891....*883 71
On the track of Ulysses; by Stillman.
  1888..883 B-2
On translating; by Arnold. 1861.......883 47
Opera et reliquiæ; rec. Monro. 1896......883 60
Origin of Homeric poems; by Bonitz.
  1880..883 40
Siege of Troy and the wanderings of
  Ulysses; by Hanson. 1883............883 51
Stories from Homer; by Church. 1878...883 38
Tale of Troy; tr. by Stewart. 1886....883 61
Truth about Homer; by Paley. '87..883 Pam.1
Wanderings of Ulysses; by Witt; tr. by
  Younghusband. 1885.....................883 54
Iamblicus. Pythagoric symbols; tr. by
  Bridgman. 1804............................*in* 888 23
Isæus. [Opera, Greek]; Dobson. 1827...885 19
Opera; interpretatio Latina; Dobson.
  1827..885 29
Speeches; tr. by Jones......................404 19
Isocrates. [Opera, Greek]; Dobson.
  1827..885 18
Opera; interpretatio Latina; Dobson.
  1827..885 29
Orations; tr. by Freese. 1894. v. 1....885 33
Longus. Dafni e Cloe; tr. in Italiani dal
  A. Caro...850 26
Daphnis and Chloe; tr. by R. Smith.
  1855..887 1
Lucanus. La Pharsale; tr. par Marmontel.
  1807. 2 v.......................................840 316
Lucian. Comedies; tr. by Maginn. '56...*in* 884 10

* Of interest to young readers.

Dialogues; tr. by Williams. 1888.........882 42
For English readers; by Collins. 1874...887 6
Six dialogues; tr. by Irwin. 1894..........887 8
  Contents: Icaromenippus.—The dream.—The ship. -
  The parasite.— The lover of falsehood.— Nigrinus.
Somnium; et Piscater; tr. by Armour.
  ....887 Pam. 1
Traveller's true tale; tr. by Church. '80..887 3
Lycurgus. [Opera, Greek]; Dobson. '27...885 19
Opera, interpretatio Latina; Dobson.
  1827..885 29
Lysias. [Opera, Greek]; Dobson. 1827...885 17
Opera, interpretatio Latina; Dobson.
  1827..885 28
Select orations; ed. by Whiton. '76......885 32
Moschus. Idyllia; tr. by Polwhele. '22...884 9
Idyls; tr. by Banks and Chapman. '64...884 8
Works; tr. by Lang. 1880..................884 14
Munk. Student's manual of Greek tragedy;
  ed. by Verrall. 1891.....................882 48
Musæus. Hero and Leander; tr. by Chapman. 1858...........................*in* 884 6
Works; tr. by Fawkes. 1822.............884 2
Orpheus. Mystical hymns; tr. by Taylor.
  1896..884 27
Paley, *tr.* Greek wit. 1881...................887 4
Phalaris, *et al.* Epistles; tr. by Francklin.
  1849..886 1
On the Epistles of; by Bentley. '36 2v...880 18
Philo Judæus. Works; tr by Yonge. 1854.
  4v..888 6
Pindar. Epinician or triumphal odes; ed.
  by Donaldson. 1868......................884 25
For English readers; by Morice. 1879...884 13
Odes; tr. by Myers. 1874....................884 4
Odes; tr. by Turner. 1868....................884 3
Odes; tr. by West, Green, and Pye. '22...884 2
Olympian and Pythian odes; ed. by Gildersleeve. 1885.................................884 19
Sicilian odes; tr. by Lloyd. 1872.........945 114
Plato. And other companions of Socrates;
  by Grote. 1867. 3v........................184 1
And the older academy; by Zeller. '76...184 16
Apology of Socrates and Crito; ed. by
  Dyer. 1885.......................................184 18
Day in Athens with Socrates. 1883......184 17
Dialogi Latine; rec. Bekker. 1826. 2v...184 28
Dialogues; tr. by Jowett. 1871. 4v......184 4
For English readers; by Collins. 1879...184 15
Scripta Græce omnia; Bekker. 9v........184 19
Talks with Athenian youths. 1891.......184 31
Talks with Socrates about life. 1886.....183 3
Trial and death of Socrates; tr. by
  Church...184 30
Works; tr. by Cary, et al. 1861. 6 v.....184 8
Plotinus. Select works; tr. by Taylor......186 2
Plutarch. For boys and girls; ed. by
  White...*920.6 13

Lives; Dryden's tr.; ed. by Clough.
  5 v...*920.6 1
Morals; tr. ed. by Goodwin. '71. 5 v......888 1
Old world worthies [selections]........*920.6 6
Our young folks' Plutarch; ed. by Kaufman. 1883....................................*920.6 12
Proclus. Fragments; tr. by Taylor. '25.....186 4
Pythagoras. Golden verses; tr. by Talbot. 1881..188 5
Sappho. Memoir, text, with tr. by Wharton. 1885...884 20
Works; tr. by Fawkes. 1822..................884 2
Sophocles. Ajax and Electra; tr. by
  Morshead. 1895............................882 59
Antigone; ed. by Humphreys. 1891....882 49
For English readers; by Collins. 1875...882 19
Œdipus Coloneus; ed. by Brasse. '29...882 39
Œdipus tyrannus; ed. by Stuart. 1837...882 37
Plays; tr. by Whitelaw. 1883...............882 32
  Contents: Œdipus the king.— Œdipus at Colonus.
  Antigone.— Electra.— Trachiniæ. — Ajax. — Philoctetes
Plays and fragments; ed. by Campbell.
  1879-81. 2 v.
  V. 1. Œdipus tyrannus.— Œdipus Coloneus.—
  Antigone..882 27
  V. 2. Ajax.—Electra.—Trachiniæ.—Philoctetes.
  —Fragments..882 28
Reference list, by Foster. v. 1.............16 55
Trachiniæ; ed. by Brasse. 1829............882 38
Tragedies; Oxford trans. 1870............882 10
  Contents: Œdipus tyrannus.— Œdipus Coloneus.—
  Electra.—Antigone.—Trachiniæ.—Ajax.—Philoctetes.
Tragedies; tr. by Coleridge. 1893........882 56
Tragedies; tr. by Francklin. 1809.........882 6
  Contents: Ajax.— Electra.— Philoctetes.—Antigone.—
  Trachiniæ.—Œdipus tyrannus.—Œdipus Coloneus.
Tragedies; tr. by Plumptre. 1890.........882 47
  Contents: Greek proper names.—Chronological table.—
  Life of Sophocles.— Œdipus the king.— Œdipus at Colonos.—Antigone.— Electra.— The maidens of Trachis.—
  Aias.— Philoctetes.— Fragments.— Appendix of rhymed
  choruses, etc.
  (See also, **Æschylus** *and* **Sophocles.**)
Theocritus. [Greek text]; rec. Wordsworth. 1877.......................................884 22
Idyllia, etc.; tr. by Polwhele. 1822........884 9
Idyls; tr. by Banks and Chapman. 1864...884 8
Selecta idyllia; rec. Edwards. 1779......884 15
Works; tr. by Calverly. 1883...............884 16
Works; tr. by Lang. 1880....................884 14
Theognis. For English readers; by
  Davies...882 11
Works; tr. by Banks, et al. 1856..........884 7
Works; tr. by Frere. 1874.....................882 26
Theophrastus. Characters; tr. by Jebb.
  1870..887 2
Thucydides. Peloponnesian war; tr. by
  Jowett. 2 v.......................................938 101
Tyrtæus. Elegies; tr. by Polwhele. '22...*in* 884 9
War-songs; tr. by Banks and Chapman.
  1864..*in* 884 8

* Of interest to young readers.

Xenophon. Anabasis; ed. by Crosby......935 17
 Cyropædia; tr. by Watson..............935 19
 Economist; tr. by Wedderburn and Collingwood. 1876....................888 11
 Expedition of Cyrus; tr. by Watson......935 18

For English readers; by Grant............935 20
History; tr. by Smith....................938 1
Memorabilia of Socrates................921.6 4
Minor works; tr. by Watson. 1857......183 2

LATIN LANGUAGE AND LITERATURE.

LANGUAGE.

Chase. Latin grammar. 1882...............475 8
Diez. Introduction to grammar of Romance languages. 1863....................475 1
Donaldson. Latin grammar. 1867......475 3
 Varronianus. 1860.....................470 1
Egbert. Introduction to the study of Latin inscriptions. 1896...................478 4
Ellis. Quantitative pronunciation. 1874.....471 2
Ferguson. Questions on Cæsar, etc. '85...475 2
Fisher. The three pronunciations. 1879....471 1
Freund. Latin-English lexicon; rev. by Andrews................................‡473 B-1
 Same; rev. by Lewis and Short. 1879.
 ....‡473 B-2
Gates. Latin word-building. 1887..........472 5
Gibson. Limen Latinum.....................475 7
Hale. Art of reading Latin. 1887....475 Pam. 1
 Sequence of tenses. 1887.......475 Pam. 2
Hall. Roots and derivations. 1861........472 2
Halsey. Etymology of Latin and Greek....472 1
Key. Latin grammar. 1871.................475 6
Leighton. Latin lessons. 1875.............475 9
Lindsay. Latin language. 1894............470 3
Lord. Roman pronunciation of Latin. 1894...471 3
Pennell. The Latin subjunctive. '81....475 Pam. 3
Roby. Grammar of Latin language. '71. 2v..475 4
Sargent, ed. Passages for tr. into Latin. '58..470 2
White, J. T. English-Latin dictionary. '69..‡473 1

MYTHOLOGY.

(See Part 3 of FINDING LIST, p. 518.)

LITERATURE.

HISTORY AND CRITICISM.

Boissier. Country of Horace and Virgil. 1896... 873 27

Cruttwell. Roman literature to death of Marcus Aurelius. 1878................. 870 4
Dunlop. Roman literature to the Augustan age. 1827. 2 v..........................870 1
Herder. Schriften zur römischen Literatur. 1820................................830 99
Hübner. Bibliographical clue to Latin literature. 1875............................870 20
Jennings and **Johnstone,** eds. Half-hours with Greek and Latin authors. 1882. 880 29
Lawrence. Primer of Latin literature........870 7
Louage. History of Greek and Roman literature. 1873..........................880 9
Mackail. Latin literature. 1895.............870 23
Middleton and **Mills.** Student's companion to Latin authors. 1896............870 24
Morris. Manual of classical literature. 1880...880 27
Nettleship. Latin literature. 1885-95.
 Series 1-2....................................870 17
Peter, ed. Specimens of poetry. 1847......881 4
Quackenbos. History of ancient literature..880 16
Ramage. Bible echoes in ancient classics..220.0 88
Sellar. Poets, Augustan age: Virgil. 1877......................................871 2
 Same: Horace and elegiac poets. '92....871 3
 Poets of the republic. 1881.................871 1
Simcox. History of Latin literature. 1883.
 2 v...870 12
Sinclair. Humanities. 1886................870 21
 Contents: A Latin tractate,— Origin of Roman race.—Latin verses and Latin pronunciation. Growth of languages.— Humanism.— Letters to England.
Spence. Polymetis. 1774.................‡871 S-1
Teuffel. History of Roman literature. 1873.
 2 v...870 14
Thompson, ed. History of Roman literature. 1882....................................870 3
Tyrrell. Latin poetry. 1895................871 4
White, C. A. Classic literature. 1877......880 8
Wilkins. Roman literature. 1890..........870 22
Wilkinson. College Latin course in English...870 25
 Preparatory Latin course in English. '83..870 16

‡ For reference.

COLLECTIONS.

Allen, *ed.* Remnants of early Latin. '80.....478 3
Cruttwell *and* **Banton,** *eds.* Specimens of
   Roman literature. 1879................870 6
Gardner, *ed.* Selections from Latin authors..870 19
Ramage, *ed.* Beautiful thoughts from
   Latin authors. 1869..................‡870 5
Scriptores rei rusticæ veteres Latini; re-
   censione J. Gesneri. 1788. 4 v. in 3.
    V. 1-2. Cato.— Varro.— Columella.........630 53
    V. 3. Palladius.— Vegetius. Gargilii Martialis
    fragmentum.— Aiison Popmae. 630 54
    V. 4. Lexicon rusticum..................630 55
Symonds, *tr.* Wine, women and song. '84..874 19
Trench, *ed.* Sacred Latin poetry. 1864....874 13
Wright, *ed.* Selection of Latin stories...821.2 451

INDIVIDUAL AUTHORS.

Apuleius. Dell' asino d'oro; tr. da Ag-
   nolo Firenzuola........................850 17
   Eros and Psyche; tr. by Bridges. '85..874 39
   Metamorphosis; tr. by Taylor. 1822..870 11B
   Works; tr. 1878.......................870 11
Aurelius Antoninus, Marcus. See Part 3 of
   FINDING LIST, p. 433.
Cæsar. Commentaries, for English readers;
   by Trollope. 1870....................937 172
   Commentaries; tr.....................937 170
   Commentarii de bello Gallico: scenes
   from books 5-6; ed. by Colbeck. '81..937 175
   Same (complete); ed. by Long. '77..937 169
   Same (books 1-7); ed. by Allen and
    Greenough. 1885....................937 170
   Same (books 2-3); ed. by Rutherford.
    1879...............................937 174
   Same (books 1-4); ed. by White. '79.937 173
Catullus. Carmina; rec. Postgate. '89....874 36
   For English readers; by Davies. '77....874 16
   Poems, etc.; tr. by Ellis. 1871........874 32
   Poems; tr. by Kelly. 1854.............874 6
   Select poems; ed. by Simpson. 1879..874 25
Cicero. Academic questions, de finibus,
   etc.; tr. by Yonge. 1853..............878 1
   Academica; ed. by Reid. 1874..........878 9
   Brutus de claris oratoribus; ed. by Kel-
    logg. 1889..........................875 24
   Correspondence; ed. by Tyrrell and
    Purser. 1894. 4v....................876 10
   De officiis; ed. by Stickney. 1885.....878 8
   De oratore; corr. P. Manutio (Aldine)....23 2
   Same (book 1); ed. by Moor. 1892....875 3A
   De senectute, etc.; ed. by Anthon. '48..878 10
    Contents: De senectute—De amicitia—Paradoxa—Som-
    nium Scipionis.
   Death no bane; tr. by Black. 1889....878 3
   For English readers; by Collins. 1875..875 8
   Letters to Quintus and Brutus; tr. by
    Watson. 1862....................*in* 875 3

Life [by Middleton] and letters; tr. by
   Melmoth and Heberden. 1892.........876 8
Offices, etc.; tr. by Edmonds. 1853....878 4
   Contents: Offices.— On friendship.— On old age.—
   Paradoxes.— Scipio's dream.— Letter to Quintus.
Opera omnia; rec. Ernesti. 1774. 8 v...875 9
Orationes; ed. by Long. 1862. 4 v.....875 17
Orationes; De senectute, etc.; edidit
   Merouille. 1814......................875 25
Orations; tr. by Yonge. 1851. 4v.....875 4
Oratory and orators; tr. by Watson. '62..875 3
Pro Cluentio; ed. by Ramsay. 1869....875 23
Second Philippic; ed. by Hahn and
   Mayor. 1867........................875 22
Selected letters; ed. by Prichard and
   Bernard. 1872.......................876 4
Speech in defence of Cluentius; tr. by
   Peterson. 1895......................875 29
Speeches: Catiline, Antony, Murena,
   Milo; tr. by Blakiston. 1894..........875 27
Treatises; tr. by Yonge. 1868.........878 2
   Contents: On the nature of the gods.—On divination.—
   On fate.—On the republic.—On the laws.—On standing
   for the consulship.
Tusculan disputations; tr. by Yonge.
   1853............................*in* 878 1
Claudian. Works; tr. by Hawkins. 1817..874 5
Epictetus. See Part 3 of FINDING LIST, p. 434.
Gellius. Attic nights; tr. by Beloe. 1795.
   3 v..................................870 8
Horace. Ars poetica, et Epistola ad
   Augustum; ed. by Hurd. '57. 2 v....874 3
   Ars poetica; verse tr. by Sibley.....874 Pam. 1
   Carminum, liber 1; ed. by Page. 1879..874 22
   Echoes from the Sabine farm; tr. by E.
    and R. M. Field. 1895..............874 41
   For English readers; by Martin. 1871..874 14
   Odes; tr. by Gladstone. 1894.........874 40
   Odes; tr. by Harrison. 1877..........874 28
   Odes and Carmen sæculare; tr. by Con-
    ington. 1874.......................874 23
   Odes and epodes, with metrical tr. by
    Lytton. 1870.......................874 2
   Opera; ed. by Desprez...............874 33
   Opera omnia; ed. by Macleane. 1881..874 21
   Satires, Epistles, and Art of poetry; tr.
    by Conington. 1872.................874 24
   Studies in odes of; by Verrall. 1884..874 20
   Works; ed. by Anthon. 1840.........874 31
   Works; tr. by Martin. 1881. 2 v.....874 17
   Works; tr. by Smart. 1858............874 1
   Works; tr. literally by Smart. 1856...874 38
Johannes Secundus. Kisses; tr. by
   Kelly. 1854..........................874 12
Julian. Select works; tr. by Duncombe.
   1784. 2 v...........................876 6
Justinus. Selections; ed. by Gardner.
   1872...........................*in* 870 19

‡For reference.

Juvenal. Fifth satire ; tr. by Chapman.......884 6
For English readers ; by Walford. '78....877 6
Satiræ 16 ; ed. by Prior. 1876...............874 29
Satiræ 16 ; rec. Ruperti. 1825. 2 v........877 1
Satires ; tr. by Dryden et al. 1822.........877 4
Same. 1754....................................877 5
Satires ; tr. by Evans and Gifford. 1867...877 3
Libanius. Selections ; tr. by Duncombe. 1784................................in 876 7
Livy. For English readers ; by Collins. 1876.............................937 168
Historiarum libri et fragmenta ; Kressig, Twiss. 1840. 4 v....................937 180
History of Rome (books 20-30) ; tr. 1828. 2 v............................937 206
Same (books 21-25) ; tr. by Church and Brodribb. 1883.................937 167
Same ; tr. by Baker. 1822. 6v......937 256
Same ; tr. by Spillan, Edmonds, and Devitte. 1849-56. 4 v............937 208
Stories from ; by Church. 1883......937 150
Lucan. First book; tr. by Marlowe......822.2 263
La Pharsale ; tr. par Marmontel..........840 316
Pharsalia ; tr. by Riley. 1853............873 4
Same ; tr. by Rowe. 1822................873 5
Lucilius. Satires ; tr. by Evans. 1867......877 3
Lucretius. De rerum natura (Oxford pocket classics)...........................187 4
Same ; tr. by Munro. 1873..............187 5
For English readers; by Mallock. 1878...187 2
On the nature of things ; tr. by Watson and Good. 1867.......................187 1
Translations from ; by Dryden.........821.2 702
Marcus Aurelius. See Part 3 of FINDING LIST, p. 433.
Martial. Epigrams ; tr. 1865.................874 7
Nepos. Selections ; ed. by Gardner. '72..in 870 19
Ovid. Elegies ; tr. by Marlowe............822.2 263
Fasti ; ed. by Hallam. 1891...............874 37
Fasti, Pontic epistles, etc.; tr. by Riley. 1851..874 11
Fastorum (book 6); ed. by Paley.......874 27
For English readers ; by Church. 1876..874 15
Heroides, amours, etc.; tr. by Riley. '69..874 10
Metamorphoseon delectus ; rec. Merkelii. 1863..................................874 35
Metamorphoses ; tr. by Garth et al. 1822...874 9
Same ; tr. by Riley. 1869................874 8
Same ; tr. by Sandys. 1640............874 B-1
Selections for schools ; ed. by Ramsay. 1868..874 26
Selections from ; by Hanson and Rolfe...478 1
Translations from ; by Dryden.........821.2 702
Persius. Satiræ 6 ; rec. Kœnig. 1825.....in 877 2
Satires ; ed. by Hart. 1875.................874 30
Same ; tr. by Dryden et al. 1754........877 5

Same ; tr. by Evans and Gifford. 1867..877 3
Same ; with tr. by Conington. 1893....877 7
Petronius Arbiter. Satyricon; ed. by Kelly. 1854...874 12
Phædrus. Fables ; tr. by Smart. 1853...in 872 10
Selections ; ed. by Gardner. 1872...in 870 19
Plautus. Comedies ; tr. by Riley. '67. 2 v..872 6
For English readers ; by Collins. 1873...872 11
Pliny, *the elder.* Chapters on the history of art ; tr. by Jex-Blake. 1896.........709 54
Pliny, *the younger.* Epistolæ ad Traianum, cum responsis ; ed. by Hardy. 1889...876 9
Letters, for English readers ; by Church and Brodribb. 1879...................876 3
Letters ; tr. by Melmoth. 1877. 2v......876 1
Selected letters ; ed. by Prichard and Bernard. 1872..............................876 5
Polybius. See FINDING LIST of History, under **Rome.**
Propertius. Elegies ; ed. by Kelly. 1854...874 12
For English readers; by Davies. 1877...874 16
Quintilian. Institutes of oratory ; tr. by Watson. 1856. 2 v.........................875 1
Institutionis oratoriæ ; rec. Bonnel.......875 21
Sallust. Florus, Paterculus; tr.by Watson...937 175
Seneca. Épitres ; tr. par Malherbe. '62...840 386
Medea and Octavia, tragedies ; tr. by Wheelwright................................821.2 746
Minor dialogues ; tr. by Stewart. 1889...878 13
Morals : prose selections ; ed. by Clode. 1888..878 12
On benefits ; tr. by Stewart. 1887........878 11
Traité des bienfaits ; tr. par Malherbe. 1862..840 386
Sulpicia. Satires ; tr. by Evans. 1867......877 3
Tacitus. Dialogus de oratoribus ; ed. by Gudeman. 1894..............................875 28
Same ; ed. by Peterson. 1893............875 26
(See also, historical works in FINDING LIST of History, under **Rome.**)
Terence. [Comedies, Latin and French.] 1770..872 8
Contents : Hecyra Phormio.
Comedies ; tr. by Riley. 1853,..............872 10
Contents : Andria.—Eunuchus (The eunuch). - Heautontimorumenos (Self-tormentor).—Adelphi (The brothers).— Hecyra (The mother-in-law).— Phormio (The scheming parasite).
Comedies ; tr. by Riley and Colman. '59..872 9
Comœdiæ ; with commentary by Parry...872 13
For English readers ; by Collins. 1873...872 11
Phormio, with tr. by Morgan. 1894......872 14
Pincerna ; ed. by Newman. 1883.........872 12
Tibullus. For English readers; by Davies. 1877..874 16
Poems ; tr. by Kelly. 1854..................874 6
Virgil. Æneid ; tr. by Conington. 1881....873 3
Same ; tr. by Cranch. 1886...............873 7

Same; tr. by Dryden. 1872..............873 2
Same; tr. by Long. 1879................873 10
Same; tr. by Morris. 1876..............873 6
Same; (book 5); ed. by Calvert. '79.....873 21
Same (book 1); tr. by Sandys. 1640.
....in 874 B-1
Same (books 1-4); ed. by White. 1879.
4 v.......................................873 17
Same; Story of; by Church. '85...in *883 65
Ancient lives, with essay; by Nettleship.
1879......................................873 25
Bucolica, Georgica, et Æneis; ed. by
Gould. 1829............................873 22
Eclogues and Æneid (books 1-6); verse
tr. by Bowen. 1887....................873 23
For English readers; by Collins. 1875..873 8

(In 'Classical writers'); by Nettleship..873 11
Opera; with notes, etc. by Cooper. '53..873 24
Selections from; by Hanson and Rolfe...478 1
Stories from; by Church..................873 9
Wanderings of Æneas; by Hanson. '84...873 16
Works; ed. by Conington and Nettleship. 1881-4. 3 v.
 V. 1. Eclogues and Georgics............873 13
 V. 2-3. Æneid............................873 14
Works; literally tr. by Bryce. 1894.....873 26
Works; prose tr. by Conington, ed. by
Symonds. 1880..........................873 12
Works; tr. by Dryden. 3 v.
 V. 1 Pastorals..........................821.2 703
 V. 2. Georgics.—Æneis, books 1-7.......821.2 704
 V. 3. Æneis, books 8-12................821.2 705

MEDIÆVAL EUROPEAN LITERATURE.

Ars moriendi. Caxton print, photo-lithograph; ed. by Nicholson..................23 4
Berington. Literary history of the middle ages...809 3
Gesta Romanorum; tr. by Swan. 1824. 2 v..813 4
Guizot. History of civilization. v. 2.....940 14
Hallam. Middle ages. v. 3...............940 110
Lacroix. Science and literature, middle ages. 1878....................................509 B-1
Lawrence. Primer of mediæval literature. 1877.....................................810 19
Maitland. The dark ages. 1853..........274 21
Paris. La poésie du moyen age. 1885-95.
2 v..841 47
Reineke fuchs; von Goethe. 1830........830 50
Same; tr. by Arnold. 1855...............831 50
Reinhart fuchs; von Grimm. 1834........831 36
Reynard the fox; from Caxton; ed. by
Arber..................................293.1 Pam. 4
Same; from Caxton, with history by
Thoms. 1844..........................821.2 455
Same; ed. by Jacobs. 1895............293.1 64
Same; from the Low German original.
1865.....................................831 11
Rowbotham. Troubadours and courts of love. 1895..............................811 99
Symonds. Latin students' songs, middle ages. 1884..............................874 19
Wright. Essays. 1861. 2 v.............571 11

MYTHOLOGY.—FOLK TALES.
(See Part 3 of FINDING LIST, pp. 519-520.)

EPICS AND ROMANCES.
(Prose and Metrical.)

Ashton. Romances of chivalry (in facsimile).
1887....................................813 30
Church. Stories of the magicians. 1887..*813 29
Cox *and* **Jones.** Popular romances of the
middle ages. 1880....................813 10
Dichtungen des deutschen Mittelalters.
8 v. 1843.
 V. 1. Der Nibelunge Nöt, und Diu Klage.....831 80
 V. 2. Tristan und Isolt. Von Gottfried von
 Strassburg; herausgegeben von Massmann.....831 81
 V. 3. Barlaam und Josaphat. Von Rudolf von
 Ems; herausgegeben von F. Pfeiffer..........831 82
 V. 4. Der Edelstein. Von Ulrich Boner; herausgegeben von Franz Pfeiffer...................831 83
 V. 5. Gudrun; herausgegeben von A. J. Vollmer
 und Albert Schott............................831 84
 V. 6. Wigalois; eine Erzählung. Von Wirnt
 von Gravenberg; herausgegeben von F. Pfeiffer..831 85
 V. 7. Mai und Beaflor; eine Erzählung aus
 dem 13ten Jahrhundert.........................831 86
 Vol. 8. Eneit Heinrich von Veldeke; herausgegeben von Ludwig Ettmüller.................831 87
Dippold. Great epics of mediæval Germany. 1882..............................831 46
Frost. Wagner story book. 1894........*813 16
Ker. Epic and romance. 1897...........811 119
Klee. Deutschen Heldensagen; ed. by
Wolstenholme. 1894..................813 44
Ludlow. Popular epics of the middle ages.
1865. 2 v.............................811 12
Pratt. Stories from old Germany. 1895..*813 54
Saintsbury. Flourishing of romance and
rise of allegory. 1897.................809 22
Simrock, *ed.* Rheinsagen. 1891.........831 103

* Of interest to young readers.

Vance, *tr.* Romantic episodes of chivalric and mediæval France. 1868..................849 5
Wägner *and* **Macdowall.** Epics and romances of the middle ages. 1883.....813 23
Ward. Catalog of romances in British museum, dept. of manuscripts. 1883. 2 v..16 B-11

THE ARTHUR CYCLE.

Alliterative romance of Joseph of Arimathie, or the Holy Grail...............820.2 324
Arthur. Life in early English verse......820.2 302
Bergman. The San Grael; an inquiry.....813 25
Borron. History of the Holy Grail; Englisht (1450) part 1...........................820.2 414
 Same; part 2............................820.2 418
 Same; part 3............................820.2 421
 Same; part 4............................820.2 423
Bulfinch. Age of chivalry....................*813 15
Eschenbach. Parcifal. 1836....................831 89
 Parzifal; tr. by Weston. 1894............831 110
Foster. Reference list, v. 2........................‡16 55
Frost. The court of King Arthur. 1896...813 59
Geoffrey *of Monmouth.* British history; tr. 1842..942.1 1
Glennie. Arthurian localities. 1869.........813 57
Gloekle. Lohengrin; herausgegeben von Görres. 1813..831 76
Gurteen. The Arthurian epic. 1895........813 50
Hanson. Stories of the days of King Arthur. 1882......................................*813 18
Heintz. Parsifal; by Wagner. 1892.........782 24
 Tristran and Isolde; by Wagner. 1892...782 25
Jackson. Legend, poem, etc., of Wagner's Lohengrin. 1881................................782 B-1
Knowles, *ed.* Legends of King Arthur. 1895...813 52
Kufferath. The Parsifal of Wagner. '92...782 23
Lancelot of the Laik.........................820.2 303
Lanier, *ed.* Boy's King Arthur. 1880.....*813 11
 Boy's Mabinogion. 1881..................,...*896 15
Layamon's Brut; ed. and tr. by Madden. 1847. 3 v.......................................821.2 B-4
Lytton. King Arthur. (Poem.) 1849. 2 v. 821.2 779
Mabinogion, *tr.* by Lady Guest. 1877...896 B-3
Maccallum. Tennyson's Idylls of the king and Arthurian story. 1894...............813 42
Malory. King Arthur (Caxton ed., 1485); introduction by Rhys. 1893. 2 v......813 45
 La mort d'Arthure; ed. by Wright. '66. 3 v...813 6
 Selections from Le morte d'Arthur; ed. by Martin. 1896.......................................813 9
Merlin. Early history of Arthur; pt. 1...820.2 305
 Same; pt. 2..820.2 309
 Same; pt. 3..820.2 318

Morte Arthur; ed. by Furnivall. 1864......821.2 490
 Morte Arthure; alliterative version...820.2 304
Nutt. Studies on the legend of the Holy Grail. 1888.......................................813 32
Rhys. Studies in the Arthurian legend. 1891...813 37
Ritson. Life of King Arthur. 1825..........811 78
Sir Gawayne and the green knight.........820.2 303
Sommer, *ed.* Roman de Merlin, or early history of King Arthur. 1894.........813 B-2
Strassburg. Tristran und Isolt. (Dichtungen des deutschen Mittelalters. v. 2)...831 81
Tennyson. Idylls of the king. See ENGLISH LITERATURE, **Tennyson.**
Three early. English metrical romances (Camden society)....................821.2 109
Contents: The anturs of Arther at the Tarnewathelan. —Sir Amadace.—The avowinge of Arthur, etc.
Waddell. The Parsifal of Wagner at Bayreuth. 1894...782 27

THE NIBELUNG CYCLE.

Baldwin. Story of Siegfried. 1882..........813 26
Barham, A. G. Foster-. Nibelungen lied. 1887..831 91
Forestier, *tr.* Echoes from mistland. 1877..831 9
Forman. Nibelung's ring. 1877...............782 18
Geibel. Brunhild; a tragedy from the Nibelung saga; tr. by Dippold. 1879......832 42
Gibb. Gudrun, etc. 1881.........................813 19
Gudrun, a mediæval epic; tr. by Nichols. 1889..831 96
Hagen. Anmerkungen zu der Nibelungen Noth. 1824....................................831 63
 Nibelungen. Lied, erneuet und erklärt. 1824..831 64
 Nordtsche Heldenromane. 1814-28. 5 v.
  V. 1-3. Wilkina- und Niflunga-Saga; oder, Dietrich von Bern und die Nibelungen.............831 70
  V. 4. Volsunga-Saga; oder, Sigurd der Fafnirstödter und die Niflungen...................831 73
  V. 5.\ Ragnar-Lodbroks-Saga, und Norna-Gests-Saga..831 74
Hands, *tr.* Golden threads from an ancient loom. 1880..........................*831 B-1
Jordan. Nibelunge, erstes Lied: Siegfridsage. 1879...831 34
 Same, zweites Lied: Hildebrant's Heimkehr. 1880................................831 35
Lettsom, *tr.* Fall of the Nibelungers. '50..831 8
Morris. Story of Sigurd the Volsung. 1879...821.2 503
Nibelungenlied. Für das deutsche Haus; nach den Quellen bearbeitet von Engelmann. 1892..........................*831 B-5
 Same; mit Holzschnitten. 1840......831 R-1
 Same; tr. by J. Birch. 1848............831 B-3
 Same; uebersetzt von Simrock. '59...831 45

* Of interest to young readers.   ‡ For reference.

LANGUAGE AND LITERATURE.

Vigfusson *and* **Powell.** Sigfred-Arminius, etc. 1886....................................830 233
Wagner. The Nibelung's ring; tr. by Forman. 1877............................782 18
Watson. The four stories of the Nibelungen ring. 1896........................782 31

THE CHARLEMAGNE CYCLE.

Baldwin. Story of Roland. 1883............813 24
Boke of Duke Huon of Burdeux; done into English by Lord Berners. pts. 1-2..820.2 430
Same; pt. 3..................................820.2 432
Bulfinch. Legends of Charlemagne........*813 27
Chanson de Roland, et le Roman de Roncevaux; Francisque Michel, ed. 1869...841 27
Chanson de Roland; tr. by Rabillon. '85..841 34
Charlemagne, an Anglo-Norman poem; ed. by Michel..................................841 60
Dahn. Kaiser Karl und seine Paladine. '87..813 31
English Charlemagne romances. 6 v....820.2 427
Four sonnes of Aymon; Englisht by Caxton. pt. 1..................................820.2 433
Lyf of Charles the Grete; tr. from the French by Caxton..........................820.2 428
Rauf Coilyear..................................820.2 429
Roland and Vernagu.—Otnel: fragments..820.2 429
Sege of Melayne.—Romance of Duke Rowlande.—Fragment of the Song of Roland..820.2 427
Sir Ferumbras..................................820.2 427
Song of Roland; tr. by O'Hagan. 1880....841 35
Sowdone of Babylone........................820.2 429
Turpin. History of Charlemagne and Orlando; tr. by Rodd..........................861 7

Way *and* **Spencer.** Song of Roland: a summary. 1895..................................841 92

MISCELLANEOUS.

Alexander and Dindimus: fragment of the alliterative romance..................820.2 400
Same; 2d fragment.........................820.2 424
Alliterative romance of the destruction of Troy; from Colonna. pt. 1............820.2 321
Same. pt. 2..................................820.2 330
Beowulf; tr. by Garnett........................821.2 96
Same; tr. by Lumsden. 1881........821.2 97
Same; tr. by Thorpe....................821.2 98
Same; tr. by Wackerbath. 1847...821.2 99
Burckhard. Lied von Tannhäuser. '90...831 100
Generydes: a romance. pt. 1............820.2 330
Same; pt. 2..................................820.2 340
Gesta Romanorum; early English versions. 820.2 426
Heintz. Master-singers of Nuremberg, by Wagner. 1892..................................782 22
King Ponthus and the fair Sidone; ed. by Mather. 1897..................................813 63
Legends of the Holy Rood................820.2 325
Reimes. Romance of Blonde of Oxford and Jehan of Dammartin..................841 9
Romance of Guy of Warwick............820.2 419
Same; in 2 parallel texts. pt. 1.....820.2 431
Romance of Kyng Horn, Floris and Blancheflour..................................820.2 306
Romance of William of Palerne........820.2 400
Romans of Partenay; or, Tale of Melusine. 820.2 310

NORSE LANGUAGES AND LITERATURE.

Boyesen. Essays on Scandinavian literature. 1895..................................898 13
Contents: Björnstjerne Björnson.—Alex. Kielland.—Jonas Lie.—Hans Christian Andersen.—Contemporary Danish literature.—Georg Brandes.—Esaias Tegnér.
Gosse. Studies in literature of northern Europe. 1879 ....898 8
Horn. History of literature of Scandinavian North. 1884..................................898 86
Howitt, Literature and romance of northern Europe. 1852. 2 v........................898 1
Larsen. Dano-Norwegian-English dictionary. 1880..................................‡498 2
Metcalfe. Englishman and Scandinavian. 1880..898 69
New pocket-dictionary, English and Swedish. 1887..................................‡498 4

Otté. Simplified grammar of Swedish. '84. 498 3
Stephens. Hand-book of old-northern Runic monuments. 1884..............‡498 R-1
Sweet. Icelandic primer. 1886.............498 1
Vigfusson *and* **Powell,** *eds.* Corpus poeticum boreale. 1883. 2 v..................898 87

THE EDDAS.—SAGAS.

Depping *and* **Michel.** Wayland Smith; a tradition of the middle ages. 1847...898 64
Faereyinga saga. Tale of Thrond of Gate; tr. by Powell. 1896..............898 96
Gould, Baring-. List of Icelandic sagas..914.8 B-1
Green, *tr.* Story of Egil Skallagrimsson. 1893..898 60

* Of interest to young readers.   ‡ For reference.

Grimm, *übers.* Altdänische Heldenlieder,
u. s. w. 1811.................................898 93
Havelok the Dane.......................820.2 402
Lloyd. Legendary tales of Sweden....*in* 914.8 18
Magnússon *and* Morris, *tr.* Three northern love stories, etc. 1875................898 95
Sæmund's edda. Aeltere Edda; übersetzt von Wenzel. 1877..............898 89
Same (the Elder Edda); tr. by Cottle. 1797..898 6
Saga library; tr. by Morris and Magnússon. 1891-5. v. 1—.............................898 14
Saga of King Olaf Tryggwason; tr. by Sephton. 1890........................898 56
Snorre's edda (the Younger Edda); ed. and tr. by Anderson. 1880................898 65
Same; tr. by Blackwell...................948 17
Story of Burnt Njal; tr. by Dasent. '61. 2v...898 61
Story of Grettir the Strong; tr. by Morris and Magnússon. 1869.................!.....898 57
Story of Viga-Glum; tr. by E. Head. '66....898 9
Sturleson, Snorre. Heimskringla............948 7
Same; ed. by Morris and Magnússon.
v. 1—...898 16
Konunga-sagor. 1816. 3 v..................898 53
Tegnér. Fridthjof's saga. 1877.............898 10
Thorgil's nursling, etc.; tr. by Baring-Gould...914.8 B-1
Vicary. Saga time. 1887.....................898 92
Vigfusson *and* Dasent, *ed.* and *tr.* Icelandic sagas. 1887-95. 4 v............898 B-2
Völsunga saga; tr. by Magnússon and Morris; ed. by Sparling. 1881..........898 68
Voluspa, The; tr. by S. Turner........*in* 942.1 5
(See also, Norse Mythology and Folk Lore, in Part 3 of FINDING LIST, pp. 518-521.)

MODERN LITERATURE.

Ahlgren. Truls Jonasson.....................S1102
Andersen. Correspondence with Dickens et al...898 58
Danish fairy legends; with memoir........039801
Fairy tales; illustrated by Lemann......039802
Ice maiden; and Story of my life............S106
Improvisatore......................................S108
Marsh king's daughter.........................039804
Northern fairy tales.............................039808
O. T..S110
Only a fiddler....................................S112
Sämmtliche Märchen............................S101
Sand-hills of Jutland..........................S114
Snow queen, etc.................................039803
Stories and fairy tales; tr. by Sommer.....S102
Stories and tales................................039806
Two baronesses...................................S116
What the moon saw..............................039809

Wonderful tales from Denmark............039807
Wonder stories...................................039805
Björnson. Arne..................................S202
Bridal march, etc. 1882........................S204
Captain Mansana, etc..........................S206
Fisher maiden....................................S208
A happy boy......................................S212
Heritage of the Kurts..........................S210
In God's way.....................................S214
Love and life (Synnöve Solbakken)......S222A
Magnhild; tr......................................S216
New tales (Nye fortaellingen).............S218
Pastor Sang: drama. 1893..................898 66
Railroad and churchyard......................S301
Sigurd Slembe: drama. 1888............898 90
Synnöve Solbakken. (Love and life in Norway)......................................S222
Blanche. Bandit...............................S1202
Bremer. A diary.— The H—— family.—
Axel and Anna..................................S402
Father and daughter............................S404
Four sisters.......................................S406
H—— family.— Tralinnam.— Axel and Anna, etc..S414
The home..S408
Letters, etc. 1868.............................928.5 15
Midnight sun....................................S410
The neighbors, etc............................S412
Buchanan, *tr.* Ballad stories. 1869.......898 11
Carlen. Brother's net..........................S504
Lavinia (One year)..............................S502
Lover's stratagem................................S506
Drachmann. Paul and Virginia of a northern zone...................................S602
Friis. Lajla.....................................S1502
Goldschmidt. Flying mail....................S301
Jacob Bendixen.................................S302
Gustaffsson. Woodland notes...............038025
Hertz. King René's daughter: drama. 1880...898 91
Ibsen. Doll's house; tr. by Lord. 1889...898 72
Same, and other plays; tr. by Archer. 1889..898 73
Contents: Introduction by E. Gosse.—A doll's house.— Pillars of society.— Ghosts.— Rosmersholm.
Emperor and Galilean. 1890.............898 74
Contents: Cæsar's apostacy.— Emperor Julian.
Ghosts.—An enemy of the people.—The wild duck; ed. by Archer. 1890......898 75
Hedda Gabler; tr. by Gosse. 1891......898 76
John Gabriel Borkman; tr. by Archer. 1897..898 77
Lady from the sea; tr. by Marx-Aveling. 1890..898 78
Lady Inger of Östråt.—The vikings at Helgeland.—The pretenders; ed. by Archer. 1890..................................898 79
League of youth.— Pillars of society.— A doll's house; ed. by Archer. 1890..898 80

Little Eyolf; tr. by Archer. 1894	898 81
On his merits; by Russell and Standing. 1897	898 97
Pillars of society, etc.; ed. by Ellis. 1888	898 82
Contents: Pillars of society.— Ghosts.— Enemies of society.	
Rosmersholm.— The lady from the sea. — Hedda Gabler; ed. by Archer. '91	898 83
Ingemann. Childhood of King Erik Menved	S1602
Jacobsen. Siren voices (Niels Lyhne)	S1402
Janson. Spell-bound fiddler	S1302
Kappey, *ed.* Songs of Scandinavia and northern Europe, with music	784 B-15
Kielland. Garman and Worse	S702
Tales of two countries	S704
Koch. Camilla	S2202
Lie. Barque Future	S802
Commodore's daughters	S804
One of life's slaves	S818
Pilot and his wife	S820
Visionary	S824
Mariager. Pictures of Hellas	S1702
Marie; tr. from Danish	S2101
Marmier, *tr.* Nouvelles danoises. 1855	898 12
Molbech. Ambrosius: play. 1879	898 67
Oehlenschläger. Aladdin. 1857	898 59
Axel and Valborg: tragedy. 1874	898 63
Correggio: a tragedy. 1854	898 70
Earl Hakon the mighty. 1874	898 94
The gods of the north. 1845	898 7
Pontoppidan. Promised land; tr. by Lucas	S1803
Prior, *tr.* Ancient Danish ballads. '60. 3 v.	898 3
Rydberg. Last Athenian	S1902
Schwartz. Birth and education	S916
Gerda, tr.	S902
Gold and name	S904
Guilt and innocence	S906
The right one	S908
Son of the organ-grinder	S910
Two family mothers	S912
Wife of a vain man	S914
Songs of Scandinavia and northern Europe; ed. by Kappey	784 B-15
Tegnér. Frithiof; tr. by Latham. 1838	898 71
Thoresen. Old Olaf	*in* S301
Thoroddsen. Sigrid	S2002
Topelius. Fairy tales from Finland	013122
Snowdrops	013120
Times of alchemy	S1002
Times of battle and of rest	S1004
Times of Charles XII	S1006
Times of Frederick I.	S1008
Times of Gustav Adolf	S1010
Times of Linnæus	S1011
Whisperings in the wood	013121

GERMAN LANGUAGE AND LITERATURE.

LANGUAGE.

Behaghel. Short historical grammar of the German language. 1891	435 4
Cutting. Difficulties of German grammar. 1891	435 Pam. 1
Eberhards. Synonymisches Handwörterbuch der deutschen Sprache. 1889	434 2
Favre. Premières leçons d'Allemand. '70	435 3
Flügel. Universal English-German and German-English dictionary. 1894. 3 v.	‡433 B-10
Follen. Practical grammar. 1831	435 2
Grieb. Dictionary, English-German and German-English. 1880. 2 v.	‡433 B-2
Grimm. Geschichte der deutschen Sprache. 1848. 2 v.	430 2
Heyne. Deutsches Wörterbuch. 1890-95. 3 v.	‡433 B-7
Klein. Rudiments of German etymology. 1875	432 1
Koop. Dictionary of English idioms, with German equivalents. 1891	‡433 1
Lüken. Fibel für den ersten Schreib- und Lese-unterricht. 1873	431 2
Otto. German conversation-grammar. '81	435 8
Rosenthal. Method of practical linguistry: German. 2v.	435 9
Sanders. Wörterbuch der deutschen Sprache. 1860. 3v.	‡433 B-4
Wörterbuch deutscher Synonymen. '82	‡434 1
Schlessing. Deutscher Wortschatz. '92	‡434 3
Sears. Selections from Luther, with philological notes. 1846	438 1
Seybold. How to speak German. 1885	435 11
Synopsis of German grammar. 1885	435 12
Stern. Studien und Plaudereien. 1st series. 1879	435 5
Strong *and* **Meyer.** Outlines of history of German language. 1886	430 1
Super. History of the German language. 1893	430 4

‡ For reference.

Victor. German pronunciation. 1885......431 1
Whitney. Compendious German grammar. 1888.......................................435 7
Woodbury. New method of learning German. 1853.................................435 1
Worman. Erstes deutsches Buch. 1880......435 6

LITERATURE.

HISTORY AND CRITICISM.

Bartels. Die deutsche Dichtung der Gegenwart. 1897....................831 121
Blaze de Bury. Les écrivains modernes de l'Allemagne. 1868....................844 11
Boyesen. Essays on German literature. 1892...830 297
  Contents: Goethe. — Schiller. — The German novel.— The romantic school in Germany.
Brümmer. Lexikon der deutschen Dichten und Prosaisten. 2 v..........830 301
Conant. Primer of German literature......830 183
Davésiés de Pontès. Poets and poetry of Germany. 1858. 2 v.............831 1
Francke. Social forces in German literature. 1896...............................830 304
Gostwick. German culture and Christianity......................................193 25
Gostwick *and* Harrison. Outlines of German literature. 1873..................830 8
Grimm. Ueber den altdeutschen Meistergesang. 1811............................831 68
Hedge. Hours with German classics. '86..830 234
  Prose writers of Germany. 1849.........830 5
Heine. The romantic school..................830 185
Hosmer. Short history of German literature..................................830 296
Japp. German life and literature. 1881...830 182
  Contents: Introduction. — Lessing. — Winckelmann.— Moses Mendelssohn.— Herder.— Goethe.— Tieck.— Novalis.
König. Deutsche Litteraturgeschichte. 1882. ....830 184
Korinski. Geschichte der deutschen Litteratur: seit dem Ausgang des Mittelalters...830 337
Lays of the minnesingers, 12-13th centuries...831 19
MacCallum. Studies in German literature.830 178
Menzel. German literature. 1840. 3v......830 1
Metcalfe. History of German literature. '58..830 6
Mielke. Der deutsche Roman des 19ten Jahrhunderts. 1897...................833 1
Passion play, Ammergau; by MacColl......832 45
  Art in the mountains; by Blackburn. 1870...832 39
  As played to-day [German and English]; by Stead. 1890.........................832 B-1
  To and from in 1871; by Doane............832 38

Passion-play at Ober-Ammergau. tr. '90..832 60
Peissner. Course of German literature. 1861...830 298
Phillipps. Short sketch of German literature..................................830 4
Scherer. Geschichte der deutschen Litteratur. 1885................................830 230
  History of German literature. 1886. 2 v...830 231
Taylor, B. Studies in German literature. 1879..830 177
Taylor, W. Historic survey of German poetry. 1830. 3 v.........................831 5
Wells. Modern German literature. 1895....830 299
Wilkinson. Classic German course in English. 1887................................830 247
Wolff. Geschichte der deutschen Litteratur in der Gegenwart. 1896..........830 303

COLLECTIONS.

MYTHOLOGY AND FOLK LITERATURE.

(For Teutonic Mythology and Folk Tales, see Part 3 of FINDING LIST, pp. 519-520. For Mediæval Epics, Romances, and Sagas, see under Mediæval Literature in this part of the FINDING LIST.)

Bernhardt, *ed.* Deutsche Novelletten-Bibliothek. 2 v.
  V. 1. Stökl: Um heiligen Abend.—Bohen: Mein erster Patient.— Werner: Der Wilddieb.— Juncker: Ein Frühlingstraum.— Wiesner: Die schwarze Dame..=11801
  V. 2. Grabowski: Vor Sonnenaufgang.— Seidel: Der gute alte Onkel; Leberecht Hühnchen.— Grabowski: Der Simpel.— Peschkau: Sphinx.— Stökl: Weihnachtsgeschichte......................=11802
Blackie. War songs of the Germans. '70...831 88
Bokum. Translations from German writers. 1836..830 7
Buchheim, *ed.* Balladen und Romanzen. 1891...831 101
Deutsche Lyrik. 1881............................831 47
Deutsches Theater. 1875-80. 3 v.
  V. 1. Benedix: Eigensinn.—Topfer: Dichter und Page.— Schlesinger: Der Hausspion.........832 49
  V. 2. Benedix: Der Prozess.— Raupach: Ein theurer Spass.— Angely; List und Phlegina.....832 50
  V. 3. Hackländer: Der geheime Agent........832 51
Short German plays. 1895....................832 54
  Contents: Wichert: Post Festum.— Benedix: Eigensinn.—Schmidt: Wie man sich bildet —Hermann von Schmidt.— Der Schlüsselbund. — Jagderfolge; nach Benedix.
Carlyle, *tr.* German romance. 4 v.
  V. 1. Musæus: Dumb love; Libussa; Melechsala.— Fouqué: Aslauga's knight...........=1416
  V. 2. Tieck: Fair-haired Eckbert; Trusty Eckart; Runenberg; The elves; The goblet.— Hoffman: The golden pot....................=1417
  V. 3. Richter: Schmelzle's journey to Flaetz; Quintus Fixlein..................................=1418
  V. 4. Goethe: Wilhelm Meister's travels......1001B

LANGUAGE AND LITERATURE.

Collection Schick. 11 v.
V. 1 (nos. 1-3). Lindau: Hans der Träumer; Verlorenes Mühen; Erste Liebe.—Lewald: Vornehme Welt; Mädchen von Oyas.—Eckstein: Die Mädchen des Pensionats; Der Besuch im Carcer.—Wilbrandt: Der Lootsencommandeur........=10901
V. 2 (nos. 4-6). Heyse: L'Arrabiata; Beppe der Sternseher; Maria Francisca. — Hopsen: Trudel's Ball; Flinserl's Glück und Ende.— Eckstein: Wider den Strom.— Franzos: Der Shylock von Barnow; Nach dem höheren Gesetz.— Droz: Das Kind..................................=10902
V. 3 (nos. 7-9). Wichert: Bekentnisse einer armen Seele.— Lindau: Tödliche Fehde. — Herr und Frau Bewer.— Rodenberg: Mein Freund der Gründer. — Rosenberg: Kunst und Natur. — Eckstein: Bonin; Eine Abendverwanderung.—Jensen: Monika Waldvogel.— Heyse: Frau von F......=10903
V. 4 (nos. 10-12). Storm: Carsten Curator.— Riehl: Der stumme Rathsherr.—Hackländer: Ein erster und ein letzter Ball.— Lindau: Im Park von Villers.—Wilbrandt: Am heiligen Damm.—Lorm: Philosophie eines Kusses.— Seidel: Der gute alte Onkel.—Heyse: Das Mädchen von Treppi; Anfang und Ende.— Sacher-Masoch: Der ewige Student.=10904
No. 17. Heyse: Der verlorene Sohn.— Keller: Frau Regel Amrain und ihr Jüngster.— Riehl: Die rechte Mutter. — Sacher-Masoch: Artaban und Pachomia.....................................=10917
No. 18. Heyse: Lottka.— Höfer: Rolof der Rekrut.—Schandorph: Stine wird Frau Bäuerin...=10918
No. 19. Auerbach: Nannchen von Mainz.— Cremer: Der Vetter aus Geldern.—Lindau: Schiffbruch.—Anzengruber: Der gottüberlegene Jakob.=10919
No. 20. Hopfen: Der verlorene Kamerad.— Keller: Kleider machen Leute.—Leander: Mährchen..=10920
No. 21. Hopfen: Die Wette Schabernacks.— Cremer: Ein Tag in der Residenz. — De Alarcon: Das Klappenhorn.—Heyse: Marion.........=10921
No. 22. Schandorph: Ein Witwenstand.— Winther: Eine Abendscene.—Kielland: Karen..=10922
No. 23. Meyer; Das Amulet; Gustav Adolf's Page.— Der Schuss von der Kanzel........=10923

Craigmyle, *tr. and ed.* German ballads..831 102
Dulcken, *tr.* Book of German songs. '71..831 10
Eden, *tr.* Fairy fancies...................=1409
Erlach, *ed.* Volkslieder der Deutschen, 1450-1833. 5 v.................................631 58
Follen. German reader. 1860................839 10
Heydenreich. Elementary German reader. 1867...839 9
Humour of Germany. 1892....................838 3
Joynes, *tr.* Songs of a revolutionary epoch. 1888..831 106
Kappey, *ed.* Songs of Germany, with music..784 B-16
Klemm, *ed.* Poesie für Haus und Schule..*831 23
Knortz, *ed.* Representative German poems [texts with English versions]............831 57
Kroeker, *tr. and ed.* Century of German lyrics. 1894..................................831 112
Love tales..=1434
Contents: Musæus: Dumb love; tr. by T. Carlyle.— Winter: Simple tale of love.– Goethe: A love tale.— The love potion.— Tieck: Love magic.— Langbein: The lady's palfrey.— Schiller: Fraternal magnanimity.— Tieck: The goblet.— Rich goldsmith of Frankfort.

Mangan, *tr.* German anthology. 2 v......831 3
Müller, *ed.* German classics, 4-19th centuries. 2 v......................................830 276
Oxenford, *tr.* Tales from the German....=1407
Contents: Musæus: Libussa. — Schiller: Criminal from lost honour.—Hauff: Cold heart; Nose, the dwarf.— Immermann: Wonders in the Spessart.— Vander Velde: Axel. — Hoffmann: Sandman; Elementary spirit; Jesuits' church in G.— Kleist: Michael Kohlhaas.— Tieck: The Klausenburg. — Richter: The moon.— Kleist: St. Cecilia.— Goethe: New Paris.—Oehlenschläger: Ali and Gulhyndi.—Zschokke: Almmontade. — Hauff: Severed hand.
Phillips, *tr.* German lyrics. 1892........831 B-2
Ramage, *ed.* Beautiful thoughts from German and Spanish authors. 1868........‡839 1
Roscoe, *tr.* German novelists..............=1420
Specimens of German romance. 3 v.
V. 1. The patricians..........................=1404
V. 2. The flea..................................=1405
V. 3. The blind passenger. — The adventurers.
—The mantle..................................=1406
Tales from Alsace............................=1402
Thompson, *tr.* German theatre. v. 2-5.
V. 2. Schiller: Don Carlos.—Kotzebue: Count Benyowsky....................................832 1
V. 3. Kotzebue: Lovers' vows; Indian exiles..832 2
V. 4. Babo: Otto of Wittelsbach; Dagobert.— Kotzebue: Adelaide of Wulfingen............832 3
V. 5. Schiller: The robbers. Kotzebue: Happy family.— Iffland: Conscience..............832 4
Tille, *ed.* German songs of to-day. 1896..831 114
Winkworth. Christian singers of Germany..245 10
Wolff. Historische Volkslieder und Gedichte der Deutschen. 1830................831 75

INDIVIDUAL AUTHORS (INCLUDING TRANSLATIONS).

Ambrosius. Gedichte. 1896.................831 117
Poems; tr. by Safford. 1896................831 118
Amelia, *princess of Saxony.* Dramas; tr. by Mrs. Jameson. 1840. 2 v.
V. 1. Introductory.—Falsehood and truth.—The uncle..832 36
V. 2. Young ward. — Princely bride. — Country cousin..832 37
Anzengruber. Der Sternsteinhof..........=1430
Appet. Gesammtabenteuer; herausgegeben von Hagen. 1850. 3 v..........831 77
Arndt. Die Mondhere........................=10401
Auer. It is the fashion.......................=4701
Auerbach. Aloys; tr........................=117
Auf der Höhe................................=102
Auf Wache...................................=138
Black forest village stories.................=139
Briefe an seinen Freund, Jakob Auerbach. 1884. 2 v...........................836 13
Brigitta (German)............................=128
Same; tr.....................................=127
Convicts......................................=113

* Of interest to young readers.   ‡ For reference.

Edelweiss ; tr............................=110
Foresters [Der Forstmeister]...............=126
Der Forstmeister......................==125
German evenings......................=123
German tales........................=124
Joseph in the snow....................=112
Das Landhaus am Rhein.   2 v...........=103
Landolin von Reutershofen..............=137
  Same ; tr..........................=136
Little Barefoot.........................=111
Lorley and Reinhard...................=121
Master Bieland.......................=133
On the heights.......................=101
Poet and merchant...................=119
Professor's lady.....................=106
  Same............................=14146
Schwarzwälder Dorfgeschichten. 10 v.
  in 5.
    V. 1-2. Der Tolpatsch.— Die Kriegspeife.— Des
    Schloszbauers Befele.— Tonelle mit der gebissenen
    Wange.— Befehlerles.— Die feindlichen Brüder.—
    Ivo, der Hajrle.— Florian und Kreszenz.— Der
    Lauterbacher.— Sträflinge.— Erdmute..........=140
    V. 3-4. Die Frau Professorin.— Luzifer.— Die
    Geschichte des Diethelm von Buchenberg.— Hopfen
    und Gerste..................................=140A
    V. 5-6. Der Lehnhold.— Der Viereckig; oder,
    Die amerikanische Kiste.— Der Geigerler.— Ein
    eigen Haus.— Barfüszele....................=140B
    V. 7-8. Joseph im Schnee.— Brosi und Moni.—
    Edelweisz...................................=140C
    V. 9-10. Das Lorles Reinhard.— Der Tolpatsch
    aus Amerika.— Das Nest an der Bahn.— Brigitta. .=140D

Spinoza ; tr.........................=131
Two stories.........................=132
Villa on the Rhine....................=104
Waldfried ; tr.......................=107
Ballestrem. Haideröslein (German) .....=10501
Bauer. Must it be?..................=1201
Baumbach. Tales from wonderland......038014
Bayer (Robert Byr, *pseud.*). Cipher despatch..............................4602
Becker, A. Tempted of the devil..........=1433
Becker, W. A. Charicles : the ancient
    Greeks..........................391 6
    Gallus ; or, Roman scenes...........391 7
Beethoven. Letters, 1790-1826. 1867. 2v...836 3
Benedix. Doktor Wespe (Lustspiel). '88..832 58
Berkow. Woe to the conquered ! ......=9590
Beyer. Arja (German)..................=7301
Biermatzki. The Hallig................=2101
Bismarck, *prince*. Letters, 1844-70. 1878...836 26
    Neue Tischgespräche und interviews ;
    herausgegeben von Poschinger. '95...839 13
    Politischen reden. 1892 —. v. 1........835 1
Blum *and* **Wahl.** Seaside and fireside
    fairies..........................038004
Bodenstedt. Aus Morgenland und Abendland (Gedichte). 1882.............831 44

Gesammelte Schriften. 1865. 12v. in 3.
    V. 1-3. Tausend und ein Tag im Orient.......831 37
    V. 4-7. Russische Dichter (Puschkin, Lermontoff, Kolzoff, und Andere)...................831 37
    V. 8. Shakespeare's Sonette, in deutscher Nachbildung..................................831 38
    V. 9-11. Alte und neue Gedichte.............831 39
    V. 12. Aus Ost und West...................831 39
Morningland.......................=6401
Songs of Mirza Schaffy. 1880......831 40
Boettcher. Gedichte................831 113
Bothmer. Poet hero..................=3701
Boy-Ed. Die Lampe der Psyche.......=13601
Brachvogel. Beaumarchais ; tr.........=2201
Brandes. Menschen und Werke. 1895.....834 5
    Contents : Goethe und Dänemark.— Ludwig Holberg.
    — Adam Oehlenschläger : Aladdin.— Friedrich Nietzsche.
    — Emile Zola.— Guy de Maupassant.— Puschkin und Lermontow.— Fjodor Dostojewski.— Leo Tolstoi.— Das Thier
    im Menschen.— Kristian Elster.— Alex. L. Kielland.— J.
    P. Jacobsen.— Aug. Strindberg.— Hermann Sudermann.
    — Gerhard Hauptmann.
Brooks, *tr.* Pieces from Schiller and others..831 14
Buersterbinder. See **Werner.**
Calm. Bella's blue book................=9546
Campe. Robinson the younger............038901
Chamisso. Peter Schlemihl (German)...=1601A
    Same ; tr........................=1601
Citizen of Prague....................=1436
Corvus. In omnibus charitas (German)....=9512
Cron. Mädchenleben.................=12701
Dahn. Die Amalungen (Gedicht). 1876..831 105
    Felicitas ; tr........................=8003
    Kleine Romane aus der Volker-wanderung. 4v.
        V. 1. Felicitas (German).................=8006
        V. 2. Bissula (German)..................=8007
        V. 3. Gelimer (German)..................=8008
        V. 4. Die schlimmen Nonnen von Poitiers......=8009
    Saga of Halfred the Sigskald..........=8005
    Skirnir (German).....................=8004
    Struggle for Rome...................=8001
Delitzsch. José and Benjamin..........=9001
Derval. Far from home............... 9502
    Perilous venture....................9503
Detlef. Russian country house............1203
Deutsch. Literary remains. 1874....204 69
Dewall, J. van, *pseud.* (A. Kühne). Auf
    verlorenem Posten..................=3307
    Ein Frühlingstraum..................=3303
    Das Geheimniss....................=3305
    Great lady..........................=3301
    Eine Schweizerpension................ 3304
De Wille. Johannes Olaf ; tr...........=3501
Dickens. See novels translated into German, cataloged with other works of **Dickens** in ENGLISH LITERATURE.
Dielitz. Hunters of the world...........=3602
    Traveller's adventures................=3601
Dingelstedt. The Amazon..............=6601
Doctor Johannes Faustus : puppet play..832 Pam. 1

LANGUAGE AND LITERATURE.

Döllinger. Addresses. 1894...............834 3
  Contents: Universities, past and present,— Founders of religions.— The empire of Charles the great and his successors.— Anagni.— Suppression of the Knights templars.- History of religious freedom.— Various estimates of the French revolution.- Part taken by North America in literature.
Ebers. Ægyptische Königstochter............=6002
  Barbara Blomberg (German)..............=6035
  Bride of the Nile. 2 v.....................=6006
  Burgomaster's wife........................=6026
  Cleopatra ; tr............................=6018
  Egyptian princess.........................=6029
  Elifën (Gedicht). 1888................831 93
  Elixir, etc...............................=6001
  Emperor...................................=6020
  Die Frau Bürgermeisterin..................=6027
  Die Gred..................................=6015
  Homo sum ; tr.............................=6008
  Im blauen Hecht...........................=6023A
  Im Schmiedefeuer. 2 v.....................=6033
  In the blue pike..........................=6023
  In the fire of the forge..................=6034
  Joshua ; tr...............................=6010
  Der Kaiser................................=6016
  Kleopatra (German)........................=6019
  Margery [Gred]............................=6022A
  Die Nilbraut. 3 v.........................=6003
  Per aspera (German).......................=6011
  A question................................=6017
  Die Schwestern............................=6014
  Serapis (German)..........................=6038
    Same ; tr...............................=6038A
  The sisters...............................=6013
  Thorny path [Per aspera]..................=6012
  Uarda (German)...........................=6028
    Same ; tr...............................=6009
  Die Unersetzlichen....................833 B-2
  A word ; only a word......................=6039
Ebner-Eschenbach. Child of the parish..=12501
Eckstein. Aphrodite ; tr.................=8907
  Chaldean magician.........................=8906
  Hertha ; tr...............................=8910
  A monk of the Aventine....................=8911
  Nero ; tr.................................=8908
  Preisgekrönt ; ed. by Wilson..............=8912
  Prusias ; tr..............................=8902
  Quintus Claudius ; tr.....................=8901
  The will..................................=8904
Edler. Baldine, etc.; tr.................=9720
Eichendorff. Aus dem Leben eines Taugenichts...........................=9534
Elizabeth, *queen of Roumania* (Carmen Sylva, *pseud.*). Edleen Vaughan ; tr..=9570
  Pilgrim sorrow............................=9501
  Shadows on love's dial....................=9571
  Songs of toil. 1888...................831 94
Elze. Essays on Shakespeare. 1874....822.3 57

Erhard. Uncle Herman....................-9519
Eschenbach. Parcival (German). 1836...831 89
  Parzival ; tr. by Weston. 1894........831 110
Eschstruth. Her little highness......... -12205
  Hofluft...................................=12202
  Princess of the stage [Hofluft]...........=12204
  Sternschnuppen............................=12203
  Wild rose of Gross-Stauffen...............-12201
Falkenhorst. With Columbus in America.*=1805
  With Cortez in Mexico....................*=1806
  With Pizarro in Peru.....................*=1807
Faustus................................=1408
Fichte. Nature of the scholar, etc. 1873...193 3
  Werke. 1845. 8 v..........................193 56
Fontane. Ellernklipp....................=8501
  Frau Jenny Treibel........................=8502
Fouqué. See **Lamotte Fouqué.**
François. The last von Reckenburg......=9532
  Letzte Reckenburgerin.....................=9532A
Franzos. Chief justice..................=8703
  For the right.............................=8702
  Jews of Barnow............................=8701
  Judith Trachtenberg ; tr..................=8704
Frapan. Bittersüsz......................=9585
  Flügel auf................................=9587
  God's will, etc...........................=9586
  Heavy laden, and Old-fashioned folk...=9584
Frederic II (*the great*). Correspondence with Voltaire............830 207
    Same (French)..........................830 221
  Œuvres posthumes. 1789. 15 v.
    V. 1. Histoire de mon temps..........830 202
    V. 2-3. Histoire de la guerre de sept ans......830 203
    V. 4. Mémoires 1763-75—Mémoires de la guerre de 1778.—Corr. au sujet de la succession de la Bavière.—Considérations sur l'état du corps politique de l'Europe.—Essai sur les formes de govt....830 205
    V. 5. Dialogues des morts.—Charles XII.—Système de la nature.—Pensées sur la religion.—Sur l'innocence des erreurs de l'esprit.—L'école du monde : comédie.—La Henriade de Voltaire.—Tâutale en procès: comédie.—Portrait de Voltaire.—Epitaph de Voltaire.—Billet de congé de Voltaire, etc..830 206
    V. 6-8. Correspondance entre Frederic et Voltaire...........................830 207
    V. 9-13. Correspondance, etc............830 210
    V. 14. Le Palladion ; poème.—La guerre des Confédérés; poème.— Odes.— Épîtres........830 215
    V. 15. Épîtres.—Discours et mélanges en verse.830 216
  Posthumous works ; tr. by Holcroft. 1789. 13 v.
    V. 1. History of my own time..........830 217
    V. 2-3. The seven years' war..........830 218
    V. 4. Memoirs from the peace of Hubertsberg to the partition of Poland..................830 220
    V. 5. Political, philosophical and satirical miscellanies...........................830 221
    V. 6-8. Correspondence with Voltaire....830 222
    V. 9-13. Other correspondence...........830 225
Freiligrath. Poems. 1871................831 41
Frenzel. Die Geschwister. 2 v...........=9301
Freytag. Aus einer kleinen Stadt........=311 5
  Die Brüder vom Deutschen Hause........=311 7

* Of interest to young readers.

Debit and credit [Soll und Haben].......=3103
Die Geschwister...............................=3108
Ingo ; tr...=3101
Ingo und Ingraban............................=3109
Ingraban ; tr.....................................=3102
Lost manuscript.................................=3112
Marcus König (German)....................=3110
Das Nest der Zaunkönige.................=3106
Soll und Haben. 2 v.........................=3104
Die verlorene Handschrift.................=3111
Friedrichs. Lost dispatch...............=7701
Galwitz. Magdalena (German)......=9511
Geibel. Brunhild: a tragedy...........832 42
Gerstaecker. Each for himself......=3001
Frank Mildman's adventures...........024502
Wife to order....................................=3002
Young whaler..................................024501
Gessner. Schriften. 1801. 3 v.
  V. 1. Tod Abels.—Der erste Schiffer.......830 278
  V. 2. Daphnis.—Evander und Alcimna.—Erast.
  —Ein Gemähld aus der Sündfluth.— Der Wunsch.
  —Die Nacht.—Die Gegend Grase.—Der Frühling..830 279
  V. 3. Idyllen....................................830 280
Glümer. Frau Domina (German)....=8805
Lutin und Lutine (German).............=8806
Noble name......................................=8801
Goethe, Catherine E. Corr. 1811......836 11
Goethe, J. W. von. Ballads, songs, etc.;
  tr. by Gibson. 1883......................831 51
Briefe an Frau von Stein ; herausgegeben
  von Schöll. 2 v. 1883.................836 20
Campaign in France.........................944.5 46
Corr. with a child. 1859..................836 6
Corr. with Carlyle; ed. by Norton. '87..826.2 47
Corr. with Schiller. 1877. 2 v.........836 9
Early and miscellaneous letters. 1884...836 12
Elective affinities..............................=1004
Faust; tr. by Anster. 1886............832 53
Same; with tr. and notes by Beta.
  1895—. v. 1..............................832 64
Same ; tr. by Blackie. 1880..........832 46
Same ; tr. by Brooks. 1878..........832 48
Same ; tr. by Filmore..................810 7
Same ; tr. by Hayward. 1874.......832 32
Same; tr. by Martin. 1877-86. 2 v...832 73
Same ; tr. by Taylor. 1881............832 33
Same. 1871. 2 v............................832 34
Same; Commentary on; by Boyesen.928.3 21
Same ; Commentary on ; by Snider.
  1886. 2 v.....................................832 55
Same : Goethe's Faust ; by Fischer.
  1895—.
  V. 1 Faust literature before Goethe......832 66
Same : Spirit of ; by Couplant. 1885..832 52
Hermann und Dorothea ; ed. by Hart.
  1887...831 22
Same ; tr. by Frothingham. 1870....831 16
Letters to Zelter ; tr. with notes by Coleridge. 1887.........................836 19

Maxims and reflections ; ed. by Saunders. 1893..................................839 11
Novels and tales..............................=1005
Opinions on the world, etc.; tr. by
  Wenckstern. 1853........................839 2
Poems ; tr. by Bowring. 1874.......831 15
Reading list (Philadelphia mercantile
  library bulletin, v.1, p.209)........16 B-18
Reynard the fox ; tr. by Arnold. 1855...831 50
Sämmtliche Werke. 1854. 6 v.
  V. 1. Gedichte.—Sprüche in Prosa.........830 B-3
  V. 2. Gedichte.—Dramen.—Theater und dramatische Poesie.................................830 B-4
  V. 3. Leiden des jungen Werther.—Briefe aus der Schweiz.—Wilhelm Meister.........830 B-5
  V. 4. Aus meinem Leben.— Italiänische Reise.—Zweiter Aufenthalt in Rom.—Ueber Italien.—Campagne in Frankreich.—Belogerung von Mainz.—Reise in der Schweiz.—Annalen, 1749-1822.....830 B-6
  V. 5. Benvenuto Cellini.— Rameau's Neffe.—Diderot's Versuch über die Malerei.—Winckelmann. — Hackert. — Die Propyläen. —Laokon.—Der Sammler und die Seinigen.—Philostrat's Gemälde.—Ferneres über Kunst.—Deutsche Literatur.—Auswartige Literatur.................830 B-7
  V. 6. Bildung und Unbildung organischer Naturen.—Metamorphose der Pflanzen.—Osteologie.— Farbenlehre. — Naturwissenschaftliche Einzelnheiten. — Mineralogie und Geologie.—Meteorologie.— Zur Naturwissenschaft im Allgemeinen.—Chronologie................................830 B-8
Wilhelm Meister (German).............=1002
Same ; tr..=1001
Werke. 1827. 55 v.
  V. 1. Zueignung.—Lieder.—Gesellige Lieder.—Balladen. — Elegien. — Episteln. — Epigramme.—Weissagungen des Bakis.— Vier Jahreszeiten....830 11
  V. 2. Sonette.—Cantaten.—Vermischte Gedichte.
— Aus Wilhelm Meister. — Antiker Form sich nähernd.—An Personen.—Kunst.—Parabolisch.—Gott, Gemüth und Welt.—Sprichwörtlich.—Epigrammatisch................................830 12
  V. 3. Lyrisches. — Loge.— Gott und Welt.—Kunst. — Epigrammatisch. — Parabolisch. — Aus fremden Sprachen.—Zahme Xenien........830 13
  V. 4. Inschriften, Denk und Sendeblätter.—Dramatisches.—Zahme Xenien..................830 14
  V. 5. Buch des Sängers; Buch Hafis; Der Liebe; Der Betrachtungen ; Des Unmuths; Der Sprüche ; Des Timur ; Suleikas ; Des Schenken ; Der Parabeln ; Des Parsen ; Des Paradieses.......830 15
  V. 6. Noten und Abhandlungen zu besserem Verständniss des West-östlichen Divans........830 16
  V. 7. Die Laune des Verliebten. · Die Mitschuldigen.— Die Geschwister. Mahomet. Tancred..830 17
  V. 8. Götz von Berlichingen mit der eisernen Hand, Schauspiel.— Egmont, Trauerspiel......830 18
  V. 9. Iphigenie auf Tauris, Schauspiel.— Torquato Tasso, Schauspiel.— Die natürliche Tochter, Trauerspiel....................................830 19
  V. 10. Elpenor, Trauerspiel.— Clavigo, Trauerspiel. - Stella, Trauerspiel · Claudine von Villa Bella, ein Singspiel. Erwin und Elmire, ein Singspiel...830 20
  V. 11. Jery und Bätely, ein Singspiel. Lila. Die Fischerin, ein Singspiel.—Scherz, List und Rache, ein Singspiel. Der Zauberflöte, zweiter Theil, Fragment.—Palaeophron und Neoterpe.—Vorspiel, 1807. Was wir bringen, Vorspiel. Theaterreden..................................830 21

LANGUAGE AND LITERATURE.

V. 12. Faust, erster Theil. — Faust, zweiter
Theil..830 22
V. 13. Puppenspiel.—Fastnachtspiel.—Bahrdt.
Parabeln.—Legende.— Hans Sachs.— Mieding.-
Künstlers Erdenwallen.— Künstlers Apotheose.-
Epilog zu Schiller's Glocke.—Die Geheimnisse.
Maskenzüge. — Caarlsbader Gedichte.— Des Epi-
menides Erwachen.......................830 23
V. 14. Der Triumph der Empfindsamkeit.—Die
Vögel.—Der Gross-Cophta.— Der Bürgergeneral...830 24
V. 15. Die Aufgeregten.—Die Ausgewanderten.
—Die guten Weiber.—Novelle.............830 25
V. 16. Inhalts- und Namen-Verzeichnisse über
sämmtliche Goethe'sche Werke..........830 26
V. 17. Die Wahlverwandtschaften.........830 27
V. 18-20. Wilhelm Meister's Lehrjahre....830 28
V. 21-23. Wilhelm Meister's Wanderjahre....830 31
V. 24-26. Aus meinem Leben, Dichtung und
Wahrheit...........................830 34
V. 27-28. Italiänische Reise...............830 37
V. 29. Zweiter Aufenthalt in Rom..........830 39
V. 30. Campagne in Frankreich, 1792.......830 40
V. 31. Tag- und Jahres-Hefte als Ergänzung
meiner sonstigen Bekenntnisse, von 1749 bis 1806 ..830 41
V. 32. Tag- und Jahres-Hefte, 1807-1822.— Zum
Andenken der Durchlauchtigsten Herzogin Anna
Amalia.— Zum Andenken des edeln Dichters,
Bruders und Freundes Wieland..............830 42
V. 33. Recensionen in die Frankfurter gelehrten
Anzeigen — Recensionen in die Jenaische allge-
meine Literaturzeitung.— Prometheus, Fragment,
1773.— Götter, Helden und Wieland, 1774.....830 43
V. 34-35. Benvenuto Cellini.................830 44
V. 36. Rameau's Neffe, ein Dialog von Diderot.
- Anmerkungen.— Diderot's Versuch über Mahl-
erei mit Noten des Uebersetzers..............830 46
V. 37. Winckelmann.— Hackert 830 47
V. 38. Einleitung in die Prophyläen.—Laokoon.
—Der Sammler und die Seinigen.— Wahrheit und
Warscheinlichkeit.— Ueber Italien.— Aeltere Ge-
mählde, Venedig, 1791.— Don Ciccio.— Neueste Ital-
iänische Literatur.....................................830 48
V. 39. Philostrats Gemählde.— Abendmahl von
Leonardo da Vinci.— Triumphzug von Mantegna.—
Kupferstich nach Tizian.— Tischbein's Idyllen.—
Handzeichnungen von Goethe.— Skizzen zu Casti's
redenden Thieren.— Blumen-Mahlerei.— Gérards
historische Portraits.—Ruisdael als Dichter.— Alt-
deutsche Gemählde in Leipzig — Bildhauerey.—
Münzen, Medaillen, geschnittene Steine.— Vor-
bilder für Fabricanten und Handwerker.— Alt-
deutsche Baukunst.........................830 49
V. 40. Reineke Fuchs.—Hermann und Dorothea
—Achilleis.—Pandora..................830 50
V. 41. Faust; der Tragödie zweiter Theil in
fünf Acten. (Vollendet im Sommer 1831.)....830 51
V. 42. Geschichte Gottfriedens von Berlichingen
mit der eisernen Hand; dramatisirt.—Götz von Ber-
lichingen mit der eisernen Hand; Shauspiel in fünf
Aufzügen.............................830 52
V. 43. Schweizerreise im Jahre 1797.—Reise am
Rhein und Main in den Jahren 1814 und 1815.....830 53
V. 44. Kunst...........................830 54
V. 45. Theater.— Deutsche Literatur..........830 55
V. 46. Auswärtige Literatur und Volkspoesie.
—Altgriechische Literatur.—Französische Litera-
tur.—Englische Literatur.—Italiänische Literatur.—
Orientalische Literatur.—Volkspoesie 830 56
V. 47. Jugendgedichte.— Lieder für Liebende.—
Chinesisch-deutsche Jahres- und Tages-Zeiten.—
Vermischte Gedichte.—Original und Nachbildung.
—Festgedichte.—Gedichte von Bildern.—Zuschriften
und Erinnerungs-Blätter. — Politica. — Zahme
Xenien.—Der neue Alcinous................830 57

V. 48. Aus meinem Leben, Dichtung und Wahr-
heit ; vierter Theil........................830 58
V. 49. Einzelheiten, Maximen und Reflexionen.830 59
V. 50. Zur Naturwissenschaft im Allgemeinen..830 60
V. 51. Mineralogie und Geologie..........830 61
V. 52. Zur Farbenlehre..................830 62
V. 53. Geschichte der Farbenlehre; erster Theil..830 63
V. 54. Geschichte der Farbenlehre; zweiter
Theil..................................830 64
V. 55. Nachträge zur Farbenlehre.—Zur Pflan-
zenlehre.— Osteologie.....................830 65
Wilhelm Meister ; tr. by Carlyle...........=1001
Wilhelm Meister's Lehrjahre..............=1002
Wilhelm Meister's Wanderjahre...........=1003
Wisdom of ; by Blackie. 1883............839 7
Gotthelf. Ulric the farm servant...........=9537
Green. See novels translated into German, cata-
loged with other works of **Anna K. Green**,
in ENGLISH LITERATURE.
Grillparzer. Sämmtliche Werke. 20 v.
V. 1-3. Gedichte..........................830 305
V. 4. Die Ahnfrau. — Sappho.............830 308
V. 5. Das goldene Vliesz................830 309
V. 6. König Ottokar's Glück und Ende.— Ein
treuer Diener seines Herren...............830 310
V. 7. Des Meeres und der Liebe Wellen.— Der
Traum.—Melusina.......................830 311
V. 8. Weh dem, der lügt !—Libussa.—Esther..830 312
V. 9. Ein Bruderzwist in Habsburg.—Die Jüdin
von Toledo............................830 313
V. 10. Blanka von Kastilien.— Die Schreibfeder.
—Wer ist schuldig?....................830 314
V. 11-12. Dramatische Fragmente, 1807-40.—
Stoffe und Charaktere...................830 315
V. 13. Dramatische Fragmente : Uebersetz-
ungen.— Satiren.— Erzählungen............830 317
V. 14. Studien zu Philosophie und Religion.—
Historische und politische Studien...........830 318
V. 15. Æsthetische Studien. — Sprächliche Stu-
dien.—Aphorismen.....................830 319
V. 16. Studien zur Litteratur............830 320
V. 17. Studien zum spanischen Theater....830 321
V. 18. Studien zur deutschen Litteratur.—Zum
eigenen Schaffen.......................830 322
V. 19. Selbstbiographie.—Tagebuch, Reise nach
Italien, 1819..........................830 323
V. 20. Ein Erlebnis.— Tagebücher.— Errinerun-
gen aus dem Jahre 1848.—Errinnerungen an Bee-
thoven.— Register zu Band 1-20............830 324
Grimm. Das Kind......................=11201
Der Landschaftsmaler..................=11202
Literature. 1886.....................834 2
Contents : Emerson.— France and Voltaire.— Voltaire
and Frederick the great.— Frederick the great and Ma-
caulay.— Dürer.— The Brothers Grimm.— Bettina Von
Arnim.— Dante in the recent Italian struggle.
Gröger. Adhimukti, etc. (German)......=13001
Groller. Prinz Klotz..................=1431
Gutzkow. Aus der Knabenzeit............=6809
Blasedow und seine Söhne................=6806
Borne's Leben, u. s. w................830 180
Fritz Elbrodt (German.)................=6812
In bunter Reihe.......................=6811
Die neuen Serapionsbrüder..............=6807
Oeffentliche Charaktere................830 179
Paris und Frankreich, 1834-74..........830 181

Die Paumgärtner. =6808
Reiseeindrücke. 1832-73. 830 180
Die Ritter vom Geiste. =6801
Saekularbilder. 830 181
Die Söhne Pestalozzi's. =6805
Through night to light. =6813
Zauberer von Rom. =6803
Zopf und Schwert (Lustspiel). 832 47
Zur Geschichte unserer Zeit. 830 179
Hackländer. Der alte Lehnstuhl, etc. =2015
Behind blue glasses. =2002
Behind the counter [Handel und Wandel]. =2003
Countess of St. Albans [Namenlose Geschichten]. =2013
Die dunkle Stunde. =2004
Enchanting and enchanted. 038030
European slave life. =2010
Forbidden fruit. =2001
Vom Haidehaus. =2014
Werke. 20 v. in 10.
  V. 1-2. Namenlose Geschichten. v. 1-2. =2107
  V. 3. Namenlose Geschichten. v. 3. =2018
  V. 4. Soldatenleben im Frieden.—Wachtstubenabenteuer. v. 1. =2018
  V. 5. Wachtstubenabenteuer. v. 2-3. =2019
  V. 6. Kleinere Erzählungen. =2019
  V. 7. Handel und Wandel. =2020
  V. 8. Reise in den Orient. v. 1. =2020
  V. 9. Reise in den Orient. v. 2. =2021
  V. 10. Eugen Stillfried v. 1. =2021
  V. 11-12. Eugen Stillfried. v. 2-3. =2022
  V. 13. Märchen: Schlosz Schwelgern.—Zwergennest.—Prinzessin Morgana.—Gesicht im Mond.—Der Zauberkrug.—Weihnachtsmärchen.—Der Leibschneider der Zwerge. =2023
  V. 14. Der Pilgerzug nach Mekka. =2023
  V. 15. Dramatische Werke. =2024
  V. 16-20. Europäisches Sklavenleben. 5 v. in 3. =2024
Zwölf Zettel. =2016
Hahn-Hahn, *countess.* Faustina; tr. =5301
Hamerling. Aspasia; tr. =8103
Hardenberg. Henry of Afterdingen. =4801
Harder. Family feud. =1101
Hartmann. Last days of a king. =2801
Hartmann von der Aue. Der arme Heinrich; ed. by Robertson. 1895. 831 120
Hartner. Severa; tr. =7801
Hauff. Constant lover. =7915
Inn in the Spessart. =7917
Die Karavane. =7904
Lichtenstein; tr. =7903
Little glass man, etc. 039002
Little Mook, etc. 039001A
Longnose the dwarf. 039001
Märchen. =7901
  Contents: Märchen als Almanach. Die Karavane. Der Scheik von Alessandria. Das Wirthshaus im Spessart
Sämmtliche Werke. 10 v. in 5.
  V. 1-2. Leben. Gedichte. Lichtenstein, v 1. 7906
  V. 3-4. Lichtenstein, v. 2. Märchen. 7907

V. 5-6. Märchen.—Memoiren des Satan. =7908
V. 7-8. Der Mann im Mond. =7909
V. 9-10. Novellen. =7910
Wine-ghosts of Bremen. =7905
Heiberg. Apotheker Heinrich. =12401
Ausgetobt. =12404
Esther's Ehe. =12405
Januskopf. =12402
Die Spinne. =12403
Heimburg. Die Andere.—Unverstanden. =6907
Ein armes Mädchen.—Das Fraulein Pate. =6904
Aus dem Leben meiner alten Freundin. =6912
Gertrude's marriage. =6919
Her only brother. =6906
Herzenskrisen. =6922
Im Banne der Musen. *in* =6920
Kloster Wendhusen. Ursula. =6909
Lore von Tollen. =6923
Lottie of the mill [Lumpenmüllers Lieschen]. =6901
Lucie's mistake [Herzenskrisen.]. =6921
Lumpenmüllers Lieschen. =6902
Magdalen's fortunes [Kloster Wendhusen]. =6910
Maiden's choice [Lumpenmüllers Lieschen]. =6901A
Misjudged [Eine unbedeutende Frau]. =6915
Miss Mistake. =6917
The pastor's daughter [Aus dem Leben meiner alten Freundin]. =6911
Penniless girl [Ein armes Mädchen]. =6902
Trudchens Heirat. Im Banne der Musen. =6920
Two daughters of one race [Die Andere]. =6908
Eine unbedeutende Frau. =6916
Unter der Linde. =6925
Unverstanden. *in* =6907
Heine. Atta Troll, etc. 1876. 831 108
Book of songs; tr. by Stratheir. 1882. 831 49
Ideas; Buch le grand; tr. by J. B. 1884. 838 2
In art and letters; tr. by Sharp 1895. 834 4
  Contents: Rossini and Meyerbeer, 1837.—Berlioz, Liszt, Chopin, 1837.—The Salon, 1831.—The Salon, 1833.—Letters from Berlin, 1822.—The old régime, 1831.—June days, 1832.—Letters from Normandy, 1832.—Letters from the Pyrénées, 1846.
Love-songs; Englished by Briggs. '88. 831 95
Pictures of travel. 914.3 6
Poems, complete; tr. by Bowring. 1866. 831 17
Poems and ballads; tr. by Martin. '78. 831 24
Prosa: selections; ed. by Buchheim. 1884. 839 8
Reisebilder. 1863. 830 66
Scintillations from; tr. by Stern. 1873. 839 3
Shakespeare heroines. 1895. 822.3 394
Werke, Sämmtliche. 1863. 7 v.
  V. 1. Reisebilder. 830 66
  V. 2. Buch der Lieder.—Neue Lieder.—Tragödien: William Ratcliff.—Almansor. 830 67
  V. 3. Salon. 830 68

V. 4. Wintermärchen.—Atta Troll.—Romanzero.
—Neueste Gedichte............................830 69
V. 5-6. Vermischte Schriften.................830 70
V. 7. Nachtrag und biographische literarische Skizze von Godfried Decker................830 72
Works; tr. by Leland. 1891-3.
  V. 1. Florentine nights.—The memoirs of Herr von Schnabelewopski.—The Rabbi of Bacharach.—Shakespeare's maidens and women............830 281
  V. 2-3. Pictures of travel. v. 1, 1823-26; v. 2, '28...830 282
  V. 4. The salon; or, Letters on art, music, popular life and politics......................830 284
  V. 5-6. Germany.........................830 285
  V. 7-8. French affairs: letters from Paris. v. 1, 1832; v. 2. Lutetia.........................830 286A

Helmholtz. Popular lectures. 1873-81. 2 v..504 36
For contents, see Part 3 of FINDING LIST, p. 351.
Henkel. Mistress of Ibichstein............=9701
Herbart. Sämmtliche Werke. 1887. 7 v...193 70
Herder. Sämmtliche Werke. 1820. 32 v.
  V. 1. Die Vorwelt........................830 73
  V. 2. Propyläen.—Philosophie der Geschichte zur Bildung der Menschheit..................830 74
  V. 3-6. Ideen zur Philosophie der Geschichte der Menschheit.........................830 75
  V. 7. Postscenien zur Geschichte der Menschheit.830 79
  V. 8. Seele und Gott.....................830 80
  V. 9. Adrastea: Begebenheiten und Charaktere des vergangenen Jahrhunderts.—Grossbritannien unter Wilhelm und Anna.—Die Grossen im Nord.—Wissenschaftliche Ereignisse und Charaktere....830 81
  V. 10. Adrastea und das 18te Jahrhundert.—Briefe zu Beförderung der Humanität..............830 82
  V. 11. Briefe zu Beförderung der Humanität...830 83
  V. 12. Sophron...........................830 84
  V. 13. Recensionen. — Nachlese historischer Schriften..................................830 85
  V. 14. Verstand und Erfahrung.—Vernunft und Sprache..................................830 86
  V. 15. Kalligone.........................830 87
  V. 16. Herder's Leben; von Ring..........830 88
  V. 17-18. Fragmente zur deutschen Literatur...830 89
  V. 19. Der Cid..........................830 91
  V. 20-21. Kritischer Wälder................830 92
  V. 22. Dramatische Stücke und Dichtungen...830 94
  V. 23. Abhandlungen und Briefe über schöne Literatur und Kunst........................830 95
  V. 24. Stimmen der Völker in Liedern......830 96
  V. 25. Blumenlese aus Morgenländischen Dichtern......................................830 97
  V. 26. Schriften zur griechischen Literatur....830 98
  V. 27. Schriften zur römischen Literatur.....830 99
  V. 28. Früchte aus den 18ten Jahrhundert...830 100
  V. 29. Nachlese zur schönen Literatur und Kunst....................................830 101
  V. 30-32. Gedichte.......................830 102

Hertza. Freeland........................=9575
Hesekiel. Two queens...................=13101
Heyse. Annina, etc. (German)...........=204
  At the ghost hour. 4 v..................=234
  Contents: The fair Abigail.—The forest laugh.—The house of the unbelieving Thomas.— Mid-day magic.
  Barbarossa (German)....................=209
  Same; tr...............................=216
  Die beiden Schwestern, etc..............=206
  Die Blinden.— Marion, etc...............=201
  Children of the world...................=212
  Dead lake..............................=215
  Divided heart, etc......................=233
  Contents: A divided heart. Minka.—Rothenburg on the Tauber.
  Die Einsamen, etc.......................=203
  Er soll dein Herr sein, etc...............=210
  Das Glück von Rothenburg...............=223
  Hans Lange.............................=224
  Himmlische und irdische Liebe...........=229
  Contents: Himmlische und irdische Liebe.—F.V.R.I.A.—Auf Tod und Leben.
  Im Paradiese. 3 v......................=213
  In paradise. 2 v.......................=217
  Incurable..............................=231
  Kinder der Welt. 3 v...................=211
  Das Mädchen von Treppi, etc............=202
  Meraner Novellen: Anheilbar, etc........=205
  Merlin (German). 3 v...................=232
  Moralische Novellen....................=208
  Mutter und Kind........................=207
  Novellen in Versen. 1873. 2 v..........831 20
  Das Räthsel des Lebens, etc............=239
  Der Roman der Stiftsdame...............=227
  Romance of the canoness................=228
  Troubadour Novellen....................=222
  Vetter Gabriel.........................=226

Hillern. Ein Arzt der Seele.............=319
  Aus eigener Kraft......................=301
  Doppelleben. 2 v.......................=304
  Elsie and her vulture [Die Geier-Wally].=311A
  Ernestine [Ein Arzt der Seele]..........=307
  Die Geier-Wally........................=312
  Graveyard flower.......................=321
  Höher als die Kirche...................=322
  The hour will come.....................=318
  On the cross, Oberammergau.............=323
  Only a girl [Ein Arzt der Seele]........=306
  A two-fold life [Doppelleben]..........=315
  Vulture maiden [Die Geier-Wally].......=311

Hofer. Die Bettelprinzess..............=2705
  Haus an Haus..........................=2703
  Land und See..........................=2704
  The old countess......................=2701

Hoffmann, E. T. W. Das Fräulein von Scuderi................................=1428
  Meister Martin........................=1425
  The Serapion brethren. 2 v............=1426
  Weird tales 2 v.......................=1427

Hoffman, F. Buried in the snow........=5405
  Dominic; tr...........................=5401
  Heute mir Morgen dir; ed. by Maude. 1894.................................=5407
  Iron age of Germany...................=5404
  Iron head.............................=5402
  Prince Wolfgang.......................=5403
  Treasure of the Inca..................=5406

Horn. Count Sylvius..................=8201
Howard, E. See novels tr. into German, cataloged under ENGLISH LITERATURE.

Humboldt, A. von. Letters to Varnhagen
 von Ense, 1827-58. 1860..................836 5
Humboldt, W. von. Thoughts and opin-
 ions of a statesman. 1849.................836 25
Immerman. Der Oberhof.....................=6301
Ingersleben. Little Heather-blossom
 (Erica)..=9579
Jean Paul. See **Richter.**
Jensen. Auf der Ganerbenburg.............=9612
 Das Asylrecht..=9604
 Die braune Erica...=9605
 Doppelleben..=9606
 Heimkunft...=9609
 Herr Senator...=9608
 Karine; tr..=9611
 Kinder vom Oedacker................................=9607
 Metamorphosen..=9603
 Die Pfeifer vom Dusenbach.................=9602
 Runic rocks...=9610
 Vom alten Stamm.......................................=9601
John, E. See **Marlitt.**
Juncker. Margarethe; tr......................=3801
Junghans. Die Brautschau................=12601
Kant. Sämmtliche Werke. 1867-8. 8 v......193 9
Keller. Der grüne Heinrich.................=8302
 Das Sinngedicht...=8301
 Züricher Novellen.....................................=8304

 Contents: Hadlaub.—Narr auf Manegg.—Landvogt
 von Greifensee.—Fähnlein der sieben Aufrechten.—Ur-
 sala.

Kinkel, G. and J. Erzählungen.............=1435
Klein. Blinde Liebe...............................=1432
Klopstock. Der Messias. 1818. 4v........831 53
 Sämmtliche Werke. 18 v. 1823-30.
  V. 1-2. Oden.............................830 248
  V. 3-6. Der Messias.................830 250
  V. 7. Oden................................830 254
  V. 8. Der Tod Adams.—Hermann's Schlacht..830 255
  V. 9. Salomo.—Hermann und die Fürsten....830 256
  V. 10. David.—Hermann's Tod...........830 257
  V. 11. Hinterlaszne Schriften von Margarethe
   Klopstock..................................830 258
  V. 12. Die deutschen Gelehrtenrepublik........830 259
  V. 13-15. Sprachwissenschäftliche Schriften..830 260
  V. 16. Ästhetische Schriften...................830 263
  V. 17. Uebersetzungen, u. s. w................830 264
  V. 18. Klopstock's Briefe......................830 265
Kohn. Gabriel; tr................................=1801
Kompert. Christian und Leah..............=9202
 Scenes from the Ghetto............................=9201
Körner. Corr. with Schiller. 1849. 3 v...836 15
 Life, with selections from poems, etc '27..830 9
 Sämmtliche werke. 1842. 2 v..........831 27
Kotzebue. Dramatic works; tr. by
 Thompson. 1802. 3 v.
  V. 1. Rolla. Pizarro. Count Benyowsky....832 25
  V. 2. The stranger.—Lovers' vows. Happy
   family....................................832 26
  V. 3. Adelaide of Wulfingen. False delicacy.
   Deaf and dumb. Indian exiles...............832 27

Lover's vows [drama]; tr by Thomp-
 son......................................*in* 822.2 147
Theatre. 1841. 40 v. in 20................832 5
Kühne, A. See **Dewall, J. van.**
Lamotte-Fouqué. Aslauga's Ritter........=907
 Four seasons...=905
 Romantic fiction..=904
 Sintram..=901
 Thiodolf, the Icelander................................=903
 Undine (German)..=902A
 Undine, etc..*=902
  Contents: Undine.—Two captains.—Aslauga's knight.
  —Sintram.
 Der Zauberring...=906
Leibniz. Œuvres. 1859-75. v. 1-7.......193 42
Lennep. Count of Talevera................=7001
 Rose of Dekama...=7002
Lessing. Ausgewählte Prosa und Briefe;
 ed. by White. 1891......................839 12
 Dramatic works; tr. by Bell. 1878. 2 v.
  V. 1. Miss Sara Sampson.— Emilia Galotti
   —Nathan the wise....................832 43
  V. 2. Damon.—The young scholar.—The old
   maid.—The woman-hater.—The Jews.—The free-
   thinker.—The treasure.—Minna von Barnhelm..832 44
 Gesammelte Werke. 1864.
  V. 1. Sinngedichte.—Anhang.—Lieder.—An-
  hang.—Oden.—Fabeln und Erzählungen.—Die Ju-
  den.—Der Freigeist.—Dokter Faust.—Werther der
  Bessere.—Miss Sara Sampson.—Philotas.—Minna
  von Barnhelm.—Emilia Galotti.—Nathan der Weise.
  —Briefe aus dem zweiten Theile der Schriften.—
  Ein Vade Mecum für den Herrn S. G. Lange, Pastor
  in Laublingen.— Rettungen des Horaz.—Abhandlungen über die Fabel.—Vorreden, etc.—Sopho-
  kles.—Wie die Alten den Tod gebildet.—Antiquar-
  ische Briefe.................................830 B-11
  V. 2. Laokoon.—Zerstreute Anmerkungen über
  das Epigramm und einige der vornehmsten Epi-
  grammatisten.—Hamburgische Dramaturgie.—
  Vom Alter der Oelmalerei aus dem Theophilus Pres-
  byter.— Zur Geschichte und Literatur—Theolog-
  ische Streitschriften.—Ernst und Falk.—Briefe, etc.
  ....830 B-12
 Laocoon; tr. by Phillimore. 1874........701 5
 Same; tr. by Frothingham. 1874.......701 6
 Nathan the wise [drama]; tr. by Froth-
  ingham, with Fischer's essay. 1878....832 40
 Same; tr. by Jacks. 1894..............832 63
Lewald, F. See **Stahr.**
Lieber. Letters. 1882....................928.3 39
Lindau, P. Die Brüder....................=10301
 Hanging moss..=10307
 Klaus Bewer's wife.....................................=10304
 Lace...=10305
 Mr. and Mrs. Bewer (Klaus Bewer's
  wife)...=10304A
 Toggenburg, und andere Geschichten..10303
Lindau, R. Der Gast.........................10320
 Gordon Baldwin, and The philosopher's
  pendulum...10325
 Gute Gesellschaft......................................10321
 Liquidated.—The seer..............................10323

* Of interest to young readers.

Liszt. Letters; ed. by La Mara. 1894. 2v..836 23
Luther. Hymns; tr. by Bacon and Allen..245 B-1
  Reading notes on; by Edmands. 1883
  ....16 Pam. 13
  Select treatises (German); ed. by Sears.
  1846...438 1
Magic ring...1412
Manteuffel. Violetta; tr.............=10801
Marlitt. Amtmann's Magd................556
  At the councillor's 506
  Bailiff's maid.................................=550
  Countess Gisela............................=521
  Das Eulenhaus..............................=509
  Das Geheimniss der alten Ma'mssell....=513
  Gold Elsie......................................508
  Goldelse..540
  Das Haideprinzesschen...................501
  Im Hause des Commerzienrathes.....=514
  Im Schillingshof.............................=549
  In the schillingscourt......................=542
  Lady with the rubies......................=564
  Little moorland princess.................=503
  Old ma'mselle's secret...................=504
  Over yonder.................................=538
  The owl's nest..............................=505
  Reichsgräfin Gisela........................=519
  Second wife.................................=507
  Thuringer Erzählungen..................=502
  Die zweite Frau............................=520
Marryatt. See novels translated into German, included with other works of **Capt. Marryatt** in ENGLISH LITERATURE.
Meinhold. The amber witch..........=9536
  Sidonia, the sorceress.................=9535
  Same (Kelmscott press)............833 B-1
Mendelssohn. Letters; tr. and ed. by
  Moscheles. 1888.......................836 22
  Letters, 1830-32; tr. by Wallace...836 7
  Same, 1833-47............................836 8
Menger. Countess Loreley............=11601
Messmer. Red Carl.......................=11501
Meyer. Angela Borgia (German)....=7405
  Georg Jenatsch (German)...........=7401
  Der Heilige.................................=7402
  The monk's wedding...................=7403
  Tempting of Pescara..................=7404
Meyr. Zwei Freier.........................=11301
Moser. Der Bibliothekar [Lustspiel]; ed. by Lange. 1886.......................832 61
Mozart. Letters, 1769-91. 1866. 2 v...836 1
Mühlbach (C. M. Mundt). Andreas
  Hofer.......................................=403
  Berlin and Sans Souci................=417
  Bernthal..................................=433
  Conspiracy of the Carbonari.......=442
  Count Mirabeau........................=2301
  Daughter of an empress.............=415

Empress Josephine............................429
Frederick the great and his court........425
Frederick the great and his family......426
Goethe and Schiller...........................402
Henry VIII and his court....................421
Joseph II and his court......................440
Louisa of Prussia..............................413
Marie Antoinette and her sons...........435
Merchant of Berlin............................419
Mohammed Ali..................................=438
Napoleon and Blücher.......................=436
Napoleon and the Queen of Prussia..=405
Old Fritz..=407
Prince Eugene and his times.............=409
Queen Hortense...............................=411
Story of a millionaire.......................=444
Müller, M. Deutsche Liebe............=6203
  Memories [Deutsche Liebe]..........=6201
Müller, O. Charlotte Ackerman; tr..=2602
  Die Förstersbraut von Neunkirchen..=2605
  Doctor Göthe's courtship..............=2601
  Der Postgraf................................=2604
  Professor von Heidelberg (German)..=2603
Mundt. See **Mühlbach.**
Nieritz. Faithful unto death...........=5701
Nietzsche. Works; ed. by Tille, tr. by
  Common. 1896.....................830 335
  V. 11. The case of Wagner.—The twilight of the idols.
  —Nietzsche contra Wagner.
Nordau. Paradoxes. 1886..........104 21
Oertel. How the French took Algiers....803
  Olaf Thorlacksen; tr.......................802
  Schoolmaster of Abbach................801
Oswald. Vain forebodings............=10201
Palzow. Godway castle................=9505
Pantenius. Im Gottesländchen.......9509
Pestalozzi. Leonard and Gertrude..9507
Pichler. Daughter of Rome...........3605
Polko. Familien-ideale.................=5004
  Getrennt...................................=5002
  Herzensfrühling und Rosenzeit...=5003
  Lulu's novel.............................=5001
  Musikalische Märchen, etc. 2 v..=5005
Postl. Cabin book......................=4901
Putlitz. Forest voices. 1886.....839 4
Raabe. Abu Telfan (German)....=11003
  Die Akten des Vogelsangs......=11004
  Der Hungerpastor..................=11001
  Unruhige Gäste.....................=11002
Raimund. From hand to hand...=6704
  Hard heart............................=6710
  New race..............................=6703
  Sought and found..................=6712
Raspe. Baron Munchausen.......=13501
Rau. Mozart; tr.........................=6101
Reichenbach. The Eichoffs.......=7501
Reuter. Hanne Nüte (Gedichte). 1868...S31 29
  In the year 1813 [Ut de Franzosentid]..=4408

Kein Hüsung (Gedichte). 1865............831 32
Läuschen un Rimels (Gedichte). '68. 2v..831 30
Old story of my farming days [Ut mine Stromtid].......................................=4402
Olle Kamellen (German)......................=4406
De Reis' nah Belligen (Gedicht). 1867...831 33
Schurr Murr (German).........................=4405
Seed time and harvest [Ut mine Stromtid]..=4401
Ut mine Stromtid..................................=4409
Richter. Campaner Thal...................=2401
Flower, fruit and thorn pieces............=2408
Hesperus (German). 2 v.................830 188
Same; tr...=2404
Invisible lodge....................................=2411
Levana; tr. 1863...............................370 25
Maria Wuz; tr.....................................=2410
Sämmtliche Werke. 1840. 33 v. in 16.
   V. 1-2. Die unsichtbare Loge................830 186
   V. 3. Quintus Fixlein.—Einige Jus de tablette für Mannpersonen.................................830 187
   V. 4. Auswahl aus des Teufels Papieren........830 187
   V. 5-8. Hesperus..830 188
   V. 9. Grönländische Prozesse...................830 189
   V. 10. Biographische Belustigungen.—Der Jubelsenior..830 190
   V. 11-12. Siebenkäs: Blumen-, Frucht- und Dornenstücke..830 190
   V. 13. Kampaner Thal und Holzschnitte.—Jean Paul's Briefe.—Konjektural-Biographie..........830 191
   V. 14. Fata und Werke vor und in Nürnberg..830 192
   V. 15-16. Titan...830 192
   V. 17. Komischer Anhang zum Titan. — Klavis Fichtiana.— Das heimliche Klaglied der jetzigen Männer.—Die Wunderbare Gesellschaft in der Neujahrsnacht...830 193
   V. 18-19. Vorschule der Æsthetik.—Kleine Bücherschau.— Kleine Nachschule zur æsthetischen Vorschule..830 194
   V. 20-21. Flegeljahre...................................830 195
   V. 22-23. Levana; oder, Erziehlehre.—Ergänzblatt zur Levana.—Freiheits-Büchlein............830 196
   V. 24. Doctor Katzenberger's Badreise.......830 197
   V. 25. Friedenspredigt an Deutschland.— Dämmerungen für Deutschland.— Mars und Phöbus Thronwechsel.— Politische Fastenpredigten........830 197
   V. 26. Leben Fibels.—Des Feldpredigers Schmelzle Reise nach Flätz................................830 198
   V. 27. Museum.—Ueber die deutschen Doppelwörter..830 198
   V. 28-29. Der Komet.— Briefe an Friedrich Heinrich Jakobi..830 199
   V. 30-31. Herbst Blumine............................830 200
   V. 32. Gesammelte Aufsätze und Dichtungen...830 201
   V. 33. Selina.— Vorlaufige Gedanken.........830 201
Titan. 2 v..830 192
Same; tr...=2402
Walt and Vult [Flegeljahre]................=2406
Riehl. Burg Neideck (German)..........=9558
Culturgeschichtliche Novellen..............=9559
Fluch der Schönheit............................=9557
Ring. John Milton and his times......=2501
Rodenberg. Grandidiers...................=7601
Roquette. Conrad Hagen's mistake...=7201

Curate of Orsières................................=7202
Der gefrorene Kuss..............................=138
Rückert. Wisdom of the Brahmin (books 1-6) [poem]; tr. by Brooks...................831 48
Rudiger. Waldtraut...........................=13301
Ruppins. Two hemispheres.............=3901
Sacher Masoch. Jewish tales...........=11904
Le legs de Caïn..................................=11905
New Job...=11901
Seraph; tr...=11903
Sirène (French)..................................=11902
Sachs. Von ihm und über ihn: Antiquarischer Anzeiger von Jos. Baer & Co., Buchhandlung. 1894............16 Pam. 66
St., W. von. In exile........................=1424
Salinger. Schicksalstragödie...........=9514
Schefer. The world-priest [poem]; tr. by Brooks. 1873....................................831 18
Scheffel. Ekkehard (German)........=1902
Same; tr...=1901
Gaudeamus (Gedichte). 1881............831 65
Same; tr. by Leland. 1872.................838 1
Frau Aventure (Gedichte). 1879........831 66
Trumpeter of Säkkingen. 1879..........831 90
Trumpeter von Säkkingen (Gedicht). 1884...831 65
Schiller. Complete works; ed., with revision and new tr., by Hempel. '70. 2v.
   V. 1. Sketch of life.— Poetical works.— The robbers.—Frisco.— Love and intrigue.— The misanthrope.— Homage of the arts.—Don Carlos.— Mary Stuart.—Maid of Orleans.—On the use of the chorus in tragedy.— Bride of Messina.— Camp of Wallenstein.—Piccolomini.—Death of Wallenstein.— Wilhelm Tell.— Posthumous works.— Demetrius.— Warbeck.—The Maltese.—Children of the house..830 B-1
   V. 2. History of the revolt of the United Netherlands.—Trial and execution of Egmont and Horn. —Siege of Antwerp, 1584-85.—History of the thirty years' war in Germany. — On the connection of man's animal and spiritual natures. — The ghostseer.— Philosophical letters. —Thoughts concerning the first human society.—Miscellaneous essays, etc..830 B-2
Corr. with Goethe. 1877. 2 v.............836 9
Corr. with Körner. 1849. 3 v............836 15
Death of Wallenstein; tr. by Coleridge...810 7
Early dramas and romances; tr. by Bohn. 1867...832 28
   Contents: The robbers.— Frisco.— Love and intrigue. — Demetrius.—Ghost-seer.—Sport of destiny.
Historical dramas; tr. 1854..............832 30
   Contents: Don Carlos.— Mary Stuart.— Maid of Orleans.— Bride of Messina.
Homage of the arts; tr. by Brooks.......831 14
Mary Stuart; tr. by Kemble............in 822.2 227
The Piccolomini; tr. by Coleridge......810 7
Poems; tr. by Bowring. 1874.............831 12
Poems and ballads; tr. by Lytton........831 13
Sämmtliche Werke. 1855. 2 v.
   V. 1. Gedichte.— Die Räuber.— Fiesco zu Genua. — Kabale und Liebe.— Der Menschenfeind.—Die

Huldigung der Kunste. Metrische Uebersetzungen. — Don Carlos.—Phädra.—Wallenstein.— Macbeth. - Wilhelm Tell. -Turandot, Prinzessin von China. -Der Parasit.—Der Neffe als Onkel.—Maria Stuart. Die Jungfrau von Orleans.—Die Braut von Messina.—Nachlass..830 II-9
V. 2. Geschichte des Abfalls der Vereinigten Niederland. — Geschichte des Dreissigjährigen Krieges—Prosaische Schriften........................830 II- 10
Wallenstein; tr. by Lockhart. 1887......832 29
Works, historical and dramatic.............832 31
Contents: Revolt of the Netherlands.—Wallenstein's camp.—The Piccolomini.— Death of Wallenstein.—Wilhelm Tell.

Schlegel, A. W. von, Sämmtliche Werke. 12 v. 1846.
V. 1-2. Gedichte...830 235
V. 3-4. Poetische Uebersetzungen und Nachbildungen...830 237
V. 5-6. Dramaturgische Vorlesungen...............830 239
V. 7-12. Vermischte und kritische Schriften......830 241

Schlegel, F. Æsthetic and miscellaneous works; tr. by Millington. 1860........834 1
Lects. on the history of literature. 1868..809 8
Sämmtliche Werke. 1822. 10 v.
V. 1-2. Geschichte der alten und neuen Litteratur...830 266
V. 3-4. Studien des classischen Alterthums........830 268
V. 5. Kritik und Theorie der alten und neuen Litteratur...830 270
V. 6. Ansichten und Ideen von der christlichen Kunst...830 271
V. 7. Romantische Sagen und Dichtungen des Mittelalters..830 272
V. 8-9. Gedichte..830 273
V. 10. Die romantische Dichtkunst.—Neue Kunst und Litteratur.—Alte Weltgeschichte...........830 275

Schmid. Habermeister.............................=4001
Schmithof. Six cups of chocolate [comedy]. 1897..832 Pam. 2
Schobert. Aschenbrödel........................=11403
Künstlerblut..=11402
Picked up in the streets..........................=11401
Schoenaich-Carolath. Melting snows...=2810
Schopenhauer. Sämmtliche Werke; herausgegeben von Frauenstädt. '91. 6v..193 79
Select essays; tr. by Droppers et al. 1881...193 88
Selected essays. 1891.............................193 89
Schröder. Isabel (German)...................=10601
Schubin. Boris Lensky (German)..........=10006
Boris Lensky; tr.....................................=10007
Closing door..=10011
Countess Erika's apprenticeship............=10008
Erlach Court...=10003
Felix Lanzberg's expiation....................=10009
Gloria victis! tr....................................=10002
Leafless spring......................................=10010
O thou, my Austria!.............................=10004
Our own set..=10001
Schulze-Smidt. Madonna of the Alps...=12901
Schumann. Jugendbriefe. 1886...........836 18
Schweichel. Camilla............................=9533

Scott, *Sir* **W.** See novels translated into German, cataloged with other works of **Scott** in ENGLISH LITERATURE.
Seidel. Gesammelte Schriften. 12 v.
V. 1. Leberecht Hünchen, und andere Geschichte. ....=12801
V. 2. Vorstadtgeschichten............................=12802
V. 3. Neues von Leberecht Hünchen und anderen Sonderlingen...=12803
V. 4. Geschichten und Skizzen aus der Heimath..=12804
V. 5. Die goldene Zeit..................................=12805
V. 6. Ein Skizzenbuch..................................=12806
V. 7. Glockenspiel......................................831 107
V. 8. Leberecht Hünchen als Grossvater........=12807
V. 9. Sonderbare Geschichten......................=12808
V. 10. Der Schatz, und Anderes...................=12809
V. 11. Neues Glockenspiel..........................831 108
V. 12. Berliner Skizzen................................=12810
Sheip. Greek maid..................................=5801
Simrock. Wieland der Schmied (Gedicht). 1851..831 104
Sperl. Die Fahrt nach der alten Urkunde..=10103
Die Söhne des Herrn Budiwoj. 2 v....=10101
Spielhagen. Allzeit voran.......................=3420
An der Heilquelle...................................=3440
Angela (German)....................................=3428
Aus meinem Skizzenbuche......................=3416
Blockhouse on the prairie.......................=3430
Breaking of the storm [Sturmflut]..........=3407
Hammer and anvil...................................=3406
Hammer und Amboltz.............................=3418
Hohensteins...=3402
In Reih' und Glied.................................=3414
Kleine Romane. 2 v.
V. 1. Clara Vere.—Auf der Düne.—In der zwölften Stunde.—Röschen vom Hofe..................=3437
V. 2. Die schönen Amerikanerinnen.—Hans und Grete.—Die Dorfcoquette,— Deutsche Pionere.=3438
Lady Clare de Vere................................=3425
Ein neuer Pharao...................................=3436
Noblesse oblige (German).....................=3435
Platt Land...=3439
Problematic characters.........................=3403
Problematische Naturen. 2 v................=3410
Quisisana (German)...............................=3426
Same; tr..=3424
Skeleton in the house............................=3427
Sturmflut. 2 v.......................................=3422
Through night to light...........................=3404
Uhlenhans...=3431
Die von Hohenstein...............................=3413
Was die Schwalbe sang..........................=3421
Was will das werden?...........................=3432
What the swallow sang..........................=3401
Spyri. Gritli's children.........................039106
Heidi; tr..039101
Red letter stories..................................039102
Rico and Stineli....................................039105
Swiss stories...039103
Uncle Titus...039104
Veronica and other friends...................039104

Stahr (F. Lewald). Hulda; tr. =601
  Josias (German). =609
  Lake house. =604
  Stella; tr. =605
Stein. Count Erbach. =9101
Stinde. Buchholz family. =9520
  Buchholzens in Italien. =9525
  Der familie Buchholz. =9523
  Frau Buchholz im Orient. =9527
  Frau Wilhelmine. =9526
  Hotel Buchholz (German). =9528
  Woodland tales. =9522
Storm. Auf der Universität. =7103
  Hans und Heinz Kuch. =7102
  Die Söhne des Senators. =7101
Strauss. Glory of the house of Israel. =4101
Streckfuss. Castle Hohenwald. =4212
  Quicksands. =4214
  Sliko (German). =4202
  Too rich. =4201
Sudermann. Dame Care. =12001
  Die Ehre (drama). 1895. 832 71
  Es war. =12003
  Frau Sorge. =12001A
  Geschwister. =12004
    Contents: Die Geschichte der stillen Mühle. — Der Wunsch.
  Heimath (drama). 1893. 832 72
  Im Zwielicht. =12007
  Iolanthes Hochzeit. =12006
  Der Katzensteg. =12005
  Magda [drama]; tr. by Winslow. 1896..832 68
  Sodoms Ende (drama). 1895. 832 70
  The wish. =12002
Suttner. Ground arms! =12301
Sweichel. Die Falkner von St. Vigil. =9401
Taylor. Antinous; tr. =8401
  Jetta (German). =8404
  Klytia (German). =8402
  Same; tr. =8403
  Through deep waters. =1411
Tieck. Sämmtliche Werke. 1837. 2v.
    V. 1. Kaiser Octavianus.—Leben und Tod der heiligen Genoveva. Der Abschied.—Leben und Tod des kleinen Rothkäppchens.—Fortunat.—Phantasus: Der blonde Eckbert.—Der getreue Eckart. — Der Runenberg. — Liebeszauber. — Liebesgeschichte der schönen Magelone.—Die Elfen.—Der Pokal.- Der Blaubart. — Der gestiefelte Kater.— Die verkehrte Welt.—Leben und Thaten des kleinen Thomas. William Lovell. Das grüne Band. 830 B-13
    V. 2. Abdallah.—Die Brüder.—Almansur.—Denkwürdige Geschichtschronik der Schildbürger.— Die sieben Weiber des Blaubart.—Leben des Kaisers Abraham Tonelli,—Das jüngste Gericht. Prinz Zerbino. Karl von Berneck.—Das Ungeheuer.—Alla-Moddin. Herr von Fuchs.—Epicoene. Die Theegesellschaft — Die Geschichte von den Heymons-Kindern Sehr wunderbare Historie von der Melusina. König Rother. Das Donauweib, erste Akt. Prologe. Der Autor. Schicksal.

— Die männliche Mutter.—Die Rechtsgelehrten.— Die Versöhnung.—Der Fremde.—Die Freunde.— Der Geheimnissvolle.—Peter Lebrecht.—Die beiden merkwürdigsten Tage aus Siegmund's Leben.— Fermer.— Der Naturfreund.—Die gelehrte Gesellschaft.—Der Psycholog.—Der Roman in Briefen.— Ein Tagebuch.—Ulrich.--Die Gemälde.—Die Verlobung.—Die Reisenden.—Der Jahrmarkt.—Musikalische Leiden und Freuden.—Pietro von Abano..830 B-14
  Tales of Fairyland. 038008
Truth, *pseud.* Hefe im Schaum. =13401
Uhland. Gedichte und Dramen. 831 116
  Songs and ballads; tr. by Skeat. '64..831 26
Ulrici. Shakespeare's dramatic art. '46..822.3 56
Velatus. Schlangenmoos. =9515
Village astronomer. =1410
Volckhausen. Why did he not die?. =5501
Vosmaer. The Amazon. =9901
Vosz. Dahiel, der Konvertit. =11701
Wagner. Letters to August Roeckel. '97..836 27
  Pilgrimage to Beethoven. =1437
  Prose works. 1893—. v. 1—. 780 95
Wald-Zedwitz. Die Schlossfrau von Scharfenstein. =9513
Walloth. King's treasure house. =9518
Walree, *Madame* von. Burgomaster's family. =3201
Walther von der Vogelweide. Gedichte; herausgegeben von Pfeiffer. 1873. 831 92
  Gedichte; uebersetzt von Simrock. 1869. 831 69
  Sämmtliche Gedichte; übersetzt von Kleber. 1894. 831 109
  Selected poems; tr. by Phillips. 1896..831 119
Werder. Roland (German). =11510
Werner, E., *pseud.* (E. Buersterbinder).
  Alpenfee. =4525
  Alpine fay. =4524
  Am Altar.—Hermann. =4531
  At a high price. =4504
  At the altar. =4540
  Clear the track! =4530
  Danira. =4538
  Der Egoist. =4515
  Ensnared and released [Banned and blessed]. =4523C
  Frühlingsboten. =4511
  Gebannt und erlöst. =4522
  Gesprengte Fesseln. =4510
  Glück auf!. =4502
  Good luck. =4501
  Ein Held der Feder.—Heimatklang. =4537
  Hermann; tr. =4507
  Hero of the pen. =4536
  Lover from across the sea. =4529
  Master of Ettersberg. =4532
  No surrender [At a high price]. =4504A
  Northern light. =4526

Saint Michael	=4519
Sankt Michael	=4520
Spell of home	=4521
Um hohen Preis	=4503
Under a charm [Vineta]. 3 v	=4505
Vineta (German)	=4506

Werner, F. L. Z. Templars in Cyprus (drama). 1886 ... 832 57
Wertmeister. Vergehens ... =9517
Wette. Theodore. 1841. 2 v ... 249 17
White, *ed.* Ruins of the Rhine ... =1414
Wichert. Eine vornehme Schwester ... =705
   Green gate ... =701
Wieland. Dialogues of the gods. 1795..324 119
   The graces. 1823 ... 831 97
   Oberon [poem]; tr. by Sotheby. 1826. 2 v ... 831 42
   Republic of fools. 1861. 2 v ... 837 2
   Sämmtliche Werke. 1814 45 v.
     V. 1-3 Agathon ... 830 132
     V. 4-5. Der neue Amadis.—Der vorklagte Amor ... 830 135
     V. 6-7. Der goldene Spiegel ... 830 137
     V. 8. Der weise Danischmend ... 830 139
     V. 9-10. Kleine poetische Schriften ... 830 140
     V. 11-12. Don Sylvio von Rosalva ... 830 142
     V. 13. Diogenes von Sinope ... 830 144
     V. 14. Beitragen zur geheimen Geschichte der Menschheit ... 830 145
     V. 15. Vermischte prosaische Aufsätze ... 830 146
     V. 16. Cyrus.—Araspes und Xanthea ... 830 147
     V. 17. Idris und Zenide ... 830 148
     V. 18. Erzählungen und Mährchen ... 830 149
     V. 19-20. Die Abderiten ... 830 150
     V. 21. Gandalin.—Klelia und Sinibald ... 830 152
     V. 22-23. Oberon ... 830 153
     V. 24. Vermischte Aufsätze ... 830 155
     V. 25. Götter-Gesprach.—Gespräche in Elysium 830 156
     V. 26. Singspiele und Abhandlungen ... 830 157
     V. 27-28. Peregrinus Proteus ... 830 158
     V. 29-30. Vermischte Aufsätze ... 830 160
     V. 31. Gespräche unter vier Augen ... 830 162
     V. 32. Agathodämon ... 830 163
     V. 33-36. Aristipp's Briefe ... 830 164
     V. 37. Eutanasia ... 830 168
     V. 38. Das Hexameron von Rosenhain ... 830 169
     V. 39. Menander und Glycerion.—Krates und Hipparchia ... 830 170
     V. 40-45. Supplemente ... 830 171
Wilbrandt, A. Adams Söhne ... =9803
   Die Eidgenossen: Schauspiel. 1896 ... 832 59
   Fridolin's mystical marriage ... =9801
   Hermann Ifinger (German) ... =9804
Wilbrandt, C. Mr. East's experiences in Mr. Bellamy's world ... =12101
Wildenbruch. Master of Tanagra ... =11101
   Noble blood ... 16128
   Heinrich und Heinrichs Geschlecht (drama). 1895 ... 832 69
Wildenhahn. Diet of Augsburg ... =8602
   Hans Sachs; tr ... =8603
   John Arndt; tr ... =8604
   Martin Luther; tr ... =8601
   Paul Gerhardt; tr ... =8605
   Philipp Jacob Spener; tr ... =8606
Wildermuth. Household stories ... 038801
   Youthful nobility ... =1415
Wister, *tr.* Alpine fay; by Werner ... =4524
   At the councillor's; by Marlitt ... =506
   Bailiff's maid; by Marlitt ... =550
   Banned and blessed; by Werner ... =4523
   Castle Hohenwald; by Streckfuss ... =4212
   Countess Erika's apprenticeship; by Schubin ... =10008
   Countess Gisela; by Marlitt ... =521
   Eichhofs; by Reichenbach ... =7501
   Enchanting and enchanted; by Hackländer ... 038030
   Erlach Court; by Schubin ... =10003
   Family feud; by Harder ... =1101
   From hand to hand; by Raimund ... =6704
   Gold Elsie; by Marlitt ... =508
   Green gate; by Wichert ... =701
   Hulda; by Stahr ... =601
   In the Schillingscourt; by Marlitt ... =542
   Lady with the rubies; by Marlitt ... =564
   Little moorland princess; by Marlitt ... =503
   Margarethe; by Juncker ... =3801
   New race; by Raimund ... =6703
   Noble name; by Glümer ... =8801
   O thou, my Austria! by Schubin ... =10004
   Old mam'selle's secret; by Marlitt ... =504
   Only a girl; by Hillern ... =306
   Owl's nest; by Marlitt ... =505
   Penniless girl; by Heimburg ... =6902
   Picked up in the streets; by Schobert ... =11401
   Quicksands; by Streckfuss ... =4214
   Saint Michael; by Werner ... =4519
   Second wife; by Marlitt ... =507
   Severa; by Hartner ... =7801
   Too rich; by Streckfuss ... =4201
   Vain forebodings; by Oswald ... =10201
   Violetta; by Manteuffel ... =10801
   Why did he not die? by Volckhausen ... =5501
Wolff. Fifty years, three months, two days ... =9542
   Das Pappenheimer (Gedicht). 1889 ... 831 99
   Rattenfänger von Hameln ... 831 98
   The robber count ... =9541
   Salt master of Lüneburg ... =9540
Zschokke. Gesammelte Schriften. 27 v.
   V. 1. Alamontade.—Harmonius.—Der Eros.—Die Herrnhuter-Familie ... 830 103
   V. 2. Diocletian in Salona.—Blätter aus dem Tagebuch des armen Pfarr-Vikars von Wiltshire—Die Verklärungen.—Kleine Ursachen.—Jonathan Frock ... 830 104
   V. 3. Ein Narr das 19ten Jahrhunderts.—Die weiblichen Stufenjahre.—Der Millionär.—Der todte Gast.—Der Fürstenblick.—Das Loch im Aermel. 830 107
   V. 4. Addrich im Moos ... 830 108
   V. 5. Der Freihof von Aarau ... 830 131

V. 6. Der Flüchtling im Jura.—Die Gründung von Maryland.—Die Irrfahrt des Philhelenen.—Florette.—Maryam in der Wüste............830 110
V. 7. Die Prinzessin von Wolfenbüttel.—Agathoklas.—Der Pflanzer in Cuba.—Hermingarda......830 111
V. 8. Der Pascha von Buda.—Der Creole.—Der Feldweibel..830 112
V. 9. Das Abenteuer der Neujahrsnacht.—Die Walpurgisnacht.—Der Blondin von Namur.—Kriegerische Abenteuer eines Friedfertigen.—Die Bohne.—Die Nacht in Brczweznicisl.—Das Bein.—Es ist sehr möglich.—Erzählungen im Nebel.—Die isländischen Briefe.............................830 113
V. 10. Rückwirkungen.—Der zerbrochene Krug.—Herrn Quints Verlobung.—Haus dampf in allen Gassen.—Tantchen Rosmarin.—Die Reise wider willen.—Der Abend vor der Hochzeit.—Das Wirthshaus zu Cransac.................................830 114

V. 11. Die Rose von Disentis.—Die Liebe der Ausgewanderten.—Schulze von Celle und Cäcilie..830 115
V. 12. Lyonel Harlington.— Die Lampe des Anaxagoras.—An Euphrasien über dem Nachrum.—Der König von Akim.—An Rosais...............830 116
V. 13. Genfer Novellen...........................830 117
V. 14. Bilder aus dem häuslichen Leben.—Schweizerskizze.—Olavides.—Der Besuch im Marienbade..830 118
V. 15. Wie Mann lieben muss.—Abällino.—Gedichte..830 119
V. 16-27. Liebensweisheit und Religion........830 120
Labor stands on golden feet................05010
Princess of Brunswick-Wolfenbüttel......=1701
Sylvester night's adventure..............=1703

DUTCH AND FLEMISH LANGUAGES AND LITERATURE.

Beets (Hildebrand, *pseud.*). Le chambre obscure.....................................=1501
Bomhoff. Dictionary, English and Dutch. 2 v..‡439 4
Boosboom-Toussaint. Major Frank......=9506
Bosworth. Origin of the Dutch. 1846......439 1
Bowring *and* Van Dyk. Batavian anthology. 1824................................831 25
Brouwer. Akbar; tr...........................=6501
Couperus. Eline Vere; tr....................=9563
Footsteps of fate...........................=9562
Majesty......................................=9564
Cummins. Grammar of old Friesic. '81...439 10
Daal. Anna, the professor's daughter......=9508
Delepierre. Sketch of the history of Flemish literature. 1860.........................830 10
Eeden. Little Johannes......................=6520
Erasmus. In praise of folly, and Letter to Sir T. More..................................837 1
Hewett. Frisian language and literature. '79..439 9
Lennep. Story of an abduction..............=7003
Liefde. Postman's bag, etc..................020702
Walter's escape............................020701
Maartens, *pseud*. God's fool................9555
Greater glory...............................9556
Joost Avelingh.............................9552
My lady nobody............................9551
Old maid's love............................9553
Question of taste...........................9554

Maeterlinck. Les aveugles (drame). '91...842 131
Plays; tr. by Hovey. 1894................842 154
Contents: Princess Maleine.—The intruder.—The blind.—The seven princesses.
Treasure of the humble. 1897............844 78
Contents: Silence.—Awakening of the soul.—The predestined.—Mystic morality.—On women.—The tragical in daily life.—The star.—The invisible goodness.—The deeper life.—The inner beauty.
Princess Maleine [drama]; tr. 1892....842 133
La Princesse Maleine. 1891...............842 130
Les sept princesses (drame). 1891......842 132
Niew volledig woordenboek der Nederduitsche, Fransche, Engelsche, etc. 1848. 2 v................................‡439 7
Perelaer. Ran away from the Dutch........=9531
Sewel. Dictionary, English and Dutch. 1754. 2 v...................................‡439 2
Tollens. The Hollanders in Nova Zembla [poem]; tr. by Van Pelt..................831 52
Wallis. In troubled times...................=9504
Royal favor................................=9516
Wermeskerken-Junius. See **Woude, Johanna van**.
Werner. Humour of Holland. 1893........838 4
Wit, John de. Fables. 1703. 2 v..........839 5
Woude, J. van, *pseud*. (Madame Van Wermeskerken-Junius). Young wife's ordeal.....................................=6510

‡ For reference.

FRENCH LANGUAGE AND LITERATURE.

LANGUAGE.

Alexandre. Le musée de la conversation. 1892.................................‡849 42
Attwell. French-English pseudo-synonyms. 1886...........................‡441 1
Bernard. Traduction oral et la prononciation française. 1894...........441 4
Bescherelle frères. Dictionnaire usuel de tous les verbes français. 2 v...............‡443 6
Bolmar, ed. Colloquial phrases (French). 1854...........................440 4
Boyer. French dictionary. 1833.............‡443 5
Brachet. Dictionnaire etymologique. '80..‡442 1
Historical grammar of French. 1884...445 10
Clapin. Dictionnaire canadien-français. 1895............................‡447 1
Darmesteter. Grammaire historique. 1891–1894.........................445 22
Diez. Introduction to grammar of Romance languages........................475 1
Ernst. Introductory French course. 1861..445 11
Fasnacht. Organic method of studying French. 1881........................445 5
Fasquelle. Course of French language. 1870............................445 15
Fivas. Introduction to French language. 1868..........................849 25
Fleming *and* Tibbins. French-English and English-French dictionary. 1851..‡443 1
French principia. pt. 1. 1878............445 19
Girard. Synonymes français, et La prosodie française; par d'Olivet. 1752......444 3
Josset. French prosody. 1884............446 1
Juenzer. Dictionnaire des gallicismes, à l'usage des Allemands. 1830............‡443 4
Hamilton *and* Legros. Dictionnaire français-anglais. 1872.............‡443 B-7
Hamilton *and* Smith. English-French dictionary. 1875.................‡443 B-8
Hatzfeld *et* Darmesteter. Dictionnaire général de la langue française. 1895. v. 1..................‡443 B-9
Keetels. Oral method with French. pt. 1. 1870............................445 20
Koschwitz. Parlers parisiens. 1893.......441 2
Lafaye. Dictionnaire des synonymes français. 1884.....................‡444 B-1
Larmoyer. Collection of French homonyms, synonyms, etc. 1896.................444 4
Larousse. Analyse grammaticale...........445 16
Grammaire élémentaire lexicologique. 1881..........................445 21
Lévizac. French grammar. 1846..........445 12
Lewis. Romance languages. 1862.........440 1
Littré. Dictionnaire de la langue française. 1873-9. 4 v...................‡443 B 2
Supp. to same....................‡443 B 6
Magill. French grammar. 1870...........445 3
Marmontel. Leçons d'un père sur la grammaire.........................840 328
Morinière. French prepositions and idioms. 1880.......................445 4
Same; rev. 1884....................445 4A
Ollendorff. New method of learning French. 1848........................445 8
Petit de Julleville. Histoire de la langue et littérature française. 1896—. v 1—..840 397
Pinney. French teacher. 1850............440 2
Plan, *ed*. Macmillan's selection of French idioms. 1896...................‡443 8
Ploetz. Grammaire française à l'usage des Allemands. 1866...............445 13
Prendergast. French (Mastery series)....445 9
Ratti. French reader...................448 1
Reynal. The French verb. 1870..........445 18
Roget. Introduction to old French. 1887..449 1
Sardou. French language with or without a teacher. 1895. 3 v...............445 23
Sicard. Prononciation française. 1893.....441 3
Spiers. English-French and French-English dictionary. 1851. 2 v..........‡443 2
Stern *and* Méras. Étude progressive de la langue française. 1883............445 17
Storr. Hints on French syntax...........445 7
Talbot. French translation. 1855.........445 14
Thurot. Prononciation française. 1881-3. 3v..441 5
Turrell. Oral exercises in French phraseology, synonymy and idioms........444 2
Wall. Practical and historical French grammar. 1878........................445 2
Williams. English into French. 1866.....440 3
Getting to Paris. 1875..............445 1
Wilson. French-English dictionary. '34..‡443 B-1

LITERATURE.

HISTORY AND CRITICISM.

Albert. Littérature française au 19me siècle. 1887. 2 v..................840 368
Astie. Louis XIV and the writers of his age. 1855......................840 7
Besant. French humorists. 1877..........848 1
Studies in early French poetry. 1877......841 4
Blaze de Bury, *Madame*. Racine and French classical drama. 1845......842 90

‡ For reference.

Brunetière. Études critiques: histoire de la littérature française. 1893-4. 4 v..840 380
Poésie lyrique, 19me siècle. 1894..........841 83
La renaissance de l'idéalisme. 1896....840 395
Cary. Early French poets. 1846..............841 2
Crane, *ed.* Le romantisme français. '87...840 346
La société française, 17me siècle. 1889..840 363
Curwen, *tr.* French love songs.................841 6
Demogeot. History of French literature.'74..840 6
Edwards. Biographical history of the French academy......................928 4 4
Egger. L'Hellenisme en France. 1869.
2 v.....................................840 108
Faguet. Dix-huitième siècle. 1890.........844 47
Fauriel. History of Provençal poetry........841 7
Fontaine. Les poètes français du 19me siècle. 1889................................841 62
Foster. Rise of French drama: reference list. v. 4...............................16 55
Fuster, *ed.* L'année des poètes. 1894—....841 91
Géruzez. Histoire de la littérature française, jusqu'à la révolution. 1876. 2 v......840 84
Histoire de la littérature française, pendant la révolution. 1869...................840 86
Gilbert. Le roman en France pendant le 19me siècle. 1896....................843 8
Hueffer. The troubadours. 1878.............841 3
James. French poets and novelists '78....824.1 103
Keene. Literature of France. 1892.........840 370
Lanson. Histoire de la littérature française. 1895....................................840 393
Martin. Nos académiciens: Académie française. 1895.........................806 1
Masson. Poets and prose writers of France. 1868........................840 195
Matthews. French dramatists, 19th century. 1881................................842 91
Mixer. Manual of French poetry. 1874.....841 5
Morillot. Roman en France....................843 6
Nisard. Essais sur l'école romantique. '91..844 48
Histoire de la littérature française. 1889. 4 v...............................840 364
Owen. Skeptics of the French renaissance. 1893.....................................840 373
Contents: Montaigne.—Peter Ramus.—Charron.—Sanchez. La Mothe-le-Vayer. Pascal.
Petit de Julleville. Histoire de la langue et littérature française. 1896—. v 1—...840 397
Preston. Troubadours and trouvères. '76..841 59
Reynolds. Modern literature of France. 1839. 2 v..............................840 4
Rosières. Recherches sur la poésie contemporaine. 1896.......................841 99
Rougemont. Manuel de la littérature française. 1893.............................840 374
Saint-Palaye. Literary history of the troubadours; abridged by Dobson. 1837...................................841 69

Saintsbury. Essays on French novelists. 1891......................................843 7
Contents: Present state of the French novel.—Anthony Hamilton.—Alain René Lesage.—A study of sensibility.—Chas. de Bernard.—Alex. Dumas.—Théophile Gautier.—Jules Sandeau.—Octave Feuillet.—Gustave Flaubert.—Henry Murger.—Victor Cherbuliez.
Primer of French literature. 1880......840 261
Short history of French literature. 1882-4................................840 263
Schuré. Les grandes légendes de France. 1892....................................813 38
Contents: Les légendes de l'Alsace.— La grande-chartreuse.— Le Mont-Saint-Michel et son histoire.— Les légendes de la Bretagne.—La génie celtique.
Staaff. La littérature française. '75. 6v...840 110
Texte. Jean Jacques Rousseau et les origines du cosmopolitisme littéraire. 1895.....840 394
Tilley, *ed.* Literature of the French renaissance. 1885.........................840 339
Van Laun. History of French literature. 1876. 3 v................................840 1
Vinet. History of French literature, 18th century..................................840 262
Vogüé. Regards historiques et littéraires..844 50
Wells. Modern French literature. 1896...840 396
Wilkinson. Classic French course in English. 1886............................840 340
Wright. Literature of the troubadours.....571 12

COLLECTIONS.

Altemont, *ed.* Choix de poésies propres à être apprises par cœur dans les écoles. 1865...........................841 58
Anthologie des poètes français, 19me siècle. 3 v. 1888.......................‡841 54
Bérard. Leçons françaises. 1848............849 33
Book of French songs; tr. by Oxenford....841 53
Chants et chansons populaires de la France [avec accompagnement de piano par H. Colet]. 2 v.......................841 B-1
Choix de contes contemporains..............X 14402
Crane, *ed.* Chansons populaires. 1891....841 74
Finod, *tr.* Thousand flashes of French wit, etc. 1880..........................849 21
Fasnacht, *ed.* Specimens, French writers, 17-19th centuries. 1894...............840 390
Fasquelle, Louis. Colloquial French reader. 1863.........................849 30
First French reading book. 1878.............849 36
Fivas, Alain *de.* Classic French reader. 1850...................................849 31
Gagnon, *ed.* Chansons populaires du Canada. 1865..........................841 98
Gatien-Arnoult. Monuments de la littérature romane. 4 v....................840 B-9
Gay. Chansons, poésies et jeux français pour les enfants. 1896................841 102
Humour of France. 1892....................848 2

‡ For reference.

Lacroix, ed. Chefs-d'œuvre de l'éloquence parlementaire. 1893–. v. 1–..............845 3
Larchey, ed. L'esprit de tout le monde. 1892................849 34
Lenient. Poésie patriotique en France. 1894. 2 v...........................841 87
  V. 1. 16me et 17me siècles.
  V. 2. 18me et 19me siècles.
Lincy. Livre des proverbes français. 2 v. 1859................................849 26
Louis, F., ed. Poésies de l'enfance........*841 72
Love songs of France. 1896............841 100
Mariette. French and English idioms and proverbs. 1896. v. 1-2..............849 45
Massacre of the innocents, etc.; by Belgian writers.........................x14428
  Contents: Maeterlinck: Massacre of the innocents.—Eekhoud: Kors Davie; Ex-voto; Hiep-Hioup.—Lemonnier: Fleur-de-blé; Saint Nicholas eve.—Jenart: Trompe-la-mort. — Delattre: Pierre-de-la-Baraque. — Richelle: The shadowy bourne. — Ganir: Jacclard.— Demolder: The denial of Saint Peter.—Krains: The mountebanks.
Masson, ed. French classics. 1877. 7 v.
  V. 1. Corneille: Cinna.— Molière: Les femmes savantes......................840 196
  V. 2. Racine: Andromaque.—Corneille: Le menteur.........................840 197
  V. 3. Molière: Les fourberies de scapin. — Racine: Athalie..................840 198
  V. 4. Selections from letters of Madame de Sevigne, etc..................840 199
  V. 5. Selections of tales by modern authors........840 200
  V. 6. Regnard: Le joueur.—Brueys et Palaprat: Le grondeur..................840 201
  V. 7. Extracts from memoirs of 17th century; Louis XIV, etc...............840 202
  La lyre française. 1881..............841 42
Mellé. Contemporary French writers. '94...840 375
Ield French romances; tr. by Morris, introduction by Jacobs. 1896...............843 9
  Contents: Tale of King Coustans the emperor. — Friendship of Amis and Amile.—Tale of King Florus and the fair Jehane.—History of over sea.
arton, ed. Le Parnasse français. 1877.....841 1
astels in prose. 1890..............844 46
ellissier. Morceaux choisis des poètes du 16me siècle. 1897............841 101
ène du Bois, tr. and ed. French folly in maxims. 1894. 3 v..............849 39
  Contents: Of art.—Of letters.—Of philosophy.
rrault, et al. Fairy tales; tr. by Planché..038003
itevin. Illustrations littéraires de la France............................849 38
Petits poëtes français. 1856. 2 v......841 B-5
lodet. Beginner's French reader. 1868...849 37
mage, ed. ‡ Beautiful thoughts from French and Italian authors. 1866...‡849 1
cueil des fabliaux; ed. by Montaiglon. 1872. 6 v......................841 63
bertson. Century of French verse. '95...841 90
intsbury, ed. French lyrics. 1882......841 43
Specimens of French literature. 1883...840 264

Songs of France, with music.........784 B 17
Stephens, ed. Principal speeches of statesmen and orators of the French revolution. 1892. 2 v....................845 1
Tales for a stormy night...............x14420
  Contents: Tourguéneff: Ghosts. — Balzac: Miracle in Flanders.—Mérimée: Venus of Ille.—Daudet: Battle of Père-Lachaise.—Balzac: Farewell.
Théâtre contemporain. 1884. 3 v........842 106
Théâtre de campagne. 1884-90. 8 v.
  V. 1 Legouvé: Ma fille et mon bien.— Meilhac: Paturel.— Bornier: Le monde renversé.—Hervilly: La soupière.—Legouvé: Autour d'un berceau - Normand: Les petits cadeaux.— Hervilly: Silence dans les rangs.—Legouvé et Mérimée: La fleur de Tlemcen.— Chazel: Avant le bal.— Edmond: Un salon d'attente......................842 122
  V. 2. Labiche: La lettre chargée.— Droz: Les crises de Monseigneur.— Gondinet: Le mari qui dort; Les convictions de papa.— Sollohub: Sa canne et son chapeau; Une sérénade.— Hervilly Vent d'ouest.— Theuriet: La vieille maison........842 123
  V. 3. Dreyfus: La gifle.— Bornier: La cage du lion.—Hervilly: De Calais à Douvres.—Normand: À la baguette.— Dupin: Le coupé jaune,— Abraham: Georges et Georgette,— Narrey: O mon Adélaïde.— Daudet: Les prunes.— Hervilly: Les revanches de l'escalier.— Meilhac: La force des femmes......................842 124
  V. 4. Labiche: L'amour de l'art.— Hervilly: Entre la soupe et les lèvres.—Guiard: Volte-face. —Verconsin: Retour de Bruxelles.— Létorière: La corbeille de mariage.—Hervilly: Notre cher insensibilisateur!— Millaud: Le collier d'or.— Decourcelle: Marie Duval.- Theuriet: Les fraises........842 125
  V. 5. Narrey: Ho! le vert!—Decourcelle: La part du lion.— Najac et Bocage: Le valet de cœur, —Raibaud: Tout chemin mène à Rome.— Guiard: La mouche.— Rieux et d'Au: Aux arrêts.— Guillimot: Les deux souspréfets de X * * *.—Verconsin: Le cap de la trentaine.— Billet: L'Andalouse.— Hervilly: Scrupules.— Dreyfus: Le confessional..842 126
  V. 6. Legouvé: L'agrément d'être laide.—Dreyfus: Un crâne sous une tempête.— Delair: Une femme bien pleurée.— Ferrier: Comme on fait son lit.— Déroulède: Le sergent.— Verconsin: Secret de Théodore.— Cros: L'homme au pieds retournés. —Hervilly: Les enfants avant tout!; Le secret d'une vaincue.—Sollohub: L'embarras du choix.— —Bocage: Vénus.—Desbeaux: Vingt mille francs.— Ceillier: Les bouquets.— Séguin: Une pluie de baisers.—Delair: Vision de Claude.—Jouan: La perle fausse.— Cros: L'homme perdu............842 127
  V. 7. Legouvé: La matinée d'une étoile.—Cros: L'ami de la maison; L'homme propre; Le pendu; L'homme qui a trouvé.— Roseaux: La souris.— Normand: Le fou rire.— Létorière: La part de butin.— Sollohub: Le premier pas; Le feu follet. —Verconsin: Adélaïde et Vermouth.— Hervilly: La Marquise de Crac.— Desbeaux: L'invention de mon grandoncle l'archevêque de Béziers.—Mendel et Cordier: La bête noire.— Cahen et Sujol: À l'essai.—Guillemot: L'heure de la liberté.—Ehrard: Madame Limaray?...........................842 128
  V. 8. Verconsin: Le rideau.— Liquier: Un amour électrique.—Manuel: Traitement thermal. —Launay: Le premier roman.—Delaporte: L'article II.— Villetard: Le thème russe.— Cortambert: Retour de voyage.—Depré et Clairville: La crémaillère.—Marthold: Un proverbe de salon.—

* Of interest to young readers.   ‡ For reference.

Cros: Le violon.—Hervilly: La laitière et le pot aux roses. — Feydeau: Notre futur. — Laluyé: Une flèche.— Roseaux: Le rigollot.— Normand: Les claqueurs..842 129

Théâtre français du 19me siècle. 1879-82. 4 v.
V. 1. Hugo: Hernani.—Scribe: La verre d'eau. — Delavigne: Les enfants d'Édouard. — Bouilly: L'abbé de L'Épée......................................842 74
V. 2, Mélesville *et* Duveyrier: Michel Perrin. —Sandeau: Mademoiselle de la Seiglière.—Scribe *et* Delavigne; Le diplomate.—Dumas: Demoiselles de Saint-Cyr..842 75
V. 3. Lebrun: Marie Stuart.—Labiche *et* Jolly: La grammaire.—Girardin: La joie fait peur.—Scribe: Valérie..842 76
V. 4. Coppée: Le luthier de Crémone; Le trésor. —Banville: Gringoire.—Scribe *et* Legouvé: Adrienne Lecouvreur.— Delavigne: Louis XI. — Moinaux: Deux sourds. — Scribe *et* Legouvé: Bataille des dames..842 77

Théâtre français moderne. 1867-70. 3 v.
V. 1. Ponsard: Charlotte Corday. — Augier: Diane.— Wafflard *et* Fulgence: Voyage à Dieppe...842 95
V. 2, Sand: Molière.—Arago: Les aristocraties..842 96
V. 3. Barrière *et* Capendu :—Les faux bonshommes.— Ponsard: L'honneur et l'argent..........842 97

Turrell. Leçons françaises......................849 28
Villemarque. Ballads and songs of Brittany; tr. by Tom Taylor. .1865..........841 8

FOLK LORE AND MEDIÆVAL LEGENDS.

(See Part 3 of FINDING LIST, pp. 519-520; and under Mediæval European Literature in this part, p. 27).

BIBLIOGRAPHY.

Annuaire de la librairie française, 1895........15 51
Bibliographie française. 1896. 6 v............15 54
Catalogue général de la librairie française..15 38
V., 9-10. Catalogue de 1876-85.
V. 11. Table des matières, t. 9-10.
V. 12. Catalogue, 1886-1890.
Le Soudier. Bibliographie française. 1896. 6 v...15 54
Librairie française. Catalogue annuel. '93..15 49
Lorenz. Catalogue mensuel de la librairie française. 1883..........................15 34
New York Mercantile Library. Findinglist, French prose fiction. 1888..........15 40
Nilsson. Catalogue mensuel de la librairie française....................................15 43
O., J. D. Some French bibliographies. '81..15 29
Thieme. La littérature française du 19me siècle. 1897...................................15 56

INDIVIDUAL AUTHORS.

À côté du bonheur....................................x4510
Abelard *and* **Eloisa.** Letters. 1802........846 43
About. Aunt's stratagem............................x622
Le buste..x620
Causeries. 1866. 2 v.........................844 12
Colonel Fouga's mistake..........................x610
Le dix-neuvième siècle. 1892.............844 52
The fellah..x617
Germaine (French)..................................x615
L'homme a l'oreille cassée...................x621
L'infâme..x606
King of the mountains..........................x612
Lawyer's nose......................................x609
Maitre Pierre..x609
Man with the broken ear.....................x601
La mère de la marquise......................x615
Mother of a marquise........................x622
New lease of life...................................x615
Le nez d'un notaire............................x607
Le roi des montagnes..........................x603
Le roman d'un brave homme..............x616
Story of an honest man.......................x613
Théatre impossible. 1864..................842 64
Contents: Guillery,—L'assassin.—L'education d'un prince.—Le chapeau de Sainte Catherine.
Tolla; tr..x602
Le Turco..x606
Les vacances de la comtesse..............x622
Achard. La toison d'or.........................x1901
Adam, *Madame.* Recits d'un paysanne.....x14501
Amazones de Paris.................................x4508
Arago. Les aristocraties [comédie]; ed. by Brette.................................842 96
Ardel. Près du bonheur........................x2805
Arène. La chèvre d'or.............................x16501
Domnine (French)..................................x16502
Golden goat..x16502
Assolant. History of the celebrated Pierrot..x6401
Aucassin and Nicolette; tr. by Bida and Macdonough. 1880....................841 48
Same; tr. by Lang. 1895.................841 93
Augier. Diane [drame]; ed. by Brette et al..842 95
Poésies. 1872.....................................841 15
Augier *and* **Sandeau.** Le gendre de M. Poirier (comédie)..........................842 107
Aulnoy, *Countess d'.* Fairy tales............03800
Balch. An author's love: unpublished letters of Mérimée's 'Inconnue.' '89...846 5
Balzac. Abbé Birotteau [English of Le curé de Tours]...............................x453A
(Same as The Vicar of Tours.)
About Catherine de' Medici..................x461A
After-dinner stories................................x434
Albert Savarus; tr..............................*in* x426
Same, etc..x426A
Contents: Albert Savarus. Paz. Madame Firmiani.
Alchemist [English of La recherche de l'absolu]...x425
(Same as 'The quest of the absolute' and 'The alkahest.')
Alkahest [Alchemist]............................x439
Atheist's mass, etc...............................x47
Béatrix; tr..x463

Brotherhood of consolation [L'envers
 de l'histoire contemporaine].................x457
 (Same as 'Love.')
Bureaucracy [Les employés].................x444
Cat and battledore [La maison du chat
 qui pelote] x422
Catherine de' Medici; tr.........................x461
César Birotteau....................................x435
Chouans; tr..x454
Comédie humaine; and its author, by
 Walker..x426
Contes drolatiques. 3 v........................x431
Correspondence. 2 v...................928.4 47
Country doctor...................................x437
Cousin Bette; tr..................................x442
Cousin Pons; tr...................................x421
Daughter of Eve.— A commission in
 lunacy.—The rural ball.....................x468
Deputy of Arcis..................................x478
Duchesse de Langeais; tr....................x430
Eugénie Grandet; tr............................x436
Fame and sorrow................................x447
Ferragus, chief of the Dévorants...........x464
(Same as ' Mystery of the rue Soly.')
Gallery of antiquities............................x470
Gobseck..x473
 Contents: Gobseck.— The secrets of the princesse de
 Cadignan.— Unconscious comedians.—Another study of
 woman.— Comedies played gratis.
La Grande Bretêche, etc.......................x472
 Contents: A study of woman.—Another study of wo-
 man.—La Grande Bretêche.—Peace in the house.—The
 imaginary mistress.—Albert Savarus.
Great man of the provinces in Paris........x456
Historical mystery [Une tenébreuse
 affaire]..x451
Juana..x475
 Contents: Juana.—Adieu.—A drama on the seashore.—
 The red inn.—The recruit.—El verdugo.—The elixir of
 life.—The hated son.—Maître Cornélius.
Last incarnation of Vautrin...................x464
Lesser bourgeoisie...............................x474
Lily of the valley.................................x448
Lost illusions......................................x455
Louis Lambert; tr...............................x443
Love [Brotherhood of consolation].........x458
Lucien de Rubempré; tr.......................x463
Magic skin [La peau de chagrin]............x441
Marriage contract, etc..........................x466
 Contents: The marriage contract. — A double
 life.—The peace of a home.
Memoirs of two young married women......x459
Modeste Mignon; tr............................x440
Mystery of the rue Soly [Ferragus].........x462
Œuvres complètes. 1866. 20 v.
 V. 1. La maison du Chat-qui-pelote.—Le bal de
 sceaux.—La bourse.—La vendetta.—Madame Fir-
 miani.—Une double famille.—La paix du ménage.—
 La fausse maîtresse.— Étude de femme.— Albert
 Savarus...x401

V. 2. Mémoires de deux jeunes mariées. Une
 fille d'Ève. Femme abandonnée.— La grenadière.
 — Le message. Gobseck.—Autre étude de femme. x402
 V. 3. La femme de trente ans.— Le contrat de
 mariage.— Béatrix, première partie....................x403
 V. 4. Béatrix, deuxième et troisième partie.—La
 Grand Bretêche; fin de Autre étude de femme.—
 Modeste Mignon.—Honorine.—Un début dans la vie. x404
 V. 5. Ursule Mirouet.— Eugénie Grandet.— Les
 célibataires: première histoire, Pierrette..............x405
 V. 6. Les célibataires: deuxième histoire, Le curé
 de Tours.—Les célibataires: troisième histoire, Un
 ménage de garçon.— Les Parisiens en province:
 première histoire, L'illustre Gaudissart. — Les
 Parisiens en province: deuxième histoire, La muse
 du département...x406
 V. 7. Les rivalités: première histoire, La vieille
 fille.— Les rivalités: deuxième histoire, Le cabinet
 des antiques.— Le lys dans la vallée...................x407
 V. 8. Illusions perdues: première partie, Les
 deux poètes; deuxième partie, Un grand homme
 de province à Paris; troisième partie, Ève et David..x408
 V. 9. Histoire des treize: premier épisode,
 Ferragus; deuxième épisode, La duchesse de
 Langeais; troisième épisode, La fille aux yeux
 d'or.—Le père Goriot..x409
 V. 10. Le Colonel Chabert.—Facino Cane.— La
 messe de l'Athée.— Sarrasine.— L'interdiction.—
 Histoire de la grandeur et de la décadence de César
 Birotteau...x410
 V. 11. La maison Nucingen.— Pierre Grassou.—
 Les secrets de la princesse Cadignan.— Les em-
 ployés.— Splendeurs et misères des courtisanes:
 première partie, Esther heureuse; deuxième
 partie, À combien l'amour revient aux vieillards....x411
 V. 12. Splendeurs et misères des courtisanes:
 troisième partie, Un prince de la Bohème.— Une
 esquisse d'homme d'affaires.—Gaudissart II.— Les
 comédiens sans le savoir.— Un épisode sous la
 terreur. — Une ténébreuse affaire.— Z. Marcas.—
 L'envers de l'histoire contemporaine: premier épisode.—Le député d'Arcis..................................x412
 V. 13. Les chouans. — Une passion dans le
 désert. — Le médecin de campagne.— Le curé de
 village..x413
 V. 14. La peau de chagrin.— Jésus-Christ en
 Flandre.— Melmoth réconcilié.— Le chef-d'œuvre
 inconnu.— Le recherche de l'absolu..................x414
 V. 15. Massimila Doni.— Gambara.— L'enfant
 maudit.— Les Marana.— Adieu.— Le réquisition-
 naire.— El verdugo.— Une drame au bord de la
 mer.— L'auberge rouge.— L'élixir de longue vie.—
 Maître Cornélius.—Sur Catherine de Médicis: pre-
 mière partie, Le martyr calviniste.......................x415
 V. 16. Sur Catherine de Médicis: deuxième
 partie.—Les proscrits.—Louis Lambert.—Séraphita.
 —Études analytiques: Physiologie du mariage......x416
 V. 17. Les parents pauvres: première partie,
 La cousine Bette; deuxième partie, Le cousin
 Pons..x417
 V. 18. Splendeurs et misères des courtisanes:
 quatrième partie, La dernière incarnation de
 Vautrin.— L'envers de l'histoire contemporaine:
 deuxième épisode, L'initié.— Les paysans.—Petites
 misères de la vie conjugale...............................x418
 V. 19. Théâtre: Vautrin.—Les ressources de
 Quinola. — Pamela Giraud. — La marâtre. — Le
 faiseur...x419
 V. 20. Des contes drolatiques. Premier dixain:
 Prologue; La belle impéria; Le péché véniel;
 La mye du roy; L'héritier du diable; Les joyeul-
 setez du roy Loys le unzïesme; Le connestable;

La pucelle de Thilhouze; Le frère d'armes; Le curé d'Azay-le-Rideau: L'apostrophe; Épilogue.—Deuxième dixain: Prologue; Les trois clerqs de Sainct-Nicholas; Le Jeusne de François premier; Les bons proupos des religieuses de Poissy; Comment feut basti le chasteau d'Azay; La faulse courtizane; Le dangier d'estre trop cocquebin; La chiere nuictée d'amour; Le prosne du ioyeulx curé de Meudon; Le succube; Dezesperance d'amour; Épilogue. — Troisiesme dixain: Prologue; Persévérance d'amour; D'un iusticiard qui ne se remembroyt les chouses; Sur le moyne amador qui feut ung glorieux abbé de Turpenay; Berthe la repentie; Comment la belle fille de Portillon quinauda son iuge; Cy est démonstré que la fortune est tousiours femelle; D'ung paouvre qui avoyt nom le Vieulx-par-chemins; Dires incongrus de trois pèlerins; Naifveté; La belle impéria mariée; Épilogue......x420
Old Goriot..x429B
The peasantry [Sons of the soil]............x477
Le père Goriot (French)......................x429A
Père Goriot; tr....................................x429
Pierrette; tr..x453
Quest of the absolute [La recherche de l'absolu]..x425A
(Same as 'Alchemist' and 'Alkahest.')
Seraphita; tr......................................x445
Shorter stories....................................x450
Sons of the soil [Les paysans]............x446
(Same as 'The peasantry')
Start in life..x465
Two brothers [Un ménage de garçon....x438
Unknown masterpiece, etc....................x476
Ursula [Ursule Mirouët]......................x449
Vendetta; tr......................................x427
Vicar of Tours....................................x453
Village rector....................................x460
Wild ass's skin [Magic skin]............x441A
Woman of thirty................................x479
Contents: A woman of thirty.—A forsaken lady.—La grenadière.—The message.—Gobseck.
Banville. Contes bourgeois...............x10002
Gringoire (drame). 1882....................842 77
Les Parisiennes de Paris......................x10001
Socrates and his wife (comedy). 1889.
....842 Pam. 3
Barancy. Implacable! (French).........x4706
Barrière *and* **Capendu.** Les faux bons-hommes (comédie)........................842 97
Bast. Contes à ma voisine...............x3601
Baudelaire. Some translations from; by H. C...841 85
Bawr. Maid of honour....................x14403
Bazin. Blot of ink........................x16002A
Humble amour..................................x16004
Les Noellet......................................x16001
Ma tante Giron................................x16003
Tache d'encre..................................x16002
Beaumarchais. Œuvres complètes. '21. 6v.
V. 1. Le genre dramatique sérieux. - Eugénie. Les deux amis. Le barbier de Séville........840 90

V. 2. Le mariage de Figaro - L'autre Tartuffe. —Tarare....................................840 91
V. 3-6. Mémoires.—Pétition, etc.—Lettres....840 92
Beaumont. El almacen de los minos........849 15
Bechard. Maurice; tr....................x5501
Belot. Article 47; tr....................x7301
Drama of the Rue de la Paix...............x7302
Le roi des Grecs..............................x7303
Belot *and* **Villetard.** Le testament de César Girodot (comédie)..............842 107
Benoit. Chronique des ducs de Normande. 3 v. 1836..............................841 B-7
Bentzon, *pseud.* See **Blanc,** *Madame.*
Béranger. Dernières chansons. 1859.....841 18
Œuvres. 1867. 2 v............................841 16
Songs; tr. by Toynbee. 1892...............841 81
Songs of France; tr. by Canby and Bowers. 1894..........................841 86
Two hundred lyrical poems; tr. by Young. 1869..............................841 10
Bergeret. Le cousin Babylas............x16401
Bernard. Fatal passion [Gerfaut]......x1305
Gerfaut (French)..............................x1302
Un homme sérieux............................x1304
Le paravent....................................x1303
La peau du lion................................x1301
Berthet. Le pacte de famine; ed. by Dickinson..................................x6905
Prehistoric world..............................x6903
Sergeant's legacy..............................x6904
Beyle (Stendhal). Abbesse de Castro....x4575
La chartreuse de Parme......................x4576
Biart. Adventures of a young naturalist.....04001
Clients of Dr. Bernagius....................x12801
Involuntary voyage............................04004
Two friends....................................04003
Blaize. La monégasque....................x4580
Blanc, *Madame,* (T. Bentzon). Un chatiment..x8809
Désirée Turpin (French)......................x8805
Un divorce....................................x8815
Expiation [Un chatiment]....................x8812
La grande saulière............................x8806
Jacqueline (French)............................x8814
Ma tante Hermine..............................x8806
La petite perle................................x8805
l'arrain d'Annette..............................x8813
Un remords....................................x8804
Remorse; tr....................................x8801
Le retour......................................x8810
Le roman d'un muet..........................x8803
Tony (French)..................................x8811
Une vie manquée..............................x8808
Le violon de Job..............................x8807
La vocation de Louise........................x8802
Blaze de Bury. Légende de Versailles...841 21
Boileau. Œuvres. 1746. 4 v.
V. 1. Vie; par Des Maizeaux.—Satires.—Épîtres..840 232

V. 2. L'art poétique.—Le lutrin.—Odes, epigrammes, etc....................................840 233
V. 3. Traité du sublime; tr. du Grec de Longin, avec réflexions critiques...............840 234
V. 4. Les héros de roman.—Lettres, etc...840 235
Works; tr. 1712. 2 v.
V. 1. Life: by Des Maizeaux.—The lutrin.—Art of poetry.—Satires..........................840 371
V. 2. Epistles.—Odes, etc.—Translations, letters, etc.—Dialogue of the dead.........840 372

Boisgobey. Golden tress...............x11802
Bornier. La fille de Roland (drame)......842 108
Bossuet. Œuvres. 1870. 4 v.
V. 1. De l'instruction de le Dauphin.—De la connaissance de Dieu et de soi-même.—Traité du libre arbitre.—Discours sur l'histoire universelle.—Politique tirée des propres paroles de l'écriture sainte.—Défense de la tradition et des saints pères.—Exposition de la doctrine de l'église catholique.—Discours à l'académie.—Sur la comédie.......840 B-3
V. 2. Oraisons funèbres.—Sermons..........840 B-4
V. 3. Sermons.— Panégyriques.— Méditations sur l'évangile....................................840 B-5
V. 4. Histoire des variations des églises protestantes.—Instructions pastorales.—Élévations sur les mystères.—Pensées...............840 B-6

Bouilly. L'abbé de l'Épée; Kastner, ed...842 74
Bourde. La fin du vieux temps..........x14301
Bourget. Cruelle enigme...............x14701
Mensonges....................................x14702
Pastels of men.
V. 1. A saint.—M. Legrimaudet.—Two little boys..x14703
V. 2. Maurice Olivier.—A gambler.—Another gambler.—Jacques Molan.—A lowly one.—Corségues...x14704
Steeple-chase.................................x14706
Terre promise................................x14705
Tragic idyll..................................x14707
Boussenard. Crusoes of Guiana..........042501
Bréhat. Bras d'Acier...................x8303
L'hotel du dragon............................x8302
Jean Belin, the French Robinson Crusoe...038201
Brueys and Palaprat. Le grondeur; ed. by Masson. 1877.........................840 201
Brunetière. Essais sur la littérature contemporaine. 1892.........................844 51
Contents: La critique impressioniste.—Alfred de Vigny.—La philosophie de Schopenhauer et les conséquences du pessimisme.—M. Sully-Prudhomme.—Alexandre Vinet.—Le symbolisme contemporain.—Critique et roman.—Le roman de l'avenir.—Les artistes littéraires.—Le naturalisme au théâtre.—La réforme du théâtre.—Apologie pour la rhétorique.—L'organisation de l'enseignement secondaire français.—Sur la littérature.
Histoire et littérature. 1892. 3 v.
V. 1. Madame de La Vallière.—Théorie du lieu commun.—Chansons historiques du 18me siècle.—Lieu commun sur l'invention.—L'enseignement primaire avant 1789.—La critique d'art au 17me siècle.—L'impératrice Marie-Thérèse et Madame de Pompadour.—La casuistique dans le roman.—Les philosophes et la révolution française.—Le personnage sympathique dans la littérature.—Le paysan sous l'ancien régime.—Le mal du siècle.—Un manuel allemand de géographie.—La déformation de la langue par l'argot.....................841 70
V. 2. La tragédie de Racine. Une figure de conventionnel. Les commencements d'un grand poète.—Trois moliéristes. Le manifeste de Brunswick. Flaubert et George Sand. Fénelon à Cambrai. Une histoire de l'émigration. Les Parnassiens.—La question du Gil Blas.—Rivarol. Les romans de Pierre Loti. Une apologie de la casuistique.—Le génie dans l'art...................844 71
V. 3. À propos du Théâtre Chinois. La jeunesse de Condé.—L'éloquence de Fléchier.—Les travaux historiques du duc de Broglie. Le théâtre de Voltaire.—Un récent historien de la révolution.—La poésie de Lamartine.—Sur Victor Hugo.—Confession d'un réfractaire.—La question du latin.—Le chansons de café-concert........844 72
Nouvelles questions de critique. 1890...844 74
Contents: La poésie française au moyen age. La fureur de l'inédit.—Les éditions originales. Le 'Dictionnaire historique de l'Académie' et 'L'histoire littéraire de la France.'—Sur l'éloquence judiciaire.—Buffon.—Le mouvement littéraire au 19me siècle.—Les métaphores de Victor Hugo.—Une définition de mots.—Symbolistes et décadents.—À propos du Disciple.—Question de morale.
Questions de critique. 1889...............844 73
Contents: Sur un buste de Rabelais.—L'influence des femmes dans la littérature française.—Madame de Maintenon.—Montesquieu.—Sur Napoléon.—La philosophie de Schopenhauer.—Le code civil et le théâtre.—Gautier.—La littérature personnelle.—Baudelaire.—Caro.—La critique scientifique.

Busnach. Le petit gosse................*x4540
Cahun. Adventures of Captain Mago.....x6201
Blue banner.................................x6202
Les pilotes d'Ango..........................x6203
Le tueuse, 1241............................x6204
Calmettes. Fisher girl of France......x4568
Calvin. Letters. 1855. 2 v............922.4 20
Cantacuzène, princesse. Carmela; tr....x11402
La mensonge de Sabine......................x11403
Poverina; tr...............................x11401
Sabine's falsehood.........................x11404
Caro. L'idole...........................x9050
Idylle nuptiale. 1897......................x9052
Carpentier. La maison fermée..........x13802
Sauvons-le!................................x13801
La tour du preux...........................x13803
Caumont. Choix de lectures. 1854. 2 v...849 13
Cauvain. Village priest................x1805
Célière. Startling exploits of Dr. J. B. Quiés...x14405
Cent nouvelles nouvelles, Les. 1884....843 2
Chabrillan, comtesse. Une méchante femme...x9801
Chandos. Le prince noir; with English tr. and notes by F. Michel. 1883.........841 B-3
Chateaubriand. Atala; tr. by Harry...843 R-1
Œuvres complètes. 1838. 36 v.
V. 1. Essais sur la vie, etc...................840 47
V. 2-3. Les révolutions. 2 v..................840 48
V. 4-7. Études historiques. 4 v...............840 50
V. 8. Mélanges littéraires....................840 54

* Of interest to young readers.

V. 9-11. Itinéraire de Paris à Jerusalem. 3 v......840 55
V. 12. Voyage en Amérique......................840 58
V. 13. Voyage en Italie..........................840 59
V. 14-17. Génie du Christianisme. 4 v..........840 60
V. 18. Atala.—René.—Le dernier Abencerage.—
Poëmes...840 64
V. 19-21. Les martyrs. 3 v.....................840 65
V. 22-23. Les Natchez. 2 v.....................840 68
V. 24. Poésies.—Moïse...........................840 70
V. 25. Mélanges historiques....................840 71
V. 26-28. Mélanges historiques. 3 v...........840 72
V. 29-31. Polémique, etc. 3 v..................840 75
V. 32. Tables des matières.....................840 78
V. 33-34. Essai sur la littérature anglaise....840 79
V. 35-36. Le Paradis perdu de Milton..........840 81

Chénier. Œuvres anciennes. 1826........329.3 4
Œuvres posthumes. 1826....................841 22
Cherbuliez. Amours fragiles.................x913
Après fortune faite.........................x929
L'aventure de Ladislas Bolski..............x917
Un cheval de Phidias.......................x910
Le comte Kostia...........................x908A
Count Kostia...............................x908
La ferme du Choquard.......................x922
Le fiancé de Mademoiselle Saint Mar........x915
Une gageure................................x926
L'idée de Jean Téterol.....................x916
Jean Téterol's idea........................x909
Joseph Noirel's revenge....................x906
King Apepi............................in x12008
Meta Holdenis (French).....................x914
Same ; tr..................................x901
Miss Rovel ; tr............................x932
Noirs et rouges............................x920
Paul Méré (French).........................x903
Phidian horse..............................x928
Le prince Vitale...........................x911
Prosper ; tr...............................x905
Prosper Randoce (French)...................x918
La revanche de Joseph Noirel...............x919
Le roi Apépi...............................x930
Roman d'une honnête femme..................x924
Saints and sinners [Noirs et rouges].......x921
Samuel Brohl and Company...................x907
Samuel Brohl et cie........................x902
Secret du précepteur......................x927A
Tutor's secret.............................x927
La vocation du comte Ghislain..............x925
Wish of his life [Jean Teterol's idea]..x909A
With fortune made.........................x929A
Chevalier. Les derniers Iroquois...........x1203
La fille des Indiens rouges...............x1205
La Huronne................................x1201
Les Nez-percés............................x1204
Peaux rouges et Peaux blanches............x1202
Les Pieds-noirs...........................x1208
Poignet-d'Acier, ou les Chippiouais.......x1206
La Tête-Plate.............................x1207
Chousy. Ignis (French)....................x14201
Cladel. Va-Nu-Pieds.......................x14601

Claretie. L'Américaine....................x10813
Boum-boum (French)........................x10810
Brichanteau, actor........................x10816
La frontière..............................x10814
La fugitive...............................x10802
Jean Mornas ; ou, L'hypnotisme............x10815
La maison vide............................x10803
Monsieur le ministre (French).............x10805
Same ; tr.................................x10804
Noris (French)............................x10806
Pierrille (French)........................x10811
Le prince Zillah..........................x10807
Same ; tr.................................x10809
Puyjoli (French)..........................x10812
Robert Burat (French).....................x10810
Le troisième dessous......................x10808
Tuyet (French).........................in x10815
Collin-Harleville. Chateaux en Espagne
(drame). 1831...............................842 2
L'optimiste (drame)..........................842 1
Colomb. Page, squire and knight..........039902
Combe. Jonquille ; tr....................x16702
Question of love..........................x16701
Condorcet. Œuvres complètes. 1804. 21 v.
V. 1-4. Éloges des académiciens..............840 21
V. 5. Vie de M. Turgot.......................840 21
V. 6-7. Vie de Voltaire......................840 21
V. 8. Progrès de l'esprit humain.............840 21
V. 9. Sur l'instruction publique.............840 21
V. 10. Lettres d'un théologien...............840 22
V. 11-18. Mélanges de politique..............840 22
V. 19-21. Mélanges d'économie politique......840 22
Conscience, H. L'année de merveilles....x1005
Le conscrit...............................x1005
Le gant perdu.............................x1005
Le gentilhomme pauvre.....................x1005
Les heures du soir........................x1005
Le jeune docteur..........................x1006
Le lion de Flandre........................x1010
Off to California.........................x1011
L'orpheline...............................x1009
Scènes de la vie Flamande.................x1005
Summer evening tales......................x1011
La tombe de fer...........................x1005
Young doctor..............................x1011
Conscience, M. Un million comptant......x1110
Constant. Adolphe (French)..............x1590
Coppée. Henriette (French)..............x1560
Same ; tr.................................x1560
Le Luthier de Crémone (drame). 1882..842 7
Mon franc parler. 4me série. 1896.........844 6
On rend l'argent ; ed. by Pronson.........x1560
Passer-by ; tr. by Luigi....................842 16
Le pater ; introduction and notes by
Sumichrast. 1896............................842 15
Rivals....................................x1560
Ten tales.................................x1560
Le trésor (drame). 1882.....................842 7
True riches...............................x1560

Coppée *and* **Maupassant**. Tales [French text]; ed. by Cameron................x15607
Cordellier-Delanoue, Jacques Cœur; tr..x16901
Corneille. Chefs-d'œuvre de. 1823. 4 v.
  V. 1-3. Same as in v. 1-3 of 'Œuvres choisies,' below..842 7
  V. 4. Ariane.— Le comte d'Essex.—Le festin de Pierre..842 10
The Cid; tr. by Mongan................842 155
Cinna; ed. by Masson. 1877...........840 196
Same; tr. by Mongan..................842 156
Horace; with tr. by Nokes............842 104
Le menteur; ed. by Masson. 1877....840 197
Œuvres; éd. par Marty-Laveaux. 1862-8. 13v.
  V. 1. Notice biographique, etc.—Mélite.—Clitandre.—La veuve.......................842 138
  V. 2. La galerie du palais.— La suivante.— La Place Royale.— La comédie des Tuileries.— Médée.—L'illusion...................................842 139
  V. 3. Le Cid.— Horace.— Cinna.— Polyeucte..842 140
  V. 4. Pompée.—Le menteur.— La suite du menteur.—Rodogune..................................842 141
  V. 5. Théodore. — Héraclius. — Audromède. — Don Sanche d'Aragon.—Nicomède.............842 142
  V. 6. Pertharite, roi des Lombards.—Œdipe.— La toison d'or.—Sertorius.—Sophonisbe.—Othon..842 143
  V. 7. Agésilas. — Attila. — Tite et Bérénice.— Psyché.— Pulchérie.— Suréna.....................842 144
  V. 8. L'imitation de Jésus-Christ.............842 145
  V. 9. Des psaumes et des cantiques............842 146
  V. 10. Poésies diverses..........................842 147
  V. 11-12. Lexique de la langue de Corneille.....842 148
  V. 13. Album.................................842 150
Œuvres choisies. 1842. 4 v.
  V. 1. Éloge; par Racine.—Vie; par Fontenelle. — Le Cid.— Horace.—Cinna......................842 3
  V. 2. Polyeucte.—Le menteur.—Pompée.—Rodogune..842 4
  V. 3. Héraclius. — Don Sanche d'Aragon.—Nicomède.— Sertorius..........................842 5
  V. 4. Sophonisbe. Othon. Discours sur l'art dramatique..842 6
Cottin. Elizabeth; or, The exiles of Siberia...07201
  Matilda; tr..................................x11502
Countess of Monte Cristo................x4505
Courcillon. Le curé manque..............x4301
Courcy. Les histoires du café de Paris...x9901
Courier. Lettres; ed. by Anderson. '94..846 57
Cournier. Une famille en 1870-1871.......x10101
Cousin. Fragments et souvenirs. 1857....844 16
Craven, *Madame*. Anne Séverin (French)..x7806
  Éliane.....................................x7807
  Same; tr..................................x7808
  Fleurange (French).........................x7804
  Same; tr..................................x7803
  Jettatrice; tr.............................x7802
  Sister's story............................x7801
Crébillon, *père*. Œuvres. 1812. 3 v.
  V. 1. Notice sur Crébillon.—Idoménée.—Atrée et Thyeste.—Électre............................842 40
  V. 2. Rhadamisthe et Zénobie.—Xerxès. Sémiramis..842 41
  V. 3. Pyrrhus.—Catilina.—Le Triumvirat. Discours académiques..............................842 42

Darmesteter. English studies. 1896....844 68
  Contents: Joan of Arc in England. The French revolution and Wordsworth. Life of George Eliot. George Eliot's letters.— Oliver Madox-Brown. The poetry of Mary Robinson.—Celtica.—Irish literature and Ossian.—Irish political ballads.—Calcutta.—Two Indian books.—A mage in Paris.
Selected essays; tr. by Jastrow. 1895..844 60
  Contents: The religions of the future.—The prophet of Israel.—Afghan life in Afghan songs.—Race and tradition.—Ernest Renan.—Essay on the history of the Jews.—The supreme God in the Indo-European mythology.
Daudet, A. L'Arlésienne [drame]. 1892..842 151
Artists' wives..............................x836
La Belle Nivernaise (French)...............x832
  Same; tr................................x831
Contes du lundi...........................x841
L'évangéliste............................x823
Fig and the idler, etc...................x839
  Contents: Fig and the idler.—My first dress coat. Three low masses.—New master.
Fromont jeune et Risler ainé............x802
L'immortel..............................x833
Jack (French)...........................x805
  Same; tr..............................x810
Kings in exile..........................x817
Letters from my mill....................x820
Lettres de mon moulin...................x828
Little good-for-nothing.................x815
Les mères (extraits)....................x811
Nabob; tr...............................x804
New Don Quixote.........................x809
Numa Roumestan (French).................x822
  Same; tr..............................x821
One of the forty (English of L'immortel).................................x834
Petite paroisse.........................x842
Pope's mule, etc........................038101
Port Salvation [L'évangeliste]..........x824
Port Tarascon; tr.......................x835
Robert Helmont; tr......................x843
Les rois en exile.......................x818
Le roman du Chaperon-Rouge..............x816
Rose and Ninette........................x837
Rose et Ninette.........................x838
Sidonie; tr.............................x801
Le siége de Berlin......................x826
Stories of Provence.....................x827
Tartarin of Tarascon....................x819
Tartarin on the Alps....................x830
Tartarin sur les Alpes..................x829
Le trésor d'Arlatan.....................x807
Daudet, E. Apostate [Défroqué].......x8906
Daniel de Kerfons (French)..............x8907
Défroqué................................x8903
Don Rafaël (French).....................x8910
Drapeaux ennemis........................x8911
Fils d'émigré...........................x8908
Le gendarme excommunié..................x8909

Henriette (French)..................................x8901
Madame Robernier; (French)..............x8902
Mademoiselle Vestris (French)............x8904
Rafael ; tr...x8910A
Les reins cassés (French).....................x8905
Debans. Sheep in wolf's clothing.......x11101
Delarbre, *Madame.* Les causeries d'une
bonne mère...*x11901
Delavigne. Les enfants d'Édouard
(drame)..842 74
Louis XI (drame)....................................842 77
Same ; ed. by Eve. 1894....................842 137
Théâtre. 1870. 3v.
V. 1. Les vêpres Siciliennes. — Les comédiens.
—Le paria.— L'école des vieillards.—La princesse
Aurélie..842 65
V. 2. Marino Faliero.— Louis XI.— Les enfants
d'Édouard.—Don Juan d' Autriche.................842 66
V. 3. Une famille au temps de Luther.— La popularité.— La fille du Cid.— Le conseiller rapporteur.
—Charles VI..842 67
Delorme, Jos., *pseud.* See **Sainte-Beuve.**
Delpit. La marquise............................x10403
Odette's marriage..................................x10401
La père de Martial................................x10402
Desbordes-Valmore. Poésies. 1872....841 13
Deschamps. Chemin fleuri..................x18601
Deslys. Compagnons de minuit..........x2701
Desmoulins. Œuvres. 1874.............329, 3 3
Diderot. Œuvres choisies. 1874. 2 v.
V. 1. Vie ; par Genin.—La religieuse.—Madame
de la Pommeraye. — Père Hudson.— L' emplâtre
de Desglands.— Les deux amis de Bourbonne.—
Lettre de M. Papin.— Ceci n'est pas un conte.—Histoire de Desroches et de Madame de la Carlière.—
Morceaux divers...840 87
V. 2. Le neveu de Rameau.—Salons.—Anecdotes détachées..840 88
Diderot *and* **Grimm.** Memoirs, etc., from
the corr. of, 1753-90. 4 v...................846 28
Didier. La petite princesse..................x10501
Dombre. Le médecin de belle-maman....x18403
Tante Rabat-Joie.................................x18401
Douze histoires pour les enfants...........*x4501
Droz. Around a spring x6601
Babolain ; tr..x6602
Bertha's baby.......................................x6604
Monsieur, madame and the baby........x6603
Du Bartas. Divine weekes and workes ;
tr. by Sylvester. 1641.......................841 B-4
Du Bois-Melly. Nicolas Muss.............x14410
Du Deffand. Lettres, 1766-80. 1812. 4v..846 47
Dudevant, *Madame* **A. L. A. D.** See **Sand,
George.**
Dudevant, J. F. M. A. See **Sand, Maurice.**
Dumanoir *and* **Lafargue.** Le gentilhomme pauvre (comédie)..................842 106
Dumas. About books, no. 1: The D'Artagnan romances................................843 Pam. 1
Adventures of a marquis......................x323

Andrée de Tavernay ; tr........................x356
Ascanio ; tr..x361
Aventures de la princesse de Monaco......x310
Beau Tancrede ; tr.................................x372
Black: the story of a dog.....................x346
Black tulip...x337
Captain Paul ; tr....................................x365
Catherine Blum ; tr................................x371
Charles le Téméraire............................x318
Chevalier de Maison Rouge ; tr............x374
Le chevalier d'Harmental (French)........x331
Same ; tr..x332
Chicot the jester [Diana of Meridor]......x395
Le collier de la reine. 3 v....................x329
Companions of Jehu............................x340
Le comte de Monte Cristo (French). 3v..x315
La comtesse de Salisbury (French)......x392
Conspirators [Chevalier d'Harmental]....x332A
Corsican brothers..................................x341
Same...*in* x343
Count of Beuzeval................................x303
Count of Monte Cristo..........................x316
Countess of Charney............................x355
La dame de Monsoreau (French).........x394
La dame de volupte..............................x397
Les demoiselles de Saint-Cyr [drame];
ed. by Tarver.....................................842 75
Les deux reines....................................x381
Diana of Meridor................................x395A
Doctor Basilius ; tr.................................x373
Edmond Dantes ; tr...............................x321
Episodes from 'Le capitaine Pamphile' ;
ed. by Morris.....................................x320
First republic [Whites and the blues]...x338
Foresters..x328
Forty-five guardsmen............................x352
Un Gil-Blas en Californie......................x399
La guerre des femmes.........................x333
Half-brothers...x370
Histoire d'une casse noisette...............x335
Ingenue ; tr...x375
Iron hand [The half brothers].............x370A
Iron mask..x350
Isabel of Bavaria..................................x391
Same...*in* x375
Jehanne la Pucelle...............................x393
Last Vendée [She-wolves of Machecoul]..x343
Louise de la Valliere ; tr.......................x351
Love and liberty....................................x339
Madame de Chamblay ; tr....................x313
Mademoiselle de Belle Isle [drama]; tr.
by Kemble.....................................*in* 822.2 227
Marguerite de Valois; tr.......................x369
Memoirs of a physician........................x301
Les Mohicans de Paris.........................x376
Nanon [La guerre des femmes]..........x334B

---
* Of interest to young readers.

Olympe de Cleves............................x322
Page of the Duke of Savoy.................x363
Paul Jones...................................x307
Queen's necklace............................x330
Regent's daughter...........................x366
Russian Gypsy...............................x364
Salvator (French)...........................x378
She-wolves of Machecoul....................x343
Six years later [Taking the Bastile].......x367
Taking the Bastile..........................x367B
Sketches in France..........................x337
Tales of the Caucasus.—The ball of snow.
  —Sultanetta...............................x345
Three musketeers [Three guardsmen].....x308
Les trois mousquetaires....................x309
La tulipe noire.............................x336
Twenty years after..........................x353
Twin captains...............................x374
Two Dianas..................................x312
Le vicomte de Bragelonne...................x347
Same; tr...................................x348
Vingt ans après.............................x354
War of women................................x334
Watchmaker..................................x317
Whites and the blues........................x338
(Historical novels arranged chronologically.)
1338. Le bâtard de Mauléon.
  Same; tr. The bastard of Mauléon.—The half-brothers.—The iron hand.—Knight of Mauléon.
1389. Isabel de Bavière.
  Same; tr. Isabel of Bavaria.
1540. Ascanio.
  Same; tr. Ascanio.
1551. Les deux Diane.
  Same; tr. The two Dianas.—Diana of Poitiers.
1555. Le page du duc de Savoie.
  Same; tr. Page of the duke of Savoy.— Emanuel Philibert.
THE VALOIS SERIES.
1572. La reine Margot (1).
  Same; tr. Queen Margot.—Marguerite of Valois,—Marguerite of Navarre.
1578. La dame de Monsoreau (2).
  Same; tr. Lady of Monsoreau.—Chicot the jester.—Diana of Méridor.
585. Les quarante-cinque (3).
  Same; tr. The forty-five.— Forty-five guardsmen.
THE D'ARTAGNAN ROMANCES; OR,
  THE GUARDSMEN SERIES.
1625. Les trois mousquetaires (1).
  Same; tr. Three musketeers.— Three guardsmen.
1648. Vingt ans après (2).
  Same; tr. Twenty years after.—Milady's son.
1660. Le vicomte de Bragelonne (3).
  Same; tr. Vicomte de Bragelonne.— Ten years later, also divided into 3 parts: Bragelonne the son of Athos, The iron mask, and Louise de la Vallière.
1650. La guerre des femmes.
  Same; tr. Woman's war.—Nanon.
1718. Le chevalier d'Harmental.
  Same; tr. The chevalier d'Harmental.—The conspirators.—Love and conspiracy.
1719. Une fille du régent.
  Same; tr. Daughter of the regent.— Regent's daughter.

MEMOIRS OF A PHYSICIAN SERIES.
1770. Mémoires d'un médicin (1).
  Same; tr. Memoirs of a physician, Joseph Balsamo.
1784. Le collier de la reine (2).
  Same; tr. Queen's necklace
1789. Ange Pitou (3).
  Same; tr. Ange Pitou.—Six years later.—Taking the Bastile.
1791. Le comtesse de Charny (4).
  Same; tr. Countess of Charny.— Also divided into 2 parts: Countess de Charny, and Andrée de Taverney.
1788-93. Ingénue.
  Same; tr. Ingénue.—Death of Marat.
1793. Le chevalier de Maison-Rouge.
  Same; tr. Chevalier de Maison-Rouge.— The chevalier.—The reign of terror.
1808. Le capitaine Richard.
  Same; tr. Captain Richard.— Twin captains Two lieutenants.
1810. Conscience l'innocent.
  Same; tr. Conscience l'innocent.— The conscript.

THE NAPOLEONIC ROMANCES.
1793-1799. Tr. The whites and the blues.— First republic.
1795-1843. Tr. She-wolves of Machecoul.—Last Vendée.

OTHER HISTORICAL TALES.
1799-1800. Tr. Companions of Jehu.—Company of Jehu.
1841. Les frères Corses.
  Same; tr. Corsican brothers.

Dupont, *ed.* Chefs-d'œuvre dramatiques
  français. 1831. 2 v.
  V. 1. Discours d'ouverture. — Épitre à Voltaire; Chénier.— Zaire; Voltaire.— Le méchant; Gresset.— L'optimiste; Collin-Harleville.— Nanine................842 1
  V. 2. Alzire ; ou, Les Americains.— La Métromanie. Piron.—Le Glorieux ; Destouches.—Les chateaux en Espagne; Collin-Harleville..................842 2

Durand, *Madame.* See Greville, H.
Duruy. Garde du corps....................x15101
Duveyrier (Mélesville). Michael Perrin
  [drame] ; ed. by Masson................842 75
Edmond. La bucheronne..................x13601
Énault. Captain's dog...................038701
Carine (French)............................x7005
Le chien du capitaine.....................*x7006
Christine ; tr.............................x7003
Pupil of the legion of honor..............x7001
Le sacrifice..............................x7007
Erckmann-Chatrian. Alsace [drame].
  1881..842 89
Alsacian schoolmaster [Histoire d'un
  sous-maitre]..............................x524
Alsaciens et Vosgiens d'autrefois.........x548
L'ami Fritz...............................x535
L'ami Fritz (drame).....................842 108
Avant 89..................................x542
Le banni..................................x541
Blockade of Phalsburg....................x503
Brigadier Frederic ; tr..................x536
Brothers Rantzau [Les deux frères].......x545
Une campagne en Kabylie..................x516
Campaign in Kabylia.......................x528

* Of interest to young readers.

Clarionet player, etc. ...x523
Conscript ...x509
Contes de la montagne ...x519
Contes des bords du Rhin ...x518
Contes populaires ...x517
Daniel Rock ; tr. ...x537
Les deux frères ...x520
Les fiancés de Grinderwald, etc. ...x543
Le fou Yégof ...x502
Friend Fritz ...x522
Le grandpère Lebigre ...x538
Great invasion of 1813-14 (English of Le fou Yégof) ...x501
La guerre [drame]; ed. by Clapin. 1883..842 94
Histoire du plébiscite ...x508
Histoire d'un paysan. 4 v.
 V. 1. Les états généraux. 1789 ...x511
 V. 2. La patrie en danger. 1792 ...x512
 V. 3. L'an de la république. 1793 ...x513
 V. 4. Le citoyen Bonaparte. 1794-1815 ...x514
Histoire d'un sous-maître ...x515
Illustrious Doctor Matheus ...x527
Madame Thérèse (French) ...x506
 Same ; tr. ...x505
La maison forestière ...x546
Maître Gaspard Fix ...x544
Man-wolf, etc. ...x529
Miller's story of the war [Histoire du plébiscite] ...x507
Polish Jew ...x530A
 Same ; dramatized, etc. ...x530
Les Rantzau [comédie] ...842 105
Stories of the Rhine ...x526
Story of a peasant. 4 v.
 V. 1. The states general. 1789 ...x531
 V. 2. The country in danger. 1792 ...x532
 V. 3. The year one of the republic. 1793 ...x533
 V. 4. Citizen Bonaparte. 1794-1815 ...x534
Strange stories ...x539
Les vieux de la vieille ...x540
Waterloo (French) ...x510
 Same ; tr. ...x521
Wild huntsman [La maison forestière] ...x525
Estaunié. Bonne-Dame ...x18501
L'empreinte ...x18502
Exauvillez, Aurélie ...x1105
Fabre. L'abbé Tigrane ...x15401
Le chevrier ...x15405
Les Courbezon ...x15404
Lucifer (French) ...x15403
Mon ami Gaffarot ...x15406
Taillevent (French) ...x15407
Toussaint Galabre (French) ...x15402
Faguet. Études littéraires. 1892-4. 4 v.
 16me siècle: Commynes.—Clément Marot.—Rabelais.- Calvin. Ronsard.— Du Bellay. D'Aubigné. Montaigne ...840 376
 17me siècle: Corneille. Pascal.— Molière.—La Rochefoucauld. La Fontaine.— Racine.— Boileau. Bossuet. Madame de Sévigné. Fénelon. Madame de Maintenon.— La Bruyère.— Saint-Simon ...840 377

18me siècle: Pierre B[?]
— Marivaux.- - Montes[?]
—Rousseau.—Buffon.—[?]
19me siècle: Chateau[?]
de Vigny.— Hugo.— A.
P. Mérimée.—Michelet.
Fénelon. Telemachu[?]
 Same ; tr. ...
Feuillet. Aliette [tr
Artist's honor ...
Bellah (French) ...
Camors ; tr. ...
Diary of a woman .
La fée (comédie) ...
Histoire de Sibylle
Histoire d'une Par[?]
Honneur d'artiste .
Journal d'une femm[?]
Julia de Trécœur (
Little countess ...
Un mariage dans le
Marriage in high lif[?]
La petite comtesse,
Le roman d'un jeu[?]
Story of Sibylle ...
Théâtre complet.
 V. 1. Un bourgeois contre.—Le crise.—Pé[?] lage.—La fée.—Le r[?] pauvre ...
La veuve ...
Feval. Chouans et B
Feydeau. Adventu[?]
Fireste ...
Sylvie (French) ...
Filon. Chemin qui m
Garrick's pupil ...
Violette Mérian (F
Flagy. Cœur d'or ...
Flammarion. Lumie[?]
Uranie ; tr. ...
Flaubert. Bouvard [?]
 Same ; tr. ...
Madame Bovary (F
Salammbô (French
 Same ; tr. ...
La tentation de Sai[?]
Fleury. Faience viol
La mascarade de la
Violon de faïence ..
Floran. Au d'épreuv
Florian. Fables ; do[?] by Perring. 189[?]
(Œuvres. 1812. 16
 V. 1. Fables ...
 V. 2. Nouvelles ...
 V. 3. Jeunesse de F
 V. 4. Galatée. Est[?]
 V. 5. Numa Pompili[?]
 V. 6-9. Don Quichott[?]
 V. 10-11. Gonzalve ...

 † Of interest to young readers.

V. 12. Guillaume Tell........................840 358
V. 13. Théâtre: Les deux billets.— Le bon ménage.— Le bon père.— Jeannot et Colin.— Les inneaux de Bergame..................................840 359
V. 14. Théâtre: La bonne mère — Le bon fils.— Myrtil et Chloé. Héro et Léandre. Le baiser.— Blanche et Vermeille...........................840 360
V. 15-16. Mélanges...............................840 361

Foa. Les petits guerriers........................x17901
Fontaines. La comtesse de Savoie. 1804..840 33
 Histoire d'Aménophis. 1804............840 303
Fontenelle. Dialogues of the dead. 1708..847 17
France, A. Balthasar, etc. (French)......x12705
 Le crime de Sylvestre Bonnard..........x12701
 Crime de Sylvestre Bonnard..............x12702
 L'étui de nacre.................................x12706
 Jardin d'épicure (essais). 1895...........844 58
 Jocaste.—Le chat maigre..................x12707
 Le livre de mon ami..........................x12710
 Le lys rouge......................................x12709
 Les opinions de M. Jérôme Coignard...x12708
 L'orme du mail..................................x12713
 Les puits de Sainte Claire..................x12711
 La rôtisserie de la reine Pédauque....x12704
 Tales from a mother-of-pearl casket..x12706A
 Thaïs (French)..................................x12703
 La vie littéraire. 1895. 4 v................844 62
France, H. L'amour au paysbleu..........x14403
Gaboriau. La corde au cou....................x7211
 La crime d'Orcival.............................x7207
 Monsieur Lecoq (French)...................x7209
Gagneur. Les vierges russes................x10701
Gandon. Jean Gigon (French)..............x4001
Gasparin. Les horizons prochains.......x15501
 Sunny fields and shady woods. 1888..x15502
Gaspé. Canadians of old....................x4701
Gaulot. Red shirts..............................x17601
Gautier, J. Usurper............................x5315
Gautier, T. Le capitaine Fracasse........x5305
 Captain Fracasse..............................x5304
 Four destinies..................................x5314
 Les grotesques (essais). 1871..........844 22
 Les Jeunes-France............................x5309
 Juancho, the bull-fighter..................x5313
 Mademoiselle De Maupan................x5306
 Nouvelles..x5311
 One of Cleopatra's nights.................x5307
 Romance of the mummy..................x5301
 Romans et contes............................x5310
 Spirite; tr......................................x5302
Gautier, T., and Mérimée. Tales before supper..................................x5312
Gautier, T., et al. Cross of Berny........x5308
Genlis, Madame de. Series of novels. 4 v.
V. 1. Mademoiselle de Clermont.—Apostasy; or, The religious fair.—The herdsmen of the Pyrenees..x4585
V. 2. The reviewer.— The castle of Kolmeras.
— The man of worth...............................x4586
V. 3. The perplexed lover.—Destiny; or, The unfortunate...x4587

V. 4. The princess of Ursins.—The green petticoat.—The husband turned tutor.—The palace and the cot.- A woman's prejudices...........x4585
Théâtre d'éducation. 1829. 5 v.
V. 1. La mort d'Adam. Agar dans le désert. Isaac. Joseph.— Ruth et Noémi La veuve de Sarepta. Retour du jeune Tobie........842 41
V. 2. La colombe. La belle et la bête. Les flacons.— L.'île heureuse. L.'enfant gâté. La curieuse. Les dangers du monde.........842 44
V. 3. L'aveugle de Spa.- Cécile. Les ennemies généreuses.— La bonne mère. L.'intrigante.842 45
V. 4. Le bal d'enfans.— Le voyageur — Vathek.
— Les faux amis.— Le magistrat.............842 46
V. 5. La rosière de Salency.— La marchande de modes.—La lingère.— Le libraire.— Le vrai sage. Le portrait...842 47

Théâtre of education. 1783. 3 v.
V. 1. Hagar in the desert.— The beauty and the monster.— The phials.— The happy island.— Spoiled child.— Effects of curiosity.— Dangers of the world.— Blind woman of Spa.—The dove — Cecilia...842 118
V. 2. Generous enemies.—The good mother. Busy body.—Children's ball.—Traveller.—Vathek.842 119
V. 3. False friends.— Judge.— Queen of the rose. — Milliner.— Linen draper.— Book-seller.— Truly wise man.— Portrait.............................842 120

Gennevraye. L'Ombra; tr................x17401
Geoffrey the knight.........................0146
Gervais. Cas de conscience...............x9015
Girardin, Madame E. La joie fait peur (comédie).................................842 Pam. 2
 Same; ed. by Gerard.....................842 76
Girardin, J. Adventures of Johnny Ironsides...040001
 Doctor's family..............................x7706
 Histoire d'un Berrichon..................x7707
 Maman (French)............................*x7702
 Mauviette (French)........................x7708
 Les millions de la tante Zéze.........x7703
 Paulette (French)..........................*x7709
 Sans-cœur.....................................x7705
 True as steel.................................x7704
Glouvet. Le berger.............................x12503
 L'étude Chandoux..........................x12507
 La famille bourgeois.....................x12504
 Le forestier..................................x12501
 L'idéal...x12505
 Le marinier..................................x12502
 Le père..x12508
 Woodman......................................x12509
Gobineau. Typhaine's abbey...............x2302
Goncourt, E. and J. Armande; tr......x6510
 Germinie Lacerteux.......................x6511
Gouraud. Peter Lipp.........................039203
 Little boy's story..........................039201
 Young mountaineer.......................039202
Gozlan. La pluie et le beau temps (drame).842 106
Grandfort. Octave (French)..............x2801
Gras. Reds of the Midi......................x18301
Gresset. Le méchant (drame). 1831..842 1

* Of interest to young readers.

Gréville (Madame Durand). Aline; tr....x6327
Bonne Marie; tr. x6308
Céphise (French).................................x6333
Clairefontaine (French)......................x6321
Cleopatra..x6322
Cléopatre..x6323
Count Xavier..x6324
Croquis (French).................................x6312
Dosia (French).....................................x6302
Same; tr. x6301
Dosia's daughter..................................x6320
Dournof; tr. x6310
Gabrielle; tr. x6303
Heiress..x6331
L'héritière...x6329
Jolie propriété......................................x6332
Louk Loukitch (French).....................x6325
Lucie Rodey; tr. x6313
Madame de Dreux (French)..............x6316
Mam'zelle Eugenie; tr. x6318
Mari d'Aurette.....................................x6330
Markoff; tr. x6311
Marrying off a daughter....................x6304
Mors aux dents....................................x6319
Un mystère...x6326
Mystery...x6326A
Noble woman [Trials of Raissa].......x6315A
Perdue (French)..................................x6317
Philomene's marriages......................x6307
Pretty little Countess Zina...............x6306
Sonia; tr. x6305
Suzanne Normis (French).................x6314
Trials of Raissa [A noble woman]....x6315
Grimm *and* **Diderot.** Selections from correspondence. 1753-90. 4 v. 846 28
Guenot. Vengeance of a Jew..............x5101
Guérin. Lettres. 1881.........................846 33
Same; tr. into English........................846 32
Guillet. Mine et contramine (drame)...842 108
Guizot, *Madame* **E. S.** L'écolier; ou, Raoul et Victor. 2 v. *x4401
Les enfants...*x4403
Une famille. 2 v. *x4405
Ten moral tales....................................039301
Guizot, F. P. G. Shakespeare and his times. 1852...822.3 9
Gyp, *pseud.* Chiffon's marriage...........x6812
Du haut en bas....................................x6810
Le journal d'un philosophe...............x6811
Petit Bob..x6814
Plus heureux de tous.........................x6815
Those good Normans.........................x6813
Halévy. L'Abbé Constantine..............x12004
Same; tr. x12002
Criquette (French)..............................x12005
Same; tr. x12009
Karikari (French)................................x12010

A love match.......................................x12008
Un mariage d'amour..........................x12006
Parisian points of view.....................x12011
Contents: Only a waltz.—The dancing-master.—The circus-charger.—Blacky.—The most beautiful woman in Paris.—The story of a ball-dress.—The insurgent.—The Chinese embassador.—In the express.
Les petites Cardinal...........................x12001
Princesse, etc. (French).....................x12007
Hamilton, *count.* Fairy tales............x4601
Hericault. 1794: a tale of the Terror...x14401
Hervieu. L'armature..........................x16202
Flirt...x16201
Hervilly. La soupière........................842 106
Vent d'ouest (drame).........................842 106
Houssaye. Les Dianes et les Vénus...x1502
L'eventail brisé. 2 v. x1504
Les filles d'Ève...................................x1503
Life in Paris. 1875.............................846 9
Mademoiselle Cléopatre....................x1501
Philosophers and actresses. 2 v. 844 8
Hugo. L'âne (poëme). 1880................841 36
L'art d'être grand-père (poésies)......841 80
Bug-Jargal; tr. x121A
By order of the king..........................x127
Claude Gueux; tr. x117
Les contemplations (poésies). 1830-45...841 23
Dramatic works; ed. by Slous and Crosland. 1887...842 111
Contents: Hernani.—King's diversion.—Ruy Blas.
La Esmerelda.— Ruy Blas.— Les burgraves. 1860..841 26
Feuilles d'automne.—Chants du crépuscule. 1857...841 25
Hans of Iceland..................................x128
Hernani (drame).................................842 108
Same; ed. by Masson........................842 74
Same; tr. by Crosland........................842 110
Inez de Castro....................................928.4 30
Jargal; tr. x121
Letters to his family, etc. 1896. 1st series...846 60
Letters to his wife, etc. 1895............846 58
The man who laughs.........................114
Les miserables....................................x112
Same (English)....................................x111
Same (Spanish). 2v. x113
Ninety-three..x106
Notre Dame (French).........................x104
Same; tr. x101
Odes et ballades.—Les orientales. '60...841 24
Outlaw of Iceland [Hans of Iceland].....x128
Les quatre vents de l'esprit. 1881. 2 v...841 39
Quatre-vingt-treize. 3 v. x108
Réligions et réligion [poëme]. 1880....841 48
Ruy Blas...x130
Select poems and tragedies; tr. by Lang, et al. 1890...841 70

* Of interest to young readers.

LANGUAGE AND LITERATURE.

Selections (poetical); tr. by various authors, ed. by Williams. 1887.............841 49
Shakespeare; tr. by Baillot. 1864.....822.3 130
Story sermons from Hugo................038601
Study of Hugo; by Swinburne. 1886..928.4 116
Things seen. 1887...........................844 44
Toilers of the sea..............................x120
Torquemada (drame). 1882..............842 93
Translations from poems; by Carrington. 1887...841 52
Les travailleurs de la mer....................x129
Huysmans. En route.........................x18801
L'inconsolée....................................x4511
Janin, Balzac, *et al.* Pictures of the French. 1840..................................849 22
Jewish Spy, The. 1739....................847 10
Joubert. Pensées; sel. and tr. by Attwell. 1896...849 44
Jules Horst....................................x14427
Julliot. Deux gloires.—Un cas d'hypnotisme.—Changement d'école............x17802
La folle du logis................................x17803
Mademoiselle Solange (French)..........x17801
Jusserand. English essays from a French pen. 1895..................................844 61
Contents: The forbidden pastimes of a recluse, England, 12th century.—A journey to Scotland in the year 1435.—Paul Scarron.—A journey to England in the year 1663.—One more document concerning Voltaire's visit to England.
Piers plowman. 1894..................821.2 929
Karr. Contes et nouvelles..................x19301
La maison close (essais). 1870.........844 23
La maison de l'ogre. 1890................844 45
Contents: La maison de l'ogre.—Legouvé.—Klmprsk. —Logographe.—Conférence sur le bonheur.— Statue de Rousseau.—Éloge de la mort.—Affaire Boulanger.— Prix de beauté.—Une femme dans un salon.— Une prophétie.— Panorama du siècle.
Ménus propos. 1859........................844 15
Pendant la pluie (essais). 1880.........844 24
Les points sur lesi (essais). 1882......844 41
Tour round my garden......................504 37
Voyage autour de mon jardin. 1861....844 14
La Bédollière. Mère Michel et son chat...*x9002
Story of a cat...................................039501
Labiche. La lettre chargée (drame).......842 108
Labiche and **Jolly.** Le grammaire (drame); ed. by Petilleau...........................842 76
Labiche and **Martin.** Le voyage de Monsieur Perichon (comédie)...........842 106
Laboulaye. Abdallah........................038402
Last fairy tales.................................038401
Paris in America; by Dr. Lefebvre. '63...847 15
Spaniel-prince...................................x3404
Yvon et Finette; ed. by Lyon..............x3403
La Brète. Mon uncle et mon curé.........x4525
Story of Reine [Mon oncle et mon curé]..x4526
(Also tr. as 'Uncle.')

La Bruyère. Characters; tr. by Van Laun. 1885..................................841 43
Lacroix. Nouveaux contes. 1881........ *815 3
La Fayette, Madame de. Œuvres complètes. 1804. 3 v.
V. 1. Zayde..849 31
V. 2. La princesse de Clèves. La comtesse de Tende.—La princesse de Montpensier. Mémoires de la cour de France. 1688-89; pt. 1 ....849 32
V. 3. Mémoires de la cour de France; pt. 2. Histoire de madame Henriette d'Angleterre. Lettres...81v 33
La princesse de Clèves......................x15001
La Fontaine. Choix de fables. 1863.....*849 32
Fables; éd. par Sauveur. 1877............849 35
Fables; tr. by Wright. 1865..................849 2
Same. 1841. 2 v...............................849 3
Œuvres. 1825. 4 v.............................849 17
Lamartine. La chute d'un ange (poème). 1845...841 31
Fior d'Aliza.......................................x2901
Geneviève..x2901
Same; tr..x2902
Graziella (French)..............................x2905
Harmonies poétiques et religieuses. '45..841 30
Jocelyn (poëme). 1847......................841 32
Lectures pour tous. 1875...................849 12
Nouvelles méditations poétiques.— Épitres.—Le dernier chant du pèlerinage d'Harold.—Chant du sacre. '45..841 29
Premières méditations poétiques.—La mort de Socrate. 1848....................841 28
Raphael; tr......................................x2907
Récueillements poétiques. 1845........841 33
Lang and **Sylvester.** The dead leman, etc..x14414
Laurie. Axel Ebersen......................038501
Captain Trafalgar.............................x1905
Crystal city under the sea.................x1910
Schoolboy days in France.................038501
Schoolboy days in Italy....................038502
Schoolboy days in Japan..................038503
Laveleye. Études et essais. 1869..........844 55
Contents: La crise religieuse au 19me siècle.—Le parti libéral et le parti catholique en Belgique.—Le voyage de la Novara.—Un roi constitutionnel.—Le mont Rose et les Alpes pennines.—Antoine Wiertz, un peintre belge contemporain.—Marina, souvenirs de la vie d'artiste à Rome.—Annexes.
Lavigne. Female nihilist..................x11601
Lebrun. Marie Stuart [drame]; ed. by Lallemand...................................842 76
Œuvres choisies. 1843......................841 20
Contents: Odes.— Épîtres— Epigrammes, etc.
Lecomte. Bouderie. 1892................842 Pam. 5
Leconte de Lisle. Derniers poèmes. '95..841 97
Poèmes antiques..............................841 96
Poèmes barbares..............................841 95
Poèmes tragiques.............................841 94

* Of interest to young readers.

Lefebvre, *Doctor.* See **Laboulaye**.
Legouvé. Autour d'un berceau (drame)...842 106
    Edith de Falsen (French)..........................x4201
    Nos filles et nos fils................................x4202
Leïla-Hanoum. Tragedy in the imperial
    harem at Constantinople....................x4512
Lemaître. Morceaux choisis. 1896......844 69
    Myrrha..x3306
    Prince Hermann, regent......................x3305
Lemoyne. Une idylle normande..............x13101
Lepelletier. Les trahisons de Marie
    Louise..x3015
Lermina. The chase............................x11301
    Three exploits of M. Parent..................x11302
Le Sage. Bachelor of Salamanca. 2 v......x2006
    Gil Blas (French)..................................x2004
    Same ; tr. 3 v......................................x2001
    Same (Spanish)....................................x2005
    Œuvres. 1840.................................840 B-7
    Contents : Le diable boiteux.— Gil Blas.— Guzman
    d'Alfarache.— Le bachelier de Salamanque.—Théâtre :
    Crispin, rival de son maître ; Turcaret.
Lesueur. Le mariage de Gabrielle............x14901
Létang. Roi s'ennuie..........................x9040
Liefde. Agnes and Karel [Galama]..........x7501A
    Galama; tr..x7501
    Maid of Stralsund................................x7502
    Postman's bag....................................020702
    Walter's escape..................................020701
Lorris *and* **Meung.** Le roman de la rose.
    1814. 2 v...841 50
Loti. Book of pity and of death...............x14015
    Child's romance..................................x14012
    Fantome d'Orient................................x14013
    From lands of exile [Propos d'exil]......x14006
    Iceland fisherman................................x14002A
    Japoneries d'automne..........................x14008
    Jean Berny, sailor [Matelot].................x14016
    Livre de la pitié et de la mort..............x14014
    Madame Chrysanthème......................x14007
    Same ; tr..x14007A
    Matelot (French)..................................x14017
    Mon frère Yves..................................x14003
    My brother Yves................................x14005
    Pecheur d'Islande................................x14002
    Phantom from the east........................x14013A
    Propos d'exil......................................x14004
    Rarahu ; or, The marriage of Loti.......x14010
    Roman d'un enfant..............................x14009
    Romance of a spahi............................x14011
    Les trois dames de la Kasbah..............x14001
Louis XVI, *of France.* Political and
    confidential correspondence. 1803. 3 v..846 5
Lubomirski. Ace of clubs....................x8705
    Safar Hadgi ; tr..................................x8701
    Tatiana ; tr..x8702

Macé. Théâtre du petit chateau..............*842 92
    Contents : L' année nouvelle.— À brebis tondue Dieu
    mesure le vent.—Une lettre.—Les ricochets.— La revolte
    des fleurs.— La larmes d'une mère.— La leçon de géo-
    graphie.— Le composition d'histoire.— Le palais du
    temps.— L'utilité de la douleur.— Souvenirs de pension.
Maël. Land of tawny beasts..................x18102
    Under the sea to the North Pole..........x18101
Mahon. Les aventures d'un jeune Gau-
    lois..x13301
Maintenon, *Madame de.* Secret corre-
    spondence. 1827. 3 v......................846 1
Mairet. Artist....................................x17001
    Tâche du petit Pierre..........................*x17003
Maistre. La jeune Sibérienne................x4514
    Journey round my room. 1883..........849 24
    Œuvres complètes. 1876..................840 265
    Contents : Notice ; par Sainte-Beuve.— Voyage au-
    tour de ma chambre. — Expédition nocturne. — Le
    lépreux de la cité d'Aoste.— Les prisonniers du Caucase.
    —La jeune Sibérienne.
Malherbe. Œuvres, poésies et prose. '70...841 20
    Contents : Odes.— Stances.— Sonnets, etc.--Lettres.
    Œuvres ; rec. par Lalanne. 1862. 5 v.
    V. 1. Poésies..................................840 385
    V. 2. Traductions de Sénèque............840 386
    V. 3. Lettres..................................840 387
    V. 4. Lettres.— Commentaires sur Des Portes.840 388
    V. 5. Portrait, facsimiles, etc.............840 389
Mallarmé. Divagations. 1897..............849 48
Malot, H. Les amours de Jacques..........x6720
    Anie (French)......................................x6723
    La belle Madame Donis ; tr..............x6717
    La Bohème-tapageuse. 3 v..............x6710
    Boy wanderer ; or, No relations [Sans
    famille]..038302
    Conscience ; tr..................................x6724
    Le docteur Claude..............................x6703
    En famille..x6725
    Une femme d'argent..........................x6711
    Her own folk [En famille].................x6725 C
    Mère..x6721
    Micheline (French)..............................x6715
    No relations [Sans famille].................038302
    Paulette (French)................................x6722
    La petite sœur....................................x6713
    Pompon (French)................................x6712
    Romain Kalbris..................................038301
    Sans famille......................................*x6705
    Zyte ; tr..x6719
Malot, *Madame.* La beauté..................x6750
Margaret *of Navarre.* Fortunate lovers ;
    from the Heptameron ; ed. by Robin-
    son. 1887..843 4
    L'Heptameron. 1615........................843 5
Margueritte. Jours d'épreuve..............x15701
    Ma grande..x15702
Marmontel. Moral tales. 3 v..............x8601
    Œuvres. 1787. 17 v.
    V. 1-3. Contes moraux. 3 v.............840 304
    V. 4. Bélisaire.— Essai sur le gout......840 307

* Of interest to young readers.

LANGUAGE AND LITERATURE.

V. 5-10. Élémens de littérature. 6v............840 308
V. 11-12. Les Incas. 2 v.......................840 314
V. 13-14. La Pharsale de Lucain. 2 v..........840 316
V. 15-16. Théâtre: Denis le tyran.— Aristomène.
— Cléopatre.—Les Héraclides.—Numitor.—Didon.
—Pénélope.—Zémire et Azor.—L'ami de la maison.
— Lucile.—Silvain.— La fausse magie.— Apologie
du théâtre. 2 v..............................840 318
V. 17. Mélanges..............................840 320

Œuvres posthumes. 1807. 13 v.
V. 1-4. Mémoires d'un père. 4 v..............840 321
V. 5-8. Leçons d'un père à ses enfans, sur la
morale, la logique, la métaphysique, et la grammaire. 4 v....................................840 325
V. 9-10. Régence du duc d' Orleans. 2 v......840 329
V. 11. Mélanges..............................840 331
V. 12-13. Nouveaux contes moraux.............840 332

Marot. Œuvres; ed. by Després. 1827...841 82
Marthold. History of a bearskin...........x17501
Mary, *queen of Scots.* Lettres et mémoires.
  1844. 7 v..................................846 21
Maupassant. Odd number....................x16102
  Pierre and Jean............................x16101
Meilhac *et* **Halévy.** L'été de la Saint-
  Martin (comédie)..........................842 Pam. 4
Mendes. Le roi vierge.....................x13001
Mérimée. Carmen (French)..................x1802
  Colomba (French)...........................x1801
  Une correspondance inédite. 1897..........846 61
  Dernières nouvelles........................x1803
  Lettres à une inconnue; ed. by Taine.
  1874. 2 v..................................846 55
  Mateo Falcone, etc. (French)...............x1804
  Théâtre de Clara Gazul. 1883..............842 109
Mérimée *and* **Gautier.** Tales before
  supper.....................................x5312
Merlet *et* **Lintilhac,** Études litteraires sur
  les classiques français. 1894.
  V. 1. Corneille.— Racine.— Molière........840 391
  V. 2. Chanson de Roland. — Villehardouin.—
  Joinville.— Froissart.— Commynes.— Montaigne.—
  Pascal.—La Fontaine.—Boileau.— Bossuet.— Fénelon.— La Bruyère.— Montesquieu.— Buffon.—Voltaire.— Rousseau.—Lettres choisies du 17me et du
  18me siècle................................840 392
Méry. Through thick and thin..............x5201
Millaud. La comédie du jour. 1887......847 B-1
Minssen, *ed.* La belle au bois dormant.
  —Le chat botté.............................x9030
  Huit contes................................x9020
Mirabeau. Œuvres. 1827. 9 v.
  V. 1-2. Lettres des prisons d'état........840 186
  V. 3-5. Lettres à Sophie...................840 188
  V. 6. Histoire de Berlin..................841 103
  V. 7-9. Discours et opinions..............840 192
Mirbeau. Sébastien Roch...................x4562
Mistral. Mireio; a Provençal poem. '72..841 11
  Le poème du Rhône. 1897...................841 103
Moinaux. Les deux sourds (drame).1882..842 77
Molière. Characters; by Clarke. 1853....842 32
  Dramatic works; tr. by Van Laun. 1878.
  3 v.

V. 1. Memoir.— The blunderer.— The love-tiff.
— The pretentious young ladies.— Sganarelle. —
Don Garcin of Navarre.— School for husbands.
The bores. — School for wives.— School for wives
criticised.— The impromptu of Versailles.— The
forced marriage..............................842 47
V. 2. Princess of Elis. Don Juan. Love is the
best doctor. The misanthrope. The physician in
spite of himself.— Melicerte.— Comic pastoral.—
The Sicilian. — Tartuffe.— Amphitryon. George
Dandin......................................842 49
V. 3. The miser. Monsieur de Pourceaugnac.—
The magnificent lovers.— The citizen who apes the
nobleman. — Psyche. — Rogueries of Scapin.
Countess of Escarbagnas. — The learned ladies.
The imaginary invalid.—Jealousy of Le Barbouille.
—The flying doctor..........................842 50

Les femmes savantes; ed. by Masson...840 196
Les fourberies de Scapin; ed. by Masson.
  ....840 198

Œuvres. 1833. 3 v. (incomplete).
V. 1. Don Garcie de Navarre.— L'école des
maris.— Les facheux.— L'école des femmes...842 29
V. 2. L'amour médecin.— Le misanthrope.— Le
médecin malgré lui. — Melicerte. — Pastorale
comique.— Le Sicilien......................842 30
V. 3. Les femmes savantes. — La comtesse
d'Escarbagnas.—Le malade imaginaire.—Le gloire
du Vol-de-Grace: poème.....................842 31

Œuvres. 1854. 2 v.
V. 1. Vie; par Voltaire.— L'étourdi.— Le dépit
amoureux.— Les précieuses ridicules.— Sganarelle.
— Don Garcie de Navarre.— L'école des maris.—
Les facheux.— L'école des femmes.— La critique
de l'école des femmes.—L'Impromptu de Versailles.
—Le mariage forcée: comédie,—Le mariage forcée:
ballet du roi.— La princesse d'Élide.— Don Juan.
— L'amour médecin.— Le misanthrope.— Le médecin malgré lui.—Mélicerte.— Pastorale comique...842 19
V. 2. Le Sicilien.— Le Tartuffe.—Amphitryon.—
L'avare.—George Dandin.— Monsieur de Pourceaugnac. — Les amants magnifiques. — Le bourgeois
gentilhomme.— Psyche.—Le fourberies de Scapin.
— La comtesse d'Escarbagnas. — Les femmes savantes.—Le malade imaginaire.—Poésies diverses...842 20

Les précieuses ridicules..................842 Pam. 1
Select comedies in French and English.
  1832. 8 v.
V. 1. The miser.— The cuckold in conceit.....842 21
V. 2. The cit turned gentleman.—Doctor and no
doctor......................................842 22
V. 3. The blunderer.— Conceited ladies......842 23
V. 4. School for husbands..................842 24
V. 5. The Imposter.— George Dandin.........842 25
V. 6. Man-hater.— Squire Lubberly..........842 26
V. 7. Amphitryon.— Forced marriage.— The Sicilian......................................842 27
V. 8. The hypochondriac.— The impertinents..842 28
Tales from Molière; by Leonard...........*x4504
[Works]; tr. by Wormeley. 1894—.
  v.1—.
V. 1. The misanthrope— Le bourgeois gentilhomme.......................................842 161
V. 2. Tartuffe.— Les précieuses ridicules...842 162
George Dandin.

Monnier. Les amours permises.............x3801
Montaigne. Essais, lettres; édition variorum. 1862. 4 v............................844 17

---
* *Of interest to young readers.*

Essays; tr. by Florio, sel. and ed. by
Chubb..844 56
Contents: Introduction.— Of his task and theme.—
Of pedantism. — Of the institution and education of
children. — It is folly to refer truth or falsehood to our
sufficiency. — Of friendship. — Of solitariness. — Of the
inequality that is between us.—Of the inconstancy of our
actions.— Of drunkenness.— Of books.— Of cruelty.—
We taste nothing purely. — Of anger and choler.— Of
profit and honesty.—Of repenting.—Of three commerces
or societies.— How one ought to govern his will.
Essays; tr. by Friswell. 1869................844 6
Shakespeare and M.; by Feis. 1884....822.3 257
Works; tr. by Hazlitt. 1845................844 1
Same; ed. by Wight. 1859. 4 v.
V. 1. Life; by Hazlitt.— Essays...............844 2
V. 2-3. Essays..844 3
V. 4. Biography; by St. John. — Journey to
Italy.— Letters..844 5
Montesquieu. Œuvres. 1822. 8 v.
V. 1. La vie de M.— Éloge; par D'Alembert.—
Éloge; par Villemain.—Grandeur et décadence des
Romains, etc..840 236
V. 2-5. Analyse de 'L'esprit des lois,' par D'Alem-
bert et Bertolini.— L'esprit des lois.— Défense de
'L'esprit des lois.'—Réponse de M. Risteau.—Com-
mentaire de Voltaire.—Lettre d'Helvetius........840 237
V. 6. Lettres persanes..............................840 241
V. 7. Arsace et Isménie.— Le temple de Gnide.
—Céphise et l'amour.—Lysimaque.—Essai sur le
gout.— Discours.— Poésies.— Lettres, etc........840 242
V. 8. Commentaire sur 'L'esprit des lois'; par le
comte Destutt de Tracy............................840 243
Œuvres choisies. 1859................................840 89
Contents: Grandeur et décadence des Romains.—Po-
litique des Romains.— Dialogue de Sylla et d'Eucrate.—
Lysimaque.— Pensées.— Lettres persanes.— Temple de
Gnide.
Spirit of laws; tr. by Nugent. 2 v........320 1
Mouton. Adventures and misadventures
Mouëzy. L'oncle de Danielle.....................x13504
of a Breton boy..................................*x17610
Murger. Le dernier rendezvous.................x3701
Les rouéries de l'ingénue..........................x3702
Scènes de la vie Bohème..........................x3703
Musset. Comédies et proverbes. 3 v....842 112
Fils du Titien.—Croisilles............................x5505
Poésies. 1867..841 12
Poet and muse [poems]; tr. by Pollock.
1880..841 44
Selections from. 1870................................840 83
Nanteuil. En esclavage........................*x4534
L'héritier des Vaubert..............................x4535
Napoleon I. Aphorismes, etc. 1848.......849 16
Confidential correspondence with Jose-
phine; ed. by Abbott. 1856..................846 8
Lettres à Josephine. 1833. 2 v..................846 51
Near to happiness; tr. by F. H. Potter....x14415
Nodier. Romans..................................x3301
Trilby, the fairy of Argyle..........................x3302
Noir. Compagnons de Buffalo................x14417
Noriac. La bêtise humaine....................x5601
Ohnet. Antoinette; tr.........................x13211
Chant du cygne....................................x13216

La comtesse Sarah................................x13204
Debt of hatred..................................x13215
Le docteur Rameau..............................x13210
Doctor Rameau; tr.............................x13210A
Edmée [Les dames de Croix-Mort]........x13213
La fille du député..............................x13217
La grande marnière............................x13207
Ironmaster [Le maître de forges]..........x13206
A last love......................................x13212
Lise Fleuron (French)........................x13205
Le maître de forges............................x13202
Le maître de forges: drame................842 107
Serge Panine..................................x13201
Same; tr..x13203
Soul of Pierre..................................x13214
Volanté..x13208
Will..x13209
Ollivier. Marie-Magdeleine (French).....x19201
Ortoli. Evening tales; tr. by Harris. 1893...848 3
Oswald. Le trésor des Bacquancourt....x15201
Ozanam. Letters; tr. by Coates. 1886....846 46
Pailleron. Le monde ou l'on ennuie
(drame)..842 108
Paris and Vienne..............................x4503
Pascal. Pensées. 1877......................204 91
Pensées, fragments et lettres; publiés
par Faugère. 1897. 2 v.....................204 129
Thoughts; tr. 1846............................204 9
Paul. Blanche Mortimer (French)..........x6001
Pelletan. Pastor of the desert............x8401
Pellissier. Literary movement in France,
19th century. 1897..........................840 405
Péronne. Veil of liberty....................x18001
Perrault. Popular tales; ed. by Lang
(French).......................................x4502
Peyrebrune. Les frères Colombo..........x15301
Pigault-Lebrun. History of Tekeli......x6101
Monsieur Botte.................................x6102
Piron. La métromanie (drame). 1831....842 2
Œuvres. 1776. 7 v.
V. 1. Vie.— L'école des pères.— Callisthène.—
L'amant mystérieux..............................842 33
V. 2. Les courses de tempé.— Gustave-Wasa.—
La métromanie.— Fernand Cortès. - La fausse
alarme..842 34
V. 3. Arlequin-Deucalion.— L'autre de Tropho-
nius.— L'endriague.— Le claperman.— Le caprice.
—L'âne d'or d'Apukè.—La rose...............842 35
V. 4. Le fâcheux veuvage.— Les chimères.— La
robe de dissention. Tirésias.....................842 36
V. 5. Le mariage de Momus.—Columbine Nitétis.
—Credit est mort.—L'enrôlement d'Arlequin.—Les
huit Mariannes.— Atis.— Philomèle.— Les enfans
de la joie..842 37
V. 6. Épitres.—Odes.—Poëme de Fontenoy, etc.
—Contes.— Épigrammes.— Fables...............842 38
V. 7. Allégories.—Satires.—Poésies diverses, etc.842 39
Ponsard. Charlotte Corday [drame]; ed.
by Brette.......................................842 95
L'homme et l'argent [comédie]; ed. by
Brette...842 97

* Of interest to young readers.

Pont-Jost. No. 13 rue Marlot..................x10901
Pontmartin. Clotilde ; tr........................x6801
Pouvillon. Césette............................x12601
   Same ; tr..........................x12602
   L'innocent..........................x12603
Pressensé, *Madame de.* Deux ans au
   lycée.............................*x2601
   Madeleine's trial, etc...............039703
   Rosa..............................039702
   Seulette ; ed. by Ingall..............*x2606
   Two years of school life.............039701
Prévost, A. F. Manon Lescaut.............x14407
Prévost, M. L'automne d'une femme......x9061
   Mademoiselle Jaufre (French)........x9060
Prudhomme. Poésies, 1865-6..............841 73
Pyat. Rag-picker of Paris..................x14416
Quinet. Lettres à sa mère ; sel. and ed.
   by Saintsbury. 1885................846 45
Rabelais. Œuvres ; nouvelle édition, par
   Lacroix. 1873......................847 16
   Readings in ; by Besant. 1883.......847 19
   Three good giants ; compiled by Dimitry.
    1888.............................847 20
   [Works, life, etc.] ; tr. with notes by
    Smith. 1893. 2 v................847 21
   Works ; tr. by Urquhart, etc. 2 v........847 1
Racine. Andromaque ; ed. by Masson...840 197
   Athalie ; ed. by Joynes. 1871..........842 158
   Athalie ; ed. by Masson. 1877........840 198
   Dramatic works ; metrical English ver-
    sion, by Boswell. 1889.
    V. 1. Biographical notice.—The Thebaïd.—Alex-
    ander the great.—Andromache.—The litigants.—
    Britannicus.—Berenice.......................842 115
    V. 2. Bajazet.—Mithridates.—Iphigenia.—Phæ-
    dra.—Esther.—Athaliah.......................842 116
   Œuvres. 1796. 7 v.
    V. 1. Vie de Racine, etc.—La Thébaïde.—Alex-
    andre le grand..............................842 11
    V. 2. Andromaque.—Les plaideurs.—Britan-
    nicus.......................................842 12
    V. 3. Bérénice.—Bajazet.—Mithridates........842 13
    V. 4. Iphigénie.—Phèdre.....................842 14
    V. 5. Esther.—Athalie.—Œuvres diversés en
    verse et en prose...........................842 15
    V. 6. Lettres sur les imaginaires.—Abrégé de
    l'histoire de Port Royal.—Fragments littéraires. etc.842 16
    V. 7. Lettres..................................842 17
   Théâtre complet ; édition variorum ; par
    Louandre. 1861....................842 18
    Contents : La Thébaïde.—Alexandre le grand.—
    Andromaque.—Les plaideurs.—Britannicus.—Bérénice.—
    Bajazet.—Mithridate.—Iphigénie en Aulide.—Phèdre.—
    Esther.—Athalie.—Plan du premier acte d'Iphigénie.
Rameau. Le cœur de Régine............x17702
   La rose de Grenade................x17701
Regnard. Le joueur ; ed. by Masson....840 201
   Œuvres. 1789. 6 v..................842 98
   Same. 1820. 6 v.
    V. 1. Voyages : Flandre, Hollande, Danemarck,
    Suède, Laponie, Pologne, Allemagne, Provence....842 68
    V. 2. La sérénade.—Le bal.—Le jouer.—Le dis-
    trait.—Attendez-moi sous l'orme.................842 69

    V. 3. Démocrite—La retour imprévu.—Les
    folies amoureuses.—Le mariage de la folie.—Les
    ménechmes.................................842 70
    V. 4. Le légataire universel. Les souhaits.
    Les vendanges—Sapor.—Carnaval de Venise.—
    Poésies diverses..............................842 71
    V. 5. Le divorce. Descente d'Arlequin aux en-
    fers.—L'homme à bonnes fortunes.—Critique de
    'L'homme à bonnes fortunes.' Les filles errantes.
    La coquette..................................842 72
    V. 6. Les chinois. Les baguette de Vulcan.
    L'augmentation de la baguette. Naissance d'Ama-
    dis.—La foire Saint-Germain.—La suite de la foire
    Saint-Germain...............................842 73
Rémusat, *Madame de.* Selections from
   letters. 1804-13...................846 41
Renan, E. *et* **H.** Lettres intimes, 1842-5 ;
   précédées de Ma sœur Henriette, par E.
   Renan. 1896......................846 59
Reybaud, *Madame C.* Le cadet de Colo-
   brières............................x3002
   Goldsmith's wife....................x3003
   Mademoiselle de Malepiere...........x3001
   Old convents of Paris...............x3006
   Thorough Bohemienne...............x3004
   Uncle Cæsar......................x3005
Reybaud, L. La comtesse de Mauleon...x9401
Richebourg. Le million du père Raclot.
   ....x17201A
   Old Raclot's million.................x17201
Richepin. Césarine (French)..............x5701
   La mer (poëme). 1890............841 71
Robert. La princesse Sophie..............x3901
Robida. Le mystère de la rue Carême-
   Prenant...........................x8001
Rochefort. Mademoiselle Bismarck ; tr....x12201
Rochefoucauld. Album, portraits, etc.,
   with Gilbert's edition of his works....840 B-8
   Moral reflections, etc. 1853...........849 11
   Œuvres ; ed. by Gilbert. 1868-83. 3v. in 5.
    V. 1. Notice biographique ; par Gourdault.—
    Reflexions ; ou, Sentences et maximes morales.—
    Appendice...................................840 334
    Appendice : V. 1. Anciens textes des maximes.—
    Notice bibliographique, etc...................840 335
    V. 2. Mémoires.—Apologie de Monsieur le
    prince de Marcillac..........................840 336
    V. 3. pt. 1. Lettres...........................840 337
    V. 3. pt. 2. Lexique ; introduction grammaticale ;
    par Regnier.................................840 338
Rochemont. Contes et nouvelles pour la
   jeunesse........................*x3405
Rocoffort. Pylade (French)................x12101
Rod. Dernier refuge......................x2206
   L'innocente.........................x2208
   Private life of an eminent politician
   [English of 'La vie privée de Michel
   Tessier']..........................x2205
   Les roches blanches.................x2207
   White rocks........................x2207A
Rodenbach. La vocation..................x17710
Rosny. L'indomptée......................x10910

---

* Of interest to young readers.

Profondeurs de Kyamo (contes)............x10911
Les Xipéhuz................................x10912
Rougeard. Strictures of Labienus.....847 Pam. 1
Rousseau, J. B. Œuvres. 1795. 4 v
  V. 1. Odes...840 104
  V. 2. Épitres.— Allégories.— Poésies diverses...840 105
  V. 3. Comédies: Le flateur.— Le capricieux.
  — Les ayeux chimériques..........................840 106
  V. 4. Le café.— La ceinture magique.— La dupe
  de soi même.— Lettres............................840 107
  Œuvres choisies. 1843............................841 20
Rousseau, J. J. Œuvres. 1817. 8 v.
  V. 1. Julie; ou, La nouvelle Héloïse.— Les
  amours de mylord Édouard Bomston............840 96
  V. 2. Émile.— Émile et Sophie...................840 97
  V. 3. Lettres politiques............................840 98
  V. 4. Dictionnaire de musique.— La musique moderne.— Origines des langues.— La musique française.— Lettre d'un symphoniste de l'académie royale de musique à ses camarades de l'orchestre....840 99
  V. 5. Lettre à D'Alembert.— De l'imitation théâtrale.— Narcisse.— Les prisonniers de guerre.— L'engagement téméraire.— Les muses galantes.— Le devin du village.— La découverte du nouveau monde.— Fragmens d' Iphis.— Courts fragmens de Lucrèce.— Quatre lettres à Malesherbes.— Rêveries du promeneur solitaire.— Fragmens pour un dictionnaire des terms d'usage en botanique.— Mélanges...840 100
  V. 6. Confessions.................................840 101
  V. 7. Rousseau juge de Jean Jacques.— Histoire du précédent écrit.— Discours sur cette question: Si le rétablissement des sciences et des arts a contribués à épurer les mœurs.— Correspondance....840 102
  V. 8. Correspondance............................840 103
  Œuvres complètes. 1788. 38 v.
  V. 1-4. Voyage à Ermenonville.— La nouvelle Héloïse. 4 v.....................................840 266
  V. 5-6. Lettres élémentaires sur la botanique. 2 v..840 270
  V. 7. L'inégalité parmi les hommes.— Lettre à M. Philopolis.— Sur l'économie politique.— Du projet de paix perpétuelle.— Polysynodie............840 272
  V. 8. Du contrat social.— Le gouvernement de Pologne.— Lettres sur la législation de la Corse....840 273
  V. 9. Lettres écrites de la montagne...............840 274
  V. 10-14. Émile. 5. v..............................840 275
  V. 15-18. Sciences, arts, et belles-lettres. 4 v...840 280
  V. 19-22. Écrits sur la musique. 4 v............840 284
  V. 23-26. Les confessions. 4 v....................840 288
  V. 27. Contestation à M. Hume..................840 292
  V. 28. Pièces diverses............................840 293
  V. 29-30. Rousseau juge de Jean Jacques. 2 v...840 294
  V. 31-35. Lettres. 5 v.............................840 296
  V. 36. Esprit, maximes, etc......................840 301
  V. 37. Musique....................................840 302
  V. 38. Récueil de plantes coloriées..............840 303
Rousselet. Drummer-boy......................040101
Le fils du connétable............................x11703
Serpent charmer..................................x11701
Son of the constable.............................x11704
Rouvre. À deux...............................x18701
Roux. Meditations of a parish priest; tr. by Hapgood. 1886...............................849 29
Saint-André. Madame Pompadour's garter..x9101
Saint-Évremond. Works; tr. by Des Maizeaux. 1728. 3 v.................................840 8

Saint-Pierre. Paul et Virginie................x2101
Paul and Virginia...............................x2102
Pablo y Virginia................................x2103
Sainte-Beuve. Causeries du Lundi. 1851-62. 16 v.
  V. 1. Cours de littérature dramatique; par Saint-Marc Girardin.— Les confidences; par Lamartine.— De la question des théâtres.— Mémoires sur Madame de Sévigné; par Walckenaer.— Raphaël; par Lamartine.— M. de Montalembert, orateur.— Hamilton.— Œuvres littéraires de Villemain et de Cousin.— Madame Récamier.— Histoire de l'empire; par Thiers.— Pensées de Joubert.— Adrienne Le Couvreur.— Campagnes d'Égypte et de Syrie; par Napoléon.— Le père Lacordaire.— Mémoires de Philippe de Commynes.— Journal de la campagne de Russie; par M. de Fezensac.— Des lectures publiques du soir.— Poésies de A. de Musset.— Discours sur l'Histoire de la révolution d'Angleterre; par Guizot.— Le livre des rois; par Firdusi.— La Mare-au-diable, La petite Fadette, François le champi; par G. Sand.— M. de Feletz et la critique littéraire sous l'empire.— Éloges académiques; par Pariset.— Lettres de Madame Du Deffand.— Mémoires d'outre-tombe; par Chateaubriand.— Lettres inédites de l'abbé de Chaulieu............844 25
  V. 2. Lettres et opuscules de Fénelon.— Œuvres de Barnave.— Pline le naturaliste.— Madame de La Tour-Franqueville et Jean J. Rousseau.— Lettres de la duchesse de Bourgogne.— La religieuse de Toulouse; par J. Janin.— Lettres de Mademoiselle de Lespinasse.— Chateaubriand romanesque et amoureux.— Huet, évêque d'Avranches.— Mémoires de Madame d'Épinay.— Lettres de Madame de Grafigny, ou Voltaire à Cirey.— Lettres de Chesterfield.— Le palais Mazarin; par L. de Laborde.— Madame Du Châtelet.— Chansons de Béranger.— Madame Geoffrin.— Lettres de Goethe et de Bettina.— Gil Blas; par Le Sage.— M. de Broglie.— Procès de Jeanne d'Arc.— L'abbé Galiani.— Balzac.— M. Bazin.— Madame de Pompadour.— Malesherbes.— Chateaubriand, homme d'état et politique............844 26
  V. 3. Rabelais; par E. Noël.— Œuvres de Madame de Genlis.— Qu'est-ce qu'un classique?— Madame de Caylus et ce qu'on appelle urbanité.— Les confessions de Rousseau.— Biographie de C. Desmoulins; par E. Fleury.— Vauvenargues.— Œuvres de Frédéric le grand. - M. Droz.— Frédéric le grand, littérateur.— La duchesse du Maine.— Florian.— Étienne Pasquier.— Les Mémoires de Saint-Simon.— Diderot.— Fontenelle; par Floureus.— Lettres de Condorcet.— Bussy-Rabutin.— Madame É. de Girardin.— Histoire du Chancelier Daguesseau; par Boullée.— L'abbé de Choisy.— Madame de la Vallière.— M. de Latouche.— La grande mademoiselle.— Théodore Leclercq..844 27
  V. 4. Mirabeau et Sophie.— H. Moreau.— Pierre Dupont.— Nouveaux documents sur Montaigne.— Correspondance entre Mirabeau et La Marck.— Mademoiselle de Scudéry.— A. Chénier, homme politique.— Saint-Évremond et Ninon.— Lettres et opuscules inédits du J. de Maistre.— Madame de Lambert.— Madame Necker.— L'abbé Maury.— Le duc de Lauzun.— Jasmin. - Marie-Antoinette.— Buffon.— Madame de Maintenon.— Histoire de la restauration; par Lamartine.— Marie Stuart; par Mignet.— M. de Bonald.— Essai sur Amyot; par Blignières.— Mémoires et correspondance de Mallet du Pan.— Mémoires de Marmontel.— Chamfort.— Rullière........844 28
  V. 5. Raynouard; par Walckenaer.— Gaîtés champêtres; par Janin.— Cardinal de Retz.— Rivarol.—

Duchesse d'Angoulême.— La Harpe.— Le Brun-Pindare. - Madame de Motteville.—Sieyès.— Fiévée. - Cardinal de Retz.— Perrault. — Patru. — Louis XIV.—Saint-Just; par Fleury.—Gourville.—De la poésie et des poètes en 1852.— La princesse des Ursins.—Portalis, Duc d'Antin.—Le comte-pacha de Bonneval..844 29
V. 6. Le maréchal Marmont.— Madame Sophie Gay.— Armand Carrel.— De la retraite de Villemain et Cousin.—Walckenaer.— La reine Marguerite.—Beaumarchais.—Rollin.— Mémoires de Cosnac.—Duchesse d'Orléans.—P. L. Courier.— Saint Anselme; par M. de Rémusat.—L'abbé Gerbet.—Les regrets.— Bernardin de Saint-Pierre.— Ducis.— Étienne.—Boileau.—Treize lettres de Saint-Pierre........844 30
V. 7. Regnard.— Michaud, de l'Académie française.— Montesquieu.—Le président de Brosses: sa vie, ses lettres sur l'Italie.—Voltaire et le président de Brosses.— Franklin.— L'abbé Barthélemy.—Le cardinal de Richelieu: ses lettres et papiers d'état.—Saint François de Sales.—Grimm.—Necker.— Les faux Démétrius; par Mérimée.—Volney.— Marguerite, reine de Navarre.— Frédéric le grand; sa correspondance.— Arnault, de l'Institut.— La Fontaine...844 31
V. 8. L'abbé de Bernis.—De l'état de la France sous Louis XV.—Le cardinal de Bernis.— Malherbe et son école.— Gui Patin.—Sully.—Mézeray.—Le prince de Ligne.—Histoire littéraire de la France, publiée par l'Institut.— Discours de Mignet, à l'Académie de science, morales, et politiques.—Le roman de Renart.—Rœderer.—Gabrielle d'Estrées.— Nouveaux voyages en zig-zag de Topffer.—Gibbon.— Histoire de la maison royale de Saint-Cyr; par Th. Lavallée.— Joinville.—Appendice aux articles sur Rœderer.......................................844 32
V. 9. Massillon.—Nouvelles lettres de Madame, mère du régent.—Froissart.—Le buste de l'abbé Prévost.— E. de la Boétie.— Le marquis de Lassay.— Duclos.— Bourdaloue.— M. de Stendhal.—Marivaux.— Geoffroy de Villehardouin.—Daru.—Madame Dacier...844 33
V. 10 Œuvres de François Arago.— Fénelon: sa correspondance spirituelle et politique.—Buffon: ses œuvres annotées par Flourens.—Chateaubriand, anniversaire du Génie du Christianisme.—Senac de Meilhan.—Le président Jeannin.—Bossuet: lettres de Poujoulat, portrait par Lamartine.—Maucroix, l'ami de La Fontaine: ses œuvres diverses; publiées par L. Paris.—Saint-Martin, le philosophe inconnu.—Vicq d'Azyr.—Agrippa d'Aubigné.— Sylvain Bailly.—Denne-Baron.—Le marquis de La Fare.—Léopold Robert: sa vie, ses œuvres, et sa correspondance; par Feuillet de Conches.—Ramond, le peintre des Pyrénées............................844 34
V. 11. Journal de Dangeau.—Œuvres de La chapelle et de Bachaumont.—Montluc.—Lettres sur l'éducation des filles; par Madame de Maintenon.—De la poésie de la nature, du foyer et de la famille; Saint-Lambert, Roucher, etc.—William Cowper.— La Divine comédie de Dante; traduite par Mesnard. —Le président Hénault.—Charron.—Instruction générale sur l'exécution du plan d'études; par Fortoul. —Werther, correspondance de Goethe et de Kestner. —Une réception académique en 1694 d'après Dangeau.— Henri IV écrivain; par Eugène Jung........844 35
V. 12. Les chants modernes; par Maxime Du Camp.—Santeul; ou La poésie latine sous Louis XIV.—Œuvres inédites de Ronsard.—Le marquis d'Argenson d'après les manuscrits.—Histoire du consulat et de l'empire; par Thiers.—Œuvres complètes de Saint-Amant.—Œuvres de Voiture.—Une petite guerre sur la tombe de Voiture. Eugénie de Guérin.—Mémoires et journal de l'abbé Le Dieu sur la vie et les ouvrages de Bossuet —Sénecé. Le duc de Rohan. Œuvres de Frédéric le grand, correspondance avec le prince Henri. La margrave de Bureith. La marquise de Crequi. Le baron de Besenval...................................844 /
V. 13. Lettres inédites de Voltaire. Le maréchale de Villars. Histoire de la querelle des anciens et des modernes; par H. Rigault, l'abbé de l'ons.—Tallemant et Bussy. - Essais de Madame de Tracy.—Histoire du règne de Henri IV; par Poirson.—Guillaume Favre de Genève. Divers écrits de Taine.- Mémoires et journal de l'abbé Le Dieu sur Bossuet.—Maine de Biran. Souvenirs militaires du Général Pelleport.—Madame Bovary; par G. Flaubert.--A. de Musset.--Les nièces de Mazarin et le duc de Nivernais. Le maréchal de Saint-Arnaud......................................844 37
V. 14. Œuvres de Vauvenargues, publiées par Gilbert. - Vie militaire du général comte Friant par le comte Friant, son fils.— Poésies complètes de Théodore de Banville.- Vie de Maupertuis; par La Beaumelle.— L'abbé de Marolles. Lettres de la mère Agnes Arnauld; publiées par P. Faugère. Fanny; par Ernest Feydeau.—Variétés: littéraires, morales, et historiques; par S. de Sacy. Histoire de l'Académie française; par Pellisson et d'Olivet, publiée par L. Livet.—Correspondance inédite de Madame Du Deffand; publiée par le marquis de Sainte-Aulaire.— Journal et mémoires du Marquis d'Argenson, publiées par Rathery.— La princesse des Ursins.—François Villon: sa vie et ses œuvres; par A. Campaux.—Souvenirs et correspondance de Madame Récamier.— Correspondance de Buffon; publiée par Nadault de Buffon.—Histoire du consulat et de l'empire; par Thiers.—Histoire de la restauration; par L. de Viel-Castel.— Mémoires du duc de Luynes, publiés par L. Dussieux et E. Soulié.—Journal de Casaubon.—Poésies inédites de Madame Desbordes-Valmore.—Charles Victor de Bonstetten; par Aimé Steinlen.....................844
V. 15. Œuvres de Maurice de Guérin.—Journal d'Olivier Lefèvre d'Ormesson.—Mélanges de critique religieuse; par E. Scherer.—Correspondance diplomatique du J. de Maistre.—Histoire du consulat et de l'empire; par Thiers.—Œuvres et correspondance de Tocqueville.— Réception du père Lacordaire.— Histoire de la littérature française, etc.; par A. Sayous.— Le général Joubert. Mémoires de Madame Elliott sur la révolution française.— Histoire de la littérature française; par D. Nisard.—Correspondance et œuvres inédites de Voltaire et Rousseau. L'abbé de Saint-Pierre.— Histoire du consulat et de l'empire, par Thiers.- Parny, poète élégiaque.— Académie française réceptions de Ponsard, de Biot, de Falloux, d'E. Augier, de J. Sandeau.—Rêves et réalités; par Madame Blanchecotte.—Sur Béranger: Sur le 'Louis XVI' d'Amédée Renée.—Lettre du Directeur gérant du Moniteur, sur la morale et l'art.—De la tradition, en littérature.— L'abbé Fléchier.— Mémoires de Saint-Simon..............................841
V. 16. Madame Tastu.—Jugements et témoignages sur Le Sage et sur Gil Blas.— Notes et remarques —Table générale et analytique: par Ch. Pierrot..844 4

Chroniques parisiennes. 1843-45..........844 21
English portraits. 1875.....................844 10
Lettres à la princesse. 1873.................846 10
Monday-chats; tr. by Mathews. 1877....844 7

Poésies. 1869..................................841 19
  Contents: Vie, poésies et pensées de Joseph Delorme.
  —Les consolations, etc.
Portraits de femmes......................920.4 5
Select essays ; tr. by Butler....................844 59
  Contents: What is a classic?—Of a literary tradition.
  —Letters of Lord Chesterfield to his son.—William Cowper.—Gibbon.—Grote's History of Greece.—Bonstettin and Gray.—M. Taine's History of English literature.
Saintine. Picciola ; tr........................*x3504
Seul (French)...................................x3502
Solitary of Juan Fernandez...................x3503
Woman's whims..................................x3501
Sales. Price of a coronet....................x17101
Sand, George, (Madame Dudevant). Antonia ; tr......................................x207
Bagpipers [Les maîtres sonneurs]............x265
Castle of Pictordu..............................x254
Le chateau des désertes........................x222
Le chêne parlant.................................x256
Cæsarine Dietrich ; tr..........................x245
La comtesse de Rudolstadt...................x259
  Same ; tr.....................................x209
La confession d'une jeune fille..............x230
Consuelo..x241
  Same ; tr.....................................x208
Correspondance. 1812-76. 6 v..............846 34
Corsair..x213
Countess of Rudolstadt........................x209
La Daniella.....................................x226
Les deux frères.................................x257
Elle et lui.....................................x255
La famille de Germandre......................x248
Fanchon the cricket............................x243
First and true love............................x212
Francis the waif...............................x246A
François le champi.............................x246
Gallant lords of Bois-Doré....................x266
Handsome Lawrence.............................x239
Haunted pool...................................x228A
L'homme de neige. 3 v..........................x217
Indiana..x247
  Same ; tr.....................................x210
Jacques (French)................................x221
Jealousy ; or, Teverino........................x214
Jean Ziska (French)............................x258
Last Aldini.....................................x212
Lavinia (French)................................x249
Lelia (French)..................................x223
Letters ; tr. and ed. by Beaufort. '86. 3v...846 40
Lucrezia Floriani (French)....................x249
Mademoiselle Merquem ; tr....................x201
Les maîtres mosaistes..........................x227
Les maîtres sonneurs...........................x235
La mare au diable...............................x228
Marianne (French)...............................x263
Le marquis de Villemer (comédie). '78..842 136
  Same ; tr.....................................x237

Master mosaic workers..........................x227A
Mauprat...x236
  Same ; tr.....................................x211
Mélanges......................................944.6 72
Miller of Angibault.............................x231
Molière ; drama in prose......................842 96
Monsieur Antoine ; tr..........................x240
  Same ; tr................................in 14139
Monsieur Sylvestre..............................x205
  Same ; tr.....................................x204
Mont-Revêche....................................x233
My sister Jeanne................................x215
Naiad...x268
Nanon (French)..................................x225
  Same ; tr....................................x225A
Narcisse (French)...............................x224
La petite Fadette...............................x229
Le Piccinino....................................x216
Rolling stone...................................x238
Simon ; tr......................................x213
Snow man..x244
Spiridion (French)..............................x264
Théâtre. 1866. 4 v. in 2.
  V. 1-2. Cosima.—Le roi attend.—François le champi.—Claudie.—Molière.—Le mariage de Victorine.—Les vacances de Pandolphe.—Le démon du foyer.—Le pressoir...........................842 62
  V. 3-4. Mauprat.—Flaminio.—Maître Favilla.—Lucie.—Françoise.—Comme il vous plaira.—Marguerite de Sainte-Gemme.—Le marquis de Villemer..842 63
Tower of Percemont..............................x232
L'Uscoque..x220
Valentine (French)..............................x267
Valvèdre...x234
La ville noir...................................x261
Wings of courage................................x253
Sand, Maurice, (J. F. M. A. Dudevant).
  Callirhoë ; tr................................x7601
Sandeau. Madame de Sommerville
  (French)......................................x1706
Mademoiselle de la Seiglière..................x1703
  Same (drame)................................842 75
Madeleine (French).............................x1705
  Same ; tr....................................x1704
La maison de Penarvon..........................x1702
Marianna (French)...............................x1701
Valcreuse (French)..............................x1707
Sarcey. Miseries of Fo-Hi. 1883.........847 18
Piano de Jeanne, and Qui perd gagne ;
  ed. by Magill.................................x5110
Sardou. Alice de Beaurepaire ; tr........x3011
La perle noire (comédie)....................842 107
Sardou, *et al.* Madame Sans-Gêne.......x3010
Scarron. Le roman comique................x14409
Schaeffer. A new year's eve...............x4725
Schultz. Jean de Kerdren.................x19105
  Same ; tr....................................x19106
Madeleine's rescue............................037701

* Of interest to young readers.

La neuvaine de Colette. 1896.............x19101
Story of Colette....................................x19102
Straight on......................................037702
Sciobert. Nouvelles scènes de la vie champêtre...x14101
Scribe. Bertrand et Raton (drame).........842 106
Russian honey-moon (comedy). 1890...842 121
Théâtre. 1828. 10 v.
V. 1. Une nuit de la garde nationale.—Le soliciteur.—La somnambule.—Le comte Ory.—Frontin mari-garçon.—L'intérieur de l'étude.—Le nouveau Pourceaugnac.—Une visite à Bedlam.—Les deux précepteurs...842 51
V. 2. Secrétaire et cuisinier.—La petite sœur.—Colonel de hussards.—Le colonel.—Gastronome sans argent.—Le mariage enfantin.—Philibert marié.—La vieux garçon.—Partie et revanche....842 52
V. 3. Le combat des montagnes.—Michel et Christine.—Maîtresse au logis.—Le café des variétés.—Demoiselle et dame.—L'héritière.—L'ours et le pacha.—L'intérieur d'un bureau.—La mansarde des artistes...842 53
V. 4. Coiffeur et perruquier.—Les grisettes.—Le plus beau jour de la vie.—La haine d'une femme.—Le baiser au porteur.—La demoiselle à marier.—L'écarté.—La quarantaine.—La loge du portier......842 54
V. 5. Le médecin des dames.—La belle-mère.—Le mariage de raison.—Le charlatanisme.—Les premières amours.—Le parrain.—Simple histoire.—Rodolphe...842 55
V. 6. La chambre à coucher.—La neige.—Le concert à la cour.—Léocadie.—La dame blanche.—Le maçon.—La vieille....................................842 56
V. 7. Les eaux du Mont d'Or.—Le bon papa.—Le menteur véridique.—Coraly.—Le confident.—L'ambassadeur.—La chatte métamorphosée en femme.—Avant, pendant et après......................842 57
V. 8. Le petit dragon.—L'ennui.—L'artiste.—Un dernier jour de fortune.—La lune de miel.—Vatel.—Le diplomate.—La marraine.—Les empériques d'autrefois..842 58
V. 9. Valérie.—Mariage d'argent.—Les manteaux.—La manie des places.—Malvina.—Les moralistes...842 59
V. 10. Fiorella.—Fra Diavolo.—La fiancée.—Louise.—La seconde année.—Philippe..............842 60
Valérie [drame]; ed. by Roulier............842 76
Le verre d'eau [drame]; ed. by Bue......842 74
Scribe et Delavigne. Le diplomate [drame]; ed. by Ragon..........................842 75
Scribe et Legouvé. Adrienne Lecouvreur [drame]. 1882......................................842 77
Bataille des dames [drame]. 1882........842 77
Scuderi. Histoire de Mathilde d' Aguilar....x9201
Second. Roman de deux bourgeois..........x10301
Ségur, *comtesse de.* Fairy tales..............038020
Memorias de un asno.............................*x3201
Les vacances.......................................*x3202
Senancour. Obermann. 1840................846 54
Seigny. Stéphanette (French)................x16301
Sévigné, *Madame de.* Lettres; nouvelle édition, par Vauxcelles. 1801. 10 v...846 11
Same; tr. and ed. by Mrs. Hale...........846 4
Selections from letters; ed. by Masson..840 199

Sophia-Adelaide x14406
Souvestre. Attic philosopher in Paris.......x1406
Brittany and La Vendée........................x1408
Confessions of a workingman................x1416
The lake shore....................................x1410
Leaves from a family journal (Le mémorial de famille).......................................x1409
Man and money..................................x1413
Le mari de Madame de Solange..............x1412
Le mat de cocagne...............................x1404
Le mémorial de famille..........................x1403
Les péchés de jeunesse.........................x1405
Un philosophe sous les toits..................x1411
Pleasures of old age [Souvenirs d'un vieillard]...x1407
Scènes et recits des Alpes......................x1402
Le serf.—Le chevrier de Lorraine............x1414
Souvenirs d'un vieillard.........................x1401
Staël, *Madame de.* Corinne...................x7401
Same; tr...x7402
Germany. 2 v...................................914.3 4
Œuvres. 1838. 2 v.
V. 1. Lettres sur Rousseau.—Procès de la reine.—Réflexions sur la paix.—Essai sur les fictions.—Mirza.—Adélaide et Théodore.—Pauline.—Zulma.—Influence des passions.—Réflexions sur le suicide.—Lady Jane Grey.—De la littérature.—Delphine.—Corinne..840 B-1
V. 2. De l'Allemagne.—M. Necker.—La révolution française.—Dix années d'exil.—Mélanges.....840 B-2
Œuvres complètes. 1820. 17 v.
V. 1. De caractère et les écrits de Madame de Staël—Lettres sur Rousseau............................840 244
V. 2. Le procès de la reine.—Les fictions.—Mirza.—Adélaide et Théodore.—Histoire de Pauline.—Zulma...840 245
V. 3. De l'influence des passions.—Sur le suicide.—Lady Jeanne Grey...............................840 246
V. 4. De la littérature dans ses rapports avec les institutions sociales....................................840 247
V. 5-7. Delphine. 3 v..................................840 248
V. 8-9. Corinne. 2 v....................................840 251
V. 10-11. De l'Allemagne. 2 v.......................840 253
V. 12-14. Sur les principaux événements de la révolution françoise. 3 v.............................840 255
V. 15. Dix années d'exil...............................840 258
V. 16. Agar dans le désert.—Geneviève de Brabant.—La Sunamite.—Le capitaine Kernadec.—La Signora Fantastici.—Le Mannequin.—Sapho.....840 259
V. 17. Du caractère de M. Necker.—Jane Grey: tragedie.—Sophie.—Mélanges.......................840 260
Stahl. Maroussia (French).....................x16601
Stanislaus, *king.* Moral sentences. 1853..849 11
Stapfer. Des réputations littéraires. 1893.
v. 1—..844 75
Stendhal, *pseud.* See **Beyle**.
Stenger. La petite Beaujard.................x13701
Stolz (Comtesse de Begon). House on wheels...039401
Sue. De Rohan; tr................................x5402
Le Juif errant. 4 v.................................x5414
Martin the foundling..............................x5401
Mysteries of Paris. 3 v..........................x5406

* Of interest to young readers.

Paula Monti ; tr............................x5412
Refugees of Martinique........................x5407
Wandering Jew.................................x5404
Woman's love..................................x5405
Swetchine, *Madame*. Writings ; tr. by
 Preston. 1869........................849 10
Taine. Derniers essais de critique et d'histoire. 1894........................844 57
 Contents: M. de Sacy.—Paul de Saint-Victor: Hommes et dieux.—Les Ardennes.—Sainte-Beuve. —É. Boutmy: Philosophie de l'architecture en Grèce.—Fondation de l'école libre des sciences politiques.—Th. Ribot : L'Hérédité.— Th. Ribot. Bain, Herbert Spencer : La philosophie de Schopenhauer, par Th. Ribot; Les sens et l'intelligence, par Bain ; L'esprit et le corps, par Bain ; Princeps de psychologie, par Herbert Spencer.—George Sand.—M. Louis de Loménie, discours prononcé par M. Taine à l'Académie française, le 15 janvier, 1880.—Mallet-du-Pan.—Marcelin: Souvenirs de ' La vie Parisienne.'—Édouard Bertin.
Tencin. Œuvres complètes. 1804. 2 v.
 V. 1. Mémoires du comte de Comminge.—Le siége de Calais.—Les malheurs de l'amour........840 344
 V. 2. Anecdotes de la cour et du règne d'Edouard II, roi d'Angleterre.—Correspondance.— Des romans........................840 345
Theuriet. L'abbé Daniel (French)..........x7922
 Same; tr.................................x7922A
 L'affaire Froidville......................x7915
 L'amoureux de la Préfète..................x7916
 Angela's fortune..........................x7907
 Antoinette ; tr...........................x7904
 La chanoinesse, 1789-93...................x7921
 Contes de la primevère....................x7924
 Contes forestiers : Tentation, etc........x7923
 Eusèbe Lombard (French)...................x7913
 Gerard's marriage.........................x7901
 Godson of a marquis.......................x7902
 Hélène (French)...........................x7914
 House of the two Barbels..................x7903
 Madame Heurteloup (French)................x7909
 Mademoiselle Roche (French)...............x7920
 Le mariage de Gérard......................x7911
 Michael Verneuil (French).................x7910
 L'oncle Scipion...........................x7917
 Raymonde; tr..............................x7905
 Reine des bois............................x7918
 Tante Aurélie (French)....................x7912
 Woodland queen............................x7919
 Young Maugars.............................x7906
Thibault, A.F. *See* **France, A.**
Tillier. Belle-Plante and Cornelius.......x4518
 Mon oncle Benjamin........................x4517
Tinseau. Bouche close (French)............x15805
 Damascus road.............................x15811
 A forgotten debt..........................x15812
 Hélène; tr................................x15804
 In quest of the ideal.....................x15813A
 Jenny's ordeal [Bouche close].............x15807
 La lampe de Psyché........................x15815
 Maître Gratien............................x15810
 Mon oncle Alcide..........................x15809
 Plus fort que la haine....................x15808
 Strass et diamants........................x15806
 Sur le seuil..............................x15803
 Vers l'idéal..............................x15813
Tissot *and* **Amiero**. Adventures of three
 fugitives................................x12302
 Exiles...................................x12301
Töpffer. Nouvelles genevoises.............x2401
Toudouze. Madame Lambelle.................x18901
Trouessart. Un rêve à deux................x4521
Uchard. Mademoiselle Blaisot (French).....x13901
Ulbach. L'enfant de la morte..............x10601
 For fifteen years........................x10604
 Papa Fortin (French).....................x10602
 The steel hammer.........................x10603
 Under the ban............................x4507
Vadier. Mon étoile........................x2501
Valbert. Hommes et choses du temps
 présent. 1883......................844 42
Vallés. Le bachelier......................x12402
 L'enfant.................................x12401
Valrey. Martha de Montbrun (French).......x8501
Verlaine. Amour (poëme). 1888.........841 76
 Bonheur (poëme). 1891..................841 78
 Chansons pour elle. 1891...............841 79
 Parallèlement (poëme). 1889............841 77
 Poems ; tr. by Hall. 1895..............841 89
 Sagesse (poëme). 1889..................841 75
Verne. Abandoned [Mysterious island;
 pt. 2]....................................x728
 Adrift in the Pacific.....................x746
 Archipelago on fire.......................x770
 Autour de la lune.........................x703
 Captain Antifer...........................x726
 Captain of the Guidara [Kéraban the
  inflexible; pt. 1].......................x705
 Castle of the Carpathians.................x717
 Claudius Bombarnac [The special correspondent]...............................x718A
 Clipper of the clouds.....................x707
 Cryptogram [Giant raft; pt. 2]............x757
 Demon of Cawnpore.........................x750
 Le désert de glace........................x711
 Dick Sands ; tr...........................x742
 Doctor Ox, etc............................x740
 Dropped from the clouds [Mysterious
  island; pt. 1]...........................x727A
 Earth to the moon.........................x701
 800 leagues on the Amazon [Giant raft;
  pt. 1]...................................x756A
 English at the North Pole [Voyages of
  Captain Hatteras; pt. 1].................x710
 Family without a name.....................x714
 Five weeks in a balloon...................x741

LANGUAGE AND LITERATURE.

Field of ice [Voyages of Captain Hatteras; pt. 2].....................................x711A
Flight to France................................x713
Floating city. x758
Foundling Mick [P'tit bonhomme]..........x719
Fur country......................................x733
Giant raft.......................................x756
Same; pt. 1, 800 leagues on the Amazon..x756A
Same; pt. 2, The cryptogram................x757
Godfrey Morgan; tr............................x763
Green ray..x723
In the land of the behemoth..................x721
Hector Servadac; tr............................x737
Journey to the center of the earth............x731
Kéraban the inflexible; pt. 1, Captain of the Guidara.................................x705
Same; pt. 2, Scarpante the spy............x706
Lottery ticket..................................x702
Mathias Sandorf; tr............................x771
Meridiana......................................x722
Michael Stroghoff; tr..........................x720
Mistress Branican..............................x716
Mysterious island...............................x727
Same; pt. 1, Dropped from the clouds...x727A
Same; pt. 2, Abandoned....................x728
Same; pt. 3, Secret of the island..........x729
Off on a comet................................x735
Purchase of the North Pole..................x715
Scarpante the spy [Kéraban the inflexible; pt. 2]..................................x706
Secret of the island [Mysterious island; pt. 3].......................................x729
Special correspondent.........................x718
Tigers and traitors............................x753
Tour round the world in 80 days............x755
Tribulations of a Chinaman..................x745
Twenty thousand leagues under the sea....x704
Underground city..............................x764
Vanished diamond..............................x769
Voyages of Captain Hatteras; pt. 1, English at the North Pole...................x710
Same; pt. 2, The field of ice................x711
Wreck of the Chancellor, etc.................x725

Vignon. Victoire Normand (French).........x4101
Vigny. Le canne de jonc.....................x3105
Cinq-Mars (French)............................x3102
Same; tr.......................................x3104
Poésies. 1874..................................841 14
Poésies complètes. 1882......................841 61
Servitude et grandeur militaires.............x3101
Stello (French)...............................x3103
Théâtre..842 61

Contents: Chatterton.—La maréchale d'Ancre.—Quitte pour la peur.—Compositions d'après Shakespeare: Othello; Shylock.

Villemain. Cours de littérature française 18me siècle. 1868. 4 v..............840 401
Lascaris (French).............................x14304
Villiers de l'Isle Adam. Akèdysséril (French)..x4545
L'amour suprême...............................x4549
Axël (drame). 1890............................842 152
L'Ève future..................................x4547
Nouveaux contes cruels; et Propos d'au dela...x4546
Tribulat Bonhomet.............................x4548
Villon. Œuvres. 1877......................841 45
Poems; tr. by Payne. 1881..................841 41
Vincent. Misé Féréol (French)..............x10202
Return of the princess.......................x10201
Vaillant, ce que femme veut..................x10203
Vogüé. Heures d'histoire. 1893............844 53
Jean d'Agrève.................................x18202
Russian portraits.............................x18201
Voltaire. Œuvres complètes. 1785-9. 70v..840 116
(For contents see printed catalogue of 1871.)
Philosophical dictionary. 1824. 6 v.......847 4
Voltairiana; tr. and ed. by Young. 1805. 4 v...849 6
Works; tr. by Smollett *et al.* 1761. 36 v.
V. 1-9. Ancient and modern history.........840 11
V. 10-11. Observations on history.—History of Charles XII.—Zadig.—The world as it goes.—Vision of Babouc.—Micromegas................840 20
V. 12. Œdipus.—Mariamne.—Brutus............840 22
V. 13. Semiramis.—Death of Cæsar.—Amelia....840 23
V. 14. Orestes.—The prodigal.—Letters........840 23
V. 15. Merope.—Nanine.—The babbler.—Letters..840 28
V. 16-17. Miscellanies in history, literature, and philosophy................................840 26
V. 18. Zara.—The prude.—Pandora.............840 27
V. 19. History of the war of 1741............840 29
V. 20-22. Annals of the empire. 3 v..........840 30
V. 23. Candid.................................840 33
V. 24. The Henriade..........................840 34
V. 25. Mahomet.—Socrates.—Alzira............840 35
V. 26. Philosophical miscellanies............840 36
V. 27. Cataline.—The coffee-house.—The orphan of China......................................840 37
V. 28. History of Russia under Peter the Great..840 38
V. 29-30. Annals of the empire. 2 v..........840 39
V. 31. Letters concerning the English.........840 41
V. 32-33. Miscellaneous poems. 2 v...........840 42
V. 34. On toleration..........................840 43
V. 35. Tales of William Vadé.................840 45
V. 36. Princess of Babylon.—Man with forty crowns..................................840 46
Zaire (drame). 1831...........................842 1
Wace. Roman de Rou; herausgegeben von Andersen. 1879. 2 v.......................841 37
Wafflard *and* **Fulgence.** Dieppe [drame]; ed. by Brette *et al.*....................842 95
Wey. Bouquet de cerises....................x8201
Witt, *Madame de.* Behind the hedges......x4808
Dames of high estate.........................03960.4
French country family........................03960.2
Heroines of Haarlem..........................039605

Marie Derville; tr..............................039603
Motherless...039601
Sur la pente.......................................x4807
Zola. Attack on the mill, etc..............x1016
Downfall..x1015
Experimental novel, etc. 1893...........813 43

Contents: The experimental novel.—A letter to the young people of France.—Naturalism on the stage.—The influence of money on literature.—The novel.—Criticism.—The influence of the republic in literature.
Lourdes ; tr..x1017
Rome ; tr...x1018
Three wars..x1016

ITALIAN LANGUAGE AND LITERATURE.

LANGUAGE.

Camerini. L'eco Italiana. 1877..............455 5
Cuore. Italian conversation-grammar........455 1
  Key to same.................................455 2
Fanfani. Vocabolario dell' uso Toscano.
  1813. 2 v....................................‡457 1
Graglia. Italian pocket dictionary.........‡453 3
Mariotti. Italian grammar. 1885............455 3
Melzi. New Italian-English and English-Italian dictionary. 1897....................453 5
Millhouse. English-Italian dictionary. '66.
  2 v...‡453 1-2
New Italian-English-French pocket dictionary..‡453 4
Ollendorff. Method of learning Italian. '76..455 4

LITERATURE.

HISTORY AND CRITICISM.

Cliffe. Manual of Italian literature. 1896...850 31
Geiger. Renaissance und Humanismus in Italien und Deutschland. 1882..........850 12
Howells. Modern Italian poets..............851 62
Lee, Vernon, (Violet Paget). Euphorion.
  1884. 2 v.
  V. 1. Introduction.— The sacrifice.—Italy of the Elizabethan dramatists.— Out-door poetry.— Symmetria prisca..850 13
  V. 2. The portrait art.— School of Boiardo.— Mediæval love. Epilogue.— Appendix......850 14
  Studies of the 18th century in Italy. 1880..850 5
Mariotti. Italy ; history and literature.
  1841. 2 v......................................850 1
Oliphant, *Mrs.* Makers of Florence. '77..920.5 4
  Makers of Venice.............................920.5 13
Owen. Skeptics of the Italian renaissance.
  1893..850 30
Paget, Violet. See **Lee, Vernon.**
Phillimore. Studies in Italian literature.
  1887..850 29
Snell. Primer of Italian literature. 1893...850 32

Symonds. Renaissance in Italy: Literature.
  1881. 2 v.....................................850 6
  Same : Revival of learning. 1877.......945 62
Yriarte. Florence : les lettres, etc. '81..914.5 R-4

COLLECTIONS.

Ferrario. Poesie pastorali e rusticali........851 47
Greene, *tr.* Italian lyrists of to-day. 1893..851 65
Hoepli. Migliori libri Italiani consigliati da cento illustri contemporanei. 1892.15 42
Hunt. Stories from Italian poets. 1846.....851 1
Ramage, *ed.* Beautiful thoughts from French and Italian authors. 1866.......‡849 1
Roscoe, *tr.* Italian novelists. 1825. 4 v...853 1
Ruskin, *ed.* Roadside songs of Tuscany.
  1885..851 B-2
Songs of Italy, with music...................784 B-18
Werner, *ed.* Humour of Italy. 1892.......858 1
(See also, Folk Lore, in Part 3 of FINDING LIST, pp. 518-521.)

INDIVIDUAL AUTHORS.

Alamanni. Della coltevazione. 1804......851 46
Alessandro. Monte Auburno. 1835...851 Pam. 2
Alfieri. Tragedie. 1819. 6 v.
  V. 1. Filippo.—Polinice.—Antigone................852 5
  V. 2. Virginia.— Agamennone.— Oreste.— Rosmunda...852 6
  V. 3. Ottavia.—Timoleone.—Merope.............852 7
  V. 4. Maria Stuarda.—La congiura de' Pazzi.— Don Garzia.— Saul.......................................852 8
  V. 5. Agide.— Sofonisba.— Bruto primo.—Mirra..852 9
  V. 6. Bruto secondo. — Alceste.— Parere dell' autore..852 10
  Tragedies; tr. by Bowring. 1876. 2 v.
  V. 1. Preface.—Philip.—Polynices.—Antigone.— Virginia.— Agamemnon.— Orestes.— Rosmunda.— Octavia.—Timoleon.—Merope.—Mary Stuart......850 11
  V. 2. Conspiracy of the Pazzi. Don Garcia.— Saul. Agis.— Sophonisba.— The first Brutus.— Myrrha. The second Brutus.—Antony and Cleopatra. Abel.—Alcestis II................................852 12
Altieri, *princess.* My Indian summer..........It101
Amicis. Alberto..It201
  Cuore...It204
  Heart (Cuore)..It204A
Anonymous letter; tr. by Nobile................It1003

‡ For reference.

Ariosto. Commedie e satire. 1856............852 4
Opere minori. 1857. 2 v................851 23
Orlando Furioso (Italian). 1639. 2v....851 32
 Same. 1846. 2 v.......................851 21
 Same; tr. by Rose. 1864. 2 v.......... 851 13
 Roland furieux; traduction par D' Ussieux. 1775. 4 v....................851 26
 Stories from; by Hollway-Calthrop.......It1001
 Tales from, for children. 1879............040201
Azeglio. Ettora Fieramosca; tr. by Lester....It302
Barrili. L'Anello di Salomone It401
 Il biancospino. 1882...................It403
 Devil's portrait; tr. by Wodehouse.........It410
 Eleventh commandment. 1882.............It406
 Fior di Mughetto. 1884.................It407
 Una notte bizzara........................It413
 Princess's private secretary.................It412
 Ritratto del diavolo......................It409
 Whimsical wooing; tr. by Bell.............It414
Basile. Pentamerone; tr. by Taylor.......038027
Beccaria. Opere diverse. 1770............850 28
Boccaccio. Il Decameron. 1857............853 7
 Same; tr..............................853 8
Bresciani. Edmondo.....................It1006
Bounarroti, Michael Angelo. See **Michael Angelo.**
Campanella. Sonnets; tr. by Symonds. 1878...................................851 34
Caro. Opere. 1807. 7 v.
 V. 1-6. Lettere........................850 20
 V. 7. Amori di Longo Sofista; tr. da Caro.—Due orazioni di Gregorio Nazianzeno.— Sermone di S. Cecilio Cipriano.—Testamento e lettere di Gregorio Nazianzeno.............................850 26
Casti. Gli animali parlanti. v. 1 and 3....851 30
Colombi. Wane of an ideal; tr. by Bell....It1102
Colonna, Vittoria. Life and poems; by Mrs. Roscoe...........................928.5 16
Dante and Catholic philosophy in the 13th century; by Ozanam. 1897.............851 74
 And his circle; by D G. Rossetti. 1876...851 16
 The banquet; tr. by Hillard. 1889......851 57
 La commedia. 1863.....................851 25
 Commedia and canzionere; tr. by Plumptre. 2 v. 1887...........................851 52
 Il convito [The banquet]; tr. by Sayer, introduction by Morley. 1887..........851 56
 The Dante collections in Boston public library and Harvard university library (Harvard university bulletin, v. 4, pp. 133, 188).............................16 B-17
 La divina commedia. 1804..............851 71
 Same; Le prime quattro edizioni per cura di Lord Vernon. 1858........‡851 R-1
 Divine comedy; tr. by Longfellow. 3v....851 8
 Same; tr. by Norton. 1891. 3v.
  V. 1. Hell............................851 59
  V. 2. Purgatory.......................851 60
  V. 3. Paradise........................851 61

 Same; tr. by Wright. 1854............851 17
 Eleven letters; by Latham. 1891..........856 1
 Handbook to; by Scartazzini. 1887.....851 54
 The Hell; tr. by Butler. 1892............851 51
 His times and his work; by Butler. 1895.
  ....928.5 40
 L'inferno; publicato da Lord Vernon. 1858.............................‡851 R-2
 Inferno; tr. by Carlyle (prose)...........851 11
 Same; tr. by Sibbald. 1884.............851 41
 Influence on modern thought; by Oelsner. 1895............................851 70
 Introduction to study; by Botta. 1886..851 63
 The new life; tr. by Norton. 1867........851 4
 Paradise; ed. with tr. by Butler. 1885..851 50
 Purgatory; ed. with tr. by Butler. 1880..851 49
 Same; with prose tr. by Dugdale. '83..851 44
 Same; tr. by Shadwell. 1892............851 64
 Readings on the Inferno: by Vernon. 1894. 2 v...........................851 67
 Shadow of; by M. F. Rossetti. 1871......851 12
 Sonnets; tr. by Garnett. 1896..........851 72
 Spiritual sense of 'Divina commedia'; by Harris. 1889......................851 58
 Studies in; by Moore. 1896. 1st series...851 73
 Study of; by Blow. 1886................851 45
 Tutte le opere. 1894...................851 69
 The vision: hell, purgatory, and paradise; tr. by Cary. 1865..................851 5
 Same. 1850. 2 v......................851 6
Dante society. Annual report, 1886....851 Pam. 1
Davanzati-Bostichi. Scisma d'Inghilterra. 1807.............................850 27
D'Azeglio. Ettore Fieramosca...............It301
Farini. Caporal Silvestro. 1884............It1201
Ferrario, rac. Poesie pastorali e rusticali...851 47
Ferrugia. Woman's folly...................It1801
Firenzuola. Opere. 1802. 5 v.
 V. 1. Vita di Firenzuola.—Dialogo della bellezza della donne.— Lettere.........................850 15
 V. 2. Ragnionamenti amorosi.— Le dieci novelle.— Lettere.— Altra del medesimo.............850 16
 V. 3. L'asino d'oro di Apulejo: tr. da Firenzuola...................................850 17
 V. 4. Lettere.— Rime...........................850 18
 V. 5. La trinuzia.— I Lucidi.....................850 19
Fogazzaro. Daniele Cortis................It501
 Same; tr................................It502
 Malombra...............................It504
 Il mistero del poeta......................It505
 Piccolo mondo antico. 1896.............It503
Garibaldi. Rule of the monk.............It1302
Giacomette. Elizabeth, queen of England: drama (Italian and English).
 ....852 Pam. 2
 Marie Antoinette: drama (Italian and English).............................852 Pam. 1
Goldoni. Comedies; ed. by Zimmern. '92.852 26
 Contents: A curious mishap.—The beneficent bear.—The fan.—The spendthrift miser.

‡ For reference.

Grossi. Marco Visconti.........................It1401
   Same ; tr..It1402
Guarini. Il pastor fido. 1807..................852 24
   Same. 1735..852 23
Guerrazzi. Beatrice Cenci ; tr. by Monti.....It602
   Isabella Orsini (Italian)......................It603
La Grange. Ferryman of the Tiber..........It1502
   Last days of Jerusalem.......................It1504
Leopardi. Essays and dialogues. 1882.....854 1
   Poems ; tr by Cliffe. 1893....................851 66
   Poems ; tr. by Townsend. 1887..........851 55
Machiavelli. Works ; tr. by Farneworth.
   1762. 2 v.
   V. 1. History of Florence.—The prince.—Anti-Machiavel ; or, Examen du Prince, by the king of Prussia.—Life of Castruccio Castracani.—Cæsar Borgia.—Affairs and constitution of France.—Affairs and constitution of Germany.....................850 3
   V. 2. Political discourses upon the first Decad of Livy.—Art of war.—Marriage of Belphegor.—Posthumous works..850 4
   Writings ; tr. by Detmold. 1882. 4 v.
   V. 1. Life.—History of Florence..................850 8
   V. 2. The prince.— Discourses on Livius. — Thoughts of a statesman............................850 9
   V. 3-4. Missions.—Miscellaneous................850 10
Mantegazza. Testa ; tr........................*It1702
Manzoni. Betrothed (I promessa sposi)......It602
   I promessa sposi................................It1601
Mazzini. Essays ; tr by Okey. 1894..........854 2
   Lettres intimes ; publiées par Melegari. 1895..856 2
Memoirs of Miss D'Arville. 1764. 2 v......853 5
Metastasio. Dramas, etc. ; tr. by Hoole. 1800. 3 v.
   V. 1. Artaxerxes.—The Olympiad.— Hypsipyle.—Titus.—Demetrius.—Dream of Scipio.—Cantatas.852 1
   V. 2. Achilles in Scyros.—Demophoon.—Adrian in Syria.—Dido.— Ætius.—Uninhabited Island.—Triumph of glory.....................................852 2
   V. 3. Zenobia.—Themistocles.—Siroes.— Regulus.—Romulus and Hersilia.—Discovery of Joseph.—Cantatas..852 3
   Poesie. 1755. 10 v.
   V. 1. Dissertazione ; Catsabigi. — Artaserse.—Adriano in Sirin.—Demetrio..............................852 13
   V. 2. Olimpiade.—Issipile.—Ezio.—Didone abbandonata.—Il sogno di Scipione.—Il natal di Giove.— La danza..852 14

V. 3. La clemenza di Tito.—Siroe.—Catone in Utica.—Demofoonte................................852 15
V. 4. Alessandro.—Achille in Sciro.—Ciro.—Temistocle.—L'isola disabitata.—Le Cinesi......852 16
V. 5. Zenobia.—Ipermestra.—Antigono.—Semiramide.—Il re pastore.—L'asilo d'amore.....852 17
V. 6. L'eroe Cinese.—Attilio Regolo.—Adriano in Siria.—Didone abbandonata.—Il tempio dell' eternità.—La contessa de' Numi................852 18
V. 7. Alessandro. — Semiramide. — Le grazie vendicate.—Il palladio conservato.—Il Parnaso.—Astrea placata.—La pace fra la virtù.—Il vero omaggio.—L'amor prigioniero.—Il Ciclope.—Cantate...852 19
V. 8. Gioas re di Giuda.—Betulia liberata.—Sant' Elena al Calvario.— Guiseppe riconosciuto.—La morte d' Abel.—La passione di Gesù Cristo.—Per la festività del SSmo. natale.— Isacco.— Canzonette.—Sonnetti.—Epitalamio....................852 20
V. 9. La Galatea.—L'Endimione.—Gli orti Esperidi.—Il Convito degli Dei.— L'Angelica.— La morte di Catone.—L'origine delle leggi.—Il ratto d'Europa.—Ode.—Giustino..............................852 21
V. 10. Nitteti.—Alcide al Bivio.—Il trionfo di Clelia.—Romolo ed Ersilia.—Partenope.—Il Parnaso confuso, etc..852 22
Michael Angelo. Sonnets, etc. ; tr. by Harford.................................in 927.5 4
   Sonnets ; tr. by Symonds. 1878........851 34
Pellico. Francesca da Rimini : tragedy....852 27
Petrarch. Rime ; con l'interpretazione di Leopardi. 1854..................................851 3
   Sonnets, etc. ; ed. by Campbell. 1869...851 2
   Sonnets ; tr. by Garnett. 1896..............851 72
Pindemonte. Arminio ; tragedia. 1819...852 25
Pulci. Il morgante Maggiore..................851 B-1
Rovetta. Il tenente dei Lancieri. 1896......It701
Rucellai. Le api. 1804..........................851 46
Serao. Fantasy..................................It802
Stampa. Sonnets ; tr. by Fletcher......in 928.5 26
Tansillo. The nurse ; tr. by Roscoe. 1804..851 15
Tasso. Gerusalemme liberata. 1853.....851 20
   Godfrey of Bulloigne ; tr. by Fairfax. 1845...851 18
   Jerusalem delivered ; tr. by Brooke...822.2 133
   Same ; tr. by Wiffen. 1868..................851 19
Verga. House by the medlar-tree............It902
   Under the shadow of Etna....................It904

SPANISH AND PORTUGUESE LANGUAGES AND LITERATURE.

LANGUAGE.

Academia Española. Diccionario. 1824.‡463 B-2
Bustamante. Dictionary of Spanish and English. 1893...‡463 4
   Same ; Inglés-Español.......................‡463 5

Carolino. New guide of the conversation in Portuguese, etc. 1883....................469 3
Harvey. Simplified grammar of Spanish language. 1890..................................465 2
Josse. Grammar of Spanish language. '32...465 3

* Of interest to young readers.   ‡ For reference.

LANGUAGE AND LITERATURE.

Neuman *and* **Baretti.** Spanish-English and English-Spanish dictionary. 1837. 2 v. ‡463 1
Sobrino. Grammaire, Espagñolle et Françoise. 1732 465 1
Velazquez. Spanish-English and English-Spanish dictionary. 1865 ‡463 3
Same. 1852 ‡463 B-1
Same; new dictionary based on. '95..‡463 6
Vieyra *and* **Aillaud.** Diccionario. Portugueza e Ingleza. 1873 ‡469 1

LITERATURE.

HISTORY AND CRITICISM.

Bouterwek. History of Spanish and Portuguese literature. 1823. 2 v.
  V. 1. Spanish literature 860 4
  V. 2. Portuguese literature 860 5
Conant. Primer of Spanish literature. '79..860 12
Gongora. [Poems; tr., with essay by Churton.] 2 v 861 17
Grillparzer. Studien zum spanischen Theater 830 321
Kennedy. Modern poets and poetry of Spain. 1852 861 4
Ramage, *ed.* Beautiful thoughts from German and Spanish authors. 1868...‡839 1
Ticknor. History of Spanish literature. 1849. 3 v 860 1

COLLECTIONS.

Boston. Public library. Catalog of Spanish and Portuguese books, Ticknor bequest. 1879 15 B-3
Bowring, *tr.* Ancient poetry and romances of Spain. 1824 861 8
Burke, *ed.* Spanish salt. 1877 ‡869 2
Lockhart, *tr.* Ancient Spanish ballads. 1842 861 1
Same; rev. ed. 1877 861 2
Portuguese songs, with music *in* 914.6 B-4
Taylor, *ed.* Humour of Spain. 1894 868 1

(See also, Folk Lore, in Part 3 of FINDING LIST, pp. 518-521.)

INDIVIDUAL AUTHORS (INCLUDING TRANSLATIONS).

Alarcon. Brunhilde Sp401
Child of the ball Sp403
Three-cornered hat Sp405
Alcaforado. Love letters of a Portuguese nun. 1890 866 1
Aleman. Guzman D'Alfarache; tr. by Le Sage SpS02
Bazán. The angular stone Sp601
Christian woman Sp607

Swan of Vilamorta Sp603
Wedding trip Sp605
Beaumont. El almacen de los minos. 1861...849 15
Calderon. Comedias. 1760. 10 v 862 5
Dramas; tr. by MacCarthy. 1870 862 1
  Contents: Love the greatest enchantment.—Sorceries of sin.—Devotion of the cross.
Teatro escogido. 1838 862 3
Camoëns. His life and Lusiads; by Burton. 1881. 2 v 861 12
Os Lusiadas; tr. by Burton. 1880. 2 v..861 10
Same; tr. by Mickle. 1877 861 5
Lyrics; tr. by Burton. 1884. 2 v 861 14
Seventy sonnets; with tr. by Aubertin. '81..861 9
Sonnets; tr. by Garnett. 1896 851 72
Cervantes. Don Quijote. 1860 Sp101
Same; English tr Sp103
Same; English tr. by Duffield. 1881. 3 v Sp103C
Same; French tr. 1827. 6 v Sp102
Same; French tr. by Florian. '12. 4v..840 352
Don Quixote: his critics, etc.; by Duffield. 1881 863 1
Same; wit and wisdom of. 1867 ‡869 1
Exemplary novels; tr. by Kelly Sp107
La Galatea. 1772 Sp105
Numantia; tr. by Gibson. 1885 862 15
Translations from; by Gyll. 1870 862 2
  Contents: Voyage to Parnassus.—Numantia—Commerce of Algiers.
Cid. Chronicle of; tr. by Southey 946 18
Poem of the; tr. by Ormsby. 1879 861 3
Echegaray. The great Galeoto, and Folly or saintliness; tr. by Lynch. 1895 862 17
Mariana; tr. by Graham. 1895 862 16
Escrich. Martyr of Golgotha Sp702
Galdos. Court of Charles IV. 1888 Sp301
Doña Perfecta Sp303
Gloria; tr. by Clara Bell. 1882 Sp305
Leon Roch. 1888. 2 v Sp307
Marianela; tr. by Clara Bell. 1883 Sp309
Trafalgar; tr. by Clara Bell. 1884 Sp311
Garcilasso de la Vega. Works; tr. by Wiffen. 1823 861 6
Goodrich. Historiettes morales Sp1101
Hurtado. Palmerin of England. 4 v 863 2
Isaacs. Marie; tr Sp1002
Isla. Friar Gerund. 1772. 2 v S67 1
Lobeira. Amadis of Gaul; tr. by Southey. 1872. 3 v 863 7
Lope de Vega. Teatro escogido. 1838...862 4
Mendoza. Lazarillo de Tormes; tr. by Roscoe SpS02
Queiros. Dragon's teeth. 1889 863 6
Quevedo Villegas. Obras. 1772. 6 v...860 6
Sanchez. La Isla Bárbara, and La guarda cuidadosa. 1896 862 18
Truebay la Quintana. The Cid Campeador Sp902

‡ For reference.

Turpin. History of Charlemagne and Orlando; tr. by Rodd. 1812	861 7
Valdés. Faith	Sp505
Grandee	Sp507
Maximina	Sp501
Sister Saint Sulpice	Sp503
Valera. Commander Mendoza	Sp201
Don Braulio	Sp203
Doña Luz	Sp205
Pepita Ximenez; tr.	Sp207
Vega. See Garcilasso de la Vega.	
Vega. See Lope de Vega.	
Villegas. See Quevedo Villegas.	
Zorilla. Album de un loco. 1867	861 16

CELTIC LANGUAGES AND LITERATURE.

Armstrong. Gaelic-English and English-Gaelic dictionary. 1825.................‡496 B-1
Arnold. Study of Celtic literature. 1867...896 1
Book of rights; tr. by O'Donovan. 1847...896 8
Catalog of collection of Celtic literature......16 19
Curry, *tr. and ed.* . Battle of Magh Leana, and Courtship of Momera. 1855........896 9
Drummond. Ancient Irish minstrelsy. '52..896 7
Gems of Welsh melody. 1873...............784 B-7
Hyde. Story of early Gaelic literature. '95..896 18
Jamieson. Dictionary of Scottish language. 1867..‡496 1
Etymological dictionary of the Scottish language; ed. by Longmuir and Donaldson. 1879-87. 5 v...............‡496 B-3
Joyce, *tr.* Old Celtic romances. 1879......896 14
Logan. Scottish Gael........................941 40
Mabinogion; tr. by Guest. 1877...........896 B-3
Boy's Mabinogion; ed. by Lanier. '81..896 15
M'Callum, *tr.* Poems of Ossian, etc........896 10
Macgregor na Ruara, Gaelic song of; tr. by Mrs. Grant................................133 2
Miller. Scenes and legends of the North of Scotland..941 53
Nash. Taliesin: bards and Druids of Britain. 1857..896 2
O'Donovan. Grammar of Irish language. 1845...496 2
Miscellany of the Celtic society. 1849...896 6
O'Reilly. Irish-English dictionary. 1864..‡496 B-2

Orrann. Poems; tr. by M'Callum. '16...*in* 896 10
Ossian. Poems in original Gaelic, and tr. by Macpherson. 1870. 2 v............896 B-1
Same; tr. by M'Callum. 1816......*in* 896 10
Same; tr. by Macpherson. 1866......896 11
Same; 1773. 2 v............................896 16
[Presentation copy, from Garrick's library, with his book plate and autograph.]
Prichard. Eastern origin of Celtic nations. 1857...496 3
Renan. Poetry of the Celtic races, etc. '96..844 67
Contents: Poetry of the Celtic races.—What is a nation?—Islamism and science.—Farewell to Tourgenief.—The deity of the bourgeois.—Intolerance in scepticism —Marcus Aurelius.—Spinoza.—Amiel.
Richards. Dictionary; Welsh-English, English-Welsh.................................‡496 6
Skene, *ed.* The four ancient books of Wales. 1868. 2 v.
V. 1. Introduction.—Translations of poems......896 12
V. 2. Texts: Black book of Caermarthen.—Book of Aneurin.—Book of Taliessin.—Red book of Hergest...896 13
Songs of Wales; ed. by Richards.........784 B-14
Stephens. Literature of the Kymry. 1849..896 3
Taliesin. Vindication of; by Turner.....942.1 7
Turner. On ancient British poems.........942.1 7
Ulin. Poems; tr. by M'Callum. 1816..*in* 896 10
Walker. Historical memoirs of Irish bards. 1818. 2v...896 4
(See also, Literature of Druidism and Celtic Folk Lore, in Part 3 of FINDING LIST, pp. 519-521.)

SLAVONIC LANGUAGES AND LITERATURE.

LANGUAGES.

Morfill. Simplified grammar of Polish. 1884..497 4
Simplified grammar of Serbian. 1887....497 5
Motti. Russian conversation-grammar. '90..497 1
Key to same. 1890..................................497 2

LITERATURE.

HISTORY, CRITICISM, AND COLLECTIONS.

Bowring, *tr.* Cheskian anthology. 1832..897 13
Servian popular poetry. 1827..............897 14
Specimens of Polish poets. 1827.........897 12

‡ For reference.

LANGUAGE AND LITERATURE.

Hapgood, *tr.* Epic songs of Russia. 1886..897 3
Leger. Littérature russe, et extraits..........897 15
Lytton, *tr.* National songs of Servia. 1866.
....821.2 396
Morfill. Dawn of Slavonic literature.
1883...897 22
Otto. History of Russian literature. 1839..897 20
Panin. Lectures on Russian literature.
1889..897 2
Ralston. Songs of the Russian people.
1872...293.1 28
Robinson (Talvi). Languages and literature of Slavic nations. 1850...............897 1
Turner. Studies in Russian literature. '82..897 19
Vogüe. Russian novelists. 1887................897 6
Voynich, *ed.* Humour of Russia. 1895....897 21
Wolkonsky. Pictures of Russian history
and literature. 1897..............................947 90
Wratislaw. Native literature of Bohemia,
14th century. 1878..................................897 16

(See also, Mythology and Folk Lore, in Part 3 of FINDING LIST, pp. 518-521.)

INDIVIDUAL AUTHORS.

Bashkirtseff. Letters..............................897 4
Danilevski. Princess Tarakanova...........R901
Dostoieffsky. Die brüder Karamásow......R501
   Crime and punishment.........................R502
   Friend of the family.............................R503
   The gambler...................................*in* R503
   The idiot...R504
Garshin. Stories from ; tr. by Voynich....R1001
Gogol. Les ames mortes........................R403B
   Saint John's eve, etc............................R401
   Taras Bulba..R402
   Tchitchikoff's journeys; or, Dead souls..R403
Gontcharoff. Common story..................R1101
Grigorovitch. Cruel city.........................R1201
Karazin. Two-legged wolf......................R1301
Kokhanovsky. Luboff Archipovna....*in* R1401
   The rusty linchpin..................................R1401
Korolenko. Blind musician.....................R601
   In two moods.......................................R602
   Contents: In two moods.—In bad society.
   The vagrant, etc....................................R603
Kostromitin. Last day of the carnival....R1501
Kovalevsky. Vera Barantzova...............R1601
Kraszewski, Joseph Ignatius. The Jew..P201
Kriloff. And his fables ; by Ralston. 1869..897 11
   Fables ; tr. by Harrison. 1883.............897 10
Lermontoff. Demon : a poem. 1875......897 23
   Hero of our time..................................R1701
Mijatovich, *tr.* Kossovo. 1881 ....897 18
Nekrasov. Red-nosed frost (Russian-English). 1886..................................897 8
Nemec. Grandmother..............................B101
Panin. Thoughts. 1887. 2 v.................897 25

Pushkin. Daughter of the commandant......R702
   Eugene Onéguine ; tr. by Spalding. '81..897 17
   Marie ; tr. by Zielinska.........................R703
   Poems ; tr. by Panin. 1888.................897 28
   Prose tales ; tr. by Keane.......................R704
   Contents: The captain's daughter. Doubrovsky. The queen of spades. An amateur peasant girl. The shot.—The snowstorm.—The postmaster. The coffinmaker.—Kirdjali. The Egyptian nights. Peter the great's negro.
   Queen of spades, etc............................R704
   Contents: Biography, by Edwards.—Queen of spades. The pistol shot.—Snowstorm. Undertaker. Postmaster. Lady rustic.—Kirdjali. History of the village of Gorohino.—Peter the great's negro.—The gypsies.
Sailhas. Kiriak ; or, The hut on ben's legs..R1801
Sienkiewicz. Children of the soil............P110
   Deluge : sequel to 'With fire and
   sword.' 2 v.......................................P103
   Lillian Morris, etc..................................P114
   Contents: Lillian Morris.—Sachem. Yamyol. The bull-fight.
   Pan Michael..P106
   Quo vadis ; time of Nero........................P116
   With fire and sword................................P102
   Without dogma......................................P108
   Yanko the musician.................................P112
   Contents: Yanko the musician.—Light-house keeper of Aspinwall.—From the diary of a tutor in Poznan.—Comedy of errors.—Bartek the victor.
Stepniak. Career of a nihilist.................R801
Tchernuishevsky. A vital question........R1901
Tolstoi, A. Prince Serebryani.................R201
Tolstoi, L. N. Anna Karénina (English)..R101
   Anna Karénine (French)......................R101D
   Childhood, boyhood, youth. 1886..........R102
   The Cossacks.......................................R103
   Dominion of darkness. 1888..................897 7
   Family happiness [Katia]......................R108C
   Gospel stories......................................R104
   Contents: If you neglect the fire, you don't put it out.—Where love is, there God is also.—A candle. The two pilgrims.—Texts for wood-cuts.—The three mendicants.—Popular legends.—The godson.—Long exile.—What men live by.
   In pursuit of happiness. 1887..............R105
   The invaders, etc..................................R106
   Contents: The invaders.—Wood-cutting expedition.—An old acquaintance.—Lost on the steppe.—Polikushka —Kholstomir: a story of a horse.
   Iván Ilyitch, etc.....................................R107
   Contents: Death of Iván Ilyitch.—If you neglect the fire, you don't put it out.—Where love is, there God is also.—A candle.—Two old men.—Texts for wood-cuts.—Three mendicants.—Popular legends.—The godson.—Skazka (Ivan the fool).
   Ivan the fool..R111
   Contents: Ivan the fool.—Lost opportunity.—Polikushka.
   Katia [My husband and I; or, Family
   happiness]..R108
   Life. 1888..897 5

Life *is* worth living, etc.............................R109
  Contents: Life *is* worth living.— Two old men.—God is love.— The candle.
Long exile, etc.................................010060
Master and man......................................R110
My husband and I [Katia], etc.............R108D
  Contents: My husband and I.— Death of Ivan Ilitch. — Políkouchka. — Two generations. — Romance of a horse.—A snowstorm.
La puissance des ténèbres [drame]. '87...897 9
Russian proprietor, etc............................R112
  Contents: Russian proprietor.— Lucerne.— Recollections of a scorer.—Albert.—Two hussars.—Three deaths.—Prisoner in the Caucasus.
Sebastopol..R113
Two pilgrims. 1887...................................R114
War and peace ; 3 pts. 6 v......................R115
What people live by................................R118
Work while ye have the light...................R119
Turgenief. Annals of a sportsman............R301
Annouchka...R302
Dimitri Roudine [Rudin].......................R308A
Fathers and children ; tr. by Garnett.....R303A

Fathers and sons ; tr. by Schuyler..........R303
First love, and Punin and Baburin..........R304
Fumée. 1874.......................................R309A
House of gentlefolk...............................R305
A Lear of the steppes.........................*in* R310
Liza..R314
Nouvelles moscovites............................R313
  Contents: Annouchka.— Le Juif.— Pétouchkoff.—Le chien.—Le brigadier.—Histoire de Lieutenant Yergounof.—Apparitions.
On the eve...R306
Poems in prose...................................R307
Rudin [Dimitri Roudine]......................R308
Smoke..R309
Spring floods.....................................R310
Unfortunate woman, and Ass'ya.............R311
Virgin soil..R312
Urbanowska. La princesse.....................P301
Vazoff. Under the yoke....................897 29
Verestchagin. War correspondent........R2001
Zagoskin. Tales of three centuries......R2101
  Contents: An evening at the Hopyor.—The three suitors.—Kuzma Roschin.

OTHER EUROPEAN LANGUAGES AND LITERATURE.

'**Ali 'Aziz Efendi.** Story of Jewād ; tr. from the Turkish................................899 10
Borrow. Romano Lavo-Lil. 1874............499 5
  Zincali ; or, Gypsies of Spain. 2 v......949x 13
Cornell University library. Catalog, Rhæto-Romanic collection. 1894....................15 47
Crawford, *tr.* The Kalevala. 2 v. 1888......899 11
Ellis. Sources of Etruscan and Basque languages. 1886.................................499 15
Gibb, *tr.* Ottoman poems. 1882.............899 5
Henderson. Lingua. 1888......................499 23
Jokai. Black diamonds..........................H102
  Doctor Dumány's wife.........................H104
  Eyes like the sea.................................H106
  Green book.......................................H108
  'Midst the wild Carpathians..................H110
  Modern Midas [Timar's two worlds].......H112
  Nameless castle..................................H114
  New landlord....................................H116
  Pretty Michal....................................H118
  There is no devil................................H120
  Timar's two worlds [A modern Midas]..H112A
Jósika. King Matthias and the beggar boy ; adapted by Gaye..................................H302

Kerckhoffs. Dictionnaire volapük-français et français-volapük. 1887...............499 16
Kirby. Hero of Esthonia, etc. 2 v..........899 13
Kirchhoff. Volapük: short course. 1888..499 22
Latham. Nationalities of Europe. v.1....940 132
  (Specimens of the literature of the Lithuanians, Esthonians, Finns, and other peoples.)
Linderfelt, *ed.* Volapük ; easy method. 1888..499 21
Magyar folk-songs ; tr. by Phillips. 1885....899 8
Murray, *tr.* National songs, Roumania. 1859..899 4
Petöfi. Selections from poems; tr. by Phillips. 1885.....................................897 27
  Translations from ; by Bowring. 1866......899 1
Redhouse. English and Turkish dictionary. 1857..‡499 3
Schleyer. Grammar of Volapük ; tr. by Seret. 1885..499 18
Singer. Simplified grammar of Hungarian. 1882..499 9
Songs of eastern Europe........................784 B-19
Sprague. Hand-book of Volapük. 1888...499 20
Szabad. Sketch of Hungarian literature. 1854..*in* 943 88

‡ For reference.

Torceanu. Simplified grammar, Roumanian language. 1883..................459 1
Vacaresco, *ed.* Bard of the Dimbovitza: Roumanian folk-songs. 1892............899 15
Van Eys. Outlines of Basque grammar. '83..499 8
Vinson. The Basque language. 1877....293.1 22
Volapük: Grundriss. 1887..............499 Pam. 3

Skizze. 1887................... 499 Pam. 2
Same; tr..................... 499 Pam. 4
W., P. Grammaire albanaise. 1887..........499 19
Wekey. Grammar of the Hungarian language. 1852........................499 1
Wohl. Sham gold.......................II202
(See also, Mythology and Folk Lore, in Part 3 of Finding List, pp. 518-521.)

AFRICAN AND OCEANIC LANGUAGES.

Crawfurd. Malayan and Polynesian languages, etc. 1848....................499 14
Cust. Sketch of modern languages of Africa. 1883. 2 v................499 11
Ellis. Polynesian researches. 4 v.........919 6 9
Gill. Myths and songs from the south Pacific. 1876..................299 22
Savage life in Polynesia. 1880.............996 8
Kessler. Language and literature of Madagascar. 1870.......................499 6

Koelle. Grammar of Bornu language. '54...499 2
Parker. Concise grammar of Malagasy. '83..199 10
Raffles. History of Java. v. 1. 1830.......992 1
Shortland. Traditions of New Zealanders. 1856..........................919.3 5
Trübner. Catalog of modern African languages....................16 Pam. 16

(See also, Folk Lore, in Part 3 of Finding List, pp. 518-521.)

ABORIGINAL AMERICAN LANGUAGES AND LITERATURE.

Boas. Chinook texts. 1894................899 2
Brinton. Ancient Nahuatl poetry. 1890....899 7
Books of Chilan Balam [Mayan].....899 Pam. 1
Primer of Mayan hieroglyphics...........499 26
The Güegüence [Nicaraguan]. 1883.....899 6
Cuoq. Lexique de la langue iroquoise. '83..499 7
Dorsey. Omaha and Ponka letters. 1891. ....499 Pam. 7
Eliot. Indian grammar begun. 1666...499 Pam. 5
Ercilla. Araucana; sketch and tr. by Molina.........................983 2

Humboldt. Philosophic grammar of American languages; ed. by Brinton. 1885...499 13
Markham. Language and literature of the Incas. 1856........................*in* 918.5 8
Mayhew. On the Indian language. 1884. ....499 Pam. 1
Ollanta [drama]; tr. from the Quichua, by Markham..........................899 3
Olmos. Grammaire de la langue Nahuatl. 1875..............................499 25

(See also, Folk Lore, in Part 3 of Finding List, pp. 519-521.)

ENGLISH LANGUAGE AND LITERATURE.

LANGUAGE.

Earle. Philology of the English tongue. 1871...............................420 11
Emerson. History of the English language. 1894...............................420 24
Hales, *ed.* Longer English poems; with philological notes. 1872..............428 2
Harrison. English language. 1848..........420 3

Lounsbury. History of the English language. 1879........................420 13
Same; revised and enlarged. 1894....420 13A
Marsh. The English language. 1860........420 2
Origin of the English language. 1871...420 10
Meiklejohn. Brief history of the English language and literature. 1887............420 21
Shepherd. History of the English language. 1874..........................420 5

Trench. English, past and present. 1855..420 4
Welsford. Origin of English language. '45..420 1

EARLY AND MIDDLE ENGLISH.

Bosworth. Anglo-Saxon and English dictionary. 1855......................‡429 2
Bright. Anglo-Saxon reader. 1894.........429 12
Carpenter. English of 14th century. 1882....428 3
Catholicon Anglicum : early English dictionary.............................820.2 344
Coleridge. Glossarial index to English literature, 13th century. 1859...........‡423 17
Cook. First book in old English. 1894.......429 7
Earle. Beginner in Anglo-Saxon. 1879.....429 9
Epinal glossary : facsimile by Griggs, ed. by Sweet. 1883.........................‡429 S-1
Leo. Anglo-Saxon names. 1852...............429 6
March. Comparative grammar, Anglo-Saxon. 1870.........................429 3
Morris. Specimens of early English. 1867..428 1
Morris and **Skeat,** eds. Early English. 1879. 2 v....................................428 4
Oliphant. Old and middle English. 1878..420 12
Shute. Anglo-Saxon. 1867..................429 5
Stratmann. Middle-English dictionary. 1891...................................‡429 11
Sweet. Anglo-Saxon primer. 1882............429 8
Middle English primer. 1884.............429 10
Student's dictionary, Anglo-Saxon. '97..‡429 13
Thorpe, ed. Analecta Anglo-Saxonica. 1846...................................429 1
Vernon. Anglo-Saxon grammar. 1846......429 4

GRAMMAR.

Abbott. Shakespearian grammar. 1870.....425 1
Alford. Plea for queen's English. 1866....420 6
Bain. English grammar......................425 5
Berry. Parsing book. 1871..................425 29
Brown. Grammar of English grammars. 1851...................................‡425 7
Institutes of English grammar. 1879...425 25
Burton. Outlines of English grammar. 1894...................................425 Pam. 1
Cobbett. English grammar ; ed. by Ayres. 1884...................................425 14
De Vere. Studies in English. 1867.........420 7
Discriminate. 1885........................425 17
English as she is wrote....................829 3
Gould. Good English. 1880................420 14
Head. 'Shall' and 'will.'..................425 2
Henry. Comparative grammar, English and German. 1891....................425 27
Hodgson. Errors in use of English 1881..425 11
Hyde. Lessons in use of English. 1891...425 23
Same ; pt. 2. 1890......................425 24
Lewis. English language. 1881............425 12

Moon. Dean's English. 1865...............425 3
Ecclesiastical English. 1886............425 20
King's English. 1881....................420 16
Revisers' English. 1882.................425 13
Morris. English grammar exercises. 1878...425 9
Mulligan. Grammatical structure of English language. 1878....................425 8
Nesbitt. Grammar-land. 1878 ....*425 10
Patterson. Advanced grammar. 1887 .....425 22
Elements of grammar. 1882.............425 21
Payne, ed. English in American universities. 1895.............................420 25
Pratt. Practical language exercises. '91....420 23
Ramsey. English language and English grammar. 1892.........................420 22
Ripley. Exercises in analysis and parsing. 1882...................................425 28
Rolfe. Elementary study of English. '96...420 27
Sievers. Old English grammar. 1885......425 18
Slip-shod English..........................425 19
Sweet. New English grammar; pt. 1. '92..425 26
Thring. Elements of grammar. 1872.......425 6
Welsh. Essentials of English. 1884........425 16
White. Every-day English. 1880............420 15
Words and their uses. 1870.............420 8
Whitney. English grammar. 1877..........425 4
Whitney and **Knox.** Lessons in English. 1884...................................425 15

SPELLING, PRONUNCIATION, ETC.

Alderson. Orthographical exercises..........421 3
American philosophical society. Report on amended orthography. 1889...421 Pam. 6
Ayres. The orthoëpist. 1880................421 7
The verbalist. 1882.....................420 17
Bigelow. Punctuation, etc. 1881............421 8
Bowen. Historical study of the ō vowel in accented syllables in English. 1895...421 19
Brewer. Errors, speech and spelling. '81..‡423 21
Chaucer. Pronunciation and spelling of Ellesmere ms.; by Hempl. 1893........421 18
Cocker. Hand-book of punctuation. 1878..421 5
Drew. Pens and types. 1872................421 2
Same; improved edition. 1889.........421 2½
Ellis. Early English pronunciation; pt. 1..820.2 401
Same; pt. 2.............................820.2 404
Same; pt. 3.............................820.2 410
Same; pt. 4.............................820.2 417
English spelling reform association. Rept. 1882...................................421 Pam. 4
Five hundred mistakes. 1873...............421 1
Grandgent. Off and on. 1893..........421 Pam. 9
Hume. On the orthographic and congruitie of the Britan tongue..................820.2 303
Meredith. Every-day errors. 1875..........421 4
Müller. On spelling........................421 Pam. 1
Murray. On spelling reform. 1880..421 Pam. 5

---
* Of interest to young readers. ‡ For reference.

LANGUAGE AND LITERATURE.

New England primer (reprint).................421 10
Patterson. Common school speller.........421 13
  Speller and analyzer..............................421 14
Phyfe. How should I pronounce? 1885....421 9
  Seven thousand words often mispronounced. 1894...‡421 15
Pitman. Applied phonetics. 1879.....421 Pam. 3
Pomeroy. Introductory reading-book........421 22
  Introductory spelling-book....................421 23
Rundell. English spellings. 1882.....421 Pam. 2
Sheldon. Further notes on the names of the letters..421 Pam. 8
  Origin of English names of letters...421 Pam. 7
Sheldon's word studies. 1886..................421 12
Smurthwaite. Comprehensive spelling book..421 11
Sweet. Primer of spoken English. 1890..421 16
Teall. Compounding of English words. 1891...421 17
Why we punctuate. 1897..............................421 21
Wilson. English punctuation....................421 6

ETYMOLOGY.

Anglo-Saxon derivations. 1854.................422 6
Anglo-Saxon root-words. 1854..................422 5
Bailey. Etymological dictionary. 1726. 2 v..‡423 1
Cockayne. Spoon and sparrow: English roots. 1861...422 16
English retraced. 1862...............................422 9
Haldeman. Etymology. 1877..................422 15
Hall. Modern English. 1873.....................422 11
  On English adjectives in -able. 1877....422 25
Hand-book of engrafted words. 1854......‡422 7
Johnson. English words. 1891..................422 24
Junius. Etymologicum Anglicanum. 1743. ....‡422 K-1
Mackay. Lost beauties of the English language...422 14
Mathews. Words, their use and abuse. 1877..422 18
Oliphant. The new English. 1886. 2 v...420 18
  Sources of English. 1873.......................422 12
Palmer. Folk-etymology. 1882...............‡422 19
  Word-hunter's note-book. 1876.............422 13
Skeat. Etymological dictionary. 1882...‡422 B-1
  Same: supp. 1884..................................‡422 B-2
  Principles of English etymology. 1st series. 1887...422 21
  Student's pastime. 1896.........................420 26
Swinton. Rambles among words. 1864...422 10
Trench. Glossary of words used formerly in senses different from their present, 1859..‡422 8
  Study of words. 1852.............................422 17
Town. Derivative words in the English language...422 23
Waites. Forgotten meanings. 1886.......‡422 20

Wedgwood. Dictionary of English etymology. 1859. 4 v...................................‡422 1

DIALECTS, ETC.

Akerman. Glossary, Wiltshire. 1842......‡427 9
American dialect society. Circular. 1895. ....427 Pam. 3
Babbitt. American dialect society. '95..427 Pam. 2
Baker. Glossary, Northamptonshire. 1854. 2 v..‡427 11
Barnes. Glossary of Dorset dialect. 1886...‡427 7
Barrère and **Leland.** Dictionary of slang. 1897. 2 v..‡427 26
Bartlett. Dictionary of Americanisms. '59..‡427 1
Brockett. Glossary of north country words. 1825..‡427 21
Bywater. Sheffield dialect. 1854.............427 18
Davies. Supplementary English glossary. 1881..‡423 23
De Vere. Americanisms. 1872.................‡427 2
Elworthy. Dialect, west Somerset. 1875..427 14
Evans. Leicestershire words, phrases and proverbs. 1881.......................................‡427 25
Galfridus *grammaticus.* Promptorium parvulorum. 1843-53. 2 v.....................‡423 15
Gaskell. Lects. on Lancashire dialect. '54..‡427 17
Gomme, *ed.* Gentleman's magazine library: Dialect, etc. 1884.......................427 6
Halliwell-Phillipps. Dictionary of archaic and provincial words. 1855. 2 v....‡423 10
Hunter. Hallamshire glossary. 1829......‡427 19
Jago. Dialect of Cornwall. 1882.............‡427 4
Jennings. Dialects in west of England. 1825..‡427 20
Kwong Ki Chin. Dictionary of English phrases. 1881...‡423 20
Leigh. Glossary, Cheshire. 1877............‡427 15
Levins. Manipulus vocabulorum. 1867....423 19
Long. Dictionary of Isle of Wight dialect. 1886..‡427 10
Maitland. American slang dictionary. '91..‡427 3
Molee. An American language. 1888.....420 20
Nares. Glossary; ed. by Halliwell *et al.* 1859. 2 v..‡423 12
Norton. Political Americanisms. 1890...‡423 27
Oxon. George Eliot's use of dialect. 1880..427 Pam. 1
Parish. Dictionary of Sussex dialect. '75. ‡427 8
Peacock. Tales and rhymes in Lindsey folk-speech. 1886..................................427 22
Ray. Collection of English words not generally used; ed. by Skeat. 1874......‡427 23
Robinson. Glossary, Mid-Yorkshire. '76..‡427 24
Wright. Dictionary of obsolete English. 1857. 2 v...‡423 8
Yorkshire glossary; by an inhabitant. 1855..‡427 16

‡ For reference.

SYNONYMS, ETC.

Crabbe. English synonyms. 1852..............424 1
Same ; with additions and corrections.
1896...‡424 1A
Fallows. Complete dictionary of synonyms
and antonyms. 1895........................‡424 5
Fernald. English synonyms and antonyms.
1896..424 6
Roget. Thesaurus of English words. '70...‡424 2
Smith. Synonyms. 1871........................‡424 3
Soule. Dictionary of English synonyms.
1871..‡424 4
Same ; revised and enlarged by Howison. 1893..‡424 4A

GENERAL DICTIONARIES.

Barclay. Universal dictionary............‡423 B-10
Barnum. Vocabulary of rhymes..............423 3
Boag. Imperial lexicon. 2 v................‡423 B-8
Century dictionary. 1889-91. 6 v....‡423 B-49
Chambers. Dictionary ; ed. by Donald.
1872...‡423 B-13
Craig. Dictionary. 1855. 2 v.............‡423 4
Hasendonck. Engelsche spraakkunst. 1815.
....423 28
Hunter *et al.* Encyclopædic dictionary.
1882-9. 14 v.................................‡423 B-22
Johnson. Dictionary. 1818. 2 v......‡423 B-1
Same ; enlarged by Latham. 1866.
4 v...‡423 B-3
Kenrick. New dictionary of the English
language. 1773............................‡423 B-58
Knowles. Critical pronouncing dictionary...‡423 B-7
Ladies' lexicon. 1828..........................423 26
Murray, *ed.* New English dictionary.
v. 1—..‡423 B-41
Ogilvie, *ed.* Imperial dictionary. 1882-3.
4 v...‡423 B-37
Phillips. New world of words. 1706..‡423 B-46
Same ; rev., with additions. 1720..‡423 B-47
Richardson. Dictionary. 1851. 2 v...‡423 B-11
Standard dictionary. 1894. 2 v......‡423 B-56
Stanford. Dictionary of Anglicised words
and phrases. 1892..........................‡423 B-55
Stormonth. Dictionary. 1884..........‡423 B-48
Supp. to same. 1895....................‡423 B-48A
Walker. Critical pronouncing dictionary.
1819...‡423 25
Same ; ed. by Sowerby....................‡423 2
Rhyming dictionary.............................‡423 7
Webster. American dictionary of English
language. 1829................................‡423 24
Same ; International dictionary. 1890.
....‡423 B-19
Williams. Readable dictionary. 1860.....‡423 6

Worcester. Dictionary. 1860............‡423 B-20
Same ; new edition. 1886..........‡423 B-20½
Wright, *ed.* Universal English dictionary.
5 v...‡423 B-14

LITERATURE.

Inclusive of the whole literature of the English language
in Great Britain and America.

HISTORY AND CRITICISM.

(For miscellaneous essays, see under Individual Authors
at the end of FINDING LIST.)

Adams. Famous books. 1879.................820 35
Adams, *ed.* Dictionary of English literature...‡820.10
American authors' guild. Constitution, etc.
1894..806 Pam. 2
Archer, T. Highway of letters [Fleet
street]. 1890....................................942 365
Archer, W. English dramatists of to-day.
....822.2 336
Arnold. English literature, 596-1832. 1879..820 36
Azarias. Development of English literature : old English. 1879................820 37
Bascom. Philosophy of English literature...820 5
Beers. From Chaucer to Tennyson. 1890..820 39
Initial studies in American letters. '91..820 144
Outline sketch of English literature. '86..820 38
Beers, *ed.* A century of American literature, 1776-1876................................820 143
Blackie. Scottish song. 1889..............821.2 833
Bourinot. Intellectual development of the
Canadian people. 1881.....................820 40
Brooke. English literature. 1878..........820 42
Same [rewritten]. 1897......................820 43
History of early English literature. '92..820 41
Buckland. Story of English literature....*820 44
Byrne *et al.* Afternoon lectures on English
literature, Dublin. 1863.....................820 25
Chasles. Anglo-American literature and
manners. 1852.............................)...820 145
Chateaubriand. Essai sur la littérature
anglaise. 2 v. 1837.........................840 79
Sketches of English literature. 1837. 2v..820 17
Cheney. The golden guess. 1892............820 82
Contents: Old notion of poetry.- Who are the great
poets?—Matthew Arnold.—What about Browning?—
Tennyson and his critics.—Six minutes with Swinburne.
—Music, or the tone poetry.—Hawthorne.
Cleveland. English literature, 19th century. 1856..820 45
Collier, J. P. History of English dramatic
poetry. 1831. 3 v........................822.2 1
Collier, W. F. History of English literature. 1877..820 46
Collins. Study of English literature. 1891..820 14

* Of interest to young readers.   ‡ For reference.

LANGUAGE AND LITERATURE.

Coppée. English literature as an interpreter of English history. 1873.........820 16
Courthope. History of English poetry. 1895. v. 1........................821.2 979
The liberal movement in English literature. 1885........................820 47
Craik. English literature and language from the conquest. 1863. 2 v.......820 48
Deshler. Afternoons with the poets.........811 59
Disraeli. Amenities of literature. 2 v......820 50
Dobson. Handbook of English literature. 1880...820 52
Donner. Chronological chart of English literature. 1890............820 Cab. 3
Dowden. French revolution and English literature. 1897....................820 159
Earle. Dawn of European literature: Anglo-Saxon. 1884.................820 53
Elze. Notes on Elizabethan dramatists. 1880. 2 v..........................822.2 265
Field. The child and his book. 1891.......820 54
Fisher. Twenty-five letters on English authors. 1895...................820 55
Fletcher. Development of, English prose style. 1881..................820 Pam. 1
Flügel, ed. Neuenglisches Lesebuch. 1895.
  V. 1. Die Zeit Heinrichs VIII................820 56
Forsyth. Novels and novelists of the 18th century. 1871..........................823 55
Garnett. The age of Dryden. 1895.........820 59
Geneste. Some account of the English stage, 1660-1830. 10 v.........822.2 12
Gilman. First steps in English literature...*820 4
Gilmore. English language and its early literature. 1880..........................820 60
Gosse. From Shakespeare to Pope. '85..821.2 750
History of 18th century literature. '89....820 61
Jacobean poets [1603-25]. 1894.......821.2 963
Gould. American criticism on American literature...40 27
Harrison. Studies in early Victorian literature. 1895............................820 62
  Contents: Characteristics of Victorian literature.— Thomas Carlyle.—Lord Macaulay.— Benjamin Disraeli.—William Makepeace Thackeray.— Charles Dickens.—Charlotte Brontë.—Charles Kingsley.— Anthony Trollope.—George Eliot.
Haweis. American humorists. 1882......828.1 4'
Hazlitt, W. Lectures on English poets.—
Book of Christmas. 1845...............821.2 4
Literature of the age of Elizabeth. 1877..822.3 103
Hazlitt, W., ed. English comic writers...828.2 7
Hazlitt, W. C., ed. English drama and stage, 1543-1664....................822.2 6
Herford. Age of Wordsworth. 1897.......820 63
Higginson. Short studies of American authors. 1880..........................820 147

Hippisley. Chapters on early English literature. 1837........................820 64
Hone. Ancient mysteries described. '23..822.2 11
Houghton, Mifflin & Co. Books by western authors. 1889..............820 Pam. 3
Hudson. Studies in interpretation: Keats, Clough, Matthew Arnold. 1896...824.1 316
Irving. History of Scottish poetry. '61..821.2 836
Jones. Renascence of the English drama 1895.......................................822.2 318
Jusserand. English novel in the time of Shakespeare. 1890..................823 111
Histoire littéraire du peuple anglais. 1894—. v. 1—...........................820 65
Literary history of English people, to renaissance. 1895..................820 66
Knapp. Lects. on American literature. 1829......................................820 148
Lawrence. English literature primers. 1879. 3 v.
  V. 1. Romance period....................820 71
  V. 2. Classical period....................820 72
  V. 3. Modern period......................820 73
Primer of American literature. 1880...820 149
Lowell. The old English dramatists. 1892.
  ....822.2 306
  Contents: Introduction.—Marlowe.- Webster. Chapman.—Beaumont and Fletcher —Massinger and Ford.
Maertz. New method for study of English literature. 1879........................820 9
Manly. Southern literature, 1579-1895....820 163
Masson. British novelists and their styles. 1859...823 56
Matthews. Introduction to the study of American literature. 1896..........820 150
Mills. Literature and literary men. 2 v...820 19
Minto. Literature of the Georgian era; ed. by Knight. 1895........................820 75
Mitchell. American lands and letters. 1897.......................................820 164
English lands, letters and kings: Celt to Tudor. 1889.......................820 76
Same: Elizabeth to Anne. 1890.......820 77
Same: Queen Anne and the Georges...820 78
Morell. Biographical history of English literature....................................820 29
Morgan. Representative names in English literature. 1876................820 8
Morley. English literature, reign of Victoria. 1881.............................820 81
English writers. 1887—. v. 1—........820 82
First sketch of English literature........820 80
Murray. Influence of Italian upon English literature. 1886................820 Pam. 2
Nichol. American literature, 1620-1880...820 151
Nicoll, H. J. Landmarks of English literature. 1895.............................820 104

* Of interest to young readers.

Nicoll, W. R., *and* **Wise, T. J.,** *eds.* Literary anecdotes of the 19th century. 1895—.
V. 1. Trial of William Blake for sedition. - Arthur Henry Hallam as advocate of Alfred and Charles Tennyson.—Midnight ; lines on the death of Alfred, Lord Tennyson; by H. Buxton Forman.—An opinion on Tennyson; by Elizabeth Barrett Browning.—Thomas Wade; the poet and his surroundings; by H. Buxton Forman.— Sonnet : To certain critics ; Fifty sonnets ; The contention of death and love; Helena; by Thomas Wade.— The Landor-Blessington papers. — Brief account of Richard Henry Horne; by H. Buxton Forman.—The ballad of Deloria; or, The passion of Andrea Como; by R. H. Horne.—Hawthorne in the shadow of Johnson, — A dramatic scene ; by Charles Wells.—A bundle of letters from Shelley to Leigh Hunt.—Materials for a bibliography of the writings in prose and verse of Robert Browning...820 15
V. 2. Letters concerning Ruskin's ' Notes on the construction of sheepfolds '; by Maurice.—Adventures of Ernest Alembert ; a fairy tale; by C. Brontë. – Elizabeth Barrett Browning and her scarcer books : a bibliographical note.—Carlyle: a disentangled essay; by E. B. Browning.—Mrs. Browning's religious opinions : letters to William Merry.—Two poetical epistles ; by George Crabbe.—George Eliot on George Meredith.—W. S. Landor : an open letter to Emerson.—The building of the Idylls ; a study in Tennyson.—John Keats : addition and substraction.—Bibliographical list of scarcer works, etc., of Swinburne.—The angel in the house; Emily A. Patmore.—Old common-place book of Edward Fitzgerald's. — William Cory, author of ' Ionica.'—Suppressed works by R. Kipling.—The author of 'Festus ' and the spasmodic school.—Tennysoniana.—Ana.................820 15A

Oliphant. Literary history, 18-19th centuries. 1882. 3 v..................820 105
Victorian age of English literature. 1893. 2 v...............................820 108
Pancoast. Introduction to English literature. 1896..................820 110
Pattee. History of American literature. 1896...........................820 152
Perry. English literature, 18th century. '83..820 111
Phelps. Beginnings of the English romantic movement. 1893.........820 112
Phillips. Popular manual of English literature. 1885. 2 v..............820 113
Raleigh. English novel : its history. '94..823 119
Reed. Lects. on English literature. 1858..820 7
Renton. Outlines of English literature. 1893...........................820 115
Reynolds. Treatment of nature in English poetry, between Pope and Wordsworth. 1896.................811 120
Richardson, A. S. Familiar talks on English literature. 1881..............*820 116
Richardson, C. F. American literature, 1607-1885. 2 v................820 154
Primer of American literature. 1878...820 153
Same; rev. edition. 1894...........820 153A

Robertson. History of English literature for secondary schools. 1894............820 117
Ross, J. D. Scottish poets in America. 1889................................928.2 401
Ross, J. W. Scottish history and literature to the reformation. 1884........941 149
Rowland. English novelists, 1700-1850. 1894..............................823 Pam. 5
Ryland. Chronological outlines of English literature. 1890...............820 118
Saintsbury. History of Elizabethan literature. 1887......................820 119
History of 19th century literature. '96.820 120
Salmon. Juvenile literature as it is. '88.....810 4
Sanborn, *ed.* Literature lessons. 1882..*820 B-11
Scherer. Essays on English literature. '91..844 49
Contents ; George Eliot : Silas Marner.— John Stuart Mill : Shakespeare.- George Eliot : Daniel Deronda.— criticism.—Milton and 'Paradise lost.'. Laurence Sterne, Taine's 'History of English literature.'—Shakespeare and or the humorist.— Wordsworth.— Thomas Carlyle.— ' Eudymion.'—George Eliot.
Scherr. History of English literature. '82..820 13
Shaw *and* **Tuckerman.** Manual of English literature. 1869..............820 3
Simonds. Introduction to study of English fiction. 1894..................823 117
Smith *and* **Tuckerman.** Smaller history, English and American literature. '70....820 6
Spalding. History of English literature. 1877...............................820 121
Spencer, *ed.* Cyclopedia of the literature of amateur journalism. 1891.........41 4
Stedman. Poets of America............824.1 211
The Victorian poets. 1876............824.1 213
Swinton. Studies in English literature. 1896..............................820 129
Symonds. Shakespeare's predecessors in English drama. 1884...........822.2 253
Taine. History of English literature. 1872. 2 v...............................820 122
Same. 1896. 4 v...................820 125
Same; abridged and ed. by Fiske. '72. ....820 124
Ten Brink. History of English literature. 1883-7.
V. 1. Early English literature...........................820 173
V. 2; pt. 1. Wyclif to renaissance....................820 174
V. 2; pt. 2. 14th century to death of Surrey.......820 175
Thackeray. English humourists, 18th century. 1854......................828.2 6
Tuckerman. History of English prose fiction. 1882......................823 90
Tyler. History of American literature, 1607-1765. 1878. 2 v............820 156
Same; rev. edition. 1897. 2 v........820 156A
Literary history of the American revolution. 1897. v. 1—..............820 158

* Of interest to young readers.

Underwood. Hand-book of English literature: American authors. 1874......820 170
Same: British authors. 1874..........820 130
Veitch. History and poetry of the Scottish border..941 24
Walker. Greater Victorian poets. '95...821.2 996
Three centuries of Scottish literature. 1893. 2 v................................820 131
Ward. History of English dramatic literature to the death of Anne. '75. 2 v..822.2 259
Warton. History of English poetry, 11-17th centuries. 1870..........821.2 1
Washburn. Studies in early English literature. 1882....................820 133
Welsh. Development of English literature and language. 1882. 2 v..........820 11
Wharton (Mrs. Thompson). Literature of society. 1862. 2 v...............820 21
Whipple. American literature, etc. '87...824.1 235
Literature of the age of Elizabeth......824.1 60
Whitcomb. Chronological outlines of American literature. 1894..........820 171
White. Outline of the philosophy of English literature. 1895—.
Contents: V. 1. The middle ages............820 134
Wright, H. C. Children's stories in American literature, 1660-1860. 1895....*820 160
Same; 1861-96. 1896................*820 161
Children's stories in English literature. 1889................................*820 137
Wright, Thomas. Essays on English literature, middle ages. 1846. 2 v..820 140
Wright, Thomas, ed. Biographia Britannica literaria. 2 v...................928.2 1
Yonge. Three centuries of English literature. 1872.........................820 142

BIBLIOGRAPHY.

Allibone. Dictionary of English literature (British and American authors). 1859-1871. 3 v.........................‡928 B-1
Supp. to same; by Kirk. 1891. 2 v...‡928 B-4
Ashton. Chap books, 18th century. 1882....29 2
British museum. Catalog of American books in; by Stevens. 1856.........15 28
Catalog of books printed in the United Kingdom to 1640. 1884. 3 v........15 35
Burt. References for students in English literature. 1887.....................‡16 77
Collier, ed. Extracts from registers of Stationers' company (Gt. Britain). 1557-1587. 2 v............................15 11
Rarest book in English language. 1865...15 13
Descriptive catalog of English plays to 1811. 4 v..............................928.2 270
Foley. American authors, 1795-1895: bibliography of first editions..........15 57
Halliwell-Phillipps. Notices of fugitive tracts, etc. (Gt. Britain). 1849.......15 27

Halliwell-Phillipps library, Notes on the. 1889................................16 Pam. 42
Harris collection of American poetry; by Stockbridge. 1886................15 39
Hartford library. Bibliography of plays, charades, etc. 1889...........16 Pam. 50
Hazlitt. Collections and notes (Gt. Britain). 1867-76..............................15 33
Hand-book to popular poetical and dramatic literature of Gt. Britain. '67......15 32
Hildeburn. A century of printing: Pennsylvania, 1685-1784. 1885-6. 2 v.....15 B 15
Issues of the press in New York, 1693-1752................................15 Pam. 3
Indiana. Descriptive catalog of official publications, 1800-90; by Howe.....15 Pam. 4
Kirk. Periodicals that pay contributors. '92..805 19
Leon & Brother, eds. First editions of American authors 1885.............15 15
Lowndes, ed. Bibliographer's manual, English literature. 1864; and appendix. 5 v..............................15 18
Roorbach, ed. Bibliotheca Americana. '49..15 B-8
Supp. to same. 1852-55..............15 B-9
Russell. Guide to British and American novels. 1894........................823 116
St. Louis novel club. Program. 1894-5..823 Pam. 6
San Francisco. Free public library. Classified English prose fiction........‡17 B-36
Slater. Early editions. 1894............15 48
Trübner, ed. Bibliographical guide to American literature. 1858..........15 30
Watt. Bibliotheca Britannica. '24. 4 v. in 2..11 B-1
Wisconsin authors. Bibliography; by Hawley. 1893....................15 50
Books by. 1893.....................15 Pam. 7

GENERAL COLLECTIONS.

Arber, ed. English garner. 1895. 8 v....42 63
English reprints, 1868-71. 14 v.
V. 1. Milton: Areopagitica.—Latimer: Sermon on the ploughers.—Gosson: Schoole of abuse....820 26
V. 2. Sidney: Apologie for poetrie.—Webbe: Travailes.—Selden: Table-talk..............820 27
V. 3. Ascham: Toxophilus.—Addison: Criticism on 'Paradise lost.'..........................820 28
V. 4. Lyly: Euphues; The anatomy of wit; Euphues and his England......................820 29
V. 5. Villiers: The rehearsal.—Gascoigne: The steele glas, etc.—Earle: Micro-cosmographie..820 30
V. 6. Latimer: Seven sermons before Edward VI.—More: Utopia............................820 31
V. 7. Puttenham: Arte of English poesie....820 32
V. 8. Howell: Instructions for forreine travell.—Udall: Roister Doister.—Revelation to the monk of Evesham.—King James I: Essays of a prentise in the divine arte of poesie; Counterblast to tobacco..820 33
V. 9. Naunton: Fragmenta regalia.—Watson: Passionate centurie of love; Eclogue, death of Sir Francis Walsingham; Teares of fancie........820 34

* Of interest to young readers.   ‡ For reference.

V. 10. Habington: Castara. — Ascham: The scholemaster..................820.2 35
V. 11. Tottel's miscellany: Songs and sonnets by Surrey, Wyat, Grimald, and uncertain authors..820.2 36
V. 12. Lever: Sermons.—Webbe: A discourse of English poetrie..................820.2 37
V. 13. Harmony of the essays of Lord Bacon..820.2 38
V. 14. Rede and be nott wrothe.—Dyaloge betwene gentillman and husbandman.—Last fight of the Revenge.—Googe's eglogs, etc..................820.2 39

Atlantic souvenir. 1830..................829.1 30
Boston book. 1850..................829.1 42
Burnett, *ed.* Specimens of English prose writers to close of 17th century. 1807.
3 v..................820 26
Camden, *ed.* Remains concerning Britain.
..................929.2 17
Chambers, *ed.* Cyclop. of English literature. 2 v..................‡820 B-7
Same. 1847. 2 v..................820 30
Chautauqua library of English history and literature. 1879. 3 v.
V. 1. To the later Norman period..................820 32
V. 2. The early Plantagenets..................820 33
V. 3. Wars of the roses..................820 34
Craik, *ed.* English prose selections. 1893-6.
5 v..................829.2 61
Duyckinck, *ed.* Cyclopedia of American literature. 1877. 2 v..................‡820 B-16
Earle *and* **Ford,** *eds.* Early prose and verse. 1893..................820 146
Early English text society publications.
1864. 82 parts in 51 vols.
V. 1, pt. 1: The pearl; Clennness; Patience: three early English alliterative poems.—pt. 2: Arthur: sketch of his life in early English verse.— pt. 3: Tractate, concernyng ye office and dewtie of kyngis, etc.; by Lander..................820.2 302
V. 2, pt. 4: Sir Gawayne and the green knight. —pt. 5: Orthographie and congruitie of the Britan tongue; by Hume.—pt. 6: Lancelot of the laik..820.2 303
V. 3, pt. 7: Story of Genesis and Exodus in English verse of about 1250 A. D.—pt. 8: Morte Arthure (alliterative version)..................820.2 304
V. 4, pt. 9: Animadversions uppon the annotacions and corrections of Chaucer's workes; by Thynne.—pt. 10: Merlin (pt. 1).—pt. 11: Sir David Lyndesay's monarchie (pt. 1)..................820.2 305
V. 5, pt. 12: The wright's chaste wife.—pt 13: Seinte Marherete (three texts, 1200-1330).—pt. 14: Romance of Kyng Horn, etc..................820.2 306
V. 6, pt. 15: Political, religious, and love poems, from the Lambeth manuscript, pt. 16: A tretice in Englisch brevely drawne out of the book of Quintis Essencijs in Latyn..................820.2 307
V. 7, pt. 17: Parallel extracts from twenty-nine Meidenhad, about 1200, pt. 19: Lyndesay's monmanuscripts of Piers plowman.— pt. 18: Hali arche (pt. 2, etc.)..................820.2 308
V. 8, pt 20: Some treatises by Richard Rolle de Hampole.—pt. 21: Merlin (pt. 2)..................820.2 309
V. 9, pt. 22: Romans of Partenay..................820.2 310
V. 10, pt. 23: Dan Michel's ayenbite of inwyt..820.2 311
V 11. pt. 24: Hymns to the Virgin and Christ, etc.—pt. 25. The stacions of Rome, etc.—pt. 26: Religious pieces, prose and verse..................820.2 312

V. 12, pt. 27: Manipulus vocabulorum (a rhyming dictionary; by Levins, 1570..................820.2 313
V. 13. pt. 28: Langland's 'Vision of Piers plowman' (pt. 1, text A)..................820.2 314
V. 14. pt. 29: Old English homilies (pt. 1)..820.2 314½
V. 15. pt. 30: Pierce the ploughman's crede.— pt. 31: Myre's 'Duties of a parish priest.'..................820.2 315
V. 16. pt. 32: The babees' boke; The children's book; Bokes of norture of J. Russell, etc..................820.2 316
V. 17. pt. 33: Knight de la Tour-Landry, 1372.— pt. 34: Old English homilies (pt. 2). — pt. 35: Lyndesay's works (pt. 3)..................820.2 317
V. 18. pt. 36: Merlin (pt. 3)..................820.2 318
V. 19. pt. 37: Lyndesay's works (pt. 4)..................820.2 319
V. 20. pt. 38: Vision of Piers plowman (pt. 2, text B)..................820.2 320
V. 21. pt. 39: Alliterative romance of the destruction of Troy (pt. 1)..................820.2 321
V. 22. pt. 40: English gilds, statutes, etc..820.2 322
V. 23. pt. 41: William Lander's minor poems.— pt. 42: Bernardus de Cura rei famularis. — pt. 43: Ratis raving, etc..................820.2 323
V. 24. pt. 44: Alliterative romance of Joseph of Arimathie; or, The holy grail.—pt. 45: King Alfred's West-Saxon version of Saint Gregory's 'Pastoral care' (pt. 1)..................820.2 324
V. 25. pt. 46: Legends of the holy rood.—pt. 47: Lyndesay's works (pt. 5)..................820.2 325
V. 26. pt. 48: The times' whistle. — pt. 49: An old English miscellany..................820.2 326
V. 27. pt. 50: King Alfred's version of Gregory (pt. 2).—pt. 51: Life of St. Juliana (2 versions)..820.2 327
V. 28. pt. 52: Palladius on husbondrie, Englisht.—pt. 53. Old English homilies (series 2)..820.2 328
V. 29. pt. 54: Vision of Piers plowman (part 3, test C)..................820.2 329
V. 30. pt. 55: Generydes: a romance.—pt. 56: Destruction of Troy (pt. 2)..................820.2 330
V. 31. pt. 57: Early English version of the 'Cursor Mundi'; 4 texts. (pt. 1)..................820.2 331
V. 32. pt. 58: The Blickling homilies (pt. 1)..820.2 332
V. 33. pt. 59: Cursor Mundi (pt. 2)..................820.2 333
V. 34. pt. 60: Meditacynns on the soper of our Lorde.—pt. 61: Thomas of Erceldoune..................820.2 334
V. 35. pt. 62: Cursor Mundi (pt. 3)..................820.2 335
V. 36. pt. 63: Blickling homilies (pt. 2).—pt. 64: Francis Thynne's emblemes and epigrams,— pt. 65: Be Domes daege, etc..................820.2 336
V. 37. pt. 66: Cursor Mundi (pt. 4)..................820.2 337
V. 38. pt. 67: Vision of Piers plowman (pt. 4, section 1. Notes)..................820.2 338
V. 39. pt. 68: Cursor Mundi (pt. 5)..................820.2 339
V. 40. pt. 69: Adam Davy's five dreams about Edward II.—Life of Saint Alexius, etc.—pt. 70: Generydes (pt. 2)..................820.2 340
V. 41. pt.71: Lay folks' mass book (4 texts)..820.2 341
V. 42. pt. 72: Palladius on husbondrie (pt. 2).— pt. 73: Blickling homilies (pt. 3)..................820.2 342
V. 43. pt. 74: English works of Wyclif, hitherto unprinted..................820.2 343
V. 44. pt. 75: Catholicon Anglicum: early English dictionary, 1483..................820.2 344
V. 45. pt. 76: Aelfric's 'Lives of saints' (pt. 1)..820.2 345
V. 46. pt. 77: Beowulf; autotypes of the unique Cotton manuscript, with transliteration, etc..820.2 346
V. 47. pt. 78: Fifty earliest English wills..................820.2 347
V. 48, pt. 79: King Alfred's Orosius' (pt. 1). (Old English text and Latin original.)..................820.2 348
V. 49. pt. 80: Life of Saint Katherine..................820.2 349
V. 50. pt. 81: Vision of Piers plowman (pt. 4, section 2).—General preface and indexes..................820.2 350
V. 51. pt. 82: Aelfric's 'Lives of saints' (pt. 2)..820.2 351

‡ For reference.

LANGUAGE AND LITERATURE.

Same; extra series. 1867. 44 parts in 34 vols.
V. 1. pt. 1: Romance of William of Palerne...820.2 400
V. 2. pt. 2: Early English pronunciation; by Ellis (pt. 1)...820.2 401
V. 3. pt. 3: Caxton's Book of curtesye.—pt. 4: Havelok the Dane..820.2 402
V. 4. pt. 5: Chaucer's Boethius.—pt. 6: Cheuelere Assigne...820.2 403
V. 5. pt. 7: Early English pronunciation; by Ellis (pt.2)...820.2 404
V. 6. pt. 8: Queene Elizabeth's achademy; a book of precedence, etc.—pt. 9: The fraternitye of vacabondes; by Awdeley.—A caveat of warening for common cursetors; by Thomas Harman.—Sermon in praise of thieves; by Parson Haben.—Groundworke of conny-catching.....................820.2 405
V. 7. pt. 10: Andrew Boorde's Introduction of knowledge and Dyetary of helth.—Barnes in the defence of the berde.—Life of Boorde..............820.2 406
V. 8. pt. 11.: The Bruce; compiled by Barbour (pt. 1)..820.2 407
V. 9. pt. 12: England in Henry VIII's time; a dialogue by Starkey (pt. 2)...........................820.2 408
V. 10. pt. 13: Supplycacyon of the beggers; by Fish, etc...820.2 409
V. 11. pt. 14: Early English pronunciation; by Ellis (pt. 3)..820.2 410
V. 12. pt. 15: Robert Crowley's epigrams, etc. —pt. 16: Chaucer on the astrolabe................820.2 411
V. 17. pts. 17-18: Complaynt of Scotlande.....820.2 412
V. 14. pt. 19: The myroure of oure Ladye.....820.2 413
V. 15. pt. 20: History of the holy grail (pt. 1).820.2 414
V. 16. pt. 21: The Bruce (pt. 2).......................820.2 415
V. 17. pt. 22: Brinklow's complaynt of Roderick Mors, and Lamentacyon of a Christen against the citye of London...820.2 416
V. 18. pt. 23: Early English pronunciation; by Ellis (pt. 4)..820.2 417
V. 19. pt. 24: History of the holy grail (pt.2)..820.2 418
V. 20. pt. 25-26: Romance of Guy of Warwick (pts. 1 and 2)..820.2 419
V. 21. pt. 27: English works of Bishop Fisher (pt. 1)...820.2 420
V. 22. pt. 28: History of the holy grail (pt. 3).—Supplement to Boorde's Dietary................820.2 421
V. 23. pt. 29: The Bruce (pt. 3).......................820.2 422
V. 24. pt. 30: History of the holy grail (pt.4).820.2 423
V. 25. pt. 31: Alexander and Dindimus.........820.2 424
V. 26. pt. 32: England in Henry VIII's time (pt. 1).—Starkey's life and letters, etc..........820.2 425
V. 27. pt. 33: Gesta Romanorum...................820.2 426
V. 28. pt. 34: English Charlemagne romances (pt. 1): Sir Fernumbras.—pt. 35: Same (pt. 2): Sege of Melayne.—Duke Rowland.—Fragment of the Song of Roland..820.2 427
V. 29. pts. 36-37: Same (pts. 3-4): Lyfe of Charles the grete; tr. from the French by Caxton.........820.2 428
V. 30. pt. 38. Same (pt. 5): The Sowdone of Babylone.—pt. 39: Same (pt. 6): Rauf Coilyear. —Fragments of Roland and Vernagu.—Otuel...820.2 429
V. 31. pts. 40-41: Same (pts. 7-8): Boke of Duke Huon of Burdeux (pts. 1-2)...........................820.2 430
V. 32. pt. 42: Romance of Guy of Warwick; two texts (pt. 1.)...820.2 431
V. 33. pt. 43: English Charlemagne romances (pt. 9): Boke of Duke Huon (pt. 3)................820.2 432
V. 34. pt. 44: Same (pt. 10): Four sonnes of Aymon; English by Caxton (pt. 1)...............820.2 433

Five centuries of English language and literature. 1860..829.2 123
Contents: Selections from Wycliffe, Chaucer, Hawes, More, Spenser, Jonson, Locke, Gray.
Gleanings from popular authors. '82. 2 v..829 B 1
Goodrich, *ed.* The token. 1839..............829.1 3
Halliday, *ed.* Savage club papers..........829.2 84
Halliwell-Phillipps, *ed.* Nursery rhymes and tales of England........................829.2 45
Harleian miscellany. 1810. 12 V............42 1
Henley *and* **Whibley.** Book of English prose, 1387-1649. '1894....................829.2 73
Home and social philosophy; from Dickens' 'Household words.' 1852.................829.2 83
Imitations of celebrated authors. 1844...829.2 85
Knickerbocker gallery. 1855................829.1 24
Library of English literature. 1847. 2 v...820 1
Lowell offering: Mind amongst the spindles. 1844..824.1 165
Minto. Manual of English prose literature. 1872..820 74
Montagu, *ed.* Selections from Taylor, Latimer, *et al.* 1845............................829.2 1
Morley, *ed.* Shorter works of English prose...820 B-9
Sketches of longer works, English verse and prose. 1881..................................820 B-10
Nebraska, University of. University studies. 1890—....................................41 Pam. 1
Overbury, *et al.* Mirror of character. 1869...829.2 2
Percy society. Early English poetry, ballads and popular literature of the middle ages, edited from original manuscripts, etc. 1840-52. 31 v.
V. 1. Collier, *ed.*: Old ballads.—Mackay, *ed.*: Songs of the London prentices and trades.—Croker, *ed.*: Historical songs of Ireland.—Pain and sorrow of evil marriage.—Parker: The king and a poor northern man..821.2 444
V. 2. Lydgate: Minor poems, selection.—Halliwell, *ed.*: Early naval ballads of England.—Rowley: Search for money.—Mad pranks and merry jests of Robin Goodfellow.......................821.2 445
V. 3. Wright, *ed.*: Political ballads during the Commonwealth. — Deloney: Strange histories.—Heywood: Marriage triumph.—History of patient Grissel...821.2 446
V. 4. Wright, *ed.*: Specimens of lyric poetry, time of Edward I.—Halliwell, *ed.*: Boke of curtasye.—Wright, *ed.*: Specimens of old Christmas carols.—Halliwell, *ed.*: Nursery rhymes of England..821.2 447
V. 5. Chettle: Kind-Heart's dream. – Dekker: Knight's conjuring.— Halliwell, *ed.*: Meeting of gallants at an ordinarie.—Porter: Two angry women of Abingdon...............................821.2 448
V. 6. Rimbault, *ed.*: Poetical tracts of the 16th century.—Rimbault, *ed.*: Cock Lorell's bote – Johnson: Crown garland of golden roses.—Wotton: Follie's anatomie.—Wotton: Poems..821.2 449
V. 7. Skelton (?): Harmony of birds.— Brampton: Paraphrase on the seven penitential Psalms.—Drayton: Harmony of the church.—Jack of Dover. —Croker, *ed.*: A Kerry pastoral...............821.2 450

V. 8. Wright, ed.: Latin stories.—Gifford: Dialogue of witches and witchcraft................821.2 451
V. 9. Rowlands: The four knaves.—Thomson: Poem to the memory of W. Congreve.— Halliwell, ed.: Pleasant conceits of old Hobson.— Rimbault, ed.: Maroccus extaticus; or, Bankes' bay horse in a trance.—Rimbault, ed.: Ballads illustrating the great frost of 1683-4................821.2 452
V. 10. Fairholt, ed.: Lord Mayor's pageants.821.2 453
V. 11. Guildford: The owl and nightingale; a poem.—Croke: Thirteen psalms, etc., in English verse.— Hall: Expostulation against the abusers of chyrurgerie and physyke.— Rich: Honestie of this age...................821.2 454
V. 12. Thoms, ed.: Reynard the fox........821.2 455
V. 13. Croke, ed.: The keen of the south of Ireland.—Goodwin, ed.: Six ballads, with burdens. — Collier, ed.: Lyrical poems, 1589-1600..........821.2 456
V. 14. Audelay: Poems. — Wright, ed.: St. Brandan; a mediæval legend of the sea.— Halliwell, ed.: Romance of the emperor Octavian......821.2 457
V. 15. Halliwell, ed.: Friar Bakon's prophesie; a satire.—Halliwell, ed.: Poetical miscellanies of the time of James I.— Chappell, W., ed.: Crown garland of golden roses (pt. 2)................821.2 458
V. 16. Wright, ed.: Seven sages, in English verse.— Halliwell, ed.: Romance of Syr Tryamoure......................821.2 459
V. 17. Dixon, ed.: Scottish traditional versions of ancient ballads.—Dixon, ed.: Ancient poems, ballads, etc., of the peasantry of England..........821.2 460
V. 18. Hawes: Pastime of pleasure: an allegorical poem................821.2 461
V. 19. Fairholt, ed.: The civic garland; Songs. – Robert of Gloucester: Life and martyrdom of Thomas Beket..................821.2 462
V. 20. Barnfield: The affectionate shepherd.— Heywood: Dialogue on wit and folly.— Denham: Collection of proverbs and popular sayings.—Halliwell, ed.: Song of Lady Bessy.................821.2 463
V. 21. Croker, ed.: Songs of the French invasion of Ireland................821.2 464
V. 22. Barclay: Cytezen and Uploudyshman.— Halliwell, ed.: An interlude of the four elements. — Ingelend: The disobedient child.—Croker, ed.: Autobiography of Mary, countess of Warwick.— Halliwell, ed.: Westward for smelts (stories).....821.2 465
V. 23. Wright, ed.: Songs and carols of the fifteenth century.—Sandes, ed.: Festive songs of the 16th and 17th centuries.—Halliwell, ed.: Descriptive notices of popular English histories..........821.2 466
V. 24-26. Chaucer: Canterbury tales, ed. by Wright. 3 v....................821.2 467
V. 27. Massinger: Believe as you list; a tragedy. —Fairholt, ed.: Songs and poems on costume....821.2 470
V. 28. Hardwick, ed.: Passion of St. George.— Hardwick, ed.: Poem on the times of Edward II. – Shoreham: Religious poems.— Halliwell, ed.: Triall of treasure.................821.2 471
V. 29. Halliwell, ed.: Notices of fugitive tracts and chap-books; Man in the moone; Manifest detection of the use of dice-play; Loyal garland, songs of the seventeenth century.— Fairholt, ed.: Poems, songs, etc., on George, duke of Buckingham......821.2 472
V. 30. Deloney: Garland of good-will.—Croker, ed.: Britannia's pastorals.— Black, ed.: Enterlude of John Bon and Mast Person...............821.2 473
V. 31. Gosson: Pleasant quippes for upstart new fangled gentlewomen. A treatise on the pride and abuse of women; by Charles Bansley......821.2 474

Read, comp. Cabinet of Irish literature. 1892. 4 v.........................820 B-12

Shaw and Smith, eds. Choice specimens of English literature. 1871...............820 23
Skeat, ed. Specimens of English literature. 1880....................820 24
Smith, H., ed. A century of American literature; selections. 1889 ....820 162
Sprague, ed. Masterpieces in English literature. 1874...............820 172
Stars and stripes in rebeldom: papers by federal prisoners. 1862................829.1 43
Stedman and Hutchinson, eds. Library of American literature. 1888-9. 11v..820 B-18
Western miscellany. 1846..............823 Pam. 2
Wintergreen, The: gift for 1844.........829.1 25
Woodworth. American miscellany. 1855...41 1

COLLECTIONS: POETICAL.

(See also, Hymnology and Sacred Music, in Part 3 of FINDING LIST, pp. 487 and 424.)

Adams, O. F., ed. Through the year with the poets. 1885-6. 12 v................811 104
Adams, W. D., ed. Songs of society. 1880..................821.2 544
Alexander, ed. Sunday book of poetry...821 27
Allingham, ed. Ballad book. 1879.....821.2 168
Auchmuty, ed. Poems of English heroism. 1882...................821.2 559
Aytoun, ed. Ballads of Scotland. 1870. 2 v..................821.2 504
Lays of Scottish cavaliers, etc. '77...821.2 506
Baby [selected poems]. 1878................821 44
Ballad minstrelsy of Scotland. 1871......821.2 78
Barney. Songs of the revolution. 1893..821.1 501
Beeton, ed. Great book of poetry. 2 v......‡821 1
Bell, ed. Early ballads. 1877...............821.2 65
Songs from the dramatists..............821.2 82
Bellew, ed. Poet's corner: a manual of English poetry...................821.2 15
Bentley ballads (from Bentley's miscellany). 1862.......................821.2 441
Bouquet, The. 1862......................811 81
Brackett and Eliot, eds. Poetry for home and school. 1894.,..............*811 117
Brock, ed. Southern amaranth: poems of the war. 1869 ....821.1 468
Brown, ed. The thistle, with music. '83...784 B-23
Browne, F. F., ed. Bugle-echoes: poems of the civil war. 1886................. 821.1 333
Golden poems. 1882.....................821 21
Bryant, ed. Library of poetry and song...‡821 4
Bullen, ed. Christmas garland: carols, etc. 1885.....................821.2 406
Poems, chiefly lyrical, of the Elizabethan age. 1890........................821.2 1009
Caine, R. H., ed. Love-songs of English poets, 1500-1800..................821.2 897

* Of interest to young readers.   ‡ For reference.

LANGUAGE AND LITERATURE.

Caine, T. H., *ed.* Sonnets of three centuries. 1882............................821 24
Campbell. Specimens of the British poets. 1819. 7 v.
  V. 1. Essay on English poetry.....................821.2 5
  V. 2. Chaucer, 1400, to Beaumont, 1628.........821.2 6
  V. 3. Drayton, 1631, to Phillips, 1664............821.2 7
  V. 4. Shirley, 1666, to Prior, 1721.................821.2 8
  V. 5. Sewell, 1726, to Carey, 1763................821.2 9
  V. 6. Churchill, 1764, to Johnson, 1784.........821.2 10
  V. 7. Whitehead, 1785, to Anstey, 1805..........821.2 11
Case, *ed.* English epithalamies. 1896...821.2 1039
Caulfield. Vocal music in Shakespear's plays. 2 v.............................784 B-5
Chambers, *ed.* English pastorals. '95...821.2 1000
Chappell, *ed.* Crown garland of golden roses, pt. 2............................*in* 821.2 458
Old English ditties............................784 B-3
Popular music of olden time. 2v........784 B-1
Child, *ed.* English and Scottish ballads. 1860. 8 v.............................821.2 51
Same. 1882—. pt. 1—...............821.2 B-10
Clarke, C. C., *ed.* Specimens of the less known British poets. 1868. 3v......821.2 12
Clarke, J. T., *ed.* Songs of the south. 1896......................................821.1 518
Clary. Our nation's history and song. '96..821.1 513
Coates, *ed.*• Fireside encyc. of poetry...‡821 B-1
Coggeshall, *ed.* Poets and poetry of the west. 1860...............................821.1 7
Collection of old ballads. 1723. 3 v.......821.2 59.
Collection of 79 black-letter ballads and broadsides, 1559-97. 1870..............821.2 83
Collier. Poetical decameron. 1820. 2 v...821.2 2
Collier, *ed.* Lyrical poems, 1589-1600...821.2 456
Old ballads..*in* 821.2 444
Collins, *ed.* Treasury of minor British poetry. 1896.............................821.2 1040
Conybeare. Illustrations of Anglo-Saxon poetry. 1826........................821.2 B-3
Crandall, *ed.* Representative sonnets, American. 1891....................821.1 445
Croker, *ed.* Historical songs of Ireland..821.2 444
Keen the south of Ireland.........*in* 821.2 456
Popular songs illustrative of French invasions of Ireland......................821.2 464
Popular songs of Ireland. 1886........821.2 800
Crow, *ed.* Elizabethan sonnet-cycles. 1896.
  v. 1-2.
  V. 1. Phillis; by Thomas Lodge.—Licia; by Giles Fletcher.................................821.2 1031
  V. 2. Delia; by Samuel Daniel.—Diana; by Henry Constable............................821.2 1032
Darley, *ed.* Selections of war lyrics. '64..821.1 316
De Leon, *ed.* South songs. 1866.........821.1 467
Denham, *ed.* Weather proverbs, etc..821.2 463
Dennis, *ed.* English sonnets. 1881......821.2 571
Dewart, *ed.* Selections from Canadian poets. 1864.............................821.2 719

Dixon, *ed.* Ancient poems of England..821.2 760
Scottish traditional versions of ancient ballads..821.2 460
Dixon *and* **Bell,** *eds.* Ballads and songs of the peasantry............................821.2 66
Dobson, A., *ed.* Old English songs. '94..821.2 594
Dobson, W. T., *ed.* Literary frivolities. 1880...................................819 47
Poetical ingenuities. 1882............811 61
Dodsley's collection of poems; by several hands. 1770. 6 v........................821.2 186
Drei altschottische Lieder; ed. and tr. by Grimm. 1813.........................821.2 Pam. 1
Drifted snowflakes. 1869..................811 19
Dumont, *ed.* Floral offering. 1868.........716 55
Eggleston, *ed.* American war ballads, etc. 1889. 2 v..................................821.1 407
Ellis, A., *ed.* Chosen English: selections from Wordsworth, Byron, Shelley, Lamb, Scott; with biographies and notes. 1896...........................821.2 1025
Ellis, G., *ed.* Specimens of early English metrical romances. 1848.............821.2 90
  Contents: Historical introduction.—Account of Peter Alphonsus and Marie's lays.—Romances relating to Arthur: Merlin; Morte Arthur.—Guy of Warwick.—Sir Bevis of Hamptoun.—Richard Cœur de Lion.—Romances relating to Charlemagne: Roland and Ferragus; Sir Otuel; Sir Ferumbras.—Seven wise masters. Florice and Blancheflour.—Robert of Cysille.—Sir Isumbras.—Sir Triamour.—Lyfe of Ipomydon.—Sir Eglamour of Artoys.—Lay le Freine.—Sir Eger, Sir Grahame and Sir Graysteel.—Sir Degoré.—Roswall and Lillian.—Amys and Amylion.
Emerson, G. D. Old time war songs: Texas, Mexico, and 1812........821.1 Pam. 14
English. Boy's book of battle lyrics...*821.1 321
Everest, *ed.* Poets of Connecticut. '43..821.1 4
Fagan, *ed.* Southern war songs. 1890. 821.1 469
Fairholt, *ed.* Lord mayor's pageants...821.2 453
Poems and songs on George, duke of Buckingham...............................821.2 472'
Satirical songs on costume...............821.2 470
Farr, *ed.* Select poetry, chiefly sacred; reign of James I. 1847...............821.2 151
Same; reign of Elizabeth. 1845. 2 v....245 2
Farrar, *ed.* With the poets. 1883........821 33
Favorite English poems and poets. '70...821.2 16
Fields *and* **Whipple,** *eds.* Family library of British poetry........................‡821.2 B-8
Franklin Square song collection. v. 1—. 784 B-8
Garland, The. 1868...........................821 8
Garrett, *ed.* Victorian songs. 1895..821.2 1001
Goodwin, *ed.* Ballads........................821.2 456
Gosse, *ed.* English odes. 1881............821.2 580
Gould, S. Baring, *ed.* English minstrelsie. 1895—. v. 1......................784 R 5
Graham, *ed.* Songs of Scotland.........784 B-4
Graves, *ed.* Irish song book. 1894.....784 10
Songs of Irish wit, etc.....................821.2 727

* Of interest to young readers.   ‡ For reference.

Griswold, *ed.* Female poets of America. 1853..................................821.1 6
Poets and poetry of America. 1847....‡821.1 5
Hale, *ed.* Poetical quotations. 1854........‡821 3
Halliwell-Phillipps, *ed.* Boke of curtasye..................................821.2 447
 Early naval ballads.....................821.2 445
 Loyal garland............................821.2 472
 Nursery rhymes of England.........821.2 447
 Poetical miscellanies...................821.2 458
 Popular English histories.............821.2 466
 The Thornton romances (metrical). 1844.
  ....821.2 89
  Contents: Sir Perceval of Galles.— Sir Isumbras.— Sir Eglamour of Artois.— Sir Degrevant.
Hamilton, J., *ed.* Our Christian classics. 4 v...................................922.2 107
Hamilton, W., *ed.* Parodies. 1884-9. 6v.
 V. 1. Parodies of poems of Tennyson, Longfellow, Bret Harte, Thomas Hood, Rev. C. Wolfe..821 B-3
 V. 2. Parodies of Shakespeare, Milton, Dryden, Watts, Tennyson, Longfellow, Hood, Bret Harte, Matthew Arnold, Poe, Wolfe's Ode, and 'My mother.'...821 B-4
 V. 3. Parodies of Burns and Scotch songs, Scott, Campbell, Goldsmith, the Anti-Jacobin, Southey, Kingsley, Swinburne, Mrs. Hemans, Moore, and Byron...821 B-5
 V. 4. Parodies of ballads, songs and odes, T. H. Bayly, Bunn, Campbell, Carey, Carroll, Cook, Dibdin, Gilbert, Herrick, Mackay, Hon. Mrs. Norton, Tennyson's jubilee ode, Swinburne's odes, Proctor, Cornwall, Payne, Sheridan, Thomson, Irish songs, Scotch songs, Welsh songs, Old English songs..821 B-6
 V. 5. Thomas Gray's 'Elegy in a country churchyard,' etc., William Cowper, William Wordsworth, S. T. Coleridge, M. G. Lewis, Leigh Hunt, Lord Macaulay, W. M. Praed, W. M. Thackeray, Lord Lytton, P. B. Shelley, Mrs. Browning, the Ingoldsby legends, J. Addison, W. Collins, S. Rogers, E. Waller, national songs of the United States, modern American poets, songs of the civil war..821 B-7
 V. 6. Swinburne, Sims, Browning, Locker-Lampson, Dobson, Rossetti, O. Wilde, Dryden, Pope, Tupper, songs in praise of tobacco, nursery rhymes, slang-songs, religious and political parodies, ballads, rondeaus, and villanelles.—A bibliography of dramatic burlesques..................821 B-8
Hannah, *ed.* The courtly poets. 1870...821.2 21
Harrison, *ed.* Cap and gown: college verse. 1894..................................821.1 475
Hatton, *ed.* Songs of England. 2 v....784 B-10
Hatton *and* **Molloy,** *eds.* Songs of Ireland.
  ....784 B-13
Hayes, *ed.* Ballads of Ireland. 2 v......821.2 79
Hazlitt, *ed.* Remains of early popular poetry of England. 1864........821.2 171
 Contents:—The king and the barker.— Kyng and hermit.—Cokwold's daunce.—Thrush and nightingale.— Vox and wolf.— Ragman roll.—Debate of the carpenter's tools.—Colyn Blowbol's testament.—Childe of Bristowe.—Merchant and son.—Ser John Mandevile and the gret Souden.—Syr Peny.— How the wise man taught his son.—How the goode wif thaught hir doughter.—How a merchaude dyd hys wyfe betray. How the plowman lernyd his paternoster. Lyfe of Roberte the Devyll. Kynge Roberd of Cysille

Helps, *ed.* Poetry for children. 1882. 3 v...*811 70
Henley, *ed.* Lyra heroica : verse for boys..*821 43
Herd, *ed.* Ancient and modern Scottish songs. 1869. 2 v...................821.2 74
Historical poems, 16th century (Camden society)...............................942 135
Hogarth. Book of British songs..........784 R-1
Hows, *ed.* Golden leaves from American poets....................................821.1 9
Hunt. Book of the sonnet. 1867. 2 v......811 14
Hunt, *ed.* Selections from English poets. 1857...................................821.2 20
Ingledew, *ed.* Ballads and songs of Yorkshire. 1860..........................821.2 72
Jack Morgan songster, no. 1 (Augusta, Ga.)...29 4
Jewett, *ed.* Ballads and songs of Derbyshire. 1867...........................821.2 73
Johnson, *ed.* Play-day poems. 1878......821 16
 Single famous poems. 1877............821 14
 (See also, Little classics.)
Joyce, *ed.* Ballads of Irish chivalry. 1872.
  ....821.2 110
Kendrick, *ed.* Our poetical favorites. 3 v..821 18
Kettell, *ed.* Specimens of American poetry. 1829. 3 v..............................821.1 1
Lamb, Charles *and* **Mary.** Poetry for children. 1878..........................*821.2 271
Lampson. See **Locker-Lampson.**
Lang, *ed.* Blue poetry book. 1891........*821 42
 Collection of ballads. 1897.........821.2 748
Langbridge, *ed.* Poets at play. 2 v......821 40
Lighthall, *ed.* Canadian poems and lays.
  ....821.2 921
 Songs of the great dominion. 1889..821.2 384
Linton, *ed.* Rare poems, 16th and 17th centuries. 1883.......................821.2 170
Linton *and* **Stoddard,** *eds.* English verse. 1883. 5 v.
 V. 1. Chaucer to Burns........................821 28
 V. 2. Lyrics of the 19th century.............821 29
 V. 3. Ballads and romances..................821 30
 V. 4. Dramatic scenes and characters....821 31
 V. 5. Translations...............................821 32
Little classics: lyrical........................821 10
 Same: narrative. 1875...................821 11
 Same: minor poems. 1875..............821 9
Living English poets, 1893................821.2 967
Locker-Lampson, *ed.* Lyra elegantiarum: social verse. 1891...................821.2 871
Lodge, *ed.* Ballads and lyrics. 1882.......821 25
Logan, *ed.* Pedlar's pack of ballads, etc. 1869..................................821.2 64
Lover, *ed.* Lyrics of Ireland. 1858.....821.2 81
Lyrics of the law. 1884......................348 6
McCabe, *ed.* Ballads of battle, etc.......821 15
MacDermott, *ed.* New spirit of 'the Nation.' 1894.......................821.2 933
 Songs and ballads of young Ireland. 1896................................821.2 1168

* Of interest to young readers. ‡ For reference.

LANGUAGE AND LITERATURE.

Mackay, *ed.* Legendary and romantic ballads of Scotland. 1861..................821.2 77
 Songs and ballads relative to London prentices...............................*in* 821.2 444
 Thousand and one gems......................821 5
Magazine of poetry. 1889-96. 8 v........821 P-1
Main, *ed.* Treasury of English sonnets...821.2 547
Major. Sagas and songs of the Norsemen. 1894...................................821.2 965
Masque of poets (No name series). '78...821.1 217
Matthews, *ed.* Poems of American patriotism. 1882..............................821.1 289
Miles, *ed.* Poets and poetry of the century. 1891-4.
  George Crabbe to S. T. Coleridge..............821.2 873
  Robert Southey to Percy Bysshe Shelley......821.2 874
  John Keats to Edward, lord Lytton............821.2 875
  Frederick Tennyson to A. H. Clough..........821.2 876
  Charles Kingsley to James Thomson...........821.2 877
  William Morris to Robert Buchanan..........821.2 878
  Robert Bridges and contemporary poets......821.2 879
  Sacred, moral and religious verse..............821.2 880
  Humour, society, parody, and occasional verse.821.2 881
  Joanna Baillie to Matilda Blind.................821.2 882
Miller. Singers and songs of the church...922 23
Moore, F., *ed.* Anecdotes, poetry, etc., of the war, 1860-65..................971.4 97
 Lyrics of loyalty. 1864...................821.1 246
 Personal and political ballads [of the rebellion]. 1864......................821.1 317
 Songs and ballads of the American revolution. 1856........................821.1 10
 Songs of the soldiers. 1864..............821.1 297
 Songs of the southern people, 1861-5...821.1 336
 Rebel rhymes and rhapsodies. 1864...821.1 313
Morley, *ed.* The king and the commons: Cavalier and Puritan songs. '69.....821.2 67
 Shorter English poems...................‡821.2 B-7
Morris, *ed.* Poet's walk: introduction to English poetry. 1882................*821.2 646
Motherwell, *ed.* Minstrelsy, ancient and modern. 1873............................821.2 95
Moulton, *ed.* In my lady's name: poems of love and beauty. 1897.............821 50
Murphy, *ed.* Anthology of New Netherland. 1865........................821.1 B-1
Murray, *ed.* Ballads and songs of Scotland. 1874............................821.2 76
New York book of poetry. 1837........821.1 314
O'Donnell, *ed.* Love poems of three centuries, 1590-1890. 1895. 2 v..........821 47
Oliphant, *ed.* La musa madrigalesca: madrigals, etc., Elizabethan age. 1837. ....821.2 71
Oxford prize poems. 1836................821.2 23
Palgrave, *ed.* Children's treasury. 1882...*821 26
 Golden treasury of songs, etc. 1880...821.2 516
Parlor muse. 1884............................821 34
Parry, *ed.* Legendary cabinet: British national ballads. 1829...............821.2 62

Patmore, *ed.* Children's garland. 1877....*821 17
Payne, *ed.* Select poetry for children......*821 22
Percy, *ed.* Boy's Percy; ed. by Lanier...821.2 653
 Folio manuscript: ballads and romances. 1868. 3 v.............................821.2 85
 Same: songs. 1867....................821.2 88
 Reliques of ancient English poetry. '45..821.2 84
Phillipps, *ed.* Book of English elegies. 1879...................................821.2 827
Pierson, *ed.* Society verse by American writers. 1887............................821.1 369
 Same; 'The merry muse,' enlarged edition...................................821.1 369A
Poems of religious sorrow, etc. 1863.........821 7
Poetry for the young. 1881..................*821 23
Powell, *ed.* Musa jocosa. 1894............821 46
Preble. History of patriotic songs of United States.......................................*in* 971 B-7
Primavera: poems [by L. Binyon, S. Phillips, A. S. Cripps, M. Ghose]. 1890..................................821.2 863
Putnam, *ed.* Singers and songs of the liberal faith. 1875..........................821.1 8
 Rhymes for you and me................*821 45
Rimbault, *ed.* Old ballads of the great frost. 1683-4.............................821.2 452
 Poetical tracts of 16th century..........821.2 449
Ritson, *ed.* Ancient popular poetry........821.2 94
 English songs, with airs. 1813. 3 v..821.2 491
 Robin Hood ballads. 1832. 2 v......923.2 320
 Scottish songs. 1869. 2 v..............784 15
Roberts, *ed.* Legendary ballads, England and Scotland............................821.2 63
Robertson, *ed.* The children of the poets..821 39
Robin Hood ballads. 2 v.................923.2 320
Robinson. The poet's birds. 1883.........598 65
Rossetti, *ed.* Humorous poems............821 35
Rowton, *ed.* Female poets of Great Britain. 1854..................................821.2 17
Sandys, *ed.* Festive songs, 16-17th centuries...................................821.2 466
Sargent, *ed.* Harper's cyclop. of poetry..‡821 B-2
Schelling, *ed.* Book of Elizabethan lyrics. 1895....................................821.2 974
Scott. Minstrelsy of the Scottish border. 1821. 3 v..........................821.2 100
Sharp, *ed.* American sonnets...........821.1 405
 Sonnets of this century. 1886........821.2 770
Sharp, *Mrs.,* *ed.* Sea-music. 1887......821 37
 Women poets of the Victorian era. 1891. ....821.2 872
 Women's voices: poems. 1887......821.2 826
Shortt. Lines and lays for wedding days..811 83
Simonds, *ed.* American song. 1894....821.1 484
Sladen, *ed.* Australian ballads and rhymes. 1888...................................821.2 880
 Australian poets. 1788-1888..........821.2 551
 Younger American poets, 1830-90....821.1 434

* Of interest to young readers. ‡ For reference.

Songs of Scotland....................784 B-12
Songs of Ireland.......................784 B-13
Spirituelles (unwritten songs of South Carolina). 1872-3....................784 Pam. 2
Stedman, *ed.* Victorian anthology. 1895.
....821.2 995A
Same..‡821.2 995
Stoddard, *ed.* The late English poets. 1867...821.2 22
Stone, *ed.* Ballads and poems, Burgoyne campaign. 1893......................821.1 462
Theta delta chi. Selected songs....821.1 Pam. 12
Songs of. 1869\..........................821.1 373
Thompson, *ed.* The humbler poets. '85...821.1 167
Thorpe, *ed.* Codex Exoniensis : Anglo-Saxon poetry ; with English translation and notes. 1842...............821.2 B-1
Three early English metrical romances. (Camden society). 1842................821.2 109
Contents: The anturs of Arther at the Tarnewathe-lan.—Sir Amadace.—The avowynge of King Arther, Sir Gawan, Sir Kaye, and Sir Bawdewyn of Bretan.
Todd, G. Eyre-, *ed.* Abbotsford series of the Scottish poets. 1891-6.
   Early Scottish poetry.................................821.2 986
   Mediæval Scottish poetry...........................821.2 987
   Scottish ballad poetry.................................821.2 988
   Scottish poetry of the 16th century..............821.2 989
   Scottish poetry of the 17th century..............821.2 990
   Scottish poetry of the 18th century. 2 v......821.2 991
Ancient Scots ballads.......................784 R-4
Tynan, *ed.* Irish love-songs. 1892......821.2 916
Universal songster. 3 v....................811 9
Veitch. History and poetry of the Scottish border................................941 24
Waddington, *ed.* English sonnets : living writers. 1881......................821.2 642
English sonnets : poets of the past. 1882...821.2 641
Waite, *ed.* Songs and poems of fairyland. 1888..821 38
Ward, A. L., *ed.* Surf and wave. 1883...811 69
Ward, T. H., *ed.* The English poets. 1880. 4 v..................................821.2 552
Warren, *ed.* Poets and poetry of Buffalo.
....821.1 487
Poets and poetry of Rochester........821.1 485
Poets and poetry of Syracuse..........821.1 486
Weber, *ed.* Metrical romances, 13-15th centuries. 1810. 3 v.
   V. 1. Introduction. Kyng Alisaunder.--Sir Cleges. Lay le Freine........................821.2 91
   V. 2. Richard Cœur de Lion. Lyfe of Ipomydon. Amis and Amiloun..................821.2 92
   V. 3. Proces of the seuyn sages. Octouian imperator Sir Amadas. The hunting of the hare.—Notes. Glossary.................................821.2 93
Weld, *ed.* Lives of the apostles..................821 12
Lives of the patriarchs.....................821 13
White, G., *ed.* Ballads and rondeaus. 1887..821 36

White, R. G., *ed.* Poetry of the civil war. 1866...821.1 11
Whittier, *ed.* Songs of three centuries......821 6
Wilkins. Political ballads. 17-18th centuries. 1860. 2v....................821.2 68
Williams. Poets and poetry of Ireland..821.2 166
Willmot, *ed.* English sacred poetry......821.2 265
Wilson, *ed.* Poets and poetry of Scotland. 1876. 2 v.............................821.2 18
Wright, K. A., *ed.* Dainty poems of the 19th century. 1895....................821 49
Wright, T., *ed.* Lyric poetry, time of Edward I....................................821.2 447
Old Christmas carols......................821.2 447
Political ballads of the commonwealth
....821.2 446
Political songs, John to Edward II. 1839...821.2 70
Songs and carols, 15th century........821.2 466
Yeats, *ed.* Book of Irish verse. 1895...821.2 978

COLLECTIONS : DRAMATIC.

(See also, Theater, in Part 3 of Finding List, p. 427.)

Bell, *ed.* British theatre. 1780. 14 v.
   V. 1. Hill: Zara.—Otway: Venice preserved.—Rowe; Jane Shore.—Hughes; Siege of Damascus.—Phillips: Distressed mother......................822.2 57
   V. 2. Vanbrugh: Provoked wife.—Jonson: Every man in his humor.—Farquhar: Beaux stratagem.—Congreve: Old bachelor.—Howard; Committee..822.2 58
   V. 3. Dryden: All for love.—Otway; Orphan.—Thompson: Tancred and Sigismunda —Lillo; George Barnwell.—Southern: Isabella......................822.2 59
   V. 4. Woods; Twins.—Dibdin; Deserter.—Foote: Commissary; Orators and patron.—Hawkesworth: Edgar and Emmeline.—Bates; Rival candidates.—Murphy; Three weeks after marriage.—Carey; Bon ton.—Milton; Comus.—Jackman; All the world's a stage.—Carey: Contrivances.—Cibber: Hob in the well.—Spirit of contradiction; by a gentleman of Cambridge...................................822.2 60
   V. 5. Rowe: Royal convert, and Lady Jane Grey.—Lee: Alexander the great ; Theodosius.—Miller: Mahomet.................................822.2 61
   V. 6. Fielding: Miser.—Vanbrugh and Cibber; Provoked husband.—Cibber: She would and she would not.—Centlivre: Busybody.—Farquhar: Sir H. Wildair..822 2 62
   V. 7. Hughes; Siege of Damascus. Hill: Merope.—Sophocles : Translation from Electra.—Mallet: Eurydice.—Glover ; Boadicea..........822.2 63
   V. 8. Farquhar ; Twin rivals. Wycherley : Country wife.—Shadwell: Fair Quaker of Deal.—Jonson ; Alchymist.—Cibber: Love's last shift......822 2 64
   V. 9. Thompson: Sophonisba - Beaumont and Fletcher: Philastre.—Crisp: Virginia.—Brooke: Gustavus Vasa.—Rowe; Ulysses........822.2 65
   V. 10. Jonson: Volpone.—Johnson: Country lasses. Vanbrugh : Mistake. — Shirley : Gamesters. Cibber; Lady's last stake....................822.2 66
   V. 11. Gay: Beggar's opera. Milton : Comus.—Wild. Jovial crew and accomplished maid.—Lionel and Clarissa...................................822.2 67

‡ For reference.

V. 12. Garrick: Guardian; High life below stairs; Lethe; Miss in her teens.—Murphy: Apprentice and upholsterer. — Ravenscraft: Antagonist.— Florizel and Perdita, altered from Shakespeare's 'Winter's tale.'— Fielding: Mock doctor. — Foote; Taste; Knights.—Colman: Deuce is in him.—Sultan.—Mendez; Chaplet...822.2 68
V. 13. (Wanting.)
V. 14. Murphy: Citizen.—Dodsley: Toy-shop.—O'Hara: Golden pippin.—Foote: Englishman in Paris; Englishman returned from Paris; Author.—Fielding: Intriguing chambermaid. — Sheridan: Brave Irishman.—Dodsley: Miller of Mansfield.—Bickerstaff: Padlock.—Garrick: Catharine and Petruchio; Cymon.—Reed: Register office...........822.2 70

Cincinnati. Public library. Catalog of dramas, etc. 1879...................16 B-5

Companion to the playhouse. 1764. 2 v...822.2 4

Crawfurd. English comic dramatists. 1883..822.2 258

Davidson. English mystery plays. '92...812 46

Dodsley, *ed.* Old English plays. 1874. 15 v.
V. 1. Interlude of four elements.—Calisto and Meliboea.— Everyman. — Hickscorner. — Heywood; Pardoner and the friar.—World and child.—God's promises.—The four P. P.—Thersites...............822.2 25
V. 2. Interlude of youth.—Wever: Lusty Juventus. — Jack Juggler. — Nice wanton. — History of Jacob and Esau.— Ingeland: Disobedient child.—Marriage of wit and science............................822.2 26
V. 3. New custom.—Udall: Ralph Roister Doister.—Gammer Gurton's needle.—Trial of treasure.—Fulwell: Like will to like..................................822.2 27
V. 4. Damon and Pithias.—Appius and Virginia. —Preston: Cambyses.—Misfortunes of Arthur.—Jeronimo 822.2 28
V. 5. Kyd: Spanish tragedy.—Cornelia.—Soliman and Perseda.—Life and death of Jack Straw........822.2 29
V. 6. Woodes: Conflict of conscience. — Rare triumphs of love and fortune.—Wilmot: Three ladies of London.—Three lords and three ladies of London.—Knack to know a knave..........................822.2 30
V. 7. Tancred and Gismunda.—Wounds of civil war.—Mucedorus.—Porter: Two angry women of Abington.—Look about you................................822.2 31
V. 8. Summer's last will and testament.—Downfall of Robert, earl of Huntington.—Death of Robert, earl of Huntington.—Contention between liberality and prodigality.—Grim, the collier of Croydon.....822.2 32
V. 9. How to choose a good wife from a bad.—Return from Parnassus.—Wily beguiled.—Lingua.—Miseries of enforced marriage.............................822.2 33
V. 10. The revenger's tragedy.—Dumb knight.—Merry devil of Edmonton.—Ram-alley.—Second maiden's tragedy.—Haughton: Englishmen for my money..822.2 34
V. 11. A woman is a weathercock.—Amends for ladies.—Green's tu quoque.—Albumazar.—The hog hath lost his pearl.—The heir...............................822.2 35
V. 12. The old cloak.—London chanticleers.—Shepherd's holiday; by Rutter. — True Trojans. — Berkley: Lost lady...822.2 36
V. 13. Match at midnight.—City nightcap.—City-match.—Queen of Arragon.—The antiquary.......822.2 37
V. 14. Rawlins: The rebellion.—Lust's dominion. — J. S.: Andromana.—Lady alimony.—Parson's wedding..822.2 38

V. 15. Elvira; or, The worst is not always true.—Falkland; Marriage night.—Adventures of five hours.—All mistaken.—Historia histrionica.........822.2 39
Dramas..812 8
Contents: Sheridan: The critic; The rivals; The school for scandal.—Ingomar. - Boucicault: London assurance.—Trowbridge: Neighbor Jackwood.—Massinger New way to pay old debts. Bulwer: Richelieu. Robertson: Society.—Taylor: Still waters run deep. To oblige Benson.

English prologues and epilogues. 1779. 4 v...822.2 7

French's minor drama. 39 v. in 13.
V. 1-3. The Irish attorney. Boots at the Swan.—How to pay the rent.—The loan of a lover.—The dead shot.—His last legs.—The invisible prince.—The golden farmer.—Pride of the market.—Used up.—The Irish tutor.—The barrack room.—Luke the laborer.—Beauty and the beast.—Saint Patrick's eve. —Captain of the watch.—The secret.—White horse of the peppers.—The Jacobite.—The bottle.—Box and Cox.—Bamboozling.—Widow's victim.—Robert Macaire..812 31
V. 4-6. Secret service.—Omnibus.—Irish lion.—Maid of Croissy.—The old guard.—Raising the wind.—Slasher and crasher.—Naval engagements. —Cockneys in California.—Who speaks first?—Bombastes furioso.—Macbeth travestie.—Irish ambassador.—Delicate ground.—The weathercock.—All that glitters is not gold.—Grimshaw, Bagshaw and Bradshaw.—Rough diamond.—Bloomer costume.—Two Bonnycastles.—Born to good luck.—Kiss in the dark. —'Twould puzzle a conjurer.—Kill or cure........812 32
V. 7-9. Box and Cox married and settled.—Saint Cupid.—Go-to-bed Tom.—The lawyers.—Jack Sheppard.—The Toodles.—The mobcap.—Ladies beware. —Morning call.—Popping the question.—Deaf as a post.—New footman.—Pleasant neighbor.—Paddy the piper.—Brian O'Linn.—Irish assurance.—Temptation. — Paddy Carey. — Two Gregories. — King Charming. — Po-ca-hon-tas. — Clockmaker's hat. —Married rake.—Love and murder..........................812 33
V. 10-12. Ireland and America.—Pretty piece of business.—Irish broom-maker.—To Paris and back for five pounds.—That blessed baby.—Our gal.—Swiss cottage.—Young widow.—O'Flannigan and the fairies.—Irish post.—My neighbor's wife.—Irish tiger.—P. P.; or, Man and tiger.—To oblige Benson. —State secrets. — Irish Yankee. — A good fellow. —Cherry and Fair Star.—Gale Breezely.—Our Jemimy. —Miller's maid.—Awkward arrival.—Crossing the line.—Conjugal lesson......................................812 34
V. 13-15. My wife's mirror.—Life in New York.—Middy ashore. — Crown prince. — Two queens. —Thumping legacy.—Unfinished gentleman.—House dog.—The demon lover.—Matrimony.—In and out of place.—I dine with my mother.—Hi-a-wa-tha.—Andy Blake.—Love in '76.—Romance under difficulties.—One coat for two suits.—A decided case.—Daughter.— No.— Coroner's inquisition.— Love in humble life.—Family jars.—Personation..........812 35
V. 16-18. Children in the wood.—Winning a husband.—Day after the fair.—Make your wills. — Rendezvous.—My wife's husband.—Monsieur Tonson.—Illustrious stranger.—Mischief-making.-A live woman in the mines.—The corsair. — Shylock.—Spoiled child.—Evil eye.—Nothing to nurse.—Wanted: a widow.—Lottery ticket.—Fortune's frolic is he jealous.—Married bachelor.—Husband at sight.—Irishman in London.— Animal magnetism.—Highways and by-ways...812 36

V. 19-21. Columbus.— Harlequin bluebeard.— Ladies at home.—Phenomenon in a smock frock.— Comedy and tragedy.—Opposite neighbors.—Dutchman's ghost.—Persecuted Dutchman.— Musard ball. —Great tragic revival.— High, low, jack, and the game.—A gentleman from Ireland.—Tom and Jerry, —Village lawyer,—Captain's not a-miss.—Amateurs and actors.—Promotion.— A fascinating individual. —Mrs. Caudle.—Shakespeare's dream.—Neptune's defeat.—Lady of the bedchamber.—Irish widow......812 37

V. 22-24. Yankee peddler.— Hiram Hireout.— Double-bedded room.—The drama defended.—Vermont wool dealer.—Ebenezer Venture.—Principles from character.—Lady of the lake.—Mad dogs.— Barney the baron.— Swiss swains.— Bachelor's bedroom.— A Roland for an Oliver.— More blunders than one.-Dumb belle.—Limerick boy.—Nature and philosophy. — Teddy the tiler. —Spectre bridegroom. — Matteo Falcone.— Jenny Lind.—Two Buzzards.—Happy man.—Betsy Baker............812 38

V. 25-27. Number 1 round the corner.—Teddy Roe. —Object of interest. — My fellow clerk. — Bengal tiger.—Laughing hyena.—The victor vanquished. —Our wife.—My husband's mirror.—Yankee land. —Nora Creina.—Good for nothing.—The first night. —The Eton boy.—Wandering minstrel.—Wanted; 1,000 milliners.—Poor Pillicoddy.—The mummy.— Don't forget your opera glasses.— Love in livery.— Antony and Cleopatra.— Trying it on.— Stage struck Yankee.—Young wife and old umbrella............812 39

V. 28-30. Crinoline.—A family failing.—Adopted child.—Turned heads.—A match in the dark.— Advice to husbands. — Siamese twins. — Sent to the tower.— Somebody else.— Ladies' battle.— Art of acting.—The lady of the lions.—The rights of man. —My husband's ghost.—Two can play at that game. —Fighting by proxy.—Unprotected female.—Pet of the petticoats. — Forty and fifty.— Who stole the pocket-book.—My son Diana.—Unwarrantable intrusion.—Mr. and Mrs. White.—A quiet family............812 40

V. 31-33. Cool as cucumber.—Sudden thoughts. —Jumbo Jum.—A blighted being.—Little toddlekins.— A lover by proxy.— Maid with the milking pail.—Perplexing predicament. Doctor Dilworth.— Out to nurse.— A lucky hit.— The dowager.— Metamora. — Dreams of delusion.— The shaker lovers. —Ticklish times.— Twenty minutes with a tiger. —Miralda; or, The justice of Tacon. A soldier's courtship.—Servants by legacy.—Dying for love.— Alarming sacrifice.— Valet de sham.— Nicholas Nickleby............812 41

V. 34-36. The last of the pigtails.— King René's daughter. The grotto nymph.—A devilish good joke. —A twice told tale.—Pas de fascination.— Revolutionary soldier.— A man without a head. -The olio.— The trumpeter's daughter.— Seeing Warren.—Green Mountain boy. - That nose.—Tom Noddy's secret.— Shocking events.— A regular fix.— Dick Turpin.— Young scamp.--Young actress. Call at No. 1-7. One touch of nature. Two b'hoys............812 42

V 37-39. All the world's a stage.- Quash; or, Nigger practice. Turn him out.— Pretty girls of Stillberg.—Angel of the attic. Circumstances alter cases.— Katty O'Sheal.—Supper in Dixie Ici on parle Français. Who killed cock robin"—Declaration of independence.— Heads or tails. Obstinate family My Aunt.—That rascal Pat. Don Paddy de Bazan. Too much for good nature. Cure for the fidgets............812 43

French's standard drama. 45 v. in 23.

V. 3-4. Colman, jr.: Poor gentleman, — Shakespeare: Hamlet; Othello; Two gentlemen of Verona. —Payne: Charles II.—Otway: Venice preserved.— Sheridan: Pizarro; Rivals.—Knowles: Love-chase; Virginius. — Morton ; Send me five shillings. — J. White: King of the commons.—Boucicault: London assurance.—Jerrold; Rent-day. — Colman: Jealous wife.—Bayly: Perfection............812 9

V. 5-6. Massinger: New way to pay old debts.— Lovell: Look before you leap.—Shakespeare; King John; Romeo and Juliet.—Bernard: Nervous man and the man of nerve.—Banim: Damon and Pythias. —Colman: Clandestine marriage.— Knowles ; William Tell; Bridal.—Mrs. C. Kemble: Day after the wedding.—Morton: Speed the plough.—J. White; Feudal times.—Planché: Charles XII; Faint heart never won fair lady; Follies of a night.—Colman, jr.: Iron chest............812 10

V. 7-8.—Holcroft: Road to ruin.— Shakespeare; Macbeth; Much ado about nothing; Twelfth night; Merchant of Venice.—Bell: Temper.—Sheil; Evadne. —Maturin: Bertram.—Sheridan; Duenna; Critic.— Shiel: Apostate.—Payne; Brutus.—Poole: Simpson & Co.—Boucicault: Old heads and young hearts.— Colman, jr.; Mountaineers. — Murphy: Three weeks after marriage............812 11

V. 9-10. Knowles: Love.--Shakespeare: As you like it; Henry IV; King Lear; Henry VIII.— Beaumont and Fletcher: Elder brother. — Byron: Werner. — Griffin: Gisippus. — Morton: Town and country.— Colman, jr.: Blue devils. — Poole: Married and single; Paul Pry. — Terry: Guy Mannering.— Renny: Sweet-hearts and wives.— Barnett: Serious family.—Goldsmith: She stoops to conquer............812 12

V. 11-12. Shakespeare: Julius Cæsar.— Coyne: Vicar of Wakefield.—Buckstone: Leap year.—Jerrold: Catspaw. — Bernard: Passing cloud. — W. H. Smith: Drunkard.— Pocock: Rob Roy Macgregor.— Lillo: George Barnwell.— Lovell; Ingomar.—Morton: Sketches in India.— Lacy: Two friends.— Rowe; Jane Shore.—Lemon: Corsican brothers; Grangé and Montépin; Mind your own business.—T. and J. M. Morton: Writing on the wall.— Colman, jr.; Heir at law............812 13

V. 13-14. Cherry: Soldier's daughter.— Home: Douglas.—Simpson: Marco Spada.—Pardey: Nature's nobleman.— Byron: Sardanapalus, king of Assyria.—Wilkins: Civilization.—Schiller: Robbers. —Shakespeare: Katherine and Petruchio; Midsummer-night's dream.—Brougham: Game of love.— Roberston: Ernestine.— Stirling: Rag-picker of Paris.— Fitzball: Flying Dutchman.—Sol. Smith: Hypocrite. —Payne: Therese, the orphan of Geneva.—La tour de Nesle; or, The chamber of death; from Hugo......812 14

V. 15-16. Amherst: Ireland as it is.—Sea of ice.— Wilks: Seven clerks. - Brougham: Game of life ; Romance and reality; Dombey and son.— Forty thieves.—Knowles: Brian Boroihme.— Booth: Ugalino,—Shakespeare: Tempest.— Fitzball: Pilot. — Jones: Carpenter of Rouen.—Taylor and Reade: King's rival.—Harris: Little treasure.—Parents and guardians.—Moncrieff: Jewess............812 15

V. 17-18. Dumas: Camille.—Buckstone: Married life; Henriette, the forsaken.—Wilks: Wenlock of Wenlock.—Lynch: Rose of Ettrick Vale.—Brougham; David Copperfield; Night and morning.— Stirling: Aline. — Pauline. — Dimond: Æthiop.— Rice : Three guardsmen.— Fitzball ; Tom Cringle. Courtney: Eustache Baudin.— Medina: Ernest Maltravers.—Barnet: Bold dragoons......812 16

V 19-20. Brougham; Dred; Red mask.—Medina: Last days of Pompeii.—Fitzball: Esmeralda; Jonathan Bradford. —Peter Wilkins.—Wilks: Ben, the boatswain. — T. Taylor; Retribution.—Plunkett: Minerali. — Haines; French spy. — Wept of Wishton-wish. —Bernard; Evil genius.—Johnstone; Ben Bolt; Sailor of France.— Boucicault: Grimaldi. — Mrs. Inchbald; Wedding day..................812 17

V. 21-22. Brougham; All's fair in love; Gunmaker of Moscow; Franklin.—Fitzball; Hofer.—Bateman: Self.—Boucicault; Phantom. — Gayler: Love of a prince; Son of the night.—Lover: Rory O'More.— Howe; Golden eagle.—Mitford; Rienzi.—Dimond: Broken sword.— Burke; Rip Van Winkle.—Buckstone: Isabelle.—Dibdin: Heart of Midlothian........812 18

V. 23-24. À Beckett; Angelo. — Ball ; Floating beacon.—Calcraft; Bride of Lammermoor.—Moncrieff: Cataract of the Ganges.— Almar; Robber of the Rhine.—Morton; School of reform.—Wandering boys. — Milner; Mazeppa. — Wilkins; Young New York.—Taylor; Victims.—Goodrich and Warden: Romance after marriage.—Planché; Brigand.—Poor of New York.—Jerrold: Ambrose Gwinnett.—Lewis: Raymond and Agnes.—Milner; Gambler's fate......812 19

V. 25-26. Fitzball; Father and son; Innkeeper of Abbeville.—Milner: Massaniello.— Rede; Sixteen string Jack; Skeleton witness.—Shannon; Youthful queen.—Pocock: The miller and his men.—Aladdin. —Oxenford: Adrienne, the actress.— Soane: Undine. —Boucicault; Jesse Brown.—Archer: Asmodeus.— English; Mormons.—Blanche of Brandywine.— Maturin; Viola.—Deseret deserted........................812 20

V. 27-28. Americans in Paris.—Buckstone; Victorine.—Haines; Wizard of the wave.—Lewis; Castle spectre. — Tayleure; Horseshoe Robinson. — *Mrs.* Ritchie; Armand.—Glance at New York. — Farquhar; Inconstant.— Aiken: Uncle Tom's cabin.— Rede; Guide to the stage.—Wallack; Veteran.— Brougham; Miller of New Jersey; Art and artifice. —Brougham and Goodrich: Dark hour before dawn. —L. Keene; Midsummer-night's dream..................812 21

V. 29-30. Feuillet; Romance of a poor young man.— Swayze: Ossawattomie Brown. — Boucicault; Pope of Rome; Pauvrette; Knight of Arva, West end.— Almar; Oliver Twist.— Lucas: Man with the iron mask.—Jones: Moll Pitcher.— Jerrold: Black-eyed Susan.—Selby; Satan in Paris.—Saunders: Rosina Meadows.—Hill; Six degrees of crime.— Dimond: Lady and the devil.—Lee; Avenger.— Taylor and Reade; Masks and faces......................................812 22

V. 31-32. Shakespeare: Merry wives of Windsor. —Miles: Mary's birthday.—Pilgrim: Shandy Maguire. — O'Keefe; Wild oats. — Wilks: Michael Erle.— Haines: Idiot witness.—Boucicault; Willow copse. —Jones: People's lawyer; Surgeon of Paris.—Tayleure: Boy martyrs.— Weston: Lucretia Borgia.— Marston; Patrician's daughter.—Hill: Shoemaker of Toulouse.—Fitzball: Momentous question.—Robson: Love and loyalty.—Pocock: Robber's wife............812 23

V. 33-34. Farrell: Dumb girl of Genoa.—Buckstone: Wreck ashore; Rural felicity; Dream at sea. —Payne: Clari,— Barrymore: Wallace.— Cunningham; Madelaine. — Johnson: Fireman. — Planché: Grist to the mill.—Taylor and Reade; Two loves and a life.—Marston; Anne Blake.—Beazley; Steward.—Jones: Captain Kyd.—Medina: Nick of the woods. — Selby: Marble heart. — Simpson: Second love..812 24

V. 35-36. Buckstone: Breach of promise; Scholar. —Colman, *jr.*: Review.—Dibdin; Lady of the Lake. — Taylor; Still waters run deep; Helping hand.—Faust and Marguerite — Pitt; Last man — Cowley; Belle's stratagem. — Salmon Old and young.— Wilks: Raffaelle the reprobate.—Williams Ruth Oakley. — Howe; British slave.—Marston Life's ransom.—Webster; Giralda.—Courtney, Time tries all..812 25

V. 37-38. Kenney; Ella Rosenberg.—Walker Warlock of the glen.—Somerset: Zelina.—Leland. Beatrice.—Trowbridge, Neighbor Jackwood.—Centlivre; Wonder.—Pilgrim; Robert Emmet.—Buckstone; Green bushes; Flowers of the forest.—Hardwicke: Bachelor of arts. — Midnight banquet. — Falconer: Husband of an hour. —Shakespeare; Love's labour's lost. — Dalrymple: Nuad queen.— Leland: Caprice.— Glover; Cradle of liberty..........................812 26

V. 39-40. Townsend; Lost ship.—Dance; Country squire. —Coyne; Fraud and its victims; Love-knot. —Bannister; Putnam, the iron son of '76. —Matidox; King and deserter. —Clapp; La fiammina. —Marston: Hard struggle.— Lemon; Gwinnette Vaughan. —Planché: Lavater, the physiognomist. — Lewes ; Noble heart.— Shakespeare: Coriolanus; Winter's tale.—Pilgrim: Eveleen Wilson.—Dibdin; Ivanhoe. —Jonathan in England..812 27

V. 41-42. Saunders: Pirate's legacy. — Almar: Charcoal burner.—Lewis: Adelgitha.—Miles: Señor Valiente. — Woodworth: Forest Rose. — Bourgeois and Feval; Duke's daughter.—Phillips: Camilla's husband.—Marston: Pure gold.—Taylor: Ticket-of-leave man; Fool's revenge. —Clarke; O'Neal the great; Pirate of the isles.—Floyd; Handy-Andy.— Waldauer; Fanchon, the cricket; Little barefoot.— Pilgrim: Wild Irish girl..812 28

V. 43-44.—Mitchell: Pearl of Savoy.—Webster: Dead heart.—Pratt: Ten nights in a bar room.— Rayner; Dumb boy of Manchester. — Webb: Belphegor, the mountebank.—Smith: Cricket on the hearth.—Planché: Printer's devil.—Craven: Meg's diversion; Chimney corner.—Pitt; Drunkard's doom. —Jerrold: Fifteen years of a drunkard's life.—Falconer: Peep o' Day. — Leguel: Identity.— Coyne: Everybody's friend.—Shakespeare: Hamlet.—Tally Rhand: Guttle and Gulpit..812 29

V. 45. Anicetus; General Grant. — Kathleen Mavourneen.—Robinson; Nick Whiffles.—Allen: Fruits of the wine cup.—Taylor; Drunkard's warning. Seymour: Temperance doctor. — Hardy: Widow Freeheart.—Walcot: Cup and the lip.—C. W. S.: Everyday life..812 30

Halliwell-Phillipps,ed. Ludus Coventriæ: mysteries, Coventry, feast of Corpus Christi. 1841.............................822.2 71

Hase. Miracle plays, etc. 1880...............812 6

Hawkins, ed. Origin of English drama. 1773. 3 v.

V. 1. Candlemas day. — Every-man.— Hyckescorner. — Lusty Juventus. — Gammer Gurton's needle.— Preston: Cambises, king of Percia......822.2 22

V. 2. Kyd: Spanish tragedy.—Peele: Love of King David and fair Bathsabe, with tragedy of Absalom.— Soliman and Perseda (attributed to Kyd).—Buckhurst and Norton: Ferrex and Porrex; or, Gorboduc...822 2 23

V. 3. Ariosto: Supposes. — Dekker: Satiro-Mastix.—Return from Parnassus.—Wily beguiled.822 2 2

Inchbald, ed. British theatre. 12 v.

V. 1. Colman: Inkle and Varico.— Colman: Jealous wife.—Massinger: New way to pay old debts. — Shakespeare: Measure for measure. — Moore; The gamester..822 2 45

V. 2. Sheridan: The duenna. — Shakespeare. Othello; Hamlet. — Kotzebue: Lovers' vows. — Cowley: The belle's stratagem.................822.2 46

V. 3. Wycherly and Garrick: The country girl. —Shakespeare: Merry wives of Windsor; King Henry V.— Murphy: Know your own mind.— Morton: Speed the plough....................822.2 47

V. 4. Home: Douglas.—Centlivre: The busy body.—Murphy: All in the wrong.—Southern: Oroonoko.— Colman and Garrick: Clandestine marriage.............................. 822.2 48

V. 5. Cumberland: The Jew.— Lillo: George Barnwell.— Lee: Rival queens. — Shakespeare: King Lear.— Lillo: Fatal curiosity..............822.2 49

V. 6. Beaumont and Fletcher: Rule a wife and have a wife; The chances.— Massinger: New way to pay old debts.—Lee: Rival queens.—Dryden: All for love.....................................822.2 50

V. 7. Morton: Cure for the heart-ache.—Shakespeare: King John; Romeo and Juliet; Julius Cæsar.—Holcroft: Deserted daughter.............822.2 51

V. 8. Shakespeare: King Henry VIII; King Richard III; Twelfth night; Much ado about nothing.—Cowley: Bold stroke for a husband....822.2 52

V. 9. Southern: Isabella.— Thomson: Tancred and Sigismunda.— Centlivre: Bold stroke for a wife.—Holcroft: Road to ruin.—Farquhar: Beaux stratagem....................................822.2 53

V. 10. Shakespeare: The tempest. — Hughes: Siege of Damascus.—Brown: Barbarossa.—Hoadly: Suspicious husband.—Baillie: De Monfort.......822.2 54

V. 11. Morton: Way to get married.— Tobin: The honey moon.—Shakespeare: King Henry IV, pt. 1.—Cumberland: The brothers.—Bickerstaff: Maid of the mill..............................822.2 55

V. 12. Racine: Distressed mother.—Miller: Mahomet. — Shakespeare: Cymbeline; Comedy of errors.—Otway: Venice preserved................822.2 56

Keltie, *ed.* British dramatists. 1870.....822.2 40
Contents: Introductory essay.—Lilly: Alexander and Campaspe.— Peele: Love of King David and fair Bethsabe.— Greene: Friar Bacon and friar Bungay.—Marlowe: Edward II; Dr. Faustus.—Jonson: Alchemist; Epicœne; Every man in his humour.—Beaumont and Fletcher: Philaster; A king and no king; Knight of the burning pestle. — Webster: Duchess of Malfi.— Marston: Antonio and Mellida; Antonio's revenge.—Massinger: Virgin martyr; Duke of Milan; New way to pay old debts.—Ford: Lady's trial.—Heywood: Woman killed with kindness.—Shirley: The traitor; The brothers.

Lamb, *ed.* Specimens of dramatic poets. 1854..822.2 82

List of miracle plays, etc. (Boston public library bulletin, v. 4)..................17 B-14

Morley, *ed.* English plays. 1879........822.2 B-1

New York drama. 10 v.
V. 1. Bulwer: Lady of Lyons; Richelieu. — Taylor: To oblige Benson.—Buckstone: A kiss in the dark. Boucicault: London assurance. — Whitty: My husband's secret.—Robinson; Mr. Joffin's hatchkey. - Coyne: An unprotected female.—Selby: The married rake—Smith, S. T.: The happy pair. Payne Brutus. - Dance: Delicate ground. Barry: Persecuted Dutchman. Shakespeare: Julius Cæsar - Dayean: The plague of my life. - Maltby: For better or worse......812 B-1

V. 2. Bulwer: Money. Becher: A crimeless criminal, and My uncle's suit. Webster: I'll tell your wife.- Talfourd: Ion. Merivale: A husband in clover.—Robertson: Caste.—Morton: Slasher and Crasher.—Hay: A lame excuse.—Sheridan: The school for scandal.—Bunn: My neighbor's wife.— Mack: The darkest hour.—Goldsmith: She stoops to conquer.—Williams: My turn next. —Marry in haste and repent at leisure.—Jerrold: The rent-day.— Edwardes and Cullerne: Used up..812 B-2

V. 3. Home: Douglas.—Planché: Captain of the watch, and Follies of a night.—The obstinate family.—Colman, *jr.*: The iron chest.—Buckstone: Good for nothing.—Love and rain.—S. T. Smith: My uncle's will, and Which is which?—Selby: Satan in Paris.—Roberts: The absent man.—Suter: Two gentlemen in a fix, and Compatibility of temper.— Dumanoix and Dennery: Don Cæsar de Bazan.— Bernard: His last legs.—Addison: Locked in with a lady.—Shakespeare: Hamlet.—Clements: Two to one..................................812 B-3

V. 4. Payne: Charles the second.—Burke: Rip Van Winkle.—Meadow: His own enemy.—Oxenford: The two orphans.—Cheltnam: A fairy's father,—Lacy: A silent woman.—Knowles: The love-chase.—Claridge and Soutar: The fast coach. —Lucas: Browne the martyr.—Robertson: Home, and David Garrick.—Gilbert: The palace of truth. —Kemble: Personation.— Morton: Woodcock's little game.—Barnett: Yankee peddler.—Dumas, *fils*: Camille.—Taming a tiger.—Townsend: The blow in the dark...................................812 B-4

V. 5. Gilbert: Charity, and Trial by jury.—Kenney: Raising the wind.—Wooler: Plots for petticoats.—Knowles: Virginius.—Phipps: My very last proposal.—Hay: Lodgers and dodgers.— Sheridan: The rivals.—Browne: A lucky sixpence.—Dubourg: Under an umbrella.— Lovell: Love's sacrifice.—Suter: A pleasant evening.— Frou-Frou.— A night of suspense.—Sam Weller's visit to his mother-in-law.—Otway: Venice preserved.—Morton: Lend me five shillings, and Box and Cox.....................................812 B-5

V. 6. Knowles: The wife.— Armstrong: Blighted love.—Suter: John Wopps.—Hugo: Ruy Blas.— Morton: My wife's bonnet.—Dance: Who speaks first?— Archer: Asmodeus.— Matthews: Little Toddlekins.—Scott: The last Illy. — Sheridan: Pizarro.—Stirling: The young scamp.—Grover: That rascal Pat.—Münch-Bellinghausen: Ingomar. —Williams: Tweedleton's tail coat.—Paul: Locked out.—Robertson: School.—Nuitter and Derley: A cup of tea.—Walton: Trott's troubles............812 B-6

V. 7. Rae: Fame.—Williams: A cure for the fidgets.— Knowles: Love.—Milman: Fazio.—Morton: A pretty piece of business.—The old guard.— Byron: Partners for life.—Buckstone: The dead shot.—Field: Extremes meet.—Tobin: The honeymoon.—Smith, S.T.: Cut off with a shilling.—Phipps: Pretty predicament.— Taylor: The fool's revenge. —Morton: A regular fix.—Maltby: Should this meet the eye. — Augier: Les Fourchambault. — Ryan: One too many.—Reeve: Obliging a friend...812 B-7

V. 8. Robertson: Ours.—Neville: The little vixens.—Dance: Kill or cure.—Cheltnham: Deborah.—Moncrieff: Monsieur Tonson.—Durivage: The stage-struck Yankee.—Colman: The jealous wife. Yates and Harrington: A night at Notting Hill. Emson: Bumble's courtship.—Wood: East Lynne.— Suter: A quiet family.—The Toodles.— Knowles: The hunchback.—Hervey: Only a flirtation. - Mack: The masquerade.—Sheil: Evadne Taylor: A blighted being.—Brough and Halliday: Going to the dogs..........................812 B-8

V. 9. O'Keefe: Wild oats.—Lemon: Go to Putney, and Gertrude's money box.—Picking up the pieces.—Massinger: A new way to pay old debts.—Maltby: Your vote and interest.—Mitford: Rienzi.—Gilbert: Sweethearts. Jerrold: Cool as a cucumber.—Edwardes: Heroes.—Planché: A peculiar position.—Stirling: Family pictures.—Shakespeare: Coriolanus.—Roberts: Forty winks.—Soutar: Sold again.—Robertson: Society.—Monroe: That blessed baby.—His novice............812 B-9
V. 10. Gilbert: Pygmalion and Galatea.—Floyd: Handy Andy.—Morton: A day's fishing.—Dumas: Gabrielle de Belle Isle.—Maltby: Mabel's holiday.—Planché: Pride of the market.—Scott: Kenilworth; adapted by Dibden.—Suter: The lost child.—Dickens and Collins: No thoroughfare.—Lancaster: The manager's daughter.—Wooler: A winning hazard.—Taylor: Henry Dunbar.—Morton: The sentinel, and Master Jones' birthday.—Byron: The Lancashire lass.—Dubois: Deeds of dreadful note..812 B-10

Pollard. English miracle plays, etc. '95..822.2 334
  Contents: Introduction.—York play: The barkers.—Chester plays: 1, Noah's flood; 2, The sacrifice of Isaac.—Towneley play: Secunda pastorum.—Coventry play: The salutation and conception.—Mary Magdalene.—The castell of perseverance.—Everyman.—Interlude of the four elements.—Skelton's 'Magnyfycence.'—Heywood's 'The pardoner and the frere.—Thersytes.—Bale's 'King John.'— Appendix: Mysterium resurrectionis D. N. Jhesu Christi; Ludus super Iconia Sancti Nicholai; The harrowing of hell; Brome play of Abraham and Isaac.—Notes.—Index.

Select collection of English plays. 1759..822.2 310
  Contents: V. 2. Dryden: The Indian emperor; All for love.— Lee: Theodosius.—Hill: King Henry V.—Southern: Oroonoko.

Webster, *ed.* Acting national drama. 1837.
  4 v.
  V. 1. Knowles: The bridal (Beaumont and Fletcher's 'Maid's tragedy').—Planché; Two Figaros.—Coyne: Queer subject.—Webster: Modern Orpheus.—Fitzball: Walter Tyrrel.—Webster: My young wife and my old umbrella.—Dance: Country squire.—Morton: Sentinel.—Planché: Peculiar position.— Blink: Tiger at large.— Peake: Middle temple.—Planché: Riquet with the tuft................822.2 41
  V. 2. Power: Saint Patrick's eve.—Peake: Quarter to nine; Blanche of Jersey; Bottle imp.—Planché: Court favour.—Morton: The spitfire.—Lover: Rory O'More.—Dance: Advice gratis.—Morton: The original; Barbers of Bassora.—Mathews: Why did you die?—Coyne: Valsha.—Planché: Bengal tiger.822.2 42
  V. 3. Planché and Dance: Puss in boots.—Mathews: Ringdoves; Black domino.—Buckstone: Our Mary Ann; Shocking events.—Bayly: The culprit; The Spitalfields weaver.—Reynolds: Confounded foreigners.—Selby: Dancing barber; Rifle brigade.—Coyne: All for love.—Haines: Angeline. Mathews: Truth..822.2 43
  V. 4. Bayly: You can't marry your grandmother.—Peake: Spring lock; The Meltonians.—Selby: Valet de Sham.—Hall: Groves of Blarney.—Planché: Hasty conclusion.—Buckstone: Weak points.—Dance: Naval engagements.—Bayly: British legion; One hour.—Buckstone: Irish lion.—Peake: Lying in ordinary..822.2 44

Wright, *ed.* Chester plays: mysteries.
  1843-7. 2 v....................................822.2 72

AMATEUR DRAMAS AND DIALOGUES.

American school dialogue book. 1875..792.1 17
Baker. Amateur dramas. 1868............792.1 11
  A baker's dozen [dialogues]..............792.1 24
  Drawing room stage. 1873..................792.1 2
  Exhibition drama. 1875......................792.1 20
  Globe dramas. 1885...........................792.1 26
  Handy dramas. 1877.........................792.1 21
  Social stage. 1875.............................792.1 23
Barmby. Plays for young people. 1879...792.1 31
Bell, *Mrs.* H. Fairy tale plays, and how
  to act them. 1896............................792.1 68
  Petit théâtre des enfants. 1888............792.1 43
Besant *and* **Pollock.** The charm, etc.
  1896...792.1 70
Bowman. Charade dramas. 1855........792.1 33
Brewster *and* **Scribner.** Parlor varieties;
  pt. 2. 1886......................................792.1 41
Burnham *and* **Root.** Christmas vision:
  cantata. 1891...................................792.1 63
  Santa Claus and company; cantata.
  1889...792.1 66
  Santa Claus' mistake: a cantata. '85...792.1 62
  Waif's Christmas: a cantata. 1886....792.1 60
Butterworth *and* **Murray.** The new Santa
  Claus: a cantata. 1888....................792.1 59
Clarke. Puck's pranks......................792.1 Pam. 2
Crosby *and* **Doane.** Wise men from the
  east: a cantata. 1893........................792.1 58
Denton. Little people's dialogues. 1893...792.1 50
Detmers. An old-time tea-party. 1896.
  ....792.1 Pam. 3
Dickens. Dialogues from; by Fette. 2v...792.1 37
Dramatic leaflets...............................815.2 73
Easy entertainments for young people. '93..792.1 54
Fitzgerald. Proverbs and comediettas.
  1869..792.1 3
Fowle. Parlor dramas. 1856...............792.1 1
Fraser. Delicate question...................792.1 77
  Merry cobbler...................................792.1 72
  Modern Ananias...............................792.1 73
  'Twixt love and money......................792.1 74
Frost. Humorous and exhibition dialogues.
  1870..792.1 15
Gabriel. Jolly Christmas: a cantata. '92..792.1 64
Griffith. School and parlor comedies.
  1894..792.1 53
Harrison. Six plays for children. 1884...792.1 40
  Theatricals and tableaux. 1882........792.1 39
Hart. Dorothy's dream: a cantata. '94..792.1 61
Healy. The home theatre. 1872............792.1 7
Hopkins. Natural history plays, dialogues,
  and recitations. 1884.......................792.1 19
Hosea *and* **Doane.** Capture of Santa
  Claus. 1894....................................792.1 67
How to 'make up.' 1877.....................792.1 30

James. What shall we act? 1882............792.1 35
Jaquith. Ma Dusenberry and her gearls...792.1 76
    Parson Poor's donation party............792.1 75
Keating. Cinderella............792.1 Pam. 5
Kohlbrand *and* Ross. Santa Claus' mistake. 1893............792.1 65
MacDonald, *Mrs.* Chamber dramas for children. 1870............792.1 5
    Contents: Cinderella.—Beauty and the beast.—Snowdrop.—The Tetterbys.
Matthews, *ed.* Comedies for amateur acting. 1880............792.1 32
Merriman. Maud Muller: burlesque.....792.1 71
Miller. Historical tableaux. 1888............792.1 22
New charades, etc............792.1 14
Nugent. Charades for acting............792.1 34
Phelps. Dramatic stories. 1874............792.1 13
Pollock. Amateur theatricals. 1879............792.1 4
Prevost. Terra-cotta plays. 1888............792.1 42
    Contents: The sleeping beauty.—The white cat.—Jack and the beanstalk.—Snowdrop and the seven dwarfs.
Pritchard. Choice dialogues. 1896............792.1 69
Prompt book. 1890-91............792.1 Pam. 1
Rook. Young folks' entertainments. '95...792.1 48
Scott, *ed.* Drawing-room plays. 1870...792.1 25
Shinn. Stories for the happy days of Christmas time. 1879............792.1 44
Shoemaker, C. C., *ed.* Holiday entertainments. 1894............792.1 49
    Humorous dialogues and dramas. '81...792.1 51
    Young folks' dialogues. 1895............792.1 47
Shoemaker, *Mrs.* J. W., *ed.* Choice dialogues. 1895............792.1 46
    Classic dialogues and dramas. 1893...792.1 52
Simpson. Drawing-room duologues. '94...792.1 45
Smith. Family theatricals............792.1 36
Steele. Drawing-room plays, etc. 1870....792.1 6
Sunday-school and church entertainments. 1895............792.1 55
T., W. L. Six acting charades. 1850...792.1 33
Tableaux, charades and pantomimes. 1895............792.1 56
Venable. Amateur actor. 1874............792.1 12
Williamson *and* Pierce. Palace of Santa Claus: a cantata. 1895............792.1 57

COLLECTIONS: ORATORICAL AND ELOCUTIONARY.

Anstey. Mr. Punch's young reciter. '92...815.2 83
Baker, *ed.* Reading club............815.2 31
Baldwin, *ed.* Harper's school speaker.
    v. 2: Graded selections. 1891............815.2 82
Baxter. Helper in school entertainments. 1890............815.2 92
Bell, D. C. Ladies' elocutionist. 1873....815.2 13
Bell, D. C. *and* A. M., *eds.* Junior elocutionist. 1873............815.2 4
Benedict. Pieces to speak. 1893............815.2 84
Benjamin, *ed.* May-time. 1889............815.2 80
Browne, *ed.* British Cicero. 1808. 3 v...825.2 4
Campbell *and* Root, *eds.* Columbian speaker. 1874............815.2 9
Carpenter, J. E., *ed.* Popular readings. 5 v............815.2 14
    Public school speaker............815.2 3
Carpenter, S. C., *ed.* Select American speeches. 1815. 2 v............825.1 2
Castle, *ed.* School entertainments. 1887. nos. 1-2............815.2 110
Cathcart, *ed.* Literary reader. 1874.....815.2 26
Chambers' readings. 1872............815.2 19
Coates, *ed.* Best authors. 1876............815.2 27
Cumnock, *ed.* Choice readings. 1878...815.2 30
Dodge *and* Burke, *eds.* Clark prize book [Hamilton college]. 1894............825.1 36
Fleming, *ed.* Readings; series 2. '70...815.2 21
Fobes, *ed.* Five-minute declamations. '86. 815.2 78
Ford. Me an' Methuselar, etc. 1895. 815.2 113
Frobisher, *ed.* Selected readings. '75...815.2 22
Garrett, *ed.* One hundred choice selections. 28 v............815.2 45
    Supp. to same: Dramatic leaflets............815.2 73
    Speaker's garland. 1881. 5 v............815.2 35
Hatch's recitals. 1895............815.2 85
Hazlitt, *ed.* Eloquence of the British senate. 1810. 2 v............329.2 70
Hentz. Flowers of elocution. 1869............815.2 11
Hood, *ed.* Cassell's illustrated readings..815.2 B-1
    Standard penny readings. 1871............815.2 20
Household book of Irish eloquence. '71...825.2 1
Hows, *ed.* Ladies' book of readings. '64..815.2 12
Humorous readings in the Norfolk dialect. 2 v............815.2 76
Kipling, *et al.* Tommy, and other poems. 1895............815.2 91
Kirkland. Patriotic eloquence. 1866............815.2 25
Larkin, *ed.* Rival collection. 1873............815.2 28
Lovell's United States speaker............815.2 8
Magoon, *ed.* Orators of American revolution............825.1 1
Mair, *ed.* Scottish readings. 1872............815.2 23
Memorial addresses and after-dinner speeches. 1892............825.1 B-3
Monroe, *ed.* Young folks' readings. 1888............815.2 40
Moore, *ed.* American eloquence. 1857. 2v............825.1 B-1
Murdoch, A. G. Scotch readings, humorous. 1889............815.2 75
Murdoch, J. E., *et al.* Patriotism in poetry and prose. 1864............815.2 2
Murray, *ed.* English reader. 1845............815.2 5
Noble, *ed.* Clover leaf series: no. 1., Child-dialect............815.2 32
    Same: no. 3, Dramatic studies.....815.2 34

LANGUAGE AND LITERATURE.

Northrop, *ed.* Peerless reciter. 1894.....815.2 88
Oldham. Humorous speaker. 1859.......815.2 6
Pattengill, *ed.* Special day exercises. '90..815.2 81
Penney, *ed.* National temperance orator..815.2 29
Pierpont. American first-class book........815.2 7
Potter, *ed.* My recitations. 1887...........815.2 44
Reception day: nos. 1-3, 5. 1882-8.......815.2 93
Same ; no. 6 ....815.2 79
Reeves. Student's own speaker. 1883...815.2 41
Relfe brothers' model reading-books ; nos. 3 and 5..................................815.2 42
Representative American orations ; ed. by Johnston. 1888. 3 v.

V. 1. Patrick Henry: Convention of delegates, March 28, 1775; On the expediency of adopting the Federal constitution, 1788.—Hamilton: On the expediency of adopting the Federal constitution, 1788.—Washington: Inaugural address, 1789.—Ames: On the British treaty.—Nicholas: On the proposed repeal of the sedition law.—Jefferson: Inaugural address, 1801.—Nott: On the death of Alexander Hamilton.—Randolph: On the militia bill.—Quincy: On the admission of Louisiana.—Clay: On the war of 1812.—Calhoun: On nullification and the force bill.—Hayne: On Mr. Foot's resolution, U. S. senate, 1830.—Webster: In reply to Hayne, 1830.................................825.1 24

V. 2. Phillips: On the murder of Lovejoy.—Calhoun: On the slavery question.—Webster: On the constitution of the Union.—Clay: On the compromise of 1850.—Phillips: On the philosophy of the abolition movement.—Chase: On the Kansas-Nebraska bill.—Sumner: On the Kansas-Nebraska bill.—Douglas: On the Kansas-Nebraska bill.—Sumner: On the crime against Kansas.—Brooks: On the Sumner assault.—Burlingame: In defence of Massachusetts.—Clingman: On 'debates' in congress..................................825.1 25

V. 3. Lincoln: On his nomination to the U.S. senate, 1858. — Douglas: In reply to Lincoln, 1861.—Breckenridge: On the Dred Scott decision.—Seward: On the irrepressible conflict.—Clingman: On secession, 1860.—Crittenden: On secession, 1860.—Iverson: On secession, 1860. — Toombs: On secession, 1861.—Hale: On secession, 1860.—Stevens: On secession, 1861.—Cox: On secession, 1861.—Lincoln: First inaugural address, 1861.—Davis: Inaugural address, 1861.—Stephens: The 'cornerstone' address.—Douglas: On the war, 1861.—Vallandigham: On the war and its conduct.—Schurz: On the democratic war policy.—Beecher: Address at Liverpool, 1863.—Lincoln: Gettysburg address, 1863; second inaugural address, 1865.—Davis: On reconstruction, 1864.—Pendleton: On reconstruction, 1864.—Sherman: On President Johnson's policy.—Stevens: On the first reconstruction bill.—Garfield: On the reaction against reconstruction.—Blackburn: Reply to Garfield, 1879.—Haywood: Thanksgiving sermon, The new South.—Clay: On the American system, 1832.—Hurd: A tariff for revenue only............................825.1 26

Representative British orations ; ed. by Adams. 1884. 3 v.

V. 1. Eliot: Condition of England under the duke of Buckingham.— Pym: On the subject of grievances in the reign of Charles I. — Lord Chatham: The right of taxing America; Address to the throne concerning affairs in America.—Lord Mansfield: Right of England to tax America.—E. Burke: Conciliation with America. 825.2 9

V. 2. W. Pitt: On his refusal to negotiate with Napoleon Bonaparte.—Fox: On the rejection of Napoleon Bonaparte's overtures of peace.—Mackintosh: In behalf of free speech.—Lord Erskine: On the limitations of free speech......................825.2 10

V. 3. Canning: On the policy of granting aid to Portugal when invaded by Spain.—Macaulay: On the reform bill of 1832.—Cobden: On the effects of protection on the agricultural interests of the country.—Bright: On the foreign policy of England.—Beaconsfield: On the principles of the conservative party.—Gladstone: On domestic and foreign affairs...825.2 11

Rice, *ed.* Holiday selections. 1895.......815.2 86
Rook *and* Goodfellow. Tiny Tot's speaker. 1895............................815.2 89
Routledge, *ed.* Modern speaker............815.2 1
Saunders, *ed.* Addresses, July 4, 1876-83, [and Columbian anniversary, 1892-3].971 206
Shoemaker, C. C., *ed.* Choice dialect, etc. 1887..............................815.2 74
Shoemaker, J. W., *ed.* Elocutionists' annual..................................815.2 24
Shoemaker, *Mrs.* J. W., *ed.* Little people's speaker. 1895..................815.2 87
Snyder, *ed.* Great speeches by great lawyers. 1881....................................340 35
Speaker's garland. See Garrett, *ed.*
Speeches of managers and counsel in trial of Warren Hastings. 1859 4 v......345.2 55
Stearns. Temperance speaker. 1872....815.2 10
Wagner, *ed.* Modern political orations. 1896..825.2 13

Contents: Brougham: Negro emancipation.- Macaulay: People's charter.— Fox: Corn laws.—O'Connell: Repeal of the Union.—Sheil: Jewish disabilities bill. Cockburn: Greek difficulty — Bulwer-Lytton: Crimean war.— Ellenborough: Polish insurrection.— Bright: Suspension of the habeas corpus act.— Lowe: Parliamentary reform. — Hardy: Irish church.—Russell: The ballot.—Butt: Home rule.—Sullivan: Irish national demands.—Beaconsfield: Berlin Congress.—Cowen: Foreign policy of England. — Gladstone: Beaconsfield ministry. — Charles Bradlaugh at the bar of the House of Commons. — McCarthy: In defence of his colleagues. — Churchill Egyptian crisis.— Chamberlain: Liberal aims.— Parnell Coercion bill.—Morley: Home rule.—Cobden: Corn laws. — The Times on 'Parnellism and crime.' — Original sources of the speeches.

Werner's readings and recitations. 1890-94. nos. 1-13....................................815.2 97
Williston, *ed.* Eloquence of the U. S. 1829. 5 v.................................825.1 18
Wood *and* Shoemaker. Treasury of humor. 1893..............................815.2 90

COLLECTIONS : ESSAYS, ETC.

Adventurer, The; ed. by Chalmers. 3 v...824.2 16
Essays illustrative of ; by Drake. 2 v...824.2 50

Afternoon lectures on literature and art;
by Napier *et al.* 1864-6. series 2-3..824.2 132
Brenton, *ed.* Voices from the press......824.1 121
British essayists; ed. by Chalmers. 30 v.
    Tatler. 4 v...824.2 6
    Guardian. 3 v.......................................824.2 10
    Rambler. 3 v..824.2 13
    Adventurer. 3 v...................................824.2 16
    World. 3 v..824.2 19
    Connoisseur. 2 v..................................824.2 22
    Idler. 1 v...824.2 24
    Mirror. 2 v..824.2 25
    Lounger. 2 v...824.2 27
    Observer. 3 v.......................................824.2 29
    Looker on. 3 v......................................824.2 32
    Index. 1 v..824.2 35
Chap-book essays. 1896..................824.1 324
    Contents: Essays by Boyesen, Burroughs, De Koven, Earle, Gates, Gosse, Guiney, Hapgood, Higginson, Jerrold, Mabie, Moulton, Simpson, Stoddard, Thompson.
Classical studies in honour of Henry
Drisler. 1894...............................824.1 137
    Contents: Ashmore: On the meaning of 'nauta' and 'viator' in Horace, Sat. I: 5, 11-23.— Butler: Anaximander on prolongation of infancy in man.—Earle: Of two.passages in Euripides' 'Medea.'— Egbert: Preliminary military service of the equestrian cursus honorum.— Gottheil: References to Zoroaster in Syriac and Arabic literature.— Gudeman: Literary frauds among the Greeks.— Hopkins: Henotheism in the Rig-Veda.— Hussey: Plato and the Attic comedy.— Jackson: Herodotus VII: 61 ; or, Ancient Persian armour.— Knapp: Archaism in Aulus Gellius.— Matthews : On certain parallelisms between ancient and modern drama.— McCrea: Ovid's use of colour and of colour-terms.— Merriam: A bronze of Polyclitan affinities in the Metropolitan museum; Geryon in Cyprus; Hercules, hydra and crab.— Peck: Anomatopoetic words in Latin.— Perry: Notes on the Vedic deity Pûsan.—Sachs: The so-called Medusa Ludovisi.— Sloane: Aristotle and the Arabs.— Woodward: Iphigenia in Greek and French tragedy.— Young: Gargettus, an Attic deme.
Connoisseur, The; ed. by Chalmers. 2 v.
    ....824.2 22
Dobson, *ed.* Eighteenth century essays...824.2 92
English essays; ed. by Lobban. 1896..824.2 506
    Contents: Introduction.— Essays by F. Bacon, Cowley, Defoe, Steele, Addison, Swift, Fielding, Pope, George Colman and Bonnel Thornton, Cowper, Earl of Chesterfield, Walpole, S. Johnson, Goldsmith, Leigh Hunt, William Hazlitt, Charles Lamb.
English literary criticism, introduction by
Vaughan. 1896...............................824.2 498
    Contents: Introduction. – Sidney, Sir P.: Apology for poetry. Dryden- Preface to the fables.—Johnson, S.: On the metaphysical poets.— Coleridge: On poetic genius and poetic diction. Hazlitt: On poetry in general. — Lamb: On the artificial comedy of the last century; On Webster's 'Duchess of Malfi'; On Ford's 'Broken heart.' Shelley: Defence of poetry Carlyle: Goethe. Pater: Sandro Botticelli.
Gladstone *et al.* Books which have influenced me. 1887...........................824 19
Guardian, The; ed. by Chalmers. 3 v.....824.2 10
    Essays illustrative of; by Drake. 3 v..824.2 47
Hale *et al.* Books that have helped me.
    1888..824 20

Idler, The; ed. by Chalmers. 1856. 1 v...824.2 24
    Essays illustrative of; by Drake. 2v...824.2 50
Looker-on, The; ed. by Chalmers. 3v...824.2 32
    Same. 1796. 2 v..............................824.2 62
Lounger, The; ed. by Chalmers. 1856. 2v.
    ....824.2 27
Mirror, The; ed. by Chalmers. 1856. 2v...824.2 25
    Same. 1803. 2 v..............................824.2 58
Monograph, The. 1882. v. 1-3................824 7
Moore's British classics. 1793. 2 v.
    V. 1. Johnson's Rambler.'—Lyttleton's 'Persian letters.'...824.2 52
    V. 2. Hawkesworth's 'Adventurer.'— Steele's 'Guardian.'..824.2 53
Morley, *ed.* Famous pamphlets. 1886...824.2 397
    Contents: Milton's 'Areopagitica.'—Killing no murder. —DeFoe's 'Shortest way with the dissenters.'— Steele's 'Crisis.'—Whateley's 'Historic doubts concerning Napoleon Buonaparte.'—Copleston's 'Advice to a young reviewer.'
Napier, J., *et al.* Afternoon readings,
Dublin, 1864..................................824.2 222
Nation, The. Critical and social essays
from. 1867.................................824.1 109
Observer, The; ed. by Chalmers. 3 v...824.2 29
Prose masterpieces from modern essayists.
1883. 3 v.
    V. 1. Irving: Mutability of literature.—Hunt: World of books.—Lamb: Imperfect sympathies.— De Quincey: Conversation.—Landor: Petition of thugs; Benefits of parliament.—Smith, S.: Fallacies of anti-reformers.—Thackeray: Nil nisi bonum.— Emerson: Compensation.— Arnold: Sweetness and light.—Morley: Popular culture..............824 16
    V. 2. Helps: Art of living with others.—Kingsley: My winter garden. – Ruskin: Work.— Lowell: On a certain condescension in foreigners. —Carlyle: History.—Macaulay: History..........824 17
    V. 3. Froude: Science of history.—Freeman: Race and language.—Gladstone: Kin beyond sea. —Newman: Private judgment. - Stephen: Apology for plain speaking.....................................824 18
Rambler, The ; ed. by Chalmers. 3 v...824.2 13
    Same by Moore. 1793........*in* 824.2 52
    Essays illustrative of ; by Drake. 2 v..824.2 50
Select American classics......................824.1 319
    Contents: Irving: The author's account of himself; The voyage; Christmas; The stagecoach; Christmas eve; Christmas day; Christmas dinner; Westminster Abbey; Legend of Sleepy Hollow; Rip Van Winkle.— Webster: Orations on Bunker Hill monument; The character of Washington; The landing at Plymouth.— Emerson: The American scholar; Self-reliance; Compensation.
Spectator, The. 1853. 4 v..................824.2 36
    Essays illustrative of; by Drake. 3 v...824.2 47
    Papers from, relating to Sir Roger de
Coverley.....................................824.2 40
Tatler, The; ed. by Chalmers. 1856. 4 v..824.2 6
    Same. 1807.....................................824.2 41
    Essays illustrative of; by Drake. 4 v...824.2 47
Topics of the time; ed. by Coan. 6 v.......824 1
Wirt *et al.* Old bachelor. 1814.........824.1 147
World, The; ed. by Chalmers. 1856. 3 v..824.2 19

COLLECTIONS: LETTERS.

Ellis, *ed.* Letters of eminent literary men, 16-18th centuries................826.2 1
Richardson, *ed.* Old love-letters. 1883...826.2 3
Scoones, *ed.* Four centuries of English letters. 1880..........................826.2 49

COLLECTIONS: HUMOR, SATIRE, ETC.

Ashton, *ed.* English caricature and satire on Napoleon I. 1884. 2 v...........944.5 43
Humour, etc., 17th century.............828.2 55
Barr, *ed.* American humorous verse. '91.828.1 58
The humour of America. 1893........828.1 79
Clemens. See **Twain, Mark.**
Haliburton, *ed.* Traits of American humour....................................828.1 63
Hunt, *ed.* Wit and humor from the poets....828.2 8
Irish diamonds..............................914.1 65
Life's comedy. Series 1—. 1897—.....827.1 R-1
The American family. 1896............827.1 B-1
Lilly. Four English humourists of 19th century. •1895..........................828.2 63
Contents: Dickens.—Thackeray.—George Eliot.—Carlyle.
Mason, *ed.* Humorous masterpieces, American literature. 1886. 3 v..............828.1 69
O'Donoghue, *ed.* Humour of Ireland. 1894. ....828.2 62
Parton, *ed.* Humorous poetry, English. 1886..828 1
Political poems and satires, reign of Henry VI...*in* 942 90
Punch. 1841—. v. 1—...............827.2 P-B-1
Pictures from. v. 1—.................827.2 B-2
Le Row, *ed.* English as she is taught....828.1 72
Sala, *ed.* More Yankee drolleries...........828 1 28
Third supply of Yankee drolleries.....828.1 29
Yankee drolleries. 1868.................828.1 27
Twain, Mark, (S. L. Clemens), *ed.* Library of humor, 1888..........................828.1 76
Vanity fair. 1860. v. 1..................827.1 P-B-1
Watterson, *ed.* Oddities in southern life..828.1 7
Wright, *ed.* Caricature history of the Georges....................................827 2, 25

COLLECTIONS: FICTION.

Blackwood, Tales from.
V. 1. Aytoun: Glenmutchkin railway.—Vanderdecken's message home.—Floating beacon.—Colonna, the painter.—Lockhart: Napoleon.—Hamley: Legend of Gibraltar.—Mudford: Iron shroud.—Hamley: Lazaro's legacy.—Story without a tail.—Faustus and Queen Elizabeth.—Aytoun: How I became a yeoman.—Southey, *Mrs.*: Devereux.—MacNish: The metempsychosis.—College theatricals............................32801

V. 2. A reading party in the long vacation.—Murray: Father Tom and the pope. Southey, *Mrs.*: La petite Madelaine.—Maginn: Bob Burke's duel with Ensign Brady.—The headsman. Galt: Wearyful woman.—Aytoun: How I stood for the Dreepdaily burghs. Mudford: First and last.—Duke's dilemma. - An old gentleman's teetotum. My college friends. Hughes: Magic lay of the one-horse chay....................................32802
V. 3. Adventures in Texas.—Aytoun: How we got possession of the Tuileries.—Lockhart: Captain Paton's lament.—D'Arbouville: Village doctor.—Hogg: Singular letter from South Africa.—Hardman: My friend the Dutchman.—My college friends: no. 2. Horace Leicester.—Aytoun: Emerald studs.—My college friends: no. 3, W. W. Hurst.—Hardman: Christine.—The man in the bell.....................................32803
V. 4. Hardman: My English acquaintance.—Doubleday: Murderer's last night.—Willis: Narration of certain uncommon things that did formerly happen to me.—The wags.—The wet wooing: a narrative of '98.—Ben-na-groich.—Aytoun: Surveyor's tale. — Forrest-race romance.—Edwards: Di Vasari. — Sigismund Fatello.—The boxes....................................32804
V. 5. Rosaura: a tale of Madrid.—Adventures in Northwest Territory.—Harry Bolton's curacy.—Florida pirate.—Pandour and his princess.—Beauty draught.—Antonio Di Carara.—Fatal repast.—Vision of Cagliostro.—First and last kiss.—Smuggler's leap.—Haunted and haunters.—The duelists....................................32805
V. 6. The Natolian story-teller.—First and last crime.—Rintoul.—Major Moss.—The premier and his wife.—Tickler among the thieves.—Bridegroom of Barna.—Involuntary experimentalist.—Le Brun's lawsuit.—Snowing-up of Strath Lucas. —A few words on social philosophy..............32806

Same; 2d series.
V. 1. Tender recollections of Irene MacGillicuddy.—Walford: Nan.—Bells of Botreaux.—Hamley: Recent confessions of an opium-eater.—Hamley: Shakespeare's funeral.—A night with the volunteers of Strathkinahan.—Philosopher's baby.—Oliphant, *Mrs.*: Secret chamber......................32808
V. 2. Battle of Dorking.—Late for the train.—Aytoun: The congress and the Agapedome.—Francillon: Grace Owen's engagement.—Aytoun: Raid of Arnaboll.—Neaves: How to make a pedigree: a new song......................................32809
V. 3. Who painted the great Murillo de la Merced.—J-nes: A parochial epic.—Military adventure in the Pyrenees.—Allardyce: Pundrapore residency. — Falsely accused. — Witch-Hampton hall....................................32810
V. 4. Railway junction. — Metamorphoses.—Cheape: Betsy Brown.—Sue-Sand: Last French hero.—Lockhart: Unlucky Tim Griffin.—Spectre of Milaggio.—Autobiography of a joint stock company (limited).—Walford: Bee or Beatrix.—Night-wanderer of an Afghan fort.—MacLeod: Ayrshire curling song..........................32811
V. 5. Hamley: Light on the hearth.—How to boil peas.—Clive's dream before the battle of Plassey.—Lever: What I did at Belgrade.—Shand: Wrecked off the Riff coast.—Dollie and the two Smiths.—Majendie: Railway journey.............32812
V. 6. Francillon: A dog without a tail.—Hamley: Wassail.—Cousin John's property.—Story: Modern magician.—Al'ardyce: Edgar Wayne's escape....................................32813

V. 7. The devil's frills.—Francillon: Story of Eulenburg.—Shadow of the door.—Wordsworth, *Mrs.*: Wreck of the Strathmore.—Lever: Hero worship and its dangers.—Annie and her master. —H. D. W.: A feuilleton............................32814

V. 8. Greg: Guy Naville's ghost.—Hardmann: The great unknown.—Easter trip of two Ochlophobists.—Aytoun: Rapping the question.—My after-dinner adventures with Peter Schlemihl.— Aunt Ann's ghost story.—Blue dragoon.—Winchilsea, *earl of*: Lord Hatton,.......................32815

V. 9. Missing bills.—Chendle: My hunt of the silver fox.—Narrative of Prince Charlie's escape. —Fenian alarm.—Lindau: Philosopher's pendulum.—Walford: Lady Adelaide.—Witcherley ways. —Lever: How Frank Thornton was cured.— Walker: In life and in death.—A cause worth trying...................................32816

V. 10. Lost secret of the Cocos group.—Two Mrs. Scudamores.—Bates' tour................32817

Same ; 3d series.

V. 1. Bourgonef. — Clifford, *Mrs.*: Thomas.— Oliphant; Brigand's bride. — Prothero.: The misogynist.—Boyle: Fetish city.—Gascon O'Driscol...32818

V. 2. Moncrieff, *Mrs.* Scott-: Elie ruby.— Gould, S. Baring-: Alexander Nesbitt, ex-schoolmaster.—Landers: King Bemba's point.—Lumsden: A vendetta.—Hartley: Master Tommy experiment.—Douglas: Matrimonial fraud...........32819

V. 3. Magendie, *Lady* M.; A French speculation.—Wellwood, *Lord*: Rufus Hickman of Saint Botolph's.— Alexis: Hans Preller.— Kingsley, M.: The puerto de Medina.— Harcourt: Jack and Minory...32820

V. 4. Lyster: My treasure.— Lorne, *marquess of*: Who were they?— Douglas: Within his danger.— Hartley: The factor's shooting.— Hamley: A magnetic mystery............................32821

V. 5. Dellenbaugh: A singular case.— Bradley: Pentock...32822

V. 6. Lewes: Dragon-tree of Telde.— Last words of Joseph Barrable.— Lumsden: How I fell among thieves.— Burton: Fiddlers three.— Stirling: Ghost of Morcar's tower.- Blackie: Ancrum Moor...32823

V. 7. Hamley: A medium of last century.— Hope: Alive, and yet dead.— Gray: An unexpected fare.— T. P. W.: Reminiscence of a march.....32824

V. 8. Burton: Don Angelo's stray sheep.— Douglas: The twins.— Bradley: The doctor.— Johnstone: The enchanted bridle..................32825

* V 9. Moncrieff, *Mrs.* Scott-: Such pity as a father hath. Russell: Coincidences?- Bird: A dead man's vengeance. Landers: Story of James Barker...32826

V. 10. Shand: Mr. Cox's protégé.—Knatchbull-Hugessen; A dramatic effect.- Cushing: A bud that lived. Coleridge: Daniel Rosqué.- Wellwood: The great unloaded.....................32827

V. 11. Cowper: Christmas eve on a haunted hulk. Dicky Dawkins, Dziewicki: Airy nothing. - Bent: Chapter from an unknown life. - Bradley: Marse Dab after the war. Cunning: Unfathomed mysteries.................................32828

V. 12. Jenner: A philanthropist. Oliphant, F R.: The grateful ghosts. Ruckland: A pickle of salt On the Wallaby track. Meldrum: Raihidei...32829

Chambers' journal, Tales from. 4 v.

V. 1. Silver lever.—Interest of a shilling.— Senside adventure. — Longest month in my life.— The brown greatcoat.— Mr. Job Samson.— Lighthouse of the Gannets.— Zekel Flint.— Monks of Cockaigne.—Unexpected blessing.—Uncle Godfrey. — My friend Ching.— Children I have met.—Cabman's story.— Narrow escape.....................32952

V. 2. Five brothers' five fixes.—Daisy's choice. —A black mare with a white star.—Hand and ring. —A gallant steed.—Bobby,—Our feather farm.— Blamyre's chambers.—Wife's secret.—Miss Fyfe's adventure.—Phantom of Deadmoor tower.—The Jamsetjee Jeejeebhoy.—Chewton.—Abbot.—Among queer people.—White Hart inn.—Flight in the dark..32953

V. 3. Without further delay.—The Arab wife.— A strange clue.—The manor house at Milford.— Story of a foundling............................32954

V. 4. The winning hazard.—A limited horizon. —Dashmarton's legacy,—A cast of the net......32955

Clifford *et al.* Grey romance, etc.............32717

Contents: Clifford: Grey romance.—Traill: Two propet prides.—Hodgson: Candidate for West Drum.— Parker: At the sign of the eagle.—Stockton: Watchmaker's wife.—Greenwood: Young genius.—Meldrum: Comedy of courtship.—Gower: For God's judgment.

Club-book, The,...............................32724

Contents: James: Bertrand de la Croix.—Galt: Haddad-Ben-Ahab: Fatal whisper; Painter; Unguarded hour; Book of life.—Power: Gipsy of the Abruzzo.— Picken: Eisenbach; Deer-stalkers of Glenskiach; Three Kearneys.—Jerdan: Sleepless woman.—Gower: Dramatic scenes, founded on Hugo's 'Hernani.'—Cunningham; Gowden Gibbie.—Moir: Bridal of Borthwick. —Hogg; Laidlaws and the Scots; Bogle o' the Brae.— Ritchie: Chenterie packman.

Eleven possible cases........................32701

Contents: Fyles: Only a girl at Overlook.—Stockton: Thing that glistened.—Miller: Lion and a lioness.— Harland: Head of death.—Thompson: Mystic Krewe.— Lockwood: Strange adventures of a million dollars.— Fawcett: Lost day.—Smith, B. G.: Tragedy of high explosives.—Munroe; Bushwhacker's gratitude.—Crinkle: End of all.—Greene, A. K.: Shall he marry her?

Fireside stories, old and new. 3 v.

V. 1. Ferguson: Father Tom and the pope.—A social failure redeemed. — Duellists. — Bulwer: Haunted and the haunters.—Clark: Story of a garden party. Balzac: Lost masterpiece.—How I won the Melbourne cup.—Willis: Lunatic's skate..32752

V. 2. Ouida: Dog of Flanders.—Attorney's revenge.—Hood; Defaulter.—Poe: Purloined letter. —How I set about paying my debts.—Leggett: Main truck.—Trollope: Christmas at Thompson Hall.—Mudford: First and last dinner.—Involuntary experimentalist.............................32753

V. 3. O'Conner: The ghost.—Bellows mender of Lyons. — Mudford: Iron shroud. — Hornung: Kenyon's innings.— Briggs: Elegant Tom Dillar.— Gellibrand; J. Cole.—O'Brien: What was it?....32754

Harrison, *ed.* Short stories....................32714

Contents: Stoddard: My own story.—Chesebro: In honor bound. Crosby: An islander.—Slosson: A speakin' ghost. Harrison: Monsieur Alcibiade.

Hazlitt, *ed.* Tales and legends, England. 1892...823 115

Henty, *ed.* Stories of history.................023334

LANGUAGE AND LITERATURE.

King, *ed.* Captain Dreams, etc..................16123
  Contents: King: Captain Dreams,—Sydenham: Ebbtide; Story of Alcatraz.—Hamilton, K.: White lilies.—Hamilton, W. H.: A strange wound.—Dene: The other fellow.—Leefe: Buttons.

Little classics; ed. by Johnson. 14 v.
  V. 1. *Exile:* Hawthorne: Ethan Brand.—Griffin: The swans of Lir.—Greenwood: A night in the workhouse.—Harte: The outcasts of Poker Flat.—Hale: The man without a country.—De Quincey: Flight of a Tartar tribe...............32901
  V. 2. *Intellect:* Bulwer-Lytton: The house and brain.—Spofford: D'outre mort.—Poe: The fall of the house of Usher.—Dickens: Chops the dwarf.—Hawthorne: Wakefield.—De Quincey: Murder considered as one of the fine arts.—Davis: The captain's story...............32902
  V. 3. *Tragedy:* Poe: The murders in the rue Morgue.—De Forest: The Lauson tragedy.—Mudford: The iron shroud.—Melville: The bell-tower.—Judson: The Kathayan slave.—Mackenzie: The story of La Roche.—De Quincey: The vision of sudden death...............32903
  V. 4. *Life:* Brown: Rab and his friends.—Howells: A romance of real life.—Harte: The luck of Roaring Camp.—Barham: Jerry Jarvis' wig.—Willis: Beauty and the beast.—Hawthorne: David Swan.—Smith: Dreamthorp.—Mitchell: A bachelor's revery.—Taylor: The grammar of life.—Curtis: My chateau.—Lamb: Dream children.—Hoffman: The man in the reservoir.—Addison: Westminster abbey.—Macaulay: The puritans.—Lincoln: Gettysburg...............32904
  V. 5. *Laughter:* Dickens: A Christmas carol.—Cooper: The haunted crust.—Lamb: A dissertation upon roast pig.—Walker: The total depravity of inanimate things.—Hale: The skeleton in the closet.—Miller: Sandy Wood's sepulchre.—Holmes: —A visit to the asylum for aged and decayed punsters.—Griffin: Mr. Tibbot O'Leary the curious.—Carleton: Neal Malone...............32905
  V. 6. *Love:* Winthrop: Love and skates.—Bulwer-Lytton: The maid of Malines.—The story of Ruth, from the Bible.—Disraeli: The rise of Iskander...............32906
  V. 7. *Romance:* Holmes: Iris.—Craik: The rosicrucian.—Spofford: The south breaker.—Wilson: The snowstorm.—Cunningham: The king of the peak...............32907
  V. 8. *Mystery:* O'Connor: The ghost.—Edwards: The four-fifteen express.—Dickens: The signal-man.—Cunningham: The haunted ships.—Lowell: A raft that no man made.—O'Connor: The invisible princess.—Crowe: The advocate's wedding day.—Hawthorne: The birthmark...............32908
  V. 9. *Comedy:* Lover: Barney O'Reirdon the navigator.—Galt: Haddad-Ben-Ahab the traveller. —Thackeray: Blubeard's ghost.—Smith, H.: The picnic party.—Ferguson: Father Tom and the pope.—Howitt: Johnny Darbyshire.—Lover: The gridiron.—Reade: The box tunnel...............32909
  V. 10. *Childhood:* Ramé: A dog of Flanders.—Ruskin: The king of the golden river.—Phelps: The lady of Shalott.—Brown: Marjorie Fleming.—De Kroyft: Little Jakey.—Kingsley: The lost child. —Neal: Goody gracious! and the forget-me-not.—Spofford: A faded leaf of history.—Dickens: A child's dream of a star...............32910
  V. 11. *Heroism:* Ludlow: Little Briggs and I. —Spofford: Ray.—Taylor: Three November days.

—Mitford: The forty seven rōnins Mayo A chance child.—Ramé: A leaf in a storm......... 32911
  V. 12. *Fortune.* Poe: The gold bug Lover: The fairy finder.—Edgeworth: Murad the unlucky —Hale: The children of the public Banim: The rival dreamers.—Hawthorne: The threefold destiny...............32912
  V. 13. *Humanity:* Stoddard: Chumming with a savage.—Dickens: Dr. Marigold.—Ludlow: A brace of boys.—Thackeray: George III Jameson: Juliet.—Mallock: Is life worth living?......32913
  V. 14. *Nature:* Warner: A-hunting of the deer.—Hamerton: Dogs.—Burroughs: In the hemlocks.—Thoreau: A winter walk.—Hawthorne: Buds and bird voices.—Kingsley: The fens.—Whymper: Ascent of the Matterhorn. King: Ascent of Mount Tyndall. Ruskin: The firmament 32914

Love tales. 5 v.
  American: Fawn's leap.—Willis: Unwritten poetry.—The tutor.—Marriage blunder.—Seaman's widow.—Paulding: Little Dutch sentinel of the Manhadoes. Marian Seaforth.—Hawthorne: Maypole of Merry Mount.—Isle of the Manito. Poe: Spectacles.—Eulalie.—Bridal ballad. Annabel Lee. 32719
  English: Bulwer: Love is the best physician.—Mitford: Freshwater fisherman.—Hook; Bride. Strickland: Love quarrel.—Warren: Broken heart —Love in a mist.—Pardoe: Virgin's fountain.—Gore: Dorathea.—Dickens: Passage in the life of Mr. Watkins Tottle.—Knowles: Widowed bride....32721
  German: Musæus: Dumb love; Carlyle, *tr.*—Winter: Simple tale of love.—Goethe: Love tale. —Love potion.—Tieck: Love magic; Goblet.—Langbein: Lady's palfrey.—Schiller: Fraternal magnanimity.—Rich goldsmith of Frankfort........=1434
  Irish: Croker: Mistletoe bough; Paddy Kelleher and his pig.—Hall: Dispensation; Annie Leslie.—Ensign O'Donoghue's 'first love.'—Lovedraught.—Carleton: Shane Fadh's wedding.—Bayly: Legend of Killarney.—Gray: Mary M'Donnell...............32722
  Scottish: Miller: Salmon-fisher of Udoll.—Moir: Mansie Waugh's calf-love; Mansie Waugh pushing his fortune.—Wilson: Lily of Lillisdale; Lover's last visit.—Macnish: Loves of the learned. —Ritchie: Maid of Neidpath; Outlaw's bride.—Margaret Carnegie.—Munroe: Bride of Loch-Ard. —Bonnie Prince Charlie.—Carne: Highland cottage.—Lauder: Legend of the floating islet.—Scott: Bridal of Janet Dalrymple...............32723

Mavericks...............32710
  Contents: Henderson: Modern Hans Sachs.—Matthews: Chesterfield's postal-cards to his son.—Bridges: Misther Handhrigan's love story.—Learned: Old Jonesy. —Cook: Romance of a spotted man.—Fish: Recollections of a busy life.—Rider: Wight that quailed.—Jessop: Biddy's dream.—Wilson: True love's triumph. —Ford: Aunt Mary's obituary.—Goodwin: Internecine comparison.—Jenks: Drawn battle.—Sidney: Magic city.—Augur: Mr. Wilkemming's hobby.—Wharton: Cashier and the burglar.—Romaine: Timely hint.—Miues: Brilliant idea.—Munkittrick: Man with the black crape mask.—Bunner: Recording spook.

Mayflower tales...............32711
  Contents: Hawthorne, J.: Modern girl's story.—Allen G.: Maisie Bowman's fate.—Dowling: The other and I. —Sims: My two wives.—Nisbet: Through the gap.

Mitford, *ed.* Stories of American life. 3v....15255

Nimmo's popular tales. 5 v...............50319

Norman, *ed.* The broken shaft..............69209
  Contents: Norman: On board the Bavaria.—Crawford: The upper berth.—Stevenson: Markheim.—Guthrie: Marjory.—Pollock: The action to the word.—Archer: My fascinating friend.—Hopkins: Riley, M. P. —Norman: Love and lightning.

Witching time, etc..............69296
  Contents: Dobson: In witching time.—Crawford: By the waters of Paradise.—Tadema: Captain's bride. —Norris: Specter of Strathannan.—Von Degen: Mystery of the Campagna.—Gosse: Witches.—Lee: Hidden door.—Archer: Pothooks and hangers.—Robinson: Vincent Hadding.—Norman: Two of a kind.—Austin: Juliet.

Outing library. v. 1, no. 3..............32718
  Contents: King: Rancho Del Muerto.—Dabney: A mighty hunter before the Lord.—Harben: A Cohotta Valley shooting match.—Sandys: Moeran's moose.— Torrance: The mystery of a Christmas hunt.— Brown: Herne the hunter.—Gilfillan: Uncle Duke's 'b'ar' story.— French: A cigarette from Carcinto.

Scribner, Stories from: Stories of Italy......32605
  Contents: Smith, F. Hopkinson: Espero Gorgoni, gondolier.—Sullivan: The anatomist of the heart.— A'Becket, J. J.: The song of the comforter.— Channing: The house on the hilltop.

Stories of New York..............32602
  Contents: Eliot, A.: From four to six: a comedietta.—Perry: Commonest possible story.—Hibbard: The end of the beginning.—Wood: A Puritan ingénue. —Wharton: Mrs. Manstey's view.

Stories of the railway..............32601
  Contents: Hibbard: As the sparks fly upward.— Davison: How I sent my aunt to Baltimore.—Page: Run to seed.—Gordon: Flandroe's Mogul.

Stories of the sea..............32604
  Contents: Spears: The port of missing ships.— Blunt: The fate of the Georgiana.— Carryl: Captain Black.—Howe: The last slave ship.

Stories of the south..............32603
  Contents: Page: No haid pawn.—Robertson: How the Derby was won.—Harris: Aunt Fountain's prisoner.—Davis, Rebecca H.: Tirar y Soult.

Short stories: magazine, July, 1890..............32703
Stories by American authors. 10 v.
  V. 1. Taylor, B.: Who was she?—Matthews and Bunner: The documents in the case.— Bishop, W. H.: One of the thirty pieces.— Davis, R. H.: Balacchi brothers.— Webster, A.: An operation in money..............32920
  V. 2. Stockton, F. R.: The transferred ghost.— Jacobi: A martyr to science. Stimson, Mrs. Knollys. Eddy: A dinner party.—Spofford: The mount of sorrow. Tincker: Sister Sylvin..............32922
  V. 3. Hale, E. E.: The spider's eye. Burnett: A story of the Latin quarter.- Lathrop: Two purse companions.—Lloyd: Ogla Moga. - Thaxter: A memorable murder Matthews: Venetian glass..............32924
  V. 4. Woolson: Miss Grief. Bunner: Love in old clothes. - Willis: Two buckets in a well. Foote: Friend Barton's concern.—DeForest: An inspired lobbyist. Brooks: Lost in the fog..............32926
  V 5. James: A light man. Millet; Yatil —Benjamin: The end of New York. Arnold, G.: Why Thomas was discharged. Mitchell, E. P.: The tachypomp..............32928

V. 6. Chaplin: The village convict.—Hayes: The Denver express.—Fairfax: The misfortunes of brother Thomas Wheatley.—Champney; The heartbreak cameo.—Webster, A.: Miss Eunice's glove. —Frederic: Brother Sebastian's friendship..............32930
V. 7. Thanet: The bishop's vagabond.—Bellamy: Lost.—Stockton, L.: Kirby's coals of fire.— Floyd, M.: Passages from the journal of a social wreck.—McKay: Stella Grayland.—Johnson: The image of San Donato..............32932
V. 8. DeForest: The brigade commander.— Beers: Split zephyr.— Phelps: Zerviah Hope.— Adee: The lie magnet.— Stoddard: Osgood's predicament..............32934
V. 9. Page: Marse Chan.— Gage: Mr. Bixby's Christmas visitor.—Chaplin: Eli.—Shinn: Young Strong of the 'The Clarion.'— Coffin: How old Wiggins wore ship.— Kip: Xmas has come..............32936
V. 10. Janvier: Pancha.—Mitchell: The ablest man in the world. — Stephens: Young Moll's peevy.— DeKay: Manmat'ha.—Boyesen: A daring fiction — Schayer: The story of two lives..............32937

Stories by English authors.
  Africa: Doyle: The mystery of Sasassa Valley. —Haggard: Long odds.—Landers: King Bemba's point—Scully: Ghamba.—Mary Musgrave.—Hemingway: Gregorio..............32730
  England: Reade: The box tunnel.— Robinson: Minions of the moon.— Edwards: The four-fifteen express.— Lewis: The wrong black bag.— Hardy: The three strangers.— Collins: Mr. Lismore and the widow.— Hope: The philosopher in the apple orchard..............32726
  France: Stevenson: A lodging for the night.— Ouida: A leaf in the storm.—Collins: A terribly strange bed.—Stretton: Michel Lorio's cross,—Weyman: A perilous amour..............32729
  Germany: Harraden: The bird on its journey. —Winter: Koosje.— Ouida: A dog of Flanders.— Stevenson: Markheim.— Black: Queen Tita's wager..............32735
  Ireland: Lover: Gridiron.—Jessop: Emergency men.—Barlow: Lost recruit.—Banim: Rival dreamers.—Carleton: Neal Malone.—The banshee..............32727
  Italy: Payn: Faithful retainer.—Norris: Bianca. — Robinson: Goneril.— Oliphant, L.: Brigand's bride.—Trollope: Mrs. General Talboys..............32731
  London: Barrie: Inconsiderate waiter.— Austey: Black poodle.— Morrison: That brute Simmons.—Zangwill: Rose of the Ghetto.—Harraden: Idle of London. — Q: Omnibus.—Corelli: The hired baby..............32728
  Orient: Kipling: Man who would be king.— Mitford: Tajima.—Douglas: Chinese girl graduate.—Beaumont: Revenge of her race.— Roberts: King Billy of Ballarat.—Syrett: Thy heart's desire.32733
  Scotland: Barrie: Courting of T'nowhead's bell.—Crockett: Heather lintie.—Maclaren: Doctor of the old school.—Scott: Wandering Willie's tale.— Aytoun: Glenmutchkin railway.— Stevenson: Thrawn Janet..............32732
  The Sea: Russell: Extraordinary adventure of a chief mate.—Besant: Quarantine island.—Rock scorpions.— O'Halloran: Master of the Chrysolite. Petrel and the Black Swan.— Allen; Melissa's tour.—Vanderdecken's message home.....32734

Stories in black and white..............32712
  Contents: Norris: Romance of Madam de Chanteloup. Russell: Memorable swim.—Hardy: To please his wife. Linton: Ghost of the past.—Payn: Rebecca's remorse. Barrie: Is it a man?—Oliphant, Mrs.: Golden rule. Allen, Grant: General Passavant's will.

Tales from Blackwood. See **Blackwood,** Tales from.

Tales from Chambers' journal. See **Chambers' journal,** Tales from.

Tales from many sources. 6 v.

V. 1. Hardy: The three strangers.—Guthrie: The black poodle.—Sturgis: Lord Richard and I. —Stevenson: The pavilion on the links.—Norris: The hermit of Saint Eugène.—Mattic.................32940

V. 2. Gerard: My Paris masters.—Ramé: Mouflou.— Martin: Beauchamp and Company.— Reade: The Knightsbridge mystery.—Archdeacon Holden's tribulations.—Smith, H.: Michel Lorio's cross.—Argles: In durance vile........................32941

V. 3. The professor and the harpy.—Shorthouse: The Marquis Jeanne Hyacinth de Saint-Pelaye. —The rock scorpions.—Black, W.: Queen Tita's wager.—King Pepin and sweet Clive.—Clerke: A film of gossamer.—The lay figure.—The Count de Rochmont..32942

V. 4. Besant, W., and Rice, J.: The ten years' tenant.—Hunt, M.: Truth triumphant.—Doyle: Bones.—Muirhead: Two plots.—Collins: She loves and lies.—Daudet: The siege of Berlin.—Payn: Patient Kitty..32943

V. 5. Ewing: Lob Lie-by-the-fire.—Wild Jack ; from Temple Bar.—Mrs. Forrester: Virginia.—Mr. Josiah Smith's balloon voyage; from Belgravia.— Peard: Number 7639.—Robinson: Goneril.—Out of season ; from Temple Bar...........................32944

V. 6. Uncle George's will; from Temple Bar.— Murray :' Fleur de lys.—Poynter: Emilia.—J. Stanley: How Quedglington was sent down.—Au pair ; from Temple Bar.—Conway : My first client. —Lady Lindsay : Gracie..............................32945

Tales of the borders. 10 v.

V. 1. Wilson: Vacant chair; Faa's revenge.— Leighton: Kate Kennedy.—Miller: Recollections of Ferguson.—Campbell: Disasters of Johnny Armstrong.—Gillespie: Mountain storm ; Fair maid of Cellardykes.—Leighton: Prescription.— Campbell: Countess of Wistonbury.—Wilson: Midside Maggy; Wife or the wuddy.—Leighton: Lord Durie and Christie's will.—Miller: Recollections of Burns.—Gillespie: Convivialists ; Philips Grey.—Campbell: Donald Gorm.—Leighton: Cured ingrate.—Wilson: Adopted son.—Howell: Fortunes of William Wighton.—Wilson: My black coat...30434

V. 2. Miller: Widow of Dunskaith.—Wilson : Whitsome tragedy.—Leighton: Diver and the bell. —Campbell: Autobiography of Willie Smith.— Gillespie: Pheebe Fortune.—Wilson: Royal bridal. —Leighton: Royal raid.—Howell: Experimenter. —Bethune: Young laird.—Campbell: Rival nightcaps.—Wilson: Solitary of the cave.—Leighton: Maiden feast of Cairnkibbie.— Gillespie: Early recollections of a son of the hills ; Suicide's grave. —Miller: Salmon-fisher of Udoll.—Leighton: Linton lairds.—Martin: Country quarters.—Campbell: Monk of Saint Anthony.—Logan: Story of Clara Douglas.—Wilson: The fair.—Howell: The slave. —Campbell: The Katheran; Monks of Dryburgh...30435

V. 3. Wilson: Bill Stanley.—Leighton: Conscience stricken; Rattling, roaring Willie.—Miller: Bill Whyte.—Gillespie: Last of the pedlars—. Leighton : Duncan Schulebred's vision of judgment. — Wilson : Archy Armstrong. — Logan : Double-bedded room.—Campbell: Highland boy.

—Howell: Major Weir's coach Muir: Divinity student.— Wilson: Guidwife of Coldingham. — Leighton: Somnambulist of Redcleugh. Richardson: Rothesay fisherman. - Wilson: Leaves from the diary of an aged spinster. Leighton: Geordie Willison, and The heiress of Castle Gower. — Campbell: Snow storm of 1825. — Guilty or not guilty.—Howell: Palatines. Peterkin The parsonage: my father's fireside.—Hethrington: Seers' cave.—Wilson: Laidley worm of Spindleston Heugh ; Sabbath wrecks........................304/6

V. 4. Wilson: Judith the Egyptian.— Leighton: Droich.— Miller : Lykewake. Campbell: Penny wedding.— Leighton : Amateur Lawyers.— Gillespie : Family incidents ; Home and the gipsy maid ; The return.— Wilson : Poor scholar.— J. H. Laird of Darnick Tower.— Wilson: Broken heart.— Maidment: Cateran of Lochloy.—Howell: John Square's voyage to India.— Wilson : Doom of Soulis.— Leighton: Harden's revenge.— Richardson ; Physiognomist's tale.— Campbell; Good man of Dryfield.—Leighton: Cherry-stone; Henwife; Artist.— Wilson : Bride; Henpecked man.—Maidment: Mortlake.—Howell: Beggar's camp.—Campbell: Leein Jamie Murdieston.—Campbell: Duncan M'Arthur..30437

V. 5. Wilson : The cripple.—Leighton : Legend of fair Helen of Kirconnel.—Richardson ; Tom Duncan's yarn.— Gillespie : Three brethren ; Mistake rectified ; Dura Den.—Campbell : Laird of Lucky's How.— Leighton : Abduction.— Wilson : Sir Patrick Hume.—Howell: Packman's journey to London.— Wilson : Charles Lawson.—Martin Mrs. Humphrey Greenwood's tea-party.—Logan Recluse of the Hebrides ; Ellen Arundel.— Campbell : Chatelard.— Leighton : Christie of the cleek. —Wilson : First-foot.—Leighton : Romance of the siege of Perth.—Gillespie : Peat-casting time ; The medal.— Richardson : Meeting at St. Boswell's.— Smith: Story of May Darling.—Wilson : I canna be fashed.—Conolly : Castle of Crail ; Legend of the church of Abercrombie ; Romance of the May. —Leighton : Caleb Crabbin.—Howell: Imprudent marriage.—Bethune: Bewildered student.—Leighton : Crooked Comyn.......................................30438

V. 6. Wilson. Dominie's class. — Leighton : Contrast of wives. — Gillespie : Social man.— Campbell : Two comrades ; The surtout.—Leighton : Suicide.—Bethune: Ghost of Howdycraigs ; Ghost of Gairyburn.—Wilson : Smuggler.—Richardson : Schoolfellows. — Wilson : Red Hall.— Miller: Scottish hunters of Hudson's Bay.—Gillespie; Wedding.— Leighton : Mike Maxwell and the Gretna Green lovers.— Wilson ; Reuben Purves. — Richardson ; Sea-storm.— Maidment: Heir of Inshannock.—Campbell: Mosstrooper; Forger.— Leighton : Three letters ; Glass back.— Wilson : We'll have another.— Howell : Scottish veteran— Maxwell: White woman of Tarras.................30439

V. 7. Wilson: The unknown.—Leighton: Trials of Menie Dempster.—Gillespie : Natural history of idiots.—Campbell : Floshend inn.—Wilson : Lottery hall ; Dominie's courtship ; Souter's wedding.—Leighton: Roseallan's daughter — Richardson : Two sailors.—Campbell : Dream.—Wilson : Coveaunting family.—Leighton : Prince of Scotland. — Campbell : Retribution. — Gillespie : The enthusiast ; Trees and burns ; Kirkyards.— Wilson : Polwarth on the green ; Festival — Leighton : Legend of Holyrood.—Richardson : Restored son.—Campbell : Skean-dhu.—Howell: Seven years' dearth.—Wilson: Order of the garter..30440

V. 8. Wilson: Recollections of a village patriarch.—Leighton: Death of James I.—Campbell: Curate of Govan.—Gillespie: Grandmother's narrative: Covenanter's march; Peden's farewell sermon; Persecution of the M'Michaels.—Richardson: Story of Tom Bertram.—Cottar's daughter.—Leighton: Case of evidence.—Bethune: Warning. —Wilson: Grizel Cochrane; Squire Ben.—Battle of Dryffe Sands.—Leighton: Clerical murderer.—Wilson: Leveller.—Leighton: Death of James III. —Gillespie: Rescue at Enterkin; Fatal mistake; Bonny Mary Gibson; Eskdalemuir story; Douglas tragedy.—Campbell: Countess of Cassilis.—Happy conclusion.—Leighton: Mr. Samuel Ramsey Thriven.—Howell: Man-of-war's man.—Richardson: Angler's tale.—Wilson: Perseverance; Irish reaper.—Campbell: Grace Cameron.—Mysterious disappearance...................................30441
V. 9. Wilson: Roger Goldie's narrative.—Leighton: Hogmanay.—Gillespie: Sergeant Wilson; Helen Palmer; Cairny cave of Gavin Muir; Porter's hole.—Campbell: Recluse; Highland tradition.—Leighton: Bereaved; Condemned.—Wilson: Unbidden guest; Simple man is the beggar's brother.—Conolly: Robbery at Pittenweem and the Porteous mob; Story of Charles Gordon and Christina Cunningham.—Howell: Legend of Calder Moor.—Leighton: Hume and the governor of Berwick.—Miller: Thomas of Chartres.—Wilson: Fugitive.—Leighton: Bride of Bramblehaugh.—Gillespie: James Renwick; Old Isbel Kirk; Curlers; Violated coffin.—Leighton: Monomaniac.—Campbell: Foundling at sea.—Campbell: Assassin.—Howell: Prisoner of war.—Wilson: Willie Wastle's account of his wife.—Campbell: Stonebreaker.—Leighton: Laird Rorieson's will..............30442
V. 10. Leighton: Domestic griefs of Gustavus M'Iver.—Wilson: First and second marriage.—Richardson: Dissolved pledge.—Campbell: Hawick Spate.—Leighton: Avenger.—Campbell: Lord of hermitage.—Gillespie: Kinaldy; Trials of the Reverend Samuel Austin.—Campbell: Curse of Scotland.—Wilson: Leaves from the life of Alexander Hamilton.—Leighton: Sportsman of Outfieldhaugh, —Sea fight.—Leighton: Dominic of St. Fillan's.—Wilson: Sayings and doings of Peter Paterson.—Leighton: Heroine.—Campbell: Barley Bannock.—Gillespie: John Govan's narrative; Old Bluntie; Thomas Harkness of Lockerben; Shoes reversed. —Thomson: Lost heir of Elphinstone.—Wilson: Trials and triumphs.—Leighton: Miser of Newabbey.—Sea skirmish.....................................30443

Tavistock tales....................................32713
Contents: Parker: March of the white guard.— Sharp: Sunshine Johnson, murderer.--Falconer. Wrong prescription. Metcalfe: Pensée.—Morrison: A Saul and David of the steppe.—Burgin: Man from the Four Corners.—Cameron: Feelers of love.—Guthrie-Smith. Tottie. —Atkinson: Miss Maloney's public-house. — Boyd: White wand and the golden star.— Cameron: A sprig of lavender.

Ten notable stories................................32716
Contents: Jordan. A rose of the mire.—Flint: Abraham's mother.—Rathbone: A pastel. Bonner: The philosophers.—Wister. The reprieve of capitalist Clyve. —Berry: Jane's holiday. —Crim: The cross-roads ghost. —Skinner: A deed with a capital D. MacGowan: The rustlers.—Taylor: When Hester came.

Thoms, *ed.* Early English prose romances.
3 v...101

Treasure trove series. 2 v.
V. 1. *Travesty:* Burnand: Treble temptation.— Thackeray: Barnwell,— Macaulay: Prophetic account of a future epic.—Paul: Saint Twel'mo.— Heresford: Lessons in biography.—Bret Harte: Mr. John Jenkins.—T. T. T.: Ho Fi of the yellow girdle.—Hood: Walton redivivus.....................57701
V. 2. *Burlesque:* Dickens: Noble savage.— Curtis: Our new livery.—Lamb: Mrs, Battles' opinion on cards.—Hood: Parish revolution.—Burnand: Day in the academy.—Sketchley: Mrs. Brown at the play.—Addison: Will of a virtuoso. —Irving: Golden age of New York.--Dodge: Insanity of Cain.—Twain: Encounter with an interviewer.—Thackeray: Painter's bargain.—Barham: Lady Rohesia................................57702

Two tales. v. 1......................................32704
Contents: Wilkins: Juliza.—Gordon: Halifax borough.—Hawthorne, J.: Inter-planetary episode.—Teal: Riparian rights. — Thompson: Shadow of love.— Doughty: Jule's light. — Harrison, *Mrs. B.:* Suit decided.—Dromgoole, W. A.: From Dan to Beersheba.— Kirk: Superfluous woman.—Scott, D. C.: Tragedy of the seignory.—Cavazza: Cirillo.—Richards: In durance vile.—Ward: Equation of a failure.—McIlvaine: Rye Rock.—Wendell: How he went to the devil.—Williams: European powers and the Major. — Howe: Kasper Craig.—Poole: Remaining Miss Smith.—Heard: Experiment with time. — Schayer: Something more than fantasy. — Catherwood: Hurricane driver. — Grant: Across the way. — Bonner: Friend of the family. —Crosby, E. R.: Ali.—McClelland: Donna Carmencita.—Thomson: Old man Savarin.

Waller. Pictures from English literature..823 B-1
Wellesley College, senior class. At Wellesley...32725
Whittier, *ed.* Child life in prose..............07136
Yeats, *ed.* Representative Irish tales. 1891.
2 v...823 112
Young folks' cyclopædia of stories...........038001

INDIVIDUAL AUTHORS.

Abbey. Ballads of good deeds. 1872....821.1 182
Poems. 1885....................................821.1 331
Abbott, C. C. Colonial wooing................35210
Days out of doors. 1889..................504 121
A naturalist's rambles about home. '84. 504 109
Outings at odd times. 1890..............504 125
Recent rambles. 1892......................504 130
Upland and meadow. 1886..............504 112
(For contents see FINDING LIST, Part 3, p. 320.)
Waste-land wanderings. 1887.........504 114
When the century was new................35211
Abbott, E. A. (A. Square, *pseud.*). Flatland...50383
Onesimus. 1882.................................249 42
Philochristus. 1878............................249 43
Abbott, Jacob. Agnes..........................010426
August and Elvie...............................010441
Beechnut..010427
Caroline..010425
Florence stories. 6 v........................010415

Harper's story books. 12 v.	010403
Hoaryhead and McDonner.	44197
Juno and Georgie.	010402
Malville.	010421
Marco Paul's voyages. 6 v.	010430
Mary Bell.	010424
Mary Erskine.	010423
Mary Osborne.	010401
Rodolphin.	010428

Rollo series. 14 v. in 7.
V. 1-2. Rollo learning to talk.— Learning to read..........010453
V. 3-4. At work.— At play..........010455
V. 5-6. At school.— Rollo's vacation..........010457
V. 7-8. Experiments.— Museum..........010459
V. 9-10. Travels. — Correspondence..........010461
V. 11-12. Fire.— Water..........010465
V. 13-14. Sky.— Air..........010466

Rollo's tour in Europe. 10 v.
V. 1. Rollo on the Atlantic..........010443
V. 2. In Paris..........010444
V. 3. In Switzerland..........010445
V. 4. In London..........010446
V. 5. On the Rhine..........010447
V. 6. In Scotland..........010448
V. 7. In Geneva..........010449
V. 8. In Holland..........010450
V. 9. In Naples..........010451
V. 10. In Rome..........010452

Stories of Rainbow and Lucky.	010436
Stuyvesant.	010429
Wallace.	010422
À Beckett. Comic Blackstone.	828.2 27
Comic history of England. 1855. 2v.	828.2 25
Comic history of Rome.	828.2 53
About babies, etc. 1867.	824.1 92
Ackerman. Price of peace.	45350
Adalet, *pseud.* Hadjira.	70560
Adams, F. C. Justice in by-ways.	15273
Story of a trooper.	15274
Von Toodleburgs.	15272

Adams, H. C. Balderscourt..........04309
Barford bridge..........04304
Boy cavaliers..........04302
Boys of Westonburg..........04316
Charlie Lucken..........04319
College days at Oxford..........04313
Encombe stories..........04310
Fighting his way..........51504
For James or George..........51503
Friend or foe..........51502
Hair-breadth escapes..........04311
In the fifteen..........04320
Mystery of Beechey grange..........04317
Perils in the Transvaal..........04321
School-boy honor..........04307
School-days at Kingscourt..........04315
Stories for Sundays..........04306
Tales of Charlton school..........04308
Tales of Walter's school-days..........04314
Tales upon texts..........51501
Who did it?..........04312
Who was Philip?..........04318
Winborough boys..........04303
Wroxby college..........04301

Adams, Mrs. J. S. Allegories of life. '72..829.2 44
Adams, J. T. White chief..........47296

Adams, John. Works. 1856. 10 v.
V. 1. Life..........329.1 4
V. 2. Diary.—Notes of debates in the Continental Congress.—Autobiography..........329.1 5
V. 3. Autobiography.—Diary.—Notes of debates —Essays..........329.1 6
V. 4. Novanglus.—Works on government..........329.1 7
V. 5-6. Works on government..........329.1 8
V. 7-9. Official letters and papers..........329.1 10
V. 10. Correspondence..........329.1 13

Adams, Mrs. John. Letters. 1848..........826.1 2
Adams, John Q. Poems of religion and society. 1854..........821.1 433

Adams, Mrs. Leith, (Mrs. Laffan). Aunt Hepsy's foundling..........42403
Bonnie Kate..........42407
Garrison romance..........42409
Geoffrey Stirling..........42404
Georgie's wooer..........42411
Louis Draycott..........42406
Madelon Lemoine..........42402
My land of Beulah..........42405
Old pastures..........42410
Peyton romance..........42408
Winstone..........42401

Adams, Mary. Honorable surrender..........62315
Adams, Samuel. Writings and life. 3v...923.1 58
Adams, W. H. D. Forest jungle..........03402
Plain living and high thinking. 1880......374 13
Scenes with the hunter..........03401
Young Marmaduke..........03403
Adams, W. T. See **Optic, Oliver.**
Adderley. Stephen Remarx..........33535
Addison. Criticism on 'Paradise lost.'...820.2 28
Poems; with life. 1822..........821.2 43
Sir Roger de Coverley. 1878..........824.2 40

Works. 1721. 4 v.
V. 1. Poems. — Rosamond. — On Virgil's Georgics. — Cato. — Poemata. — Dialogues on ancient medals..........820.2 184
V. 2. Remarks on Italy.—Tatler.—Spectator...820.2 155
V. 3-4. Spectator. — Guardian. — Lover. — Freeholder.—Christian religion, etc..........820.2 186

Works. 1873. 3 v.
V. 1-2. Spectator..........820.2 181
V. 3. Tatler.—Guardian. — Freeholder.— Whig examiner. — The lover. — Dialogues on ancient medals.—Remarks on Italy.—Present state of the war. — Trial of Count Tariff. — Evidences of the Christian religion.—On Virgil's Georgics.—Poems. —Translations from Ovid.—Poemata.—Rosamond. —Cato.—The drummer..........820.2 182

Addison and Steele. Papers from the Spectator relating to Sir Roger de Coverley..........824.2 40

Selected papers from The Spectator; ed.
by Habberton. 1876......................824.2 229
(See also, Guardian, Spectator, Tatler; p. 100.)

Ade. Artie."...58180
Adeler, Max, (C. H. Clark). Fortunate is-
land, etc..65101
Out of the hurly burly. 1880............828.1 41
Random shots.......................................65102
Adventures in the moon, etc. 1836......827.2 20
Aguilar. Days of Bruce............................7605
Home influence......................................7601
Home scenes...7613
Mother's recompense.............................7610
Vale of cedars..7612
Woman's friendship...............................7611
Aïdé. Carr of Carrlyon...........................13603
Cliff mystery..13608
Elizabeth's pretenders.........................13610
In that state of life..............................13602
Introduced to society...........................13606
Morals and mysteries..........................13605
Penruddock..13604
Voyage of discovery...........................13609
Aikin. Corr. with Channing. 1874........826.1 4
Ainslie, Herbert, *pseud.* See **Maitland, E.**
Ainslie, P. Priceless orchid..................22005
Ainsworth. Beau Nash........................7334
Boscobel..7332
Cardinal Pole.......................................7315
Chetwynd Calverley.............................7322
Constable de Bourbon.........................7311
Crichton..7331
Fall of Somerset..................................7328
Good old times....................................7318
Guy Fawkes..7321
Hilary St. Ives....................................7303
John Law..7304
Lancashire witches.............................7301
Lord mayor of London.......................7313
Manchester rebels..............................7333
Merry England...................................7317
Mervyn Clitheroe...............................7306
Old St. Paul's....................................7316
Ovingdean grange..............................7309
Preston fight......................................7325
Saint James's....................................7335
South sea bubble...............................7305
Spanish match...................................7310
Spendthrift..7312
Star-chamber.....................................7308
Tower of London................................7320
Windsor Castle..................................7307
Akenside. Poems; with life. 1822......821.2 36
Akers. The high-top sweeting, etc. (poems).
1891..821.1 436

Alberg. Night in a church-spire............in 038025
Albert, *prince consort.* Principal speeches,
etc. 1866...825.2 2
Albertson. Four-footed lovers..............010640
Alcestis..55274
Alcock. Roman students......................62318
Alcott, A. B. Concord days 1872......824.1 67
New Connecticut: an autobiographical
poem..821.1 360
Sonnets and canzonets. 1882..........821.1 296
Table-talk. 1877...............................829.1 22
Tablets. 1868...................................824.1 66
Alcott, L. M. Aunt Jo's scrapbag..........08808
Eight cousins.....................................08815
Garland for girls................................52603
Hospital sketches..............................52601
Jack and Jill......................................08838
Jo's boys...08809
Little men...08803
Little women.....................................08801
Lulu's library....................................08802
Modern Mephistopheles....................52604
Moods..52602
Morning-glories................................08813
Old-fashioned girl.............................08806
Rose in bloom..................................08820
Silver pitchers..................................52608
Spinning-wheel stories.....................08847
Three proverb stories.......................52605
Under the lilacs................................08829
Work..52606
Alcott, L. M., *et al.* Comic tragedies.
1893..822.1 34
Alden, *Mrs.* I. M. See **Pansy,** *pseud.*
Alden, J. Studies in Bryant. 1878......821.1 282
Alden, W. L. Among the freaks..........25132
Cruise of the canoe club...................025104
Cruise of the Ghost..........................025103
Domestic explosives. 1877..............828.1 59
His daughter....................................25134
Loss of the Swansea.......................025106
Lost soul...25130
Moral pirates..................................025101
Mystery of Elias G. Roebuck, etc...25133
A new Robinson Crusoe..................025105
Shooting stars................................828.1 64
Told by the colonel........................25131
Contents: An ornithological romance.—Jewseppy.—
That little Frenchman.—Thompson's tombstone.—Union
meeting.—Clerical romance.—A mystery.—My brother
Elijah.—Saint Bernard myth.—A matrimonial romance.—
Hoskins' pets.—Cat's revenge.—Silver-plated.

Aldrich, Anne Reeve. Songs about life,
love, and death. 1893....................821.1 460
Aldrich, T. B. Cloth of gold, and other
poems. 1874..................................821.1 559
Flower and thorn: later poems. '77..821.1 560

LANGUAGE AND LITERATURE.

Friar Jerome's beautiful book, etc., from
'Cloth of gold,' and 'Flower and
thorn.' 1881....................821.1 565
Judith and Holofernes: a poem. '96...821.1 566
Marjorie Daw, etc......................11101
   Contents: Marjorie Daw.— Rivermouth romance. – Quite so.—Young desperado.—Miss Mehetabel's son.— Struggle for life.—Friend of my youth.—Mademoiselle Olympe Zabriski.—Père Antoine's date-palm.
Mercedes, and later lyrics. 1884......821.1 561
Out of his head........................11103
Prudence Palfrey......................11107
Queen of Sheba.........................11104
The sister's tragedy, with other poems.
   1891..............................821.1 563
Stillwater tragedy....................11108
Story of a bad boy.....................010302
Two bites at a cherry, etc............11102
   Contents: Two bites at a cherry.—' For bravery on the field of battle.'—The Chevalier de Resseguier.—Goliath.—My cousin the colonel.—A Christmas fantasy.—Her dying words.
Unguarded gates, and other poems.
   1894..............................821.1 564
Wyndham towers (poem). 1890......821.1 562

Aldrich, T. B., *and* **M. O. W. Oliphant.**
   Second son................................3101

Alexander, *Mrs., pseud.* (Mrs. Annie F.
   Hector). Admiral's ward..............5238
   At bay...................................5250
   Beaton's bargain.........................5253
   Blind fate...............................5213
   Broken links.............................5219
   By special wire......................*in* 32715
   By woman's wit...........................5201
   Crooked path.............................5210
   Executor.................................5241
   Fight with fate..........................5224
   For his sake.............................5216
   Forging the fetters......................5205
   Found wanting............................5217
   Freres...................................5228
   Golden autumn............................5223
   Her dearest foe..........................5204
   Heritage of Langdale.....................5214
   Life interest............................5207
   Look before you leap.....................5234
   Maid, wife or widow......................5220
   Mammon...................................5208
   Mona's choice............................5206
   Ralph Wilton's weird.....................5209
   Second life..............................5246
   Snare of the fowler......................5215
   Valerie's fate...........................5222
   Ward in chancery.........................5218
   Well won.................................5202
   What gold cannot buy.....................5221
   Which shall it be?.......................5225

   Woman's heart............................5212
   Winning hazard...........................5251
   Wooing o't...............................5211

Alexander, W. J. Introduction to poetry
   of Browning. 1889................821.2 1111
Alford, E. M. Netherton-on-sea............17289
Alford, Henry. Poetical works. '43...821.2 478
Alfred *the great.* Orosius; old English
   text and Latin original............820.2 348
   Proverbs of........................820.2 326
   West-Saxon version of Saint Gregory's 'Pastoral care'; pt. 1...820.2 324
   Same; pt. 2........................820.2 327
   Whole works; jubilee edition. 1852.
   3 v. in 2.
   V. 1. Harmony of the chroniclers; by Dr. Giles. —Anglo-Saxon mint; by Akerman.—Coins of King Alfred; by Haigh. — Metrical version of King Alfred's poems; by Tupper. — Europe in the 9th century; by Forester. — King Alfred's jewel; by Giles. — The Danes; by Hook. — King Alfred's charters; by Giles.— King Alfred's will; by Giles. —Decline and fall of the heptarchy; by Giles.—Domestic manners of the Anglo-Saxons; by Soane, —Traces of the Danes in England; by Forester.—Grimbald's crypt; by Giles......................820.2 17
   V. 2. English translation of Alfred's Anglo-Saxon of the historian Orosius; by Bosworth. — Alfred's version of Bede's ' Ecclesiastical history '; tr. by Thomson.— Alfred's version of Boethius; tr. by Fox...820.2 18
   V. 3. Alfred's handbook; by Pauli. — On the geography of King Alfred; by Hampson.— Anglo-Saxon version of Gregory's 'Pastoral care'; by Norman. — English version of Alfred's blossom-gatherings from Saint Augustine.— Laws of King Alfred; by Giles.— Alfred's preface to Gregory's dialogues; by Fox. (Bound with v. 2).........820.2 18
Alger. School of life. 1881..............374 12
Alice Thorne...........................07133
Alison. Miscellaneous essays. 1870...*in* 824.2 72
All for greed..........................50356
All the world over.....................0133
Allardyce. Balmoral....................53103
   City of sunshine.........................53102
   Earlscourt...............................53101
Allen, Charles. Papier mâché (stories)...69960
Allen, E. Washington; or, The revolution:
   drama. 1895. 2 v...................822.1 42
Allen, F. M. Little green man............034301
   Pinches of salt..........................32460
   Voyage of the ark. 1888............828.2 54
Allen, Grant. Colin Clout's calendar.
   1883..................................504 97
   Common sense science. 1886..........504 113
   Vignettes from nature. 1881..........504 92
Allen, J. L. Aftermath...................27004
   Choir invisible..........................27006
   Flute and violin, etc....................27001
   John Gray................................27002
   Kentucky cardinal........................27003
   Summer in Arcady.........................27005

Allen, L. W. Abraham Lincoln : a poem.
1896..821.1 522
Allen, Richard. Miss Eaton's romance.....25893
Allen, W. A decade of addresses, 1820-29.
....824.1 244
Allen, W. B. Great island.....................032706
John Brownlow's folks.......................032703
Lion city of Africa................................032701
Lost on Umbagog...............................032704
Mammoth hunters..............................032705
Silver rags..032702
Allingham. Blackberries (verse.) 1884..821.2 726
Songs, ballads, and stories. 1877......821.2 520
Allston. Lects. and poems. 1850..............704 5
Monaldi...56826
Alma Tadema. Love's martyr..................21801
Wings of Icarus......................................21802
Almack's. 2 v..50391
Almy et al. Frilby. 1895....................822.1 47
Orpheus and Eurydice........................822.1 72
Altsheler. Sun of Saratoga.....................10140
American coin..69051
American convent..................................50348
American girl in a boys' college..............50301
Ames, Fisher. Works. 1854. 2 v.......329.1 92
Same. 1809..329.1 94
Ames, L. T. Memoirs of a millionaire......28301
Ames, Mary Clemmer. See Clemmer,
Mary.
Among the Alps......................................07102
Among the chosen.................................58995
Anderson, F. Zenaida............................47281
Anderson, M. B. Papers and addresses.
1895. 2 v.
V. 1 Educational papers and addresses: End and means of a liberal education; The university of the 19th century; Art training in American colleges; Voluntaryism in higher education; Commencement addresses: The scholar's relation to practical life; The issues of the civil war; Right conduct of life; Elements of success; Administrative capacity; The tests of character; Demands of modern life; Moral ideals; The law of self-sacrifice.—Religious papers and addresses: Work of foreign missions; Skepticism with respect to a personal creator; Evolution and its religious bearings; The right use of wealth; The laity of the Baptist church; Christianity and our country: The lessons of fifty years............................824.1 209
V. 2. Philosophical and scientific papers: Origin and political life of the English race; Language as a means of classifying man; Sir William Hamilton's lectures; Growth and relation of the sciences; The Arabian philosophy; Christianity and the common law —Miscellaneous papers and addresses Alexander von Humboldt; Prof. Morse and the electric telegraph Pauperism and organized charity ; Means of relief from foreign paupers; Political economy and its ethical relations; Currency legislation..................824.1 302
Anderson, Mary. Othello's occupation...43320
Andreae. Stanhope of Chester..............31080
Vanished emperor................................31081

Andrews, F., (Elzey Hay, pseud.). Prince
Hal..56835
Andrews, Jane. Each and all............572 49
Only a year and what it brought..........032241
Seven little sisters...............................*572 48
Ten boys...*904 55
Angelina Gushington's thoughts...............55223
Annals of a fishing village.......................19164
Anstey (F. Anstey Guthrie). Black poodle...67310
Giant's robe..67307
Lyre and lancet...................................67306
Man from Blankley's, etc. 1893........828.2 61
Pariah...67302
Puppets at large................................. 67313
Statement of Stella Maberly...............67312
Talking horse, etc...............................67304
Contents: Talking horse.—Good little girl.—Matter of taste.—Don.—Taken by surprise.—Paleface and Redskin.—Shut out.—Tommy's hero.—Canine Ishmael.—Marjory.
Tinted Venus.......................................67311
Tourmalin's time cheques...................67303
Travelling companions.......................67308
Under the rose....................................67309
Vice versa..67301
Appleton, G. W. Frozen hearts..............62802
Jack Allyn's friends............................62801
Appleton, T. G. Chequer-work (essays).
1879..824.1 145
A sheaf of papers. 1875.................824.1 117
Arab wife..55249
Arblay, Madame D', (F. Burney). Camilla....403
Cecilia..402
Evelina..401
Archer, E. M. Christina North..............62521
Archer, T. By fire and sword..................69226
Archie Mason...07111
Arey. Household songs. 1855..........821.1 49
Argles, Mrs. See Hungerford.
Argyle, A., pseud. Olive Lacey..............20443
Argyll, duke of. Highland nurse..............15515
Aristocracy...69050
Armin. Nest of ninnies, 1608. 1842......828.2 5
Armitt. In shallow waters......................69223
Armstrong, G.F. Garland from Greece.821.2 650
Armstrong, J. Poems ; with life. 1822. 821.2 45
Armstrong, W. American nobleman......69325
Thekla..69322
Arnold, Sir Edwin. Adzuma : a play.
1893..822.2 307
In my lady's praise ; poems. 1889....821.2 761
Light of Asia...................................821.2 759
Light of the world. 1891.................821.2 760
Pearls of the faith (poems). 1883....821.2 762
Poems. 1880....................................821.2 766
Potiphar's wife, and other poems. '92.821.2 763
Secret of death, etc. (poems). 1885....821.2 764
Tenth muse, and other poems. 1895...821.2 765

* Of interest to young readers.

Arnold, Edwin L. Constable of St.
  Nicholas..47002
  Phra the Phœnician.........................47001
  Story of Ulla, etc..............................47003
Arnold, Ethel M. Platonics...............31065
Arnold, F. Farm on the mountain............09801
Arnold, George. Poems. 1871..........821.1 456
Arnold, Matthew. Alaric at Rome, and
  other poems. 1896.................821.2 1035
  Bibliographical note (Boston public
    library bulletin, v. 6, p. 84)............17 B-14
  Civilization in the U. S....................917.1 157
  Culture and anarchy. 1869.................301 9
  Discourses in America. 1885..........824.2 372
    Contents: Numbers.—Literature and science of Emerson.
  Essays in criticism. 1865................824.2 259
    Contents: Function of criticism.—Literary influence of academies.—Maurice de Guérin.—Eugenie de Guérin.—Heine.—Pagan and mediæval religious sentiment.—Joubert.—Spinoza.—Marcus Aurelius.—On translating Homer.—A French Eton.
  Same; 2d series. 1888................824.2 260
    Contents: Study of poetry.—Milton.—Gray.—Keats.—Wordsworth.—Byron.—Shelley.—Tolstoi.—Amiel.
  A French Eton......................................378 43
  Friendship's garland. 1871................304 23
  God and the Bible..............................231 24
  Higher schools of Germany...............373 6
  Irish essays, etc. 1882..................824.2 323
    Contents: The incompatibles.—An unregarded Irish grievance.—Ecce convertimur ad gentes.—Future of liberalism.—Speech at Eton.—French play in London.—Copyright.—Prefaces to poems.
  Isaiah XL-LXVI..................................224 37
  Isaiah of Jerusalem............................224 53
  Last essays on church, etc. 1877......204 56
  Letters, 1848-88; ed. by Russell. 1895.
    2 v..826.2 120
  Literature and dogma....................220.0 74
  Mixed essays. 1879.......................824.2 261
    Contents: Democracy.—Equality.—Irish catholicism and British liberalism.—Porro unum est necessarium.—Guide to English literature.—Falkland.—French critic on Milton.—French critic on Gœthe.—George Sand.
  New poems. 1867...........................821.2 711
  On translating Homer. 1861..............883 47
  Passages from prose writings. 1880...829.2 54
  Poems. 1882.....................................821.2 712
  Poetical works. 1896........................821.2 710
  Popular education of France............370 84
  Saint Paul and protestantism.............227 31
  Schools and universities on the continent.370 20
Arnold, W. T. Modern Xanthippe......43501
Arr, E. H., (Mrs. E. H. Rollins). New
  England bygones. 1880.............824.1 151
  Old-time child-life. 1881..............824.1 157
Arthur. Angel and demon......................8201
  Bar-rooms at Brantley..........................8210
  Friends and neighbors.........................8219
  Home heroes, saints, and martyrs......8206
  Home lights and shadows...................8227
  Latimer family.......................................8211
  Light on shadowed paths....................8209
  Lizzie Glen...8222
  Love in high life..................................8225
  Married life..8213
  Our neighbors, etc..............................8207
  Out in the world..................................8223
  Seedtime and harvest.........................8218
  Steps toward heaven..........................8204
  Stories for young housekeepers........8217
  Ten nights in a bar-room...................8220
  Three years in a man-trap.................8226
  Tom Blinn's temperance society, etc...8224
  Two wives..8214
  Wedding guest....................................8203
  What came afterwards........................8208
  Woman to the rescue..........................8221
  Words for the wise, etc.......................8216
Asbjornson and Andersen. Northern
  fairy tales..03986S
Ascham. The scholemaster............820.2 35
  Toxophilus....................................820.2 28
• Whole works; ed. by Giles. 3 v. in 4.
  V. 1 (2 pts.). Life; by Dr. Giles. — Letters.
    Glossary...820.2 44
  V. 2. Letters, continued. — Toxophilus.— Glossary...820.2 46
  V. 3. Report and discourse of affairs and state of Germany. — The schoolmaster. — Poemata.—Edward Grant's oration on Ascham. — Letters of Giles Ascham.— Glossary...................820.2 47
Asmodeus in New York.....................50350
Aspinwall. Short stories for short people..037101
Astor, J. J. Journey in other worlds......46201
Astor, W. W. Sforza...........................69190
  Valentino..69189
Atherton. Doomswoman......................69710
Atkinson, B. Commonplace girl........20280
Atkinson, J. C. Play hours and half-
  holidays..04902
  Walks, talks, etc., of two schoolboys..04901
Atkinson, M. E. Ivy leaves (poems).
  1870...821.1 178
Atkinson, W. P. Right use of books.
  1878...374 9
Aubrey. Devil-tree of El Dorado.........71280
Audelay. Poems............................821.2 457
Austen, Jane. Emma..............................702
  Lady Susan, etc....................................707
  Same.......................................in 928.2 165
  Mansfield park.......................................706
  Northanger abbey.—Persuasion...........704
  Persuasion...705
  Pride and prejudice..............................703
  Sense and sensibility.—Mansfield park.....701
Austin, Alfred. At the gate of the convent,
  and other poems. 1885..............821.2 740

Conversion of Winckelmann, and other
poems. 1897...................821.2 860
England's darling (drama). 1896......822.2 333
English lyrics ; ed. by Watson. 1890..821.2 859
Human tragedy (poem). 1886.........821.2 799
Love's widowhood, etc. (poems). '89..821.2 838
Poetry of the period. 1870................811 18
Savonarola : a tragedy. 1881............822 2 126
The season : a satire. 1861............821.2 798
Soliloquies in song. 1882.............821.2 656
Tower of Babel: drama. 1874......822.2 289
Austin, Arthur W. Floral tribute. 1876.
....821.1 Pam. 33
Austin, B., *and* Abbott, L. Cone-cut corners....................................15271
Austin, Jane G. Betty Alden 9208
Cipher.......................................9203
David Alden's daughter, etc 9209
Desmond Hundred...........................9211
Doctor LeBaron and his daughters..........9207
Dora Darling.................................9205
Mrs. Beauchamp Brown....................9212
Moonfolk....................................027701
Nameless nobleman........................9210
Outpost......................................9204
Shadow of Moloch mountain................9201
Standish of Standish........................9206
Twelve great diamonds.....................9202
Awdeley. Fraternitye of vacabondes...820 2 405
Aytoun, W. E., (T. P. Jones). Bothwell:
a poem. 1856............................821.2 440
Firmilian. 1867...............................828.2 37
Aytoun *and* Martin. Book of ballads...828.2 37
Azarias, *Brother.* Books and reading. '90...374 8
Essays, miscellaneous. 1896............824.1 330
Contents: Literature: its nature and influence.—Religion in education.—Sonnets and plays of Shakespeare.—Culture of the spiritual sense.—Our Catholic school system.—What is the outlook for our colleges?—Church and state.
Essays, philosophical. 1896.................104 35
Contents: Aristotle and the Christian church.—The nature and synthetic principle of philosophy.—Symbolism of the cosmos.—Psychological aspects of education.—Ethical aspects of the papal encyclical.
Babcock. An invention of the enemy......56844
Baby John. (See **Laddie**.)....................17911
Bache. Young wrecker......................032232
Bacheller. Master of silence 56420
Bacon, D. Philosophy of the plays of Shakespeare. 1857......................822 3 78
Bacon, *Sir* F. Essays ; ed. by Selby. '89..824.2 416
Same ; ed. by West. 1897................824.2 2A
Same; ed. by Whately and Heard. 1873...824.2 2
Harmony of essays ; by Arber..........820.2 38
Promus of formularies ; ed. by Pott...822.3 210
Works; ed. by Montagu. 1825 17 v.
V. 1. Essays. Tracts. Apothegms, etc........192 5
V. 2. Advancement of learning. New Atlantis...192 6

V. 3. Wisdom of the ancients.—Henry VII.—State of Europe.—Felicities of Queen Elizabeth.—Julius Cæsar.................................192 7
V. 4. Sylva sylvarum........................192 8
V. 5. Tracts relating to England and Scotland....192 9
V. 6. Speeches.—Charges.—Papers relating to earl of Essex.
V. 7. Theological tracts.....................192 10
V. 8-11. De augmentis scientiarum.—Instauratio magna, and other works in Latin.......192 12
V. 12-13. Letters, law tracts, etc..........192 16
V. 14-15. Translations: Novum organum; Natural history ; Fifth part of great instauration; On the nature of things, etc................192 18
V. 16. Life of Bacon..........................192 20
Bacot. Mrs. Thorndale's cousin.............31045
Baddeley. Death of Antar, etc. (verse.) 1881.....................................821.2 586
Badeau. Conspiracy.........................69179
Bagby. Miss Träumerei......................30380
Bagehot. Estimates of some Englishmen, etc. 1858................................824.2 262
(Contents included in 'Literary studies.')
Literary studies ; by Hutton 1879. 2 v.
V. 1. Memoir of the author ; by Hutton.—The first Edinburgh reviewers.—Hartley Coleridge.—Shelley. — Shakespeare. — Milton. — Lady Mary Wortley Montagu. — Cowper. — Letters on the French coup d'état, 1851.— Cæsarism in 1865.—Memoir of right honorable James Wilson........824.2 239
V. 2. Gibbon. — Bishop Butler. — Sterne and Thackeray. — Waverley novels. — Dickens. — Macaulay.—Béranger.--Clough's poems.--Henry Crabb Robinson.—Wordsworth, Tennyson, and Browning.—Ignorance of man.—Emotion of conviction.—Metaphysical basis of toleration.—Public worship regulation bill..................................824.2 240
Bailey, *Mrs.* A. W. Mark Heffron..........70101
Bailey, J. M. Life in Danbury. 1873...828.1 54
Mr. Phillips' governess......................56846
Bailey, P. J. The age : a satire. 1858...821.2 334
Festus : a poem. 1864....................822.2 158
Baillie. Paraguayan treasure..................69355
Bain, Alexander. Practical essays. '84..824.2 358
Bain, F. W. Dmitri............................11420
Baker, G. A., *jr.* Point-lace and diamonds (poems). 1875...........................821.1 205
Baker, James. By the western sea..........34202
Gleaming dawn...............................34204
John Westacott...............................34201
Mark Tillotson................................34203
Baker, *Sir* Samuel W. Cast up by the sea...02502
True tales for my grandsons................02503
Baker, W. M. Blessed Saint Certainty.....34714
Colonel Dunwoodie, millionaire...........34718
His majesty, myself.........................34707
Making of a man............................34720
Mose Evans..................................34702
New Timothy.................................34701
Virginians in Texas.........................34704
Year worth living............................34703
Balch. Peculiar people.......................62552

Baldwin, *Mrs.* **A.** Story of a marriage......13021
    Where town and country meet..............13020
Baldwin, James. Horse fair.................010010
Baldwin, Joseph G. Flush times of Alabama...44151
Baldwin, Lydia W. Yankee school teacher in Virginia..................................69102
Baldy. Romance of a Spanish nun...........14220
Bale. Kynge Johan: play; ed. by Collier. 1838..822.2 79
Balestier. Average woman....................62705
   Contents: Reffey.—A common story.— 'Captain, my Captain!'
    Benefits forgot.................................62706
    Victorious defeat..............................62707
Balestier *and* **Kipling.** Naulahka.........31412
Balfour, A. J. Essays and addresses. 1893.
    ....824.2 455
   Contents: The pleasures of reading.—Bishop Berkeley's life and letters.—Handel.—Cobden and the Manchester school.— Politics and political economy. — A fragment on progress.—The religion of humanity.
    Pleasures of reading. 1887......... 374 Pam. 3
Balfour, F. H. Cherryfield Hall..............28707
Balfour, M. C. Maris Stella..................56061
    White sand......................................56060
Ballantyne. Away in the wilderness........02642
    Battery and boiler............................02635
    Big otter...02647
    Black ivory.....................................02622
    Blown to bits..................................02650
    Blue lights......................................02649
    Buffalo runners...............................02653
    Coral island....................................02601
    Crew of the Water Wagtail..............02652
    Deep down....................................02608
    Digging for gold.............................02643
    Dog Crusoe....................................02626
    Eagle cliff......................................02651
    Erling the bold...............................02609
    Fighting the flames.........................02639
    Floating light.................................02621
    Freaks on the fells..........................02619
    Gascoyne......................................02612
    Giant city of the north....................02633
    Golden dream................................02634
    Gorilla hunters...............................02611
    Hunted and harried........................02654
    In the track of the troops................02638
    Iron horse......................................02606
    Island queen..................................02646
    Life boat..02603
    Life in the red brigade....................02665
    Lighthouse....................................02607
    Lonely island.................................02630
    Lost in the forest............................02631
    Martin Rattler...............................02614
    Middy and the Moors.....................02648

    Norseman in the west.....................02605
    Over the Rocky mountains..............02632
    Philosopher Jack............................02624
    Pioneers..02641
    Post haste......................................02623
    Rivers of ice..................................02602
    Rover of the Andes........................02645
    Settler and savage..........................02636
    Shifting winds...............................02620
    Six months at the cape....................02628
    Sunk at sea....................................02629
    Under the waves............................02618
    Ungava..02613
    World of ice..................................02604
    Young fur-traders..........................02640
    Young trawler................................02644
Bampfylde. Poems. 1822..............*in* 821.2 46
Bancroft, G. Literary and historical miscellanies...824.1 29
Bancroft, H. H. Essays and miscellany. 1890...978 89
Bandelier. Delight makers..................14005
Bangs. The bicyclers, and other farces. 1896..822.1 39
   Contents: The bicyclers.—A dramatic evening.—The fatal message.—A proposal under difficulties.
    Coffee and repartee. 1893..........827.1 35
    Half-hours with Jimmieboy..............06350
    House-boat on the Styx. 1896.......828.1 81
    The idiot. 1895...........................827.1 36
    Mantel-piece minstrels, etc...............06351
    Mr. Bonaparte of Corsica. 1895.....827.1 37
    Pursuit of the house-boat. 1897.....828.1 82
    Rebellious heroine 6351
    Three weeks in politics. 1894.......827.1 34
    Water ghost, etc...............................6350
   Contents: The water ghost of Harrowby hall.—The spectre cook of Bangletop.—The speck on the lens—A midnight visitor.—A quicksilver Cassandra.—The ghost club.—A psychical prank.—The literary remains of Thomas Bragdon.
Banim. Bit o' writin'..........................12028
    Mayor of Wind-gap........................12027
Banks, Alice. Cheep and chatter............031601
Banks, *Mrs.* **G. L.** Bond slaves............64512
    Bridge of beauty.............................64513
    Caleb Booth's clerk........................64503
    From the same nest........................64510
    Glory...64502
    In his own hand.............................64509
    Manchester man.............................64501
    Miss Pringle's pearls.......................64511
    Rough road....................................06450
    Stung to the quick..........................64504
    Sybilla, etc....................................64508
    Watchmaker's daughter, etc............64506
    Wooers and winners.......................64505
Banks, Mary Ross. Bright days in old plantation times...............................62577

Bansley. Pride and abuse of women...821.2 474
Bar-sinister...69022
Barbauld, *Mrs.* Tales, poems and essays.824.2 355
  Works : 1825. 2 v.
    V. 1. Memoir; by Lucy Aikin.— Poems........821.2 281
    V. 2. Correspondence.— Miscellany................821.2 282
Barbour. The Bruce: metrical history;
    ed. by Jamieson............................821.2 111
  Same ; ed. by Skeat. pt. 1............820.2 407
  Same. pt. 2................................820.2 415
  Same. pt. 3................................820.2 422
Barclay, Alex. Cytezen and uplondysh-
  man...821.2 465
Barham. Ingoldsby legends. 1864. 2 v..828.2 49
  Miscellaneous poems..................*in* 928.2 171
Baring-Gould. See **Gould, S. Baring-.**
Barker, *Lady.* Boys.............................011104
  Christmas cake in four quarters............011101
  Holiday stories...................................011105
  Spring comedies.................................15270
  Stories about....................................011102
  White rat..011103
Barkley. My boyhood........................05930
Barlow, Jane. Bog-land studies (verse).
  1894...821.2 928
  End of Elfintown (verse). 1894........821.2 968
  Irish idylls...37905
  Kerrigan's quality................................37906
  Maureen's fairing................................37907
  Mrs. Martin's company, etc....................37909
  Strangers at Lisconnel.........................37908
Barlow, Joel. The Columbiad. 1809..821.1 231
  Political writings. 1796....................329.1 142
  Vision of Columbus : a poem. 1787..821.1 340
Barnard, C., (Jane Kingsford, *pseud.*).
  Knights of to-day..............................30410
  Money and music 30408
  Soprano...30407
  Whistling buoy..................................30409
Barnes, James. For king or country........70020
  Loyal traitor......................................07021
  Midshipman Farragut..........................07020
  Princetonian 70021
Barnes, Josiah. Green mountain travellers.12058
Barnes, William. Poems in the Dorset
  dialect..821.2 407
  Poems of rural life, in the Dorset dialect.
  1879..821.2 540
Barnfield. Affectionate shepherd........828.2 463
Barr, Amelia E. Beads of Tasmer...........19221
  Bernicia...19235
  Between two loves 19206
  Border shepherdess...........................19209
  Bow of orange ribbon........................19208
  Christopher, etc.................................19213
    Contents: Christopher. — Crowther and Thirsk.— Master of Rushen. — Rex Macarthy. — Our Joe.— Jonathan Yeadon's justification.—Seed by the way-side.— Heart of Sam Naylor.

  Cluny Macpherson...............................19201
  Daughter of Fife.................................19205
  Feet of clay......................................19217
  Flower of Gala Water..........................19234
  Friend Olivia.....................................19220
  Girls of a feather................................19231
  Hallam succession..............................19229
  Harvest of the wind, etc......................19212
    Contents: Harvest of the wind.—Preacher's daughter. —Rex Macarthy.
  Household of McNeil..........................19216
  In spite of himself..............................19214
  Jan Vedder's wife...............................19202
  Knight of the nets..............................19236
  Last of the Macallisters......................19204
  Lone house.......................................19233
  Lost silver of Briffault.........................19203
  Love for an hour is love forever...........19226
  Master of his fate...............................19211
  Mate of the Easter Bell, etc................19230
    Contents: Mate of the Easter Bell. — Harvest of faith and constancy. — Consequences of a mistake.— Agnes Stirling.—A horse for a wife.—Tale of two brothers. —Romance of two pictures.—Story of a wedding.—A discovered life. — The true Delzel. — Earning one's capital. — Brave girl.— Just as it happened.— Druid's moss. — I meant no harm. — Here of Saltham pit.— Only Jones. — Blue Wesley teapot. — Not for gold. — One pair of gloves.— A dishonored bill.— The belle of the Orkney isles. — Nap Fontaine's duel. — Tom Burleson's love affair. — Davie's shoulder-straps. — More than two at a bargain.— Housewife and wife. — Only my lord's brother.— Gypsy lady. — Saving of Eshold. — It's guid to be honest and true.
  Michael and Theodora........................019220
  Paul and Christina.............................19210
  Preacher's daughter...........................19228
  Same...*in* 19212
  Prisoners of conscience......................19237
  Remember the Alamo (Woven of love
    and glory)....................................19218
  Rose of a hundred leaves....................19224
  Scottish sketches...............................19219
    Contents: Crawford's sair strait.—James Blackie's revenge.— Facing his enemy.— Andrew Cargill's confession. — One wrong step. — Lile Davie.
  She loved a sailor..............................19222
  Short stories.....................................19225
    Contents: Femmetia's strange experience.—Marrying for money.—Out of Egypt.—John Taggert's trial.—The Forsyth will case.— Luck.—Mary's marriage. — Only this once.— A southern temper.— A man and his own way.—A romance of labor.—A faithful woman.— Kate Dalrymple.—With her eyes open.— James Macharg's temper.— I don't care. — The Kennedys' good fortune.— Paid in his own coin.— Roy of Airlie.—The Udaler's daughter.—How I said 'yes.'—Smitten with remorse.— Ike Brennan's watch.— Sold for naught. — A young man saved. — Anything for peace. — The good-for-nothing.— The parents' mistake.— The ruined house.— For better, for worse.
  Singer from the sea...........................19232
  Sister to Esau..................................19223

Squire of Sandal-Side	19207
Woven of love and glory (Remember the Alamo)	19218
Young people of Shakespeare's dramas. 1882	*822 3 204
r, Robert. Face and the mask	43291
From whose bourne?	43293
In the midst of alarms	43290
One day's courtship.—The heralds of fame	43294
Revenge (stories)	43295

Contents: An Alpine divorce.—Which was the murderer?—A dynamite explosion.—An electrical ship.—The vengeance of the dead.—Over the Stelvia pass.—The hour and the man.— And the rigour of the game.—The Bromley Gibberl's story.—Not according to the code.—A modern Samson.—A deal on 'change.— Transformation. —The shadow of the greenback.—The understudy.— Out of Thun.— A dramatic point.—Two Florentine balconies. —The exposure of Lord Stansford.—Purification.

Woman intervenes	43292
rett, E. S., (Cervantes Hogg). The rising sun. 1809. 3 v.	827.2 14
rett, Frank. Folly Morrison	53802
Great Hesper	53803
His helpmate	53806
John Ford.—His helpmate	53810
Justification of Andrew Lebrun	53809
Kitty's father	53808
Lieutenant Barnabas. 3 v	53801
Olga's crime	53812
Out of the jaws of death	53807
Recoiling vengeance	53804
Set of rogues	53811
Smuggler's secret	53805
rett, Wilson. Sign of the cross	58240
rie. Auld Licht idylls	33201
Auld Licht manse, etc	33207

Contents: J. M. Barrie; by Henderson.—An Auld Licht manse.—Dite Deuchars.—Biggest box in the world. Our new servant.—Shutting a map.—Result of a tramp. —Other ' Times.'—My husband's book.—An invalid in lodgings.— Mending the clock.—Fox-terrier Frisky.— Reminiscences of an umbrella.—Ndint-pile pont (?).— Humor of Dickens.—What is Scott's best novel?—Q.— Man from Nowhere.— Woodland path.

Better dead	33205
Same	*in* 33203A
A holiday in bed, etc. 1892	824.2 450
Lady's shoe	*in* 32715
Little minister	33206
My lady Nicotine	33203
Sentimental Tommy	33210
Tillyloss scandal.— Life in a country manse	33208
Two of them	33209

Contents: Two of them.— Our new servant.— Reminiscences of an umbrella.—Inconsiderate waiter.— Playwright and the fowl.— Fox-terrier Frisky.— Family honor.—Wicked cigar.—Result of a tramp in Surrey.— My husband's book.—A lady's shoe.—Was it a watch?—Man from nowhere.— Holiday in bed.— is it a man?— Woodland path.—Woman and the press.—Plea for smaller books.—Boys' books : their glorification.—Lost works of George Meredith.--Humor of Dickens.—Gretna Green revisited.— Thoughtful boys make thoughtful men.— Ndintpile pont (?).—To the influenza.— Four-in-hand novelists. — Q. — Rules for carving. — What is Scott's best novel?—My favorite authoress.

Window in Thrums	33202
Barrington, Mrs. Helen's ordeal	37311
Lena's picture	37310
Barry. Intriguers	70860
Bartlett, G. H. Commercial trip with an uncommercial ending	22790
Water tramps	22791
Bartlett, J. Concordance to Shakespeare. 1894	‡822.3 B-35
Bartlett, Mrs. J. M. D. Until daybreak	47291
Bartol. Principles and portraits. 1880	824.1 148
Barton. Memoir, letters, etc. 1850	826.2 33
Basil. Drawn game	23501
Bassett. Hippolyte.—Goldenbeak	15625
Bates, Arlo. Albrecht	16008
Book o' nine tales	16010
In the bundle of time	16011
Lad's love	16009
Berries of the brier. 1886	821.1 357
Pagans	16003
Patty's perversities	16013
Philistines	16007
Sonnets in shadow. 1887	821.1 361
Told in the gate (poems). 1892	821.1 448
Wheel of fire	16012
Bates, Arlo, *and* **Putnam, E.** Prince Vance	040901
Bates, J. W. Blind lead	69387
Bates, Mrs. L. W. Bunch-grass stories	31520
Bates, Lizzie. Stories from the Moorland	25859
Bathurst. Essays in The Adventurer. 3v.	824.2 16
Batson. Dark	38501
Battershall, Daughter of this world	43221
Mists	43220
Battle of Dorking; by Chesney. 1871	827.2 Pam. 2
Battle of Berlin. 1871	827.2 Pam. 13
Siege of London. 1871	827.2 Pam. 4
What happened after	827.2 Pam. 3
Baylor. Behind the Blue Ridge	69166
Claudia Hyde	69165
On both sides	69167
Shocking example, etc	69160
Bayly, A. E. See **Lyall, Edna.**	
Bayly, E. B. Zachary Brough's venture	43310
Bayne. Days of Jezebel: drama. 1872	822.2 165
Essays in biography, etc. 1858. 2 v.	

V. 1. De Quincey.— Tennyson and his teachers.— Mrs. Browning.— Recent British art.—Ruskin and his critics.—Hugh Miller.—The modern novel. —Currer Bell..................824.2 115
V. 2. Kingsley.— Macaulay.— Sir A. Alison.— Coleridge.— Wellington.— Bonaparte.— Plato.— Christian civilization.— The modern university.— Pulpit and press.—Testimony of the rocks......824.2 116

* Of interest to young readers.   ‡ For reference.

Lessons from my masters. 1879......824.2 266
   Contents: Carlyle.—Tennyson.—Ruskin.
Baynes. Shakespeare studies. 1896....822.3 386
Beach, C. A. Now or never...................021201
Beach, R. G. Puritan and the Quaker......55205
Beaconsfield, *earl of.* See Disraeli, Benjamin.
Beal. Boys of Clovernook.......................034901
Beale, A. Farm on the down.— Old Gwen..38604
   Gladys the reaper................................38602
   Simplicity and fascination....................38601
Beale, Maria. Jack o' Doon....................9340
Bean. Doctor Mortimer's patient..............52284
Beard. Moonblight.................................30540
Beattie. Dissertations. 1809. 3 v............104 1
   Essays. 1809. 3 v................................104 4
   Minstrel, etc. (poems). 1809..........821.2 207
   Poems; with life. 1822....................821.2 48
   Poetical works. 1831.....................821.2 206
Beaumont, F., *and* Fletcher, J. Works.
   1840. 2 v..822.2 103
Beaumont, Mary. Joan Seaton...............13921
   Ringby lass, etc..................................13920
Becke. By reef and palm (stories)............43230
   Ebbing of the tide................................43231
   His native wife....................................43234
Becke *and* Jeffery. First Fleet family....43232
   Mystery of the Laughlin islands............43233
Becket, A. Shakespeare's himself again.
   1815. 2 v..822.3 70
Becket, Thomas à. See Thomas à Becket.
Beckett, C. H. Who is John Noman?......69306
Beckett, *Mrs.* S. Corinthia Marazion.........2650
Beckford. History of Caliph Vathek. '83...823 88
   Same; Vathek......................................12035
Beckman. Pax and Carlino....................034401
Beckonings from little hands. 1895..........137 4
Beddoes. Letters; ed. by Gosse. 1894..826.2 111
   Poems. 1851. 2 v.............................821.2 715
Bede, *The venerable.* Be Domes dæge..820.2 336
   Miscellaneous works. 1843. 6 v.
      V. 1. Life.—Poemata—Epistolæ..................820.2 20
      V. 2-3. Historia ecclesiasticæ......................820.2 21
      V. 4. Opuscula historica............................820.2 23
      V. 5. Homilies...820.2 24
      V. 6. Scientific tracts.—Appendix................820.2 25
Bede, Cuthbert, *pseud.* (E. Bradley).
   Nearer and dearer................................12032
   Verdant Green.....................................12030
Beebee. Edmund Dawn..........................47244
Beechenhurst..55218
Beecher, H. W. Metaphors, similes, etc.;
   comp. by Ellinwood. 1895..............829.1 39
   Norwood..8801
   Star papers. 1873...........................824.1 99
Beecher, L. Autobiography and correspondence. 2 v.............................922.1 69

Beerbohm. Happy hypocrite...................55020
Beers, E. L. All quiet along the Potomac,
   and other poems. 1879..................821.1 229
Beers, H. A. Odds and ends: verses.
   1878..821.1 207
   Suburban pastoral, etc..........................31055
   Contents: A suburban pastoral.—A midwinter night's dream.—A comedy of errors.—Declaration of independence.—Split zephyr.—A graveyard idyl.—Eric the wild and the witch wife.—The wine-flower.
Beesly. Ballads, etc. 1895.................821.2 977
Behn, *Mrs.* Plays, histories and novels.
   1871. 6 v...822.2 218
Belial..14104
Bell, E. M. Poems. 1872...................821.1 191
Bell, *Mrs.* Hugh. Story of Ursula...........52540
Bell, Lilian. Little sister to the wilderness...30606
   Love affairs of an old maid....................30605
   Under side of things.............................30607
Bell, *Mrs.* Martin. See Martin, *Mrs.* Bell.
Bell, William. Shakespeare's Puck and his
   folkslore. 1852.................................822.3 141
Bellamy, C. J. Breton Mills..................58701
   Six to one...58702
Bellamy, E. Dr. Heidenhoff's process.....17103
   Equality..17104
   Looking backward, 2000-1887..............17102
   Miss Ludington's sister.........................17101
Bellamy, E. W. Old man Gilbert............69490
Bellew. Memoirs of a griffin...................30404
Belloc. In a walled garden. 1895........920.2 93
   A passing world...................................59310
Belsham. Essays. 1799. 2 v............824.2 65
Beman. Intellectual position of our country...40 27
Benedict, F. L. Her friend Laurence.......8023
   John Worthington's name......................8001
   Madame..8012
   Price she paid.....................................8027
   'Twixt hammer and anvil......................8008
Benedict, H. A. Fagots (verse). '95...821.1 494
Benedict, H. E. Poems...............821.1 Pam. 24
Bengough. In a promised land..............13625
Benjamin. Choice of Paris....................30601
   Sea-spray...30602
Benoni Blake, M. D................................50328
Benson, A. C. Essays. 1896............824.2 509
   Contents: The ever-memorable John Hales.— A minute philosopher.—Henry More, the Platonist. —Andrew Marvell.— Vincent Bourne. — Thomas Gray.— William Blake.— The poetry of Keble.—E. B. Browning.— The late master of Trinity.—Henry Bradshaw. — Christina Rossetti. — The poetry of Edmund Gosse.— Epilogue.
Benson, E. F. The babe, B. A...........15528
   Dodo..15525
   Rubicon..15526
   Six common things..............................15527

LANGUAGE AND LITERATURE.

Beowulf. Autotypes of the Cotton ms., with transliteration and notes by Zupitza....................820.2 346
Same; tr. by Wackerbath. 1849....821.2 99
Same; tr. by Lumsden. 1881........821.2 97
Same (with 'The fight at Finnsburg'); tr. by Garnett................821.2 96
Same (with 'The Scop; or, Gleeman's tale,' and 'The fight at Finnsburg'); ed. and tr. by B. Thorpe............821.2 98
Berdoe. Browning and the Christian faith. 1896..................821.2 1113
Browning cyclopædia. 1892..........821.2 1112
Berdoe, *ed.* Browning studies. 1895..821.2 1114
Berkeley. Essays in The Guardian. 3 v...824.2 10
Works; ed. by Fraser. 1871. 4 v.
   V. 1-2. Philosophical works.........................192 56
   V. 3. Miscellaneous works............................192 58
   V. 4. Life and letters...................................192 59
Berquin. Children's friend. 6 v..............037901
Berringer. New virtue........................36780
Bertz. French prisoners......................032202
Berwick. The secret of Saint Florel..........54680
Besant. All in a garden fair..............42625
All sorts and conditions of men...............42615
Armorel of Lyonesse......................42623
The art of fiction. 1884...................813 41
Bell of St. Paul's........................42622
Beyond the dreams of avarice...............42635
Children of Gibeon......................42610
City of refuge..........................42638
Demoniac..............................42628
Dorothy Forster........................42624
Doubts of Dives........................42621
For faith and freedom...................42618
Fountain sealed........................42641
Herr Paulus............................42640
Holy Rose, etc..........................42626
   Contents: The holy rose.—The last mass.—Inner house.—Even with this.—Camilla's last string.
In deacon's orders, etc..................42636
   Contents: In deacon's orders.—Peer and heiress.—The equal woman.—The shrinking shoe.—Quarantine island.—In three weeks.—One and two.—A night with Tantalus.—The Solid gold reef company, limited.—To the third and fourth generation.—King David's friend.
Inner house............................42617
Same...............................*in* 42626
Ivory gate..............................42633
Let nothing you dismay.................*in* 42627
Master craftsman.......................42637
Rebel queen...........................42634
Revolt of man..........................42616
St. Katherine's by the tower..............42631
They were married......................42627
To call her mine, etc....................42620
   Contents: To call her mine.—Katharine regina.—Self or bearer.

Uncle Jack, etc..........................42629
   Contents: Uncle Jack.—Julia.—Sir Jocelyn's cup.—A glorious fortune.—In luck at last.
Verbena Camellia Stephanotis, etc.........42632
   Contents: Verbena Camellia Stephanotis. Doubts of Dives.—Demoniac.—Doll's house—and after.
World went very well then..............42639
Besant *and* **Pollock.** The charm, etc.: plays.................................792.1 70
Besant *and* **Rice.** By Celia's arbor..........42601
Case of Mr. Lucraft, etc.................42605
   Contents: From the supernatural: The case of Mr. Lucraft; The mystery of Joe Morgan; An old, old story; Lady Kitty; The old four-poster; My own experience. —From fairyland: Titania's farewell.—From fact: On the Goodwin; Edelweis; Love finds the way; The death of S. Pickwick; When the ship comes home.
Captain's room, etc....................42619
   Contents: Captain's room.—Let nothing you dismay. —They were married.—Humbling of the Memblings.—Murder of Nick Vedder.
Chaplain of the fleet....................42613
Golden butterfly........................42607
Monks of Thelema......................42604
My little girl............................42603
Novels of; by A. E. Barr. 1888......823 Pam. 3
Ready-money Mortiboy...................42602
Seamy side.............................42609
Shepherds all and maidens fair..........*in* 42630
Ten years' tenant.......................42612
This son of Vulcan......................42608
'Twas in Trafalgar's bay, etc...............42630
   Contents: 'Twas in Trafalgar's bay.—Shepherds all and maidens fair.—Such a good man.—Le chien d'or.
When the ship comes home.............42611
Same................................*in* 42605
With harp and crown....................42606
Bethel. Millicent and her cousins...........022401
Bickerdyke. Banished beauty..............36530
Bickerstaff, Isaac. See **Steele,** *Sir* **R.**
Bickersteth. The two brothers, and other poems..................................821.2 411
The reef, and other parables............06701
Yesterday, to-day and forever (poem)..821.2 410
Bierce. Can such things be?................30547
In the midst of life.......................30546
Bigelow, A. G. 'Cello player................41775
Bigelow, E. Diplomatic disenchantments...29980
Bigelow, E. E. Beautiful Mrs. Thorndyke...69405
Bigelow, J. Eolopoesis: American rejected addresses (verse.) 1855......821.1 509
Bigelow, W. S. Holly leaves: Christmas poem............................821.1 Pam. 34
Bigot, *Mrs.* See **Healy, Mary.**
Billings, E. E. Marking the boundary.....06705
Billings, Josh, (H. W. Shaw). His sayings. 1866................................828.1 39
On ice.................................828.1 40
Works, complete. 1887..................828.1 38
Bingham. L'envoi (poem)................821.1 503

Birchenough, *Mrs.* Disturbing elements...6980I
Bird, R. M. Nick of the woods.................56809
Bird, R. M. *and* **F. M.** Belated revenge....56808
Birrell, A. Obiter dicta. 1884............824.2 400
  Contents: Carlyle.— Alleged obscurity of some of Mr. Browning's poetry.—Truth hunting.—Actors.—A rogue's memoirs (Cellini).—The via media.—Falstaff.
  Same. 2d series. 1887................824.2 401
  Contents: Milton.— Pope.— Johnson.— Burke.— The muse of history.—Charles Lamb.—Emerson.— The office of literature. — Worn-out types. — Cambridge and the poets.— Book-buying.
  Essays about men, women and books. 1894..824.2 466
  Contents: Dean Swift.— Lord Bolingbroke.— Sterne. —Dr. Johnson.—Richard Cumberland.—Alexander Knox and Thomas De Quincey.— Hannah More.—Marie Bashkirtseff. — Sir John Vanbrugh. — John Gay. — Roger North's autobiography.— Books, old and new. — Bookbinding.— Poets laureate.—Parliamentary candidates.— The bona-fide traveller.— Hours in a library. — Americanisms and Briticisms.—Authors and critics.
  Res judicatæ. 1892.......................824.2 445
  Contents: Samuel Richardson. — Edward Gibbon.— William Cowper.—George Borrow.—Cardinal Newman.— Matthew Arnold.—William Hazlitt.— Letters of Charles Lamb.— Authors in court.— Nationality.— The Reformation.— Sainte-Beuve.
Birrell, O. Anthony Langsyde.................34615
Biscoe. Katharine's experience...............20431
Bishop, A. W. Oration, Fayetteville, Ark., 1865.............................825.1 Pam. 2
Bishop, W. H. Brown-stone boy............67803
  Choy Susan..67807
  House of a merchant prince...................67801
  Golden justice....................................67802
  Pound of cure....................................67805
  Yellow snake.....................................67804
  Writing to Rosina................................67806
Bisland *and* **Broughton.** Widower indeed...7905
Black, Alexander. Miss Jerry..............20250
Black, Clementina. Agitator...............21630
Black, Ivory, *pseud.* See **Janvier, T. A.**
Black, William. Adventures in Thule...027802
  Briseis..2318
  Daughter of Heth..............................2383
  Donald Ross of Heimra......................2314
  Four Macnicols................................027801
  Green pastures and Piccadilly..............2309
  Handsome Humes............................2317
  Highland cousins..............................2308
  In far Lochaber................................2306
  In silk attire...................................2312
  Judith Shakspeare............................2376
  Kilmeny...2301
  Lady Silverdale's sweetheart, etc..........2340
  Contents: Lady Silverdale's sweetheart.—Maid of Killeena.—Fight for a wife.
  Love or marriage..............................2319
  MacLeod of Dare..............................2328
  Madcap Violet.................................2302
  Magic ink, etc.................................2315
  Contents: Magic ink.—A Hallowe'en wraith.—Nanciebel.
  Maid of Killeena..............................2364
  Monarch of Mincing lane....................2342
  Penance of John Logan, etc.,..............2310
  Contents: Penance of John Logan.— Romeo and Juliet.—A snow idyll.
  Prince Fortunatus.............................2307
  Princess of Thule.............................2313
  Sabina Zembra................................2303
  Shandon bells..................................2366
  Stand fast, Craig-Royston!.................2311
  Strange adventures of a house-boat.......2305
  Strange adventures of a phaeton..........2320
  Sunrise..2356
  That beautiful wretch........................2361
  Three feathers................................2304
  White heather.................................2386
  White wings....................................2343
  Wise women of Inverness..................2384
  Wolfenberg....................................2316
  Yolande...2371
Blackburn. Young Calvin in Paris..........30462
Blackford, *Mrs.* Orphan of Waterloo.....019301
Blackie. Ideal of humanity. 1895..........204 127
  Contents: David, king of Israel.—Christian unity.— Wisdom.—Women.—Saint Paul and the Epistle to the Romans.—The Scottish Covenanters.
  Lays and legends of ancient Greece. 1880...821.2 572
  Musa Burchicosa: songs for students. 1869...821.2 809
  On self-culture. 1874........................374 3
  Songs of religion and life. 1876.......821.2 425
  Wise men of Greece (drama). 1877...822.2 203
  Wisdom of Goethe. 1883..................839 7
Blackmore, *Sir* **R.** Creation: a poem...821.2 176
  Poems; with life. 1822..................821.2 47
Blackmore, R. D. Alice Lorraine..........26018
  Christowell.....................................26019
  Clara Vaughan................................26005
  Cradock Nowell...............................26010
  Cripps the carrier............................26006
  Erema..26004
  Kit and Kitty..................................26003
  Lorna Doone..................................26001
  Maid of Sker..................................26009
  Mary Anerley.................................26015
  Perlycross.....................................26008
  Slain by the Doones, etc. [Tales from the telling-house]..............................26011
  Contents: Slain by the Doones.— Frida.— George Bowring.—Crocker's hole.
  Springhaven..................................26002
Blackwell. Island neighbors.................14161
Blagden, Isa. Nora and Archibald Lee....12069
  Woman I loved................................12070

LANGUAGE AND LITERATURE.

Blagden, S. Some sweet poems, etc. '95..821.2 492
Blair, E. N. Lisbeth Wilson........................58220
Blair, Robert. Poems; with life. '22...*in* 821.2 39
Blake, F. Oration at Worcester, July 4.
    1812..40 22
Blake, Lilian D. Fettered for life..........44188
Blake, M. M. Courtship by command......41001
Blake, William. Bibliographical note
    (Boston public library bulletin, v.4, p.
    335)...17 B-14
    Poems; ed. by Skipsey. 1885........821.2 816
    Poetical works; ed., with memoir, by
    Rossetti. 1875..............................821.2 290
    Selections from writings. 1893..........821.2 915
Blanchard. Sketches from life. 1846...824.2 177
Bland, *Mrs.* H. See Nesbit.
Blatchford. Tommy Atkins of the Ramchunders..27041
    Son of the forge......................................27040
Blessington, *countess of.* Country quarters..10001
    Desultory thoughts, etc......................829.2 12
    Marmaduke Herbert.................................10003
    Meredith..10005
Blind. Heather on fire (verse). 1886...821.2 801
    Tarantella..69107
Bloede. See Sterne, Stuart, *pseud.*
Bloomfield. Farmer's boy (verse). 1811.
    ....821.2 530
    Wild flowers: poetry. 1806.............821.2 137
    Works..821.2 408
Blossom. Checkers....................................36801
Blundell, *Mrs.* See Francis, M. E.
Boalt. Owl biddeth good-bye to Bromley.
    ....828.1 Pam. 1
Boisgilbert, E., *pseud.* See Donnelly, I.
Boit. Eustis......................................62364
Boker. Book of the dead (verse). 1882.
    ....821.1 277
    Königsmark, and other poems. 1869...822.1 11
    Plays and poems. 1856. 2 v.
    V. 1. Calaynos.—Anne Boleyn.—Leonor de Guzman.—Francesca da Rimini......................822.1 20
    V. 2. The betrothal.—The widow's marriage.—
    Poems...822.1 21
    Poems of the war. 1864................821.1 307
Boldrewood, Rolf, *pseud.* (T.A. Browne).
    Crooked stick................................69547
    Miner's right..................................69542
    Modern buccaneer........................69545
    My run home................................69550
    Nevermore....................................69544
    Robbery under arms......................69548
    Sealskin cloak................................69549
    Sphinx of Eaglehawk......................69546
    Squatter's dream............................69543
Bolingbroke, *Lord.* Works. 1841. 4 v....192 60
    (For contents, see FINDING LIST, Part 3, p. 436).
Bolingbroke *et al.* The craftsman. 14 v...329.2 48

Bolton, C. K. Love story of Ursula Wolcott: verse. 1895......................821.1 500
Bolton, S. K. Present problem................44174
Bonar. Hymns of faith and hope. 3 v...821.2 294
Bonner, Sherwood, *pseud.* (Mrs. K. S.
    McDowell). Dialect tales..................44147
    Suwanee river tales.............................44148
Booth. See Rita, *pseud.*
Boothby. The beautiful white devil.........53744
    Bid for fortune..................................53743
    Dr. Nikola..53745
    In strange company............................53740
    Lost endeavor..................................53742
    Marriage of Esther.............................53741
Border lances; by author of 'Belt and
    spur.'..20201
Borlase. Stirring tales of colonial adventure..43140
Borrow. Lavengro...................................30423
    Romany rye. 2 v................................30421
Borrow, *tr.* Gypsy songs and poetry......949x 14
Botta, *Mrs.* See Lynch, A. C.
Boulger. See Gift, Theo.
Boulton. Bess.......................................13641
    Josephine Crewe................................13640
Bourne. Mystery of the Cordillera............32001
Bouton. Round the block.........................44141
Bouvé. Centuries apart...........................21220
Bouvet. Child of Tuscany.......................09712
    My lady...9750
    Pierrette..9751
    Prince Tip-Top................................09711
    Sweet William.................................09710
Bowen, F. Gleanings from a literary life...104 15
Bowen, H. M. Daughter of Cuba..............70660
Bower. Paynton Jacks, gentleman............19410
    The story of Mollie...........................04040f
Bowles, John. Stormy petrel..................31701
Bowles, W. L. Poetical works. 1855. 2v.
    V. 1. Sonnets.—Miscellaneous poems.—Spirit of
    discovery.—The missionary......................821.2 260
    V. 2. Memoir; by Gilfillan.—Banwell Hill.—
    Grave of the last Saxon.—Saint John in Patmos.—
    Sorrows of Switzerland.—Villager's verse-book,
    etc...821.2 270
Bowman. Among the Tartar tents...........07409
    Boy pilgrims..................................07414
    Clever Jack, and other tales................07415
    How to make the best of it.................07412
    Laura Temple................................07411
    Rector's daughter...........................07406
    Sunshine and clouds.......................07407
    Young exiles..................................07402
    Young Nile voyagers.......................07413
Bowne. A girl's life 80 years ago: letters.
    1887...923.1 558
Boyd. Autumn holidays of a country parson..824.2 204

    Critical essays of a country parson.....824.2 208
    Everyday philosopher. 1863............824.2 206
    Leisure hours in town. 1862............824.2 207
    Our little life: essays. 1882............824.2 205
    Recreations of a country parson. '62..824.2 203
    Towards the sunset. 1883................824.2 335
    What set him right, etc. 1885..........824.2 370
Boydell. Illustrations of Shakespeare; ed.
    by Spooner. 1852. 2 v.............822.3 Cab. 3
Boyesen. Against heavy odds...................25610
    Boyhood in Norway........................025605
    Daughter of the Philistines.....................25614
    Falconberg...25604
    Golden calf...25612
    Gunnar..25602
    Idyls of Norway, and other poems. 1882.
    ....821.1 286
    Ilka on the hill-top, etc........................25605
        Contents: Ilka on the hill-top.—Annunciata.—Under the glacier.—Knight of Dannebrog.—Mabel and I.—How Mr. Storm met his destiny.
    Light of her countenance......................25609
    Literary and social silhouettes. 1894...824.1 286
    Mammon of unrighteousness..................25611
    Modern vikings..................................25607
    Norseland tales................................025606
    Norseman's pilgrimage........................25601
    Queen Titania...................................25606
    Social strugglers................................25613
    Tales from two hemispheres..................25603
        Contents: Man who lost his name.—Story of an outcast.—Good-for-nothing.—Scientific vagabond.—Truls the nameless.—Asathor's vengeance.
    Vagabond tales..................................25608
        Contents: Crooked John.—Child of the age.—Monk Tellenbach's exile.—Disastrous partnership.—Liberty's victim.—Perilous incognito.—Charity.
Boyle. Chronicles of No-Man's Land........57501
    From the frontier...............................57506
    Legends from my bungalow..................57503
    On the border land............................57504
    Prophet John....................................57505
    Savage life......................................57502
Boyle *and* **Russan.** Orchid seekers........57520
    The riders.......................................57522
    Through forest and plain......................57521
Boylston. John Charáxes.........................20451
    Boys' and girls' book of enchantment........0127
    Boys' and girls' book of story..................0126
    Boys' and girls' book of travel................0128
    Boys' kingdom...................................0124
Boyse. Poems; with life. 1822............821.2 35
Brabourne, *Lord.* See **Hugessen, E. H. K.**
Brace. Fawn of the Pale Faces.................52285
Brackenridge. Adventures of Captain
    Farrago..12067
    Adventures of Major O'Regan.................12066
    Modern chivalry................................12064

Braddon (Mrs. Maxwell). All along the
    river..4028
    Asphodel..4058
    Aurora Floyd.....................................4003
    Birds of prey.....................................4042
    Captain of the Vulture.........................4007
    Charlotte's inheritance.........................4014
    Christmas hirelings..............................4068
    Cloven foot......................................4046
    Cut by the county..............................4076
    The day will come..............................4017
    Dead men's shoes...............................4039
    Dead sea fruit...................................4035
    Doctor's wife....................................4019
    Eleanor's victory................................4013
    Fatal three.......................................4009
    Fenton's quest..................................4059
    Flower and weed................................4065
    Golden calf......................................4064
    Henry Dunbar...................................4006
    Hostages to fortune............................4060
    Ishmael...4069
    Ishmaelite..4071
    John Marchmont's legacy.....................4018
    Joshua Haggard's daughter...................4005
    Just as I am.....................................4056
    Lady Audley's secret...........................4016
    Lady Lisle.......................................4051
    Lady's mile......................................4024
    Like and unlike.................................4011
    London pride....................................4033
    Lost for love.....................................4061
    Lovels of Arden.................................4015
    Lucius Davoreen................................4047
    Milly Darrell.....................................4048
    Mohawks...4020
    Mount Royal....................................4063
    Octoroon, The..................................4021
    One life, one love...............................4023
    One thing needful...............................4002
    Only a clod......................................4032
    Open verdict....................................4030
    Phantom fortune................................4066
    Publicans and sinners..........................4001
    Ralph the bailiff.................................4041
    Robert Ainsleigh................................4008
    Run to earth....................................4049
    Rupert Godwin..................................4012
    Sir Jasper's tenant..............................4010
    Sons of fire.....................................4031
    Strange world...................................4050
    Strangers and pilgrims.........................4026
    Story of Barbara................................4055
    Taken at the flood..............................4094
    To the bitter end................................4034
    Trail of the serpent.............................4038
    Under love's rule...............................4078

Under the red flag	4067
Venetians	4027
Vixen	4044
Weavers and weft	4029
Whose was the hand?	4022
World, the flesh and the devil	4025
Wyllard's weird	4077

Bradford, G., *jr.* Types of American character. 1895............824.1 307
Bradford, S. D. Works. 1858............820.1 29
Bradley. See **Bede, Cuthbert.**
Bradnack. Doctor Case's handbill. 1888.
....827.1 Pam. 1
Sonnets............................821.1 Pam. 23
Bradshaw. Goddess of Atvatabar............22720
Bradstreet. Works, in prose and verse;
ed. by Ellis. 1867............820.1 B-2
Bragg. Tekel............52270
Brainerd. Robert Atterbury............69860
Brampton (?). Paraphrase on the seven penitential psalms............821.2 450
Bramston. Blue bell............59404
Carbridges	59401
Cat and a cake during 30 years' war	59409
Heroine of a basket van	59407
Home and school	024204
Missy and master	024203
Pair of cousins	59408
Panelled house	59403
Rosamund Ferrars	024202
Shaven crown	59410
Snowball society	024201
Thorn fortress	59402
Uncle Ivan	59406
Woman of business	59405

Branch. Kanter girls............041501
Brave dame Mary............50387
Bray, Anna E. Courtenay of Walreddon..11904
De Foix	11908
Fitz of Fitzford	11905
Henry de Pomeroy	11902
Protestant	11906
The Talba	11903
Trelawny of Trelawne	11901
Trials of the heart	11910
Warleigh	11909
White hoods	11907

Bray, C. Ivanda............019710
King's revenge............19750
Bread-winners............15801
Brearley, W. H., *pseud.* Wanted, a copyist............14560
Breitmann, Hans. See **Leland, C. G.**
Brenda, *pseud.* Uncle Steve's locker............037801
Brennan (D. O'K. Branden). Heart-tones, and other poems. 1897............821.1 582
Brereton. Some famous Hamlets. 1884...822.3 95

Brewer. Love, too, is vanity............69231
Brewster, A. M. H. Compensation............37902
Saint Martin's summer............37901
Brewster, M. Under the water-oaks............012205
Brick, T. A., *pseud.* See **De Mille.**
Bridges, *Mrs. Colonel.* See **Forrester,** *Mrs.*
Bridges, R. Overheard in Arcady. 1894..827.1 33
Return of Ulysses; drama. 1890......822.2 314
Shorter poems. 1891............821.2 931
Suppressed chapters, etc. 1895............824.2 182
Contents: Suppressed chapters.—Arcadian letters. Novels that everybody read. The literary partition of Scotland.—Friends in Arcady. Arcadian opinions.
Brierley. Tales and sketches of Lancashire life. 1884. 2 v............824.2 368
Bright, *Mrs.* **A. M.** Three Bernices............52210
Bright, John. Speeches. 1868. 2 v...329.2 40
Speeches on the American question....971 4 73
Bright, M. A., (Lyndon, *pseud.*) Margaret..47298
Brimley. Essays. 1868............824.2 175
Brinckle. Poems. 1872............821.1 201
Brine. Bessie and Bee............030107
Boys and girls of Marble Dale	030104
Dan	030105
A dozen and one	030103
Grandma's attic treasures. 1893	821.1 166
Little lad Jamie	030106
Margaret Arnold's Christmas, etc.	30120
Papa's little daughters	030101
Stories grandma told	030102
Story of aunt Patience (poem). '93	821.1 465

Brinkerhoff. Nah-nee-ta............69235
Brinklow. Complaynt of Roderyck Mors. 1542............820.2 416
Lamentacyon of a Christen agaynst the cytye of London. 1545............820.2 416
Brinton. Maria Candelaria; drama. '97..822.1 73
Briton. Amyot Brough............35902
Face of death............35901
Sue............35903
Britton. Essays on Shakespeare. 1849..822.3 B-1
Brock. Hattie and Nellie............48202
Penny-wise and pound-foolish............48203
Broderip. Whisperings of a shell............017302
Brodhead, Eva Wilder (McGlasson).
Bound in shallows	15601
Diana's livery	15604
Earthly paragon	15605
Ministers of grace	15606
One of the Visconti	15607

Brome. Dramatic works. 3v............822.2 191
Brontë, Anne, (Acton Bell). Agnes Grey.
....*in* 6101B
Tenant of Wildfel hall............6201
Brontë, Charlotte, (Currer Bell). Jane Eyre............6001
Poems. 1882............821.2 661
Professor............6003

Shirley..6005
Villette..6006
Bronte, E. Wuthering heights....................6101
Brook. Fool of quality.............................12004
Brooke, A. Romeus and Iuliet. (New
   Shakespeare society, 1875)............822.3 B-5
Brooke, E. F. Life the accuser.................20762
   Transition..20761
   Superfluous woman....................................20760
Brooke, Henry. Poetical works. 1792. 4 v.
   V. 1. Life.—Jack the giant queller.— Contend-
   ing brothers.—Female officer.—Marriage contract.
   —Ruth.—Epilogues aud poems.........................822.2 132
   V. 2. Universal beauty.—Jerusalem delivered; tr.
   from Tasso.—Constantia.................................822.2 133
   V. 3. The impostor.—Earl of Westmorland.—
   Cymbeline.—Montezuma..................................822.2 134
   V. 4. Temple of Hymen.—Sparrow and the
   dove.—Female seducers.—Love and vanity.—Last
   speech of John Good.—Gustavus Vasa.—Earl of
   Essex.—Conrade..822.2 135
Brooke, L. Three fair daughters...............62340
Brooke, Stopford A. Poems. 1889.....821.2 657
   Theology in the English poets : Cowper,
   Coleridge, Wordsworth, Burns. '75..824 2 281
Brooks, Byron A. Those children.............62592
Brooks, C. S. Sooner or later.................12025
Brooks, C. T. Poems ; with memoir..821.1 332
Brooks, E. S. Boy of the first empire.....032323
   Chivalric days..032322
   Historic boys..032320
   Historic girls..032321
   In Leisler's times....................................*33802
   Son of Issachar..33801
   Under the tamaracks...............................032325
Brooks, E. S., and Alden, J. The long
   walls..032324
Brooks, Noah. Boy emigrants..................07903
   Boy settlers...07904
   Fairport nine...07902
   Our baseball club.....................................07905
   Tales of the Maine coast............................7950
Brooks, Phillips. Addresses 1893......204 124
   Essays and addresses. 1894............824.1 288
Broome. The stranger of Seriphos :
   poem. 1869...821.2 412
Brougham, Lord Henry. Albert Lunel...14107
   Contributions to the Edinburgh review.
   1856. 3 v..824.2 287
   Speeches. 1857. 2 v............................329.2 64
Brougham, John. Bunsby papers............12076
   Marine residence, etc.............................12077
Broughton. Beginner................................7906
   Belinda...7921
   Cometh up as a flower.............................7901
   Dear Faustina..7912
   Doctor Cupid..7902
   Good-bye, sweetheart...............................7908
   Joan..7910

Mrs. Bligh...7903
Nancy...7904
Not wisely, but too well...........................7909
Red as a rose is she................................7907
Scylla or Charybdis ?..............................7911
Second thoughts......................................7919
Twilight stories..7918
Broughton and Bisland. Widower indeed..7905
Brown, Alice. Day of his youth............43332
   Fools of nature.......................................43330
   Meadow-grass : tales.............................43331
Brown, Anna. Sir Mark.........................70520
Brown, C. A. Shakespeare's autobio-
   graphical poems. 1838...................822.3 8
Brown, C. B. Arthur Mervyn................11602
   Edgar Huntley...11604
   Jane Talbot...11605
   Wieland...11601
Brown, E. Trial of Cain (verse). 1832.
   ....821.1 Pam. 11
Brown, Helen D. Little Miss Phœbe Gay..032410
   Petrie estate...32401
   Two college girls....................................32402
Brown, Helen E. Good catch................69128
Brown, Henry. Sonnets of Shakespeare
   solved. 1870......................................822.3 81
Brown, John, *D. D.* Essays on Shaftes-
   bury's ' Characteristics.' 1751.......824.2 57
Brown, John, *M. D.* Horæ subsecivæ.
   1882. 3 v.
   1st series. Prefaces.—Locke and Sydenham.
   —Andrew Combe.— Dr. H. Marshall and military
   hygiene.— Art and science,— Our Gideon Grays.—
   Dr. Andrew Brown and Sydenham.— Free compe-
   tition in medicine.— Edward Forbes.— Dr. Adams
   of Banchory.—Henry Vaughan.—Excursus ethicus.
   —Dr. John Scott and his son, etc.—Health.........824.2 327
   2d series. Letter to John Cairns.—Dr. Chalmers.
   —Dr. George Wilson.—Her last half-crown.—Queen
   Mary's child-garden.— Our dogs.— Notes on art.—
   Oh, I'm wat, wat !—Education through the senses.
   —Presence of mind and happy guessing.— Black
   dwarf's bones.—Rab and his friends.—With brains,
   sir.— Arthur H. Hallam..................................824.2 328
   3d series. John Leech.- A Jacobite family.—Mystifications. — Miss Stirling Graham of Duntrune.—
   Thackeray's death.— Marjorie Fleming. · Minchmoor.— In clear dream and solemn vision.—Jeems
   the doorkeeper.—Landseer's picture 'There's life
   in the old dog yet.'—The enterkin.—Duke of Athole.
   —Struan.- Dick Mihi.—E. V. K. to his friend in
   town.—Sir H. Raeburn..................................824.2 329
   Rab and his friends................................32480
   Same ; in N. Y. point, for the blind.
   ....362.4 N-Y-18
   Spare hours. 1862................................824.2 325
   (Contents same as ' Horæ subsecivæ,' second series
   with following additional papers: Mystery of black and
   tan.—My father's memoir.— Mystifications —Vaughan's
   poems.—St. Paul's thorn in the flesh.)

* Of interest to young readers.

Spare hours. 1866.....................824.2 326
  Contents: Leech. – Marjorie Fleming. – Jeems the doorkeeper. – Minchmoor. – The enterkin. – Health. – Duke of Athole. – Struan. – Thackeray's death. – Thackeray's literary career. – More of our dogs. – Plea for a dog home. – Bibliomania. – In clear dream and solemn vision. – A Jacobite family.

Brown, T. A. See **Boldrewood, R.,** *pseud.*
Brown, Vincent. My brother................71080
Browne, C. F. See **Ward, Artemus.**
Browne, Irving. House of the heart (poems). 1897.....................821.1 514
  Iconoclasm and whitewash (essays). 1885.....................824.1 214
Browne, *Sir* Thomas. Miscellaneous works.....................242 1
  Contents: Religio medici. – Urn-burial. – Letter to a friend. – Vulgar errors.
  Works; ed. by Wilkin. 1852. 3 v.
    V. 1. Life of Sir Thomas Browne; by Doctor Johnson. – Supplementary memoir; by the editor. – Mrs. Lyttleton's communication to Bishop Kennet. – Pseudoxia epidemica.....................820.2 40
    V. 2. Pseudoxia epidemica continued. Religio medici. – Garden of Cyrus.....................820.2 41
    V. 3. Hydriotaphia. – Letter to a friend. – Christian morals. – Miscellany. – Correspondence, etc.820.2 42
Browne, W. Britannia's pastorals; 3d book 821.2 473
  Poems; ed. by Goodwin. 1894. 2v...821.2 1002
  Whole works. 1868. 2 v.
    V. 1. Memoir. – Britannia's pastorals.....................821.2 149
    V. 2. Britannia's pastorals. – Shepheard's pipe. – The inner temple masque. – Miscellaneous poems.....................821.2 150
Brownell. War lyrics and other poems.821.1 300
Browning, *Mrs.* **E. B.** Aurora Leigh, and other poems. 1866.....................821.2 1050
  Drama of exile, etc. 1845. 2 v......821.2 1047
  Earlier poems, 1826-33.....................821.2 1049
    Contents: Essay on mind. – Miscellaneous poems.
  The Greek Christian poets and the English poets. 1863.....................824.2 168
  Lady Geraldine's courtship; with essay by Stedman. 1881.....................821.2 1051
  Letters; with memoir by Stoddard.....826.2 39
  Poems; ed. by Tuckerman. 1867. 3 v.
    V. 1. The seraphim. – Miscellaneous poems. – Sonnets from the Portuguese. – Translations.....821.2 1044
    V. 2. Drama of exile. – Romaunt of the page. – Lay of the brown rosary. – Lady Geraldine's courtship. – Vision of poets. – Rhyme of the Duchess May. – Miscellaneous poems. – Casa Guidi windows. – Napoleon III in Italy, etc.....................821.2 1045
    V. 3. Aurora Leigh. – Last poems.....821.2 1046
Browning, Robert. And the Christian faith; by Berdoe. 1896.....................821.2 1113
  Aristophanes' apology.....................821.2 1080
  As a philosophical and religious teacher; by Jones. 1896.....................821.2 1121
  Asolando. 1890.....................821.2 1081
  Balaustion's adventure. 1871.....821.2 1082
  Bibliography, 1833-81; by Furnivall........16 42

Blot in the 'scutcheon, etc.; ed. by Rolfe. 1887.....................821.2 1100
  Contents: A blot in the 'scutcheon. – Colombe's birthday. – A soul's tragedy.
Browning cyclopædia; by Berdoe. 1892. ....821.2 1112
Browning studies; ed. by Berdoe. '95.821.2 1114
Browning's women; by Burt. 1887..821.2 1115
Complete poetic and dramatic works. 1895.....................821.2 1076
Dramatic idyls. 1879.....................821.2 1083
  Contents: Martin Relph. – Pheidippides. Halbert and Hob. – Ivan Ivanovitch. – Tray. – Ned Bratts.
Dramatic idyls. Series 2. 1880.....821.2 1084
  Contents: Echetlos. – Clive. Muléykeh. – Pietro of Abino. – Doctor. – Pan and Luna.
Essays on; by Nettleship. 1868......821.2 1123
Favorite poems. 1881.....................821.2 1051
Ferishtah's fancies. 1884.....................821.2 1085
Fifine at the fair, etc. 1872.....................821.2 1086
Guide book to works of; by Cooke. 1891.....................821.2 1117
Handbook to; by Orr. 1885..........821.2 1124
The inn album. 1876.....................821.2 1087
Introduction to the poetry of; by W. J. Alexander. 1889.....................821.2 1111
Introduction to the study of; by Corson. 1886.....................821.2 1118
Jocoseria. 1883.....................821.2 1088
  Contents: Wanting is – what? – Donald. – Solomon and Balkis. – Christini and Monaldeschi. – Mary Wollstonecraft and Fuseli. – Adam, Lilith and Eve. – Ixion. – Jochanan Hakkadosh. – Never the time and place. Pambo.
La Saisiaz. – Two poets of Croisic. 1878. ....821.2 1097
Lyrics of life. 1865.....................821.2 1089
Men and women. 1876.....................821.2 1090
On the poet.....................16 42
Pacchiarotto, etc. 1877.....................821.2 1091
Phrase book; by Molineux. 1896....821.2 1099
Parleyings. 1887.....................821.2 1092
Poems. 1866. 2 v.
  V. 1. Paracelsus. – Pippa passes. – King Victor and King Charles. – Colombe's birthday.........821.2 1055
  V. 2. A blot in the 'scutcheon. – Return of the Druses. – Luria. – A soul's tragedy. – Dramatic romances and lyrics.....................821.2 1056
Poetical works. 1886. 8 v.
  V. 1. Men and women. – Sordello.....821.2 1057
  V. 2. Dramatis personæ. – Dramatic romances and lyrics. – Strafford. – Christmas eve. – Easter day.....................821.2 1058
  V. 3. Fifine at the fair. – Red cotton night-cap country. – Prince Hohenstiel-Schwangau. – Hervé Riel. – Inn album.....................821.2 1059
  V. 4. Balaustion's adventure. – Aristophanes' apology. – Pacchiarotto, and other poems.....821.2 1060
  V. 5. Agamemnon of Æschylus. – La Saisiaz. – Two poets of Croisic. – Pauline. – Dramatic idyls: 1st and 2d series. – Jocoseria.....................821.2 1061
  V. 6. The ring and the book.....................821.2 1062

‡ For reference.

V. 7. *Dramas:* Paracelsus. — Pippa passes. King Victor and King Charles.—Colombe's birthday.—A blot in the 'scutcheon.—Return of the Druses.—Luria.—A soul's tragedy............821.2 1063
V. 8. Ferishtah's fancies.........................821.2 1064

Poetical works. 1894. 9 v.
V. 1. Pauline.—Sordello.—Paracelsus.—Strafford.........................821.2 1065
V. 2. Pippa passes.—King Victor and King Charles.--Return of the Druses.—A soul's tragedy. —A blot in the 'scutcheon.—Colombe's birthday. —Men and women........................821.2 1066
V. 3. Dramatic romances.—Christmas-eve and Easter-day.—Dramatic lyrics.—Luria.......821.2 1067
V. 4. In a balcony.—Dramatis personæ.—The ring and the book; v. 1.........................821.2 1068
V. 5. The ring and the book; v. 2-3........821.2 1069
V. 6. Balaustion's adventure.—Prince Hohenstiel-Schwangau.—Fifine at the fair.—Red cotton night-cap country.—The inn album..........821.2 1070
V. 7. Aristophanes' apology.—The Agamemnon of Æschylus.—Pacchiarotto.—Other poems....821.2 1071
V. 8. Dramatic idylls.—Jocoseria.—Ferishtah's fancies.—Parleyings with certain people........821.2 1072
V. 9. Asolando. — Biographical and historical notes to the poems........................821.2 1073

Poetical works; ed. by Birrell. 1896.
2 v...821.2 1074
Poetry of: outline studies. 1886....821.2 1116
Prince Hohenstiel-Schwangau. '71 ..821.2 1093
Red cotton night-cap country. '73..821.2 1094
The ring and the book. 1869. 2 v...821.2 1095
Select poems; ed. by Rolfe. 1886....821.2 1077
Selections from. 1884. 2 v............821.2 1078
Sermons from; by Ealand. 1892......821.2 1119
Sordello; analysis of, by Morison. 1889.
....821.2 1122
Sordello, Strafford, Christmas eve, and
Easter day. 1864.................821.2 1098
Stories from; by Holland. 1882.....821.2 1120
Browning, R. *and* **Mrs. E. B.** The Brownings for the young; ed. by Kenyon. 1896..........................821.2 1054
Browning society. How [it] came into being; by Furnivall. 1884..........806 Pam. 1
Bruce. Poems; with life. 1822......*in* 821.2 39
Brunton. Self-control..................14164
Brush. Colonel's opera cloak...............23802
Inside our gate.............................23801
Bryan. Manch.............................60101
Wild work..................................60102
Bryant, Marguerite. Morton Verlost....16540
Bryant, W. C. Orations and addresses.
1873............................825.1 38
Poems. 1834........................821.1 278
Poetical works. 1879................821.1 279
Poetical works. 1883. 2 v.
V. 1. Thanatopsis, and other earlier poems. Poems of the middle period..............821.1 280
V. 2. Later poems. Hymns written at various times. Translations of various dates. Unpublished or uncollected poems..........821.1 281

Prose writings. 1884. 2 v.
V. 1. Lectures on poetry. — Early American verse. — On trisyllabic feet in iambic measure. — Nostradamus' Provençal poets. — Moriscan romances.—Female troubadours.—Oldham's poets.— Cowley.—Poets and poetry of the English language. — The whirlwind. — Indian spring. — Marriage blunder.—Skeleton's cave.— Story of Cuba.— Commemorative discourses on Cooper, Irving, Halleck, and Verplanck............................824.1 196
V. 2. Illinois 50 years ago. — Tour in the old South. —The early northwest.--Glimpses of Europe. —Cuba and the Cubans. —Visit to Mexico.—Occasional addresses.— Editorial comments, etc.......824.1 197

Studies in; by Alden. 1878.........821.1 282
Translation of the Iliad. 1870. 2 v......883 23
Translation of the Odyssey. 1871-2. 2 v..883 25
Bryce. Dream of conquest..................23901
Friends in exile..........................23902
Bryden. Tales of South Africa..........70780
Brydges. Fortnight in heaven..........69270
Buchan. Sir Quixote of the moors......15690
Buchanan, Robert. Tragic dramas from history. 1868. 2v.
V. 1. Wallace.—James I of Scotland.—British brothers......................................822.2 177
V. 2. Gaston Phœbus.— Edburga.— Legendary and other poems.................822.2 178

Buchanan, Robert W. Annan water......42209
Ballads of life, love, etc..............821.2 643
Book of Orm (poem). 1870........821.2 403
Child of nature............................42202
The city of Dream: poem. 1888......821.2 821
Come, live with me........................42218
The coming terror, etc. 1891.........824.2 437
Contents: The coming terror. — Are men born free and equal? — On descending into hell: a protest against over-legislation in matters literary. — Modern young man as a critic.--Is chivalry still possible?—Imperial Cockneydom.—Is the marriage contract eternal?—Flotsam and jetsam.—Final words.

Diana's hunting............................42220
Drama of kings. 1871..............822.2 175
Contents: pt. 1: Buonaparte.—pt. 2: Napoleon fallen. —pt. 3: Teuton against Paris.

The earthquake. 1885...............821.2 754
Effie Hetherington.....................42223
Foxglove manor.........................42212
God and the man.......................42206
Heir of Linne.............................42216
Lady Kilpatrick.........................42221
A look round literature. 1887......824.2 396
Love me forever........................42207
Marriage by capture....................42224
Master of mine..........................42213
Matt..42211
Moment after............................42217
Napoleon fallen. 1871..............822.2 176
New Abelard.............................42210
Piper of Hamelin: opera. 1893.....822.2 313

Poetical works. 1874. 2 v.
  V. 1. Ballads and romances.—Ballads and poems of life..821.2 400
  V. 2. Ballads and poems of life.—Lyrical poems, etc.—Songs of the terrible year (1870).—Faces on the wall...821.2 401
Red and white heather: tales and ballads..42219
Shadow of the sword...............................42201
Stormy waters......................................42215
That winter night..................................42214
Undertones (poems). 1863...............821.2 402
The wandering Jew: carol. 1893........821.2 906
Buchanan, tr. Ballad stories. 1869.......898 11
Buchanan *and* **Murray.** Charlatan......42222
Bucke. Beauties, etc., of nature. 3 v..824.2 105
Buckle. Essays. 1863.........................824.2 174
  Contents : Biographical sketch of the author.—Mill on liberty.— Influence of women on the progress of knowledge.
Buckley. Edith Moreton. 1853...............40 13
Bucknill. Mad-folk of Shakespeare. 1867.
....822.3 126
Buckstone. Rough diamond: farce. 1895.
....822.2 332
Buddington. Can the old love?............44105
Budgell. Essays in The Guardian. 3v....824.2 10
  Essays in The Spectator. 4 v............824.2 36
  Essays in The Tatler. 4 v..................824.2 6
Bullock. By Thrasna river....................20270
Bulwer. See **Lytton.**
Bumont tragedy...................................69047
Bunce. Bachelor Bluff.......................824.1 167
  Story of Happinolande........................69118
  Timias Terrystone..............................69117
Bunner. Airs from Arcady and elsewhere. 1884..821.1 308
  Jersey street and Jersey lane. 1896....824.1 314
  Contents : Jersey and Mulberry.— Tiemann's to Tubby Hook.—The Bowery and Bohemia.— The story of a path.—The lost child.—A letter to town.
  Love in old cloathes, etc....................21910
  Contents : Love in old cloathes.—A letter and a paragraph.— As one having authority.— Crazy wife's ship.—French for a fortnight.—The red silk handkerchief.—Our aromatic uncle.
  Made in France ; French tales............21907
  Contents : Tony.— Prize of propriety.—Dennis.— The minuet.—A pint's a pound.—A capture.—Uncle Atticus.—The Pettibone brolly.—Joke on Monsieur Peplonneau.—Father Dominick's convert.
  The Midge...21901
  More 'Short sixes.'.............................21908
  Contents : Cumbersome horse.—Mr. Vincent Egg and the wage of sin.—The ghoollah.—Cutwater of Seneca.—Mr. Wick's aunt.—What Mrs. Fortescue did.—The man with the pink pants.— Third figure in the cotillion.—Samantha Boom-de-ay.—My dear Mrs. Billington.
  Poems. 1896.....................................821.1 520
  Runaway Browns................................21906
  Short sixes..21905

  Contents : The tenor.— Colonel Brereton's early round-up. Two churches of 'Quawket. Love-letters of Smith.— Zenobia's infidelity.— Nine cent girls. Nice people.—Mr. Copernicus and the proletariat. Hector A sisterly scheme - Zozo. An old, old story.
  Story of a New York house...................21903
  Suburban sage...................................21909
  Woman of honor................................21902
  Zadoc Pine, etc..................................21904
  Contents : Zadoc Pine labor union. Natural selection.— Casperl.— A second-hand story. Mrs. Tom spree.—Squire Five-Fathom.
Bunner *and* **Matthews.** In partnership...17701
  (For contents, see **Matthews, B.**)
Buntling ball, The : satire. 1885..........827.1 23
Bunyan. Pilgrim's progress...................*249 16
  Same ; ed. by Offor. 1847....................249 38
  Same ; ed. by Offor. 1892....................*249 15
  Same ; ed. by Venables. 1879.............249 39
  Works ; ed. by Offor. 1852. 3 v.
    V. 1-2. Experimental, doctrinal and practical.249 B-9
    V. 3. Allegorical : Pilgrim's progress ; Holy war ; Heavenly footman ; Holy city ; Solomon's temple ; House of the forest of Lebanon ; Water of life ; Barren fig tree ; Mr. Badman ; A few sighs from hell ; One thing is needful ; Ebal and Gerizzim ; Book for boys and girls.............249 B-9
Burbury. Florence Sackville..............*in* 14156
Burdett. Margaret Moncrieffe...............56816
Burgess, J. J. H. Viking path...............53340
Burgess, J. T. Harry Hope's holidays...020401
Burgin. At Tuxter's.............................31540
  Gascoigne's 'ghost.'..........................31543
  Judge of the Four Corners...................31541
  Tomalyn's quest.................................31542
Burke, C. E. Value of life. 1897..........170 115
Burke, E. Celebrated speeches. 1845.*in* 825.2 12
  Correspondence. 1744-97. 4 v........826.2 11
  Selections from. 1893.....................820.2 246
  Speeches. 1816. 4 v........................329.2 10
  Works. 1864. 6 v.
    V. 1. Natural society.—The sublime and beautiful.—Political miscellanies...........................820.2 25
    V. 2. Political miscellanies.—Reflections on the French revolution.— Letter to a member of the national assembly.............................820.2 26
    V. 3. Appeal from new to old whigs.—Speech on the nabob of Arcot's debts.—Thoughts on French affairs, etc..............................820.2 27
    V. 4. Reports on affairs in India.—Articles against Warren Hastings............................820.2 28
    V. 5. Charges against Hastings, concluded.—Political letters.....................................820.2 29
    V. 6. Letters, notes, fragments, etc.—Abridgment of English history.—Index................820.2 30
  Works ; rev. ed. 1865. 12 v.
    V. 1. To the reader.—Vindication of 'Natural society.'—The sublime and beautiful.—Short account of a late short administration.—Observations on 'The present state of the nation.'—Thoughts on the cause of the present discontents..........820.2
    V. 2. Speech on American taxation.—Speeches at Bristol, etc..820.2

* Of interest to young readers.

V. 3. Speech on nabob of Arcot's debts.— Speech on army estimates. 1790.—Reflections on the revolution in France........................820.2 249
V. 4. Letter to a member of the national assembly.—Appeal from new to old whigs.—Letter to a peer of Ireland.—Thoughts on French affairs, etc........................820.2 250
V. 5. On the conduct of the minority.—Three letters on the proposals for peace with the regicide directory of France, etc........................820.2 251
V. 6. Fourth letter on the proposals for peace.— Letter to Fox on the American war, 1777.— Letter to the Marquis of Rockingham, etc........................820.2 252
V. 7. Fragments and notes of speeches in parliament.—Essay towards an abridgment of English history........................820.2 253
V. 8. Ninth and eleventh reports of com. on affairs of India.—Articles against Warren Hastings........................820.2 254
V. 9-12. Articles against Hastings, concluded.— Speeches in the impeachment of Hastings.—General table of contents.—Index........................820.2 255

Burke, Chatham, *and* **Erskine.** Celebrated speeches. 1845....................825.2 12
Burke, T. A., *ed.* Polly Peablossom's wedding........................47279
Burleigh. Poems; with life. 1871........821.1 64
Burnaby. Our radicals........................69265
Burnand. Chikkin Hazard........................27302
  Gone wrong........................27303
  Happy-thought hall. 1872..............828.2 36
  Happy thoughts. 1869....................828.2 43
  My health. 1872........................828.2 44
  My time and what I've done with it........27301
Burnett. Dolly [Vagabondia]................14908
  Earlier stories. 2 v.
    V. 1. Lindsay's luck.—Miss Crespigny.—Theo...14916
    V. 2. Kathleen Mavourneen.—Pretty Polly Pemberton........................14917
  Editha's burglar........................025503
  Fair barbarian........................14933
  Fortunes of Philippa Fairfax...........14905
  Giovanni, etc........................025505
  Haworth's........................14914
  Jarl's daughter, etc........................14913
    Contents: Jarl's daughter.— The men who loved Elizabeth.—Wanted: a young person.
  Kathleen Mavourneen........................14910
  Lady of quality........................14918
  Little Lord Fauntleroy...................025501
  Little Saint Elizabeth, etc..............025504
  Lindsay's luck........................14912
  Louisiana........................14922
  Miss Crespigny........................14907
  Miss Defarge........................14902
  Piccino, etc........................025506
    Contents: Two days in the life of Piccino.— The captain's youngest. Little Betty's kitten tells her story.— How Fauntleroy occurred.
  Pretty Polly Pemberton....................14911
  Pretty sister of José...................14915
  Quiet life........................14909

Sara Crewe........................025502
Same (reserved copy). 1891..........823.1 1
Surly Tim, etc........................14901
  Contents: Surly Tim. — Le Monsieur et la petite dame.— Smethurstses.—One day at Arle.—Esmeralda.— Mère Giraud's little daughter.—Lodusky.—Seth.
That lass o' Lowrie's........................14904
Theo........................14903
Through one administration................14941
Tide on the moaning bar................*in* 14909
Two little pilgrims' progress..........025507
Vagabondia........................14908
Burney, F. See **Arblay,** *Madame D'.*
Burnham (Edith Douglas, *pseud.*). Dearly bought........................66707
  Doctor Latimer........................66706
  Miss Archer Archer......................66712
  Miss Bagg's secretary...................66703
  Mistress of Beech Knoll................66705
  Next door........................66708
  No gentlemen........................66704
  Sane lunatic........................66701
  Sweet Clover........................66709
  Young maids and old....................66702
  We, Von Arldens........................66711
  Wise woman........................66710
Burns. In drama; by Stirling. 1878...824.2 292
  In other tongues; [with] review of translations of Burns; by Jacks. 1896...821.2 637
  Life and works; ed. by Currie and Peterkin. 1815. 4 v............821.2 627
  Poems (fac-simile of Kilmarnock edition.) 821.2 632
  Poetical works; ed. by Currie. 1868..821.2 633
  Poetical works; with life. 1850........821.2 634
  Selected poems; ed. by Robertson. 1889. ....821.2 635
  Selected poems; introduction by Lang. 1896........................821.2 636
  Works; with life by Lockhart. 1832..821.2 631
  Same; self-interpreting edition. 1886. 6 v........................821.2 621
Burrell. Man with seven hearts, etc..........11930
Burritt. Chips from many blocks. '78..824.1 155
  Lects. and speeches. 1869..............825 1 15
  Old Burchell's pocket. 1877..........*824.2 351
  Thoughts and things. 1854............824.1 35
Burroughs, E., *pseud.* See **Jewett, Sophie.**
Burroughs, John. Birds and bees. 1887. ....*824.1 198
  Birds and poets, etc. 1895...........824.1 199
    Contents: Birds and poets.—Touches of nature.- A bird medley.—April.—Spring poems.—Our rural divinity.— Before genius.— Before beauty.—Emerson.— The flight of the eagle.—Index.
  A bunch of herbs, etc.................*824.1 200
    Contents: Biographical sketch.- A bunch of herbs.- Strawberries.—A March chronicle. A spray of pine.— A spring relish.— English woods: a contrast.—Autumn tides.

* Of interest to young readers.

Fresh fields. 1885..................824.1 201
  Contents: Nature in England.—English woods. In Carlyle's country.—Hunt for the nightingale.—English and American song-birds.—Impressions of some English birds.—In Wordsworth's country.—Glance at British wild flowers. - British fertility. — Sunday in Cheyne row.—At sea.
Indoor studies. 1889...............824.1 202
  Contents: Henry D. Thoreau.—Science and literature.—Science and the poets.—Matthew Arnold's criticism.—Arnold's view of Emerson and Carlyle.—Gilbert White's book.—A malformed giant.—Brief essays. An egotistical chapter.
Locusts and wild honey. 1879......*824.1 203
  Contents: Pastoral bees.—Sharp eyes.—Strawberries.—Is it going to rain?—Speckled trout.—Birds and birds.—A bed of boughs.—Bird's-nesting.—The halcyon in Canada.
Pepacton. 1881...................*824.1 204
  Contents: Pepacton: a summer voyage.—Springs.—Idyl of the honey-bee.—Nature and the poets.—Notes by the way.—Foot-paths.—A bunch of herbs.—Winter pictures.
Riverby. 1894....................824.1 205
  Contents: Among the wild-flowers. — The heart of the southern Catskills. — Birds' eggs. — Bird courtship.—Notes from the prairie. — Eye-beams.—A young marsh hawk. — The chipmunk.—Spring jottings. — Glimpses of wild life. — A life of fear.—Lovers of nature. — A taste of Kentucky blue-grass.—In Mammoth cave.—Hasty observation.—Bird life in an old apple-tree. — The ways of sportsmen.—Talks with young observers.
Signs and seasons. 1886..........*824.1 206
  Contents: A sharp lookout.—A spray of pine.— Hard fare. — The tragedies of the nests. — A snow-storm.— A taste of Maine birch.—Winter neighbors.—A salt breeze.—A spring relish.—A river view.—Bird enemies.—Phases of farm life.—Roof-tree.
Wake-robin. 1871..................598 37
  Contents: Return of the birds.—In the hemlocks.— Adirondac.—Birds' nests.—Spring at the capital. — Birch browsings.— The invitation.
Winter sunshine. 1876.............824.1 207
  Contents: Winter sunshine. — Exhilarations of the road.—Snow-walkers. — The fox.—A March chronicle.—The apple.—An October abroad.
Year in the fields: selections. 1896..824.1 208
  Contents: A snow-storm. — Winter neighbors. — A spring relish. — April. — Birch browsings. — A bunch of herbs; Fragrant wild flowers; Weeds.—Autumn tides.— A sharp outlook.
Burt. Browning's women. 1887......821.2 1115
Burton, Mrs. H. S. Who would have thought it?...............................50352
Burton, J. Bloundelle-. Denounced.....14192
  Desert ship............................014105
  Gentleman adventurer...................14190
  Hispaniola plate.......................014106
  In the day of adversity................14191
Burton, Mina E. Ruling the planets....16530
Burton, W. E. Yankee among the mermaids.................................47274
Bushe. Painted bird...................012601
Bushnell. Work and play; varieties. 1864.
  ....824.1 153
Butcher. Armenosa of Egypt............54430

Butler, Frances A. Kemble. See Kemble, F. A.
Butler, Samuel. (1612-80.) Hudibras.
  1806.................................827.2 3A
  Same; ed. by Bohn. 1859..............827.2 3
  Poems; with life. 1822...............821.2 30
Butler, Samuel. (1835—.) Erewhon.....62352
Butler, W. A. Domesticus..............38702
  Mrs. Limber's raffle.................38701
  Oberammergau (poem). 1890.........821.1 B 4
  Poems. 1871..........................821.1 238
  Contents: Virginia's virgin. Poems of travel. Nothing to wear.—The sexton and the thermometer.—Broadway.—The equestrian statue of Washington. Two millions. — General average. - Miscellaneous poems. Uhland. — Translations from Uhland. Two cities.
  Two millions (poems). 1858........821.1 237
Butt, B. M. Delicia...................26402
  Eugenie..............................26401
  Geraldine Hawthorne..................26404
  Keith Deramore.......................26406
  Miss Molly...........................A 26403
Butt, Geraldine. Time of roses........58313
Butt, M. H. Leisure moments..........12086
Butterworth. Boys of Greenway court...024908
  In old New England...................24960
  Contents: Pardon Ponder, pedagogue. The haunted oven.—Wych Hazel, the Jew.—Captain Tut-Tut-Tuttle and the miracle clock. — The inn of the good woman —The bewitched clambake.—The miraculous basket.—No room in the inn.— Nix's mate.—Old 'Bunker Hill.' Milo Mill's fourth of July poem.—Husking stories, songs and fiddlers.—King Philip's last hunt.
  In the boyhood of Lincoln............024907
  Knight of liberty....................024910
  Patriot schoolmaster.................024909
  Wampum belt..........................024911
  Zigzag journeys in Acadia..........*917.6 51
  Zigzag journeys in classic lands...*914 126
  Zigzag journeys in Europe..........*914 125
  Zigzag journeys in northern lands..*914 127
  Zigzag journeys in the Occident....*917.1 158
  Zigzag journeys in the Orient......*914 128
Buxton, B. H. From the wings..........64904
  Great Grenfel gardens................64902
  Jennie of the Prince's...............64901
  Nell on and off the stage............64903
Buxton, H. J. Wilmot-. Sweet o' the year.69312
Bynner. Agnes Surriage................22804
  Begum's daughter.....................22802
  Chase of the Meteor..................022820
  Contents: Chase of the Meteor.—Jammer's ghost. Extra train.—Discontented dowager.—Hercules Jack. - Our special artist.— Tramp's dinner party — Black Beard's last struggle.—Cruise in a soap-bubble.
  Damen's ghost........................22805
  Penelope's suitors...................22801
  Zachary Phips........................22803
Byrn. See Rattlehead, D.

* Of interest to young readers.

Byron. Childe Harold; ed. by Rolfe.
1886..821.2 1143
Œuvres complètes; traduites par La-
roche. 1851. 4 v.........................821.2 1138
Poems [sel.]..821.2 1135
Poetical works.....................................821.2 1136
Poetical works. 1879. 10 v.
   V. 1. Hours of idleness.—Edinburgh Review on same.—Occasional pieces.—English bards and Scottish reviewers...................................821.2 1125
   V. 2. Childe Harold's pilgrimage............821.2 1126
   V. 3. Occasional pieces.—Hints from Horace.—Curse of Minerva.—The waltz.—The Giaour.—Bride of Abydos.—The Corsair...............821.2 1127
   V. 4. Ode to Napoleon.—Lara.—Hebrew melodies.—Siege of Corinth.—Parisini.—Domestic pieces.—Monody on the death of Sheridan.—Prisoner of Chillon.—The dream.—Occasional pieces..821.2 1128
   V. 5. Manfred.—Lament of Tasso.—Mazeppa.—Morgante Maggiore of Pulci.—Prophecy of Dante.—Occasional pieces................................821.2 1129
   V. 6. Francesca of Rimini.—Stanzas to the Po, etc.—The blues.—Marino Faliero.—Vision of judgment.—Occasional pieces......................821.2 1130
   V. 7.* Heaven and earth.—Sardanapalus.—The two Foscari.—The deformed transformed..........821.2 1131
   V. 8. Cain.—Werner.—Age of bronze.—The island.—Stanzas.—Lines...........................821.2 1132
   V. 9-10. Don Juan..................................821.2 1133
Poetry; chosen by Matthew Arnold.
1881..821.2 1142
Selections from; ed. by Ellis. 1896.
....in 821.2 1025
Vindicated; by Manfred..................821.2 442
Works. 1874..................................821.2 1137
   Contents: Poems.—Letters.—Review articles.—Parliamentary speeches, etc.
Works; ed. by Henley.
   V. 1. Letters. 1804-13.........................826.2 101
   (Others to come.)
C. and C. Two gentlemen of Gotham.........69292
C., S. T. Harleys of Chelsea place...............07128
Cable. Bonaventure.....................................54503
Doctor Sevier..54525
Grandissimes...54502
John March, southerner.............................54506
Madame Delphine.......................................54504
Old Creole days...54501
Strange true stories of Louisiana..............54505
Cabot. In plain air......................................54740
Cadell. Worthy..56862
Caedmon. Metrical paraphrase of parts of Holy Scripture; ed., with English tr., by Thorpe..226.4 B-5
Caffyn, Mrs. See Iota, pseud.
Cahan. Yekl..70640
Caine. Bondman...42904
Captain Davy's honeymoon.......................42906
Cobwebs of criticism. 1883.............824.2 353
   Contents: The Lake school: Wordsworth, Southey, Coleridge. The Satanic school: Byron. The Cockney school: Leigh Hunt, Keats, Shelley. Quarrels of critics, etc.

Deemster...42903
Last confession.—Blind mother................42907
Manxman..42908
Scapegoat...42905
Shadow of a crime......................................42901
She's all the world to me..........................42909
Son of Hagar...42902
Caird, E. Essays on literature and philosophy. 1892. 2 v.
   V. 1. Dante in his relation to the theology and ethics of the middle ages.—Goethe and philosophy.—Rousseau.—Wordsworth.—Problem of philosophy at the present time.—Genius of Carlyle...824.2 448
   V. 2. Cartesianism.—Metaphysic.................824.2 449
Caird, Mona. Romance of the moors......29480
Calder. Miriam's heritage..........................52237
Caldwell, Mrs. Marsh-. Aubrey..............14207
Castle Avon..14208
Emilia Wyndham...14205
Father Darcy..in 14201
Heiress of Haughton.................................14209*
Lettice Arnold.......................................in 14201
Mordaunt hall...14210
Mount Sorel..14204
Norman's bridge...14202
Ravenscliffe...14203
Rose of Ashurst...14206
Time the avenger..................................in 14202
Triumphs of time.......................................14201
Calhoun. Speeches. 1843.....................329.1 68
Works. 1852. 6 v...................................329.1 69
Callwell. Champion of the faith...............035301
Calmire..21310
Calmour. Facts and fiction about Shakespeare...822.3 B-36
Calverley. Fly leaves. 1872..................828.2 46
Literary remains. 1885.........................821.2 771
Verses and translations. 1884.............821.2 720
Calvert. Arnold and Andre: drama. '64..822.1 5
Brief essays, etc. 1874..........................824.1 72
Essays æsthetical. 1875........................824.1 73
Maid of Orleans: a tragedy. 1874......822.1 6
Shakespeare: a study. 1879................822.3 145
Cambridge, Ada, (Mrs. G. F. Cross).
Fidelis...18126
Humble enterprise......................................18127
Little minx..18124
Marked man..18121
Marriage ceremony.....................................18125
My guardian..18123
Not all in vain...18122
Three Miss Kings..18120
Cambridge, R. O. Essays in The World.
3 v...824.2 19
Camden. Remains concerning Britain...929.2 17
   Contents: Names.—Proverbs.—Epigrams, etc.

Cameron, *Mrs.* H. L. Bad lot....................19616
    Cost of a lie..19608
    Daughter's heart...................................19611
    Deceivers ever.......................................19612
    Devout lover...19607
    Hard lesson...19610
    In a grass country................................19604
    Jack's secret...19609
    Life's mistake.......................................19606
    Lodge by the sea..................................19602
    North country maid............................19601
    Pure gold..19605
    This wicked world..............................19615
    Tragic blunder.....................................19613
    Vera Nevill..19603
    Worth winning....................................19614
Cameron, V. L. Cruise of the Black Prince
    privateer..032902
    Harry Raymond..032901
Camp of refuge...58923
Campbell, Helen. His grandmothers......46420
    Miss Melinda's opportunity....................46426
    Mrs. Herndon's income..........................46423
    Roger Berkeley's probation....................46424
    Under green apple boughs 46421
    Unto the third and fourth generations......46422
    What to do club..46425
Campbell, Thomas. Poetical works; with
    memoir by Aytoun. 1873..............821.2 278
Campbell, W. L. Civitas (poem). '86. 821.1 362
Campbell, William. Dread voyage:
    poems. 1893.................................821.2 926
Campion, T. Lyric poems; ed. by Rhys.
    1896..821.2 1017
Canning. Select speeches and writings..329.2 21
Canton. Invisible playmate, etc. 1894......137 1
    A lost epic, etc. 1887.....................821.2 825
    W. V., her book; and various verses.
    1896..829.2 79
Captain Wolf..07193
Carew, Rachel. Tangled.........................44171
Carew, Thomas. Poems; with memoir.
    1870..821.2 152
Carey, Annie. Autobiography of a lump
    of coal..014501
    School girls.......................................014502
Carey, Rosa N. Aunt Diana...................50212
    Averil...50219
    Barbara Heathcote's trial......................50211
    But men must work............................50221
    Cousin Mona.....................................50225
    Doctor Luttrell's first patient. 1897......50227
    Esther..50205
    For Lilias..50209
    Heriot's choice..................................50215
    Little Miss Muffet............................50222
    Lover or friend?................................50216

    Mary St. John....................................50217
    Merle's crusade..................................50213
    Mistress of Brae Farm........................50226
    Mrs. Romney....................................50223
    Nellie's memories...............................50202
    Not like other girls.............................50206
    Old, old story....................................50224
    Only the governess............................50210
    Our Bessie...50218
    Queenie's whim.................................50203
    Robert Ord's atonement.....................50207
    Search for Basil Lyndhurst.................50214
    Sir Godfrey's grand-daughters............50220
    Uncle Max...50204
    Wee wifie..50208
    Wooed and married............................50201
Carleton, *pseud.* See Coffin, C. C.
Carleton, Will. City ballads. 1886......821.1 541
    City festivals. 1892.....................821.1 542
    City legends. 1889.....................821.1 543
    Farm ballads. 1874.....................821.1 544
    Farm festivals. 1881...................821.1 545
    Farm legends. 1876...................821.1 546
    Old infant, etc..................................30840
    Contents: The old infant.—The vestal virgin.—Lost
    two young ladies.—The one-ring circus.—The Christmas
    car.—A business flirtation.—Oldbottle's burglars.
    Rhymes of our planet. 1895............821.1 547
    Young folks' centennial rhymes. '76..821.1 540
Carleton, William. Art Maguire............11008
    Black prophet....................................11004
    Emigrants of Ahadarra........................11003
    Evil eye...11005
    Fardorougha the miser.......................11011
    Parra Sastha......................................11009
    Poor scholar......................................11007
    Redmond, count O'Hanlon................11006
    Traits and stories of Irish peasantry.....11001
    Willy Reilly......................................11010
Carlyle, *Mrs.* Jane W. Early letters. '89..826.2 75
    Letters; ed. by Froude. 1883. 2 v.....826.2 72
    Same; 2 v. in 1...............................826.2 74
Carlyle, Thomas. Bibliographical note
    (Boston public library bulletin, v. 4,
    p. 334)..17 B-14
    Carlyle anthology; ed. by Barrett. '76.829.2 8
    Characteristics. 1881.....................*in* 821.2 238
    Corr. with Emerson, 1834-72. 2 v.......826 1
    Same; supplementary letters. 1886....826 3
    Corr. with Goethe; ed. by Norton.
    1887...826.2 47
    Early letters, 1814-26; ed. by Norton.
    1886...826.2 88
    Essays. 1860. 4 v.
    V. 1. Richter.—State of German literature.—
    Werner.—Goethe's Helena.—Goethe.—Burns.—
    Heine.—German playwrights...............824.2 137

V. 2. Voltaire.—Novalis.—Signs of the times.—
Richter again.— History.— Luther's psalm.—Schiller.— The Nibelungen lied. — German literature,
14-15th centuries. — Taylor's German poetry.—
Appendix..824.2 138
V. 3. Characteristics.—Goethe's portrait.—Biography. — Boswell's Johnson. — Death of Goethe.
—Goethe's works. — Corn-law rhymes. — History,
again.—Diderot. — Cagliostro. — Death of Edward
Irving.—Appendix................................824.2 139
V. 4. The diamond necklace.— Mirabeau. — Parliamentary history of the French revolution.—Sir W.
Scott. — Von Ense's memoirs.— Copyright bill.—
Sinking of the Vengeur.—Baillie the Covenanter.—
Dr. Francia.—An election to the long parliament.—
Two hundred and fifty years ago. — The opera.—
Scottish portraits.—The prinzenraub............824.2 140
Heroes and hero-worship.................233 15
Last words. 1892............................820.2 299
Contents: Wotton Reinfred: a romance. — Excursion
(futile enough) to Paris.—Letters.
Latter-day pamphlets...................824.2 141
Contents: The present time.— Model prisons.— Downing street.—New Downing street.—Stump-orator.—Parliaments.—Hudson's statue.—Jesuitism.
Letters, 1826-36; ed. by Norton.........826.2 99
On the choice of books. 1881..............374 14
Past and present. 1844....................301 10
Reference list; by Foster. v.1...........16 55
Sartor resartus.............................827.2 33
 Same; ed. by MacMechan. 1896....827.2 32
Thoughts on life; sel. by Duncan. '95..829.2 76
Works. 1869. 34 v.
V. 1. Sartor resartus............................820.2 265
V. 2-4. French revolution........................820.2 266
V. 5. Life of Schiller............................820.2 269
V. 6-11. Essays..................................820.2 270
V. 12. Heroes and hero-worship..................820.2 276
V. 13. Past and present..........................820.2 277
V. 14-18. Cromwell's letters and speeches......820.2 278
V. 19. Latter-day pamphlets.....................820.2 283
V. 20. Life of John Sterling....................820.2 284
V. 21-30. History of Frederick the great.—Index..820.2 285
Translations. V. 1-2. Goethe's Wilhelm Meister.
....820.2 295
V. 3. Musæus.—Tieck.— Richter..................820.2 297
General index....................................820.2 298
Carman. Low tide on Grand Pré: lyrics.
 1893.......................................821.2 920
Carman and Hovey. More songs from
 Vagabondia. 1896......................821.2 1043
Songs from Vagabondia. 1894........821.2 969
Carmen Sylva, pseud. See Elizabeth, queen
 of Roumania.
Carpenter, Edith. Your money or your
 life..69880
Carpenter, E. J. Woman of Shawmut.........8130
Carr, Alaric. Treherne's temptation.........15401
Carr, Alice C. Margaret Maliphant..........55301
Carr, Mrs. Comyns. Cottage folk.............55302
Contents: The hoppers.— A retrospect. — The breadwinner.—His little maid. — A farm tragedy. — A broken
tryst. An only son. A woman's wager. A ne'er-do-weel.
Carr, J. C. King Arthur: drama. 1895..822.2 325

Carrel. The city................................58140
Carrington. Aschenbroedel...................15081
Carroll, Lewis, pseud. (C. L. Dodgson.)
 Alice in wonderland.......................0902
 Hunting of the snark. 1876...........828.2 35
 Rhyme? and reason? 1883............828.2 56
 Sylvie and Bruno..........................0906
 Tangled tale.................................0905
 Through the looking-glass..............0901
Carruth. Adventures of Jones...............35270
 Voyage of the Rattletrap.................35271
Carryl. Admiral's caravan..................041901
 Davy and the goblin......................041902
Carus. Karma: a story of early Buddhism..294 89
Cary, Alice. Ballads, etc. 1869............821.1 50
 Bishop's son.................................20360
 Clovernook..................................20362
 Pictures of country life..................20361
Cary, Alice and Phœbe. Last poems;
 ed. by Ames. 1873......................821.1 52
 Poetical works. 1895....................821.1 53
Cary, Gillie. Uncle Jerry's platform, etc...30496
Cary, Phœbe. Poems. 1868.................821.1 51
Case. Forward house.........................15650
Case of Mohammed Benani..................69046
Cass. Address, Hamilton college. 1830...40 24
Casseday. Hortons.............................44111
Castle. Consequences........................29450
 La Bella......................................29451
 Light of Scarthey..........................29452
 My little Lady Anne......................29459
Catherwood. Chase of Saint-Castin, etc...28206
Contents: Chase of Saint-Castin. — Beauport loupgarou.—Mill at Petit Cap.—Wolfe's cove.—Windigo.—
Kidnapped bride.—Pontiac's lookout.
 Craque o' doom............................28207
 Lady of Fort St. John....................28203
 Little Renault..............................in 28209
 Old caravan days.........................028202
 Old Kaskaskia..............................28204
 Rocky Fork..................................028201
 Romance of Dollard......................28201
 Spirit of an Illinois town................28209
 Story of Tonty.............................28202
 White islander..............................28205
Caulfield, ed. Vocal music in Shakespeare's
 plays. 2 v.................................784 B-5
Caunter. Romance of history: India......47256
Cavazza. Don Finimondone..................20220
Cawthorn. Poems; with life. 1822....in 821.2 39
Centlivre, Mrs. Dramatic works. 1872.
 3 v..822.2 198
Cervus. Model wife...........................69140
 White feathers..............................69139
Chadwick, J. H. Whole truth...............69291
Chadwick, J. W. Book of poems. '81...821.1 287
Chalmers, James. Renegade.................22020
Chalmers, T. Selections from corr. '53...826.2 28

Chamberlain, C. Servant girl of the period..44181
Chamberlain, N. H. New England farm house..30140
 Sphinx in Aubrey parish................30141
Chamberlain, W. M. Manuela Parèdes...15069
Chambers, Julius. Lovers four and maidens five...22301
 Missing (In Sargasso)...........................22303
 On a margin..22302
Chambers, Robert. Essays from Chambers' journal. 2 v.....................824.2 159
Chambers, R. W. In the quarter............31351
 King and a few dukes............................31353
 King in yellow.......................................31350
 Maker of moons, etc..............................31354
  Contents: Maker of moons.— Silent land. — Black water.—In the name of the most high.—The boy's sister.—The crime.—Pleasant evening.—Man at the next table.
 Red republic..31352
 With the band (verses). 1896............821.2 538
Chambers, William. Ailie Gilroy...........15297
Chamier. South-sea siren......................67060
Champfleury, *pseud.* See **Fleury, Jules.**
Champney. Bubbling teapot 028806
 Howling Wolf and his trick pony.........028809
 Three Vassar girls abroad....................028801
 Three Vassar girls at home..................028808
 Three Vassar girls in England.............028803
 Three Vassar girls in France................028810
 Three Vassar girls in Italy...................028805
 Three Vassar girls in South America....028804
 Three Vassar girls on the Rhine..........028807
Chandler, Bessie. Woman who failed.....41720
  Contents: Woman who failed.— Silent soul.— Esther Godwin's geese. — Margaret's romance. — Victim of prejudice. — Middle Miss Tallman. — Thanksgiving wedding.—Miss Polly Atherton's bell. — Uncle Nathan's ear-trumpet.—Turning of the worm.
Chandler, *Mrs.* G. W. Anthè................69120
Channing, G. E. Sister of a saint, etc.....60130
Channing, W. E., *the elder.* Correspondence with Lucy Aikin. 1874............826.1 4
 Note-book. 1887...........................829.1 27
 Self-culture.................................374 16
 Works. 4 v..................................240 48
Channing, W. E., *the younger.* Eliot: a poem. 1885.........................821.1 328
 John Brown (drama). 1886............822.1 23
 The wanderer: a poem. 1871........821.1 181
Chanter. Witch of Withyford 36760
Chapel of St. Mary...............................50388
Chaperoned...14790
Chapman, George. Comedies and tragedies. 1873. 3 v.......................822.2 182
 Translation of the Iliad. 1865. 2 v.....883 6
 Translation of the Odyssey. 1857. 2 v....883 8
 Translations. 1858............................884 6
  Contents: Homer: Batrachomyomachia; Hymns; Epigrams.—Hesiod: Works; Days.—Musœus: Hero and Leander.—Juvenal: Fifth satire.

Chapman, J. M. Translations of Theocritus, Bion, and Moschus. 1864.........884 8
Chapone. Works. 1809. 2 v............826.2 37
Chapple. Minor chord..........................57310
Chard. Across the sea, and other poems. 1875..................................821.1 245
Charles, *Mrs.* E. Against the stream........3713
 Attila and his conquerors.....................3702
 Conquering and to conquer..................3715
 Cripple of Antioch..............................3712
 Diary of Kitty Trevelyan......................3709
 Draytons and Davenants.......................3707
 Early dawn..3704
 Joan the maid...................................3716
 Lapsed but not lost............................3714
 Liberation of Holland.........................3711
 Martyrs of Spain................................3711
 On both sides of the sea.....................3708
 Schoenberg Cotta family......................3701
 Victory of the vanquished....................3706
 Winifred Bertram...............................3710
Charles, H. F. Young Sir Richard........032235
Charlesworth. England's yeomen...........19143
 Ministry of life.................................19144
 Oliver of the mill..............................19145
Charlotte, Elizabeth. See **Tonna,** *Mrs.*
Chatelaine, *Madame de.* Truly noble......020201
Chatfield. The tin trumpet. 1859........829.2 19
Chatham, *earl of.* See **Pitt, William,** *earl of Chatham.*
Chatterton. Poetical works. 1842. 2 v...821.2 117
 Works. 1803. 3 v.
  V. 1. Life; by Gregory.—Miscellaneous poems.821.2 114
  V. 2. Poems attributed to Rowley....................821.2 115
  V. 3. Miscellaneous pieces in prose.................821.2 116
Chaucer. Animadversions upon the corrections of; by F. Thynne...........820.2 305
 Canterbury tales..............................821.2 954
 Same; annotated and accented by Saunders. 1889.........................821.2 955
 Same; new text; ed. by Wright. 3 v.
 ....821.2 467
 Chaucer's England; by Browne. 2 v......394 8
 Complete works; ed. by Skeat. 1894.
  V. 1. Life of Chaucer. — Romaunt of the rose.
  —Minor poems..821.2 931
  V. 2. Boethius and Troilus..............................821.2 934
  V. 3. House of fame.—Legend of good women.
  —Treatise on the astrolabe.—Account of the sources of the Canterbury tales...........................821.2 940
  V. 4. Canterbury tales: text..............................821.2 941
  V. 5. Notes to Canterbury tales........................821.2 942
  V. 6. Introduction.—Glossary.—Indexes........821.2 943
 Fables and tales from; by Dryden....821.2 701
 For children; by Mrs. Haweis. '82...*821.2 959
 Illustrations of; by Todd. 1810......928.2 B-1
 Legend of good women; ed. by Skeat. 1889..821.2 957
 Minor poems; ed. by Skeat. 1888....821.2 958

* Of interest to young readers.

Notes, grammatical and philological; by
  Carpenter...428 3
Parliament of foules; ed. by Lounsbury.
  ....821.2 956
Poems modernized; by Horne, Wordsworth, Hunt, *et al.* 1841............821.2 952
Poetical works; ed. by Bell. 1861. 8 v.
  V. 1-3. Canterbury tales............................821.2 944
  V. 4. Canterbury tales, concluded. -- Court of love.—Assembly of foules.--Of the cuckow and the nightingale.—The flower and the leaf..............821.2 947
  V. 5-6. Troilus and Cryseyde.—Chauceres dreme. —Chauceres A B C — Boke of the duchesse.—Of Queen Anelyda and false Arcyte. — The house of fame...821.2 948
  V. 7. Romaunt of the rose.............................821.2 950
  V. 8. Compleynte of a loveres life.—Compleynte of Mars and Venus. — Legende of goode women. —Minor poems...821.2 951
The riches of; by Clarke. 1835........821.2 953
Selections from; by Wordsworth......821.2 674
Specimens of; by Leigh Hunt......*in* 824.2 242
Studies in; by Lounsbury. 1892. 3v..821.2 960
Tales from; by Pope........................821.2 608
Translation of Bœthius' 'De consolatione philosophiæ.'..........................820.2 403

Chellis. Revere estate...................................68601
  Temperance doctor.....................................68602
Cheney, *Mrs.* **E. D.** Child of the tide......19194
  Sally Williams..19195
Cheney, J. V. Old doctor...........................69150
  Queen Helen, and other poems. '95..821.1 498
  That dome in air: thoughts on poetry and poets. 1895..............................824.1 306
Chesebro'. Foe in the household................19120
  Peter Carradine..19121
Chesney. Battle of Dorking. 1881..827.2 Pam. 2
  Dilemma..65801
Chester, A. G. Story of Miriam Grey (verse). 1869.......................821.1 Pam. 22
Chester, Eliza. Chats with girls on self-culture. 1891..374 20
Chester, G. J. Julian Cloughton............62526
Chester, Robert. Love's martyr (poem).
  ....821.2 B-9
Chester, Sarah. Sir Genevieve................04401
Chesterfield. Essays in The World. 3 v..824.2 19
  Letters, maxims, etc. 1870................829.2 42
  Letters to his godson. 1889. 2 v......826.2 7
  Letters to his son; ed. by Carey. 1872.
   2 v..826.2 9
  Letters; with the Characters; ed. by Bradshaw. 1892. 3 v..................826.2 10
Chestnutwood. See **Perkins,** *Mrs.* **E. B.**
Chettle. Kind-heart's dream.................821.2 448
Chetwode. Marble city...............................03570l
Chetwynd. Brilliant woman......................18720
Chetwynd *and* **Wilkins.** John Ellicombe's temptation.....................................18721

Child, *Mrs.* Letters. 1883....................826 1 10
  Romance of the republic.........................41114
Childer. Future marquis..............................62556
Children of Issachar.......................................69001
Children's journey...02480l
Choate. Writings and life. 1862. 2 v..923.1 302
Cholmondeléy. Danvers jewels. Sir Charles Danvers..55287
  A devotee...55289
  Diana Tempest...55288
Chopin. Bayou folk (stories).......................36001
Chorley. Prodigy. 3 v...................................56847
Christian. Persis Yorke..............................36521
  Sarah...36520
Church, A. J. Burning of Rome................2205
  Callias..2206
  Chantry priest of Barnet.............................2208
  Count of the Saxon shore............................2201
  Fall of Athens..2207
  Greek Gulliver (Traveller's true tale; by Lucian).......................................*887 3A
  Heroes and kings. 1883.........................*883 50
  Stories of the Iliad and the Æneid. '85..*883 65
  Stories of the magicians. 1887...............*893 54
  Story of the Illiad. 1891........................*883 70
  Story of the Odyssey. 1891..................*883 71
  Three Greek children..............................*2202
  To the lions...2203
  Translation of Traveller's true tale; by Lucian. 1880..887 3
  Two thousand years ago............................2209
  With the king at Oxford............................2211
  Young Macedonian.....................................2204
Church, A. J., *and* **Seeley, R.** The hammer..2210
Church, *Mrs.* **L. D.** Right spirit..........41860
Church, *Mrs.* **R.** See **Marryat, Florence.**
Church, R. W. Dante, and other essays. 1888..824.2 417
  Contents: Dante.—William Wordsworth — Sordello.
  Gifts of civilisation. 1891.......................204 123
  Contents: Gifts of civilisation.—Civilisation before and after Christianity.—On some influences of Christianity upon national character. — The sacred poetry of early religion.
  Miscellaneous essays. 1888..................824.2 409
  Contents: Essays of Montaigne. — Brittany. - Cassiodorus.—Letters of Pope Gregory I. --The early Ottomans.
  Occasional papers. 1897. 2 v........824.2 518
Churcher. Mystery of Shakespeare revealed. 1886..822.3 341
Churchill, C. Poems; with life. 1822......821.2 40
  Poetical works; ed. by Gilfillan. 1855.
  ....821.2 185
  Poetical works; with memoir by Hannay, notes by Tooke. 1892. 2 v..821.2 183
Churchill, *Lord* **R.** Speeches and life..923.2 576

* Of interest to young readers.

Churchill, William. Princess of Fiji........16305
Churchward. Jem Peterkin's daughter......35705
Clark, Alexander. Old log school-house....52272
Clark, Alfred. Finding of Lot's wife........52580
Clark, C. H. See **Adeler, Max.**
Clark, *Mrs.* **C. M.** See **Clay, Charles M.,** *pseud.*
Clark, F. E. Mossback correspondence. 1889..824.1 246
Clark, F. T. Mexican girl........................16650
    Mistress of the ranch............................16652
    On Cloud mountain...............................16651
Clark, Imogen. Las' day.........................22405
    Victory of Ezra Gardner.......................22406
Clark, Kate E. Dominant seventh...........69535
Clark, *Mrs.* **S. R. G.** Our street...............56876
Clark, W. G. Literary remains. 1844...824.1 13
Clarke, Charles Carlos. Beauclercs........52278
    Which is the winner?.............................52279
Clarke, Charles Cowden. Riches of Chaucer. 1835........ ....821.2 953
    Shakespeare characters. 1863.........822.3 132
Clarke, Charles Cowden *and* **M. C.** The Shakespeare key. 1879................822.3 128
Clarke, Charles H., *and* **Ross, A.** Story of a honeymoon............................828.2 47
Clarke, *Mrs.* **H.** Roscorla farm.................56101
Clarke, J. F. Legend of Thomas Didymus. 1881....................................249 40
    Memorial and biographical sketches. 1878...824.1 75
    Contents: John A. Andrew.—James Freeman.—Charles Sumner.— Theodore Parker.—S. G. Howe.—W. E. Channing.— W. Channing. — Ezra S. Gannett. — Samuel J. May.—Susan Dimock.— George Keats.— R. J. Breckenridge.—George D. Prentice. — Junius Brutus Booth, the elder.— Washington.— Rousseau.—Heroes of one country town.—William Hall.
    Oration, July 5, 1875..................329.1 Pam. 42
    Self-culture. 1880..........................374 11
Clarke, Marcus. Chidiock Tichbourne...34101
    Heavy odds..34103
    His natural life......................................34104
    'Twixt shadow and shine.....................34102
Clarke, Mary Cowden. Complete concordance to Shakespeare............‡822.3 B-3
    Girlhood of Shakespeare's heroines. 3 v..822.3 212
    Same; abridged......................*822.3 211
    Iron cousin..19104
    Rambling story 19103
    The trust, etc.: stories in metred prose. 1874..821.2 419
    Yarns of an old mariner........................06001
Clarke, McDonald. Poems. 1836.....821.1 271
Clarke, R. S. See **May, Sophie,** *pseud.*
Clarke, S. M. Our country (verse). 1864. ....821.1 Pam. 1

Clarkson. Shadow of John Wallace 62392
Clay, C. M. Baby Rue..............................68203
    Daughter of the gods............................68204
    Modern Hagar.......................................68201
Clay, Henry. Corr. and speeches. 3v..329.1 105
    Speeches. 1844. 2 v...................329.1 87
Clemens. See **Twain, Mark.**
Clement, Eleanor Maitland................62547
Clemmer, Mary Ames. His two wives....29502
    Outlines of men, women and things. 1873..824.1 135
    Poems. 1883...........................821.1 290
Cleveland. George Eliot's poetry, etc. 1885..821.1 161
    Long run..69243
Clifford, *Mrs.* **W. K.** Anyhow stories.....03040A
    Aunt Anne...30505
    Dominant note, etc. (Mere stories).... ..30510A
    Contents: The dominant note Mr Webster.—Lady Margrave. In case of discovery.—The woman and the Philistine.— John Alwyn.— Julie.— A woman who had genius.
    Flash of summer....................................30509
    Last touches, etc....................................30508
    Contents: Last touches.— An interlude. On the way to the sea.—Sorry love-affair.— Ridiculous tragedy. Sad comedy.—Thomas.—Last scene of the play. Wooden Tony.
    Marie May..30507
    Mere stories (Dominant note)............30510
    Wild proxy..30506
Clifford family...50366
Cline. Henry Cortland............................44112
Clinton, De Witt. Discourse before Literary and philosophical society, New York. 1814................................825.1 4
    Speeches and addresses. 7 pamphlets. ....329 Pam. 33
Clinton, G. W. Address, Albany normal school. 1856........................825.1 9
    Address, I. O. of Rechabites. 1845.........40 27
    Catalogue of papers and addresses of, to be found in the state library, Albany. ....16 Pam. 4
    Historical address, Young men's association, Buffalo. 1862............95.2x Pam. 6
    List of papers and addresses which are in the N. Y. state library...............16 Pam. 4
    Oration, Schenectady, 1857.........825.1 Pam. 10
Clive. Paul Ferroll..................................18515
Clough. Poems; with memoir. 1871...821.2 329
    Prose remains. 1888.......................826.2 95
    Selections from poems. 1894..........821.1 328
Clouston. Literary coincidences. 1892...824.2 147
Clowes. Double emperor........................3064
Clyde. Under foot...................................14152
Coann *and* **Noble.** Love and shawl-straps..6550 7
Cobb, J. B. Leisure labors. 1858........824.1 30

---

* Of interest to young readers.   ‡ For reference.

Cobb, J. F. Feast of stories from foreign
lands..030602
Martin the skipper..............................030601
Silent Jim...59602
Watchers on the longships...................59603
Workman and soldier..........................59601
Cobb, Thomas. Westlakes.................27910
Cobban. Avenger of blood...................24007
Burden of Isabel..................................24005
Horned cat..24003
Julius Courtney...................................24001
King of Andaman.................................24008
Nemesis..24009
Red sultan..24004
Reverend gentleman............................24002
Soldier and a gentleman.......................24006
Tyrants of Kool-Sim.............................024011
White kaid of the Atlas.........................024010
Wilt thou have this woman?..................24010
Cobbe. Darwinism in morals, etc. 1883...204 93
Italics. 1864..................................914.5 90
The peak in Darien, etc. 1882.............211 64
Studies, new and old. 1865.................170 25
Cobbett. Porcupine's works. 12 v.......329.1 48
Cobbleigh, Tom, *pseud.* See **Raymond, Walter.**
Cock Lorell's bote; ed. by Rimbault......821.2 449
Cockton. Fatal marriages....................10904
George Julian......................................10908
Love match...10901
Sylvester Sound...................................10907
Valentine Vox......................................10906
Cody. In the heart of the hills...............70180
Coffin, C. C., (Carleton, *pseud.*). Caleb
Krinkle...22852
Dan of Millbrook.................................22850
Daughters of the revolution..................22851
Winning his way..................................022801
Coffin, R. B., (Barry Gray, *pseud.*). Cakes
and ale..19138
Matrimonial infelicities.........................19136
My married life, etc..............................19137
Coghill (A. L. Walker). Trial of Mary
Broom..10430
Cogswell. Regicides............................70940
Cokain. Dramatic works; with memoir.
1874...822.2 234
Coleman. Curly..................................69156
Coleridge, C. R. Amethyst...................66906
Bag of farthings..................................041701
Colt from the heather..........................66911
English squire.....................................66903
Gertrude's lover..................................66908
Hanbury Mills.....................................66902
Jack O'Lanthorn..................................66905
Lady Betty...66901
Minstrel Dick......................................66910

Plunge into troubled waters..................66904
Tender mercies of the good..................66907
Coleridge, C. R., *and* **Shipton, H.**
Ravenstone.......................................66909
Coleridge, Hartley. Poems; with life.
1851. 2 v..................................821.2 174
Coleridge, M. E. Seven sleepers of Ephesus..32140
Coleridge, S. T. Anima poetæ, from notebooks; ed. by Coleridge. 1895......829.2 77
Christabel, and lyrical and imaginative
poems; ed., with essay, by Swinburne..821.2 569
Complete works; ed. by Shedd. 1860.
7 v.
V. 1. Introductory essays; by Shedd.— Aids to
reflection.—Statesman's manual...................820.2 140
V. 2. The friend..820.2 141
V. 3. Biographia literaria..............................820.2 142
V. 4. Notes and lectures upon Shakespeare, etc.
—Literary remains...820.2 143
V. 5. Literary remains....................................820.2 144
V. 6. Constitution of church and state............820.2 145
V. 7. Poetical and dramatic works...................820.2 146
Lects. and notes on Shakspere, etc..822.3 217
Letters; ed. by Coleridge. 1895......826.2 115
Letters, etc. 1836.............................826.2 81
Letters to the Beaumonts. 2 v......*in* 826.2 90
Miscellanies. 1885............................824.2 380
Contents: Essays on the fine arts. — On the Prometheus of Æschylus.— Fragments and notes: The middle ages; Cervantes; Wit and humor; Dante; Mythology; Style.—Over the Brocken.—On unmeasured language and intolerance.—Allegoric vision.— The improvisatore.—On the choice of a husband.—On literary praise.—On thinking and reflection. — Historic and gests of Maxilian.— Miscellaneous notes.—Theory of life.
Passages from prose and 'Table talk';
ed. by Dircks................................829.2 75
Poetical and dramatic works. 1880. 4 v.
V. 1. Memoir.—Juvenile poems, sonnets, etc..821.2 565
V. 2. France: an ode.—Frost at midnight. — Fears in solitude.—The nightingale.—Ancient mariner.—Sibylline leaves: Christabel, etc.—Epigrams.—Appendix..821.2 566
V. 3. Fall of Robespierre: a drama.—Translation of Schiller's 'Wallenstein.'..............................821.2 567
V. 4. Remorse: a tragedy.—Zapolya............821.2 568
Rime of the ancient mariner; ed. by
Bates. 1896...............................821.2 1169
Specimens of table talk. 1851........829.2 50
Table talk.—Omniana. 1884...........829.2 86
Coleridge, S. T., *and* **Wordsworth, W.**
Lyrical ballads: reprint; ed. by Dowden. 1890......................................821.2 684
Coleridge, Sara. Phantasmion..............08101
Coles. The microcosm, etc. (poems)....821.1 396
National hymns..........................821.1 Pam. 17
Collier, J. P., *ed.* Ghost of Richard III:
poem, 1614. (Shakespeare society,
1844.)..822.3 49
Mad pranks and merry jests of Robin
Goodfellow..................................821.2 445

LANGUAGE AND LITERATURE.

Reply to Hamilton's 'Inquiry' into Shakespeare forgeries............822.3 Pam. 12
Shakespeare's library. 1843. 2 v......822.3 41
Collier, W. F. Marjorie Dudingstoune.....53911
   Tales of old English life........................53910
Collingwood, Harry, *pseud.* (W. J. C. Lancaster.) Log of a privateersman..036101
Collingwood, H. W. Andersonville violets..69516
Collingwood, W. G. Thorstein of the Mere..32340
Collins, C. A. Bar sinister.......................47204
   Cruise upon wheels................................47205
Collins, J. C. Essays and studies. 1895..824.2 479
   Contents: John Dryden.— Predecessors of Shakspeare.— Lord Chesterfield's letters. — The Porson of Shakspearian criticism.—Menander.
   Illustrations of Tennyson. 1891......821.2 375
Collins, J. L. See **Jonquil.**
Collins, Mabel. Ida................*in* 53805
   Star sapphire..56180
Collins, Mortimer. Fight with fortune.....52302
   Sweet and twenty..................................52304
   Sweet Anne Page..................................52305
   Transformation.....................................52306
   Two plunges for a pearl........................52301
   Vivian romance....................................52303
Collins, Mortimer *and* **Frances.** Blacksmith and scholar..................................52307
Collins, Wilkie. After dark..................1912
   Antonina...1916
   Armadale..1906
   Basil..1927
   Black robe...1946
   Blind love..1909
   Dead alive...1914
   Dead secret...1931
   Evil genius..1956
   Fallen leaves..1941
   Haunted hotel......................................1935
   Heart and science................................1950
   Frozen deep...1920
   Guilty river..1902
   I say no..1952
   Hide and seek......................................1930
   Jezebel's daughter...............................1943
   Law and the lady................................1905
   Legacy of Cain....................................1904
   Man and wife.......................................1907
   Miss or Mrs.?......................................1942
   Moonstone...1903
   My lady's money.................................1932
   New Magdalen....................................1908
   No name...1923
   Percy and the prophet..........................1933
   Plot in private life................................1921
   Poor Miss Finch..................................1910
   Queen of hearts....................................1948

   Rogue's life..1938
   Sister Rose..1911
   Two destinies......................................1918
   Woman in white..................................1901
   Yellow mask..1939
Collins, William. Poems; with life. '22..821.2 32
Colman, G., *the elder.* Prose, with some verse. 1787. 3 v.................821.2 256
Colman, G., *the younger.* Broad grins...828.2 10
   Mountaineers: a play..........*in* 822.2 147
Colmore. Daughter of music................41510
Colomb. The Miss Crusoes..................032236
Colton, C. C. Lacon. 1836...............829.2 15
   Modern antiquity, and other poems. 1835...821.1 171
Colton, G. H. Tecumseh: a poem. '42...821.1 19
Combe. Doctor Syntax's three tours.......828.2 9
Comic natural history of the human race. ....828.1 B 1
Comins. Hartwell farm........................47301
   Marion Berkley..................................47304
Compton. Free lance in a far land........34570
Comyn. Atherston priory...................66101
   Elena: an Italian tale..........................66102
Cone. Oberon and Puck: verses........821.1 233
   The ride to the lady, etc. (poems). '91.821.1 435
Confessions of Amos Todd, adventurer......55402
Congdon, C. M. The guardian angel, etc. (verse). 1856.................................821.1 423
Congdon, C. T. Tribune essays. 1869..329.1 101
Congreve. Dramatic works. 1860......822.2 180
Connelly. Tilting at windmills..............69416
   Under the surface................................69417
Conrad. Almayer's folly......................13350
   Outcast of the islands..........................13351
Conscience, B., *pseud.* (S. W. Cooper). Confessions of a society man..............69324
Constance of Acadia..............................69032
Converse. Lost gold mine....................036901
Conway, H. Bound together................17209
   Called back...17201
   Cardinal sin..17220
   Carriston's gift, etc.............................17215
   Dark days..17210
   Family affair......................................17217
   Living or dead....................................17222
   Slings and arrows...............................17219
Conway, K. E. A lady and her letters. 1895..816 11
Conway, M. D. Prisons of air..............30102
   Necklace of stories..............................30103
   Pine and palm....................................30101
Conyngham. Eunice Quince..................67010
Cook, Dutton. Doubleday's children.....56807
Cook, Eliza. Melaia, and other poems. 821.2 269
   Poetical works. 1858...................821.2 298

Cooke, G. W. Guide to works of Browning. 1891...............................821.2 1117
Poets and problems. 1886..............824.1 132
Cooke, J. E. Canolles...........................33611
  Doctor Vandyke...........................33601
  Fanchette.....................................33619
  Hammer and rapier......................33614
  Henry St. John............................33606
  Her majesty the queen................33613
  Justin Harley...............................33607
  Leather stocking and silk...........33610
  Maurice mystery..........................33616
  Mr. Grantley's idea....................33618
  Mohun..33609
  My lady Pokahontas..................33615
  Pretty Mrs. Gaston.....................33605
  Professor Pressensee..................33617
  Surrey of Eagle's Nest..............33608
  Virginia Bohemians....................33612
  Virginia comedians....................33602
Cooke, Rose Terry. Happy Dodd.........21703
  Huckleberries..............................21705
  Somebody's neighbors...............21701
  Sphinx's children........................21702
  Steadfast.....................................21704
Coolidge, J. I. T. Address, Boston young men's Christian union. 1853........*in* 825.1 17
Coolidge, Susan, *pseud.* (Sarah C. Woolsey). Barberry bush, etc................011214
  Clover..011211
  Cross patch, etc..........................011205
  Eyebright....................................011203
  A few more verses. 1889..........821.1 404
  For summer afternoons.............28401
  Guernsey lily.............................011204
  In the high valley....................011213
  Just sixteen (stories)................011212
  Little country girl...................011208
  Mischief's Thanksgiving.........011210
  New year's bargain..................011206
  Nine little goslings..................011216
  Not quite eighteen (stories)....011215
  Old convent school in Paris. 1895......824.1 305
    Contents: An old convent school in Paris.—Countess Potocki.—Girlhood of an autocrat.—Miss Eden.—Duc de Saint-Simon.
  Round dozen..............................011207
  Verses. 1880..............................821.1 254
  What Katy did..........................011201
  What Katy did at school.........011202
  What Katy did next.................011209
Coombs. As common mortals..........69041
  Game of chance........................69039
  Garden of Armida...................69040
Cooper, E. H. Enemies...................34606
  Richard Escott..........................34605
Cooper, J. F. Afloat and ashore.......1032
  Die Ansiedler [German of 'The pioneers']..1005

Autobiography of a pocket-handkerchief...1040
Die beiden Admirale [German of 'The two admirals']......................1027
Bravo...1058
Chainbearer...1011
Crater..1016
Deerslayer...1001
Eve Effingham....................................1082
Headsman..1015
Heidenmauer.......................................1063
Home as found....................................1036
Homeward bound................................1057
Jack Tier..1029
Last of the Mohicans..........................1002
Leather-stocking tales (reserved copy). 1876. 5 v.
  Deerslayer..1823 91
  Last of the Mohicans......................1823 92
  Pathfinder..1823 93
  Pioneers..1823 94
  Prairie..1823 95
  Same [abridged]................................1007
Lionel Lincoln....................................1065
Der Lootse [German of 'The pilot']...1071
Mercedes of Castile...........................1046
Miles Wallingford..............................1034
Monikins..1017
Ned Myers...1033
Oak openings......................................1013
Pathfinder...1055
Der Pfadfinder [German of 'The pathfinder']..1056
Pilot...1070
Pioneers...1004
Prairie..1006
Precaution...1083
Red rover..1024
Red skins..1003
Satanstoe..1043
Sea lions..1030
Sea tales (reserved copy). 1859. 5 v.
  Pilot..1823 99
  Red rover..1823 100
  Water-witch....................................1823 101
  Sea-lions...1823 102
  Crater..1823 103
Der Spion [German of 'The spy']...1010
Spy...1009
Stories of the sea................................0301
Two admirals.....................................1026
Water-witch.......................................1019
Ways of the hour................................1037
Wept of Wish-ton-wish.....................1045
Wing and wing...................................1021
Wyandotte..1012
Cooper, J. G. Poems; with life........821.2 31
Cooper, S. F. Rhyme and reason of country life. 1855......................819 11
  Rural hours. 1851............................829.1 5

‡ For reference.

LANGUAGE AND LITERATURE.

Cooper, S. W. See **Conscience, Blanche,** *pseud.*
Copsley annals.....................................50318
Copway. Ojibway conquest (poem). 1850.
....821.1 216
Corbet. Holiday camp...........................07801
Corbett. Business in great waters..........23603
   Fall of Asgard......................................23601
   Kophetua the thirteenth.....................23602
Corbin. The Elizabethan Hamlet. 1895..822.3 392
Corcoran. Pickings from the portfolio......47276
Corelli. Ardath....................................51004
   Barabbas...51007
   Cameos..51011
   Jane...51013
   Mighty atom..51010
   Murder of Delicia................................51012
   Romance of two worlds......................51003
   Silence of the Maharajah....................51008
   Sorrows of Satan.................................51009
   Soul of Lilith......................................51006
   Thelma..51002
   Vendetta!..51001
   Wormwood..51005
   Ziska...51014
Corkran. Bessie Lang............................44126
Cornford. Captain Jacobus....................71120
   Master-beggars....................................71121
Cornwall, Barry. See **Proctor, B. W.**
Cornwall, C. M. Free, yet forging their own chains...52212
Cornwallis, C. F. Small books on great subjects. 1847...104 7
Cornwallis, K. Adrift with a vengeance...44113
Corrie. In scorn of consequence..............69279
Corry O'Lanus (J. H. Howard). His views, etc. 1867...................................828.1 52
Corson. Introduction to study of Browning. 1886...821.2 1118
   Introduction to study of Shakespeare. 1889..822.3 216
Coryell. Diego Pinzon.............................010840
Cossins. Isban-Israel..............................43350
Costello, F. H. Master Ardick, buccaneer..71060
Costello, L. S. Catherine de' Medici.s......44115
Cotes, *Mrs.* E. See **Duncan, Sara J.**
Cotes, V. C. Two girls on a barge............29485
Cotterell. Tempe..................................51406
Cotton. Poems; with life. 1822............821.2 31
Couch, A. T. Quiller-. See **Q.**
Coulson. Ghost of Redbrook...................58501
Country parson, A. See **Boyd, A. K. H.**
County, The..55286
Courtenay. Commentaries on historical plays of Shakspeare. 1840. 2 v......822.3 63
Couvreur, *Madame.* See **Tasma,** *pseud.*
Cove. Susan de L'Orme..........................07107

Coventry. After his kind........................69196
Coverdale. Fall of the great republic......69019
Cowan. Daybreak..................................70920
Cowen *and* Zangwill. Premier and the painter..22523
Cowley. Essays; ed. by Hurd, *et al.* '69...824.2 5
   Poems; with life. 1822. 2 v........821.2 24
   Works. 1707. 3 v.
   V. 1. Life; by Clifford.—Miscellanies.—Anacreontiques.—The mistress.—Pindaric odes.—Davideis..821.2 541
   V. 2. Davideis, concluded.—Davideidos.—Verses on several occasions.—Proposition for advancement of experimental philosophy.—Government of Cromwell.—Essays in verse and prose.—Cutter of Coleman street..........................821.2 542
   V. 3. Constantia and Philetus.—Piramus and Thisbe.—Sylva.—Love's riddle.—Naufragium joculare.—Six books of plants.....................821.2 543
Cowper, F. Hunting of the auk..............035401
Cowper, William. Favorite poems, '81.821.2 595
   Letters; ed. by Benham. 1884........826.2 592
   Poems; with life. 1822..................821.2 49
   Translation of the Iliad. 1809..........883 36
   Translation of the Odyssey. 1809.......883 30
   Works; ed. by Southey. 1853. 8 v.
   V. 1-4. Life, by Southey.—Letters........821.2 198
   V. 5. Miscellaneous poems.—Olney hymns.—Table talk.—Progress of error.—Truth.—Expostulation.—Hope.—Charity.—Conversation.—Retirement.—Miscellaneous poems and translations..821.2 201
   V. 6. The task.—Tirocinium.—John Gilpin.—Miscellaneous poems.—Adam: a sacred drama..821.2 203
   V. 7. Translation of Homer's Iliad..........821.2 204
   V. 8. Translation of Homer's Odyssey......821.2 205
Cox, M. B. Left on the prairie...............040450
Cox, Maria McI. Raymond Kershaw......69428
Coxe, A. C. Athanasion, etc. (poems).
   1842...821.1 570
   Christian ballads. 1849..................821.1 571
   Same; 1865.......................................821.1 572
   Halloween: a romaunt. 1869..........821.1 573
   Ladye Chace: a ballad. 1877..........821.1 574
   Paschal: poems. 1889....................821.1 575
   Saul: a mystery (drama). 1845......822.1 46
Coxwell. Knight of the air.....................20290
Cozzens, F. S., *pseud.* (Haywarde, R.)
   Prismatics. 1853............................824.1 26
   Sayings of Doctor Bushwhacker, etc. 1867..829.1 7
   Sparrowgrass papers.........................29405
Cozzens, S. W. Young trail hunters.......022302
Crabbe. Poetical works, letters, etc. 8 v.
   V. 1. Life; by his son........................821.2 210
   V. 2. Letters and journals, etc........821.2 211
   V. 3. The borough.............................821.2 212
   V. 4. The borough, concluded.—Occasional pieces.—The world of dreams.—Tales..821.2 213
   V. 5. Tales.—Flirtation.—Occasional pieces.821.2 214
   V. 6-7. Tales of the hall.......................821.2 215
   V. 8. Posthumous tales........................821.2 217
Cracker Joe..15004
Cracroft. Essays. 1868. 2 v..............824.2 171

Craddock. Despot of Broomsedge Cove...16205
   Down the ravine.................................016250
   His vanished star...............................16207
   In the clouds.....................................16203
   In the 'Stranger people's' country.........16206
   In the Tennessee mountains..................16201
   Mystery of Witch-Face mountain, etc...16209
     Contents: Mystery of Witch-Face mountain.—Taking the blue ribbon at the county fair.—The casting vote.
   Phantoms of the foot-bridge, etc............16208
     Contents: Phantoms of the foot-bridge.—His day in court.—'Way down in Lonesome cove.—Moonshiners at Hoho-Hebee falls.—Riddle of the rocks.
   Prophet of Great Smoky mountains........16213
   Story of Keedon bluffs........................016251
   Where the battle was fought..................16202
Craig. Sacrifice of fools. 1896..................71240
Craig-Knox. See **Knox.**
Craigie, C. Old man's romance.................23310
Craigie, Mary E. John Anderson and I.....69420
Craigie, Pearl. See **Hobbes, J. O.**
Craik, A. D. Alfgar, the Dane.................61301
   Camp on the Severn...........................61305
   Doomed city......................................61307
   Edwy the fair....................................61302
   Fairleigh Hall....................................61306
   Last abbott of Glastonbury..................61304
   Rival heirs.......................................61303
Craik, *Mrs.* **D. M.** See **Mulock.**
Craik, G. M. Anne Warwick..................13706
   Cousin from India..............................06502
   Dorcas...13714
   Esther Hill's secret.............................13705
   Faith Unwin......................................13701
   Hard to bear....................................13720
   Hero Trevelyan.................................13707
   Hilary's love story.............................13710
   Leslie Tyrell.—Mildred.......................13703
   Lost and won...................................13712
   Mildred...13719
   Miss Moore......................................06501
   Only a butterfly................................13711
   Sydney..13716
   Sylvia's choice..................................13715
   Theresa..*in* 13715
   Two women......................................13708
   Winifred's wooing.............................13702
   Without kith or kin............................13713
Cranch. Ariel and Caliban, with other poems. 1887..........................821.1 356
   The bird and the bell, with other poems. 1875..................................821.1 345
   Last of the Huggermuggers.................033001
   Kobboltozo.....................................033002
Crane, E. Nisida..................................56867
Crane, S. The black riders, etc. (verse). 1895....................................821.1 502
   Little regiment, etc............................29963

   Contents: The little regiment.—Three miraculous soldiers.—A mystery of heroism.—An Indiana campaign.—A gray sleeve.—The veteran.
   Red badge of courage........................29960
   The third violet................................29964
Crashaw. Complete works. 1858......821.2 181
   Contents: Steps to the temple.—Delights of the muses.—Sacred poems.—Poemata Latina.—Epigrammata sacra.
Crawford, E. (Mrs. J. A. Crawford). Jo of Auchendorass..............................31940
Crawford, F. M. Adam Johnstone's son..68023
   American politician............................68043
   By the waters of Paradise................*in* 68018
   Casa Braccio....................................68022
   Children of the king..........................68014
   Cigarette-maker's romance...................68012
   Doctor Claudius................................68008
   Don Orsino.....................................68013
   Greifenstein.....................................68010
   Katharine Lauderdale.........................68017
   Khaled..68006
   Love in idleness................................68019
   Marion Darche.................................68016
   Marzio's crucifix...............................68003
   Mr. Isaacs.......................................68001
   Paul Patoff......................................68004
   Pietro Ghisleri..................................68015
   The Ralstons...................................68020
   Roman singer...................................68031
   Rose of yesterday.............................68025
   Sant' Ilario......................................68011
   Saracinesca.....................................68002
   Tale of a lonely parish.......................68055
   Taquisara.......................................68024
   Three fates.....................................68009
   To leeward......................................68021
   Upper berth....................................68018
     Same..*in* 69209
   Witch of Prague...............................68007
   With the immortals...........................68005
   Zoroaster.......................................68050
Crawfurd. Beyond the seas.....................17303
   Sylvia Arden...................................17304
   White feather, etc.............................17305
   The world we live in.........................17301
Crayon, Geoffrey, *pseud.* See **Irving, Washington.**
Crellin. Romances of the old seraglio........53720
   Contents: The old seraglio.—The new sultan.—Hassan, the barber.—Game of chess.—Harem tragedy.—Sultan's fate.—Vizier's doom.—Lost girdle.—Missing bride.—Fatal draught.—Dream fulfilled.
   Tales of the caliph............................53721
Cresswell, Henry. Modern Greek heroine..58928
   Without issue..................................58926
   Wooing of fortune............................58927
Crim. Adventures of a fair rebel...............16630
   Elizabeth, Christian scientist................16632
   In Beaver cove and elsewhere...............16631

LANGUAGE AND LITERATURE.

Crockett. Bog-myrtle and peat..................32210
   Contents: Adventures.— Intimacies.— Histories.—
   Idylls.—Tales of the kirk.—In praise of Galloway.
   Cleg Kelly...32214
   Galloway herd......................................32211
   Gray man...32215
   Lads' love...32216
   Lilac sunbonnet....................................32208
   Mad Sir Uchtred of the hills..................32207
   Men of the moss-hags...........................32212
   Play-actress..32209
   Raiders..32206
   Stickit minister....................................32205
   Sweetheart travellers............................32213
Crockett *et al.* Tales of our coast............32750
   Contents: Crockett: The smugglers of the Clone.—
   Parker: There is sorrow on the sea.—Frederic: The
   path of Murtogh.—Q: The roll-call of the reef.—Russell:
   That there mason.
Croke, *Sir* A. Poems. 1841. 2 v.
   V. 1. Progress of idolatry.—Fragments.—Plates.
   —Notes..821.2 291
   V. 2. Three ordeals. — Ballads. — Prologues.—
   Epigrams, etc.—Studley priory...............821.2 292
Croke. Psalms, etc., versified...............821.2 454
Croker, B. M. Beyond the pale............33015
   Bird of passage.....................................33001
   Diana Barrington..................................33003
   Family likeness.....................................33006
   In the kingdom of Kerry, etc.................33012
   Interference 33005
   Mr. Jervis..33009
   Pretty Miss Neville..............................33014
   Proper pride...33013
   Real Lady Hilda...................................33011
   Some one else.......................................33002
   Third person..33008
   To let, etc...33007
   Two masters...33004
   Village tales and jungle tragedies...........33010
Croker, T. C., *ed.* A Kerry pastoral...821.2 450
Croly. Poetical works. 2 v.
   V. 1. Paris in 1815.—Death of Leonidas.—The
   angel of the world.—Miscellaneous poems.—Gems
   from the antique....................................821.2 267
   V. 2. Catiline: a dramatic poem.—Sebastian.—
   Miscellaneous poems.............................821.2 268
   Salathiel..25829
Cromarty. Under God's sky..................35725
Cromie. Next crusade...........................10921
   Plunge into space.................................10920
Crommelin. Dead men's dollars.............24301
   Dust before the wind............................24306
   For the sake of the family....................24305
   Freaks of Lady Fortune.......................24304
   Goblin gold..24307
   Love, the pilgrim.................................24302
   Midge..24303
Crompton. Friday's child....................012312
   Gentle heritage....................................012310
   Master Bartlemy..................................012311

Crosby. Violin obligato, etc...................26701
Cross, *Mrs.* J. W. See Eliot, George.
Cross, M. B. Blind bats..........................64720
Crossland. English tales and sketches......44136
   Hubert Freeth's prosperity....................44137
Crowfield, Christopher. See Stowe, *Mrs.*
   H. B.
Crowley. Epigrams, etc. 1550............820.2 411
Crowne. Dramatic works. 1873. 4 v.
   V. 1. Juliana. — Charles VIII, of France. —
   Calisto.—Notices of performers in Calisto.—Pro-
   logue to Horace...................................822.2 115
   V. 2. Thyestes.—City politicks.—Destruction of
   Jerusalem; pts. 1-2..............................822.2 116
   V. 3. Country wit. — Ambitious statesman.— Sir
   Courtly Nice,—Darius..........................822.2 117
   V. 4. English friar.— Regulus.—Married beau.—
   Caligula..822.2 118
Crowninshield, M. B. All among the
   lighthouses......................................*656 41
Crowninshield, *Mrs.* S. Ignoramuses.....69386
Crowquill, A., (Forrester, A. H.). Sey-
   mour's humorous sketches. 1872....828.2 32
Crowquill, Christopher, *pseud.* See Stowe,
   Mrs. H. B.
Cruger. Brotherhood..............................14420
   Hyperæsthesia.....................................14421
Cruikshank, George. Three courses and
   a dessert...25845
Cruikshank, R. Cruikshank at home......25843
Cumberland. Posthumous dramatic works.
   1813. 2 v.
   V. 1. The Sybil.— The Walloons.— The con-
   fession.— Passive husband.— Torrendal.— Lover's
   resolutions..822.2 140
   V. 2. Alcanor.— Eccentric lover.— Tiberius in
   Capreæ.—Last of the family.—Don Pedro.—False
   Demetrius...822.2 141
Cummins. El Fureides............................44603
   Lamplighter..44601
   Mabel Vaughan...................................44604
Cunningham, Allan. Traditional tales....52293
Cunningham, *Mrs.* B. S. In Sancho Pan-
   za's pit...67601
Cunningham, *Sir* H. S. Cœruleans..........9521
   Heriots...9520
   Sibylla..9523
   Wheat and tares....................................9522
Cunningham, J. Poems; with life 1822.
   ....*in* 821.2 41
Cunningham, R. The observer. 3 v...824.2 29
Cupples, George. Cupples Howe, mar-
   iner..69176
   Deserted ship......................................69177
   Green hand...69175
Cupples, *Mrs.* **George.** Norrie Seaton...012801
   Singular creatures..............................012804
   Woodfords 012802
Curran, J. E. Miss Frances Merley..........69406
Curran, J. P. Select speeches. 1831....329.2 22
   Speeches. 1815..................................329.2 23

* Of interest to young readers.

Curse of intellect....................................55405
Cursor mundi in four texts; pt. 1..........820.2 331
   Same; pt. 2.............................820.2 333
   Same; pt. 3.............................820.2 335
   Same; pt. 4.............................820.2 337
   Same; pt. 5.............................820.2 339
Curtis, *Mrs.* D. Spirit of seventy-six, etc.
   (dramas). 1868........................822.1 4
Curtis, G. W. American oratory; by
   Fleischmann. 1893..............825.1 Pam. 11
   From the Easy chair. 1892..........824.1 327
   Same; 3d series. 1894...............824.1 329
   Literary and social essays. 1894......824.1 291
     Contents: Emerson.— Hawthorne.— Works of Nathaniel Hawthorne.— Rachel.—Thackeray in America.— Sir Philip Sidney.— Longfellow.— Oliver W. Holmes.— Washington Irving.
   Orations and adresses; ed. by Norton.
   1893-4. 3 v..............................825.1 31
   Other essays from the Easy chair. '93..824.1 328
   Our best society. 1889................827.1 28
   Potiphar papers. 1860................827.1 3
   Prue and I.................................11301
   Trumps.....................................11303
Curtois. Jenny.................................10820
Cushing. Blacksmith of Voe................20320
   Cut with his own diamond.................20321
   Great chin episode.......................20322
Cutts. Nuthurst...............................10841
   Villa of Claudius.........................10840
Cynewulf. Elene: poem (Latin); ed. by
   Kent. 1889...........................821.2 839
Czeika. Operetta in profile..................69345
Dabney. Little daughter of the sun..........70980
Dagonet the jester.............................69030
Dahlgren. Washington winter..................62330
Daintrey. King of Alberia.....................40110
Dalin, Talmage, *pseud.* European relations....................................14720
Dall. Patty Gray's journey: At Mount
   Vernon......................................030803
   Patty Gray's journey: Baltimore to
   Washington................................030802
   Patty Gray's journey: Boston to Baltimore....................................030801
   What we really know about Shakespeare. 1886.........................822.3 94
Dallas. Billtry.................................29920
Dalton. Lost among the wild men.............013601
   Tiger prince................................15291
   Wasps of the ocean........................013602
   Will Adams..................................15290
   Wolf boy of China..........................15292
Daly. Adventures of Roger L'Estrange.....32020
Dame Europa's school. The fight in; by
   Pullen. 1871......................827.2 Pam. 6
   Dame Europa's report. 1871.....827.2 Pam. 7
   John justified: a reply. 1871....827.2 Pam. 8
   John's governor visits the school..827.2 Pam. 10
   Why Johnny didn't interfere. 1871.
   ....827.2 Pam. 9
   Which should John have helped?..827.2 Pam. 11
Damon. Old New-England days..............69367
Dana, F. Leonora of the Yawmish..........54001
Dana, K. F. Our Phil, etc...................69471
Dana, R. H. Essays and reviews. 1850..821.1 34
   Poems. 1850..............................821.1 33
Dane. Vengeance is mine........................9920
Danforth. Not in the prospectus...........69247
Daniel, George. Merrie England in the
   olden time..................................25842
Daniel, *Mrs.* M. Heiress in the family......25869
Daniel, Samuel. Complete works; ed. by
   Grosart. 1885-96. 5 v.
   V. 1. Verse..............................820.2 176
   V. 2. Civile wars between Lancaster and Yorke.
   ....820.2 177
   V. 3. Dramatic works................820.2 178
   V. 4. Epistles before Paulus Iouius.—Defence of ryme.— Collection of the history of England, from William I to Henry II....................820.2 179
   V. 5. History of England, Richard I to Edward III.—Index...............................820.2 180
   Poetical works. 1718. 2 v............821.2 917
   Selections from poetical works; with
   biography. 1855.......................821.2 864
Daniels. Sardia................................36501
Danish parsonage.............................58999
D'Arcy. Monochromes.........................31290
Dark year of Dundee..........................55248
Darmesteter, *Madame,* (A. Mary F. Robinson). Arden..................................38506
   Marguerites du temps passé..............38505
   New Arcadia, and other poems. 1884..821.2 718
   Songs, ballads, etc. 1888..........821.2 824
Darnell. Craze of Christian Engelhart.......20020
   A nation's thanksgiving (poem). '86..821.1 376
   Philip Hazelbrook...........................20021
D'Arron. Elia..................................52202
Darrow. Iphigenia, and other poems.
   1888......................................821.1 387
Dartmouth sketches. 1893................824.1 275
Darwin. The botanic garden: a poem.
   1807......................................821.2 208
   Temple of nature: poem. 1804.......821.2 209
Dasent. Annals of an eventful life..........19171
   Jest and earnest. 1873. 2 v.
     V. 1. A fortnight in Faroe.—Wildbad and its water.—England and Norway in the 11th century.—Origin of the English language..................824.2 212
     V. 2. Latham's Johnson's dictionary.—The Greek and English quarrel.—Story of free-trade.—How we were all vaccinated.— Magnus the good and Harold Hardradn.— Harold Hardrada, king of Norway.—Pickings from Poggio.................824.2 213
   Lady Sweetapple..........................19170
Daugé. Fair philosopher......................67201
Daunt. Frank Redcliffe......................029102
   In the land of the moose................029103

Three trappers..................................029101
  With pack and rifle in the far southwest..029104
D'Avenant. Dramatic works. 1872. 5 v.
  V. 1. Memoir.—Albovine.—Cruel brother.—Just
  Italian.—Temple of love.—Prince D'Amour........822.2 228
  V. 2. Platonic lovers.—The wits.— Britannia
  triumphans.—Salmacida spolia....................822.2 229
  V. 3. Unfortunate lovers.—Love and honour.—
  Entertainment at Rutland House.—Siege of
  Rhodes..822.2 230
  V. 4. Playhouse to be let.—News from Plymouth.
  —The fair favourite.—The distresses.—The siege.
  ....822.2 231
  V. 5. Man's the master.—Law against lovers.—
  The rivals.—Macbeth.—The tempest................822.2 232
Davenport. Constance and Nellie..........019001
Davidson, H. C. Old Adam...................36301
  Mr. Sadler's daughters........................36302
Davidson, J. Ballads and songs. 1894.
  ....821.2 970
  Baptist lake..................................46506
  Fleet street eclogues. 1893...............821.2 733
  Same ; 2d series.............................821.2 734
  New ballads. 1897.........................821.2 1042
  Random itinerary. 1894...................824.2 480
    Contents: The 38th of March.—In expectation of
    rain.—Parks and squares. — A suburban tour.—Among
    the Chilterns.—By way of epilogue.
  Wonderful mission of Earl Lavender.......46507
Davidson, L. M. Poems. 1871............821.1 15
Davies, G. C. Peter Penniless.................04007
  Swan and her crew............................04002
  Wildcat tower................................04006
Davies, Sir J. Complete poems. 1869..821.2 218
Davies, T. Dramatic miscellanies. 3 v...822.3 74
Davis, *Mrs.* **C. E. K.** Granny Bright's
  blanket......................................011602
Davis, Ethel. When love is done...........60210
Davis, H. R. Gilbert Elgar's son...........11620
  In sight of the goddess.....................11621
Davis, J. A. Chinese slave girl..............56896
Davis, L. C. Stranded ship....................56880
Davis, *Mrs.* **M. E. M.** Elephant's track,
  etc...15642
    Contents: Along Jim-Ned creek.—Flying threads.—
    From the quarter.
  In war times at La Rose Blanche..........15640
  Under the man-fig............................15641
Davis, R. E. As it may happen..............55273
Davis, Rebecca H. Dallas Galbraith....43105
  Doctor Warrick's daughters................43102
  Frances Waldeaux...........................43103
  John Andross.................................43107
  Kent Hampden...............................04330
  Law unto herself............................43106
  Natasqua....................................43104
  Silhouettes of American life..............43101
  Waiting for the verdict....................43108
Davis, Richard H. Cinderella, etc.........24524
    Contents: Cinderella.—Miss Delamar's under-study.
    —Editor's story.—An assisted emigrant.—Reporter who
    made himself king.

  Exiles, etc...................................24522
    Contents: The exiles.—The writing on the wall.—The
    right of way.—His bad angel. — The boy orator of
    Zepata city.—The romance in the life of Hefty Burke.
    An anonymous letter.
  Gallegher, etc...............................24520
    Contents: Gallegher.—Walk up the avenue.—My dis-
    reputable friend Mr. Raegen.—The other woman.—
    Trailer for room number 8.—There were ninety and nine.
    —Cynical Miss Catherwaight.—Van Bibber and the swan-
    boats.—Van Bibber's burglar.— Van Bibber as best man
  Princess Aline................................24523
  Soldiers of fortune...........................24525
  Stories for boys.............................011010
    Contents: Reporter who made himself king —Mid-
    summer pirates.—Richard Carr's baby.—Great tri-club
    tennis tournament.—The jump at Corey's slip.— Van
    Bibber baseball club.—The story of a jockey.
  Van Bibber and others......................24521
    Contents: Her first appearance.—Van Bibber's man-
    servant.—Hungry man was fed.—Van Bibber at the
    races.— Experiment in economy.—Mr. Travers's first
    hunt.—Love me, love my dog.— Eleonore Cuyler.—
    Recruit at Christmas.—Patron of art.—Andy M'Gee's
    chorus girl.—Leander of the East river.— How Hefty
    Burke got even.—Outside the prison.—Unfinished story.
Davis, Thomas. Poems. 1872.........821.2 307
Davis, V. A. J. Veiled doctor..................33120
Dawe. Mount Desolation.......................47601
Dawes, Geraldine, and other poems. '39..821.1 18
Dawning, The.................................69023
Dawson, E. Fountain of youth...............29490
Dawson, W. J. London idylls.................34130
  Makers of modern English. 1890.....824.2 426
  Quest and vision. 1892...................824.2 463
    Contents: Shelley.—Wordsworth and his message.—
    Religious doubt and modern poetry.—Longfellow.—
    George Eliot.—George Meredith.—The new realism;
    Olive Schreiner; Mark Rutherford; R. Kipling; J. M.
    Barrie.—The poetry of despair.
  Story of Hannah............................34131
Day, Lal Behari. Govinda Sâmenta......25825
Day, Thomas. Desolation of America
  (poem). 1822.........................*in* 821.2 46
  Poems ; with life. 1822..............*in* 821.2 39
  Sandford and Merton........................012301
Days of Knox..................................50379
Dean, Amos. Lect., Albany Young men's
  association. 1839...........................40 23
Dean, *Mrs.* **Andrew.** Grasshoppers.........14841
  Lesser's daughter...........................14840
Dear. (See **Laddie.**)........................17910
Debenham. Whispering winds...............0940
Deepdale vicarage..............................58924
De Falbe. Where Hamlet came from.
  1885....................................822.3 Pam. 15
Defoe. Captain Singleton........................306
  Colonel Jack..................................310
  Due preparations for the plague..............315
  Duncan Campbell...............................304
  Journal of the plague year....................309
  King of pirates, etc..........................316

Contents: The king of pirates: Captain Avery.— The Cartoucheans in France.—Life, robberies, etc., of John Sheppard.—Jonathan Wild.—Captain John Gow.—Lives of six notorious street-robbers.
Life of Colonel Jack..................................08509
Memoirs of a cavalier..............................305
New voyage round the world....................314
Novels and miscellaneous works. '67. 7v.
  V. 1. Captain Singleton.—Colonel Jack........820.2 78
  V. 2. Memoirs of a cavalier.— Captain Carleton.—Dickory Cronke.— Everybody's business is nobody's business...................................820.2 79
  V. 3. Moll Flanders.— History of the devil.
....820.2 80
  V. 4. Roxana.—Mrs. Christian Davies..........820.2 81
  V. 5. The plague in London.—The storm, 1703.—The true-born Englishman........................820.2 82
  V. 6. Duncan Campbell.— New voyage round the world.—Political tracts.........................820.2 83
  V. 7. Robinson Crusoe.............................820.2 84
Robinson Crusoe....................................301
Same...08501
Same. 1882. 2 v..................................823 84
Uncollected writings ; ed. by Lee. 2v.
....928.2 282
Writings, newly discovered ; ed. by Lee.
2 v..928.2 282

DeForest. Bloody chasm....................17505
Honest John Vane..................................17501
Kate Beaumont.......................................17504
Overland..17503
De Kay. Bohemian................................56825
Hesperus, and other poems. 1880...821.1 244
Dekker. Dramatic works. 1873. 4 v...822.2 194
A knight's conjuring.............................821.2 448
Non-dramatic works ; ed. by Grosart. 1884. 5 v.
  V. 1. Memorial introduction.—Canaan's calamitie.—The wonderful yeare (1603).—The batchelar's banquet...820.2 12
  V. 2. The seven deadly sinnes of London.— Newes from hell. — The double P. P. — The gulls horne-booke.—Jests to make you merrie.........820.2 13
  V. 3. Dekker, his dreame. — The belman of London.—Lanthorne and candle-light.—A strange horse-race..820.2 14
  V. 4. The dead terme.—Worke for armourours. —The ravens almanacke.—A rod for runawayes..820.2 15
  V. 5. Foure birdes of Noah's arke. — Patient Grissill.—Index......................................820.2 16
Dekker, Chettle, *and* **Haughton.** Patient Grissil: comedy. 1841..........822.2 75
Same.............................*in* 822.2 77
De Koven, J. Dorchester polytechnic academy..07901
De Koven, *Mrs.* **R.** Sawdust doll............18530
De Kroyft. A place in thy memory. '52...826.1 7
Deland, E. D. In the old Herrick house, etc..018381
Oakleigh...018380
Deland, Margaret. John Ward, preacher...35401
Mr. Tommy Dove, etc..............................35404
Contents: Mr. Tommy Dove.— Face on the wall. Elizabeth.—At whose door?—A fourth-class appointment.

The old garden, and other verses. '89..821.1 403
Philip and his wife...................................35405
Sidney..35402
Story of a child.......................................35403
Wisdom of fools......................................35406
Contents: Where ignorance is bliss, 'tis folly to be wise.—House of Rimmon.—Counting the cost.— The law or the Gospel?
De Leon, E. Askaros Kasis......................52207
De Leon, T. C. Creole and Puritan..........30707
Cross purposes.......................................30706
John Holden, unionist..............................30705
Delepierre. Macaronéana. 1852............811 79
Deloney. Garland of good-will...........821.2 473
Strange histories.................................821.2 446
Demage. Plunge into the Sahara............041801
De Mille. Among the brigands................0803
The B. O. W. C......................................0810
Babes in the woods................................7005
Boys of the Grand Pré school..................0808
Castle in Spain......................................7015
Comedy of terrors..................................7008
Cord and crease....................................7012
Cryptogram...7013
Dodge club..7007
Fire in the woods...................................0807
Helena's household................................7009
Lily and the cross..................................7010
Living link..7014
Lost in the fog......................................0806
Open question......................................7003
Seven hills..0801
Shaving them [Dodge club]....................7007A
Strange manuscript found in a copper cylinder..7001
Treasure of the sea................................0809
Winged lion...0805
Deming. Adirondack stories...................61001
Tompkins and other folks........................61002
Democracy..58909
De Montauban. Cruise of a woman hater..69308
De Morgan, A. A budget of paradoxes..824.2 214
De Morgan, Mary. Necklace of Princess Fiorimonde..025601
Dempster. Blue roses. 2 v....................55104
Hotel du Petit Saint Jean.......................55101
Iseulte...55103
Ninette..55102
Vera..55105
Denham, *Sir* **J.** Poems ; with life..........821.2 27
Denison, M. A. Grandmother Normandy..23101
His triumph..23109
Old slip warehouse................................23108
Master..23103
That husband of mine............................23110
That wife of mine..................................23113
Victor Norman......................................23102

Denison, T. S. Iron crown. 69045
Dennis. Andrew. 69261
Dennison. Orcadian sketch-book. 106
Depew. Addresses, 1895-6. ....825.1 Pam. 4
  Addresses: Columbus statue, New York,
    and University of Virginia. 1894.825.1 Pam. 1
  Orations and after-dinner speeches. 1890.
    ....825.1 23
  Our Chauncey; by Bromley. 1891......828.1 78
De Quincey. The avenger, etc. 1859...824.2 83
  Contents: The avenger.—Additions to 'Confessions of an English opium-eater.'—The Essenes.—Supplementary. —Aellus Lamia.—China.— Traditions of the rabbins.
  Beauties from. 1868. ....829.2 9
  Collected writings; ed. by Masson. 1889-1890.
    V. 1. Autobiography, 1785-1803.................820.2 524
    V. 2. Autobiography, 1803-8. — Lake reminiscences. 820.2 525
    V. 3. London reminiscences. — Confessions of an English opium-eater. 820.2 526
    V. 4-5. Biographies and biographic sketches..820.2 527
    V. 6-7. Historical essays and researches.......820.2 529
    V. 8. Speculative and theological essays......820.2 531
    V. 9. Political economy and politics..............820.2 532
    V. 10-11. Literary theory and criticism..........820.2 533
    V. 12-13. Tales, romances and prose phantasies.820.2 535
    V. 14. Miscellanea and index............................820.2 537
  Confessions of an English opium-eater;
    and Suspiria de profundis. 615.9 14
  Same, etc. 1876..........................615.9 15
  Same..615.9 16
  Contents: Confessions.—Suspiria de profundis.—Additions to the 'Confessions.'— Coleridge and opium-eating.—The English mail-coach.—Notes.
  Essays on the poets, etc. 1867............824.2 77
  Contents: Wordsworth.— Shelley. — Keats. — Goldsmith.—Pope.—Godwin.—Foster.—Hazlitt.—Landor.
  Historical and critical essays. 1866. 2 v.
    V. 1. Philosophy of Roman history.-- The Essenes. — Philosophy of Herodotus. — Plato's 'Republic.'—Homer and the Homeridae.......824.2 75
    V. 2. Cicero. — Style.— Rhetoric.— Secret societies. 824.2 76
  Letters to a young man, etc. 1854.....824.2 82
    Contents: Letters to a young man.—Theory of Greek tragedy.—Conversation.—Language.—French and English manners.—California and the gold mania.—Presence of mind.
  Memorials, etc. 1856. 2 v.
    V. 1. Explanatory.—The orphan heiress.—Oxford.—Pagan oracles.—The revolution of Greece..824.2 80
    V. 2. Klosterheim.— Sphinx's riddle.— Templars' dialogues. 824.2 81
  Miscellaneous essays. 1851. ....824.2 74
  Miscellanous essays. 1867..................824.2 73
    Contents: On the knocking at the gate, in 'Macbeth.' —Murder, considered as one of the fine arts. — Supplementary paper on murder.—Joan of Arc.— The English mail-coach: Glory of motion; Vision of sudden death; Dream-fugue.--Dinner, real and reputed.--Orthographic mutineers. — Sortilege on behalf of the Glasgow athenæum.
  Narrative and micellaneous papers. 2 v.
    V. 1. The household wreck.—The Spanish nun. —Flight of a Tartar tribe. 824.2 78

V. 2. System of the heavens as revealed by Rosse's telescope.—Modern superstition. – Coleridge and opium-eating.—Temperance movement. —War.—Last days of Kant. 824.2 79
Note-book of an English opium-eater..824.2 84
On philosophical writers, etc. 1854. 2 v.
  V. 1. Hamilton.—Mackintosh.—Kant.—Herder. --Richter.—Lessing. 104 10
  V. 2. Bentley.—Parr. 104 11
Select essays; ed. by Masson. 1888. 2 v..
  V. 1. On murder, considered as one of the fine arts. — Early memorials of Grasmere. — Revolt of the Tartars. 824.2 414
  V. 2. Spanish military nun. — English mail-coach.—Suspiria de profundis. 824.2 415
Theological essays, etc. 1854. 2 v.
  V. 1. Christianity as an organ of political movement. — Protestantism.—On the supposed Scriptural expression for 'eternity.'—Judas Iscariot.— Hume's argument against miracles.—Casuistry.— Greece under the Romans. 204 12
  V. 2. Secession from the Church of Scotland.— Toilette of the Hebrew lady. — Milton. — Charlemagne.—Modern Greece.—Lord Carlisle on Pope..204 13
Derby, G. H. See Phœnix, John.
Dering, R. G., *pseud.* See Balfour, F. H.
Derwent. Circe's lovers. 16301
Descendant, The. 69084
Deslonde. Miller of Silcott mill. 25846
Despard, M. C. Chaste as ice. 52260
Despard, Matilda. Kilrogan cottage......56805
Detmers. Last of the Tories (drama).
  1897. ....822.1 Pam. 1
  Old-time tea-party: a play. 1895......822.1 48
De Vere. Antar and Zara, and other poems.
  1877. ....821.2 789
  Essays, chiefly on poetry. 1887. 2 v...824.2 412
  Fall of Rora, and other poems. 1877...821.2 790
  Foray of Queen Meave, etc. (poems)...821.2 792
  Julian the apostate; The duke of Mercia:
    dramas. 1858. ....822.1 280
  Legends of Saxon saints (poems). '79..821.2 791
  Mary Tudor: a drama. 1884............822.1 264
  May carols. 1881.............................821.2 793
  Saint Thomas of Canterbury: poem.
    1876. ....821.2 788
  Search after Proserpine, etc. (poems).
    1843. ....821.2 794
Devereaux. Sam Shirk. 52203
De Witt. Kate Weston. 25880
Diane Coryval. 15028
Diary of a désennuyée. 50367
Diaz. Bybury to Beacon street. 46502
  Chronicles of the Stimpcett family.........013305
  John Spicer lectures. 013307
  King Grimalkin. 013303
  Lucy Maria. 46501
  Polly Cologne. 013304
  William Henry and his friends. 013301
  William Henry letters. 013306
Dickens, Charles. Barnaby Rudge........1109
  Same (German). 1110

Bibliography; by Cook. 1879..............16 22
Bibliography; by Shepherd. 1834-80....16 139
Bleak House..1119
Boy Joe...010806
Bozland: Dickens' places and people;
    by Fitzgerald. 1895.............................1197
Child-wife, etc....................................010801
Children's stories from; retold by his
    grand-daughter, et al.; ed. by Vredenburg...010807
Christmas carol, in modified Braille, for
    the blind.............................362.4 M-B-3
Christmas stories; 1st series....................1133
    Contents: A Christmas carol.—The chimes.—The cricket on the hearth.—The battle of life.—The haunted man.
Christmas stories; 2d series, etc...............1134
    Contents: Christmas stories: Seven poor travellers; Holly-tree; Wreck of the Golden Mary; Perils of certain English prisoners; Going into society; Haunted house; Message from the sea; Tom Tiddler's ground; Somebody's luggage; Mrs. Lirriper's lodgings; Mrs. Lirriper's legacy; Doctor Marigold; Two ghost stories; Mugby junction; No thoroughfare.— Master Humphrey's clock.—Hunted down.—Holiday romance.—George Silverman's explanation.
Cricket on the hearth; drama. 1895..822.2 329
Dame Durden......................................010805
David Copperfield....................................1103
    Same; abridged....................................1104
Dickens dictionary; by Pierce....................1140
Dickensiana: bibliography; by Kitton.
    1886..16 73
Doctor Marigold's prescriptions................1125
Dombey and son....................................1189
    Same; abridged..................................1190
    Same (German).................................1191
Edwin Drood..1114
    Same..in 1123B
Watched by the dead: study of same;
    by R. A. Proctor..................................1113
Florence Dombey..................................010802
Great expectations..................................1115
Hard times..1126
    Same..in 1123B
    Same..in 1142B
John Jasper's secret................................1112
Lamplighter: a farce. 1879............822.2 212
Letters, 1833-70.............................826.2 100
Letters. 1879-81. 3 v....................826.2 44
Letters to Wilkie Collins. 1892......826.2 106
Little Dorrit..1122
Martin Chuzzlewit..................................1116
    Same..in 1183G
Master Humphrey's clock, etc..................1143
    Contents: Master Humphrey's clock.— Seven poor travellers.—Holly tree inn.—Somebody's luggage.—Mrs. Lirriper's lodgings.—Mrs. Lirriper's legacy. — Doctor Marigold's prescriptions. — Mugby junction. — General index of characters.—Familiar sayings from Dickens.

Master Humphrey's Wanduhr..................1144
Mudfog papers......................................1199
    Contents: The public life of Mr. Tulrumble.—Full report of the first meeting of the Mudfog Association for the advancement of everything.—Same, second meeting. —The pantomime of life.—Some particulars concerning a lion.—Mr. Robert Bolton.
Mugby junction................................in 1125
Nicholas Nickleby..................................1183
Nicolaus Nickleby (German)....................1184
No thoroughfare....................................1152
Novels of: bibliography; by Kitton. '97..1141
Old curiosity shop..................................1107
    Same; abridged..................................1108
Oliver Twist..1105
    Same (German)..................................1106
Oliver Twist condensed by Kirk..........010808
Our mutual friend..................................1111
Pen photographs of Dickens' readings;
    by K. Field............................824.1 124
Pickwick club..1101
Pictures from Italy........................in 1115C
    Same................................in 1133 E, F
    Same................................in 1183G
Plays and poems; ed. by Shepherd. 2 v.
    V. 1. Introduction.—Plays: The strange gentleman. — Village coquettes.— Is she his wife?—The lamplighter.—Lamplighter's story...............822.2 268
    V. 2. Mr. Nightingale's diary. — Sketches of young gentlemen.—Sketches of young couples.— Poems.— Sunday under three heads. — Threatening letter to Thomas Hood.— Preface to John Over's 'Evenings of a working man.'—To be read at dusk.—Fechter's acting.—Bibliography of Dickens.—Index......................................822.2 269
Raritätenladen [German of 'Old curiosity
    shop']..in 1144
Readings; condensed by himself..............1151
Schools and schoolmasters......................1160
Sissy Jupe..010803
Sketches by Boz....................................1139
Skizzen aus dem Londoner, alltagsleben
    [German of 'Sketches by Boz ']..........1138
Smike..010804
Speeches. 1880............................825.2 7
Strange gentleman: comic burletta..822.2 207
Tale of two cities..................................1142
    Same................................in 1105 D, F
Uncommercial traveller, etc....................1123
    Same..in 1115A
Village coquettes: comic opera. '36..822.2 208
With Dickens in Kent; by Frost. 1880.
    ....914.2 111
Works (reserved copy). 1870. 30 v.
    V. 1-2. Pickwick papers...................[823 26
    V. 3-4. David Copperfield................[823 28
    V. 5. Oliver Twist..........................[823 30
    V. 6-7. Old curiosity shop.—The long voyage. —The begging letter-writer. — A child's dream of a star.—Our English watering-place. — Our French watering-place.- Bill-sticking.- Births: Mrs. Meeks, of a son. — Sketches by Boz..................[823 31

‡ For reference.

V 8. Master Humphrey's clock.—Seven poor travellers. Holly tree inn.—Somebody's luggage.—Mrs. Lirriper's lodgings.—Mrs. Lirriper's legacy —Doctor Marigold's prescriptions.—Mugby junction.—General index of characters in Dickens' works.—Familiar sayings from Dickens...............1823 33
V. 9-10. Barnaby Rudge.—Sketches by Boz......1823 34
V. 11-12. Nicholas Nickleby................................1823 36
V. 13. Pictures from Italy.—American notes......1823 38
V. 14-15. Martin Chuzzlewit..............................1823 39
V. 16-17. Dombey and son..................................1823 41
V. 18. Christmas stories: Christmas carol.—Chimes.—Cricket on the hearth.—Battle of life.—Haunted man.—Christmas tree................................1823 43
V. 19. Hard times.—Reprinted pieces...............1823 44
Reprinted pieces.—Lazy tour of two idle apprentices...1823 44A
V. 20-21. Bleak house..1823 45
V. 22-23. Little Dorrit...1823 47
V. 24. A tale of two cities.....................................1823 49
V. 25. Uncommercial traveller............................1823 50
V. 26. Great expectations....................................1823 51
V. 27-28. Our mutual friend................................1823 52
V. 29. The mystery of Edwin Drood..................1823 54

Dickens, Charles, *and* **Collins, Wilkie.** Lazy tour of two idle apprentices, etc...1153
Contents: Lazy tour of two idle apprentices.—No thoroughfare.—The perils of certain English prisoners.

Dickens, Charles, *et al.* Tuggs's at Ramsgate, etc..47206

Dickens, Mary A. Cross currents............31601
Mere cipher..31602
Prisoners of silence...................................31604
Some women's ways (stories)...................31605
Valiant ignorance......................................31603

Dickinson, A. E. What answer?..............20487

Dickinson, D. S. Address, Queens county agricultural society...................................40 23

Dickinson, Emily. Letters. 1894. 2v...826.1 16
Poems; ed. by Todd and Higginson. 1891-6. 3 v....................................821.1 430

Dickinson, J. Writings; ed. by Ford. 1895—. v. 1—......................................329.1 B-2

Dickinson, J. *and* **E. E.,** *and* **Dowd, S. E.** Winter picnic..............................69418

Diehl. Doctor Paull's theory.................12305

Diekenga *and* **Ashworth.** Tom Chips....52242

Dilke. Papers of a critic. 1875. 2 v.
V. 1. Memoir of the author.—Pope's writings.—Lady Mary Wortley Montagu.—Swift, etc.........824.2 300
V. 2. Junius.—Wilkes.—Grenville, etc.—Burke. 824.2 301

Dillon. See Roscommon, *earl of.*

Dillwyn, E. A. Jill....................................69109
Jill and Jack..69108

Dillwyn, George. Occasional reflections. 1815..829.1 28

Diman. Orations and essays. 1882......824.1 169

Dimitry. House in Balfour street............52206

Dimmick. Anna Clayton........................52201

Disosway. South meadow......................25826

Disraeli, B., *earl of Beaconsfield.* Alroy.....5605
Coningsby...5603
Contarini Fleming....................................5609

Corr. with his sister. 1832-52..........923.2 579
Count Alarcos: a tragedy.......................5615
Endymion..5623
Henrietta Temple...................................5608
Same......................................*in* 5605B
Ixion in heaven..5615
Lothair..5619
Reference list; by Foster. v. 1...........16 55
Selected speeches. 1882. 2 v........329.2 68
Sybil...5614
Tancred...5601
Venetia..5616
Vivian Grey...5613
Wit and wisdom of. 1881...........829.2 55
Young Duke..5618

Disraeli, I. Amenities of literature. 1841. 2 v..820 50
Calamities of authors. 1859.........928.2 263
The literary character. 1818..............928 5

Distant cousins......................................07119

Ditchfield. Sorceress of Paris................31920

Dix. Girl from the farm........................32250

Dixie. Young castaways........................011620

Dixon, Charles. Fifteen hundred miles an hour...34590

Dixon, E. H. Story of a modern woman...31060

Dixon, H. Broken columns..................52204

Doane. Songs by the way. 1860......*in* 922.1 24

Dobell. Poetical works. 1875. 2 v.
V. 1. Memoir; by Nichol.—The Roman.—Miscellaneous poems.—Sonnets on the war (Crimean). —England in time of war.................................821.2 508
V. 2. Balder.—Later miscellaneous poems.—Sonnets, etc.—England's day.—Fragments............821.2 509

Dobson. At the sign of the lyre. 1885...821.2 738
Ballad of Beau Brocade, etc. 1892...821.2 914
(From 'Old world idylls' and 'At the sign of the lyre.')
Eighteenth century vignettes. 1893-6. 3 v.
V. 1. Steele's letters.—Prior's 'Kitty.'—Spence's 'Anecdotes.'—Captain Coram's charity.—The female Quixote.—Fielding's 'Voyage to Lisbon.'—Hanway's travels.—A garret in Gough square.—Hogarth's 'Sigismunda.'—The citizen of the world. —An old London bookseller.—Gray's library.—The new Chesterfield.—A day at Strawberry hill.—Goldsmith's library.—In Cowper's arbour.—The Quaker of art.—Bewick's tailpieces.—A German in England.—Old Vauxhall gardens......................824.2 459
V. 2. The journal to Stella.—At Tully's head. —Richardson at home.—Little Roubillac.—Nivernais in England.—Topography of 'Humphrey Clinker.'—The prisoners' chaplain.—Johnson's library.—The two Paynes.—The Berlin Hogarth.—Lady Mary Coke.—Ranelagh.—Epilogue......824.2 460
V. 3. Prologue.—Exit Roscius.—Doctor Mead's library.—Grosley's 'Londres.'—Polly Honeycombe. —Thomas Gent, printer.—The adventures of five days.—A rival of Reynolds.—Fielding's library.—'Cambridge, the everything.'—The officina arbuteana.—Matthew Prior.—Puckle's 'Club.'—Mary Lepel, lady Hervey.—The tour of Covent Garden..824.2 461

‡ For reference.

Poems on several occasions. 1895. 2 v.
  V. 1. Old-world idylls. — Proverbs in porcelain.—Vignettes in rhyme.—Miscellaneous pieces.—Essays in old French forms..................821.2 1004
  V. 2. At the sign of the lyre.—Memorial verses.—Fables of literature and art.—Tales in rhyme.—Vers de société.—Varia.—Prologues and epilogues.
....821.2 1005
  Proverbs in porcelain, etc. 1893......822.2 311
  Story of Rosina, and other verses. 1895.
....821.2 1007
  Vignettes in rhyme. 1880................821.2 545
Doctor Faustus.....................................*in* 103
Doctor Hermione.....................................42502
Doctor Quodlibet.....................................52315
Doctor's ward..55225
Dodd, A. B. Glorinda................................34903
  Republic of the future..............................34901
  Struthers.—Comedy of the masked musicians.......................................34902
Dodd, W. Beauties of Shakspeare. '54..822.3 342
Dodge, L. Question of identity......................15002
Dodge, L., *and* Preston, H. W. Guardians.......................................26604
Dodge, Mary A. See Hamilton, Gail.
Dodge, Mary Mapes. Along the way (verse). 1879..............................821.1 232
  Donald and Dorothy..................................08303
  Hans Brinker...08301
  Land of pluck, etc. 1894..................*949 24
  Rhymes and jingles. 1875..............*821.1 202
  Theophilus and others................................25701
  When life is young (verses). 1894..*821.1 479
Dodgson. See Carroll, Lewis, *pseud.*
Doe. Buffets.......................................56829
Doesticks (M. Thomson). Elephant club..828.1 36
Doings in Maryland..................................50349
Dole, E. P. Stand-by................................39040
Dole, N. H. On the Point.............................33130
Dolly's kettle-drum...................................0135
Don. (See Laddie.)..................................17914
Donne, John. Poems; ed. by Chambers, introduction by Saintsbury. 1896.
  2 v..821.2 1011
Donnelly. Cæsar's column...........................10510
  Golden bottle...10511
  The great cryptogram. 1888..............822.3 348
Dorothy Wallis.......................................42660
Dorr. Afternoon songs. 1885...........821.1 213
  Expiation..25864
  Friar Anselmo, and other poems. '79..821.1 227
  Poems. 1872................................821.1 203
Dorsey, *Mrs.* A. H. Flemmings.....................47121
  Nora Brady's vow....................................47120
Dorsey, S. A. Athalie...............................25856
Dorsheimer. Addresses and speeches. 1884...............................825.1 39
Dot and Dime.......................................07198

Doten. Poems from the inner life. '64. 821.1 364
Douce. Illustrations of Shakespeare. 2 v..822.3 68
Doudney. Michaelmas daisy.........................67001
  Stepping stones......................................67002
  Strangers yet..67003
Dougall, L. Beggars all............................30515
  Madonna of a day....................................30520
  Mermaid..30517
  Question of faith....................................30519
  What necessity knows................................30516
  Zeit-geist...30518
Doughty. Mirrikh; or, A woman from Mars.......................................30550
Douglas, Amanda M. Bethia Wray's new name.......................................10715
  Claudia..10730
  Floyd Grandon's honor...............................10742
  Foes of her household...............................10703
  Fortunes of the Faradays...........................10704
  From hand to mouth..................................10710
  Heirs of Bradley House..............................10712
  Home nook...10706
  Hope Mills..10733
  In the King's country...............................10718
  In trust...10714
  In wild rose time...................................10721
  Kathie series :
    Kathie's three wishes..............................01411
    Kathie's aunt Ruth.................................01404
    Kathie's summer at Cedarwood......................01405
    Kathie's soldiers..................................01414
    In the ranks.......................................01408
    Kathie's harvest days..............................01406
  Larry..10716
  A little girl in old New York........................01403
  Lost in a great city.................................10736
  Lucia..10701
  Lyndell Sherburne....................................10717
  Midnight marriage....................................10708
  Mistress of Sherburne................................10723
  Modern Adam and Eve in the garden......10709
  Nellie Kinnard's kingdom.............................10705
  Old woman who lived in a shoe.....................10726
  Osborne of Arrochar..................................10711
  Our wedding gifts....................................10719
  Out of the wreck.....................................10748
  Santa Claus land.....................................01417
  Seven daughters......................................01409
  Sherburne cousins....................................10720
  Sherburne house......................................10713
  Sherburne romance....................................10722
  Stephen Dane...10702
  Sydnie Adriance......................................10724
  Whom Kathie married..................................10725
  Woman's inheritance..................................10707
Douglas, Edith, *pseud.* See Burnham, Clara L.
Douglas, Theodore. Iras: a mystery........44401
Dow, *jr.* Patent sermons. 4 v............828.1 17

* Of interest to young readers.

Dowd *and* Dickinson. Winter picnic.......69418
Dowden. Introduction to Shakespeare.
    1893..822.3 383
    New studies in literature. 1895..........824.2 483
    Contents : Mr. Meredith in his poems.—The poetry of Robert Bridges.—The poetry of John Donne.—Amours de voyage.—Goethe.—Coleridge as a poet.—Edmond Scherer. —Literary criticism in France.—The teaching of English literature.
    Shakespeare : a study. 1879............822.3 138
    Shakspere (literature primer). 1878..822.3 102
    Studies in literature. 1887................824.2 403
    Transcripts and studies. 1888.........824.2 407
Dowie. Gallia..53330
    Some whims of fate (stories)..................53331
Dowling, Richard. Baffling quest..........55003
    Catmur's caves.....................................55004
    Mystery of Killard..................................55002
    Tempest driven.....................................55001
    Under St. Paul's....................................55005
Dowling, Thomas. Wreckers................69233
Down the river......................................55235
Downey. In one town.............................69286
Downing, Jack, (Seba Smith). Life and writings. 1834...........................827.1 1
Downing, M. Young Gascarillero..........041101
Downs. The mountain decameron..........30418
Dowson. Dilemmas.................................69379
Dowson *and* Moore. Comedy of masks....69378
Doyle. Adventures of Sherlock Holmes.....51311
    Beyond the city....................................51308
    Captain of the Pole-Star, etc..................51304
    Contents: The captain of the Pole-Star.—J. Habakuk Jephson's statement.—The great Keinplatz experiment.— The man from Archangel.—That little square box.— John Huxford's hiatus.—A literary mosaic.—John Barrington Cowles.—The parson of Jackman's gulch.—The ring of Thoth.
    Doings of Raffles Haw..........................51309
    The exploits of Brigadier Gerard............51321
    Firm of Girdlestone..............................51305
    Great Keinplatz experiment, etc............51317
    Contents : Great Keinplatz experiment.—Captain of the Pole-Star.—J, Habakuk Jephson's statement—John Huxford's hiatus.—A literary mosaic.—John Barrington Cowles.—The ring of Thoth.
    Great shadow......................................51312
    Gully of Bluemansdyke, etc..................51310
    Memoirs of Sherlock Holmes................51315
    Micah Clarke.......................................51301
    My friend the murderer.........................51314
    Mystery of Cloomber.............................51306
    Parasite..51318
    Refugees..51313
    Rodney Stone......................................51322
    Round the red lamp.............................51316
    Sign of the four...................................51303
    The Stark Munro letters........................51319
    Study in scarlet...................................51302
    Surgeon of Gaster Fell.........................51320

Uncle Bernac..51323
White company....................................51307
Drage. Cyril..29439
Drake, Jeanie. In old St. Stephen's........43201
    Metropolitans....................................43202
Drake, Joseph R. The American flag (poem). 1861.....................821.1 B 2
    The culprit fay. 1859......................821.1 25
Drake, Nathan. Essays illustrative of the Tatler, Spectator, etc. 1814. 5v..824.2 47
    Literary hours. 1800. 3v................824.2 101
    Shakspeare and his times. 1817. 2v..822.3 B-31
Drake, S. A. Captain Nelson................56822
    Watch fires of '76. 1895....................033801
Drayson. Diamond hunters of South Africa..56834
    Hans Sterk...56833
    White chief of the Caffres..................032233
Drayton. England's heroical epistles...821.2 519
    Harmony of the church.....................821.2 450
    Works ; ed. by Hooper. 1876. v. 1-3..821.2 561
    Contents: Poly-olbion.—Harmony of the church.
Drew. Lutaniste of St. Jacobi's..............64301
Drinkwater. Miss Prudence..................59003
    Rue's helps..59002
    Tessa Wadsworth's discipline..............59001
    Uncle Seth's will.................................59004
Drosenes, G., *pseud.* Amaryllis..............30901
Drummond, Henry. Baxter's second innings...010620
Drummond, William, *of Hawthornden.*
    Poetical works. 1856.................821.2 143
Drury. Deep waters.............................34301
    Eastbury...34302
Dryden. Poetical works. 1854. 5 v.
    V. 1. Life; by Mitford.—On the death of Cromwell.—Astrea redux and other poems. — Annus mirabilis. — Essay upon satire. — Absalom and Achitophel ; pt. 1.............................821.2 686
    V. 2. Absalom and Achitophel; pt. 2. — The medal.—Religio laici.—Threnodia Augustalis.— Hind and panther. — Britannia rediviva. — MacFlecknoe.—Epistles.—Elegies and epitaphs..821.2 687
    V. 3. Songs, odes and mask. — Prologues and epilogues. — Translations, etc. — Palamon and Arcite.—The cock and the fox......................821.2 688
    V. 4. Flower and leaf.— Wife of Bath. — Character of a good parson.—Translations from Boccaccio and Ovid..821.2 689
    V. 5. Translations from Ovid, Juvenal, Persius and Homer.— The art of poetry.— Miscellaneous...821.2 690
    Works; ed. by Scott and Saintsbury. 1882-93. 18 v.
    V. 1. Life; by Sir W. Scott.....................821.2 691
    V. 2. Preface to dramas. — The wild gallant.— Rival ladies.— Indian queen. — Indian emperor.— Secret love..821.2 692
    V. 3. Sir Martin Mar-all. — The tempest. — An evening's love.—Tyrannic love....................821.2 693
    V. 4. Almanzor and Almahide.—Essay on heroic plays.—Marriage à la mode. — The assignation..821.2 694
    V. 5. Amboyna.—State of innocence and fall of man,—Aureng-Zebe.— All for love..............821.2 695

V. 6. Limberham. — Œdipus. — Troilus and Cressida.—The Spanish friar..................821.2 696
V. 7. Duke of Guise. — Albion and Albanius.— Don Sebastian..........................821.2 697
V. 8. Amphitryon.—King Arthur.—Cleomenes. —Love triumphant.—Prologue for ' The Pilgrim.'—Doubtful plays: The mall; The mistaken husband..821.2 698
V. 9. Poems, historical and political: Cromwell; Astrea redux; Annus mirabilis; Absalom and Achitophel: The medal, etc...............821.2 699
V. 10. Religio laici.—Threnodia Augustalis.— Hind and panther. — Britannia rediviva. — Prologues and epilogues.—MacFlecknoe........821.2 700
V. 11. Epistles.—Elegies and epitaphs.—Odes, songs, etc.—Fables and tales from Chaucer.— Fables from Boccaccio....................821.2 701
V. 12. Appendix to 'Fables and tales from Chaucer.'—Translations from Ovid, Theocritus, Lucretius, Horace and Homer..............821.2 702
V. 13. Translations from Juvenal, Persius, and Virgil.—Pastorals........................821.2 703
V. 14-15. The Georgics and Æneis, translated. —Poems ascribed to Dryden.—Original prose works....................................821.2 704
V. 16. Life of Saint Francis Xavier.......821.2 706
V. 17. Life of Plutarch. — Translation of History of the League.—Controversy between Dryden and Stillingfleet.—Art of Painting....821.2 707
V. 18. Character of Saint-Evremont and Polybius.—Letters.—Appendices.—Index......821.2 708
Drysdale. Mystery of Abel Forefinger.....03805
Du Bois, C. G. Martha Corey................16620
  Modern pagan..................................16621
Du Bois, H. P. Princesses in love...........60160
Du Chaillu. Ivar the viking.................40201
Duchess, The, *pseud.* See **Hungerford, Mrs.**
Duff, H. A. Virginia.........................58350
Duff, M. E. G. Miscellanies. 1878......824.2 243
Duhring. Philosophers and fools : a study.
  ....824.1 131
Dulac. Before the dawn.....................69377
Du Maurier. The Martian....................29905
  Peter Ibbetson................................29901
  Trilby..29902
  Trilbyana......................................29903
Dumont. Life sketches, etc.................47229
Dunbar. Lyrics of lowly life. 1896....821.1 558
Duncan, F. I. Ye last sweet thing in corners : drama...............................822.1 18
Duncan, Sara J. American girl in London...8620
  Daughter of to-day............................8622
  Simple adventures of a memsahib............8621
  Story of Sonny Sahib..........................8624
  Vernon's aunt.................................8623
Dunmore, *earl of.* Ormisdal.................22780
Dunn. Red cap and blue jacket..............35610
Dunning. Cabin and gondola (stories)......21681
  Step aside....................................21682
  Upon a cast..................................21680
Dunstan. Quita..............................22250
Dunster. Historical tales, Lancastrian times..19119
Dunton. Athenianism. 1710............824.2 46

Durivage *and* **Burnham.** Stray subjects...47277
Du Tertre (Denzil Vane, *pseud.*). Polish conspiracy....................................23420
Dutton. Wisdom's folly......................70620
Dyer. Poems ; with life...................821.2 36
E., A. L. O., *pseud.* See **Tucker, Charlotte M.**
E., O. A. Cruise under six flags...........62302
Ealand. Sermons from Browning. '92..821.2 1119
Earle, A. R. Her great ambition............22270
Earle, J. Micro-cosmographie...........820.2 30
  Same ; ed. by Bliss. 1867...............824.2 4
Earle, Mary T. Wonderful wheel..........036501
Eastman, Julia A. Kitty Kent's troubles..023201
  Romneys of Ridgemont.......................023203
  Schooldays of Beulah Romney...............023202
Eastman, M. H. Fashionable society......20434
Eastwick. The new centurion...............54310
Eastwood. Geoffrey the Lollard............30460
  Marcella......................................30459
Eddy. Percy family. 5 v...................015207
  Walter's tour in the east. 6 v.............015201
Eden, C. H. Fortunes of the Fletchers....59702
  Guinea gold...................................023402
  Philip Vandeleur's victory...................023401
  Prisoner of the Pampas.......................023403
  Ula...59701
Eden, Eleanor. Dumbleton Common........19176
Edgar. Runnymede............................12095
Edgeworth. The absentee......................613
  Classic tales...................................612
  Early lessons..................................0402
  Ormond..614
  Parent's assistant.............................0401
  Patronage.......................................611
  Tales and novels. 20 v. in 10.
V. 1-2. Castle Rackrent.—Essay on Irish bulls.— Essay on the noble science of self-justification.— Moral tales: Forrester; The Prussian vase ; The good aunt...601
V. 3-4. Moral Tales: Angelina; The good French governess; Mademoiselle Panache, pt. 2 ; The knapsack. — Popular tales : Lame Jervas; The will; The Limerick gloves; Out of debt, out of danger; The lottery; Rosanna..................602
V. 5-6. Popular tales : Murad the unlucky ; The manufacturers ; The contrast ; The grateful negro ; To-morrow. — Tales of fashionable life: Ennui; The dun......................................603
V. 7-8. Tales of fashionable life: Manœuvering; Almeria ; Vivian..................................604
V. 9-10. Tales of fashionable life: The absentee; Madame de Fleury; Emilie de Coulanges.—The modern Griselda....................................605
V. 11-12. Belinda...................................606
V. 13-14. Leonora.— Letters on various subjects. —Patronage, pt. 1..................................607
V. 15-16. Patronage, pt. 2. — Comic dramas: Love and law ; The rose, thistle and shamrock....608
V. 17-18. Harrington. - Thoughts on horses; Ormond...609
V. 19-20. Helen.....................................610

Edmonds, *Mrs.* Amygdala.........................45310
Edwardes, *Mrs.* **Annie.** Adventuress......3403
    Archie Lovell..3411
    At the eleventh hour...........................3426
    Ballroom repentance............................3427
    Blue stocking..3414
    Jet..3419
    Leah..3402
    Miss Forrester.......................................3412
    Ought we to visit her?........................3404
    Pearl-powder..3401
    Playwright's daughter..........................3428
    Point of honor......................................3407
    Stephen Lawrence.................................3410
    Susan Fielding.......................................3418
    Vagabond heroine.................................3422
    Vivian the beauty.................................3423
Edwards, C. New house-master...........035501
Edwards, Adeline. Muriel.....................69229
Edwards, Amelia B. Barbara's history....3308
    Debenham's vow..................................3305
    Half a million of money....................3314
    Hand and glove....................................3304
    In the days of my youth....................3301
    Ladder of life..3302
    Lord Brackenbury................................3313
    Miss Carew...3306
    Monsieur Maurice.................................3312
    My brother's wife..................................3307
Edwards, *Mrs.* **C. M.** Itinerant side........44149
    Rainbow side...44150
Edwards, G. W. Break o' day, etc..........12532
    Contents: A watch and chain.— A mole or not.— Manley.—A protégé.—Pop's yaller fiddle.—Break o' day —A matter of will.
    P'tit Matinic', etc..................................12530
    Contents: Arrival of the mail.—The wreck.—Drusil's Fair!'.—The new justice.—The head of ol' Gull.—The wooing of Hise.—The prodigal.—Old Grimes's masterpiece.—A disturber of faith.
    Rivalries of long and short codiac..........12531
    Contents: Ambition o' women.—The new store.—The rivals. — Old Quigley's bequest. — Hanse's keg hat.— Rodney's fambly.—Jimsey Demsey.—Sam's surrender.—The treasure of Pigeon Head.—Unc' Sime's faith.
Edwards, H. S. Sons and fathers............30802
    Two runaways, etc................................30801
    Contents: Two runaways. — Elder Brown's backslide.— An idyl of Sinkin' mount'in. —'Ole Miss' and 'Sweetheart.'—Sister Todhunter's heart.— De valley an' de shadder.— Minc: a plot.— A born inventor.— Tom's strategy.
Edwards, Henry. A mingled yarn: sketches. 1883........................S24.1 116
Edwards, M. Betham-. Brother Gabriel..54902
    Curb of honour....................................54917
    Disarmed...54905
    Doctor Jacob..54901
    Dream-Charlotte....................................54919
    Felicia..54903
    Flower of doom....................................54907
    For one and the world......................54909
    Forestalled..54910
    Half-way...54912
    Kitty...54906
    Love and mirage..................................54904
    North country comedy......................54911
    Parting of the ways............................54908
    Pearla..54915
    Romance of a French parsonage......... 54916
    Romance of Dijon................................54918
    Two aunts and a nephew..................54914
    White house by the sea....................54913
Edwin. East and west. 1896...........824.2 490
    Contents: The Egyptian thief.— Aspects of life. A flight of locusts.— Astronomy and religion.— In the Indian woods.—Love the preserver.—A real thirst.—The Indian Upanishads.—The two bridges.—Indian viceroys. —Under the sunshine. -Jungle kingdoms.- A fisherman's wife,— An engine of fate.—In the stone trade. The triumph of Japan.—Lost and found.—Buddha-Gya.—The garden of repose.—The sword of Japan.— Limpets.- A delicate entertainment.
Egerton. Keynotes.....................................51701
Eggleston, Edward. Circuit rider.........11206
    Duffels..11207
    End of the world................................11203
    Faith doctor...11205
    Graysons...11202
    Hoosier schoolboy................................01703
    Hoosier schoolmaster..........................11204
    Mystery of Metropolisville.................11201
    Queer stories for boys and girls.........01705
    Roxy...11210
    Schoolmaster's stories..........................01701
Eggleston, G. C. Big brother...................02001
    Captain Sam...02002
    Signal boys...02003
    Wreck of the Redbird........................02004
Eggleston, G. C., *and* **Marbourg, D.**
    Juggernaut..11720
Eiloart. Boy with an idea......................05401
    Dean's wife...66501
    Ernie at school......................................05403
    Some of our girls................................66503
Elbon, Barbara, *pseud.* (L. B. Halstead.)
    Bethesda..62309
Elder. Periscopics (essays). 1854........S24.1 19
Elia. See **Lamb, Charles.**
Eliot, Annie. White birches...................30590
Eliot, George, *pseud.* (Marian Evans, Mrs. Lewes, Mrs. Cross.) Adam Bede...1426
    And her heroines ; by Woolson. 1886.
    ....928.2 483
    Brother Jacob.—The lifted veil................1445
    Daniel Deronda.......................................1417
    Essays, etc. 1884...................S24.2 354
    Contents: Worldliness and other-worldliness - German wit : Heine.— Evangelical teaching : Dr. Cumming.— Influence of rationalism : Lecky's history.—

Natural history of German life: Riehl.—Three months in Weimar.—Address to workingmen by Felix Holt.—Leaves from a note-book.
Essays; ed. by N. Sheppard. 1883...824.2 340
   Contents: Carlyle's 'Life of Sterling.'—Woman in France: Madame de Sablé.—Evangelical teaching: Dr. Cumming.—German wit: Heine.— Natural history of German life.—Silly novels by lady novelists.—Worldliness and other-worldliness.—Influence of rationalism.—Address to workingmen by Felix Holt.
Felix Holt..1411
Gwendolin (sequel to 'Daniel Deronda')..1441
Impressions of Theophrastus Such....824.2 194
In Derbyshire; by Roslyn. 1876..........823 57
Legend of Jubal, and other poems. 1874.
   ....821.2 735
Life, in her letters and journals; ed. by Cross. 1885. 3 v....................928.2 478
Lifted veil...1445
Middlemarch..1413
Mill on the Floss.....................................1406
Reference list; by Foster. v. 1..........16 55
Romola..1412
Scenes of clerical life.—Silas Marner......1405
   Contents: The sad fortunes of the Reverend Amos Barton.—Mr. Gilfil's love story.—Janet's repentance.—Silas Marner.
Silas Marner..1401
The Spanish gypsy: a poem. 1868...821.2 736
Wit and wisdom of. 1875.................829.2 43
Ellerton, Vincent, *pseud.* See **Logan, M. C.**
Ellet. Poems. 1835........................821.1 17
Elliot, Anne. Evelyn's career................35608
   Lord Harborough.................................35607
   Winning of May...................................35606
Elliot, C. W., (T. White, *pseud.*). Wind and whirlwind........................20435
Elliot, Frances. Italians......................20380
   Red cardinal..20381
   Romance of old court life in France......20382
Elliott, Ebenezer. Splendid village; Corn law rhymes, etc. 1833........821.2 744
Elliott, H. R. Bassett claim.................62395
Elliott, S. B. Felmeres......................10422
   Jerry..10420
   John Paget..10421
Ellis. New Britain. 1820.................827.2 18
Ellis, Havelock. The new spirit. '93..824.2 458
   Contents: Diderot.—Heine.—Whitman.—Ibsen.—Tolstoi.
Ellis, *Mrs.* **S. S.** Brewer's family.........19192
   Temper and temperament....................19193
Ellis, T. Mullett. Beauty of Boscastle...31050
Ellwanger. Idyllists of the country-side.
   1896..824.1 309
   Contents: The wand of Walton Gilbert White's pastoral. The landscape of Thomas Hardy. Afield with Jefferies.—The sphere of Thoreau. A ramble with Burroughs.
Story of my house. 1891..................728 41

Elmslie. His life's magnet................22510
Elsie..55233
Elton. Below the surface................20433
Elwell. Boys of thirty-five..............62342
Emerson, N. S. Thanksgiving story. '73.
   ....821.1 159
Emerson, P. H. Caóba.....................71102
   Son of the fens...................................71101
Emerson, R. W. Conduct of life.......824.1 52
   Contents: Fate.—Power.—Wealth.—Culture.—Behavior.—Worship.—Considerations by the way.—Beauty.—Illusions.
Culture, etc. 1880......................824.1 4½
   Contents: Culture.—Behavior.—Beauty.—Books.—Art.—Eloquence.—Power.—Wealth.—Illusions.
Correspondence with Carlyle, 1834-72....826 1
   Same; supplementary letters. 1886....826 3
Essays. 2 v. in 1.........................824.1 50
Essays; 1st series........................824.1 48
   Contents: History.—Self-reliance.—Compensation.—Spiritual laws.—Love.—Friendship.—Prudence.—Heroism.—The over-soul.—Circles.—Intellect.—Art.
Essays; 2d series.........................824.1 49
   Contents: The Poet.—Experience.—Character.—Manners.—Gifts.—Nature.—Politics.—Nominalist and realist.—New England reformers.
Lectures and biographical sketches......824.1 56
   Contents: Demonology.—Aristocracy.—Perpetual forces.—Character.—Education.—The superlative.—Sovereignty of ethics.—The preacher.—The man of letters.—The scholar.—Plutarch.—Historic notes of life and letters in New England.—Chardon street convention.—Ezra Ripley.—Mary Moody Emerson.—Samuel Hoar.—Thoreau.—Carlyle.
Letters and social aims..................824.1 55
   Contents: Poetry and imagination.—Social aims.—Eloquence.—Resources.—The comic.—Quotation and originality.—Progress of culture.—Persian poetry.—Inspiration.—Greatness.—Immortality.
May-day, and other pieces. 1867......821.1 70
Miscellanies. 1865......................824.1 53
   Contents: Same as 'Nature, addresses, etc.'
Miscellanies. 1884......................824.1 57
   Contents: The Lord's supper.—Historical discourse in Concord.—Address at dedication of soldiers' monument.—Address on emancipation in British West Indies.—War.—The fugitive slave law.—Assault on Mr. Sumner.—Speech on affairs in Kansas.—Remarks at meeting for relief of John Brown's family.—John Brown.—Theodore Parker.—American civilization.—Emancipation proclamation.—Abraham Lincoln.—Harvard commemoration speech.—Editors' address: Massachusetts Quarterly review.—Woman.—Address to Kossuth.—Burns.—Scott.—Remarks at organization of Free religious association.—Speech at annual meeting of same.—Fortune of the republic.
Natural history of intellect, etc. '93.....824.1 59
   Contents: Natural history of intellect.—Memory.—Boston. Michael Angelo.—Milton.—Papers from the Dial: Thoughts on modern literature; Landor; Prayers; Agriculture of Massachusetts; Europe and European books; Past and present; A letter; The tragic.
Nature, addresses, and lectures........824.1 53

LANGUAGE AND LITERATURE. 151

Contents: Nature.—The American scholar.—Address, Divinity college, Cambridge, 1838. — Literary ethics.— Method of nature.— Man the reformer. — Introductory lect. on the times.' — The conservative. — The transcendentalist.—The young American.

Poems. 1856.................................821.1 71
Poems ; Riverside edition, complete. 1896...821.1 72
Prose works. 1870. 2 v.
  V. 1. Miscellanies.—Essays....................824.1 46
  V. 2. Representative men. — English traits.— Conduct of life...824.1 47
Prose works. 1883. 3 v.
  V. 1. Miscellanies (lects. and addresses).—Essays..824.1 43
  V. 2. Representative men. — English traits.— Conduct of life...824.1 44
  V. 3. Society and solitude.—Letters and social aims.—Fortune of the republic........................824.1 45
Reference list; by Foster. v. 2.............16 55
Representative men......................................824.1 54
  Contents: Uses of great men. — Plato. — Plato: New readings.—Swedenborg.—Montaigne. — Shakespeare.— Napoleon.—Goethe.
Society and solitude................................824.1 51
Two unpublished essays. 1896........824.1 58
  Contents: The character of Socrates. — The present state of ethical philosophy.
Emery, E. Myself.....................................52283
Emery, E. B. Queens...............................47216
Emery, Sarah A. Three generations......47211
Emmons. The Fredoniad : poem on the war of 1812. 1832. 4 v..............821.1 309
Emory. Told at Tuxedo..........................52420
End of the beginning................................59101
Engle. Story of four acorns....................027201
English. American ballads. 1880....821.1 266
Enterlude of John Bon and Mast Person ; ed. by W. H. Black.......................821.2 473
Erasmus. Life and letters ; by Froude. 1894..922.5 45
Erma's engagement..................................55219
Erroll. Ugly duckling..............................69532
Erskine, *Mrs.* T. Wyncote......................25827
Erskine, Thomas. Letters. 1878......922.2 159
  Speeches ; with memoir. 4 v..............345.2 6
Erskine, Chatham, *and* Burke. Celebrated speeches. 1845....................825.2 12
Esler. Maid of the manse........................30621
  'Mid green pastures...............................30622
  Wardlaws...30624
  Way of transgressors..............................30623
  Way they loved at Grimpat...................30620
Estvan. Harry Delaware,.........................47284
Eustaphieve. Demetrius, hero of the Don. 1818..821.1 14
Evans, A. E. Curse of immortality (drama). 1873......................................822.2 159
Evans, Augusta. See Wilson, *Mrs.* Augusta Evans.

Evans, E. E. Laura...............................62336
Evans, Marian. See Eliot, George.
Evans, R. W. Rectory of Valehead.......249 25
Evelyn. Silva. 1825. 2 v...............715 B-2
Evening and the morning..........................55251
Evenings at Haddon hall..........................58974
Everett, C. C. Poetry, comedy, and duty. 1888..811 89
Everett, E. Great issues. 1861.........825.1 11
  Orations and speeches. 1850. 3 v.....825.1 7
  Same ; v. 1. 1836..................................825.1 10
Everett, H. L. People's program.............41790
Everhart. The fox chase (poem). 1874. ....821.1 200
Ewing, Hugh. Castle in the air...............69396
Ewing, *Mrs.* J. H. Blue bells on the lea, etc..02724
  Brothers of pity..02706
  Brownies, etc..02702
    Contents: The land of lost toys.—Three Christmas trees.—An idyll of the wood.—Christmas crackers.— Amelia and the dwarfs.
  Daddy Darwin's dovecot.........................24803
  Same ; In New York point, for the blind...362.4 N-Y-17
  Dandelion clocks, and other tales........02721
  Flat-iron for a farthing...........................24804
  Great emergency......................................02701
  Jackanapes...02709
  Jan of the windmill.................................24802
  Last words..02725
  Lob Lie-by-the-fire..................................02711
  Mary's meadow..02719
  Melchior's dream, etc.............................02718
  Miscellanea..24805
  Mrs. Overtheway's remembrances.....02705
  Mother's birthday review, etc..............02717
  Peace egg, etc..02720
  Six to sixteen..*24801
  Snap dragons, etc....................................02722
  Soldier's children, etc............................02723
  Story of a short life...............................02710
  We and the world..................................02703
  Week in a glass pond............................02707
Exciting stories of London society. v. 2...50330
Expatriation..69052
Exquisite fool..69072
Eyster. On the wing.................................020801
  Sunny hours..020802
Eytinge. Ball of the vegetables............031001
Faber. Ugly heroine.................................15282
Fadette, *pseud.* See Rodney, *Mrs.* M. R.
Faithful. A reed shaken with the wind....44164
Falconer, Lanoe, *pseud.* (Mary Hawker.)
  Cecilia de Noël.......................................14712
  Hotel d'Angleterre.................................14711
  Mademoiselle Ixe....................................14710

* Of interest to young readers.

Falconer, William. Poems; with life.
   1822..*in* 821.2 39
  Poetic works; ed. with memoir by Mitford.
   1895..821.2 414
  The shipwreck: poem. 1868............821.2 413
Falkner, J. M. Lost Stradivarius..............22010
Falkner, W. C. Little brick church..........62576
Fall of Paris..................................827.2 Pam. 12
Family pride...22903
Famous victory...58913
Fane. Collected verses. 1880............821.2 585
  Story of Helen Davenant.........................66402
Far and near...0117
Fargus. See Conway, Hugh.
Farjeon. Aaron the Jew..................................10232
  Betrayal of John Fordham........................10233
  Blade o' grass...10204
  Bread and cheese and kisses....................10212
  Bright star of life.....................................10219
  Christmas angel..10215
  Duchess of Rosemary Lane......................10209
  Fair Jewess...10231
  For the defense...10228
  Gautran...10210
  Golden grain..10207
  Golden land..10218
  Great Porter square..................................10211
  Grif..10205
  House of white shadows...........................10213
  Jessie Trim...10202
  Joshua Marvel..10201
  King of No-land..10222
  Last tenant...10230
  London's heart...10206
  Love's victory...10223
  Mystery of Monsieur Felix........................10225
  Nine of hearts..10220
  Peril of Richard Pardon............................10224
  Sacred nugget..10217
  Self-doomed...10214
  Something occurred.................................10229
  Ties, human and divine............................10226
  Toilers of Babylon....................................10227
  Tragedy of Featherstone..........................10221
Farmer of Inglewood forest.........................14168
Farquhar, A. Singer's heart...........................39101
Farquhar, George. Dramatic works.
   1860..*in* 822.2 180
Farrar, C. A. J. Down the west branch..024402
  Eastward ho!...024401
  Through the wilds....................................024405
  Up the north branch................................024403
  Wild woods life..024404
Farrar, F. W. Darkness and dawn..........59903
  Eric...02101
  Gathering clouds: days of Saint Chrysostom 59904

  Julian Home..59902
  St. Winifred's...02103
  Three homes..02104
Farrington, M. V. Fra Lippo Lippi.......18520
Father's coming home...............................07132
Favenc, E. Marooned on Australia.........31980
Favorite narratives....................................0105
Fawcett, E. D. Hartmann the anarchist....34601
Fawcett, Edgar. Adventures of a widow..60813
  Ambitious woman..................................60806
  Confessions of Claud.............................60805
  Fantasy and passion (verse). 1878...821.1 225
  Gentleman of leisure..............................60803
  Hopeless case..60801
  House at High Bridge............................60804
  Mild barbarian.......................................60809
  Olivia Delaplaine...................................60807
  Purple and fine linen.............................60802
  Social silhouettes..................................60815
  Solarion...60808
  Song and story: later poems. 1884...821.1 315
  Tinkling cymbals...................................60812
Fawcett, H. Essays and lectures. 1872...304 4
Fawcett, Millicent G. Janet Doncaster...56831
Fay (C. G. H., *pseud.*). Constance Lyndsay..15218
  Dreams and reveries of a quiet man.
   1832. 2 v...824.1 173
  Norman Leslie......................................15219
Fayette in prison; drama........................40 12
Featherstone. It's a way love has.........69313
Feis. Shakespeare and Montaigne.'84..822..3 257
Feltham. Resolves. 1832................824.2 112
Female minister................................*in* 14156
Fenn. Bag of diamonds...........................63913
  Black Tor..019618
  Brownsmith's boy.................................019605
  Chaplain's craze....................................63910
  Clerk of Portwick..................................63901
  Commodore Junk..................................63918
  Cormorant Crag....................................63927
  Crystal hunters.....................................019609
  Dark house...63908
  Devon boys...019607
  Diamond dyke......................................019616
  Dingo boys...019611
  Double cunning....................................63917
  Eli's children...63919
  Fire island..019613
  First in the field...................................019615
  Fluttered dovecote...............................63920
  Golden dream......................................63922
  Golden magnet....................................63904
  Grand Chaco..019610
  Hollowdell grange................................019601
  In marine armor...................................019614
  In the king's name...............................019603
  Master of the ceremonies....................63911

Menhardoc 63905
Mint of money...63921
Nat the naturalist.......................................019604
New mistress..63923
Off to the wilds...019602
One maid's mischief......................................63915
Original penny readings..................................63912
Parson o' Dumford..63902
Poverty corner..63906
Rajah of Dah...019608
Real gold..019612
Star-gazers..63925
Story of Antony Grace.....................................63914
Sweet mace..63907
Tiger lily...63926
Treasure hunters...63916
Vicar's people...63903
Witness to the deed..63924
Young castellan..019617
Fenn *et al.* Seven frozen sailors.................63928
Fennell. Calico printer..............................69760
Fenton. Poems; with life. 1822..........821.2 50
Ferguson, Samuel. Hibernian nights entertainments.......47214
Ferguson, V. Munro, (V., *pseud.*). Betsy...30535
Music hath charms..30536
Fern, Fanny, (*Mrs.* J. Parton). Fern leaves. 1853......................824.1 95
Folly as it flies (essays). 1868............824.1 74
Ginger-snaps (essays). 1870.................824.1 76
Ruth Hall...25881
Selected writings........................in 928.1 47
Fernald. The cat and the cherub, etc........57040
Ferres. His first kangaroo............................035901
Ferrier. Destiny......................................25811
Inheritance..25812
Marriage...25810
Ferry boy and the financier...............................0122
Field, C. L. Unseen king, etc. (verse). 1887.................................821.1 371
Field, *Mrs.* **E. M.** Denis........................35250
Master Magnus...035201
Field, Eugene. Culture's garland. 1887..828.1 66
Field flowers (poems). 1896..............821.1 B-5
Holy cross, etc..13806
Contents: Holy cross.—Rose and the thrush.—Seal-wife.—Flail, Trask, and Bisland.—Touch in the heart.—Daniel and the devil.—Methuselah.—Félice and Petit-Poulain.—The river.—Franz Abt.—Mistress Merciless.
The house...13807
Little book of profitable tales.............................13805
Contents: First Christmas tree.—Symbol and the saint.—Coming of the prince.—Mouse and the moonbeam.—Divell's Chrystmasse.—Mountain and the sea.—Robin and the violet.—Oak-tree and the ivy.—Margaret: a pearl.—Springtime.—Rodolph and his king.—Hampshire hills.—Ezra's thanksgivin' out west.—Ludwig and Eloise.—Fido's little friend.—Old man.—Bill, the lokil editor.—Little yaller baby.—The cyclopeedy.—Dock Stebbins.—Fairies of Pesth.

Little book of western verse. 1890...821.1 551
Love affairs of a bibliomaniac...............10 28
Love-songs of childhood. 1894........*821.1 551
Second book of tales.........................13808
Contents: Humin natur' on the Han'bul 'nd St. Jo.—Mother in Paradise.—Mr. and Mrs. Blossom.—Death and the soldier.—'Jinn' farms.—Angel and the flowers.—Child's letter.—Singer mother.—Two wives.—Wooing of Miss Woppit.—The talisman.—George's birthday.—Sweet-one-darling and the dream fairies.—Sweet-one-darling and the moon-garden.—Samuel Cowles and his horse Royal.—The werewolf.—Marvellous invention.—Story of Xanthippe.—Baked beans and culture.—Mademoiselle Prud'homme's book.—Demand for condensed music.—Learning and literature.—' Die Walkure' und der boomerangelungen.—Works of Sappho.
Second book of verse. 1893..............821.1 552
Songs and other verse. 1896..............821.1 553
With trumpet and drum. 1895........*821.1 555
Field, Eugene *and* **R. M.,** *trs.* Echoes from the Sabine farm. 1895...............874 41
Field, J. M. Drama in Pokerville.............47268
Field, Kate. Hap-hazard (essays). '73..824.1 123
Pen photographs of Dickens' readings. 824.1 124
Field, Margaret. Secret of Fontaine-La-Croix..69445
Field, Michael. Brutus ultor (drama). 1886..822.2 286
Callirhoë.—Fair Rosamond. (Dramas.) 1884..822.2 257
Canute the great.—The cup of water. (Dramas.) 1887............................822.2 298
Father's tragedy.— William Rufus.— Loyalty or love? (Dramas.) 1885. 822.2 279
Stephania: a trialogue. 1892..........822.2 309
The tragic Mary [Marie Stuart] (drama). 1890..822.2 181
Fielding. Miscellanies and poems; ed. by Browne. 1872............................820.2 216
Contents: Case of Elizabeth Canning.—Case of Boscavern Penlez.—Poems.
Select works; with life. 5 v.
V. 1. Life.—Joseph Andrews...............820.2 217
V. 2-3. History of a foundling.............820.2 218
V. 4. History of a foundling (continued).— Amelia..820.2 220
V. 5. Amelia (continued).—Jonathan Wild...820.2 221
Tom Jones....................................820.2 234
Works. 1824. 12 v.
V. 1-3. Dramatic works.....................820.2 222
V. 4. Dramatic works.—Jonathan Wild.....820.2 225
V. 5. Journey to the next world.—Joseph Andrews..820.2 226
V. 6. Joseph Andrews.—Tom Jones...........820.2 227
V. 7-9. Tom Jones.— Miscellaneous.........820.2 228
V. 10-11. Amelia.............................820.2 231
V. 12. Increase of robbers.—On conversation.— On the characters of men.—Covent-garden journal.— Voyage to Lisbon, etc........................820.2 233
Works; ed. by Murphy. 1821. 10 v.
V. 1. Essay; by A. Murphy.—Dramatic works. 820.2 200

* Of interest to young readers.

V. 2-3. Dramatic works..................820.2 207
V. 4. The fathers: a comedy.—Jonathan Wild.—
Journey from this world to the next..............820.2 209
V. 6-7. Tom Jones..................820.2 211
V. 8. Miscellaneous pieces.—Amelia..............820.2 213
V. 9. Amelia (concluded).— On conversation.—
On the knowledge of the characters of men.......820.2 214
V. 10. Covent-garden journal.—Essay on nothing.—Charge to grand jury.—Voyage to Lisbon.—
On Bolingbroke's essays.—Increase of robbers...820.2 215

Fields, Annie, (*Mrs.* J. T.). Shelf of old
    books. 1894..........................824.1 290
    Contents: Leigh Hunt.—Edinburgh.—From Milton
    to Thackeray.
    Under the olive (verse). 1881..........821.1 330
Fields, J. T. Ballads, etc. 1881........821.1 329
    Underbrush (essays). 1877..............824.1 105
    Yesterdays with authors....................824.1 85
Fight at Finnsburg (poem); tr. by Garnett.
    ....*in* 821.2 96
    Same; ed. and tr. by Thorpe..........821.2 98
Filluel. Pendower............................62583
Findlater. Green graves of Balgowrie..:....70240
Findlay. Michael Lamont, schoolmaster...59705
Finn. Home in the Holy Land..............30445
    Third year in Jerusalem....................30446
Firth. Kind hearts...........................62598
Fish. Supplycacyon of the beggers (1528),
    etc. 820.2 409
Fisher, F. C. See **Reid, Christian.**
Fisher, G. P., *jr.* Out of the woods.........70680
Fisher, L. H. Figures and flowers (verse).
    1888.................................821.1 385
Fiske, John. Darwinism, etc. 1879.....824.1 146
    Contents: Darwinism verified.—Mivart on Darwinism.—Bateman on same.—Büchner on same.—A crumb
    for the modern symposium.—Chauncey Wright.—What
    is inspiration?—Doctor Hammond and the table-tippers.
    —Buckle's fallacies.—Races of the Danube.—A librarian's
    work.
    Excursions of an evolutionist. 1884.....575 56
    Contents: Europe before the arrival of man.—The
    arrival of man in Europe.—Our Aryan forefathers.—
    What we learn from old Aryan words.—Was there a
    primeval mother-tongue?—Sociology and hero-worship.
    —Heroes of industry.—The causes of persecution.—The
    origins of Protestantism.—The true lesson of Protestantism.—Evolution and religion.—The meaning of infancy.
    —A universe of mind-stuff.—In memoriam: Charles
    Darwin.
    The unseen world, etc. 1876...........824.1 104
    Contents: The unseen world.—The to-morrow of
    death.—The Jesus of history.—The Christ of dogma.—
    Miracles.—Draper on science and religion.—Nathan the
    wise.—Historical difficulties. Famine of 1770 in Bengal.
    Spain and the Netherlands. Longfellow's 'Dante.'—
    Paine's 'Saint Peter.' Philosophy of art.—Athenian and
    American life.
Fiske, S. Mr. Dunn Brown's experiences
    in the army............................52250
Fitch, A. M. Bound down.................15245
Fitch, C. Some corr. and six conversations..57410
Fittis. Gilderoy..............................15244

Fitzgerald, E. Letters and literary remains. 1889. 3 v.
    V. 1. Letters, and index to same..............820.2 521
    V. 2. Euphranor.—Six dramas from Calderon.
    —The bird parliament (from the Persian of Farid-
    Uddin Attar).—The two generals...............820.2 522
    V. 3. The mighty magician, and Such stuff as
    dreams are made of (from Calderon).—Downfall
    and death of King Œdipus (from Sophocles).—
    Agamemnon (from Æschylus).—Rubáiyát of Omar
    Khayyám.—Salámán and Absál (from the Persian
    of Jámi).—Bredfield hall.—Chronomoros.—Virgil's
    garden.—Translations from Petrarch, etc..........820.2 523
    Letters to Fanny Kemble. 1895......826.2 117
Fitzgerald, Percy. Second Mrs. Tillotson. 1889......................................19173
Fitz-Gibbon. New river....................69204
Fitzpatrick, J. P. The outspan: tales
    of South Africa..........................58601
Five hundred pounds reward..............14156
Five, ten, and fifteen....................017920
Flagg, W. J. Good investment..............21660
    Wall street and the woods..................21661
Flagg, Wilson. Studies in field and forest.
    1857..................................504 58
Flanders, *Mrs.* G. M. Ebony idol..........15214
Fleischmann, S. American oratory: G.
    W. Curtis........................825.1 Pam. 11
Fleming, Alice M. Pinchbeck goddess...31450
Fleming, George, *pseud.* (Julia C.
    Fletcher.) Andromeda...................62021
    For plain women only..................136 80
    Head of Medusa..........................62001
    Kismet..................................62008
    Mirage..................................62012
    Truth about Clement Ker...............62002
    Vestigia.................................62015
Fleming, Keith. At the eleventh hour.....61510
Flemming, Harford, *pseud.* Broken
    chords..................................15720
    Carpet knight...........................15722
    Cupid and the sphinx...................15721
Fletcher, A., (Sheelah). Mother's request..52271
Fletcher, Giles. Complete poems; ed.
    by Grosart. 1876..................821.2 476
Fletcher, J. S. At the gate of the fold.....27413
    Mistress Spitfire........................27414
    Quarry farm............................27410
    When Charles the first was king.........27411
    Where highways cross..................27412
Fletcher, Julia C. See **Fleming, George.**
Fletcher, P. Poems. 1869. 4 v.
    V. 1. Memoir and essay; by Grosart. — Who
    wrote Brittain's 'Ida'?—Brittain's 'Ida.'—Notes..821.2 521
    V. 2. Locustæ. — Apollyonists. — Notes, etc..—
    Piscatorie eclogues.—Notes....................821.2 522
    V. 3. Sicelides: a piscatory. — Elisa. — Poetical
    miscellanies.—Minor poems.—Sylva poetica....821.2 523
    V. 4. Purple Island; with notes, etc.—Indices..821.2 524
Fletcher, R. H. Johnstown stage, etc......30485
Florentine tales (verse). 1847..........821.2 1028

Floyd. See **Forest, Neil**.
Fo'c's'le yarns: Betsy Lee, etc. (verse).
    1881....................................821.2 583
Fogerty. Countess Irene..................25882
    Mr. Jocko....................................25883
Follen, *Mrs.* C. Poems (copy presented to Harriet Martineau by the author). 1839....................................821.1 341
Follen, Charles. Works. 1842. 5 v.,......204 4
    (For contents, see FINDING LIST, pt. 3, p. 450.)
Fonblanque. Bad luck.....................20303
    Family tree..................................20302
    Filthy lucre..................................20306
    Pious frauds...............................20307
    Tangled skein.............................20301
Fondey. Oration, July 4, 1838............40 27
Foote, Mary Hallock. Chosen valley......15303
    Cœur d'Alene...............................15305
    Cup of trembling, etc...................15307
        Contents: Cup of trembling.—Maverick.—On a side track.—The trumpeter.
    Fate of a voice...................*in* 15302
    In exile, etc................................15304
        Contents: In exile.—Friend Barton's ' concern.'—The story of the Alcázar.—A cloud of the mountain.—The rapture of Hetty.—The watchman.
    John Bodewin's testimony............15306
    Last assembly ball.......................15302
    Led horse claim..........................15301
Foote, S. Bon-mots; ed. by Jerrold. '94...829.2 69
    Dramatic works. 2 v.
        V. 1. Taste.—Englishman at Paris.—The author.—Englishman returned from Paris.— Knights. — Mayor of Garrat.—Orators.— The minor.— The lyar.—The patron.........................822.2 130
        V. 2. The commissary. — Lame lover. — The bankrupt. — The cozeners.—Maid of Bath.— The nabob.—Devil upon two sticks.—Trip to Calais.— The Capuchin...............................822.2 131
Foote, T. M. Address, Hamilton College. 1848.....................................320 Pam. 6
For the fourth time of asking (See '**Laddie.**')..17912
Foran. The other side.......................69243
Forbes. Camps, quarters, and casual places. 1896............................824.2 503
    Contents: Matrimony under fire.— Reverencing the golden feet.—German war prayers.—Miss Priest's bride-cake.—A version of Balaclava.—How I 'saved France.'—Christmas in a cavalry regiment.—The mystery of Monsieur Regnier.—Railway Lizz.—My native salmon river.—The Cawnpore of to-day.—Bismarck before and during the Franco-German war.— The Inverness 'character' fair.—The warfare of the future.—George Martell's band-obast.—The Lucknow of to-day.—The military courage of royalty.—Parade of the commissionaires.— The inner history of the Waterloo campaign.
    Czar and sultan..............................13340
    Glimpses through the cannon-smoke. 1880....................................824.2 283
    Soldiering and scribbling. 1872.....824.2 227
    Souvenirs of some continents. 1885...824.2 374
Forbes *et al.* Camps and quarters,............13341

Ford, Harriet. Me an' Methuselar, etc. 1895.................................815.2 113
Ford, Helen J. Will it be?................12059
Ford, Isabella O. Miss Blake of Monkshalton......................................30530
    On the threshold...........................30531
Ford, J. L. Doctor Dodd's school........028820
    Dolly Dillenbeck............................28811
    Hypnotic tales...............................28810
    Literary shop, and other tales. 1894...824.1 296
Ford, John. Dramatic works; ed. by H. Coleridge. 1840......................822.2 105
    Works; ed. by Gifford and Dyce. 1895. 3 v..................................822.2 320
Ford, Mary H. Otto's inspiration.........15560
Ford, P. L. Great K. and A. robbery....43241
    Honorable Peter Stirling................43240
Ford, Sallie R. Raids and romance of Morgan and his men................15293
Ford, Theodosia. Christmas fairies......016801
Forde, Gertrude. Only a coral girl......69376
Forde, John. Honour triumphant, and A line of life: tracts......................824.2 3
Foreign marriage................................58905
Forest, Neil, *pseud.* (Cornelia Floyd.)
    Mice at play.................................09101
Forman. Our living poets. 1871.........824.2 224
    Contents: Introduction.—Idyllic school: Tennyson; Smedley; Ingelow.—Psychological school: Browning; Story; Webster.—Preraphaelite group: The Rossettis; Patmore; Woolner; Scott.—Renaissance group: M. Arnold; Swinburne; Morris; Horne; Taylor; George Eliot.—Appendix: Payne; O'Shaughnessy.
Forney. New nobility.........................62503
Forrest. Eight days...........................30579
Forrester, *Mrs.* Dearest....................45702
    Diana Carew................................45706
    I have lived and loved..................45728
    June..45729
    Light of other days.......................45707
    Mignon...45705
    My hero..45714
    My lord and my lady....................45727
    Of the world, worldly...................45703
    Omnia vanitas..............................45731
    Once again...................................45701
    Rhona..45708
    Roy and Viola..............................45722
    Viva..45704
Forrester, A. See **Crowquill, A.**
Forrester, Frank, *pseud.* (H. W. Herbert.) Deer stalkers................33709
    Fair Puritan.................................33705
    Life and writings. 1882. v. 1-2......824.2 320
    My shooting box..........................33707
    Quorndon hounds........................33710
    Roman traitor..............................33706
    Sporting scenes...........................33701
    Warwick woodlands....................33708

Forster, Francis. Major Joshua............30810
Forster, John. Historical and biographical essays. 2 v.
  V. 1. Debates on the grand remonstrance.—Plantagenets and Tudors.—The civil wars and Cromwell................824.2 304
  V. 2. De Foe.— Steele.— Charles Churchill.—Samuel Foote................824.2 305
Forsyth, Jean. Making of Mary............31320
Fortunes of Hassan............58922
Foster, Hannah. Coquette............15243
Foster, Isabella H. See Huntington, Faye.
Foster, J. Critical essays. 1856. 2 v..824.2 302
  Essays............824.2 306
Foster, M. F. Doty Dontcare............31390
Fothergill, Caroline. Comedy of Cecilia..69525
  Diana Wentworth............69524
  Question of degree............69526
Fothergill, Jessie. Aldyth............59215
  Borderland............59204
  First violin............59202
  From Moor isles............59206
  Healy............59213
  Kith and kin............59209
  Lasses of Levermore............59205
  March in the ranks............59210
  One of three............59208
  Orioles' daughter............59207
  Peril............59214
  Probation............59201
  Wellfields............59203
Found afloat............07141
Fourdrinier. Our new parish............15251
Fowell. Wreck of the Argo............011720
Fowler. Young pretenders............034001
Fox, C. J. Speeches. 1815. 6 v............329.2 75
Fox, Mrs. Emily, (Toler King, pseud.).
  Gemini............62573
  Off the rocks............62572
Fox, H. J. Student's Shakespeare. '80..‡822.3 B-2
Fox, John, jr. Cumberland vendetta, etc..20240
Franc. Marian............62303
  Vermont vale............62304
Francillon. A Christmas rose............55812
  Dog and his shadow............55817
  Earl's Dene............55819
  Golden bells............55809
  Jack Doyle's daughter............55818
  King or knave?............55813
  Olympia............55806
  One by one............55805
  Pearl and emerald............55810
  Queen Cophetua............55804
  Real queen............55807
  Romances of the law............55814
  Ropes of sand............55816
  Seal of the snake............55811
  Under Slieve Ban............55802

Francillon et al. Wooing, etc............55815
Francis, Francis. Wild Rose............21080
Francis, M. E., (Mrs. F. Blundell). Among the untrodden ways (stories)............28223
  Daughter of the soil............28221
  Frieze and fustian............28222
  In a north country village............28224
  Story of Dan............28220
Franklin. Bibliographical note (Boston public library bulletin, v. 5., pp. 217, 276, 420)............17 B-14
  Familiar letters, etc. 1833............826.1 1
  Sayings of Poor Richard; ed. by Ford. 1890............829.1 31
  Works; ed. by Sparks. 10 v.
    V. 1. Autobiography; continued by Sparks......820.1 4
    V. 2. Essays on religious and moral subjects and the economy of life.—Bagatelles.—Essays on general politics, commerce and political economy......820.1 5
    V. 3-4. Essays and tracts, historical and political, before the American revolution......820.1 6
    V. 5. Political papers during and after the revolution.—Letters and papers on electricity.—Appendix......820.1 8
    V. 6. Letters and papers on philosophical subjects......820.1 9
    V. 7-10. Correspondence.—Index......820.1 10
Fraser, Mrs. Hugh. Brown ambassador..31380
  Palladia............31381
Fraser, Sir William. Hic et ubique. 1893............824.2 363
Fraser-Tytler. See Tytler.
Fraternity............69048
Frazer, D. Perseverance Island............032301
Frazer, R. W. Silent gods and sunsteeped lands............69980
Frederic. Copperhead............50905
  Damnation of Theron Ware............50907
  In the sixties............50909
  Contents: The copperhead. — Marsena.— The war widow.—The eve of the Fourth.—My aunt Susan.
  In the valley............50903
  The Lawton girl............50902
  March hares............50908
  Marsena, etc............50906
  Contents: Marsena.—The war widow.—The eve of the Fourth.—My aunt Susan.
  Mrs. Albert Grundy. 1896............827.1 40
  Return of the O'Mahony............50904
  Seth's brother's wife............50901
French, Alice. See Thanet, Octave.
French, H. W. Castle Foam............62103
  Colonel Thorndike's adventures........in 041101
  Ego............62101
  Lance of Kanana............028703
  Nuna the Brahmin girl............62102
  The only one............62104
  Oscar Peterson............028704
  Our boys in China............*915.1 98
  Our boys in India............*915.4 54

* Of interest to young readers.   ‡ For reference.

French, Virginia L. My roses..............12048
Freneau. Poems. 1861......................821.1 12
Frere. Original works and minor translations. 1874..........................821.2 578
> Contents: Contributions to The Microcosm.—Miscellanies.—Contributions to The Anti-Jacobin.—Remarks on book IX of the Iliad, etc.—Whistlecraft's 'King Arthur.'—Fables and other miscellanies.—Translations from 'The Cid.'—Miscellaneous translations.—Translations of the Psalms.

Translations from Aristophanes and Theognis. 1874...................................882 26
Frier Bacon..*in* 101
Frier Rush...*in* 101
Frisbie. Address, Cambridge. 1817.........40 22
Friswell, J. H. Burden of life: essays. 1897..170 62
Essays on English writers................824.2 191
> Contents: Study of history.—History and historical biography.—English poets.—Essayists.—Rise of the drama.—Dramatic literature.—The Bible and its translators.—Theologians.—Letters and letter-writing.—Satirists.—Scottish poets.—Political and metaphysical writers.—Novelists.—Periodical essayists.—Poets of the present century.

The gentle life: essays. 1869. 2 v..824.2 192
A man's thoughts. 1880..................824.2 276
Modern men of letters honestly criticised. 1870.............................824.2 190
> Contents: Dickens.—Lemon.—Hugo.—Reade.—Ruskin.—Browning.—Trollope.—Tennyson.—Sala.—Lever.—Grote.—Disraeli.—Lytton.—Ainsworth.—Carlyle.—Longfellow.—Swinburne.—Kingsley.—Emerson.—Robertson.—About.

One of two......................................15230
Other people's windows................15229
Out and about...............................023801
Frith, H. Escape from Siberia...........032217
Frith, W. In search of quiet..............50440
Frolics of Puck...............................50389
Frothingham, N. L. Metrical pieces. 1855-70. 2 v.............................821.1 342
Frothingham, W. Martel papers..........15269
Froude, J. A. Short studies on great subjects. 1868-83. 4 v.
> V. 1. Science of history.—Erasmus and Luther.—Influence of the reformation on Scottish character.—Philosophy of Catholicism.—Free discussion of theological difficulties.—Criticism and gospel history.—Job.—Spinoza.—Dissolution of the monasteries.—England's forgotten worthies.—Homer.—Lives of the saints.—Representative men.—Reynard, the fox.—The cat's pilgrimage.—Fables.—Parable of the bread-fruit tree.—Compensation..824.2 186
> V. 2. Calvinism.—A bishop of the 12th century.—Newman on the grammar of assent.—Condition and prospects of Protestantism.—England and her colonies.—A fortnight in Kerry; pts. 1-2.—Duties of state and subject.—The merchant and his wife.—Progress.—The colonies once more.—Education.—England's war.—Eastern question.—Scientific method applied to history...........824.2 187

V. 3. Annals of an English abbey.—Revival of Romanism.—Sea studies.—Society in Italy in the last days of the republic.—Lucian. Divus Caesar.—Uses of a landed gentry.—Party politics.—South African journal...........................824.2 188
V. 4. Becket.—Oxford counter-reformation.—Origen and Celsus.—A Cagliostro of the 2d century.—Cheneys and the house of Russell.—A siding at a railway station...............824.2 189
Two chiefs of Dunboy....................69501
Froude, R. H. Letters. 1838.........*in* 230 140
Remains. 1838. 4 v.
> V. 1. Journal.—Letters.—Poems, etc..........230 140
> V. 2. Sermons...230 141
> V. 3. Theological miscellany..........................230 142
> V. 4. History of Thomas à Becket................230 143

Fry. Listener.....................................44160
Fuller, A. M. A. D. 2000....................29001
Fuller, Anna. Literary courtship.......31803
Peak and prairie (stories).................31803
Pratt portraits...................................31802
Venetian June..................................31804
Fuller, E. Complaining millions of men...26810
Forever and a day...........................26811
Fuller, H. Grand transformation scenes..824.1 126
Fuller, H.B., (Stanton Page, *pseud.*). Chatelaine de La Trinité..........................69565
Chevalier of Pensieri-Vani...............69564
Cliff-dwellers....................................69566
Puppet-booth: plays. 1896...........822.1 41
> Contents: The cure of souls.—On the whirlwind.—The love of love.—Afterglow.—The ship comes in.—At St. Judas's.—The light that always is.—The dead-and-alive.—Northern lights.—The story-spinner.—The stranger within the gates.—In such a night.

With the procession...........................69567
Fuller, Lydia. Mistaken......................15220
Fuller, Margaret. See Ossoli, S. M. F.
Fuller, Martha. Righted at last.........44155
Fuller, Metta V. Senator's son..........44184
Fuller, S. R. Address on death of Grant. 1885.................................923.1 Pam. 100
Fuller, T. Fulleriana....................*in* 922.2 103
Wise words, etc.; ed., with life, by Jessopp. 1892....................................829.2 81
Fullerton. Constance Sherwood.........13302
Stormy life...13304
Too strange not to be true................13301
Fullom. Daughter of the night..........14137
Furman, A. A. Philip of Pokanoket: drama. 1894............................822.1 38
Furman, L. S. Stories of a sanctified town...57060
Furness. Concordance to Shakespeare's poems. 1874.........................‡822.3 98
Furniss. Farce-comedies. 1891........822.1 28
> Contents: A box of monkeys.—The Jack trust.—The veneered savage.—Tulu.

Furnivall. Succession of Shakspeare's works. 1874.....................822.3 Pam. 8
Fush. Won at West Point...................58992
Gage. Steps upward...........................20458

‡ For reference.

Gale. Country muse. 1892.................821.2 757
    Same ; 2d series. 1893................821.2 758
    Cricket songs. 1894........................821.2 922
    June romance..45301
    Orchard songs. 1893.....................821.2 923
    Songs for little people. 1896........*821.2 1036
Galetti. Some annals of an Italian village..70840
Gallagher. Miami woods, etc. (poems).
    1881..821.1 348
Gallatin. Writings. 1879. 3 v............329.1 132
Gallon. Tatterley..71201
Galpin *et al.* Children's history book..........0143
Galt. Annals of the parish............................7503
    The entail...7501
    Miscellanies. 2 v..............................928 2 206
    The provost, etc...7502
    Contents: The provost.—The steam-boat.—The omen.
    —Illustrations, anecdotes, and critical remarks.
    Sir Andrew Wylie..7504
Galton. Urbana scripta. 1885. ....824.2 373
    Contents: English poetry in 1885.—Tennyson.—Browning. — Matthew Arnold. — Swinburne. — W. Morris.— Merchant of Venice. — An overlooked characteristic of Julius Cæsar.—Mark Pattison.—Horace Walpole.
Gannett. Studies in Longfellow......928.1 Pam. 5
Gardiner. Essays. 1803. 2 v..........................304 12
Gardner, C. E. Broken dreams (poems).821.1 187
    Compensation (verse). 1880............821.1 243
    Every inch a king...50112
    Rich Medway's two loves..........................50103
    Stolen waters (poems). 1874...........821.1 188
    Terrace roses..50101
    Tested...50102
    A twisted skein (verse). 1884..........821.1 269
    Uncle Ralph...50116
    Woman's wiles..50111
Gardner, *Mrs.* H. C. Discontent, etc......19540
    Glimpses of our lake region.......................19541
Gardner, Sarah M. H. Quaker idyls.....27030
Garfield. Words of; ed. by Balch. 1881.829.1 23
    Works. 1882. 2 v.................................329.1 138
Garland. Crumbling idols. 1894........824.1 284
    Contents: Provincialism.—New fields.—The question of success.—Literary prophecy.—Local color in art.—The local novel.—The drift of the drama.— The influence of Ibsen.—Impressionism.—Literary centres.—Literary masters.—A recapitulatory afterword.
    Jason Edwards..30475
    Little Norsk...30477
    Main-travelled roads..................................30474
    Contents: Branch-road.—Up the Coulé.—Among the corn rows.—Return of a private. Under the lion's paw. Mrs. Ripley's trip.
    Member of the third house......................30476
    Prairie folks..30479
    Contents: Uncle Ethan's speculation. Test of Elder Pill. William Bacon's hired man. Sim Burns's wife. Saturday night on the farm. Village cronies.—Drifting Crane Old Daddy Deering Sociable at Dudley's.
    Prairie songs. 1893......................821.1 466

Rose of Dutcher's Coolly................30480
Spoil of office...30478
Garrett, Edward, *pseud.* (Isabella F. Mayo). Capel girls............................20612
    Chance child..*in* 20610
    Crooked places..20608
    Crust and the cake....................................20602
    Daughter of the Klephts.........................20618
    Dead sin, etc..20607
    Doing and dreaming...............................20605
    Equal to the occasion............................20615
    Family fortunes.......................................20613
    Gold and dross..20609
    House by the works...............................20611
    John Winter...20616
    Not by bread alone...............................20617
    Occupations of a retired life................20601
    Premiums paid to experience.............20606
    Quiet Miss Godolphin............................20610
    White as snow..20603
Garrick. Correspondence. 1835. 2 v...826.2 B-1
Dramatic works. 1798.
    V. 1. Lethe.—Lying valet.—Miss in her teens.— Romeo and Juliet.—Every man in his humour.—The fairies.— Florizel and Perdita.—Catharine and Petruchio..822.2 123
    V. 2. Lilliput. — Male coquette. — Gamesters.— Isabella.— Guardian.— Enchanter.— Cymbeline.— Farmer's return from London.....................822.2 124
    V. 3. Clandestine marriage.—A peep behind the curtain.—Arthur and Emmeline.—Bon ton.—High life below stairs.—Irish widow. — Mayday.—Theatrical candidates.......................................822.2 125
Garrigues. Summer boarders...............56893
Garry. Out of bounds.............................70301
Garth. Poems ; with life. 1822............821.2 42
Garver. Brother of the third degree..........30370
Gascoigne. Complete poems ; ed. by Hazlitt. 1869. 2 v.
    V. 1. The posies.—Supposes: a comedie (from Ariosto).—Iocasta: a tragedy (from Euripides).— Hearbes.—Weedes.—Ferdinando Ieronimi........821.2 140
    V. 2. The glasse of governement.—Princelye pleasures at the courte at Kenelwoorth.—Hermit's tale.—The steele glas.—Complaynt of Phylomene.— The grief of joye.—Noble art of venerie.........821.2 141
The steele glas. — Complaynt of Philomene...820.2 30
Gaskell. Cousin Phillis............................5314
    Same..*in* 5310B
    Cranford, and other tales......................5305
    Dark night's work...................................5308
    Grey woman, etc..................................5313
    Contents: The grey woman.—Curious if true.—Six weeks at Heppenheim.—Libbie Marsh's three eras.— Christmas storms and sunshine.—Hand and heart.— Bessy's troubles at home.—Disappearances.
    Lizzie Leigh, etc.......................................5312
    Contents: Lizzie Leigh.—The well of Pen-Morfa.— The heart of John Middleton.—The old nurse's story.— Traits and stories of the Huguenots.—Morton Hall.— My French master.—The squire's story.

---

* Of interest to young readers.

Lois the witch	5307
Mary Barton	5301
Same, and other tales	5301B
Contents: Mary Barton.—Cousin Phillis.—My French master.—The old nurse's story.—Bessie's troubles at home.—Christmas storms and sunshine.	
Moorland cottage	5304
My lady Ludlow	5315
North and south	5302
Right at last	5310
Ruth, etc	5303
Contents: Ruth.—The grey woman.—Morton Hall.—Mr. Harrison's confessions.—Hand and heart.	
Sylvia's lovers	5306
Widow of Windsor	5320
Wives and daughters	5311

Gasquet. Old English Bible, and other essays. 1897 ... 220.0 268
Contents: Mediæval monastic libraries.—The monastic scriptorium.—A forgotten English preacher.—Pre-reformation English Bible.—Religious instruction in England, 14th and 15th centuries.—A royal Christmas in the 15th century.—Canterbury claustral school in the 15th century.—Note books of William Worcester.—Hampshire recusants.

Gatchell. See **King, Thorold,** *pseud.*
Gatty, A. Key to 'In memoriam.' ... 821.2 361
Gatty, *Mrs.* **A.** Aunt Judy's letters ... 025904
Parables from nature. 1879. 2 v	*829.2 51
Aunt Judy's tales	025901
Domestic pictures and tales	025907
Fairy godmothers	025902
Human face divine	20450
Hundredth birthday, etc	20449
Legendary tales	20448
Proverbs illustrated	025906

Gaunt. Dave's sweetheart ... 45320
Moving finger ... 45321
Gay. Fables. 1746. 2 v ... 829.2 22
Poems; with life. 1822 ... 821.2 29
Gayarré. Aubert Dubayet ... 52244
Fernando De Lemos ... 52245
Gaye. Coming ... 13801
Geddie. Beyond the Himalayas ... 62562
Gedge. Sunflowers ... 62382
Geldart. Mary Leigh ... 52290
Gellie. Fearless Frank ... 028502
New girl ... 028501
Stephen the schoolmaster ... 59501
Genin. Selections from writings; with biography. 1869 ... 820.1 30
Genone. Bellona's husband ... 19561
Inquirendo island ... 19560
George A Green ... *in* 102
Geraldine [by A. A. Hopkins] ... 821.1 261
Gerard, Dorothea. Angela's lover ... 62618
Arranged marriage	62614
Etelka's vow	62610
Lady Baby	62605
Lot 13	62612
On the way through, etc	62608
Orthodox	62603
Queen of curds and cream	62609
Recha	62606
Rich Miss Riddell	62613
Spotless reputation	62617
Wrong man	62615

Gerard, Dorothea *and* **E.** Sensitive plant. 62607
Gerard, E. D., (Mrs. Emily Gerard Laszowska). Beggar my neighbor ... 62602
Foreigner	62616
Reata	62601
Voice of a flower	62611
Waters of Hercules	62604

Gervinus. Shakespeare commentaries ... 822.3 54
Giant ... 07120
Gibbon, C. Braes of Yarrow ... 60406
By mead and stream	60416
Dead heart	60414
Flower of the forest	60412
For lack of gold	60405
For the king	60419
Golden shaft	60415
Hard knot	60407
Heart's delight	60410
In honor bound	60418
In pastures green	60411
Loving a dream.—One of his inventions	60408
Margaret Carmichael [Princess of Jutedom]	60409A
Of high degree	60413
Princess of Jutedom [Margaret Carmichael]	60409
Queen of the meadow	60402
Robin Grey	60404
Was ever woman in this humor wooed?	60417

Gibbon, E. Miscellaneous works. '37. 928.2 486
Private letters. 1896. 2 v ... 928.2 488
Gibbs. If love be love ... 69255
Giberne. Andersons ... 50010
Curate's home	50001
Dalrymples	50009
Detained in France	50002
Duties and duties	50003
Father Aldur	040301
Girl at the Dower house, and afterward	50012
Miss Devereux, spinster	50011
Nigel Browning	50008
Number 3 Winfred place	50007
Old comrades	50013
Sweetbriar	50004

Gibson. Sharp eyes. 1893 ... 504 134
Gifford. Dialogue of witches ... 821.2 451
Gift, Theo, *pseud.* (Dora Havers, now Mrs. Boulger.) Cape Town Dicky ... 032241
Dishonored ... 20214

* Of interest to young readers.

Garden of girls..................................26205
Innocent maiden...............................26210
Island princess..................................26215
Lil Lorimer..26212
Maid Ellice.......................................26203
Matter-of-fact girl.............................26207
Pretty Miss Bellew............................26202
Victims...26213
Visited on the children.....................26211
Wrecked at the outset......................26216

Gilbert, William. Clara Levesque..........20504
King George's middy.........................20503
Magic mirror.....................................04801
Modern wonders of the world..............04802
Monomaniac.....................................20501
Wizard of the mountain......................20505

Gilbert, W. S. Bab ballads............828.2 45
Foggerty's fairy, etc............................25838
Iolanthe; or, The peer and the peri:
  opera...822.2 Pam. 3
Original comic operas. 1886............822.2 281
  Contents: The sorcerer.—H. M. S. Pinafore.—Pirates of Penzance.—Iolanthe.—Patience.—Princess Ida.—The mikado.—Trial by jury.
Same; 2d series....,......................822.2 282
  Contents: The gondoliers.—The grand duke.—Yeomen of the guard.—His excellency.—Utopia, limited.—Ruddigore.—The mountebanks.—Haste to the wedding.
Original plays. 1876.......................822.2 179
  Contents: Wicked world.—Pygmalion and Galatea.—Charity.—The princess.—Palace of truth.—Trial by jury.
Same; 2d series. 1881................822.2 179A
  Contents: Broken hearts.—Engaged.—Sweethearts.—Daniel Druce.—Gretchen.—Tom Cobb.—Sorcerer.—H. M. S. Pinafore.—Pirates of Penzance.
Same; 3d series. 1895................822.2 179B
  Contents: Comedy and tragedy.—Foggerty's fairy.—Rosencrantz and Guildenstern.—Patience.—Princess Ida.—The mikado.—Ruddigore.—The yeomen of the guard.—The gondoliers.—The mountebanks.—Utopia, limited.

Gilchrist. Stone dragon, etc............31070
Gildehaus. In rhyme and time. 1895....821.1 504
Gilder. The celestial passion (verse)....821.1 440
Five books of song. 1894................821.1 480
  Contents: The new day:—The celestial passion.—Lyrics.—Two worlds.—The great remembrance.
For the country (poems). 1897........821.1 161
Great remembrance, etc. (poems).
  1893..821.1 464
Lyrics and other poems. 1885.........821.1 158
The new day; a poem. 1876...........821.1 169
The poet and his master, and other
  poems, 1878................................821.1 221

Gildersleeve, B. L. Essays and studies.
  1890...824.1 255
  Contents: Limits of culture.—Classics and colleges.—University work in America and classical philology.—Grammar and æsthetics.—The legend of Venus.—Xanthippe and Socrates.—Apollonius of Tyana. Lucian.—Emperor Julian. Platen's poems. Maximilian: his travels and his tragedy. Occasional addresses.

Gildersleeve, *Mrs.* **C. H.** Remy St.
  Remy..41750
Giles, Ella A. Maiden Rachel................56836
Giles, H. Illustrations of genius. 1854...824.1 27
Lects. and essays. 1850. 2 v.
  V. 1. Falstaff.—Crabbe.— Moral philosophy of Byron's life. — Moral spirit of Byron's genius.— Ebenezer Elliott. — Goldsmith. — Spirit of Irish history..824.1 247
  V. 2. Ireland and the Irish.—Worth of liberty.—True manhood.—The pulpit.—Patriotism.—Economies. — Music. — The young musician. — A day in Springfield.—Chatterton.—Carlyle. — Savage and Dermody..824.1 248

Gilfillan. Modern literature and literary
  men. 1851.................................824.2 169
Gilkes. The thing that hath been..........21030
Gilliat. Dragonnades..........................22180
John Standish....................................22181
Gillmore. Amphibious voyage...............032206
Gilman, A. Seven historic ages............05201
Gilman, C. Recollections of a New England
  bride and of a southern matron......20402
Gilmore, J. R. *See* **Kirke, Edmund.**
Girl's birthday book............................07167
Gissing. Born in exile.........................15417
Demos..15410
Denzil Quarrier.................................15415
Emancipated....................................15418
Eve's ransom...................................15419
In the year of jubilee..........................15420
Life's morning..................................15413
Nether world...................................15411
New Grub street...............................15414
Odd women....................................15416
Paying guest...................................15422
Sleeping fires..................................15423
Thyrza...15412
Unclassed......................................15421
Whirlpool.......................................15425
Workers in the dawn........................15424

Gladden. Santa Claus on a lark...........011511
Gladstone. Gleanings of past years. 1879.
  7 v.
  V. 1. The prince consort.—The county franchise.—Kin beyond sea........................824.2 245
  V. 2. Blanco White.—Leopardi.—Tennyson.—Wedgwood.—Bishop Patteson.—Macaulay.—Norman Macleod..................................824.2 246
  V. 3. Theses of Erastus and Scottish church establishment.—On 'Ecce Homo.'—Courses of religious thought. — Influence of authority in matters of opinion.—The 16th century before the 19th...824.2 247
  V. 4. State prosecutions of the Neapolitan government.—Parini on the States of the church.—Germany, France, and England, 1870.—The Hellenic factor in the eastern problem.—Montenegro.—Aggression on Egypt and freedom in the east..824.2 248
  V. 5. Present aspect of the church, 1843. —Ward's ideal of a Christian church. Royal supremacy..824.2 249

LANGUAGE AND LITERATURE.

V. 6. Laymen in the church.—Bill for divorce.—
Church of England and ritualism.—Italy and her
church..824.2 230
V. 7. The work of universities.—Ancient Greece
in the providential order.—Chapter of autobi-
ography.— Law of probable evidence. — Evan-
gelical movement..824.2 251
Homer. 1878...883 37.
Homeric synchronism. 1876...............................881 6
Juventus mundi..938 26
Landmarks of Homeric study. 1890.....883 67
Later gleanings. 1897. v. 1—..........824.2 252
'Robert Elsmere' and the battle of be-
lief..824.2 Pam. 1
Speeches. 1885...329.2 74
Studies on Homer. 1858. 3 v.........................883 1
Thoughts from writings and speeches;
ed. by G. Barnett Smith. 1894........829.2 74
Glaister. Constant woman......................................56860
Glanville. Fair colonist..61112
    Fossicker..61111
    Golden rock..61113
    Lost heiress...61110
Glapthorne. Plays and poems. '74. 2v..822.2 201
Gleason. Anniversary poem, Boston, 1855.
....in 825.1 17
Gleig. Hussar..20485
    Self-devotion 20484
    Subaltern...20486
Glenn. Cousin Paul..20415
Glimpses of Nineveh, B. C. 690...................50335
Glover. Poems; with life. 1822........821.2 44
Glyn. Fifty pounds for a wife.........................14520
    Pearl of the realm..14521
Glyndon, Howard, *pseud.* See **Redden.**
Glynn. Poems; with life. 1822........*in* 821.2 39
Goddard. Search for the grael....................20479
Godkin, E. L. Reflections and comments.
1865-95...824.1 304
Godkin, G. S. Il mal occhio; or, The evil
eye..31075
Godwin, Mary W. Letters to Imlay...826.2 43
Posthumous works. 1798. 4 v.
    V. 1-2. Wrongs of woman.—Lessons................820.2 129
    V. 3-4. Letters.—Extract of the cave of fancy.
    —On poetry.—Hints..820.2 131
Godwin, P. Commemorative addresses,
1895...824.1 292
    Contents: George William Curtis.—Edwin Booth.—
    Louis Kossuth.— John James Audubon.—William Cullen
    Bryant.
Out of the past (essays). 1870.........824.1 102
Political essays. 1856..........................329.1 81
Godwin, William. Brother's secret...........12040
    Caleb Williams...12037
    The enquirer: reflections. 1797......824.2 390
    Fleetwood...12041
    Mandeville..12038
    St. Leon..12042
Goetz. Kallirrhoe: a dramatic poem. '96..822.1 49

Gold stories of '49. 1896....................821.1 526
Goldsmith, H. Euancondit.....................227.10
Goldsmith, O. Citizen of the world. 1794..827.2 5
The deserted village, in N. Y. point, for
the blind. 1895..............................362.4 N-Y-14
Deserted village.—Traveller. 1881...821.2 395
Essays and poems; with memoir. 1807.
....820.2 101
Poems; with life. 1822................*in* 821.2 41
She stoops to conquer (drama). 1895..822.2 324
Vicar of Wakefield.................................20408
    Same...820.2 95
    Same...820.2 97
Works; ed. by Cunningham. 1854. 4 v.
    V. 1. Poetical works.—Dramas.—Vicar of Wake-
    field...820.2 97
    V. 2. Enquiry into the state of polite learning.
    —The citizen of the world.......................................820.2 98
    V. 3. The bee.—Essays.—Unacknowledged es-
    says.—Prefaces, etc..820.2 99
    V. 4. Memoirs of Voltaire.—Life of Beau Nash.
    —Life of Thomas Parnell.—Life of Bolingbroke.—
    Reviews.— Extracts from 'Animated nature.'—
    Cock Lane ghost.—Translation of Vida's 'Chess.'—
    Letters..820.2 100
Works; ed. by Prior. 1856. 4 v.
    V. 1. The bee.— Essays.— Inquiry into the state
    of polite learning in Europe.—Prefaces.......820.2 93
    V. 2. Citizen of the world..............................820.2 94
    V. 3. Vicar of Wakefield................................820.2 95
    V. 4. Poems, dramas, etc..............................820.2 96
Goodale, E. Journal of a farmer's daugh-
ter. 1881..824.1 163
Goodale, E. *and* **D. R.** All round the year.
—In Berkshire with the wild flowers.
(Verses.) 1881..................................821.1 250
Apple blossoms (verses). 1878......821.1 224
Goodloe. College girls.............................30680
Goodman. Too curious...........................69399
Goodrich. Fireside education. 1838......374 19
Goodwin, Christina. How they learned
housework..032229
Goodwin, *Mrs.* **H. B.** See **Talcot,** *Mrs.* **H. B.**
Goodwin, M. W. Head of a hundred....15660
    White aprons..15661
Googe. Eglogs, sonnettes, etc...........820.2 39
Gordon, A. Northward ho!....................22760
Gordon, A. C., *and* **Page, T. N.** Befo'
de war (poems). 1888.....................821.1 370
Gordon, C., (Vieux Moustache, *pseud.*).
    Boarding-school days..................................25850
    Two lives in one...25849
Gordon, H. L. Feast of the virgins, etc.
(verse). 1891....................................821.1 446
Gordon, Janet. Jacob Jennings...........032207
Gordon, Julien, *pseud.* (Mrs. Van Rensse-
laer Cruger.) Diplomat's diary......12920
    Poppæa..12924
    Puritan pagan..12922
    Marionettes..12923

Successful man.................................12921
Wedding, etc...................................12925
Gordon, W. J. Englishman's haven..........03305
Gore. Banker's wife.........................*in* 14809
  Birthright......................................14809
  Dean's daughter.............................14803
  Hecklington...................................14801
  Life's lessons................................14806
  Mammon.......................................14808
  Progress and prejudice......................14807
  Queen of Denmark..........................*in* 14809
  Self..14804
  Two aristocracies............................14805
Goss. Jack Alden.............................033403
  Jed...033401
  Tom Clifton....................................033402
Gosse, E. Critical kit-kats. 1896.......824.2 492
  Contents: The sonnets from the Portuguese.—Keats in 1894.—T. L. Beddoes.—Edward Fitz Gerald.—Walt Whitman.—Tolstoi.—Christina Rossetti.—Lord De Tabley.—Toru Dutt.—M. José.—Maria de Heredia.—Walter Pater.—R. L. Stevenson.
  Firdausi in exile, and other poems. 1885.
  ....821.2 753
  From Shakespeare to Pope. 1885....821.2 750
  Gossip in a library. 1892..................824.2 444
  Contents: Camden's 'Britannia.'—A mirror for magistrates.—A poet in prison.—Death's duel.—Gerard's 'Herbal.'—Pharamond.—A volume of old plays.—A censor of poets.—Lady Winchelsea's poems.—Amasia.—Love and business.—What Ann Lang read.—Cats.—Smart's poems. —Pompey the little.—John Buncle.— Beau Nash.— Diary of a lover of literature.—Peter Bell.—The fancy.—Ultracrepidarius.— Duke of Rutland's poems.— Ionica.— The shaving of Shagpat.
  In russet and silver (poems). 1894...821.2 964
  Jacobean poets. 1894......................821.2 963
  King Erik : a tragedy. 1893.............822.2 312
  On viol and flute. 1876...................821.2 652
  Questions at issue. 1893..................824.2 457
  Contents: Tyranny of the novel.—Influence of democracy on literature.—Has America produced a poet?—What is a great poet?—Making a name in literature.—Limits of realism in fiction.—Is verse in danger?—Tennyson, and after.—Shelley in 1892.—Symbolism and M. Stéphane Mallarmé.—Two pastels: R. L. Stevenson as a poet; Kipling's short stories.—An election at the English academy.
  Secret of Narcisse................................43301
  Seventeenth century studies. 1883...824.2 347
  Studies in literature of northern Europe. 1879..898 8
Gosse, P. H. Land and sea. 1865...........504 53
  Contents: Lundy Island.—Ramble to Brandy Cove.—The sea—Highwater mark.—Babbicombe to Hope's Nose.—An hour among the Torbay sponges.—Goby hunting.—Meadfoot and the starfish.—A day in the woods of Jamaica.—Ferns. Dartmoor and the dart.
  Romance of natural history. 1881. 2 v...504 90
Gosson. Newfangled gentlewomen......821.2 474
  Schoole of abuse............................820.2 26
Gould, G. M. An autumn singer (verse). 1897..821.1 524

Gould, Jennie T. Marjorie's quest..........56701
Gould, S. Baring-. Arminell...............18310
  Broom-squire.................................18321
  Cheap Jack Zita..............................18317
  Court Royal...................................18303
  Dartmoor idylls..............................18322
  Eve..18309
  Gaverocks.....................................18307
  Grettir the outlaw...........................033501
  Guavas the tinner. 1897..................18323
  Icelander's sword............................033503
  In exitu Israel................................18304
  In the roar of the sea......................18315
  Jacquetta, etc................................18311
  John Herring.................................18302
  Kitty alone....................................18319
  Margery of Quether, etc..................18314
  Mehallah......................................18301
  Mrs. Curgenven of Curgenven.........18316
  My Prague pig, etc.........................033502
  Noémi..18320
  Pennycomequicks...........................18312
  Queen of love................................18318
  Red spider....................................18306
  Richard Cable................................18308
  The silver store (poems).................821.2 409
  Story of Jael................................*in* 10228
  Urith..18313
Goulding. Boy life among Indians..........03206
  Marooner's island...........................03201
  Nacoochee....................................03204
  Sal-o-quah....................................03203
  Sapeloo...03205
Gower. Confessio amantis. 1857. 3 v...821.2 123
  Illustrations of ; by Todd. 1810......928.2 B-1
  Readings in ; by Easton. 1895........821.2 1027
Graeme. Poems ; with life. 1822......*in* 821.2 41
Graham, Ennis, *pseud.* See Molesworth, *Mrs.*
Graham, *Mrs.* H. See Marshall, Emma.
Graham, J. W. Neæra........................69281
Graham, M. C. Stories of the foot-hills....22730
  Contents: The Withrow water right.—Alex Randall's conversion.—Idy.—Complicity of Enoch Embody.—Em. —Colonel Bob Jarvis.—Brice.
Graham, P. A. The red scaur.................54330
Graham, S. Golden milestone................25140
Grahame, J. Birds of Scotland, with other poems. 1807...................................821.2 306
Grahame, K. Golden age (stories)..........21060
Grail. Nameless city...........................15520
Grainger. Poems ; with life................821.2 35
Grand. Heavenly twins........................34305
  Ideala...34306
  Our manifold nature.........................34308
  Contents: Eugenia. — The yellow leaf. — Janey, a humble administrator. — Boomellen. — Kane, a soldier servant.—Ah Man.
  Singularly deluded...........................34307

Grant, A. C. Bush-life in Queensland........62527
Grant, Mrs. Anne, of Laggan. Correspondence. 1845. 3 v................826.2 20
.Letters from the mountain. 1845. 2 v..826.2 23
 Same. 1809. 3 v.....................826.2 25
Grant, Charles. Stories of Naples and the Camorra............................62356
Grant, James. Adventures of an aide-de-camp...................................6413
 The Cameronians........................6427
 Captain of the guard....................6412
 Dick Rodney.............................6420
 First love and last love................6409
 Frank Hilton............................6423
 Girl he married.........................6411
 Jack Manley.............................6416
 Jane Seton..............................6415
 Laura Everingham.......................6408
 Legends of the black watch..............6401
 Letty Hyde's lovers.....................6410
 Mary of Lorraine........................6421
 Phantom regiment........................6406
 Phillip Rollo...........................6425
 Rob Roy.................................6422
 Second to none..........................6404
 Yellow frigate..........................6426
Grant, Maria M. Artiste.....................37506
 My heart's in the highlands.............37503
 Prince Hugo.............................37504
 Sun maid................................37502
 Victor Lescar...........................37501
Grant, R. Average man.......................60908
 Bachelor's Christmas, etc...............60905
  Contents: Bachelor's Christmas.—An eye for an eye. In fly time. — Richard and Robin. — The Matrimonial tontine benefit association.— By hook or crook.
 Confessions of a frivolous girl.........60901
 Face to face............................60906
 Jack Hall...............................042701
 Jack in the bush........................042702
 Knave of hearts.........................60910
 The lambs: a tragedy. 1883..........827.1 2
 Little tin gods-on-wheels. 1880......827.1 17
 Mrs. Harold Stagg.......................60904
 Opinions of philosopher.................60912
 Reflections of a married man............60909
 Romantic young lady.....................60911
Grant, R., *et al.* King's men..............62373
Granville, C. Sapphire ring.................31150
Granville, Harriet, *countess.* Letters, 1810-45; ed. by Gower. 1894. 2v...826.2 113
Grattan, H. Miscellaneous works. 1822...329.2 63
 Select speeches. 1831................*in* 329.2 22
 Select speeches. 1845...................329.2 24
Grattan, T. C. Jacqueline of Holland......62568
Graves, C. L. The Hawarden Horace. 1895...................................827.2 47
 More Hawarden Horace. 1896........827.2 48

Graves, Clo. Field of tares................22260
Gray, A. Letters. 1893. 2 v..............925.1 15
Gray, Barry, *pseud.* See Coffin, R. B.
Gray, David, (*Buffalo*). Last of the Kah-Kwahs: poem....................821.1 Pam. 29
 Letters, poems, etc.; ed. by Larned. 1888..............................821.1 578
 Ministry of art : poem. 1864....821.1 Pam. 28
 New year's item in verse. 1870..821.1 Pam. 27
 Poem ; N. Y. state editorial association. 1885...............................821.1 Pam. 30
Gray, David, (*Glasgow*). Poetical works. 821.2 495
Gray, E. McQ. Elsa.......................23020
 My stewardship..........................23021
Gray, Maxwell, *pseud.* (M. G. Tuttiett.)
 Costly freak............................23206
 In the heart of the storm...............23203
 Innocent impostor, etc..................23205
 Last sentence...........................23204
 Reproach of Annesley....................23202
 Silence of Dean Maitland................23201
Gray, Thomas. Elegy, and other poems. 821.2 163
 Elegy, etc., in N. Y. point, for the blind. 1896............................362.4 N-Y-15
  Contents: Elegy in a country churchyard.—Odes on the pleasure arising from vicissitude.—A distant prospect of Eton college.—The bard.
 Poems. 1775.........................821.2 182
 Same. 1871..........................821.2 182A
 Same ; with life. 1822..............821.2 37
 Works ; ed. by Gosse. 1884. 4 v.
  V. 1. Poems.—Journals.—Essays.....820.2 119
  V. 2-3. Letters...................820.2 120
  V. 4. Notes on Aristophanes and Plato.....820.2 122
Gray, W. T. Bad boy abroad................62331
Graydon. In the days of Washington......036201
Grayson. Standish the Puritan.............20412
Great Britain. The lords and the franchise bill: debates. 1884..........329.2 72
Greeley. Address, Hamilton college......40 23
 Hints toward reforms. 1857..........824.1 70
Green, Anna K., (*Mrs.* Rohlfs). Behind closed doors............................63505
 Cynthia Wakeham's money................63511
 Defence of the bride, etc. (verse). 1882. ....821.1 384
 Doctor, his wife, and the clock.........63516
 Doctor Izard............................63517
 Forsaken inn............................63508
 Hand and ring...........................63510
 Hand und Ring (German).................63509
 Hinter verschlossenen Thüren [Behind closed doors]........................63505K
 Leavenworth case........................63504
 Marked. 'Personal.'.....................63514
 Matter of millions......................63512
 Mill mystery............................63522

Miss Hurd..63515
Old stone house, etc.....................................63513
Risifi's daughter : a drama. 1887.......822.1 25
Schein und Schuld [The Leavenworth
   case]..63504G
7 to 12...63501
Strange disappearance...............................63503
Sword of Damocles....................................63502
That affair next door....................................63518
Verlassene Gasthaus [The forsaken inn]..63507
X. Y. Z..63506
Green, E. E. Arnold Inglehurst...............31008
   Dominique's vengeance..........................031007
   Golden Gwendolyn.................................31005
   Mistress of Lydgate priory......................31004
   Secret chamber at Chad.........................031005
   Shut in..31007
   Tom Heron of Sax...................................31006
   Young pioneers..031006
Green, H. Shakespeare and the emblem
   writers. 1870.......................................822.3 77
Green, J. R. Stray studies, England and
   Italy..824.2 278
Green, M. Poems ; with life................821.2 37
Greene, A. D. Peter and Polly..................56901
Greene, Batchelder, *pseud.* Reflections.
   1886..829.1 26
Greene, Belle C. New England conscience..69131
Greene, G. W. Historical studies. '50....824.1 33
Greene, H. Blind brother............................09520
   Burnham breaker.....................................09521
   Riverpark rebellion..................................09522
Greene, L. L. Burtons of Burton hall........07602
   Cushions, and corners...........................07605
   Filling up the chinks................................07606
   Gray house on the hill............................07601
   Little castle maiden................................07603
   School-boy baronet................................07604
Greene, R. Dramatic and poetical works;
   ed. by Dyce. 1861............................822.2 101
   Contents : Life, etc.—Orlando Furioso.—Looking-
   glass for London and England.—Friar Bacon and Friar
   Bungay.—James IV.—Alphonsus, king of Arragon.—
   George-a-Greene, Pinner of Wakefield.—Ballads and
   poems.
   Green pastures : extracts made by Gro-
      sart. 1894......................................829.2 72
   Life and works ; ed. by Grosart. 1881-6.
      15 v.
      V. 1. Storojenko's ' Life of Greene '..........820.2 492
      V. 2. Mamillia.—Anatomie of flatterie..........820.2 493
      V. 3. A myrrour of modestie.— Morando.—
         Arbasto..820.2 494
      V. 4. The carde of fancie. Debate betweene
         Follie and Love.— Pandosto................820.2 495
      V. 5. Planetomachin. Penelope's web. The
         Spanish masquerado.........................820.2 496
      V. 6. Menaphon : Camilla's alarum to slumber-
         ing Euphues. Euphues, his censure to Philautus.
         ....820.2 497

V. 7. Perimedes the black-smithe.—Ciceronis
   amor.—The royal exchange.....................820.2 498
V. 8. Greene's ' Never too late.'— Francesco's
   fortunes..820.2 499
V. 9. Alcida.—Greene's 'Mourning garment.'— •
   Greene's ' Farewell to folly '........................820.2 500
V. 10. A notable discovery of coosnage.—'Conny-
   catching '; pts. 2-3,— A disputation betweene a
   hee and shee conny-catcher.....................820.2 501
V. 11. The blacke booke's messenger.—Defence
   of conny-catching.— Philomela.— A quippe for an
   upstart courtier..820.2 502
Plays. 2 v...820.2 504
Greene, *Mrs.* Sarah P. McLean. See Mc-
   Lean, Sarah P.
Greenleaf. King Sham, etc. 1868........828.1 44
Greenough, *Mrs.* R. Mary Magdalene :
   poem. 1882...821.1 447
Greenough, *Mrs.* S. D. In extremis..........20445
Greenwell. Essays. 1866........................204 21
   Poems ; with biography by Dorling...821.2 837
Greenwood, F. W. P. Miscellaneous
   writings..824.1 69
Greenwood, Fred. Lover's lexicon. '94.....819 61
Greenwood, Grace, (*Mrs.* S. J. Lippin-
   cott). Forest tragedy, etc..........................30414
   Greenwood leaves....................................30413
   Records of five years. 1867.........824.1 139
   Stories from famous ballads..................018801
Greenwood, J. Fair Phyllis of Lavender
   Wharf..53640
   In strange company............................824.2 228
Greer, *Mrs.* J. R. Society of Friends........20414
Greer, T. Modern Dædalus......................62350
Greey. Bear-worshippers of Yezo..........027103
   Wonderful city of Tokio.......................*915.2 21
   Young Americans in Japan....................027101
Greg, Percy. Across the zodiac..............61101
Greg, W. R. Enigmas of life. 1873.........304 6
   Literary and social judgments. 1873..824.2 201
   Miscellaneous essays. 1882.................824.2 143
   Same ; 2d series. 1884.......................824.2 144
   Political and social science. 1853. 2 v...329.2 46
   Political problems. 1870......................329.2 44
   Rocks ahead. 1875.................................304 5
Grendel. Contrasts....................................62520
Greville, *Lady* V. Faiths and fashions..824.2 284
Grey, *Mrs.* E. C. Bosom friend.—Gam-
   bler's wife.—Young husband.................14130
Grey, R. Story of Chris...........................28010
Greyson, R. E. H. See Rogers, H.
Gribble. Things that matter.....................69840
Grier. His excellency's English governess...31901
   Uncrowned king......................................31902
Griffin, G. W. Studies in literature. '71..824.1 107
Griffin, Gerald. Colleen bawn ; or, The
   collegians..21204
   Poetical works, etc............................821.2 120
   Tales of the five senses..........................21203

* Of interest to young readers.

Tales of the Munster-festivals............21202
Talis qualis..................................21201
Griffith, Cecil, *pseud.* See **Becket, Mrs. S.**
Griffiths. Lola..............................44124
Grimoald. Poems................*in* 821.2 146
    Songs and sonnets.................820.2 36
Griswold. Hugo Blanc.....................52248
Groome. Kriegspiel, the war game.......36701
Grote, A. R. Rip Van Winkle, and other poems. 1882....................821.1 189
Grote, G. Minor works. 1873......824.2 145
    Contents: Critical estimate of character and writings; by Alexander Bain. — Parliamentary reform. — Molesworth's edition of Hobbes.—Grecian legends and early history.— Review of Boeckh.— Addresses.— Review of Lewis on the credibility of early Roman history.—Plato on the rotation of the earth.—Review of Mill on Hamilton.—Philosophy.
Grove. Mexican mystery....................20425
Grundy. Days of his vanity................31040
Guernsey. Chevalier's daughter..........20720
    Loveday's history...........................20721
    Through unknown ways..................20722
Guildford. Owl and nightingale......821.2 454
Guiney. Goose-quill papers. 1885....824.1 122
    Lovers' Saint Ruth's, etc....................55601
    Contents: Lovers' Saint Ruth's. — Our lady of the Union.—An event on the river.—The provider.
    Patrins. 1897...........................824.1 320
    The white sail, etc. (poems). 1888....821.1 383
Gunsaulus, Phidias, and other poems. 1891.................................821.1 442
Gurney. Tertium quid: chapters on disputed questions. 1887. 2 v........824.2 410
Gurteen. The epic of the fall of man: Cædmon, Dante, Milton. 1896......821.2 1021
Guthrie. See **Anstey, F.**
H., C. G., *pseud.* See **Fay, T. S.**
H., H. See **Hunt, Helen.**
Habberton. All he knew...................52803
    Barton experiment..........................52806
    Bowsham puzzle............................52822
    Brueton's bayou.............................52802
    Chautauquans................................52807
    Country luck..................................52823
    Helen's babies................................52801
    Jericho road...................................52811
    Just one day..................................52820
    Little Guzzy...................................52819
    Other people's children....................52815
    Out at Twinnett's............................52824
    Scripture club of Valley Rest.............52814
    Some folks....................................52818
    Who was Paul Grayson?...................026201
    Worst boy in town..........................52821
Habington. Castara....................820.2 35
Hack. Winter evenings....................05001
Hackett. Essay on Falstaff...............40 27
Haddock. Addresses, etc. 1846......825.1 16

Hadermann (Mrs. J. R. Walworth). Dead men's shoes.................................21104
    Forgiven at last..............................21105
    New man at Rossmere....................21108
    Nobody's business..........................21106
    Old Fulkerson's clerk......................21107
    Scruples..21103
    Without a blemish..........................21102
Haggard. Allan Quatermain.............17020
    Allen's wife, etc.............................17021
    Contents: Allen's wife.—Hunter Quatermain's story. —A tale of three lions.—Long odds.
    Beatrice...17022
    Cleopatra......................................17023
    Colonel Quaritch, V. C....................17024
    Dawn...17025
    Eric Brighteyes...............................17026
    Heart of the world..........................17037
    Jess...17027
    Joan Haste.....................................17038
    King Solomon's mines....................17028
    Maiwa's revenge............................17029
    Mr. Meeson's will...........................17030
    Montezuma's daughter...................17031
    Nada the lily..................................17032
    People of the mist..........................17036
    She...17033
    Witch's head...................................17034
    Wizard..17039
Haggard *and* **Lang.** World's desire...17035
Hains. Captain Gore's courtship........43901
Hake. Within sound of the weir.........35910
Haldane. Chord from a violin...........36720
Hale, E. E. Back to back..................15130
    Christmas eve and Christmas day....15111
    Christmas in Narragansett...............15117
    Crusoe in New York........................15114
    Daily bread.....................................15119
    East and west................................15126
    Fortunes of Rachel........................15116
    Four and five..................................15123
    G. T. T..15103
    His level best, etc...........................15102
    Contents: The brick moon.—Water talk.—Mouse and lion.—The modern Sindbad.—A tale of a salamander.—The queen of California.—Confidence.
    How they lived at Hampton.............15120
    If Jesus came to Boston...................15127
    If, yes and perhaps........................15109
    Contents: The children of the public.—A piece of possible history.—The South American editor.—The old and the new, face to face.—The dot and line alphabet.—The last voyage of the Resolute.—My double and how he undid me.— The man without a country.—The last of the Florida.—The skeleton in the closet.—Christmas waits in Boston.
    In his name....................................*15105
    Ingham papers...............................15107

* Of interest to young readers.

Contents: Memoir of Captain Ingham.—The good-natured pendulum.— Paul Jones and Denis Duval.— Round the world in a hack.—Friends' meeting.—Did he take the prince to ride?—How Mr. Frye would have preached it.—The rag-man and the rag-woman.—Dinner speaking.—Good society.—Daily bread.

Man without a country..........................*15122
Same...*in* 15109
Mr. Tangier's vacations.........................15118
Mrs. Merriam's scholars.........................15113
My friend the boss..............................15121
Our Christmas in a palace.......................15115
Our new crusade.................................15106
Philip Nolan's friends..........................15101
Sunday-school stories...........................15128
Susan's escort, etc.............................15131
Sybaris and other homes.........................15108
Sybil Knox......................................15124
Ten times one is ten...........................*15112
Ups and downs...................................15110

Hale, E. E. *and* **L. P.** New Harry and Lucy...15125
Hale, Lucretia P. Last of the Peterkins..030702
Peterkin papers................................030701
Hale, Sarah J. Liberia.......................19146
Hales. Folia litteraria. 1893..........824.2 464
Notes and essays on Shakespeare.......822.3 256
Haliburton. Nature and human nature.....19160
Old judge......................................19159
Sam Slick's wise saws.....................828.2 34
Season ticket..................................19158
Yankee stories.................................19161
Yankee yarns...................................19163
Hall, Alice C. Miss Leighton's perplexities..62595
Hall, Captain C. W. Adrift in the ice fields..04601
Drifting around the world......................04602
Twice taken....................................19172
Hall, Gertrude. Far from to-day.............15710
Foam of the sea, etc...........................15711
Hall, G. S. Aspects of German culture..824.1 160
Hall, John. Historical expostulation...821.2 454
Hall, Joseph. Works. 1837. 12 v........230 262
(For contents, see FINDING LIST, pt. 3, p. 473.)
Hall, Marie S. Andrew Marvel and his friends...55650
Hall, Mary L. Live coals: poems. '78..821.1 512
Hall, R. Works. 1861. 6 v...............240 42
(For contents, see FINDING LIST, pt. 3, p. 483.)
Hall, Mrs. S. C. Kate Kemp................017701
Midsummer eve..................................25102
Tales of woman's trials........................25101
White boy......................................25104
Hallam, A. H. Remains, verse and prose......................................821.2 318
Halleck. Alnwick Castle, etc. 1836....821.1 31
Fanny (poem). 1819.........................821.1 437
Poetical works. 1852.......................821.1 32

Halliday. Sunnyside papers. 1866......824.2 176
Halliwell-Phillips. Curiosities of modern Shaksperian criticism...............822.3 Pam. 9
Dictionary of old English plays. '60..822.2 211
Memoranda on 'All's well that ends well,' 'Two gentlemen of Verona,' 'Much ado about nothing,' 'Titus Andronicus.' 1879....................822.3 352
Memoranda on 'Hamlet.' 1879.........822.3 353
Memoranda on 'Love's labour's lost,' 'King John,' 'Othello,' 'Romeo and Juliet.' 1879.........................822.3 355
Memoranda on 'Midsummer night's dream.' 1879.........................822.3 354
Outlines of the life of Shakespeare. '86. 2 v....................................822.3 B-33
Shakesperiana: catalogue. 1841......822.3 161
Which shall it be—Shaxpeare or Shakespeare? 1879....................822.3 Pam. 18
Halliwell-Phillips, *ed.* Illustrations of fairy mythology of 'Midsummer night's dream.' (Shakespeare society, 1845.)
....822.3 47
Interlude of the four elements........821.2 465
Man in the moone.........................821.2 472
Marriage of wit and wisdom. 1846....822.3 46
Meetings of gallants at an ordinarie..821.2 448
Moral play of wit and science..........822.2 74
Notices of fugitive tracts..............821.2 472
Pleasant conceits of old Hobson......821.2 452
Romance of Syr Tryamoure.............821.2 459
Romance of the Emperor Octavian...821.2 457
Song of Lady Bessy.....................821.2 463
Triall of treasure......................821.2 471
Use of dice-play........................821.2 472
Westward for smelts, stories..........821.2 465
Halpin. Oberon's vision. (Shakespeare society, 1843.)..........................822.3 48
Halpine. See **O'Reilly, Miles.**
Halsey. Two of us.........................56840
Halstead. See **Elbon, Barbara.**
Hamerton, Eugenie. Golden mediocrity...69250
Mirror of truth................................03501
Hamerton, P. G. Art essays. 1881........704 18
Chapters on animals........................*596 5
Harry Blount..................................03502
Human intercourse. 1884.........824.2 362
Intellectual life. 1873....................374 5
Isles of Loch Awe, and other poems. '85.
....821.2 620
Marmorne....................................12056
Portfolio papers. 1889....................704 30
(For contents, see FINDING LIST, pt. 3, p. 412.)
Round my house. 1876...................914.4 58
Sylvan year. 1876.........................829.2 36
Same; and Unknown river..............829.2 37
Thoughts about art. 1871................704 12

* Of interest to young readers.

Unknown river	829.2 37
Wenderholme	12055
Hamilton, A. K. One of the Duanes	69121
Hamilton, Alexander. Federalist, etc.	
1810. 3 v.	329.1 37
Papers	329.1 40
Reference list; by Foster. v. 1	16 55
Works. 1851. 7 v.	329.1 27
Same. 1810. 3 v.	329.1 34
Hamilton, C. B. Ropes of sand	20477
Woven of many threads	20478
Hamilton, C. V. Crown from a spear	25847
Hamilton, E. Lee-. Apollo and Marsyas, and other poems. 1884	821.2 741
Hamilton, Gail, *pseud.* (Mary A. Dodge).	
Child world	023101
Country living and country thinking. 1877	824.1 91
First love is best	20480
Gala days. 1863	917 64
Little folk life	023102
Sermons to the clergy. 1876	204 55
Skirmishes and sketches. 1865	824.1 88
Summer rest. 1866	824.1 90
Twelve miles from a lemon. 1874	824.1 89
Hamilton, Janet. Poems, essays, etc.	821.2 649
Hamilton, K. W. Parson's proxy	69591
Rachel's share of the road	69590
Hamilton, M. Across an Ulster bog	57021
McLeod of the Camerons	57022
A self-denying ordinance	57020
Hamilton, T. Cyril Thornton	44120
Hamilton, William. Poems; with life	821.2 38
Hamlen. Chats	032501
Hamley, E. B. Lady Lee's widowhood	54301
Hamley, W. G. Guilty or not guilty	54302
Traseaden hall	54303
Hamlin, Myra S. Nan at Camp Chicopee	037301
Politician's daughter	69254
Hammond, *Mrs.* **E. H.** The Georgians	63407
Hammond, J. Poems. 1822	*in* 821.2 46
Hammond, W. A. Doctor Grattan	18401
Lal	18408
Mr. Oldmixon	18403
On the Susquehanna	18406
Robert Severne	18407
Strong-minded woman	18404
Hammond, W. A., *and* **Lanza, C.** Tales of eccentric life	18405
Hancock. Montanas	44101
Hanna. Essays. 1861	824.2 146
Hannah Hewitt. 3 v.	50337
Hannah Tarne	58991
Hannay. Singleton Fontenoy	14154
Hansen. Legend of Hamlet. 1887	822.3 Pam. 16
Hanson. Old Greek stories. 1883	*883 51
Harben. Land of the changing sun	43280
Harding. Jack Stapleton	58101
Hardman. Peninsular scenes and sketches	19115
Hardwick, *ed.* Passion of Saint George	821.2 471
Poem on the times of Edward II.	821.2 471
Hardy, A. S. F. Princess and priest. — Mademoiselle Étienne	21330
Hardy, A. S. But yet a woman	12101
Justina	12104
Passe Rose	12102
Wind of destiny	12107
Hardy, Iza D. Love, honor and obey. 3 v.	65301
New Othello	65304
Hardy, R. F. Tom Telfer's shadow	69278
Hardy, Thomas. Art of; by L. Johnson. 1894	823 118
Desperate remedies	13111
Distracted young preacher	13114
Far from the madding crowd	13101
Fellow-townsmen	13116
Group of noble dames, etc.	13103
Contents: The first countess of Wessex.—Barbara, of the house of Grebe.—The marchioness of Stonehenge.—Lady Mottisfont.—The Lady Icenway.—Squire Petrick's lady.—Anna, Lady Baxby.—The Lady Penelope.—The duchess of Hamptonshire. — The honorable Laura.	
Hand of Ethelberta	13104
Jude the obscure (Hearts insurgent)	13109
Laodicean	13118
Life's little ironies, etc.	13105
Contents: The son's veto.—For conscience's sake.—A tragedy of two ambitions.—On the western circuit.—To please his wife.—The melancholy hussar of the German legion.—The fiddler of the reels.—A tradition of 1804. —A few crusted characters.	
Mayor of Casterbridge	13125
Pair of blue eyes	13106
Return of the native	13112
Romantic adventures of a milkmaid	13124
Tess of the D'Urberville's	13107
Trumpet major	13115
Two on a tower	13121
Under the greenwood tree	13108
The well-beloved	13110
Wessex tales, etc.	13113
Contents: The three strangers.—The withered arm.—Fellow-townsmen.—Interlopers at the Knap.—The distracted preacher.	
Woodlanders	13102
Hardy, T. D. Present state of the Shakesperian controversy. 1860	822.3 Pam. 13
Hare, J. C. *and* **A. W.** Guesses at truth	829.2 17
Hargreaves. Paul Romer	41401
Poste restante	41402
Harlan. Fate of Marcel	62332
Harland, Harry. See **Luska, Sidney.**	
Harland, Marion. See **Terhune,** *Mrs.* **M. V.**	
Harman. Caveat of warening for commen cursetors	820.2 405

* Of interest to young readers.

Harraden. Hilda Strafford...................32303
  In varying moods (stories).................32302
  Ships that pass in the night..............32301
  Things will take a turn....................041001
Harris, F. Elder Conklin, etc..............43120
Harris, J. C. (Uncle Remus, *pseud.*).
  Balaam and his master, etc................16703
    Contents: Balaam and his master.—Conscript's Christmas.—Ananias.—Where's Duncan?—Mom Bi.—The old Bascom place.
  Daddy Jake the runaway...................016714
  Free Joe, etc...............................16702
    Contents: Free Joe.—Little Compton.—Aunt Fountain's prisoner.—Trouble on Lost mountain.—Azalia.
  Little Mr. Thimblefinger..................016711
  Mingo, etc..................................16701
    Contents: Mingo.—At Teague Poteet's.—Blue Dave.—A piece of land.
  Mr. Rabbit at home........................016712
  Nights with Uncle Remus. 1883......*828.1 68
  On the plantation..........................016710
  Sister Jane..................................16704
  Story of Aaron.............................016713
  Uncle Remus and his friends. 1892...*828.1 61
  Uncle Remus, his songs and sayings..*828.1 60
Harris, Miriam C. Frank Warrington.......9816
  Happy Go Lucky............................9831
  Louie's last term at St. Mary's............9809
  Missy..9821
  Perfect Adonis..............................9805
  Phœbe..9835
  Richard Vandermarck......................9817
  Roundhearts, etc...........................01601
  Rutledge....................................9801
  St. Phillip's.................................9802
  Sutherlands.................................9804
  Utter failure................................9803
Harrison, A. Martha's vineyard...............56882
Harrison, *Mrs.* B. The Anglomaniacs......10020
  Bachelor maid..............................10027
  Bar Harbor days...........................10022
  Belhaven tales, etc........................10025
    Contents: Belhaven tales.—Crow's nest.—Una and King David.
  Bric-a-brac stories.........................032210
  Daughter of the south, etc................10023
    Contents: Daughter of the south.—Thorn in his cushion.—Mr. Clendenning Piper.—Jenny, the débutante.—Wife's love.—Harp unstrung.—Suit decided.
  Edelweiss of the Sierras, etc..............10024
    Contents: Edelweiss of the Sierras.—Golden-rod.—Under the convent wall.—Cherrycote.—Shattered violin.—House built upon the sand.—On a hill-top.
  Errant wooing..............................10028
  Flower de Hundred.......................10021
  Merry maid of Arcady, etc................10030
    Contents: The merry maid of Arcady.—Worrosquoyacke.—Leaves from the diary of Ruth Marchmont, spinster.—Thirteen at table.—At a winter house-party.—The secret of San Juan.—The stranger within thy gate.—His lordship.

Son of the Old Dominion...................10031
Sweet bells out of tune.....................10026
Virginia cousin, etc.........................10029
  Contents: Virginia cousin. — Out of season. —On Frenchman's bay.
Harrison, F. B. Brothers in arms...........032208
  Masaniello..................................69294
Harrison, F. Choice of books, etc..824.2 384
  Studies in early Victorian literature. '95...820 62
Harrison, J. A. A group of poets. '75..824.1 133
Harrison, J. B. Certain dangerous tendencies in American life, etc. 1880...824.1 150
Harrison, Joanna. Northern lily............69262
Harrison, *Major* S. Queen of the arena..69211
Harrison, *Mrs.* W. See **Malet, Lucas.**
Harry and his homes.........................07140
Harsha. Timid brave.........................69234
Hart, *Mrs.* F. Harry (verse). 1877....821.2 429
  Miss Hitchcock's wedding dress..........53301
  Mrs. Jerningham's journal. 1876......821.2 430
  Very genteel................................53304
  Very young couple........................53307
Hart, G. In the rapids.......................44104
Hart, J. C. Marian Coffin....................56872
Hart, Mabel. From harvest to hay-time...14821
  Two English girls..........................14820
Harte, Bret. Argonauts of North Liberty....12807
  Barker's luck, etc..........................12833
    Contents: Barker's luck.—A yellow dog.—Mother of five.—Bulger's reputation.—In the tules.—Convert of the mission.—Indiscretion of Elsbeth.—Devotion of Enriquez.
  Bell-ringer of Angel's, etc.................12824
    Contents: The bell-ringer of Angel's.—Johnnyboy.—Young Robin Gray.—The sheriff of Siskyon.—A rose of Glenbogie.—The mystery of the hacienda.—Chu Chu.—My first book.
  By shore and sedge.......................12829
    Contents: An apostle of the tules.—Sarah Walker.—A ship of '49.
  Clarence....................................12827
  Colonel Starbottle's client, etc............12820
    Contents: Colonel Starbottle's client.— Post-mistress of Laurel Run. — Night at 'Hays.' — Johuson's old woman.—New assistant at Pine Clearing school.—In a pioneer restaurant.—Treasure of the galleon.—Out of a pioneer's trunk.—Ghosts of Stukeley castle.
  Condensed novels........................12801
  Cressy.......................................12810
  Crusade of the Excelsior..................12809
  Devil's ford.................................*in* 12802
  Drift from Redwood camp................*in* 12806
  Drift from two shores.....................12815
    Contents: The man on the beach.—Two saints of the foot-hills.—Jinny.—Roger Catron's friend.—Who was my quiet friend?—A ghost of the Sierras.—The hoodlum band : a condensed novel.—The man whose yoke was not easy.— My friend the tramp.—The man from Solano.—The office seeker.—A sleeping car experience.— Five o'clock in the morning.—With the entrées.
  East and west: poems. 1871..........821.1 148
  Echoes of the foot-hills. 1875..........821.1 149

* Of interest to young readers.

First family of Tasajara............................12818
Flip.—Found at Blazing Star...................12819
Gabriel Conroy..12825
Heritage of Dedlow marsh, etc..............12811
   Contents: Heritage of Dedlow marsh.— Knight errant of the foot-hills.—Secret of Telegraph hill. Captain Jim's friend.
In a hollow of the hills...........................12831
In the Carquinez woods..........................12826
Luck of Roaring camp, etc......................12808
   Contents: The outcasts of Poker Flat. Miggles.—Tennessee's pardner.—The idyl of Red Gulch.—Brown of Calaveras.— High-water mark.—A lonely ride.—The man of no account.—M'liss.—The right eye of the commander.—Notes by flood and field.—Mission Dolores.—John Chinaman.—From a back window.—Boonder.
Maruja..12830
Millionaire of Rough-and-Ready............12802
Mrs. Skagg's husbands............................12803
   Contents: Mrs. Skagg's husbands.— How Santa Claus came to Simpson's Bar.—The princess Bob and her friends.—The Iliad of Sandy Bar.—Mr. Thompson's prodigal.—The romance of Madroño Hollow.—The poet of Sierra Flat.—The Christmas gift that came to Rupert.—Urban sketches.—Legends and tales.
On the frontier..12828
   Contents: At the mission of San Carmel.—A blue grass Penelope.—Left out on Lone Star mountain.
Phyllis of the Sierras..............................12806
Poems. 1871...................................821.1 146
Poetical works. 1882......................821.1 147
Protégée of Jack Hamlin's, etc...............12823
   Contents: A protégée of Jack Hamlin's.—An ingénue of the Sierras.—The reformation of James Reddy.—The heir of the McHulishes.—An episode of West Woodlands.—The home-coming of Jim Wilkes.
Queen of the pirate isle........................032236
Sally Dows, etc.......................................12822
   Contents: Sally Dows.—Conspiracy of Mrs. Bunker.—Transformation of Buckeye camp.—Their uncle from California.
Sappho of Green Springs, etc................12816
   Contents: Sappho of Green Springs.—Chatelaine of Burnt Ridge.—Through the Santa Clara wheat.—A Mæcenas of the Pacific slope.
Snow-bound at Eagle's...........................12832
Story of a mine......................................12805
Susy..12821
Tales of the Argonauts, etc....................12812
   Contents: The rose of Tuolumne.—A passage in the life of Mr. John Oakhurst.—Wan Lee, the pagan.—How old man Plunkett went home.—The fool of Five Forks.—Baby Sylvester.—An episode of Fiddletown.—A Jersey centenarian.
Thankful Blossom....................................12804
Twins of Table mountain........................12817
Two men of Sandy Bar: drama. 1876..822.1 15
   Same. 1882.................................821.1 147
Waif of the plains...................................12813
Ward of the Golden Gate.......................12814
Hartley, *Mrs.* W. N. See Laffan, May.
Hartzell. Application and achievement.
   1891...824.1 36
Wanderings on Parnassus. 1884......821.1 379

Harvey, G. Works; ed. by Grosart. 3v...820.2 9
Harvey, J. C., *and* Wilson, T. B. After
   many days..58810
Harwood, Isabella. Kathleen...............14169
   Raymond's heroine................................14170
Harwood, J. B. Lady Egeria....................56711
Haskins. Essays and lects....................824.1 171
   Miscellaneous writings......................824.1 171
Hassaurek. Secret of the Andes...............56828
Hastings, Elizabeth, *pseud.* See Sherwood, M.
Hatch. Under the cedars..........................52261
Hatton. Banishment of Jessop Blythe........61411
   Christopher Kenrick................................61405
   Cigarette papers......................................61408
   Clytie..61403
   John Needham's double..........................61406
   Old house at Sandwich...........................61407
   Princess Mazaroff....................................61409
   Tallants of Barton...................................61404
   Three recruits..61401
   Under the great seal................................61410
   When Greek meets Greek......................61412
Havelok the Dane, Lay of; tr. by Wyatt..821.2 858
Haven. Coopers..44131
   Loss and gain..44132
Havergal. Life echoes (poems). '83....821.2 714
   Poems. 1881..................................821.2 582
Havers. See Gift, Theo.
Haweis. Poets in the pulpit. 1880......824.2 282
   Contents: Longfellow. — Tennyson. — Browning.—Keble.—George Herbert.—Wordsworth.—Gleanings.
Hawes. Pastime of pleasure...............821.2 461
Hawker, Mary. See Falconer, Lanoe, *pseud.*
Hawkes. Footprints of former men in
   far Cornwall. 1870......................824.2 220
Hawkesworth. Adventurer. 1793...*in* 824.2 53
   Same. 3 v......................................824.2 16
   See also, Adventurer, p. 99.
Hawley. Address, Young men's association,
   Buffalo. 1836.....................................40 27
Hawthorne, J. American penman..............9711
   Archibald Malmaison...............................9707
   Beatrix Randolph.....................................9722
   Bressant..9702
   Confessions and criticisms. 1887......824.1 221
   David Poindexter's disappearance..........9712
   Dream and a forgetting...........................9715
   Dust..9714
   Fool of nature...9719
   Fortune's fool..9718
   Garth..9704
   Golden fleece..9717
   Great bank robbery.................................9709
   Idolatry..9701
   John Parmelee's curse............................9728
   Judith Armytage..............................*in* 32715

Laughing mill	9713
Love is a spirit	9720
Love—or a name	9727
Millicent and Rosalind	9716
Mrs. Gainsborough's diamonds	9706
Noble blood	9724
Prince Sarony's wife, etc.	9708
Sebastian Strome	9710
Sinfire	9703
Tragic mystery	9705

Hawthorne, N. American note-books. 1881. 2 v.............917.1 129
Blithedale romance.................7709
Doctor Grimshawe's secret............7711
Dolliver romance..................7715
English note-books. 1866. 2 v......914.2 56
Fanshawe, etc....................7723
French and Italian note-books. 1876...914.5 29
Grandfather's chair...............972 51
    Same............................*in* 1001
House of seven gables...............7708
Marble Faun.......................7713
Mosses from an old manse.............7705
    Contents: The old manse.—The birthmark.—A select party.—Young goodman Brown.—Rappaccini's daughter.—Mrs. Bullfrog.—Fire worship.—Buds and bird voices.—Monsieur du Miroir.—The hall of fantasy.—The celestial railroad.—The procession of life.—Feathertop: a moralized legend.—The new Adam and Eve.—Egotism, or the bosom serpent.—The Christmas banquet.—Drowne's wooden image.—The intelligence office.—Roger Malvin's burial.—P.'s correspondence.—Earth's holocaust.—Passages from a relinquished work.—Sketches from memory.—The old apple dealer.— The artist of the beautiful.—A virtuoso's collection.

Our old home. 1863..............914.2 54
Scarlet letter.—Blithedale romance.........7724
Septimius Felton..................7722
Sketches and studies..............824.1 191
    Contents: Life of Franklin Pierce.—Chiefly about war matters.— Alice Doane's appeal.— The ancestral footstep.—Appendix.

Snow image, etc...................7710
    Contents: The snow image.—The great stone face.—Main street.—Ethan Brand.—A belle's biography.—Sylph Etherege.—The Canterbury pilgrims.—Old news.—The man of adamant.—The devil in manuscript.—John Inglefield's thanksgiving.—Old Ticonderoga.—The wives of the dead.—Little Daffydowndilly.—Major Molineux.

Tanglewood tales...................01002
Twice-told tales....................7701
    Contents: The gray champion.—Sunday at home.—The wedding knell.—The minister's black veil.—The May-pole of Merry Mount.—The gentle boy.—Mr. Higginbotham's catastrophe.—Little Annie's ramble.—Wakefield.—A rill from the town pump.—The great carbuncle.—The prophetic pictures.—David Swan.—Sights from a steeple.—The hollow of the three hills.—The toll-gatherer's day.—The vision of the fountain.—Fancy's show box.—Dr. Heidegger's experiment.—Legends of the Province house: Howe's masquerade; Edward Randolph's portrait; Lady Eleanore's mantle;

Old Esther Dudley.—The haunted mind.—The village uncle.—The ambitious guest.—The sister years.—Snowflakes.—The seven vagabonds.—The whiteold maid.—Peter Goldthwaite's treasure.—Chippings with a chisel.—The Shaker bridal.— Night sketches.— Endicott and the red cross,—The lily's quest.—Foot-prints on the seashore.— Edward Fane's rosebud.— The three-fold destiny.

Wonder book, etc..................01001
Hawtrey. Corydalis (verse). 1880........821.2 564
Hay, Elzey, *pseud.* See **Andrews, Fannie.**
Hay, J. Pike county ballads, etc. 1878....821.1 215
    Poems. 1890....................821.1 418
Hay, M. C. Among the ruins, etc...........2608
    Arundel motto.....................2607
    Back to the old home..............2612
    Bid me discourse, etc.............2602
    Brenda Yorke, etc.................2633
    Dark inheritance..................2611
    Dorothy's venture.................2630
    For her dear sake.................2623
    He stoops to conquer...........*in* 2633
    Hidden perils.....................2604
    Lady Carmichael's will...........32755
    Lester's secret...................2637
    Missing...........................2601
    Nora's love test..................2606
    Old Myddleton's money.............2605
    Reaping the whirlwind.............2613
    Sorrow of a secret................2614
    Squire's legacy...................2603
    Under the will....................2629
    Victor and vanquished.............2610
    Wicked girl.......................2639

Haydn, and other poems. 1870..........821.1 57
Hayes, Henry, *pseud.* See **Kirk, Ellen Olney.**
Hayley. Poems and plays. 1785. 6 v.
    V. 1. Essays on painting.—Epistles, odes, sonnets, etc........................821.2 191
    V. 2. Essay on history............821.2 192
    V. 3. Essay on epic poetry........821.2 193
    V. 4. Notes to epistles 3-5 of above.....821.2 194
    V. 5. Triumphs of temper. — The happy prescription....................821.2 195
    V. 6. Marcella.— The two connoisseurs.— Lord Russel.—The mausoleum..........821.2 196

    Triumphs of temper: poem. 1781...821.2 197
Hayne. Avolio, etc.; poems...........821.1 58
    Legends and lyrics. 1872..........821.1 59
    Poems. 1882......................821.1 301
Haynes. Farm-house cobweb.............45370
Hays. Prince Lazybones.................023602
    Princess Idleways..................023601
Hayward. Biographical and critical essays.
    New series, 1873. 2 v............824.2 215
    Selected essays. 1878. 2 v.......824.2 217
Haywarde, R. See **Cozzens, F. S.**
Hazeltine. Chats about books. 1883...824.1 181

Hazlitt, W. English comic writers. '45.....828.2 7
 Essays on the fine arts. 1873.................704 13
 Literature of the age of Elizabeth.—
  Characters of Shakespeare. 1877...822.3 103
 Men and manners: sketches. 1852...824.2 371
 Plain speaker: opinions. 1870............824.2 99
 Round table. — Northcote's conversa-
  tions.—Characteristics. 1871.........824.2 202
 Table-talk. 1845................................824.2 98
Hazlitt, W. C., *ed.* Inedited tracts; 16th-
  17th centuries. 1868........................824.2 1
  Contents: Cyulle and uncyulle life.— A health to the
  gentlemanly profession of servingmen.—The court and
  country.
Headley, H. Poems. 1822..............*in* 821.2 46
Headley, J. T. Miscellaneous works. 2 v.
  ....824.1 178
Healy (Mrs. Bigot). Foreign match............51204
 Lakeville..51201
 Summer's romance..................................51202
Heard, F. F. Shakespeare as a lawyer.
  1883...822.3 215
Heard, J., *jr.* Charge for France, etc..........9950
Hearn. Chita..51102
 Youma..51101
Heart of the west.....................................55240
Heaton, J. L. The quilting bee, etc.
  (verse). 1896..................................821.1 515
Heaton, William. Story of Robin Hood...012701
Heavysege. Saul: a drama. 1857......822.2 256
Heber. Poems and translations. 1829...821.2 745
Hector, *Mrs. A. F.* See **Alexander,** *Mrs.*
Heighway. Leila Ada..............................44109
Heir of Malreward...................................50373
Helder. Chronicles of a health resort........34110
Heldman. Belton scholarship................029502
 Mutiny on board the Leander................029501
Helen Brent, M. D...................................50340
Helena Bertram.....................................07127
Hellis. Where the brook and river meet....56940
Helps, *Sir Arthur.* Animals and their
  masters..179 2
 Brevia: essays, etc. 1871.................829.2 20
 Cassimir Maremma................................12019
 Companions of my solitude (essays)..824.2 198
 Essays written in intervals of business.
  ....824.2 195
 Friends in council. 1869. 2 v........824.2 196
 Ivan de Biron..12020
 Organization in daily life. 1862..........304 19
 Oulita, the serf: a tragedy. 1858......822.2 251
 Realmah...12018
 Social pressure. 1875........................304 18
 Thoughts in the cloister and the crowd.
  ....829.2 58
Helyas, knight of the swan...................*in* 103
Hemans, *Mrs.* Favorite poems. 1881...821.2 595
 Poetical works..................................821.2 584

 Works. 1844. 7 v.
  V. 1. Essay; by Mrs. Sigourney. — Memoir, by
  a sister. England and Spain. · Wallace's invo-
  cation..821.2 283
  V. 2. Tales and historic scenes. — Restoration
  of works of art to Italy.—Modern Greece.—Translations. — Miscellaneous poems. — Italian literature...821.2 284
  V. 3. The sceptic. — Tale of the secret tribunal.
  —Miscellaneous poems. — The siege of Valencia:
  a dramatic poem.................................821.2 285
  V. 4. Forest sanctuary.—Lays of many lands.—
  Miscellaneous pieces. — Dartmoor. — Welsh melodies. — Hymns for childhood. — De Chatillon; a
  tragedy.—Miscellaneous......................821.2 286
  V. 5. Vespers of Palermo: a tragedy.— Songs of
  the Cid.—Records of woman.—Miscellaneous po-
  ems..821.2 287
  V. 6. Songs of the affections. — Miscellaneous
  poems.--National lyrics........................821.2 288
  V. 7. Lyrics and songs for music. — League of
  the Alps. — Scenes and hymns of life. — Female
  characters of Scripture. — Sonnets, etc. — General
  index..821.2 289
Henderson. Shenac's work at home.........52291
Henderson, I. Agatha Page....................69218
 Prelate..69219
Henderson, W. J. Afloat with the flag...033611
 Sea yarns for boys...............................033610
Henley. Book of verses. 1888.........821.2 822
 Song of the sword, etc. 1892......821.2 894
 Views and reviews. 1890............824.2 425
Henley *and* **Stevenson.** Deacon Brodie:
  a melodrama. 1897.....................822.2 338
Henry, C. S. Doctor Oldham.................44134
Henry, E. '89..62320
Henty. At Agincourt..............................023356
 Beric the Briton...................................023344
 Bonnie Prince Charlie...........................023326
 Boy knight..023308
 Bravest of the brave.............................023319
 By England's aid..................................023338
 By pike and dyke.................................023332
 By right of conquest.............................023335
 By sheer pluck....................................023311
 Captain Bayley's heir............................023331
 Cat of Bubastes...................................023330
 Chapter of adventures...........................023336
 Condemned as a Nihilist.......................023343
 Cornet of horse...................................023303
 Curse of Carne's hold...........................13330
 Dash for Khartoum..............................023340
 Dragon and raven................................023314
 Facing death......................................023306
 Final reckoning...................................023321
 For name and fame..............................023316
 For the temple....................................023324
 Friends, though divided.......................023312
 Held fast for England...........................023342
 In freedom's cause..............................023320
 In Greek waters..................................023345
 In the days of the mutiny......................13331

In the heart of the Rockies..................023351
In the night of terror..........................023323
In times of peril.................................023304
Jack Archer..023310
Jacobite exile.....................................023346
Knight of the white cross....................023352
Lion of St. Mark................................023329
Lion of the north...............................023315
Maori and settler................................023337
On the Irrawaddy...............................023357
One of the 28th..................................023333
Orange and green...............................023325
Out on the pampas.............................023301
Redskin and cow-boy........................023341
Saint Bartholomew's eve.....................023348
Saint George for England....................023313
Through Russian snows......................023353
Through the fray................................023327
Through the Sikh war........................023347
Tiger of Mysore.................................023354
True to the old flag............................023322
Under Drake's flag.............................023307
When London burned........................023350
Winning his spurs..............................023328
With Clive in India............................023309
With Cochrane the dauntless..............023355
With Lee in Virginia..........................023339
With Wolfe in Canada.......................023318
Woman of the Commune....................13332
Wulf the Saxon..................................023349
Young buglers....................................023302
Young Carthaginian............................023317
Young franc-tireurs.............................023305
Henty, *ed.* Stories of history...............023334
Hepworth. !!!.....................................29140
  Brown studies..................................29141
  Farmer and the Lord........................29142
Her crime..15083
Her picture..15077
Her sacrifice..55232
Heraud. Shakspere, his inner life. '65.....822.3 79
Herbert, *Lord* E., *of Cherbury.* Poems..821.2 593
Herbert, George. Works; ed. by Willmott...820.2 118

  Contents: Life.—The church.—The church militant.—Miscellaneous poems.—A priest to the temple.—Jacula prudentum.—English letters.—Latin letters.—Latin and Greek poems.

Herbert, H. W. See Forrester, Frank.
Herbert Tracy......................................50395
Herman. Great Beckleswaithe mystery.....68444
  His angel..68441
  King in Bohemia................................68442
  Scarlet fortune....................................68440
  Woman, the mystery..........................68443
Herman *and* Murray. See Murray, D. C., *and* Herman, H.

Herrick, Robert, (1591-1674). Poems and other remains. 2 v................821.2 147
  Contents: Hesperides.—Noble numbers.—Appendix.
  Selections from his poetry; ed. by Hale. 1895...821.2 539
Herrick, Robert, (19th century). Man who wins...71180
Hertz-Garten, T., *pseud.* Through the red-litten windows.—The old river house...14730
Hervey, E. L. Rock light......................020101
Hervey, M. H. Amyas Egerton, cavalier..13061
  Dartmoor..13060
  Reef of gold...042001
Hetherington *and* Burton. Paul Nugent, materialist................................53660
Hetty's boarder.....................................55281
Hewett. The votary. 1867................821.1 198
Hewlett. Earthwork out of Tuscany. 1896..704 34
  (For contents, see Finding List, pt. 3, p. 412.)
Heywood, J. Dialogue on wit and folly..821.2 463
Heywood, T. Dramatic works. 1874. 6 v...822.2 185
  Fair maid of the exchange.—Fortune by land and sea. (Dramas.) 1845......822.2 88
  Fair maid of the west: comedy. '50....822.2 86
  Golden age.—Silver age.(Dramas.) 1851.
  ....822.2 89
  King Edward IV (drama.) 1842......822.2 87
  Marriage triumph..............................821.2 446
  Royal king and loyal subject.—Woman killed with kindness. (Dramas.) '50..822.2 85
  Two plays on the life of Queen Elizabeth...822.2 84
Hibbard. Dark horse..............................41822
  Governor, etc......................................41820
  Contents: Governor.— Deedless drama. — As the sparks fly upward.— A matter of fact.— Fresh-water romance.—End of the beginning.
  Iduna, etc...41821
  Contents: Iduna.—Woman in the case.—Papoose.—Would Dick do that?—The dragoness.— In maiden meditation.
  Nowadays, etc....................................41823
  Contents: Nowadays.— There's nothing half so sweet in life.—A mad world, my masters.—Guilty Sir Guy.—In the midst of life.—A flirt.
Hickling. Rector of Roxburgh..............44166
Hickmott. A man: lect. 1864........824.1 Pam. 1
Hickok. Address, Buffalo Young men's association. 1847.............................40 23
Hicks. Man from Oshkosh......................30650
Hickson. Cuckoo songs. 1894..........821.2 976
Higginson, E. W. From the land of the snow-pearls.....................................71401
Higginson, Mary T. Room for one more..023501
Higginson, *Mrs.* S. J. Princess of Java....69330
Higginson, T. W. Afternoon landscape (poems). 1889...............................821.1 398
  Atlantic essays. 1871..........................824.1 260

Book and heart: essays. 1897........824.1 263
Concerning all of us. 1892...............824.1 265
Contents: Pillars of the republic.—Good society and the best society.—Ancestors who come after us.—Lilliputian theory of women.—Little social circles. — The merely conventional.—Easy lessons in caste.—The theory of universal vulgarity.—Feminine conquerors.—Future of small country towns.—Transplantation of wealth.—Domestic service in the millenium.—One of Thackeray's women.—Habit of prostration.—A home-made dialect.—Processes. — English and American health.—Advantage of reasonable expectations.
Malbone...44901
Monarch of dreams..............................44902
The new world and the new book, etc.
 1892..824.1 262
Oldport days. 1873............................824.1 84
Out-door papers. 1863.......................824.1 83
Procession of the flowers, etc. 1897...824.1 261
Contents: The procession of the flowers.—April days.—Water-lilies.—My out-door studies.—The life of birds.—A moonglade.
High lights...62536
Higham. Cloverly................................26101
 Other house......................................26103
Hildreth. White slave..........................69260
Hill, A. Poems; with life. 1822........*in* 821.2 39
Hill, B. Story of a cañon....................32230
Hill, F. S. Twenty years at sea..........05505
Hill, G. B. Writers and readers. 1892...824.2 439
Hill, G. C. Cap sheaf..........................44123
 Homespun...824.1 111
Hillhouse. Iola....................................43260
Hilliard. Under the black eagle..........034801
Hillyard. Little trapper........................06101
Hillyer. Marable family.......................56845
Himes. Study of 'Paradise lost.'......821.2 164
Hinkson, H. A. O'Grady of Trinity....56110
Hinkson, *Mrs.* H. A. See Tynan, K.
Hinton, C. H. Stella.—An unfinished
 communication...................................60140
Hinton, H. My comrades....................52249
Hinton, J. Art of thinking, etc. 1879...824.2 142
Hitchcock, Edward. Religious bearings
 of man's creation. 1856............*in* 825.1 17
Hitchcock, E. A. Spenser's 'Colin Clout'
 explained, etc. 1865..................821.2 138
Hoare. Brave fight..............................22191
 Mike : a tale of the Irish famine.....22193
 Paths in the great waters................22192
 Turbulent town..................................22190
Hobbes, J. O., *pseud.* (Pearl Craigie.)
 Bundle of life....................................14743
 Gods, some mortals, and Lord Wickenham...14744
 Herb-moon..14746
 Some emotions and a moral............14741
 Some good intentions and a blunder....14745
 Sinner's comedy...............................14740
 Study in temptations........................14742

Hobbes, T. English works. 1839. 11 v...192 23
Hobbs, Aspasia, *pseud.* See Hubbard, E.
Hocking, J. 'All men are liars.'..........31212
 The birthright...................................31217
 Fields of fair renown.......................31215
 Ishmael Pengelly..............................31210
 Mist on the moors............................31214
 Monk of Mar-Saba.—Elrad the Hic....31211
 Story of Andrew Fairfax..................31216
 Zillah..31213
Hocking, S. K. For such is life..........5017
 Heart of man....................................5016
 Son of Reuben.................................5015
 Where duty lies................................5014
Hodder. Thrown on the world............020502
 Tossed on the waves........................020501
Hodgetts. Champion of Odin..............032216
Hodgson. Outcast essays and verse translations. 1881............................824.2 293
Hoey. Blossoming of an aloe............51603
 Lover's creed....................................51604
 Out of court......................................51602
Hoffman, C. F. Poems. 1873..........821.1 241
 Contents: Forest musings. — Lays of the Hudson.—Love poems.—Songs and occasional poems.
Hoffman, D. Chronicles of Cartaphilus,
 the wandering Jew.............................30429
Hoffman, Mary I. Agnes Hilton.........44140
Hofland. Cumberland statesman......*in* 14150
 Czarina..14149
 Daniel Dennison..............................14150
Hogan. Lost explorer.........................8720
Hogarth. Hogarth's frolic..................828.2 11
Hogg, Cervantes. See Barrett, E. S.
Hogg, J., (*the Ettrick shepherd*). Mountain
 bard: ballads and songs. 1807...821.2 935
 Songs by the Ettrick shepherd. 1831..821.2 936
 Tales and sketches............................30431
 Works. 1869......................................821.2 B-2
 Contents: Life; by Thomson.— The queen's wake.—Mountain bard. — Mador of the moor. — Pilgrims of the sun.—Poetic mirror.—Queen Hynde.— Forest minstrel; songs.—Poetical tales and ballads.—Miscellaneous poems and songs.—Autobiography.
Holcombe. In both worlds..................19127
Holding. Little Corporal......................05820
Holdsworth. Joanna Traill, spinster...35620
 Spindles and oars.............................35622
 Years that the locust hath eaten......35621
Hole. Memories of Dean Hole. 1893..922.2 230
 More memories. 1894......................824.2 475
 Contents: Personal.—Ecclesiastical. — Preaching and preachers.—Church services and missions.—Our perplexities. — Observance of Sunday. — Church progress.—Education.—Marriage.—Our aristocracy.—Workingmen.—Politics.—Why are speakers so many and orators so few?—Flowers and florists.—Design and the delights of a garden. — About roses. — My verses. — The drama.—Bores.—Impostors.—Our sports and games. Horses and racing.

Holgate. Noachidæ...44122
Holiday time at Forrest House......................0132
Holland, C. My Japanese wife.................29990
Holland, D. Donal Dun O'Byrne...........44194
Holland, F. M. Stories from Browning.
    1882..821.2 1120
Holland, *Dr.* J. G. Arthur Bonnicastle......6708
    Bay-path..6701
    Bitter-sweet. 1868..........................821.1 137
    Complete poetical writings. 1879......821.1 141
      Contents: Bitter-sweet.—The puritan's guest.— Kathrina. — Jacob Hurd's child. — Mistress of the manse.— Heart of the war. — The marble prophecy. — Shorter poems.
    Every-day topics 824.1 80
    Gold-foil (essays). 1864......................824.1 79
    Kathrina. 1867..................................821.1 138
    Lessons in life. 1873.............................*170 37
    Letters to the Joneses. 1863................170 22
    Letters to young people.......................*170 21
    Marble prophecy, and other poems.
      1872...821.1 139
    Miss Gilbert's career................................6703
    Mistress of the manse (poem). 1874......821.1 140
    Nicholas Minturn.....................................6710
    Plain talks....................................824.1 78
    Sevenoaks...6705
Holley. Josiah Allen's wife........................62204
    Josiah's alarm.—Abel Perry's funeral......62210
    Miss Richards' boy................................62214
    My opinions and Betsy Bobbitt's.........62209
    My wayward partner.............................62201
    Samantha among the brethren..............62203
    Samantha at Saratoga..........................62202
    Samantha at the World's Fair................62205
    Sweet Cicely..62215
Hollister. Kinley Hollow...........................40802
    Mount Hope..40801
Holloway. Scenes of youth, with other poems......................................821.2 315
Holm, Saxe, *pseud.* Stories, 1st and 2d series.
    V. 1. Draxy Miller's dowry.—The elder's wife.— Whose wife was she?—The one-legged dance.— How one woman kept her husband. — Esther Wynn's love-letters.....................................55901
    V. 2. A four-leaved clover.—Farmer Bassett's romance.—My tourmaline.—Joe Hale's red stockings.—Susan Lawton's escape.......................55902
Holmes, Eleanor. Price of a pearl...........15740
Holmes, Margaret. Chamber over the gate.69271
Holmes, *Mrs.* M. H. Scenes in our parish..44103
Holmes, N. Authorship of Shakespeare..822.3 10
Holmes, O. W. Autocrat of the breakfast table......................................829.1 11
    Before the curfew, and other poems.
      1888..821.1 128
    Elsie Venner..43701
    Guardian angel....................................43705

The iron gate, and other poems. '80..821.1 127
Mechanism in thought, etc..........................150 4
Medical essays. 1842-82...........................610 30
Mortal antipathy..43708
Over the tea-cups. 1890..........................829.1 14
Pages from an old volume of life. '83..824.1 190
  Contents: Bread and the newspapers. — My hunt after the captain.—The inevitable trial.—Physiology of walking.—The seasons.— The human body.—Cinders from the ashes.—Mechanism in thought and morals.— Physiology of versification.—Crime and automatism.— Jonathan Edwards.—Pulpit and pew.
Poet at the breakfast table..................829.1 13
Poetical works....................................821.1 126
Professor at the breakfast table.........829.1 12
Songs in many keys. 1864..................821.1 124
Songs of many seasons, 1862-74........821.1 125
Soundings from the Atlantic. 1864...824.1 189
  Contents: Bread and the newspaper.—My hunt after the captain. — Stereoscope and stereograph. — Sun-painting and sun-sculpture.—Doings of the sunbeam.— The human wheel.—Visit to the autocrat's landlady.— Visit to the asylum for aged and decayed punsters.—The great instrument.—The inevitable trial.
Holroyd, C. C. Seething days..................32120
Holroyd, D. Within the shadow................69421
Holt, E. S. All for the best.....................50517
    At ye Green Griffin..............................50506
    Behind the veil...................................50515
    Earl Hubert's daughter......................50504
    Joyce Morrell's harvest......................50505
    King's daughters.................................50513
    Lady Sybil's choice............................50518
    Lettice Eden......................................50502
    Lord mayor..50509
    Lord of the marches...........................50510
    One snowy night................................50516
    Out in the forty-five..........................50514
    Red and white...................................50507
    Sister Rose..50503
    Tangled web......................................50511
    Wearyholme......................................50508
    White rose of Langley.......................50501
Holt, J. S. Abraham Page........................25848
Home. Works. 1822. 3 v.
    V. 1. Life. — Agis. — Douglas............822.2 144
    V. 2. • Siege of Aquileia. — Fatal discovery. — Alonzo.—Alfred.—History of rebellion, 1745.....822.2 145
    V. 3. History of rebellion, concluded..822.2 146
Home and foreign service.........................55206
Home stretch..58943
Honor Ormthwaite.....................................35716
Honorable Stanbury, etc; by Two...........14855
Hood, P. Self-formation. 1883................374 15
Hood, Thomas. From nowhere to the north pole...026701
    Hood's own. 1871. 1st series..........828.2 28
    Same. 2d series..................................828.2 29
    Poetical works. 1873......................821.2 313
    Prose and verse. 1857....................821.2 314

* Of interest to young readers.

Tales, romances, etc..................................19129
   Contents: Our family.— Mr. Withering's consumption and its cure.— Camberwell beauty.— Confessions of a phœnix.— Mrs. Burrage.— Mrs. Peck's pudding.— Schoolmistress abroad.— Tower of Lahneck.— A sea-totaller.— Fatal bath.— The character.— New lodger.— Patronage.— Mrs. Gardiner.— Tale of terror.— Mr. Chubb.— The happiest man in England.
Tylney hall...19130
Whimsicalities. 1857......................828.2 30
Hood, Tom, *jr.* Golden heart...............15203
  Love and valor.......................................15201
Hook, J. Pen Owen..................................19112
Hook, T. E. All in the wrong..................31104
  Bon-mots; ed. by Jerrold. 1894........829.2 69
  Choice humorous works...............828.2 48
  Fathers and sons....................................31103
  Gilbert Gurney......................................31101
  Gurney married....................................31105
  Jack Brag...31115
  Life and remains; by Barham.........928.2 298
  Sayings and doings. 9 v.......................31106
  Widow and marquess............................31102
Hooper, *Mrs.* House of Roby.................62379
Hooper, J. J. Captain Simon Suggs........47267
  Widow Rugby's husband......................47266
Hooper, L. H. Tsar's window.................23441
  Under the tri-color..............................23440
Hope, A. J. B. B. Brandreths................14002
  Strictly tied up....................................14001
Hope, Anthony, *pseud.* Change of air......38003
  Chronicles of Count Antonio..................38012
  Comedies of courtship............................38013
    Contents: Wheel of love.— Lady of the pool.— Curate of Poltons.— Three-volume novel.— Philosopher in the apple orchard.— Decree of Duke Deodonato.
  Dolly dialogues...................................38008
  Father Stafford....................................38001
  God in the car.....................................38006
  Half a hero..38004
  Heart of the princess Osra.....................38014
  Indiscretion of the duchess...................38007
  Man and his model...............................38011
  Man of mark.......................................38009
  Mr. Witt's widow................................38002
  Phroso...38015
  Prisoner of Zenda................................38005
  Sport royal, etc....................................38010
    Contents: Sport royal.— Tragedy in outline.— Malapropos parent.— How they spoiled the Run.— Little joke.— Guardian of morality.— Not a bad deal.— Middleton's model.— My astral body.— Nebraska loadstone.— Successful rehearsal.
Hope, Ascott R., *pseud.* (A. R. H. Moncrieff.) Black and blue.....................019812
  Buttons..019805
  Evenings away from home...................019808
  Homespun stories................................019807
  Stories about boys..............................019803
  Stories about old folks and young ones...019806

Stories of French school life................019802
Stories of old renown. 1883..............*813 21
Stories of school life..........................019801
Stories out of school time....................019810
Texts from The Times. 1870..........824.2 225
Young traveller's tales........................019811
Hope, Ascott R., *ed.* Stories of long ago..019813
Hope, S. New Godiva..............................47255
Hope, T. Anastasius...............................44128
Hopkins, A. A. Geraldine: a souvenir of the St. Lawrence (poem). 1887.....821.1 261
Hopkins, L. Comic history of U. S. '80..828.1 8
Hopkins, Mark. Science and religion: a sermon. 1856...........................*in* 825.1 17
Hopkins, Mark, *jr.* World's verdict........69375
Hopkins, S. R. Young prince of commerce...040801
Hopkins, T. Incomplete adventurer, etc...21241
  Lady Bonnie's experiment....................21242
  Nell Haffenden...................................21243
  Nugents of Carriconna.........................21240
  'Twixt love and duty...........................21244
Hopper. Dutch pilgrim fathers, and other poems. 1865.............................821.1 199
  One wife too many (poem). 1867.....821.1 211
Hoppin, A. Fashionable sufferer...........62324
  Two Compton boys.............................032203
Hoppin, J. M. Notes of a theological student..824.1 20
Hoppus (Mrs. A. Marks). David Pannell......15503
  Great treason......................................15501
  Story of carnival.................................15502
Horace Hazelwood.................................07116
Hornaday. Man who became a savage....41880
Horne. Ballad romances. 1846..........821.2 749
  Bible tragedies...........................822.2 283
    Contents: John the Baptist.— Rahman.— Judas Iscariot.
  Cosmo de' Medici: a tragedy. 1875..822.2 284
  Laura Dibalzo: a tragedy. 1880......822.2 285
  Orion: an epic. 1872....................821.2 305
  Prometheus (poem). 1864.............821.2 797
Hornung. Boss of Taroomba..................38203
  Bride from the bush.............................38201
  Irralie's bushranger.............................38205
  My lord duke......................................38207
  Rogue's march....................................38206
  Tiny Luttrell......................................38202
  Unbidden guest..................................38204
Horsley. Blue balloon............................034201
Hort. Tiari..51401
Horton, G. Constantine.........................70760
Horton, *Mrs.* M. B. Wife's messenger......44135
Hosmer, B. G. Poems. 1868........821.1 196
Hosmer, G. W. As we went marching on..69146
Hosmer, J. K. How Thankful was bewitched..41841
  The thinking bayonet...........................41840

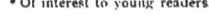
* Of interest to young readers.

Hosmer, W. H. C. Later lays and lyrics..821.1 45
　Months. 1847......................................821.1 44
　Pioneers of western N. Y. 1838..821.1 Pam. 7
　Poetical works. 1854. 2 v...............821.1 41
　Yonnondio : a poem. 1844..............821.1 43
Hotchkiss. In defiance of the king............29970
Hough. Dr. Joliffe's boys.........................031401
　For fortune and glory..............................031402
Houghton, *Lord,* (R. M. Milnes). Poems
　of many years. 1846.........................821.2 312
House. Midnight warning, etc...................06905
　Yone Santo...69480
Household verses on health and happiness..821.2 499
Housman. Farm in fairyland........................0930
Houston. Barbara's warning.....................56409
　Done in the dark.....................................56404
　First in the field......................................56407
　Fixed as fate...56408
　Recommended to mercy........................56401
　Sink or swim...56410
　Taken upon trust....................................56411
　Zoe's brand...56402
Hovey. Launcelot and Guenevere (drama).
　..822.1 29
Howard, Blanche W. Aulney Tower.....28130
　Aunt Serena..28105
　Battle and a boy....................................028110
　Guenn...28115
　No heroes..028111
　One summer..28101
　Open door...28103
　Tony the maid..28102
Howard, Blanche W., *and* **Sharp,
　William.** Fellowe and his wife..........28106
Howard, E. Der alte Commodore.............38324
　Ardent Troughton [Outward bound].
　　(German)..38321
　Outward bound.......................................38320
　Sir Henry Morgan, buccaneer...............38322
　Same (German).......................................38323
Howard, H. See **Surrey,** *earl of.*
Howard, J. H. See **Corry O'Lanus.**
Howard, J. H. W. Bond and free..............41780
Howe, E. W. Ante-mortem statement......17603
　Man story..17602
　Moonlight boy...17610
　Mystery of the locks..............................17605
　Story of a country town........................17601
Howe, *Mrs.* **J. W.** Is polite society polite?
　etc. 1895..824.1 308
　Contents: Is polite society polite? — Paris. — Greece revisited. — The salon in America. — Aristophanes. — The halfness of nature. — Dante and Beatrice.
　Passion-flowers (poems). 1854..........821.1 183
　Words for the hour (poems). 1857....821.1 177
　The world's own (drama). 1857........822.1 26
Howe, Mary A. Merchant mechanic..........15289

Howe, Maud. Atlanta in the south............16402
　Mammon..16407
　Newport aquarelle...................................16403
　Phillida..16408
　San Rosario ranch...................................16401
Howell, James. Epistolæ Ho-Elianæ.
　1678..826.2 4
　Same ; ed. by Jacobs. 1892. 2 v......826.2 5
Howell, Jane L. Justine's lovers...............50313
Howell, J. E. Poems. 1867. 2 v..........821.1 62
Howells, W. D. Albany depot (farce).
　1892...822.1 51
　Annie Kilburn..10611
　April hopes..10603
　Chance acquaintance..............................10601
　Christmas every day, etc......................010630
　Coast of Bohemia....................................10620
　Counterfeit presentment : comedy. 1877.
　...822.1 52
　Day of their wedding..............................10660
　Day's pleasure, etc.: sketches...........824.1 162
　Doctor Breen's practice..........................10639
　Elevator: farce. 1896.........................822.1 53
　Evening dress: farce. 1893................822.1 54
　Fearful responsibility..............................10636
　Five o'clock tea : farce. 1894............822.1 55
　Foregone conclusion...............................10604
　Garroters : farce..................................822.1 56
　Hazard of new fortunes..........................10606
　Imperative duty......................................10613
　Indian summer...10686
　Lady of the Aroostook............................10614
　Landlord at Lion's head. 1897.............10609
　Letter of introduction : farce. 1892....822.1 58
　Likely story : farce.............................822.1 57
　Minister's charge....................................10602
　Modern instance.....................................10645
　Modern Italian poets...........................851 62
　Mouse-trap: farce. 1894.....................822.1 59
　　Same ; and other farces. 1889.......822.1 67
　　Contents: The garroters. — Five o'clock tea. — The mouse-trap. — A likely story.
　My literary passions. 1895................824.1 298
　Out of the question : comedy. 1877..822.1 60
　Parlor car: farce. 1894......................822.1 68
　Parting and a meeting.............................10624
　Poems. 1873.......................................821.1 495
　Previous engagement : comedy. 1897..822.1 61
　Quality of mercy....................................10615
　Register : farce. 1884........................822.1 62
　Rise of Silas Lapham...............................10673
　Sea-change : farce. 1888...................822.1 63
　Shadow of a dream.................................10607
　Sleeping-car : farce............................822.1 64
　　Same ; and other farces. 1889.......822.1 66
　　Contents: The parlor-car. — The sleeping-car. — The register. — The elevator.
　Stops of various quills (poems). 1895.
　..821.1 496

Suburban sketches. 1871..............824.1 134
  Contents: Mrs. Johnson—Door-step acquaintance.—
  A pedestrian tour.—By horse-car to Boston.—A day's
  pleasure.—Romance of real life.—Scene.—Jubilee days.
  —Flitting.
Their wedding journey.........................10608
Three villages. 1884......................824.1 195
  Contents: Lexington.—Shirley.—Gnadenhütten.
Traveler from Altruria.......................10621
Undiscovered country.........................10629
Unexpected guests : farce. 1893........822.1 65
Woman's reason...................................10659
World of chance..................................10617
Howitt, Anna M., (Mrs. A. M. Watts).
  School of life...............................44106
Howitt, Mary. Angel unawares..............01304
  Ballads, etc. 1847....................821.2 297
  Honest Gabriel...............................01305
  Lillieslea 01306
  New story book................................01301
  Peter Drake's dream, etc....................01302
  Pleasant life................................01303
  Songs of animal life..................821.2 588
  Who shall be greatest?............. 10506
Howitt, Mary, *ed.* Pictorial calendar.
  1854₁...829.2 39
Howitt, William. Country year-book.
  1850...829.2 38
  Jack of the mill...............................10501
  Stories of English and foreign life...........10505
Howland. From out of the past..........31705
Howliston. Cat-tails, and other tales........05020
Hoyland. Poems. 1822..................*in* 821.2 46
Hubback. Love and duty....................30454
  Stage and the company......................30455
Hubbard, E., (Aspasia Hobbs, *pseud.*).
  Forbes of Harvard............................41905
  The man......................................41901
  No enemy (but himself).....................41902
  One day.......................................41904
  Story of the legacy...........................41903
Hubbell. Various verses. 1896..........821.1 539
Hudson, H. N. Lects. on Shakespeare.
  1857. 2 v.............................822.3 153
  Same. 1848. 2 v..................822.3 153A
  Studies in Wordsworth, etc. 1884...824.1 252
Hudson, H. R. Poems. 1874............821.1 195
Hudson, W. C., (Barclay North, *pseud.*).
  Jack Gordon, knight errant................29701
  Man with a thumb....................... 29703
  Vivier...29702
Hueffer, F. Italian and other studies...824.2 352
Hueffer, H. F. M. Queen who flew...........0920
  Shifting of the fire............................30180
Hugessen (Lord Brabourne). Crackers
  for Christmas.................................03602
  Ferdinand's adventures......................03605
  Friends and foes from fairyland..............03606
Other stories..................................03604
Stories for my children........................03601
Whispers from fairyland.......................03603
Hughes. The ashen faggot...............*in* 44306
  Scouring of the white horse. — Ashen
    faggot.....................................44305
  Tom Brown at Oxford.......................44301
  Tom Brown at Rugby........................*44307
  Same ; in raised letters, for the blind.
    2 v..362.4 L-5
Huidekoper. Meadowside musings. '85..821.1 400
Huldah. Lion battalion, etc...............032221
Hume, D. Essays ; ed. by Green and
  Grose. 1875. 2 v.............................192 97
Hume, F. Aladdin in London..............28905
  Black carnation...............................28906
  Carbuncle clue................................28910
  Creature of the night........................28903
  Crime of the Liza Jane.......................28911
  Expedition of Captain Flick................28909
  Harlequin opal...............................28907
  Island of Fantasy............................28904
  Lone inn : a mystery.........................28908
  Monsieur Judas...............................28902
  Mystery of a hansom cab....................28901
  Tracked by a tattoo..........................28912
Humphrey, F. A. Children of old Park's
  tavern.......................................69249
Humphrey, F. P. New England cactus,
  etc..14540
Humphreys. Miscellaneous works. 1804.820.1 28
Hungerford, J. Old plantation...........44130
Hungerford, Mrs. M., (The Duchess).
  Airy Fairy Lilian.............................57810
  April's lady...................................57834
  Beauty's daughters...........................57830
  Coming of Chloe............................ 57818
  Conquering heroine..........................57813
  Doris..57859
  Duchess......................................57805
  Faith and unfaith.............................57841
  Her first appearance.........................57853
  Her last throw................................57835
  Honorable Mrs. Vereker.....................57807
  Hoyden.......................................57814
  In durance vile, etc..........................57861
  Jerry, etc.....................................57832
  Lady Branksmere.............................57870
  Lady Patty....................................57811
  Lady Valworth's diamonds..................57802
  Life's remorse................................57831
  Little Irish girl, etc..........................57809
  Lonely maid..................................57817
  Lovice. 1897.................................57842
  Loys, Lord Beresford.........................57852
  Maiden all forlorn............................57865
  Marvel.......................................57804

* Of interest to young readers.

Mental struggle..57873
Mrs. Geoffrey...57833
Modern Circe..57803
Molly Bawn..57806
O tender Dolores..57866
O'Connors of Ballinahinch..............................57812
Peter's wife...57815
Phyllis..57801
Portia...57847
Rossmoyne..57854
Undercurrents..57808
Unsatisfactory lover.......................................57816

Hunt, *Mrs.* **A. W.** Barrington's fate.........63007
Black squire...63006
Leaden casket...63001
Mrs. Juliet..63005
Self-condemned..63003
That other person..63004
Thornicroft's model..63002

Hunt, Helen., (H. H., Mrs. H. H. Jackson). Between whiles........................18102
Bits of talk for young folks..............*829.1 21
Cat stories..023704
Hetty's strange history..................................18112
Hunter cats..023703
Letters from a cat...023701
Mammy Tittleback..023702
Mercy Philbrick's choice.................................18111
Nellie's silver mine..023705
Ramona..18101
Sonnets and lyrics. 1886...................821.1 358
Story of Boon (verse). 1875...............821.1 305
Verses. 1877......................................821.1 208
Zeph..18117

Hunt, *Mrs.* **Holman.** Children at Jerusalem..026301

Hunt, Leigh. As poet and essayist : passages; ed. by Kent. 1889..............824.2 419
Book for a corner. 1857.......................810 15
Book of the sonnet. 1867. 2 v...........811 14
Correspondence. 1862. 2 v.............826.2 31
Day by the fire, and other papers......824.2 97
Essays and miscellanies. 1857..........824.2 94
Essays; sel. and ed. by Johnson. '91..824.2 438
Feast of the poets. 1815......................827 2 43
Imagination and fancy. 1875..................811 68
The Indicator : miscellany. 1845.....824.2 96
Jar of honey from Mount Hybla. 1883..824.2 361
Men, women and books. 1876........824.2 275
The months. 1897............................824.2 232
Poems ; sel. and ed. by Johnson. '91..821.2 883
Poetical works.................................821.2 773
Religion of the heart............................241 79
The seer. 1878................................824.2 242
Story of Rimini : poem. 1819..........821.2 796
Stories from Italian poets. 1846............851 1
Table-talk. 1879.................................829.2 48

Wishing-cap papers. 1873................824.2 95
Wit and humour..................................828.2 8

Hunt, Leigh, *ed.* Dramatic works of Wycherley, Congreve, Vanbrugh, and Farquhar..822.2 180
Hunt, M. B. Two Hardcastles...............032213
Hunt, Violet. Hard woman.....................30631
Maiden's progress...................................30630

Hunter, J. New illustrations of Shakespeare. 1845. 2 v......................822.3 5
Hunter, P. H. James Inwick.................30504
John Armiger's revenge.........................30503
Hunter, P. H., *and* **Whyte, W.** Crime of Christmas day................................30502
My ducats and my daughter..................30501

Huntington, F. D. Addresses.........*in* 825.1 17
Huntington, Faye, *pseud.* (Isabella H. Foster.) Echoing and re-echoing........59801
Huntington, J. V., (John Vincent, *pseud.*).
Lady Alice..21351
Rosemary...21350
Huntington, L. S. Professor Conant....62369
Hurst. Stephen Lescombe.....................53140
Hutcheson, J. C. Fritz and Eric............23610
White squall..23612
Wreck of the Nancy Bell.......................23611
Hutcheson, M. Bardossi's daughter......55501
Hutchinson, H. Fairway island............18140
Hutton, H. Follie's anatomie..........821.2 449
Hutton, L. From the books of. 1892..824.1 267
Other times and other seasons. '95..824.1 301
  Contents : Foot-ball.—Prize-fights.—Tennis.—Golf.—Boat-races. — Transportation. — Tobacco. — Coffee. — A gammon of bacon.—Saint Valentine's day.—April-fool's day.—Good-Friday.—May-day.—The fifth of November. Christmas day.
Hutton, R. H. Contemporary thought and thinkers. 1894. 2 v......................824.2 468
Essays, literary. 1871.....................824.2 280
  Contents : Goethe and his influence.—Wordsworth and his genius.—Shelley's poetical mysticism.—Browning.—Poetry of the Old Testament.—George Eliot.—Clough.—Hawthorne.
Essays, theological and literary, v. 1. 1871..204 66
Modern guides of English thought in matters of faith. 1887................824.2 406
Hutton, S. K. Dessie Fennimore..........032220
Huxley, T. H. Critiques and addresses. 1873...504 38
  (For contents, see FINDING LIST, pt. 3, p. 313.)
Discourses, biological and geological...590 130
  (For contents, see FINDING LIST, pt. 3, p. 317.)
Essays upon some controverted questions. 1892...................................215 75
  (For contents, see FINDING LIST. pt. 3, p. 470.)
Lay sermons. 1870..............................504 61
  (For contents, see FINDING LIST, pt. 3, p. 313.)
Method and results. 1894....................504 135
  (For contents, see FINDING LIST, pt. 3, p. 313.)

*Of interest to young readers.

Science and culture. 1881.....................504 88
(For contents, see FINDING LIST, pt. 3, p. 313.)
Huxley, *Mrs.* **T. H.** My wife's relations..032223
Hyde, D., *tr.* Love songs of Connacht.
1893..821.2 924
Hyde, M. C. Under the stable floor.........010020
Van and Nochie of Tappan sea.............010021
Hyne. Honour of thieves.......................25513
Recipe for diamonds..............................25512
Sandy Carmichael..................................25511
Iddesleigh (Sir Stafford H. Northcote).
Desultory reading. 1885....................374 17
Ignorant essays. 1887......................824.2 408
In a silent world : the love story of a deaf
mute..69080
In duty bound....................................58925
Inchbald. Simple story, etc...................56884
Incredulity of Saint Thomas (miracle
play)...942 136
Inderwick. Prisoner of war...................43020
Influence of example. 1896............823 Pam. 7
Ingelend. Disobedient child.............821.2 465
Ingelow. Don John..............................25306
Fated to be free.....................................25304
John Jerome...25301
Monitions of the unseen. — Poems of
love and childhood. 1871............821.2 388
Mopsa the fairy....................................03901
Motto changed....................................25302
Off the Skelligs...................................25303
Poems..821.2 385
Poems of the old days and the new.
1885..821.2 386
Quite another story..............................25305
Sarah de Berenger...............................25311
Sister's bye-hours................................25309
Stories told to a child. 2 v...................03902
Story of doom, and other poems. '67..821.2 387
Studies for stories................................25308
Ingersoll, E. Country cousins, 1884......*590 108
Friends worth knowing. 1881...........*590 96
Ice queen..032001
Silver caves..032002
Ingersoll, R. G. The gods, and other
lectures...211 38
Ingleby. Shakspere allusion books; pt. 1.
1874...822.3 164
Ingleby *and* **Smith.** Shakespeare's cen-
turie of prayse. 1879......................822.3 B-6
Ingraham. Percival Mayberry..................10805
Pillar of fire..10803
Prince of the house of David................10801
Throne of David..................................10804
Innsly, Owen, *pseud.* See **Jennison, L. W.**
Iota, *pseud.* (Mrs. Caffyn.) Children of
circumstance.....................................36102
Yellow aster.......................................36101
Ireland, *Mrs.* **M. E.** Timothy.................62589

Ireland, W. H. Confessions of. 1805..822.3 149
Scribbleomania; by Anser Pen-drag-on.827.2 17
Irene the missionary....................................58902
Iron, Ralph, *pseud.* See **Schreiner, O.**
Irving. Adventures of Captain Bonneville.
....917.5 119
The Alhambra...............................*914.6 53
Astoria..*917.5 118
Beauties of Irving. 1866..................829.1 4
Bracebridge hall...............................12902
Same. 1822. 2 v............................823 108
Crayon miscellany. 1854................917.5 135
Knickerbocker's history of New York..828.1 1
Same. 2 v.....................................828.1 2
Old Christmas. 1882......................*394 38
Readings from Irving. 1887..........*829.1 29
Rip Van Winkle, as played by Joseph
Jefferson. 1895............................822.1 40
Sketch-book of Geoffrey Crayon......*824.1 10
Spanish papers. 1866. 2 v............824.1 11
Stories and legends. 1896.............*824.1 9
Contents: Dolph Heyliger.—The legend of the storm-
ship.—Kidd the pirate.—The devil and Tom Walker.—
Rip Van Winkle.—The legend of Sleepy Hollow.—Philip
of Pokanoket.—The early experiences of Ralph Ring-
wood.—The phantom island.—The adalantado of the
seven cities.
Tales of a traveller............................12901
Contents: Strange stories by a nervous gentleman.—
Buckthorne and his friends. — Italian banditti. — The
money-diggers.
Wolfert's roost, etc............................12907
Irving *and* **Paulding.** Salmagundi........824.1 8
Same. 2 v...................................824.1 6
Irwin. Man of honour..............................41640
Jack of Dover.................................821.2 450
Jackson, E. P. Demigod..........................69035
Jackson, G. A. Son of a prophet...............46715
Jackson, *Mrs.* **H. H.** See **Hunt, Helen.**
Jackson, Henry. Gilbert Rugge..............14145
Jackson, Z. Shakespeare's genius justified.
1819..822.3 73
Jacob. Gate of Paradise. 1882............249 46
Jacob Schuyler's millions..........................69028
Jacobi, Mary Putnam-. Found and lost.....15540
Jacobs, J. As others saw him...................55403
Literary studies. 1896.................824.2 504
Contents: Introduction. — George Eliot. — Matthew
Arnold. — Browning. — Newman. — Tennyson. — Steven-
son.—Seeley.
Jacobs, W. W. Many cargoes..................63701
Jacox. The literary life......................824.2 134
Jago. Poems ; with life. 1822............821.2 37
Jäk. Professor Johnny.............................0144
James I, *king of England.* Essays of a
prentice in the divine arte of poesie...820.2 33
James, Charles. At the sign of the os-
trich...56020
Where Thames is wide......................56021

* Of interest to young readers.

James, C. T. C. Worker in iron............43150
James, G. P. R. Agincourt.......................5417
  Ancient regime....................................5402
  Arabella Stuart...................................5429
  Arrah Neil..5428
  Attila..5427
  Beauchamp.....................................*in* 5421
  Book of the passions.........................5434
  Brigand...5409
  Castle of Ehrenstein..........................5421
  Charles Tyrrell...................................5401
  Darnley..*in* 5418
  De L'Orme..5404
  Desultory man.....................................5403
  False heir...5430
  Forest days..5416
  Forgery...5423
  Gentleman of the old school..............5412
  Gipsy..5420
  Heidelberg.—Darnley..........................5418
  Henry Masterson.................................5408
  Henry of Guise....................................5406
  Huguenot..5410
  John Marston Hall..............................5411
    Same..*in* 5429
  King's highway....................................5407
  Man at arms..5424
  Man in black.......................................5433
  Mary of Burgundy...............................5426
  Morley Ernstein..................................5415
  One in a thousand...............................5425
  Philip Augustus...................................5432
  Richelieu..5431
  Rose d'Albret......................................5413
  Russell...5414
  Sir Theodore Broughton......................5422
  Stepmother..5419
  String of pearls....................................5405
James, Rev. Henry. Literary remains.....204 97
James, Henry, *jr.* American.....................8503
  Aspern papers......................................8509
  Author of Beltraffio, etc....................8537
    Contents: Pandora.—Georgina's reasons.—The path of duty.—Four meetings.
  Bostonians...8538
  Bundle of letters.................................8522
    Same..*in* 8524
  Confidence...8516
  Daisy Miller...8521
  Daisy Miller: a comedy....................822.1 19
  Diary of a man of fifty.......................8524
  Embarrassments..................................8518
    Contents: The figure in the carpet.—Next time.—The way it came.
  Essays in London, etc. 1893...........824.1 280
    Contents: London.—J. R. Lowell.—Frances Anne Kemble.—Gustave Flaubert.—Pierre Loti.—Journal of the brothers de Goncourt. Browning in Westminster abbey.—Henrik Ibsen,—Mrs. Humphry Ward.—Criticism,—An animated conversation.

  Europeans..8508
  French poets and novelists. 1878.....824.1 103
  International episode.........................8513
  Lesson of the master.........!...............8511
    Contents: Lesson of the master.—The marriages.—The pupil.—Brooksmith.—The solution.—Sir Edmund Orme.
  London life, etc..................................8507
    Contents: A London life.—The Patagonia.—The liar.—Mrs. Temperly.
  Other house..8520
  Partial portraits. 1888....................824.1 237
    Contents: Emerson.— The life of George Eliot.—Daniel Deronda : a conversation.—Anthony Trollope.—Robert Louis Stevenson.—Miss Woolson.—A. Daudet.—Guy de Maupassant.—Turgenieff.—George Du Maurier.—The art of fiction.
  Passionate pilgrim, etc.......................8505
    Contents: The last of the Valerii.—Eugene Pickering.—The Madonna of the future.—The romance of certain old clothes.—Madame de Mauves.
  Portrait of a lady...............................8523
  Princess Casamassima.........................8504
  Private life, etc..................................8514
    Contents: The private life.— Lord Beaupré.— The visits.
  Real thing, etc....................................8512
    Contents: Real thing.—Sir Dominick Ferrand.—Nona Vincent.—The chaperone.—Greville Fane.
  Reverberator......................................8506
  Roderick Hudson................................8502
  Siege of London.................................8531
  Spoils of Poynton...............................8525
  Tales of three cities...........................8534
    Contents: The impressions of a cousin.—Lady Barberina.—A New England winter.
  Terminations......................................8517
    Contents: The death of the lion.—The Coxon fund.—The middle years.—The altar of the dead.
  Theatricals : Tenants; Disengaged. 1894.
    ....822.1 36
  Theatricals; 2d series : The album; The
    reprobate. 1895..........................822.1 37
  Tragic muse..8510
  Washington square.............................8519
  Watch and ward.................................8501
  Wheel of time.— Collaboration.—Owen
    Wingrave.....................................8515
James, Marian. Diamond on the hearth..44157
Jameson, *Mrs.* **A. M.** Characteristics of
  women. 1846. 2 v...........................822.3 84
  Commonplace book. 1855..............829.2 16
  Memoirs and essays. 1846...............824.2 100
Jamison, *Mrs.* **C. V.** Lady Jane............010820
  Toinette's Philip...............................010821
Janney. Alton Thorpe............................61501
Janvier, Margaret. See **Vandegrift,** Margaret.
Janvier, T. A. Aztec treasure-house.........24201
  Color studies......................................24202
    Contents: Rose Madder.—Jaune d'Antimoine.— Orpiment & Gamboge.— Roberson's medium.

Stories of old New Spain	24202
Uncle of an angel, etc.	24203

Contents: Uncle of an angel. — A border ruffian. — Our pirate hoard.—Temporary deadlock.—For the honor of France.—Romance of Tompkins square.— An idyl of the east side.

Jarvis. Geoffrey Hampstead...................8820
Jay, Harriet. My Connaught cousins........67102
   Through the stage door.....................67103
   Two men and a maid........................67101
Jay, J. Writings and life. 2 v............923.1 93
Jay, W. M. L., *pseud.* See **Woodruff, J. L. M.**
Jayne. Lost in the wilderness..............07006
   Through Apache land........................07005
Jeaffreson. Lottie Darling.................14602
   Woman in spite of herself..................14603
Jeans. Always in the way..................20420
Jebb, *Mrs.* Some unconventional people...54401
Jefferies. After London....................60302
   Amaryllis at the fair......................60305
   Amateur poacher. 1879.................799 91
   Dewy morn..................................60304
   Field and hedgerow. 1889.............504 122
   Game-keeper at home. 1879............799 59
   Greene Ferne farm..........................60301
   Hodge and his masters. 1880. 2 v....630 48
   Life of the fields. 1884............824.2 360
   Nature near London. 1883.............504 101
   Open air...................................60303
   Round about a great estate. 1880....590 95
   Wild life in a southern county. 1879...590 88
   Wood magic................................026401
Jefferson. Memoir, correspondence and miscellanies. 4 v........................329.1 23
   Writings. 1853. 9 v.
     V. 1. Autobiography and correspondence......329.1 14
     V. 2-7. Correspondence..............................329.1 15
     V. 7-8. Official papers..............................329.1 20
     V. 8. Notes on Virginia.-Biographical sketches 329.1 21
     V. 9. Manual of parliamentary practice.—The Anas.—Miscellaneous papers..........................329.1 22
   Writings; ed. by Ford. 1892—. v. 1—..329.1 156
Jeffrey, F. Contributions to the Edinburgh Review. 1844. 4 v........824.2 268
Jeffrey, Rosa V. Marah.....................62353
Jeffrey, W., *and* **Becke, L.** First Fleet family....................................43232
   Mystery of the Laughlin islands...........43233
Jenkin, *Mrs.* C. Jupiter's daughters........18506
   Madame de Beaupré.........................18502
   Once and again............................18504
   Psyche of to-day...........................18505
   Skirmishing................................18503
   Who breaks, pays...........................18501
   Within an ace..............................18507
Jenkins. Captain's cabin....................26302
   Devil's chain..............................26301
   Ginx's baby. 1871......................827.2 28
   Jobson's enemies...........................26305

Lisa Lena	26303
Lord Bantam: a satire. 1872	827.2 30
Paladin of finance	26304
Pantalas	26307
Secret of her life	26306

Jenkinson. God's winepress..................31960
Jenks. Imaginations........................027901
Jenness. Piokee and her people.............06211
   Two young homesteaders...................06210
Jennings, H. Childishness and brutality of the time. 1883....................824.2 337
Jennings, L. J. Millionaire................29434
   Philadelphian.............................29433
Jennison (Owen Innisly, *pseud.*). Love poems and sonnets. 1881............821.1 276
Jenyns. Poems; with life. 1822.......*in* 821.2 41
   Summary and free reflections. 1798...824.2 64
Jephson. Pink wedding......................64101
Jerome. Diary of a pilgrimage. 1891....828.2 59
   Idle thoughts of an idle fellow. 1890...824.2 465
   John Ingerfield, etc......................43402

Contents: In remembrance of John Ingerfield and of Anne, his wife.— The woman of the saeter.— Variety patter.—Silhouettes.—The lease of the Cross Keys.

   Novel notes..............................43401
   Sketches in lavender, blue and green......43403
   Stage-land............................792 58
   Three men in a boat. 1890..........828.2 60
Jerrold, D. Bon-mots. 1893.............829.2 67
   Comedies. 1853........................822.2 209
   Fireside saints, etc......................18604
   History of Saint Giles and Saint James...18601
   Men of character..........................18602
   Mrs. Caudle's curtain lectures. 1875...828.2 39
   Punch's letters to his son. 1853......828.2 40
   Works. 4 v.
     V. 1. Memoir; by his son.—Saint Giles and Saint James.—Punch's letters to his son......827.2 21
     V. 2. Story of a feather.—Cakes and ale......827.2 22
     V. 3. Mrs. Caudle's curtain lectures.—Men of character.—Punch's complete letter-writer.....827.2 23
     V. 4. Man made of money.—Sketches of the English.—Chronicles of Clovernook.—Sick giant and Doctor Dwarf.................................827.2 24
Jerrold, W. B. Cent per cent................20436
   Christian vagabond........................20437
   Chronicles of the crutch. 1860......829.2 34
   Cockaynes in Paris........................20439
   Disgrace to the family...................20438
   Story of Madge, etc......................06601
Jersey, *countess of.* Eric, prince of Lorlonia..................................035001
Jervis. Dictionary of the language of Shakespeare. 1868...................‡822.3 B-7
Jessop, G. H., *and* **Matthews, B.** Check and counter-check......................17705
   Tale of twenty-five hours.................17709
Jessopp. Frivola. 1896..............824.2 500

Contents: An antiquary's ghost story.—Queen Mary's fool.—Ups and downs of an old nunnery.—A country

‡ For reference.

cousin in London.—The dying out of the marvellous.—Clocks and watches.—The phenomena of doubles.—Dreams.—A night of waking.—The phantom coach.—Books that have helped me.
Random roaming, etc. 1894............824.2 471
  Contents: Random roaming.—Castle acre.—Hill-digging and magic.—A 14th-century parson,—A rustic retrospect, 1799.—A scheme for clergy pensions.—Something about village almshouses.
Simon Ryan the Peterite......................70220
Trials of a country parson. 1890......824.2 435

Jeune, *Lady.* Lesser questions. 1895...824.2 481
  Contents: Introduction—A Highland seer and Scotch superstitions.—London society.—Dinners and diners.—Conversation.—The revolt of the daughters.—The woman of to-day.—Extravagance in dress.—The crinoline.—Helping the fallen.—Saving the innocent.—Technical education for women.—The homes of the poor.—The Salvation Army.—The domestic servant.—The creed of the poor.

Jewett, Sarah O. Betty Leicester..........023002
Country by-ways (sketches). 1881....824.1 168
Country doctor......................................36909
Country of the pointed firs...................36913
Deephaven..36901
King of Folly Island, etc......................36903
  Contents: King of Folly Island.—Courting of Sister Wisby.—The landscape chamber.—Law lane.—Miss Peck's promotion.—Miss Tempe's watchers.—A village shop.—Mère Pochette.
Life of Nancy......................................36910
  Contents: Life of Nancy.—Fame's little day.—War debt.—Hiltons' holiday.—The only rose.—Second spring.—Little French Mary.—Guests of Mrs. Timms.—Neighbor's landmark.—All my sad captains.
Marsh island.......................................36914
Mate of the Daylight, etc....................36908
  Contents: Mate of the Daylight.—Landless farmer.—New parishioner.—An only son.—Miss Debby's neighbors.—Tom's husband.—Confession of a house-breaker.—Little traveler.
Native of Winby, etc............................36907
  Contents: A native of Winby.—Decoration day.—Jim's little woman.—The failure of David Berry.—The passing of Sister Barsett.—Miss Esther's guest.—The flight of Betsey Lane.--Between mass and vespers.—A little captive maid.
Old friends and new.............................36906
  Contents: Lost lover.—Sorrowful guest.—A late supper.--Mr. Bruce.—Miss Sydney's flowers.—Lady Ferry.—Bit of shore life.
Play days..023001
Strangers and wayfarers......................36905
  Contents: Winter courtship.—Mistress of Sydenham plantation.—Town poor.—Quest of Mr. Teaby.—Luck of the Bogans.—Fair day.—Going to Shrewsbury.—Taking of Captain Ball.—By the morning boat.—In dark New England days.—White rose road.
Tales of New England..........................36904
  Contents: Miss Tempy's watchers.—Dulham ladies.—An only son.—Marsh rosemary.—A white heron.—Law lane.—Lost lover.—Courting of Sister Wisby.
White heron, etc..................................36902
  Contents: White heron.—Gray man.—Farmer Finch.—Marsh rosemary.—Dulham ladies.—Business man.—Mary and Martha.—News from Petersham.—Two Browns.

Jewett, Sophie, (Ellen Burroughs, *pseud.*).
  The pilgrim, and other poems. '96..821.1 444
Jewett, Susan W. Fourteen to four score...47243
Jewsbury, Geraldine E. Zoe..............*in* 14141
Jocelyn, *Mrs.* Big stake......................37001
Joe Lambert's ferry, etc..........................0139
John-a-dreams....................................55254
John Barlow's ward..............................58939
Johnson, B. F., of Boone, *pseud.* See **Riley, J. W.**
Johnson, C. F. Three Americans and three Englishmen. 1886............824.1 216
  Contents: Wordsworth.—Coleridge.—Shelley.—Hawthorne.—Emerson.—Longfellow.
Johnson, Clifton. The farmer's boy. 1894..*137 2
Johnson, D. Political comedy of Europe.
....827.1 18
Johnson, E. Judge's pets......................012001
Johnson, H. K. Raleigh Westgate...........69472
Johnson, J. Ruth's life work..................032214
Johnson, L. Poems. 1895.................821.2 972
Johnson, Richard. Crown garland of golden roses......................................821.2 449
Johnson, Rossiter. End of a rainbow...026902
  Idler and poet (verse). 1883............821.1 291
  Phaeton Rogers..................................026901
Johnson, S. Essays in The Adventurer.
  3 v..824.2 16
Johnsoniana; ed. by Croker. 1842......829.2 4
Letters; ed. by Hill. 1892. 2 v........826.2 107
Poems; with life. 1822.....................821.2 45
Rasselas..30403
  Same. 1883..............................*in* 823 88
Reference list by Foster. v. 4............16 55
Wit and wisdom; sel. by Hill. 1888...829.2 82
Works; ed. by Murphy. 1825. 6 v.
  V. 1. Life.—Philological tracts.—Political and miscellaneous essays.........................820.2 87
  V. 2. On Greek comedy.—Dedications.—Adventurer.—Rambler.............................820.2 88
  V. 3. Rambler, (continued).................820.2 89
  V. 4. Idler.—Essays.—Political tracts.—Journey to western islands of Scotland............820.2 90
  V. 5-6. Lives of the poets....................820.2 91
Works; ed. by Murphy. 1835. 2 v.
  V. 1. Life and genius; by Murphy.—The Rambler.—The Adventurer.—The Idler.—Rasselas.—Tales of the imagination.—Letters.—Miscellaneous poems..820.2 B-2
  V. 2. Lives of the poets.—Lives of eminent persons; viz., Paul Sarpi, Boerhaave, Robert Blake, Sir Francis Drake, Barretier, Lewis Morin, Peter Burman, Thomas Sydenham, Francis Cheynel, Edward Cave, Charles Frederick, king of Prussia, Sir Thomas Browne, Roger Ascham.—Political, philological and miscellaneous tracts.—Dedications.—Opinions on questions of law.—Reviews and criticisms.—Journey to the western islands of Scotland.—Prayers and meditations........820.2 B-3
  (See also, **Idler,** and **Rambler,** p. 100.)
Johnson, Virginia W. Fainalls of Tipton.66602
Joseph the Jew....................................66605

* Of interest to young readers.

Treasure tower of Malta......66603
Tulip place......66604
What the world made them......66601
Johnston, Annie Fellows-. Big brother...041201
Joel, a boy of Galilee......041202
Little colonel......041203
Johnston, Grace K. See Keith, Leslie.
Johnston, H. Doctor Congalton's legacy...61450
Johnston, R. M. Dukesborough tales: chronicles of Mr. Bill Williams......15907
Contents: The goosepond school.— How Mr. Bill Williams took the responsibility.— Investigations concerning Mr. Jonas Lively.— Old friends and new.— The expensive treat of Colonel Moses Grice.— King William and his armies.
Little Ike Templin, etc......15910
Contents: Little Ike Templin.— Oby Griffin.— Black spirits and white.— The bee-hunters. — Poor Mr. Brown. — Len Cane about dogs.— Buck and old Billy.— The two Woollys. — The stress of Tobe. — The quick recovery of Mr. Nathan Swint.— The campaign of Potiphar McCray. — Careful pleadings.— A stepson's recollection.
Mr. Absalom Billingslea, etc......15903
Contents: Critical accident to Mr. Absalom Billingslea. — Brief embarrassment of Mr. Iverson Blount.— Reverend Rainford Gunn and the Arab chief.— Martha Reid's lovers. — Suicidal tendencies of Mr. Ephrodtus Twilley.— Dr. Hinson's degree. — Meditations of Mr. Archie Kittrell.— Rivalries of Mr. Toby Gillam.— Hotel experience of Mr. Pink Fluker.— Wimpy adoptions. — Stubblefield contingents. — Historic doubts of Riley Hood. — Mr. Thomas Chiver's boarder.— Moll and Virgil.
Mr. Billy Downs and his likes......15909
Mr. Fortner's marital claims, etc......15908
Contents: Mr. Fortner's marital claims. — Old Gus Lawson.— Adventure of Mr. Joel Bozzle. — A moccasin among the hobbys.— A surprise to Mr. Thompson Byers.
Ogeechee Cross-firings......15904
Old Mark Langston......15901
Old times in middle Georgia......15911
Primes and their neighbors......15906
Contents: Durance of Mr. Dickerson Prime.— Combustion of Jim Rakestraw.— Self-protection of Mr. Littleberry Roach.— Humors of Jack Bundle.— Experiment of Miss Sally Cash. — Travis and Major Jonathan Wilby.— New discipline at Rock Spring.— Mr. Joseph Pate and his people.— Mr. Gibble Colt's ducks. — The pursuit of the Martyns.
Widow Guthrie......15905
Johnstone, A. A. Unlucky lie......62525
Johnstone, *Mrs.* **C. J.** Edinburgh tales......47285
Johnstone, D. L. Brotherhood of the coast.53321
Rebel commodore......53320
Jolly. Caste......50403
Colonel Dacre......50402
Entanglements......50404
Mr. Arle......50407
My son's wife......50401
Pearl......50405
Jones, A. I. Beatrice of Bayou Têche......23030
Jones, Amanda T. Poems. 1867......821.1 257
A prairie idyl, and other poems. '82..821.1 258
Ulah, and other poems. 1861......821.1 256

Jones, C. C. Negro myths. 1888......828.1 75
Jones, E. Studies of sensation and event: poems. 1879......821.2 721
Jones, H. Browning as a teacher. '96..821.2 1121
Jones, H. A. Michael and his lost angel: play. 1896......822.2 335
Jones, J. B. Life and adventures of a country merchant......22106
Rival belles......22102
Wild western scenes......22109
Jones, J. H. Dominie's son......19102
Jones, J. R. Quaker soldier......30453
Jones, R. Growth of the 'Idylls of the king.' 1895......821.2 351
Jones, T. P., *pseud.* See Aytoun, W. E.
Jones, *Sir* **William.** Poems; with life. 1822......821.2 47
Jonquil, *pseud.* (J. L. Collins.) Was she engaged?......47201
Jonson, Ben. A study of; by Swinburne. 1889......822.2 250
Workes; 1st edition. 1616......822.2 B 3
Works; ed. by Gifford and Cunningham. 1875. 9 v.
V. 1. Memoir; by Gifford. — Commendatory verses, etc.— Every man in his humour.— Notes.822.2 241
V. 2. Every man out of his humour.— Cynthia's revels.— The poetaster.— Notes......822.2 242
V. 3. Sejanus, his fall.— Volpone.— Epicœne.— Notes......822.2 243
V. 4. The alchemist.— Catiline.— Bartholomew Fair.— Notes......822.2 244
V. 5. The divil is an ass.— The staple of news. — The new inn.— Ode to himself, and answers to the same......822.2 245
V. 6. The magnetic lady.— Tale of a tub.— The sad shepherd.— Fall of Mortimer.— The case is altered.— King James's entertainment, etc.— The satyr.— The penates. — Entertainments of two kings, etc.— Notes......822.2 246
V. 7. Masques at court.— Notes......822.2 247
V. 8. Time vindicated.— Neptune's triumph.— Pan's anniversary.— Masque of owls.— Fortunate isles.— Love's triumph thro' Callipolis.— Chloridia.— Expostulation with Inigo Jones.— Love's welcome at Welbeck.— Love's welcome at Bolsover.— Epigrams.— Notes......822.2 248
V. 9. Underwood: Miscellaneous poems. — Translations from Latin poets.— Explorata.— The English grammar.— Miscellaneous pieces and conversations.— Interlude, etc.— Conversations with William Drummond.— Jonsonus virbius.— Notes. 822.2 249
Jonson, Ben, *and* **Marston, J.** Five court masques. 1848......822.2 81
Jordan, *Mrs.* **D. M.** Rosemary leaves (verse). 1873......821.1 439
Jordan, D. S. The story of the innumerable company, etc. 1896......824.1 315
Contents: The story of the innumerable company.— The story of the passion.— The California of the padre — The conquest of Jupiter Pen.— The last of the Puritans.— A knight of the order of poets.— Nature study and moral culture.— The higher sacrifice.— The bubbles of Saki.

Josiah Allen's Wife. See **Holley, Marietta.**
Joyce, Blanid (poem). 1879..............821.1 228
  Deirdrè (poem). 1876..................821.1 219
Judd, C. F. Lilies from the vale of thought (verse). 1878.........821.1 499
  Zaida Eversey............................41760
Judd, S. Margaret........................20429
  Philo: an evangeliad. 1850..............821.1 30
  Richard Edney............................20430
Judith: an old English epic fragment; ed. by Cook. 1888..........821.2 832
Judson, *Mrs.* E. C. Alderbrook...........15283
  Olio of domestic verses. 1852........821.1 29
Junius. Letters of; ed. by Woodfall. 1836. 2 v.........................329.2 3
  Same; ed. by Wade. 1881. 2 v.......329.2 1
Junius, E., *pseud.* Critical dialogue between Aboo and Caboo on a new book. (Satire on G. W. Cable.) '80..827.1 39
K., A. H. Our two lives....................62596
Kaler. See **Otis, James,** *pseud.*
Kate Marstone..............................50378
Katy's birthday..............................0136
Kavanagh, Julia. Adele....................3806
  Beatrice..................................3827
  Bessie...................................3818
  Daisy Burns..............................3805
  Dora.....................................3815
  Forget-me-nots...........................3824
  Grace Lee................................3816
  John Dorrien.............................3802
  Madelaine................................3812
  Nathalie.................................3814
  Queen Mab................................3817
  Rachel Gray..............................3803
  Seven years, etc.........................3822
  Silvia...................................3829
  Sybil's second love......................3807
  Two Lilies...............................3809
Kavanagh, *Rev.* M. Shemus Dhu..........15246
Kaye. Essays of an optimist. 1871......824.2 209
Keary, Annie. Castle Daly................26801
  Clemency Franklin........................26806
  Doubting heart...........................26804
  Janet's home.............................26805
  Oldbury..................................26803
  Sidney Grey..............................031201
  York and a Lancaster Rose................26802
Keary, C. F. Herbert Vanlennert.........17522
  Mariage de convenance...................17520
  Two Lancrofts............................17521
Keats. Eve of St. Agnes, etc....*in* 821.2 238
  Letters to Fanny Brawne, 1819-20....826.2 41
  Letters to his family and friends. '91...826.2 105
  Poems; ed. by Drury, introduction by Bridges. 1896. 2 v.
    V. 1. Poems (1817).—Sonnets. Sleep and poetry. Endymion............821.2 247

  V. 2. Lamia, etc.—Posthumous and fugitive poems.—Otho the great.—King Stephen.—The cap and bells.........................821.2 248
  Poetical works. 1846..................821.2 244
  Same. 1857............................821.2 245
  Poetical works. 1869..................821.2 246
  Poetical works and other writings; ed. by Forman. 1883. 4 v.
    V. 1. Editor's preface, note on portraits of Keats, etc.—Poems published in 1817.—Endymion. —Appendix......................821.2 223
    V. 2. Lamia.—Isabella.—Eve of St. Agnes.—Ode to a nightingale.—Hyperion.—Posthumous and fugitive poems.— Otho the great: a tragedy.— King Stephen: a dramatic fragment.—The cap and bells............................821.2 224
    V. 3. Notes on Shakespeare, etc.—Notes on 'Paradise lost.'—A vow.—Miscellaneous letters.821.2 225
    V. 4. Miscellaneous letters.--Letters to Fanny Browne.— Appendix................821.2 226
  Poetry and prose; ed. by Forman. '90..821.2 227
Keble. Miscellaneous poems. 1869.....821.2 424
Keddie. See **Tytler, Sarah.**
Keeler. Gloverson.........................52219
Keeling. Old maids and young............32102
  Orchardscroft............................32101
  Three sisters............................32103
Keenan. Aliens...........................18906
  Iron game................................18902
  Trajan...................................18901
Keene. Guy's life lesson................011501
  Lyle MacDonald..........................011502
  Orient boys.............................011504
Keightley, S. R. Cavaliers...............34541
  Crimson sign.............................34540
  Last recruit of Clare's..................34542
Keightley, T. Shakespeare expositor. 1867............................822.3 86
Keith, A. Y. Spinster's leaflets..........30610
Keith, Leslie, *pseud.* (C. K. Johnston.)
  For love of Prue........................11523
  Indian uncle............................11524
  'Lisbeth................................11522
  Lost illusion...........................11520
  Our street..............................11521
Kelley. Desperate chance.................69225
Kellogg, E. Elm Island stories:
  1. Lion Ben of Elm Island..............011901
  2. Charlie Bell........................011902
  3. Ark of Elm Island...................011903
  4. Boy farmer..........................011904
  5. Young shipbuilders..................011905
  6. Hard scrabble.......................011906
  Forest Glen series:
  1. Sowed by the wind...................011907
  2. Wolf run............................011908
  3. Brought to the front................011909
  4. Black Rifle's mission...............011910
  5. Forest Glen.........................011911
  6. Burying the hatchet.................011912
  Good old times series:
  1. Good old times......................011925
  2. Strong arm..........................011926

3. Unseen hand............011927
4. Live oak boys..........011928

Pleasant Cove series:
1. Arthur Brown...........011913
2. Young deliverers.......011914
3. Cruise of the Casco....011915
4. Child of the Island Glen....011916
5. John Godsoe's legacy...011917
6. Fisher-boys of Pleasant Cove....011918

Whispering pine series:
1. Spark of genius........011919
2. Sophomores of Radcliffe....011920
3. Whispering pine........011921
4. Winning his spurs......011922
5. Turning of the tide....011923
6. Stout heart............011924

Kelly. Edwin Lloyd......09902
Kelso. Stars and bars......25813
Kemble, Adelaide. See **Sartoris, Adelaide.**
Kemble, Mrs. F. A. Far away and long ago......25803
  Notes on some of Shakespeare's plays. 1882........822.3 209
  Plays. 1863........822.2 227
  Poems. 1844........821.2 556
Kemble, J. P. 'Macbeth' and 'Richard III': an essay. 1817......822.3 133
  'Macbeth' reconsidered. 1776...822.3 Pam. 1
Kendall. Such is life......35230
Kenealy. Doctor Janet of Harley street.....34610
Kennard. Right sort......62381
Kennedy, E. B. Out of the groove......18145
Kennedy, Grace. Dunallen......19175
Kennedy, Jane. Young men and old men..52218
Kennedy, J. P. At home and abroad...824.1 94
  Horseshoe Robinson......9901
  Rob of the bowl......9902
  Swallow barn......9903
Kennedy, W. In the dwellings of silence..47801
Kent, J. Johnson manor......44173
  Sibyl Spencer......44172
Kent, W. Tale of a handkerchief (verse). ..821.1 Pam. 21
Kenyon. Story of John Coles......32425
Ker. Boy slave......032602
  Cossack and czar......032605
  Into unknown seas......032603
  Lost among white Africans......032604
  Lost city......032601
  Prisoner among pirates......032606
  Swept out to sea......032608
  Vanished !......032607
  Wizard king......46401
Kernahan. Captain Shannon......51820
Kerr, Orpheus C., *pseud.* See **Newell, R. H.**
Kettle. Falls of the Loder......22222
  Magic of the pine woods......22221
  Old hall among the water meadows......22220
Key. Poems. 1857......821.1 349

Keyser. On the borderland......29120
  Thorns in your sides......29121
Kimball. Henry Powers......8401
  Romance of student life......8410
  St. Leger......8404
  To-day......8411
  Undercurrents of Wall street......8406
  Was he successful?......8412
Kincaid. Selecta poemata. 1727....821.2 165
King, Alice. Queen of herself......62586
King, Anna E. Brown's retreat, etc......32110
  Contents: Brown's retreat.—Odelia Blynn.—Heart story of Miss Jack.—Father Sterling's courtship.—Professor of Döllingen.—A trifle of information.—Mr. Carmichael's conversion.—Jacinth.—Freak of fate.—Monsieur Pampalon's repentance.—Legend of old New York.
  Kitwyk stories......32111
King, Captain Charles. Army Portia......16115
  Same......in 16117
  Army wife......16127
  Between the lines......16107
  Cadet days......016120
  Captain Blake......16116
  Captain Close.—Sergeant Crœsus......16121
  Colonel's daughter......16101
  Deserter......16102
  Dunraven ranch......16105
  Foes in ambush......16118
  From the ranks......16103
  Garrison tangle......16126
  Kitty's conquest......16108
  Laramie......16106
  Marion's faith......16112
  Sergeant Crœsus......in 16121
  Soldier's secret.—Army Portia......16117
  Starlight ranch, etc......16109
  Contents: Starlight ranch.—Well won.—From the Point to the plains.—The worst man in the troop.—Van.
  Story of Fort Frayne......16122
  Sunset pass......16111
  Trooper Ross.—Signal butte......16124
  Trumpeter Fred......16125
  Two soldiers......16110
  Under fire......16120
  Waring's peril......16119
  War-time wooing......16104
  West Point parallel......16128
King, Charles, *ed.* By land and sea......16114
  Captain Dreams, etc......16123
  Colonel's Christmas dinner......16113
King, E. Gentle savage......68301
  Golden spike......68304
  Joseph Zalmonah......68305
  Kentucky's love......68302
King, Grace. Balcony stories......59453
  Earthlings......59452

Monsieur Motte..59450
Tales of a time and place........................59451
  Contents: Bayou L'Ombre.— Bonne maman. — Madrilène.—Christmas story of a little church.
King, H. C. Phantom column: poem.
....821.1 Pam. 20
King, H. E. H. Ugo Bassi's sermon in the hospital (poem). 1891...... 821.1 Pam. 15
King, K. D. Scripture reader of St. Mark's..56040
King, Katharine. Bubble reputation........33305
  Lost for gold..33304
  Off the roll..33301
  Queen of the regiment..............................33302
King, Pauline. Alida Craig.....................70540
  Christine's career.......................................037201
King, T. S. Substance and show, and other lects. 1877...........................824.1 180
King, Thorold, *pseud.* (Charles Gatchell.)
  Haschisch..69236
King, Toler, *pseud.* See **Fox, E.**
King's service....69025
Kingsford, Jane, *pseud.* See **Barnard, C.**
Kingsley, C. Alton Locke.........................5702
  Andromeda, and other poems. 1858...821.2 381
  At last..917.9 10
  Discipline, and other sermons...............254 51
  From death to life....................................237 61
  Glaucus. 1855..590 73
  Good news of God...................................254 43
  Health and education. 1874............824.2 184
    Contents: Science of health.—Two breaths.—Tree of knowledge.—Nausicaa in London.—Air mothers.—Thrift. —Study of natural history.— Bio-geology.— Heroism.— Superstition. — Science.—Grots and groves.— George Buchanan, scholar.—Rondelet, Huguenot naturalist.— Vesalius.
  Hereward..5704
  The hermits...922.6 5
  The heroes...*292 13
  Hypatia...5707
  Lectures in America. 1875................824.2 272
    Contents: Westminster Abbey.— The stage as it was. —First discovery of America.—The servant of the Lord. —Ancient civilization.
  Letters and memories. 1877. 2 v....928.2 288
  Limits of exact science applied to history..901 13
  Madam How and Lady Why..............*553 23
  Miscellanies. 1859. 2 v.
    V. 1. Raleigh and his times.—A mad world, my masters. My winter garden. — Chalk-stream studies. Tennyson.—Poetry of sacred and legendary art. — Alexander Smith and Alexander Pope.— Shelley and Byron. — Hours with the mystics.— Burns and his school...........................824.2 181
    V. 2. Mansfield's 'Paraguay,' etc. — Froude's 'England.' -Plays and Puritans.— The agricultural crisis. Water-supply of London – North Devon.— Speech, Ladies' sanitary association, 1859. — Great cities and their influence – Study of natural history. —Thoughts in a gravel pit.........................824.2 182

New miscellanies. 1860.................824.2 183
  Contents (Same as Miscellanies,' with the following added): John Tauler.— Henry Brooke and 'The fool of quality.'—'Pilgrim's progress' illustrated.
Out of the deep (selections)...................243 21
Phaethon..241 85
Poems. 1856..821.2 380
Same. 1884. 2 v.
  V. 1. The saint's tragedy..........................821.2 382
  V. 2. Andromeda.—Miscellaneous poems...821.2 383
Prose idyls. 1880...............................824.2 279
  Contents: A charm of birds.—Chalk-stream studies. —The fens.— My winter garden. — From ocean to sea.— North Devon.
The Roman and the Teuton.................940 23
Saint's tragedy: Elizabeth of Hungary.822.2 164
Selections from. 1873.......................829.2 7
Sermons for the times...........................254 44
Sir Walter Raleigh and his time, etc.
  1859..824.2 185
  Contents: Raleigh and his time. — Plays and Puritans. — Burns and his school.—Hours with the mystics.— Tennyson—Poetry of sacred and legendary art. — North Devon. — Phaethon. — Alexandria and her schools.— My winter garden.—England from Wolsey to Elizabeth.
Three lectures on the ancient regime.....322 14
Town geology...550 38
Two years ago. 5703
Water babies..0601
Westward ho!..5709
Yeast..5701
Kingsley, F. M. Paul, a herald of the cross..58122
  Stephen, a soldier of the cross...............58121
  Titus, a comrade of the cross................58120
Kingsley, H. Austin Elliot....................5805
  Boy in grey, etc...5821
  Geoffrey Hamlin..5806
  Grange garden..5814
  The Harveys..5809
  Hetty, etc..5820
    Contents: Hetty.—The two cadets.—Our brown passenger.—Seeking your fortune.
  Hillyars and the Burtons..........................5808
  Hornby mills...5818
  Leighton court..5804
  Mademoiselle Mathilde..........................5819
  Mystery of the island...............................5811
  Number 17...5816
  Oakshott castle..5815
  Old Margaret...5817
  Ravenshoe..5802
  Reginald Hetherege.................................5813
  Silcote of Silcotes....................................5801
  Stretton..5807
  Valentine...5812
Kingston. Adrift in a boat....................05329
  Adventures in Africa...............................05352
  Afar in the forest.....................................05342
  African trader..05306

* Of interest to young readers.

At the south pole.........................05324
Dick Cheveley............................05350
Fire ship..................................05323
Foxholme Hall...........................05302
Fred Markham in Russia..............05326
Frontier fort..............................05337
Gentlemen adventurers................05338
Golden grasshopper.....................05357
Harry Skipwith..........................05318
Hendricks the hunter...................05340
Hurricane Hurry.........................05344
In New Granada.........................05339
In the eastern seas......................05303
In the Rocky mountains...............05353
In the wilds of Florida.................05355
James Braithwaite, the supercargo...05351
John Deane of Nottingham............05345
Little Ben Haddon......................05315
Manco......................................05309
Mark Seaworth..........................05347
Michael Penguyne.......................05308
Missing ship..............................05348
Off to sea..................................05317
Old Jack...................................05327
On the banks of the Amazon.........05316
Our fresh and salt water tutors.......05311
Peter the ship boy.......................05333
Peter the whaler.........................05328
Rival Crusoes............................05346
Salt water.................................05343
Settlers....................................05349
Seven champions of Christendom...05336
Snow-shoes and canoes................05356
Sunshine Bill.............................05310
Taking tales for cottage homes. 2 v...05330
Three admirals...........................05335
Three commanders......................05312
Three lieutenants........................05301
Three midshipmen......................05341
Trapper's son.............................05313
True blue..................................05325
Twice lost.................................05314
Voyage round the world...............05304
Will Weatherhelm.......................05322
Won from the waves...................05354
Young rajah..............................05332

Kinkead. Young Greer of Kentucky.......60170
Kinney. Felicita: metrical romance. 1855.
....821.1 24
Kinney-Réno. See Réno.
Kinsman. Cadet life at West Point......52255
Kip, L. Ænone..............................63204
Dead marquis............................63202
Under the bells..........................63203
Kip, W. F. Would you have left her?......41730
Kipling. Courting of Dinah Shadd, etc....31405
Contents: Biographical sketch.—Courting of Dinah Shadd.—The man who was.—A conference of the powers.—Without benefit of clergy.—On Greenhow Hill.—Incarnation of Krishna Mulvaney.

Departmental ditties, etc. 1890........821.2 866
Same; barrack-room ballads, etc. '90.
....821.2 867
Jungle book...............................031410
Same; in N. Y. point, for the blind.
....362.4 N Y-11
In black and white.......................31406
Contents: Dray Wara Yow Dee.—Judgment of Dungara.—At Howli Thana.—Gemini.—At twenty-two.—In flood time.—Sending of Dana Da.—On the city wall.
Life's handicap...........................31411
Contents: Lang men o' Larut.—Reingelder and the German flag.—Wandering Jew.—Through the fire.—Finances of the gods.—Amir's homily.—Jews in Shushan.—Limitations of Pambé Serang.—Little Tobrah.—Bubbling well road.—City of dreadful night.—Georgie Porgie.—Naboth.—Dream of Duncan Parrenness.—Mine own people (which see).
Light that failed.........................31409
Many inventions.........................31413
Contents: Disturber of traffic.—Conference of the powers.—My lord the elephant.—One view of the question.—Finest story in the world.—His private honor.—Matter of fact.—Lost legion.—In the Rukh.—Brugglesmith.—Love-o'-women.—Record of Badalia Herodsfoot.—Judson and the empire.—Children of the zodiac.—Envoy.
Mine own people..........................31410
Contents: Binji.—Namgay Doola.—Recrudescence of Imray.—Moti Guj, mutineer.—Mutiny of the Mavericks.—At the end of the passage.—Incarnation of Krishna Mulvaney.—Courting of Dinah Shadd.—The man who was.—Conference of the powers.—On Greenhow Hill.—Without benefit of clergy.
Phantom 'rickshaw, etc..................31404
Contents: The phantom 'rickshaw.—My own true ghost story.—The strange ride of Morrowbie Jukes.—The man who would be king.
Plain tales from the hills................31401
Contents: Lisbeth.—Three and—an extra.—Thrown away.—Miss Youghal's Sais.—Yoked with an unbeliever.—False dawn.—Rescue of Pluffles.—Cupid's arrows.—Three musketeers.—His chance of life.—Watches of the night.—Other man.—Consequences.—Conversion of Aurelian McGoggin.—Taking of Lungtungpen.—Germ destroyer.—Kidnapper.—Arrest of Lieutenant Golightly.—In the house of Suddhoo.—His wedded wife.—Broken-link handicap.—Beyond the pale.—In error.—Bank fraud.—Tods' amendment.—Daughter of the regiment.—In the pride of his youth.—Pig.—Rout of the White Hussars.—Bronckhorst divorce case.—Venus Annodomini.—Bisara of Pooree.—Gate of the hundred sorrows.—Madness of Private Ortheris.—Story of Muhammad Din.—On the strength of a likeness.—Wressley on the foreign office.—By word of mouth.—To be filed for reference.
Second jungle book.....................031411
Seven seas (poems). 1896.............821.2 868
Soldier stories.............................31414
Contents: With the main guard.—Drums of the fore and aft.—The man who was.—Courting of Dinah Shadd.—Incarnation of Krishna Mulvaney.—Taking of Lungtungpen.—Madness of Private Ortheris.

Soldiers three..................................31402
  Contents: The god from the machine.— Private Learoyd's story.—The big drunk draf.—The solid Muldoon.—With the main guard.—In the matter of a private.—Black Jack.—Only a subaltern.
Story of the Gadsbys.......................31403
Under the Deodars.........................31407
  Contents: The education of Otis Yeere.—At the pit's mouth.—A wayside comedy.—The hill of illusion.—A second-rate woman.—Only a subaltern.
Wee Willie Winkie, etc....................31408
  Contents: Wee Willie Winkie.—Baa, baa, black sheep.—His majesty the king.—Drums of the fore and aft.
Kipling *and* Balestier. Naulahka..........31412
Kirby, M. *and* E. Bundle of sticks........014101
Kirby, William. Golden dog.................69289
Kirk, Eleanor. Up Broadway.................44175
Kirk, *Mrs.* E. O., (Henry Hayes, *pseud.*).
  Better times...............................20804
  Ciphers....................................20807
  Clare and Bébé.............................20811
  Daughter of Eve............................20805
  Fairy gold.................................20812
  Lesson in love.............................20809
  Midsummer madness..........................20810
  Queen money................................20803
  Sons and daughters.........................20802
  Story of Lawrence Garthe...................20808
  Story of Margaret Kent.....................20801
  Walford....................................20806
Kirke, Edmund, *pseud.* (J. R. Gilmore.)
  Adrift in Dixie............................21605
  Among the guerrillas.......................21606
  Among the pines............................21601
  Down in Tennessee..........................21603
  Mountain-white heroine.....................21607
  My southern friends........................21604
Kirkland, *Mrs.* C. M. Evening book.
  1852....................................824.1 18
Kirkland, Joseph. McVeys...................69430
  Zury.....................................69431
Knight, A. L. Rajah of Monkey island....018305
Knight, C. Glimpses of the past........824.2 147
  Once upon a time (essays). 1865.....824.2 162
  Studies in Shakespeare. 1868...........822.3 99
Knight, E. F. Save me from my friends...20210
Knight, F. A. By leafy ways. 1889......504 120
Knight, H. B. F. Girl with a temper.......23505
Knight, W. The lake district as interpreted in Wordsworth. 1878.........821.2 664
  Studies in philosophy and literature...824.2 274
Knight, W., *ed.* Memorials of Coleorton. 1887. 2 v.........................826.2 90
Knowles. Dramatic works. 1859......822.2 157
  Contents: Caius Gracchus. Virginius. William Tell. Alfred the great. The hunchback. The wife. Beggar of Bethnal Green. The daughter.—Love chase.—Woman's wit. Maid of Mariendorpt. Love. John of Procida.—Old maids.—Rose of Arragon. Secretary.

Fortescue 14140
Hunchback.—Love-chase. (Dramas.) 1887 ....822.2 297
Knox, I. Craig-, Esther West..............61701
Knox, T. W. Boy travellers in Africa...*916 15
  Boy travellers in Australasia..........*919.3 10
  Boy travellers in central Europe.......*914 123
  Boy travellers in Ceylon and India....*915.4 53
  Boy travellers in Egypt................*916.2 104
  Boy travellers in Gt. Britain and Ireland..................................*914.2 53
  Boy travellers in Japan and China.....*915.2 20
  Boy travellers in Mexico...............*917.8 45
  Boy travellers in Northern Europe.....*914 122
  Boy travellers in South America....... *918 48
  Boy travellers in Siam and Java.......*915.12 13
  Boy travellers in southern Europe.....*914 124
  Boy travellers in the Levant..........*916.1 7
  Boy travellers in the Russian empire..*914.7 99
  Boy travellers on the Congo...........*916.7 32
  Captain John Crane........................029023
  Close shave...............................029014
  Hunters three.............................029021
  In wild Africa............................029022
  John Boyd's adventures....................029017
  Land of the kangaroo......................029024
  Lost army.................................029019
  Siberian exiles............................29020
  Talking handkerchief, etc.................029018
  Voyage of the Vivian....................*919.8 67
Knox, V. Essays. 1785. v. 2.........824.2 61
Knutt. Snow angel..........................07137
Kolson. Walden Stanyer, boy and man....60150
Koopman. Mastery of books. 1896....374 23
Kouns. Arius the Libyan....................62328
  Dorcas...................................62327
Künst, Hermann. See Smith, *Rev.* W. C.
Kuppord. Rickerton medal.................010040
L. Letters to eminent hands. 1892......824.2 440
L., C. E. Lily and her brothers............62345
Lackland, T. See Hill, G. C.
Lacy. Dramatic works; with memoir. 1875.
  ....822.2 236
Ladd. Cherry-bloom; verse. 1896......821,1 519
Laddie, *Author of.* Baby John...............17911
  Dear 17910
  Don......................................17914
  For the fourth time of asking............17912
  Laddie..................................*in* 17909
  Lil......................................17906
  Miss Toosey's misson.....................17904
  My honey.................................17915
  Our little Ann...........................17902
  Pen......................................17905
  Pomona...................................17913
  Pris.....................................17909
  Rose and lavender........................17908

* Of interest to young readers.

Tip cat.....17901
Zoe.....17907
Lady Bluebeard.....42501
Lady Jean's vagaries.....35715
Lafargue. New judgment of Paris.....69415
  Salt of the earth.....69414
Laffan, *Mrs.* **B.** See **Adams,** *Mrs.* **Leith.**
Laffan, M., (Mrs. W. N. Hartley). Christy Carew.....60201
  Flitters, Tatters, and the counsellor, etc...60205
  Hogan, M. P.....60203
  Honorable Miss Ferrard.....60204
  Ismay's children.....60207
  Singer's story.....60206
Lagutry. Love conquereth: poems. '90..821.1 259
Laing. Problems of the future, and essays...504 124
Laird of Logan. 1868.....828.2 13
Lakeman. Pretty Lucy Mervyn.....62396
Lamb, Charles. Bon-mots; ed. by Jerrold. 1893.....829.2 67
  Eliana. 1864.....824 2 316
  Contents: Essays and sketches.—Pawnbroker's daughter.—Adventures of Ulysses.—Tales.—Poems.—Letters.
  Essays of Elia. 1859.....824.2 313
  Same; 1st series.....824.2 314
  Final memorials; by Talfourd. 1859..826.2 29
  Same, entitled 'Literary sketches and letters.' 1848.....826.2 30
  Last essays of Elia. 1897.....824.2 315
  Letters. 1859.....*in* 928.2 300
  Letters; ed. by Ainger. 1888. 2 v...826.2 92
  Life, letters and writings; ed. by Fitzgerald. 1876. 6 v.
    V. 1. Life, and final memorials; by Talfourd.—Correspondence with Coleridge.....824.2 307
    V. 2. Correspondence with Coleridge, Southey, Wordsworth and others.....824.2 308
    V. 3. Miscellaneous correspondence.—Essays of Elia.—Last essays of Elia.—Notes.....824.2 309
    V. 4. Last essays of Elia, concluded. Miscellaneous essays.—Letters in The Reflector.—Rosamund Gray.....824.2 310
    V. 5. Tales from Shakespeare.—Stories contributed to Mrs. Leicester's school.—Dramatic works: The defeat of time; John Woodvil; Mr. H—; The pawnbroker's daughter.—Sketches, etc.....824.2 311
    V. 6. Sketches, etc.—Contributions to Hone's Everyday book.—Criticisms.—Poems—Sonnets, etc.....824.2 312
  Selections from; ed. by Ellis. '96..*in* 821.2 1025
  Works; ed. by Ainger. 1884. 4 v.
    V. 1. Essays of Elia.....820.2 488
    V. 2. Plays.—Poems.—Miscellaneous essays..820.2 489
    V. 3. Mrs. Leicester's school.—Adventures of Ulysses.....820.2 490
    V. 4. Tales from Shakespeare.....820.2 491
Lamb, Charles *and* **Mary.** Tales from Shakespeare. 1868.....*822.3 93
Lamb, *Mrs.* **M. J.** Snow and sunshine.....028301
Lampman. Among the millet, etc. (poems). 1888.....821.2 830
Lampson. See **Locker-Lampson.**

Lancaster, A. E. All's dross but love.....62387
Lancaster, A. E., *and* **Vincent, F.** Lady of Cawnpore.....16520
Landon. Complete works. 1853.....821.2 279
Landor. Andrea of Hungary.—Giovanna of Naples. (Dramas.) 1839.....822.2 156
  Imaginary conversations: Greeks and Romans. 1853.....829.2 28
  Same. 1876.....829.2 28A
  Same; literary men and statesmen. 3 v.....829.2 25
  Pericles and Aspasia. 1871.....829.2 29
  Selections from; ed. by Hilliard. '56..829.2 30
  Selections from; ed. by Colvin. 1882..829.2 31
  Works and life. 1876. 8 v.
    V. 1. Life; by Forster.....820.2 147
    V. 2. Imaginary conversations: Classical.—Citation and examination of William Shakespeare touching deer-stealing.....820.2 148
    V. 3. Dialogues of sovereigns and statesmen.—The Pentameron.....820.2 149
    V. 4-5. Dialogues of literary men.—Dialogues of famous women.—Pericles and Aspasia.—Minor prose pieces.....820.2 150
    V. 6. Miscellaneous dialogues.....820.2 152
    V. Gebir.—Acts and scenes: Count Julian; Andrea of Hungary; Giovanna of Naples; Fra Rupert; Siege of Ancona; Ines de Castro, etc.—Hellenics.....820.2 153
    V. 8. Miscellaneous poems.—Criticisms on Theocritus, Catullus and Petrarca.....820.2 154
Lane. Dresden romance.....62518
  Ella's mistake.....030301
  My sister's keeper.....62519
Lang, Alice. From prison to Paradise.....69441
Lang, Andrew. Ballades and verses vain. 1884.....821.2 717
  Ban and arrière ban: rhymes. '94....821.2 932
  Essays in little. 1891.....824.2 434
  Contents: Dumas.—Mr. Stevenson's works.—Thomas Haynes Bayly.—Théodore de Banville.—Homer and the study of Greek.—The last fashionable novel.—Thackeray.—Dickens.—Adventures of buccaneers.—The sagas.—Charles Kingsley.—Lever.—Poems of Sir Walter Scott —Bunyan.—Letter to a young journalist.—Mr. Kipling's stories.
  Gold of Fairnilee.....024108
  Grass of Parnassus: rhymes. 1888..821.2 831
  Helen of Troy (poem). 1882.....821.2 654
  Homer and the epic. 1893.....883 75
  In the wrong Paradise, etc.....21502
  Letters in literature. 1889.....824.2 418
  Letters to dead authors. 1886.....824.2 383
  Mark of Cain.....21501
  Monk of Fife.....21503
  My own fairy book.....024107
  Old friends: epistolary parody. 1890...828.2 58
  Prince Prigio.....024105
  Prince Ricardo of Pantouflia.....024106
  Princess Nobody.....024109
  Rhymes à la mode. 1885.....821.2 742
  XXXII ballades in blue china. 1881..821.2 618

* Of interest to young readers.

Lang, Andrew, *and* **Haggard, R.** World's desire..17035
Lang, *Mrs.* **Andrew.** Dissolving views.....68901
Langbridge. Miss Honoria.......................35601
Langhorne. Poems; with life. 1822....821.2 42
Langille. Snail Shell harbor....................41770
Langland. Richard the Redeles.— The crowned king (imitation of Piers)...820.2 329
Vision of Piers ploughman: parallel extracts from 29 manuscripts..........820.2 308
Same; text A.................................820.2 314
Same; text B.................................820.2 320
Same; text C.................................820.2 329
Same; notes..................................820.2 338
Same; general preface and indexes..820.2 350
Same; tr. and ed. by Warren. '95..821.2 971
Same; ed. by Wright. 1856. 2v.....821.2 107
Same: English mysticism; by Jusserand. 1894...............................821.2 929
See also, **Piers** plowman's creed.
Lanier. The English novel. 1897............813 22
Poems; ed. by his wife. 1884..........821.1 320
Science of English verse.........................426 3
Lanman. Recollections. 1881............824.1 172
Lanza. Mr. Perkin's daughter.....................63601
Righteous apostate..............................63603
Tit for tat...63602
Lanza *and* **Hammond.** Tales of eccentric life...18405
Larcom. Childhood songs. 1875.......*821.1 262
Easter gleams (poems). 1890.........821.1 414
An idyl of work (poem). 1875.........821.1 176
Wild roses of Cape Ann, and other poems. 1881................................821.1 252
Larned, Augusta. Village photographs. 1887...824.1 222
Larned, J. N. Address, death of Grant. ....923.1 Pam. 100
Address, birthday of Lincoln, 1873 (?). ....923.1 Pam. 98
Address, decoration day, 1875.....971.4 Pam. 43
Addresses, Academy of fine arts. 2 pamphlets..95.3 Pam. 9-10
Bases of morality...........................98.4 Pam. 62
Brief address on Washington and Lincoln................................*in* 971.4 Pam. 41
A talk about books. 1897....................374 24
Larned, W. C. Arnaud's masterpiece.....52930
Larremore. Mother Carey's chickens. 1888. ....821.1 409
Last days at Apswich..................................69026
Laszowska. See **Gerard.**
Latham. The Hamlet of Saxo grammaticus and of Shakespear. 1872..............822.3 162
Lathrop, G. P. Afterglow......................53409
Echo of passion..................................53403
Behind time..03280I

Gold of pleasure.................................53408
In the distance...................................53402
Newport...53404
Somebody else..................................53401
True, and other stories....................53405
Two sides of a story.........................53406
Would you kill him?..........................53407
Lathrop, Rose H. Along the shore. '88..821.1 288
Latimer. Chain of errors........................24101
My wife and my wife's sister..........24104
Princess Amélie................................24103
Salvage..24102
Latter-day saint..................................16001
Lauder. Minor poems.......................820.2 323
Lavante, *pseud.* (E. A. Poe or A. Wilmer?) Poets and poetry of America. 1887..821.1 368
Lawless. Chelsea householder.............19801
Grania..19805
Hurrish..19804
Maelcho...19808
Major Lawrence................................19806
Millionaire's cousin..........................19803
With Essex in Ireland.......................19807
Lawrence, G. E. Anteros.....................12414
Barren honor.....................................12409
Border and Bastile, etc....................12402
Brakespeare......................................12403
Breaking a butterfly.........................12404
Guy Livingstone...............................12401
Hagarene...12405
Sans merci..12407
Sword and gown...............................12413
Lawrence, Uncle, *pseud.* See **Walsh, W. S.**
Lawton. The three dramas of Euripides. 1889...882 45
Layamon. Brut; ed., with translation, by Madden. 1847. 3 v....................821.2 B-4
Layard. Poems. 1890........................821.2 889
Lazarus. Poems. 1889. 2 v............821.1 394
Leadbeater. Mss. and correspondence. 1862. 2 v......................................826.2 35
Lean, *Mrs.* **F.** See **Marryatt, Florence.**
Lear. Nonsense books. 1888..........*828.2 14
Learned. Between times (poems). '89....821.1 413
Leathes. Actor's wife............................62701
Leavitt. American cardinal. 2 v..........52267
Le Clerc. Mistress Beatrice Cope.......69521
Rainbow at night...............................69522
Robert Carroll...................................69523
Lee, Albert. Tommy Toddles..............034501
Lee, Aubrey. John Darker..................30750
Lee, D. K. Merrimack..........................12091
Lee, Harriet. Canterbury tales.
V. 1. Introduction.—The landlady's tale: Mary Lawson. · The friend's tale: Stanhope.—The wife's tale: Julia.—The traveller's tale: Montford.--The poet's tale: Arundel.—The old woman's tale: Luthaire, a legend...12085

* Of interest to young readers.

LANGUAGE AND LITERATURE.

V. 2. The German's tale: Kruitzner. — The Scotsman's tale: Claudine. — The Frenchman's tale: Constance.—The officer's tale: Cavendish..12085A

Lee, Holme, *pseud.* See **Parr, Harriet.**

Lee, Katharine. Katharine Blythe..........21020
   Love or money......................................21021

Lee, M. and C. Oak staircase....................62599
   Rosamund Fane...................................020601
   St. Dunstan's fair.................................020603

Lee, Margaret. Divorce..........................59511
   Doctor Wilmer's love.............................59510
   One touch of nature..............................59512

Lee, Mary C. In the cheering-up business..69485
   Quaker girl of Nantucket.......................69484
   Soulless singer.....................................69486

Lee, N. Dramatic works. 1734. 3 v.
   V. 1. Œdipus.—Theodosius.—Princess of Cleve.
   —Lucius Brutus................................822.2 127
   V. 2. Mithridates. — Cæsar Borgia.—Constantine the Great.—Duke of Guise.............822.2 128
   V. 3. Sophonisba. — Nero. — Gloriana. — Rival queens.—Massacre of Paris................822.2 129
   Lucius Junius Brutus : tragedy. 1763.
   ....822.2 Pam. 1

Lee, Mrs. R. Adventures in Australia........06804
   African wanderers................................06801
   Cape Coast castle.................................06806

Lee, Sophia. Canterbury tales.................12087
   Contents: The clergyman's tale: Pembroke. — The young lady's tale: The two Emilys.

Lee, Vernon, *pseud.* (Violet Paget.) Althea: 2d book of dialogues. '94..824.2 472
   Contents: Value of the individual.—Orpheus in Rome.—On friendship.—About the social question.—The spiritual life.—The use of the soul.
   Baldwin; being dialogues. 1886......824.2 388
   Contents: Responsibilities of unbelief. — Consolations of belief,—Honour and evolution.—Novels.—Value of the ideal.—Doubts and pessimism.
   Belcaro..704 23
   Contents: The book and its title. — The child in the Vatican.—Orpheus and Eurydice.—Faustus and Helena.—Chapelmaster Kreisler. — Cherubino. — In Umbria.—Ruskinism.—Poetic morality.—Postscript.
   Hauntings......................................12504
   Juvenilia. 1887.............................704 29
   (For contents, see FINDING LIST, pt. 3, p. 412.)
   Limbo; and other essays. 1897......824.2 324
   Contents: Limbo.—In praise of old houses. — The lie of the land. — Tuscan midsummer magic. — Of modern travelling.—Old Italian gardens.—About leisure.
   Miss Brown..................................12506
   Ottilie..12502
   Phantom lover..............................12503
   Prince of a hundred soups...............12501
   Renaissance fancies and studies. '95..824.2 487
   Contents: The love of the saints. — The imaginative art of the renaissance.—Tuscan sculpture. — A seeker of pagan perfection, being the life of Domenico Neroni, pictor sacrilegus.—Valedictory.
   Vanitas: polite stories...................12505

Lees. Stronbuy..................................58936

Le Fanu. Bird of passage......................14404
   Cock and anchor................................14410
   Fortunes of Colonel Torlogh O'Brien......14412
   Guy Deverell.....................................14402
   House by the churchyard.....................14403
   In a glass darkly................................14409
   Purcell papers...................................14407
   Uncle Silas.......................................14406
   Wylder's hand...................................14405

Le Fanu *et al.* Stable for nightmares........14411

Leffingwell, A. Mystery of Bar Harbor...69327

Leffingwell, W. B. Manulito................11310

Le Gallienne. Book-bills of Narcissus......6325
   Prose fancies. 1894........................824.2 473
   Same. 2d series. 1896...................824.2 474
   Quest of the golden girl......................6326
   Retrospective reviews. 1896. 2 v.....824.2 495
   Robert Louis Stevenson, and other poems. 1895..........................821.2 985

Legaré. Writings. 2 v.
   V. 1. Biography.—Diary of Brussels. — Journal of the Rhine. — Diplomatic correspondence.—Private correspondence.—Speeches and addresses.
   ....824.1 141
   V. 2. Contributions to the Southern review..824.1 142

Legge. Richardus Tertius: Latin play...822.2 76

Le Grange. Salted with fire....................12047

Leigh. Lives that came to nothing...........32440

Leighton, R. Olaf the glorious.............017008
   Pilots of Pomona.............................017005
   Thirsty sword..................................017006
   Wreck of the Golden Fleece..............017007

Leighton, W. At the court of King Edwin: drama..........................822.1 14
   Change (verse). 1879...................821.1 220

Leland, C. G. Hans Breitmann about town. 1869..828.1 74
   Hans Breitmann in Germany — Tyrol. 1895..828.1 45
   Hans Breitmann's ballads................828.1 21
   Hans Breitmann's party. 1869.........828.1 73
   Meister Karl's sketch-book. 1872.....828.1 23
   Songs of the sea, and Lays of the land. 1895..821.1 489

Leland, C. G., *tr.* Gaudeamus: humorous poems from the German of Scheffel. 1872..838 1

Leland, H. P. The grey-bay mare, etc....828.1 24

Lemon. Falkner Lyle............................12009
   Golden fetters...................................12006
   Leyton hall.......................................12008
   Wait for the end................................12007

Lemore. Covenant with the dead...........28801

Leo. Shakespeare-notes. 1885..........822.3 318

Leofwine the monk..............................58905

Leppere. Rainbow creed........................52223

Le Queux. Devil's dice..........................67043
   Great white queen.............................67044

Guilty bonds..67040
Secret service...67042
Zoraida...67041
Le Row, Caroline, *ed.* English as she is taught. 1887.................................828.1 72
Lesdernier, *Madame* De. Headland home..12098
Leslie, Eliza. Pencil sketches.................12090
Leslie, Emma. Harry Lawley............010002
Saxby..62399
Leslie, *Mrs.* M. Juliette...........................12094
Let well alone..50371
Letters from Rome, A. D. 138....................50336
Lever. Arthur O'Leary..............................1635
Barrington.......................................1640
Bramleighs of Bishop's folly.................1629
Charles O'Malley...................................1601
Confessions of Con Cregan....................1627
Cornelius O'Dowd upon men and women, etc. 1873............................824.2 263
The Daltons...1614
Davenport Dunn.....................................1651
Day's ride...1636
Dodd family abroad..............................1642
Fortunes of Glencore..............................1645
Gerald Fitzgerald...................................1652
Harry Lorrequer.....................................1605
Horace Templeton.................................1622
Jack Hinton..1612
Knight of Gwynne..................................1623
Lord Kilgobbin..1624
Luttrell of Arran.....................................1634
Martins of Cro' Martin.........................1637
Maurice Tiernay...................................1610
Nuts and nutcrackers.........................827.2 26
The O'Donoghue....................................1628
One of them..1650
Paul Gosslett's confessions.................1633
Same..*in* 1632
Rent in a cloud.....................................1630
Roland Cashel.......................................1648
St. Patrick's eve....................................1632
Sir Brooke Fosbrooke..........................1638
Sir Jasper Carew..................................1616
That boy of Norcott's............................1631
Tom Burke of ' ours '..........................1607
Tony Butler..1619
Le Voleur. By order of the brotherhood...69920
Levy. Miss Meredith..................................22242
Reuben Sachs.......................................22241
Romance of a shop..............................22240
Lewes, G. H. Ranthorpe........................14166
Three sisters...14167
Lewes, *Mrs.* G. H. See Eliot, George.
Lewes, L. Women of Shakespeare. 1895.
....822.3 390
Lewis, C. B. See Quad, M.
Lewis, *Sir* G. C. Letters. 1870............826.2 42

Lewis, *Mrs.* H. Amber the adopted..........56894
Lewis, Mary A. Two pretty girls.............65501
Lewis, S. A. King's stratagem (drama). 1874..822.2 163
Leyland *and* Robinson. For the honour of the flag......................................43030
Leys. Lawyer's secret................................36020
Liddell. Jasmine Leigh............................25205
Jonathan..25202
Making or marring................................25206
Mistress Judith......................................25201
Liddon. Essays and addresses. 1892...824.2 452
Contents: Lects. on Buddhism.—Lects. on the life of Saint Paul.—Papers on Dante.
Lieber. Miscellaneous writings. 1881. 2 v..304 21
Life and death..50368
Life below : seven poems. 1868............821.1 56
Life in Italy..55204
Life in Normandy..50369
Life of a lawyer..50333
Life of a prig; by one................................69029
Life of Jefferson S. Batkins....................50343
Lifting the veil...50345
Lights and shadows of English life. 2 v......50363
Lil. (See Laddie.)....................................17906
Liljencrantz, O. J. The scrape that Jack built..036701
Lillie, Lucy C. Colonel's money............029705
Elinor Belden...66005
Esther's fortune....................................029707
False witness..................................*in* 029708
Family dilemma....................................66006
Household of Glen Holly.....................029706
Jo's opportunity...................................029704
Kenyon's wife..66002
Mildred's bargain................................029701
My mother's enemy.............................66003
Nan...029702
Phil and the baby...............................029708
Prudence...66001
Rolf house...029703
Roslyn's trust..66004
Lilio. Dramatic works. 1810. 2 v.
V. 1. Life of Lillo.—Silvia.—George Barnwell. —Life of Scanderbeg.—Christian hero............822.2 121
V. 2. Fatal curiosity.— Marina. — Elmerick.— Britannia and Batavia.—Arden of Feversham...822.2 122
Lilly, J. Dramatic works. 1858. 2 v.
V. 1. Life. — Endimion. — Campaspe. — Sapho and Phao.—Gallathea...................................822.2 95
V. 2. Midas.—Mother Bombie.—Woman in the moone.—Love's metamorphosis..................822.2 96
Lilly, W. S. Essays and speeches. 1897.
....824.2 515
Contents: Alexander Pope.—Professor Green.—John Henry Newman.—Temporal power of the pope.—Making of Germany.—Literature and national life.—The new spirit in history.
Lin. What dreams may come..................69447

Lincoln, A. Complete works. 1894. 2v..329.1 171
    Lost speech; reported by Whitney. 1856.
    ....329.1 Pam. 133
    Pen and voice: letters and addresses.
    1890..329.1 98
    Political debates with Douglas. 1858..329.1 140
    Table talk; ed. by Stoddard. 1894....829.1 36
Lincoln, F. W. Address. 1844................40 27
Lincoln, J. G. A genuine girl.................56703
    Her Washington season.....................56702
Linden. Gold....................................70801
Lindley. Log of the Fortuna..................30426
Lindsay. Rhoda Roberts......................31140
Lindsey. Cinder-path tales...................70960
Linskill. Between the heather and the
    northern sea..................................20005
    Cleveden.......................................20007
    Glover's daughter............................20001
    Hagar..20002
    Haven under the hill........................20006
    In exchange for a soul.....................20004
    Lost son.—The glover's daughter.........20001
    Robert Holt's illusion.......................20003
    Tales of the North Riding................20008
Linton. Atonement of Leam Dundas........53507
    Dulcie Everton................................53523
    The girl of the period, etc. 2 v........824.2 349
    Ione..53515
    Lizzie Lorton..................................53521
    Mad Willoughbys............................53509
    Misericordia...................................53501
    My love...53513
    New woman in haste and at leisure....53519
    Our professor.................................53522
    Paston Carew.................................53516
    Patricia Kemble..............................53502
    Rebel of the family.........................53510
    Sowing the wind.............................53518
    Through the long night....................53517
    Todhunters at Loanin' head..............53511
    True history of Joshua Davidson........53514
    'Twixt cup and lip, etc....................53520
    Under which lord?..........................53508
    With a silken thread, etc.................53512
    World well lost. 2 v.......................53503
Lippard. Blanche of Brandywine............20459
    Legends of the revolution................20461
    Paul Ardenheim.............................20460
Lippincott, *Mrs.* **S. J.** See **Greenwood, Grace.**
Lipsett. Where the Atlantic meets the
    land..56140
Lisle. Self and self-sacrifice.................52280
Litchfield. Criss-cross.........................19304
    Hard-won victory............................19305
    In the crucible................................19307
    Knight of the Black Forest..............19301

Little he and she.............................619320
Little Venice, etc...........................19306
    Contents: Little Venice.—Selina's singular marriage. Myrtle.—One chapter.—An American flirtation. La Rochefoucauld's saying.—Hilary's husband.—The price I paid for a set of Ruskin.
Little German drummer-boy..............07165
Littledale. On Tennyson's 'Idylls of the
    king.' 1893..............................821.2 350
Livingston *and* **Alden.** John Remington,
    martyr...4908
    Profiles...4905
Llewellyn. Title hunting......................44152
Locke, D. R., (Petroleum V. Nasby, *pseud.*).
    Morals of Abou Ben Adhem. '75....827.1 9
    Ekkoes from Kentucky. 1868..........827.1 8
    Hannah Jane (verse). 1882..........821.1 264
    Nasby in exile. 1882....................914 148
    Paper city......................................56819
    Swingin' round the cirkle. 1867.....827.1 6
Locke, J. Works. 1801. 10 v..............192 39
    (For contents, see FINDING LIST, pt. 3, p. 436.)
Locke, *Mrs.* **M.** In far Dakota..............20444
Locke, W. J. At the gate of Samaria.....43270
    Demagogue and Lady Phayre.............43271
    Study in shadows...........................43272
Locker, A. Stephen Scudamore.............56801
Locker-Lampson. London lyrics. '70..821.2 428
    Poems. 1884..............................821.2 731
Lockhart, J. G. Reginald Dalton..........25835
    Some passages in the life of Mr. Adam
    Blair...25833
    Valerius..25834
Lockhart, L. W. M. Doubles and quits...61901
    Fair to see....................................61902
    Mine is thine.................................61903
Lodge. Forbonius and Prisceria............175 2
    Rosalind...69326
Logan, J. Poems; with life. 1822......821.2 45
Logan, M. C., (Vincent Ellerton, *pseud.*).
    Artist's dream...............................25871
Logan, Olive, (Mrs. Sikes). Apropos of
    women and theatres. 1869.........824.1 115
    Chateau Frissac..............................40101
    Get thee behind me, Satan...............40102
    They met by chance........................40103
Loggerville literary society transactions.
    ....828.2 41
London Times; Essays from the. 1852...824.2 178
Long, J. D. After-dinner speeches, etc.
    1895..825.1 37
Long, J. L. Miss Cherry-Blossom of Tôkyô.51415
Long, Lily A. Squire of low degree........9905
Longfellow, H. W. Aftermath. 1873...821.1 90
    Bibliography of first editions. 1885........16 63
    Complete poetical works: Cambridge
    edition......................................821.1 92
    Courtship of Miles Standish, etc. 1859..821.1 91

Divine tragedy. 1871.....................822.1 10
Evangeline. 1869.........................821.1 85
Golden legend. 1859....................821.1 86
Hyperion...................................12021
In the harbor: Ultima Thule, pt. 2......821.1 84
Kavanagh...................................12022
Kéramos, and other poems. 1878......821.1 88
Masque of Pandora, etc. 1875..........821.1 75
New England tragedies. 1868..........822.1 16
Contents: John Endicott.—Giles Corey of the Salem farms.
Outre-mer..................................914 44
Poetical works. 1866. v. 1, 3, and 4.
V. 1. Voices of the night.—Ballads, etc.—Poems on slavery.—Spanish student......................821.1 79
V. 3. Golden legend.—Courtship of Miles Standish.—Birds of passage...............................821.1 80
V. 4. Song of Hiawatha.—Tales of a wayside inn.—Birds of passage.................................821.1 81
Poetical works. 1883...................821.1 87
Contents: Voices of the night. — Earlier poems.—Translations. — Ballads, etc.— Children of the Lord's supper.—Poems of slavery.—Spanish student,—Belfry of Bruges, etc.—Songs.—Sonnets.—Curfew.—Evangeline.—Seaside and fireside.—Song of Hiawatha.—Courtship of Miles Standish.—Birds of passage.—Tales of a wayside inn.—Flower de luce.—Judas Maccabæus.—Masque of Pandora,—Hanging of the crane.—Morituri salutamus. — Kéramos. — Ultima Thule. — Folk-songs. — L'envoi. — Notes.—Index.
Poetical works. 1885...................821.1 87A
(Contents same as above, with following additions: In the harbor.—Personal poems.—Michael Angelo.—Notes. —Index.)
Reference list; by Foster. v. 2..............16 55
Seaside and fireside. 1850.............821.1 76
Selections from poetical works, in New York point, for the blind. 1883...362.4 N-Y-6
Song of Hiawatha. 1856................821.1 77
Studies in; by Gannett. 1886.....928.1 Pam. 5
Tales of a wayside inn. 1864...........821.1 89
Three books of song. 1872.............821.1 78
Contents: Tales of a wayside inn, second day.—Judas Maccabæus.—A handful of translations.
Translation of Dante's 'Divine comedy.' 1871. 3 v..................................851 8
Ultima Thule. 1880......................821.1 83
Same; pt. 2...............................821.1 84

Longfellow, S. Hymns and verses. '94..821.1 483
Longstreet. Georgia scenes..............15275
Loomis. Mental and social culture. 1873....374 6
Lord, E. B. Hymn for the voiceless..821.1 Pam. 32
Lord, J. C. Lectures. 1851....................204 67
Occasional poems. 1869..........821.1 375
Oration, Buffalo, July 5, 1858......825.1 Pam. 12
Sonnets ....821.1 Pam. 31
Lord, *Mrs.* **J. C.** Travels of the Du Le Telle family. 1869..................828.1 Pam. 3
Lord, W. W. Christ in Hades; poem...821.1 28
Lorimer. Messages of to-day. 1896......170 111
Loring. The Boston dip, etc. (verse). 1871...821.1 453

Lorne, *marquis of.* Memories of Canada and Scotland. 1883......................825.2 8
Lost beauty.................................50329
Lost in Pompeii...............................0138
Loth. Forgiving kiss.........................30452
Lothrop, H. M. See **Sidney, Margaret,** *pseud.*
Lotos-leaves..................................55272
Loudon, *Mrs.* Mummy.....................52286
Loughead, Flora H. Abandoned claim...22502
Man from nowhere......................22503
Man who was guilty....................22501
Lovejoy. Agricultural poem. 1859..821.1 Pam. 8
Lovelace. Lucasta: poems; ed. by Hazlitt.......................................821.2 596
Lovell. Poems. 1822.................*in* 821.2 46
Lover. Handy Andy.........................1704
Same; dramatized by Floyd. 1895..822.2 331
He would be a gentleman 1706
Irish sketches.— American sketches.—Poetry......................................*in* 928.2 169
Legends and stories of Ireland..............1707
Poetical works.........................821.2 319
Rory O'More................................1701
Lovibond. Poems. 1822.............*in* 821.2 46
Low. Tales of old ocean....................012901
Lowe. Fallen star............................34580
Lowell, J. R. Among my books. 2 v.
V. 1. Dryden.—Witchcraft.—Shakespeare once more.—New England two centuries ago.—Lessing.—Rousseau and the sentimentalists.............824.1 184
V. 2. Dante.—Spenser.—Wordsworth.—Milton. —Keats..824.1 185
Biglow papers...........................827.1 19
Same; 2d series. 1882..................827.1 20
The cathedral. 1870....................821.1 101
Complete poetical works; Cambridge edition. 1896..........................821.1 100B
Democracy, etc. 1887.................824.1 183
Contents: Democracy.—Garfield.—Stanley.—Fielding. — Coleridge.— Books and libraries. — Wordsworth. — Don Quixote.—Harvard anniversary.
Fireside travels. 1864.................824.1 182
Contents: Cambridge 30 years ago.—A Moosehead journal.—Leaves from my journal in Italy and elsewhere.
Heartsease and rue. 1888.............821.1 95
Last poems. 1895......................821.1 103
Latest literary essays, etc. 1892........824.1 187
Contents: Gray.—Some letters of Landor.—Walton. —Milton's 'Areopagitica.'—Shakespeare's 'Richard III.' —The study of modern languages.—The progress of the world.
Letters; ed. by Norton. 1894. 2 v...826.1 12
My study windows. 1871................824.1 186
Contents: My garden acquaintance.—A good word for winter.—On a certain condescension in foreigners.—A great public character. — Carlyle.— Lincoln.—J. G. Percival.- Thoreau.—Swinburne's tragedies.—Chaucer. —Library of old authors. Emerson the lecturer. Pope

Poems. 1857. 2 v.
  V. 1. Legend of Brittany —Miscellaneous poems.
  —Sonnets.—L'envoi..........................821.1 98
  V. 2. Miscellaneous..............................821.1 99
Poetical works. 1871. 2 v.
  V. 1. Miscellaneous poems.—Memorial verses.
  —Sonnets...821.1 96
  V. 2. Fable for critics.— Biglow papers.—Unhappy lot of Mr. Knott.—Oriental apologue........821.1 97
Poetical works. 1890.......................821.1 100
Under the willows, and other poems.
  1869...821.1 102
Lowell, R. T. S.   Antony Brade............40504
  Fresh hearts, etc. (verse). 1860.......821.1 454
  New priest of Conception Bay................40501
  Story or two from an old Dutch town......40505
Lowry. Women's tragedies.....................13380
Luard. Clare Saville..................................12089
Lubbock. Pleasures of life. '87. 2 v...*824.2 512
Lucas, Anne. Leonie.............................62584
Lucas, R. Felix Dorrien...........................69660
Lucretia..50390
Lucy. Gideon Fleyce................................68701
  Miller's niece, etc..............................68702
Ludlow. Captain of the Janizaries............27603
  King of Tyre....................................27601
  That angelic woman.............................27602
Lummis. Gold fish of Gran Chimú............36601
Lunt. Poems. 1839...........................821.1 338
  Three eras of New England, etc. '57...824.1 98
Lushington. Over the seas and far away...66301
Luska, Sidney, *pseud.* (Henry Harland.)
  As it was written. 21402
  Grandison Mather.............................21408
  Land of love..................................21405
  Latin-quarter courtship......................21407
  Mademoiselle Miss, etc........................21412
    Contents: Mademoiselle Miss.—The funeral march of a marionette.—The prodigal father.—A sleeveless errand. —A light sovereign.
  Mea culpa....................................21411
  Mrs. Peixada.................................21401
  My uncle Florimond..........................21406
  Two voices...................................21409
  Two women or one?..........................21410
  Yoke of the Thorah..........................21404
Luxton. New house that Jack built.........029201
Lyall, A. Agonistes (essays). 1856.....824.2 113
Lyall, D. Land o' the leal........................39060
Lyall, Edna. Autobiography of a slander..19704
  Autobiography of a truth....................19711
  Derrick Vaughan, novelist...................19706
  Donovan 19701
  Doreen......................................19710
  Hardy Norseman.............................19708
  In the golden days..........................19705
  Knight-errant...............................19703
  To right the wrong..........................19709
  We two......................................19702
  Won by waiting..............................19707

Lydgate. Minor poems..................821.2 445
  The assembly of gods; ed. by Triggs.
  1895...821.2 1022
Lyly. Endymion [drama] ; ed., with biography, by Baker. 1894................822.2 317
  Euphues.— Anatomy of wit.— Euphues
  and his England..............................820.2 29
Lynch, A. C., (Mrs. Botta). Poems. '49..821.1 170
Lynch, Hannah. Daughters of men........29010
  Doctor Vermont's fantasy....................29011
  Odd experiment..............................29012
Lyndesay, Sir D. Works ; pt. 1........820.2 305
  Same ; pt. 2..................................820.2 308
  Same ; pt. 3..................................820.2 317
  Same ; pt. 4..................................820.2 319
  Same ; pt. 5..................................820.2 325
Lyndon, J. W. Ninety-three....................44183
Lyndon, *pseud.* See **Bright, M. A.**
Lyndsay. Dramas of the ancient world..822.2 142
    Contents: The deluge.—Plague of darkness.— Last plague.— Rizpah.—Sardanapalus.— Destiny of Cain.— Death of Cain.—The Nereid's love.
Lyon, Anna E. West-. My first harvest
  (verse). 1893................................821.1 481
Lys. Doctor's idol...................................21510
Lysaght, E. J. Over the border................56859
Lysaght, S. R. Marplot.........................30595
Lyster. Alone in crowds............................22141
  Two old maids................................22140
Lytle. Poems; with memoir by Venable.
  1894...821.1 550
Lyttelton. Ephemera. 1865.............824.2 114
  Persian letters. 1793...................*in* 824.2 52
  Poems ; with life. 1822.................821.2 44
Lytton, E. Bulwer, *baron.* Alice............1308
  Calderon......................................1345
  Caxtoniana : essays. 824.2 155
  Caxtons.......................................1327
  Coming race...................................1351
  Critical and miscellaneous writings. 2 v.
  ....824.2 151
  Devereaux.....................................1309
  Disowned 1314
  Earnest Maltravers.............................1307
  Eugene Aram...................................1304
  Falkland.—Zicci...............................1390
  Godolphin.....................................1317
  Harold..1325
  Kenelm Chillingly.............................1346
  King Arthur (poem). 1849. 2 v......821.2 779
  Lady of Lyons.................................1397
    Same ; acting edition.........822.2 225
    Same ; adapted to the stage by Booth.
  ....822.4 330
  Last days of Pompeii..........................1355
  Last of the barons............................1322
  Leila..1345

* Of interest to young readers.

Lost tales of Miletus. 1866............821.2 787
Lucretia..1312
Miscellaneous prose works. '68. 3 v..824.2 148
  Same. 1868. 2 v......................824.2 153
My novel...1334
New Timon (poem). 1846................821.2 786
New Timon.—St. Stephen's. 1860...821.2 787
Night and morning...........................1356
Parisians..1353
Paul Clifford.....................................1301
Pausanias the Spartan....................1349
Pelham..1302
Pilgrims of the Rhine.......................1343
  Same...*in* 1345
Poetical and dramatic works. 1852. 5 v.
  V. 1. The new Timon.—Constance.—Milton.—Eva.—The fairy bride.—The beacon.—The lay of the minstrel heart.—Narrative lyrics...........821.2 781
  V. 2. King Arthur; books 1-9..............821.2 782
  V. 3. King Arthur; books 10-12.—Corn flowers. —Earlier poems...................................821.2 783
  V. 4. Duchesse de la Vallière.—Lady of Lyons. —Richelieu...821.2 784
  V. 5. Money.—Not so bad as we seem......821.2 785
Richelieu: a play............................822.2 224
Rienzi..1352
Strange story...................................1338
What will he do with it?..................1336
Zanoni..1319
Zicci..1390

Lytton, R. Bulwer, *earl,* (Owen Meredith. After paradise, with other poems. 1887........................821.2 394
  Fables in song. 1874......................829.2 24
  Glenaveril: a poem. 1885..............821.2 399
  Lucile (poem). 1880........................821.2 398
  Marah. 1892....................................821.2 393
  Poems. 1866. 2 v.
    V. 1. The wanderer.—Tannhäuser............821.2 395
    V. 2. Clytemnestra.—Minor poems.— National songs of Servia..................................821.2 396
  Poetical works. 1875.....................821.2 397
    Contents: Lucile.—Apple of life.—Clytemnestra.— Wanderer, etc.
  Ring of Amasis..............................15263

Lytton, *Lady* **Rosina.** Lady Chevely.......15264
  School for husbands.....................15265

M., *Mr.* Shen's pigtail, etc.................14830
Mabel's stepmother............................0131
Maberly. Leontine...............................14122
Mabie. Books and culture. 1896........824.1 321
  Contents: Material and method.—Time and place.— Meditation and imagination.—The first delight.—The feeling for literature.—The books of life.—From the book to the reader.—By way of illustration.—Personality. —Liberation through ideas. The logic of free life.— The imagination, Breadth of life. Racial expression. —Freshness of feeling. Liberation from one's time.— Liberation from one's place.—The unconscious element. —The teaching of tragedy. The culture element in fiction. Culture through action—The interpretation of idealism. The vision of perfection.—Retrospect.

Essays on nature and culture. 1896...824.1 313
  Contents: The art of arts.—Education.—Time and tide.—Man and nature.—The race memory.—The discovery to the senses.—The discovery to the imagination. —The poetic interpretation.—The moral impress.—The record in language.—The individual approach.— Personal intimacy. — Fundamental correspondences. — Creative force. — The great revelation. — Form and vitality.—The method.—Distinctness of individuality.— Vital selection. — Repose. — The universal life. — The unconscious life. — Solitude and silence. — Unhasting, unresting. — Health. — Work and play. — Work and beauty.—The rhythmic movement.—Law of harmony.— Prophecy of nature.
Under the trees, and elsewhere. 1891..824.1 257
Macalpine. Joel Marsh, etc................22321
  Man's conscience..............................22320
Macaulay, *Miss* **E.** Tales from the drama...30401
Macaulay, T. B. Critical and historical essays (Trevelyan edition). 1890. 2 v.
  V. 1. Milton.—Machiavelli.—Hallam's constitutional history.—Southey's colloquies on society. —Mr. Robert Montgomery's poems.—Moore's Life of Lord Byron.'— Southey's edition of 'The pilgrim's progress.'— Civil disabilities of the Jews.— Boswell's 'Life of Johnson.'— Lord Nugent's ' Memorials of Hampden.'—Burleigh and his times. — War of the succession in Spain.— Horace Walpole.— William Pitt, earl of Chatham.—Sir James Mackintosh.—Lord Bacon.........................824.2 130
  V. 2. Sir William Temple. — Gladstone on church and state.— Lord Clive.— Von Ranke.— Leigh Hunt.—Lord Holland.—Warren Hastings. —Frederic the great.—Madame D'Arblay.— Life and writings of Addison.— The earl of Chatham. 824.2 131
Essays. 1843. 4 v..........................824.2 118
  Same. 1860. 6 v.
    V. 1. Fragments of a Roman tale. — Royal society of literature. — Scenes from ' Athenian revels.'— Dante. — Petrarch.—;The great lawsuit between the parishes of St. Dennis and St. George in the water.—Conversation between Cowley and Milton. — The Athenian orators. — Prophetic account of ' The Wellingtoniad.'—Mitford's 'Greece.' —Milton. — Machiavelli. — Dryden. — History.— Hallam's constitutional history........................824.2 122
    V. 2. Mill on govt.— Westminster Reviewer's defence of Mill. — Utilitarian theory of govt.— Southey's colloquies. — Robert Montgomery's poems.—Sadler's law of population.— Pilgrim's progress. — Sadler's refutation refuted. — Civil disabilities of the Jews.— Moore's life of Byron. —Croker's Boswell's 'Johnson.'—Nugent's 'Memorials of Hampden.'...................................824.2 123
    V. 3. Burleigh and his times.—Mirabeau.—War of the succession in Spain.— Horace Walpole.— Chatham.—Sir James Mackintosh.—Bacon........824.2 124
    V. 4. Sir William Temple.—Gladstone on church and state.—Lord Clive.—Ranke's 'History of the popes.'—Comic dramatists of the restoration.— Lord Holland...824.2 125
    V. 5. Warren Hastings.—Frederic the great. —Madame D'Arblay.—Addison.—Barère........824.2 126
    V. 6. Chatham. Atterbury.—Bunyan.— Goldsmith.— Samuel Johnson. — Pitt.—The West Indies. — London university. — Capacities of negroes. The present administration.—Index...............824.2 127

Lays of ancient Rome......................*821.2 326
Miscellaneous writings and speeches..824.2 420
Contents: Fragments of a Roman tale.—On the royal society of literature.—Scenes from 'Athenian revels.'—Criticisms on the principal Italian writers.—Great lawsuit between the parishes of St. Dennis and St. George in, the water.—Conversation between Mr. Abraham Cowley and Mr. John Milton touching the great civil war.—On the Athenian orators.- Prophetic account of a grand national epic poem to be entitled 'The Wellingtoniad.' — On Mitford's 'History of Greece.'—John Dryden.— History.— Mill on govt. — Westminster Reviewer's defence of Mill. — Utilitarian theory of govt. Sadler's law of population.—Sadler's refutation refuted. —Mirabeau.— Barère.— Francis Atterbury.—John Bunyan.— Oliver Goldsmith.— Samuel Johnson.-- William Pitt.—Miscellaneous poems, etc.

Selections from ; ed. by Trevelyan. '77.
....829.2 41
Selections from essays and speeches. 2v.
V. 1. Warren Hastings. — Clive. — Chatham.— Ranke's 'History of the popes.' — Gladstone on church and state.-- Addison.— Horace Walpole.— Johnson...824.2 128
V. 2. Bacon. — Byron. — Comic dramatists. — Frederick the great.— Hallam's constitutional history.—Speeches on parliamentary reform..........824.2 129

McCabe, J. D. Our young folks abroad...027401
  Our young folks in Africa......................027402
McCabe, J. D., *jr.* Planting the wilderness..032227
McCall, G. A. Letters from the frontiers. 1868..826.1 9
McCallum, Mrs. M. C. See **Stirling, M. C.**
McCarthy, Justin. Camiola....................33425
  Comet of a season.................................33412
  Commander's statue.............................*in* 32755
  Dear Lady Disdain...............................33402
  Dictator..33406
  Donna Quixote....................................33410
  Fair Saxon..33403
  Lady Judith..33401
  Linley Rocheford.................................33405
  Maid of Athens...................................33420
  Miss Misanthrope.................................33409
  My enemy's daughter...........................33423
  Red diamonds.....................................33414
  Riddle ring...33416
  Roland Oliver.....................................33411
  Waterdale neighbors............................33407
McCarthy, Justin, *and* **Praed,** *Mrs.* **C.**
  Ladies' gallery....................................33408
  The right honourable...........................33404
  Rival princess.....................................33413
McCarthy, Justin H. Dolly...................33452
  Hafiz in London (verse). 1886..........821.2 772
  Lily lass..33450
  London legend [Woman of impulse]......33454
  Our sensation novel.............................33451
  Royal Christopher...............................33455
  Woman of impulse [London legend]......33453

McChesney. Miriam Cromwell, royalist. ..53601
McClellan. See **Flemming, Harford.**
McClelland. Broadoaks........................42808
  Jean Monteith....................................42803
  Madame Silva....................................42804
  Mammy Mystic..................................42811
  Manitou island..................................42807
  Nameless novel..................................42806
  Oblivion..42812
  Old post road....................................42809
  Princess..42801
  St. John's wooing...............................42810
  Self-made man 42802
  Ten minutes to twelve........................42805
MacColl. Bide a wee, and other poems. 1880..821.1 265
McConaughy. Fire fighters...................02401
McConnell, Annie Bliss. Half married...34801
MacConnell, J. L. Talbot and Vernon.....50310
McCook. Old farm fairies......................020010
McCosh. Bibliography; by Dulles. 1895.
....16 Pam. 77
McCray *and* **Smith.** Wheels and whims...58931
Macdonald, George. Adela Cathcart........5913
  Alec Forbes..5914
  Annals of a quiet neighborhood............5920
  At the back of the north wind..............0701
  Book of strife (verse). 1885...........821.2 739
  Cross purposes, etc..............................0708
    Contents: Cross purposes. — The golden key. — The carasoyn.—Little daylight.
  Cruel painter, etc................................5904
    Contents: Cruel painter. — The castle. — The wow o' Rivven.— Broken swords.— Gray wolf.— Uncle Cornelius, his story.
  David Elginbrod.................................5901
  The disciple, and other poems. '68...821.2 404
  Donal Grant......................................5950
  Double story.....................................0702
  Elect lady...5910
  Flight of the shadow.........................5919
  Gifts of the child Christ.....................5947
  Guild court......................................5943
  Heather and snow.............................5922
  Hidden life, and other poems. 1872..821.2 405
  Home again.....................................5912
  The imagination, and other essays.....824.2 333A
    Same, under the title 'Orts.' '82...824.2 333
  Light princess, etc.............................0707
    Contents: The light princess. — The giant's heart.—The shadows.
  Lilith...5951
  Malcolm..5921
  Marquis of Lossie..............................5918
  Mary Marston..................................5939
  Paul Faber......................................5930
  Phantastes.......................................5915

* Of interest to young readers.

Poetical works. 1893. 2 v. 821.2 911
Portent..5946
Princess and Curdie.................................0705
Princess and the goblin..........................0703
Ranald Bannerman's boyhood...............0704
Robert Falconer..5903
Rough shaking..0706
St. George and St. Michael....................5917
Seaboard parish.......................................5911
Sir Gibbie..5935
Stephen Archer, etc................................5949
There and back..5916
Thomas Wingfold, curate........................5907
Tragedie of Hamlet........................822.4 336
Vicar's daughter.......................................5909
Warlock o' Glenwarlock...........................5944
Weighed and wanting..............................5948
What's mine's mine..................................5952
Wilfrid Cumbermede................................5905
Within and without.—A hidden life.
  (Poems.) 1884...............................821.2 1018
Macdonald, J. M. Thunderbolt...............32320
McDonnell. Heathens of the heath..........47238
McDougall. Hidden city...........................10830
McDowell. See **Bonner, Sherwood.**
McElroy. Red acorn....................................68801
Macfarlane. Romance of history: Italy....47226
MacGahan. Xenia Repninà.....................25897
McGee. Poems. 1869......................821.2 423
McGlasson, Eva Wilder. See **Brodhead, Eva Wilder.**
McGloin. Norodom..................................62587
McGrath. Pictures from Ireland.............62502
Macgregor. John Ward's governess......22150
  Professor's wife.....................................22151
Machar. Marjorie's Canadian winter......010003
Machen. Three impostors.......................60180
McIlrain. Ebon and gold..........................52265
McIntosh. Charms and countercharms......9402
  Evenings at Donaldson manor..................9410
  Lofty and lonely..9404
  Two lives..9403
  Two pictures..9408
Mackarness. Mingled yarn......................54804
  Old saws new set..................................017403
  Peerless wife..54805
  Sunbeam stories....................................54801
  Trap to catch a sunbeam.....................017402
Mackarness *et al.* Hope rewarded.......017401
Mackay, *Mrs.* Clifford castle...................47290
Mackay, Eric. Love-letters of a violinist,
  etc. (poems). 1892.........................821.2 896
  Lover's missal (verse). 1897..........821.2 1026
  Song of the sea. 1895.......................821.2 557
Mackay, K. The yellow wave...................50430
Mackay, Minnie. See **Corelli, Marie.**
Mackaye, S. Appalling passion...............12099

McKeever. Maude and Miriam................19123
  Silver threads..19126
  Twice crowned.....................................19124
  Westbrook parsonage.........................19125
McKellar. In Oban town..........................52520
Mackenzie, *Mrs.* **A. S.** Aureola...........12049
Mackenzie, H. Miscellaneous works.
  1836...824.2 60
  Contents: Man of feeling.—Papers from The Lounger.
  —Man of the world.—Julia de Roubigne.—Papers from The Mirror.
  Works. 1808. 8 v.
  V. 1-2. Man of feeling.—Man of the world...820.2 108
  V. 3. Julia de Roubigne......................820.2 110
  V. 4-7. Papers from The Mirror, Lounger, etc.
  ....820.2 111
  V. 8. Poems.—Dramatic pieces.........820.2 115
Mackenzie, H., *ed.* The Lounger. 2v..824.2 27
  The Mirror. 2 v...............................824.2 25
  Same. 1803. 2v..............................824.2 58
Mackenzie, R. S. Tressilian....................12050
Mackie. Devil's playground....................30720
  Sinners twain.......................................30721
  They that sit in darkness...................30722
Mackintosh. Miscellaneous works. '50..824.2 108
McKnight. Old Fort Duquesne..............44185
Maclachlan. William Blacklock, journalist..30820
McLain, Mary W. Wedding garments...19118
Maclaren, Ian, *pseud.* (John Maclaren
  Watson.) Beside the bonnie brier
  bush...45330
  Days of auld lang syne.......................45331
  Kate Carnegie.....................................45332
McLaren, J. F. True patriotism............40 27
McLaughlin, *ed.* Literary criticism for
  students. 1893............................824.2 467
  Contents: Introduction.—Sir Philip Sidney.—Ben Jonson.—John Dryden.—Joseph Addison.—Jonathan Swift.—Samuel Johnson.—William Wordsworth.—Samuel Taylor Coleridge.—Charles Lamb.—Thomas De Quincey.—Thomas Carlyle.—Matthew Arnold.—James Russell Lowell.—John Ruskin.—Richard Holt Hutton.—Walter Pater.
Maclean, Maggie. Romance of Skye......41201
McLean, Sarah P., (Mrs. Greene). Cape
  Cod folks..64801
  Lastchance Junction...........................64802
  Some other folks.................................64813
  Towhead...64808
  Vesty of the Basins.............................64803
McLellan. Poems of the rod and gun...821.1 346
Macleod, *Mrs.* **A.** Silent sea.................27010
McLeod, D. Bloodstone.........................52236
Macleod, F. Green fire............................14418
  Mountain lovers....................................14415
  Sin-eater, etc...14416
  Washer of the ford, etc........................14417
Macleod, N. Character sketches............28602
  The gold thread................................032243

Old lieutenant and his son	28003
The starling	28001

MacMahon, Ella. Modern man............31170
    Pitiless passion............31171
McManus. Red star............60120
    Silk of the kine............60121
MacNab. Relics............29205
McNaughton. Onnalinda (poem). 1888.
    ....821.1 B-3
McNulty. Misther O'Ryan............57370
Macon. Uncle Gabe Tucker. 1883........828.1 65
Macquoid, Katherine S. Appledore farm..13531
    At an old chateau............13529
    At the Red Glove............13504
    Awakening............13518
    Berkshire lady............13510
    Berris............13532
    Beside the river............13514
    Cosette............13527
    Diane'............13509
    Esau Runswick............13520
    Fisherman of Auge............13508
    Gone............13534
    Haunted fountain............13528
    Her sailor love............13522
    Hester Kirton............13507
    His last card............13536
    In an orchard............13535
    In the sweet spring time............13512
    Joan Wentworth............13525
    Louisa............13523
    Maisie Derrick............13502
    Miss Eyon of Eyon court............13533
    My story............13503
    Old courtyard............13530
    Patty............13517
    Pictures across the channel............13501
    Rookstone............13505
    Story of Yves............13526
    Too soon............13506
McVickar. Purple light of love............41601
Macy. There she blows............56812
Madame Lucas............63414
Madge Dunraven............50304
Madison. Letters, etc. 1865. 4 v............329.1 44
    Papers. 1841. 3 v............329.1 41
Madoc. Story of Melicent............62321
Mag.............50314
Maginn. Miscellanies, prose and verse.
    1885. 2 v............824.2 381
Magnay. The fall of a star............54640
Magnet stories. 8 v............07150
Magruder, Julia. Across the chasm............71020
    At anchor............71021
    Child Amy............025625
    Honored in the breach............71023
    Magnificent plebeian............71022
    Miss Ayr of Virginia, etc............71027
    Princess Sonia............71024
    The violet............71026
Mahoney, F. See **Prout,** *Father.*
Maine. Scarscliffe rocks............12068
Maitland, E., (Herbert Ainslie, *pseud.*).
    By and by............19154
    Higher law............19156
    Pilgrim and the shrine............19157
Maitland, E. F. Pages from the day-book
    of Bethia Hardacre............69820
    The Saltonstall gazette. 1896............824.2 508
Maitland, J. A. Diary of a physician............8702
    Old patroon............8706
    Wanderer............8705
    Watchman............8701
Majendie, *Lady.* Dita............12044
    Gianette............12043
    Once more............12045
Ma-ka-tai-me-she-kia-kiak, or Black
    Hawk : a poem. 1848............821.1 441
Malcolm. Fifty thousand dollars ransom...57010
Malet, Lucas, *pseud.* (Mrs. W. Harrison.)
    Carissima............68103
    Colonel Enderby's wife............68104
    Counsel of perfection............68105
    Little Peter............032242
    Mrs. Lorimer............68101
    Wages of sin............68102
Mallary. Horace Wilde............52211
Mallet. Poems ; with life............821.2 34
Mallock. Atheism and the value of life..824.2 367
    Every man his own poet. 1879......827.2 Pam. 1
    Heart of life............57204
    Human document............57203
    New Paul and Virginia. 1878............827.2 29
    New republic............57206
    The old order changes............57202
    Poems. 1880............821.2 549
    Romance of the 19th century............57201
    Studies of contemporary superstition.
    1895............204 126
    (For contents, see FINDING LIST, pt. 3, p. 451.)
Malone. Inquiry into the [Ireland forger-
    ies]. 1796............822.3 152
Man proposes............58912
Manfred, *pseud.* Byron vindicated............821.2 442
Mangan. Poems ; with memoir. 1870...821.2 308
    Selected poems ; ed. by Guiney............821.2 737
Manigault. Saint Cecilia ; pt. 1............52266
Manley. Some children of Adam............69720
Mann, *Mrs.* F. Parish of Hilby............62355
Mann, H. Lects. on various subjects.
    1850............170 11
Mann, Mary. Juanita............69299
Mann, Mary E. In summer shade............69601
    Susannah............69602

Manning, Anne. Cherry and violet..........40613
  Chronicle of Ethelfled..........................40606
  Colloquies of Edward Osborne............40612
  Diary of Lady Willoughby.....................40614
  Faire Gospeller......................................40611
  Family pictures.....................................40605
  Good old times....................................40604
  Household of Sir Thomas More.............40603
  Mary Powell..40602
  Mrs. Clarissa Singleheart......................40601
  Moravian life..40608
  One trip more, etc...............................40609
  Provocations of Madame Pallisy............40610
Manning, H. E. Essays read before the Academia. 1865.................................204 60
Man's a man for a' that.........................55280
Manton. Man's wrongs..........................47231
Mapes. Latin poems attributed to. 1841..821.2 105
Marbourg *and* **Eggleston.** Juggernaut....11720
March. Love on the wing......................47245
Marchmont. Parson Thring's secret........32330
Marcy. Border reminiscences.................47202
Marguerite's journal...............................07117
Marjory Graham...................................58966
Markham, C. R. Paladins of Edwin the great...036001
Markham, R. Colonial days..................029601
Markoe. My lady's heart.......................56160
Marks, *Mrs.* **Alfred.** See **Hoppus, M. A. M.**
Marlowe. Works; ed. by Bullen. 3 v.
  V. 1. Introduction. — Tamburlaine. — Doctor Faustus..822.2 261
  V. 2. Jew of Malta.—Edward II.—Massacre at Paris.—Dido...822.2 262
  V. 3. Hero and Leander.—Ovid's elegies.— Epigrams.—First book of Lucan.—Passionate shepherd.—Fragment, etc......................822.2 263
  Works; ed. by Cunningham. 1870..820.2 86
  Contents: Introductory. — Tamburlane. — Doctor Faustus.—Jew of Malta.—Edward II.—Massacre at Paris. Dido.—Hero and Leander.—Ovid's elegies. — Miscellaneous poems.—First book of Lucan.—Doctor Faustus, from folio of 1604.—Notes.
Marmion. Dramatic works; with memoir. 1875...822.2 235
Maroccus Extaticus; ed. by Rimbault...821.2 452
Married for fun......................................69021
Marryat, Florence, (Mrs. F. Lean). Broken blossom...7221
  Facing the footlights..............................7243
  Fair haired Alda......................................7230
  Fatal silence...7253
  Fighting the air......................................7226
  For ever and ever...................................7229
  Gerald Estcourt.......................................7204
  Ghost of Charlotte Cray, etc....................7245
  Girls of Feversham................................7211
  Harvest of wild oats...............................7202
  Heart of Jane Warner............................7249
  Her lord and master..............................7208
  Little stepson..7215
  Love's conflict.......................................7213
  Madame Dumaresq................................7227
  Moment of madness..............................7244
  Mount Eden..7251
  My own child..7201
  My sister the actress..............................7237
  Nelly Brooke...7209
  Nobler sex...7254
  On circumstantial evidence....................7250
  Open sesame..7207
  Out of his reckoning.............................7214
  Parson Jones..7255
  Petronel...7203
  Phillyda..7241
  Poison of asps, etc................................7210
  Prey of the gods...................................7212
  Risen dead..7252
  Star and a heart....................................7235
  Under the lilies and roses......................7248
  Veronique...7205
  Written in fire.......................................7224
Marryat, *Captain* **F.** Children of the forest.....1516
  Dog fiend..1519
  Die drei Kutter [The three cutters]......*in* 1533
  Frank Mildmay......................................1509
  Same (German)....................................1510
  Jacob Faithful......................................1515
  Japhet in search of a father..................1514
  Same (German)....................................1513
  Joseph Rushbrook: Wilddieb [The poacher]...1507
  King's own..1517
  Little savage...1536
  Masterman Ready.................................1529
  The mission..1539
  Mr. Midshipman Easy............................1522
  Same (German)....................................1523
  Monsieur Violet....................................1520
  Newton Forster....................................1504
  Same (German)....................................1505
  Pacha of many tales..............................1512
  Percival Keene......................................1537
  Same (German)....................................1538
  Peter Simple...1501
  Same (German)....................................1502
  Phantom ship.......................................1506
  Der Pirat..1533
  Pirate.—Three cutters............................1534
  Poacher..1508
  Poor Jack...1524
  Privateersman......................................1521
  Settlers in Canada................................1539
  Valerie...1511
Marsden. Milady Monte Cristo...............56080
Marsh, C. Memory's pictures (verse). 1871...821.2 443

Marsh, J. B. Robin Hood............47251
Marsh, R. Mrs. Musgrave—and her husband............24980
Marsh-Caldwell. See **Caldwell,** *Mrs.* **Marsh-.**
Marshall, Emma, (Mrs. H. Graham).
    Abigail Templeton............012110
    Alma............012106
    Benvenuta............47408
    Bristol bells............47425
    Bristol diamonds............47421
    By the North sea............47432
    Cassandra's casket............47416
    Castle meadow............47436
    Close of St. Christopher's............012108
    Constantia Carew............47410
    Court and cottage............012103
    Daphne's decision............012105
    Dorothy's daughters............47405
    Dulcibel's day-dreams............47422
    Edward's wife............47401
    Escape from the tower............47433
    First light on the Eddystone............47428
    Haunt of ancient peace............47434
    Heights and valleys............47407
    In Colston's days............47412
    In the east country............47414
    In the service of Rachel, Lady Russell...47426
    Joanna's inheritance............012102
    Job Singleton's heir, etc............47409
    Kensington palace, days of Queen Mary II............47429
    Life's aftermath............47403
    Lizette and her mission............012109
    Master of the musicians............47431
    Memories of troublous times............47404
    Mrs. Mainwaring's journal............47406
    Mistress of Tayne court............47415
    Mrs. Willoughby's octave............47413
    New relations............012107
    Now-a-days............47424
    No. 13: a story of the lost vestal............47417
    Old gateway............47402
    On the banks of the Ouse............47420
    Only Susan............47435
    Penshurst castle in the time of Sir Philip Sidney............47427
    Poppies and pansies............012104
    Stellafont abbey............012101
    Tower on the cliff............47419
    Under Salisbury spire............47423
    Under the mendips............47418
    White King's daughter............47430
Marshall, F. It happened yesterday............18610
Marshall, Nelly. As by fire............52229
Marshall, W. H. Old Vauxhall. 3 v............52225
Marston, J. Works. 1856. 3 v.
    V. 1. Antonio and Mellida.—Wonder of women.—What you will............822.2 106

    V. 2. Parasitaster.—Dutch courtezan—Malcontent............822.2 107
    V. 3. Eastward ho!—Insatiate countesse.—Metamorphosis of Pigmalion's image, etc.—Scourge of villanie.—Lord and Lady Huntingdon's entertainment.—City pageant.—Verses by Marston............822.2 108

    Works; ed. by Bullen. 1887. 3 v....822.2 293
Marston, J., *and* **Jonson, B.** Five court masques. 1848............822.2 81
Marston, P. B. For a song's sake, etc......69333
    Song-tide, and other poems. 1871....821.2 427
    Wind voices (poems)............821.2 730
Martin, *Mrs.* **Bell.** Julia Howard........*in* 14156
Martin, E. S. Cousin Anthony and I. 1895............824.1 303
    Contents: Cousin Anthony and his book.—Readers and reading.—Work and the Yankee.—Chores.—Considerations matrimonial.—Love, friendship, and gossip.—Woman suffrage.—The knowledge of good and evil.—Civilization and culture.—Arcadia and Belgravia.—Ourselves and other people.—Profit and loss.—Certain assets of age.—The after-dinner speech.—Cousin Anthony's address to the trained nurses.

    A little brother of the rich, etc. (verses). 1890............821.1 427
    Sly ballades in Harvard china. '82..821.1 285
    Windfalls of observation (essays). 1894............824.1 282
Martin, Elizabeth G. Whom God hath joined............69239
Martin, *Mrs.* **H.** Bonnie Leslie............61201
    For a dream's sake............61202
    Gentleman George............61206
    Guide, philosopher and friend............61203
    Lindsay's girl............61204
    Out of the workhouse............61205
    Two Dorothys............06120
Martin, J. Placidio: a drama........*in* 928.2 219
Martin, Kate B. Belgian days............62571
Martin, *Sir* **T.** Shakespeare or Bacon? 1888............822.3 351
    Translation of Goethe's 'Faust.' 1877–1886. 2 v............832 73
    Translation of Oehlenschlaeger's 'Correggio.' 1854............898 70
    (See, also, **Aytoun** *and* **Martin.**)

Martineau, Harriet. Deerbrook............11802
    Feats on the Fiord............11819
    Five years of youth............01802
    Forest and game-law tales. 3v.
    V. 1. Merdhin.—The manor and the eyrie.—The staunch and their work.—Old landmarks and old laws............11820
    V. 2. The bishop's flock and the bishop's herd.—Heathendom in Christendom.—Four years at Maude-Chapel farm............11821
    V. 3. Gentle and simple............11822
    Hampdens............11818
    Hour and man............11801

Illustrations of political economy.
  No. 4. Demerara..11803
  No. 7. Cousin Marshall..................................11805
  No. 8. A Manchester strike...............................11806
  No. 12. French wines and politics........................11807
Letter on woman's rights. 1851.........*in* 40 1
The peasant and the prince....................01803
Playfellow..01801
Popular tales.
  V. 1. Demerara.—Ella of Garveloch.—Weal and woe in Garveloch..................................11810
  V. 2. Messrs. Vanderput and Snoek.—The loom and the lugger.......................................11811
  V. 3. Briery creek.— The three ages.—The farrers of Budge row.—The moral of many fables........11812
  V. 4. Homes abroad.— For each and for all.—French wines and politics..............................11813
  V. 5. Life in the wilds.—The hill and the valley.—Brooke and Brooke farm............................11814
  V. 8. The charmed sea.—Berkeley the banker....11817
Martineau, Harriet, *ed.* Traditions of Palestine...249 37
Martineau, J. Essays, philosophical and theological. 1870. 2 v.........................104 12
Essays, reviews and addresses. 1890.
  V. 1. Personal sketches: Joseph Priestley; Arnold; Channing; Theodore Parker; Lessing; Personal influence on present theology—Newman, Coleridge, Carlyle; Schleiermacher; Comte; J. J. Tayler; John Kenrick.—Political essays: International duties and the present crisis; Foreign policy for 1856; Slave empire of the west..........824.2 430
  V. 2. Ecclesiastical, historical: Church and state; Church of England; Battle of the churches; Philosophical Christianity in France; Letter and spirit; Europe since the reformation; Phaethon; Alexandria and her schools; Professional religion; The Unitarian position; Church-life or sect-life? Tracts for priests and people; Crisis of faith; Way out of the Trinitarian controversy; National church as a federal union.......................824.2 431
  V. 3. Theological: Francis William Newman; Hans Christian Oersted, 'One mind in nature'; Henry Longueville Mansel, 'Limits of religious thought'; Nature and God; Science, nescience and faith; Early history of Messianic ideas; Ernest Renan, 'Vie de Jesus.'— Philosophical: William Whewell; Samuel Bailey, 'Theory of reasoning'; Sir William Hamilton's philosophy; John Stuart Mill's philosophy; Alexander Bain's psychology; Is there any axiom of causality?..................824.2 432
Martyn, *Mrs.* George. Liberal education...41406
Marvel, Ik, *pseud.* See **Mitchell, Donald G.**
Marvell, A. Poetical works..................821.2 169
Marzials. Gallery of pigeons, etc. (verse).
....821.2 1171
Mason, A. E. W. Courtship of Morrice Buckler...69940
The philanderers..................................69941
Mason, C. W. Rape of the gamp............14117
Mason, William. Poems; with life. '22...821.2 48
Works. 1811 4 v.
  V. 1. Odes, elegies, sonnets, etc...............820.2 125
  V. 2. Dramatic writings. Letters on the drama.
  ....820.2 126
  V. 3. Du Fresnoy's 'Art of painting'; tr. into English verse, with notes by Sir Joshua Reynolds, etc.—Essays on church music..................820.2 127
  V. 4. Sermons, etc..............................820.2 128
Massey. Shakespeare's sonnets. 1866...822.3 80
Massinger. Believe as you list: tragedy..821.2 470
Dramatic works; ed. by H. Coleridge..822.2 105
Masson. Edinburgh sketches and memories...941 212
The three devils, etc. 1874.............824.2 199
  Contents: The three devils: Luther's, Milton's, Goethe's.—Shakespeare and Goethe.—Milton's youth.—Dryden and the literature of the restoration.—Swift.—How literature may illustrate history.
Wordsworth, Shelley and Keats, etc..824.2 200
  Contents: Wordsworth.—Scottish influence in British literature. — Shelley. — Keats. — Theories of poetry.—Prose and verse: De Quincey.
Masterman. Devoted couple...................35625
Masters. Duchess lass.............................69781
Shuttle of fate......................................69780
Mather. Lancashire idylls.....................36740
Sign of the wooden shoon........................36741
Mathers, Helen B., (Mrs. H. Reeves). As he comes up the stair..........................25007
Blind justice [Hedri].............................25014
Cherry ripe..25004
Comin' thro' the Rye.............................25001
Eyre's acquittal....................................25011
Fashion of this world............................25013
Hedri [Blind justice]..............................25014
Jock o' Hazelgreen................................25012
Land o' the leal...................................25006
Lovely Malincourt.................................25020
Man of to-day.....................................25019
My Jo, John..25016
My lady Greensleeves............................25009
Mystery of number 13...........................25015
Rebel...25021
Sam's sweetheart.................................25010
Sin of Hagar.......................................25022
Token of the silver lily (verse)......821.2 496
T'other dear charmer............................25017
Wrostella's weird..................................25018
Mathers, Helen, *et al.* Fate of Fenella.....32702
Mathew, F. At the rising of the moon....70202
Wood of the brambles...........................70201
Mathews, A. See **Siegvolk, Paul.**
Mathews, C. Chanticleer.........................30428
Various writings...................................30427
Mathews, Joanna H. Bessie among the mountains..09004
Bessie and her friends...........................09003
Bessie at school...................................09005
Bessie at the seaside............................09001
Bessie Bradford's secret.........................09012
Bessie in the city.................................09002
Bessie on her travels............................09006
Breakfast for two.................................09011

Fred Bradford's debt..................09013
Harry Bradford's crusade................09014
Uncle Rutherford's attic...............09015
Mathews, Julia A. Bessie Harrington's
   venture...............................03002
Jack Granger's cousin...................03001
Mathews, M. H. Doctor Gilbert's daughters..62542
Mathews, William. Getting on in the
   world. 1876..........................*170 17
The great conversers, etc...........824.1 127
Hours with men and books. 1877....824.1 128
Literary style, etc. 1881..............824.1 164
Men, places and things. 1887........824.1 231
Nugæ litterariæ : brief essays. '96...824.1 325
Matthews, B. Americanisms and Briticisms, etc. 1892..........................824.1 289
   Contents: Americanisms and Briticisms. — As to American spelling.—Literary independence of the U. S.—Centenary of Fenimore Cooper. — Ignorance and insularity.—The whole duty of critics.—Three American essayists.—Dissolving views: Twain's best story; Zola; Women's novels; Two latter-day humorists.
Aspects of fiction, etc. 1896..........824.1 318
   Contents: American literature. — Two studies of the south. — The penalty of humor. — On pleasing the taste of the public. — On certain parallelisms between the ancient drama and the modern. — Two Scotsmen of letters: Lang; Stevenson. — Aspects of fiction: The gift of story-telling; Cervantes, Zola, Kipling & Co.; Prose tales of Monsieur François Coppée; Short stories of Monsieur Ludovic Halévy; Mr. Charles Dudley Warner as a writer of fiction ; Text-books of fiction.
Decision of the court: comedy. '93......822.1 33
Family tree, etc..........................17706
   Contents: Family tree.—Memories.—Idle notes of an uneventful voyage. — On the battlefield. — Scherzi and Skizzen.
His father's son..........................17713
In the vestibule limited.................17708
Last meeting.............................17703
Pen and ink. 1888......................824.1 245
   Contents: Pen and ink ; by A. Lang.— Antiquity of jests. — Ethics of plagiarism. — True theory of the preface. — Philosophy of the short-story. — Two latter-day lyrists. — Songs of the civil war. — On the French spoken by those who do not speak French.—Poker talk.—Epistle to the author ; by H. C. Bunner.
Royal marine.............................17712
Story of a story, etc....................17710
   Contents: The story of a story.—A cameo and a pastel.—Two letters. — The new member of the club.— Etelka Talmeyr.
Tales of fantasy and fact..............17714
   Contents: Primer of imaginary geography.—Kinetoscope of time. — Dream-gown of the Japanese ambassador. — Rival ghosts. — Sixteen years without a birthday.—Twinkling of an eye.—Confidential postscript.
This picture and that: comedy. '94......822.1 35
Tom Paulding............................017710
Vignettes of Manhattan................17711
   Contents: In the little church down the street.—Twenty-ninth of February. — At a private view.—Spring in a side street. — Decoration-day revery.—In search of local color.— Before the break of day. — Midsummer midnight. — Vista in Central park. — Speech of the evening.—Thanksgiving-day dinner. — In the midst of life.

Matthews, Brander, *and* **Bunner, H. C.**
   In partnership.......................17701
   Contents: Documents in the case.—Venetian glass.—Red silk handkerchief. — Seven conversations of dear Jones and baby Van Rensselaer.—Rival ghosts. A letter and a paragraph.—Playing a part.—Love in old clothes.
Matthews, Brander, *and* **Jessop, G. H.**
   Check and counter-check............17705
   Tale of twenty-five hours..........17709
Matthews, B., *et al.* With my friends.......17707
   Contents: Art and mystery of collaboration.—Documents in the case.— Seven conversations of dear Jones and baby Van Rensselaer.—Edged tools.—Mated by magic.—One story is good till another is told.—Three wishes.
Matthews, Margaret H. Dame Prism..012330
Matthews, S. Address, Wooster....825.1 Pam. 6
Mattison. White wave (verse). '75..821.1 Pam. 2
Maturin. Bertram : tragedy. 1818......822.2 143
Maud, C. Wagner's heroines. 1896......813 66
Maude. Merciful divorce....................18820
Maurice, C. E. Richard de Lacy : Lollards..28715
Maurice, F. D. Friendship of books, etc.
....824.2 163
   Contents: Friendship of books.—Words.—Books.—Use and abuse of newspapers.—Christian civilization.—Ancient history.— English history.— Spenser's ' Faerie queene.'—Milton.—Milton as a schoolmaster.—Burke.—Acquisition and illumination.
Max Victor's schooldays....................0141
Maxwell, C. Story of three sisters........57301
Maxwell, Sir H. Duke of Britain.........22330
   Rainy days in a library. 1896..........824.2 505
   Contents: Adam Petrie's rules.—Baldassare's perfect courtier. — The oldest sporting journal.— Firmilian.—Bulwer's 'Artificial changeling.' — Hayward's 'Art of dining,—Jonston's 'Wonders.'—St. John's 'Highland sport.'—Tallemant des Réaux.—Acts of the Scottish parliament.—Captain Topham's letters.—Pitcairn's 'Criminal trials.'—Blaeu's atlas.
Maxwell, *Mrs.* **M. E.** See **Braddon, M. E.**
Maxwell, W. H. Adventures of Captain
   Blake..................................28609
Bivouac.....................................28604
Hector O'Halloran.........................28605
Stories of Waterloo.......................28602
Wild sports in the west...................28601
May, E. J. Dashwood priory.............08901
Louis' school days.........................08903
Saxelford...................................08904
May, G. T. The ever-living life. 1883.
....821.1 Pam. 4
May, Sophie, *pseud.* (R. S. Clarke).
   Dotty Dimple series.
   1. At her grandmother's.............026101
   2. At home............................026102
   3. Out west............................026103
   4. At play..............................026104
   5. At school...........................026105
   6. Flyaway............................026106

* Of interest to young readers.

Drone's honey.....................................25402
Flaxie Frizzle series.
  1. Flaxie Frizzle..........................026119
  2. Doctor Papa.............................026120
  3. Little pitchers..........................026121
  4. Twin cousins............................026122
  5. Kittyleen.................................026123
  6. Flaxie growing up....................026124
Little Prudy series.
  1. Little Prudy.............................026107
  2. Sister Susy..............................026108
  3. Captain Horace........................026109
  4. Cousin Grace...........................026110
  5. Fairy book...............................026112
  6. Dotty Dimple...........................026111
Little Prudy's children series.
  1. Wee Lucy................................026125
  2. Jimmy boy..............................026126
  3. Kyzie Dunlee...........................026127
Little Prudy's Flyaway series.
  1. Little folks astray.....................026113
  2. Prudy keeping house................026114
  3. Aunt Madge's story..................026115
  4. Little grandmother...................026116
  5. Little grandfather.....................026117
  6. Miss Thistledown.....................026118
Quinnebasset series.
  1. Doctor's daughter....................25408
  2. Our Helen...............................25404
  3. Asbury twins...........................25401
  4. Quinnebasset girls...................25406
  5. Janet......................................25410
  6. In old Quinnebasset.................25403
Mayfield. Carrie Harrington..................20446
Mayhew, A. Faces for fortunes..............10302
  Paved with gold............................10301
Mayhew, A. *and* **H.** Greatest plague of life...10401
Mayhew, H. Peasant boy philosopher......01901
  Young Benjamin Franklin...............01903
Mayo, Isabella F. See **Garrett, Edward** *and* **Ruth.**
Mayo, W. S. The Berber.......................9502
  Kaloolah......................................9501
  Never again.................................9504
  Romance dust..............................9503
Mayor Roger S. Potter........................50334
Me!...55266
Meade. Bashful fifteen........................013017
  Betty, a school girl......................013015
  Catalina.....................................013020
  Daddy's boy...............................013014
  David's little lad..........................50603
  Four on an island........................013011
  Girl in ten thousand....................013021
  Girls, new and old.......................013019
  Good luck...................................50616
  Heart of gold..............................50606
  Honorable miss..........................50605
  The house of surprises...............013010
  In an iron grip............................50612
  Lady of the forest......................013012

Life for a love......................................50602
Little mother to the others..................013022
Medicine lady......................................50609
Out of the fashion..............................50607
Palace Beautiful..................................50601
Polly, a new-fashioned girl.................013018
Princess of the gutter..........................50613
Red rose and tiger lily........................013016
Ring of rubies.....................................50608
Soldier of fortune...............................50611
Son of Ishmael....................................50615
Voice of the charmer..........................50617
World of girls.....................................013013
Meade *and* **Halifax.** Doctor Rumsey's patient...50614
  Stories from the diary of a doctor...........50610
Meadows. Heads of the people. 1840.
  2 v...827.2 34
Meeker. Life in the west......................52216
Meekins. Robb's island wreck, etc........21620
Meirion. Cause and effect....................31190
Meisner. Terrace de Mon Desir............69297
Meldrum. Grey mantle and gold fringe.....70260
  Story of Margrédel.......................70261
Melville, G. J. Whyte-. Black but comely..6625
  Brooks of Bridlemere...................6603
  Cerise..6601
  Contraband.................................6612
  Digby Grand...............................6610
  General Bounce...........................6617
  Gladiators...................................6611
  Good for nothing........................6627
  Holmby house.............................6626
  Inside the bar.........................*in* 6616
  Interpreter..................................6609
  Kate Coventry......................*in* 6610
  Katerfelto...................................6613
  M. or N......................................6608
  Market Harborough, etc..............6616
  Queen's Maries...........................6607
  Rosine..6615
  Roy's wife...................................6622
  Sarchedon...................................6605
  Satanella....................................6620
  Sister Louise...............................6624
  Songs and verses.................821.2 439
  Tilbury Nogo..............................6618
  Uncle John..................................6614
  White Rose.................................6606
Melville, H. Battle pieces. 1866........821.1 46
  Confidence man..........................6509
  Israel Potter [Refugee]................6506
  Mardi..6510
  Moby Dick..................................6503
  Omoo..6502
  Pierre..6508
  Redburn......................................6512

Refugee [Israel Potter].............................6506
Typee..6501
White Jacket..6505
Mercier. Campanelle..........................021101
Meredith, G. Amazing marriage..............53216
Beauchamp's career...............................53212
Case of General Ople and Lady Camper...53213
Diana of the crossways.........................53206
The egoist..53203
Evan Harrington....................................53205
Harry Richmond....................................53207
Lord Ormont and his Aminta..................53215
Modern love, etc. (verse). 1892........821.2 891
One of our conquerors..........................53214
Ordeal of Richard Feveril......................53202
Poems and lyrics of the joy of the earth.
  1883..821.2 512
A reading of earth (poems). 1888.....821.2 828
Rhoda Fleming......................................53210
Sandra Belloni.......................................53208
Shaving of Shagpat...............................53201
Tale of Chloe..53211
Tragic comedians..................................53204
Vittoria...53209
Meredith, K. M. C. Green gates............70380
Meredith, Owen. See Lytton, R. B., *earl.*
Merington, M. Daphne (drama). 1896...822.1 44
Merivale, H. C. Binko's blues................17801
Faucit of Balliol...................................17802
Merriman, H. S., (H. S. Scott). Christian
  Vellacott ; or, The slave of the lamp...2951A
Flotsam...2956
From one generation to another..............2952
Grey lady..2955
Phantom future.....................................2950
Slave of the lamp (Christian Vellacott).....2951
Sowers...2954
With edged tools...................................2953
Merriman *and* Tallentyre. From wis-
  dom court (essays). 1893.............824.2 364
Money-spinner, etc................................2957
Merron. As the wind blows...................21070
Meteyard. Lilian's golden hours...........018102
Meynell. The children. 1897..............137 10
Colour of life : essays. 1896.........824.2 502
Poems. 1896............................821.2 1016
The rhythm of life, etc. 1896........824.2 491
  Contents: The rhythm of life.—Decivilized.—A re-
  membrance.—The sun.—The flower.—Unstable equilib-
  rium.—The unit of the world.—By the railway side.—
  Pocket vocabularies.—Pathos.—The point of honour.—
  Composure.—O. W. Holmes.—J. R. Lowell.—Domus
  Angusta.—Rejection.— The lesson of landscape.— Mr.
  Patmore's odes.—Innocence and experience.— Penulti-
  mate caricature.

Michel. Ayenbite of inwyt (1340)........820.2 311
Michell. Spirits of the past: poem. '53..821.2 420
Mickle. Poems ; with life...................821.2 38

Middlemass. Dandy................................62337
The Maddoxes,....................................62336
Middlemore. Round a posada fire............62317
Middleton, J. Love vs. law....................56710
Middleton, T. A tragi-coomodie : the
  witch..822.2 270
Works ; ed. by Bullen. 1885. v. 1-8.
  V. 1. Blurt, master-constable.— The phœnix -
  Michaelmas term...............................822.2 271
  V. 2. Mayor of Queenborough. - The old law.
  —Trick to catch the old one................822.2 272
  V. 3. Family of love.—Your five gallants.—A
  mad world.......................................822.2 273
  V. 4. The roaring girl.—A fair quarrel.—No wit,
  no help like a woman's......................822.2 274
  V. 5. Chaste maid in Cheapside. — The widow.
  —Anything for a quiet life.—The witch....822.2 275
  V. 6. The changeling.—Spanish gipsy.—Women
  beware women.—More dissemblers.........822.2 276
  V. 7. Game at chess.—World lost at tennis.—
  Inner temple masque.—Civic entertainments, etc.
  ....822.2 277
  V. 8. The black book.—Father Hubbard's tales.
  — Micro-cynicon. — Wisdom of Solomon para-
  phrased.—Peacemaker.—Index, etc......822.2 278
Miles, A. H., *ed.* Fifty-two stories for
  boys..0306
Fifty-two stories for girls........................0305
Miles, G. H. Christine, etc. 1866........821.1 54
Mohammed : a tragedy. 1850...........822.1 7
Milford. Ned Stafford's experiences in the
  U. S..69230
Mill. Dissertations and discussions. 2 v.
  V. 1. State interference with corporation and
  church property.—The currency juggle.— French
  revolution.—Poetry and its varieties.— Professor
  Sedgwick on the studies of Cambridge.—Civiliza-
  tion.—Aphorisms.—Armand Carrell.—A prophecy.
  —Writings of Alfred de Vigny.—Bentham.—Cole-
  ridge..824.2 375
  V. 2. De Tocqueville on 'Democracy in America.'
  —Bailey on Berkley's 'Theory of vision.'-Michelet's
  'History of France.'—Claims of labour.—Guizot's es-
  say's, etc.— Early Grecian history and legend.
  — Vindication of French revolution of 1848.— En-
  franchisement of women.—Whewell on moral phil-
  osophy.—Grote's 'History of Greece.'—Appendix.824.2 376
Early essays. 1897........................824.2 511
  Contents: Essays on some unsettled questions of po-
  litical economy.—Corporation and church property.—
  What is poetry?—The two kinds of poetry.—Tennyson's
  poems.—Carlyle's 'French revolution.'—Bentham.
Inaugural addresses. 1867................373 3
Mill agent...55247
Milledulcia. 1857............................‡40 16
Miller, Annie J. Barbara Thayer.........22171
'Twixt love and law.............................22170
Miller, Emily H. Royal road to fortune...02201
Miller, H. Essays. 1865..................824.2 158
Leading articles. 1870..................824.2 157
Miller, J. Baroness of New York, '77...821.1 192
Building of the city beautiful.................21385
Destruction of Gotham..........................21384
'49: Gold-seeker of the Sierras..............21383

‡ For reference.

Memorie and rime. 1884.................824.1 193
One fair woman...................................21380
Shadows of Shasta..............................21381
Ship in the desert. 1875...............821.1 156
Songs of Italy. 1878........................821.1 151
Songs of the Mexican seas. 1887......821.1 153
Songs of the Sierras. 1871.............821.1 154
Songs of the soul. 1896..................821.1 157
Songs of the sun-lands. 1873.........821.1 155
Miller, O. T. Nimpo's troubles..............041401
Miller, S. F. Wylkins Wylder...................52213
Miller, Thomas. My father's garden........44198
Millet. Capillary crime, etc......................69363
Millington. Ship Daphne......................67020
Mills. Belle of the village.......................25867
Christmas in olden time....................25868
Milman, E. H. Arthur Conway...............14134
Milman, Helen. Boy.............................011311
Little ladies...011310
Uncle Bill's children............................011312
Milman, H. H. Poetical works. 1839. 3 v.
  V. 1. Fall of Jerusalem.—Martyr of Antioch.—Belshazzar...............821.2 309
  V. 2. Samor, lord of the bright city.— Miscellaneous poems...........821.2 310
  V. 3. Anne Boleyn: a drama.—Fazio: a tragedy.—Nala and Damayanti.—Death of Yajnadatta.—Extracts from the Mahabharata.—Descent of the Ganges.—The deluge.—Stanzas...........821.2 311
Savonarola and essays. 1870................204 64
Milman, R. Mitslav..................................62579
Milner. Country pleasures. 1881........824.2 357
Milnes. See **Houghton, Lord.**
Milton. L'allegro, Il penseroso, etc.; with essay by Macaulay.........................821.2 163
And Vondel; by Edmundson..........928.2 501
Areopagitica....................................820.2 26
Concordance to poetical works; by Bradshaw. 1894.................................‡821.2 165
Concordance to poetical works; by Cleveland. 1867...........................‡821.2 160
Milton's prosody; by Bridges. 1893......426 4
Minor poems; ed. by Rolfe. 1887.....821.2 162
On education; ed. by Browning............370 144
Le paradis perdu; tr. par Chateaubriand. 2 v...840 81
Paradise lost. 1875..........................821.2 156
Same, books 1-2; ed. by Sprague. 1883.
....821.2 155
Same: criticism on; by Addison.....820.2 28
Same: study of; by Himes. 1878...821.2 164
Poetical works: ed. by Masson. 3 v.
  V. 1. Essay on Milton's English.—Paradise lost...821.2 157
  V. 2. Paradise regained.—Samson Agonistes.—Minor poems. - L'allegro. — Il penseroso. — Arcades.—Comus. Lycidas.—Sonnets, etc..........821.2 158
  V. 3. Translations.—Latin poems.—Notes......821.2 159
Poetical works; ed. by Masson. '87...821.2 153

Same; ed. by Montgomery. 1861. v.2.
....821.2 154
Contents: Paradise regained.—Samson Agonistes.—Comus.— Arcades.—Lycidas.— L'allegro.— Il penseroso.—Sonnets.—Odes, etc.
Prose; sel. and ed. by Garnett..........829.2 70
Prose works; ed. by Fletcher. 1835..820.2 B-1
Same; ed. by St. John. 5 v.
  V. 1. Preface.—Defence of the people of England.—Second defence.—Eikonoklastes..............820.2 48
  V. 2. Tenure of kings and magistrates.—Areopagitica.—Letter to a friend.—Letter to General Monk.—Ready and easy way to establish a free commonwealth.—On the articles of peace.—Letters of state.—Manifesto of the lord protector.—Notes upon a late sermon.—Of reformation in England.—Of prelatical episcopacy.—The reason of church govt...820.2 49
  V. 3. To remove hirelings out of the church.—Animadversions upon the remonstrant's defence against Smectymnuus. — Apology for Smectymnuus.—Doctrine and discipline of divorce.—Judgment of Martin Bucer concerning divorce.—Tetrachordon.—Colasterion.—On education.—Declaration for the election of the king of Poland.—Familiar letters.................................820.2 50
  V. 4-5. Treatise on Christian doctrine.—History of Britain to the Norman conquest.—Brief history of Moscovia. — Accedence commenced grammar.—Index...................................820.2 51
Selected prose writings; ed. by E. Myers...824.2 359
Contents: Introduction.—Reformation in England.—Reason of church government.—Animadversions upon the remonstrant's defence against Smectymnuus. — Apology for Smectymnuus.—Doctrine and discipline of divorce.— On education.— Areopagitica.— Tenure of kings, etc.—Eikonoklastes.—Ready and easy way to establish a free commonwealth.
Sonnets; ed. by Pattison. 1883........821.2 161
Sonnets of; by Sampson. 1886...821.2 Pam. 3
Minelli. Alfio Balzani.............................52230
Minor. Bietigheim. 1886....................827.1 26
Minto. Mediation of Ralph Hardelot........69446
Minturn. Last of the Kerdrecs................60501
Mishaps of Mr. Ezekiel Pelter... 55229
Miss Bayle's romance............................69038
Miss Columbia's public school. 1871....827.1 10
Miss Mallows among the publishers....823 Pam. 1
Miss Matty...07105
Miss Toosey's mission. (See **Laddie.**).....17904
Mr. and Mrs. Morton.............................58987
Mr. Magnus..55265
Mitchel, F. A. Sweet revenge................57901
Mitchell, D. G., (Ik Marvel). About old story-tellers....................................*928 14
Bound together. 1884..................824.1 194
Contents: Washington Irving.—Titian and his times.—Procession of the months.—Beginnings of an old town.—Two college talks.—In-doors and out-of-doors.
Doctor Johns..9603
Dream life..9605
Fudge doings..9601
The lorgnette. 2 v...........................827.1 13

* Of interest to young readers.   ‡ For reference.

My farm of Edgewood. 1872..............630 16
Reveries of a bachelor............................9606
Rural studies................................712 4
Seven stories, etc.................................9607
   Contents: Wet day at an Irish inn.—Account of a consulate.—The petit soulier.—The bride of the Ice-king.—The cabriolet.—The Count Pesaro.—Emile Roque.—Under the roof.
Wet days at Edgewood.....................630 45
Mitchell, J. Female pilgrim. 1814.........249 36
Mitchell, J. A. Amos Judd....................18421
Last American...................................18420
That first affair, etc..............................18422
   Contents: That first affair.—Mrs. Lofter's pride.—Two portraits.—Man who vanished.—A bachelor's supper.
Mitchell, L. E. Love in the backwoods....58160
   Contents: Two Mormons from Muddlety.—Alfred's wife.
Mitchell, S. Weir. Characteristics...........18204
Cup of youth, etc. (poems). 1889..821.1 399
Far in the forest..................................18203
Hephzibah Guinness, etc.......................18207
   Contents: Hephzibah Guinness.—Thee and thou.—Draft on the bank of Spain.
In war time......................................18201
Madeira party....................................18206
A masque, and other poems. 1887.....821.1 382
Mr. Kris Kringle...............................018205
Philip Vernon: a tale in prose and verse. 1895...821.1 493
Psalm of death, and other poems. '90..821.1 428
Roland Blake....................................18202
When all the woods are green................18205
Mitchell, W. Bryan Maurice....................20331
Two strings to his bow.........................20330
Mitford, B. Gun-runner.........................34501
King's assegal...................................34503
Luck of Gerard Ridgeley.......................34502
Sign of the spider..............................34505
'Tween snow and fire..........................34506
White shield.....................................34504
Mitford, Mary R. Country stories............60110
Friendships, as recorded in letters. 1882.
   2 v...826.2 69
Our village. 1882. 2 v....................824.2 345
Recollections of a literary life. '72...824.2 104
Works, in prose and verse. 1854......820.2 300
   Contents: Our village. — Belford Regis. — Country stories.—Finden's tableaux.—Foscari.—Julian.— Rienzi.—Charles I.
Modern heretic....................................55257
Modern minister...................................55244
Moffat. Not without honor.......................38901
Moffett. Crown jewels.............................52217
Moir. Mansie Wauch..............................19116
Molesworth, *Mrs.* (EnnisGraham, *pseud.*).
   Adventures of Herr Baby..................024702
   Blanche.......................................024732
   Boys and I....................................024706

Carrots..024709
Carved lions....................................024736
The children of the castle....................024725
Christmas-tree land............................024710
Cuckoo clock...................................024704
Farthings..024730
Four winds farm...............................024715
Grandmother dear.............................024714
Green casket, etc..............................024722
Hathercourt....................................42701
Hermy...024712
Leona..42708
Lettice...42704
Little Miss Peggy..............................024718
Little Mother Bunch...........................024723
Little old portrait..............................024711
Mary..024733
Miss Bouverie..................................42703
My new home..................................024734
Neighbours.....................................42706
Next-door house...............................024728
Nurse Heatherdale's story...................024726
Old pincushion.................................024721
Olivia..42709
Oriel window...................................024737
Palace in the garden..........................024717
Philippa...42711
Rectory children...............................024720
Red Grange....................................42707
Robin Redbreast..............................024729
Rosy...024707
Sheila's mystery...............................024735
Silverthorns....................................024716
Story of a spring morning....................024724
Summer stories................................024703
Sweet content..................................024727
Tapestry room.................................024701
Tell me a story.................................024705
That girl in black.—Bronzie..................42705
Third Miss St. Quentin.......................42713
Two little waifs................................024708
Uncanny tales..................................42712
Us..024713
White turrets..................................42710

Molloy. Excellent knave........................20511
Sweet is revenge...............................20510
Moncreiff, F. Provost-marshal................53620
Moncrieff, R. H. See **Hope, Ascott R.,** *pseud.*
Moncrieff, W. T. Selections from dramatic works. 1851. 3 v.
   V. 1. Gisella.—Scamps of London.—Tarnation strange.—Monsieur Mallet.—One fault.—Heart of London.—Bringing home the bride.—Borrowing a husband......................................822.2 151
   V. 2. Sam Weller. — Peer and the peasant.—Somnambulist.— The Tobit's dogs.—The winterbottoms.—Kiss and the rose.—How to take up a bill.—Birthday dinner.......................822.2 152

V. 3. Tom and Jerry.—Rochester.—Giovanni in London.—Monsieur Tonson.—All at Coventry.—Zoroaster.—Home for the holidays.—The secret..822.2 153
Money-makers..69006
Monk. Altar of earth..11950
Monkland, *Mrs.* Nabob at home...............14148
Monroe. Columbian ode. 1893...........821.1 461
Montagu, *Mrs.* E. Letters. 1810. 4v...826.2 84
  Writings, etc., of Shakespeare. 1777...822.3 62
  Same. 1810..................................822.3 62A
Montagu, *Lady* **Mary W.** Letters; ed. by Hale. 1856..............................826.2 17
  Letters and works; ed. by Wharncliffe. 1861. 2 v...........................826.2 15
Montague, C. The vigil: story of Zululand..70601
Montague, C. H., *and* **Dyar, C. W.** Written in red..............................56705
Montesole *and* **Roberts.** Circassian......29415
Montgomery, Florence. Blue veil....031301
  Colonel Norton...29609
  Fisherman's daughter..................................29608
  Misunderstood..29602
  Seaforth...29601
  Thrown together...29604
  Thwarted..29605
  Town-crier..031302
  Transformed..29607
  Very simple story..29603
  Wild Mike..29606
Montgomery, J. Poetical works. 4 v.
  V. 1. Wanderer of Switzerland.— The West Indies. — Miscellaneous poems. — Prison amusements...821.2 532
  V. 2. The world before the flood.—Miscellaneous poems.— Thoughts on wheels.— Climbing boy's soliloquies.—Songs of Zion.................821.2 533
  V. 3. Greenland.—Miscellaneous poems.—Narratives.—Translations from Dante..............821.2 534
  V. 4. Pelican island. — Miscellanies. — Sacred and Scriptural subjects, etc...........................821.2 535
Montgomery, R. Luther: a poem......821.2 303
Monti (S. Stapleton, *pseud.*). Adventures of a consul abroad......................................62557
  Leone...62558
Montrésor. False coin or true?...............13362
  Into the highways and hedges................13360
  One who looked on....................................13361
  Worth while...13363
Moodey. Tragedy of Brinkwater..............69298
Moore, A., *and* **Dowson, E.** Comedy of masks..69378
Moore, B. H. On dangerous ground..12053
Moore, C. L. Book of day-dreams (verse). 1892..821.1 459
  Poems, antique and modern. 1883..821.1 458
Moore, E. Poems; with life. 1822......821.2 44
Moore, F., *ed.* The world. 3 v..............824.2 19
Moore, George. Impressions and opinions. 1891..824.2 348

Moore, *Mrs.* **J. F.** Losses and gains.........25861
Moore, J. Edward..7406
  Mordaunt..7401
  Zeluco...7404
Moore, *Sir* **J. H.** Poems. 1822.........*in* 821.2 46
Moore, Susan T. Ryle's open gate..........26120
Moore, T. Epicurean...................................69301
  Lalla Rookh. 1826..........................821.2 249
  Memoirs of Captain Rock. 1824.......|.827.2 13
  Poetical works.................................821.2 250
  Same..821.2 252
  Poetical works.—The epicurean.........821.2 251
  Prose and verse; ed. by Shepherd. 1878...820.2 205
  Translation of odes of Anacreon. 1820. 2 v...884 17
Moore, *Rev.* **W. B.** Six sisters of the valley...12071
More, Hannah. Cœlebs in search of a wife..52235
  Same...240 37
  Works. 1853. 11 v.
  V. 1. Stories for persons in the middle ranks.....240 31
  V. 2. Tales.—On the manners of the great, etc...240 32
  V. 3. Modern system of female education........240 33
  V. 4. Hints toward forming the character of a young princess...240 34
  V. 5. Tragedies: The inflexible captive. —Percy.—Fatal falsehood.—Poems................240 35
  V. 6. Turn the carpet.—Epitaphs, etc.—Hymns.—Ballads.—Sacred dramas: Moses in the bulrushes; David and Goliath; Belshazzar; Daniel.—Reflections of King Hezekiah.—Search after happiness.—Ode to charity.—Essays.—Moriana......240 36
  V. 7. Cœlebs in search of a wife.......................240 37
  V. 8. Practical piety......................................240 38
  V. 9. Christian morals..................................240 39
  V. 10. Saint Paul.—Spirit of prayer.................240 40
  V. 11. Moral sketches, etc..............................240 41
More, P. E. Great refusal. 1894..........829.1 38
More, *Sir* **Thomas.** Utopia..............820.2 31
  Same...324 55
  Same; with history of Richard III.....324 54
Moredun...58958
Morford. Coward.......................................52231
  Days of Shoddy..52232
  Shoulder straps...52233
Morgan, A. The Shakesperian myth. '81..822.3 197
Morgan, C. L. Animal sketches. 1895...590 107
Morgan, George. John Littlejohn of J.....58201
Morgan, H. H. Topical Shakespeariana. 1879...822.3 142
Morgan, *Mrs.* **M.** Keeping the vow.........62567
Morgan, *Lady* **S.** Dramatic scenes from real life. 1833...............................822.2 155
  O'Donnel..19501
Morgann, M. Dramatic character of Falstaff. 1777................................822.3 11
Morier. Adventures of Hajji Baba............20492
  Zohrab..20493

LANGUAGE AND LITERATURE.

Morison, Jeanie. Sordello: analysis of. 1889.................................821.2 1122
Morison, J. H. Great poets as religious teachers. 1886...................................241 90
Morley, H. Journal of a London playgoer. 1866...................................792 23
Oberon's horn...................................011701
Morley, J. Critical miscellanies. 2 v.
  V. 1. Vauvenargues.—Condorcet.—Joseph de Maistre.—Carlyle.—Byron.—Some Greek conceptions of social growth.—On the development of morals.—Appendix.....................824.2 237
  V. 2. France in the 18th century.—Robespierre. —Turgot.—Death of Mill.—Mill's autobiography. —Mill on religion.—Popular culture.—Macaulay.
...................................824.2 238
On the study of literature. 1887...........374 18
Studies in literature. 1891..............824.2 516
  Contents: Wordsworth. — Aphorisms. — Maine on popular govt.—A few words on French models.—On the study of literature.—Victor Hugo's ' Ninety-three.'—On ' The ring and the book.'—Memorials of a man of letters. —Valedictory.
Morley, Susan. Aileen Ferrers..............14115
Morrah. Faithful city...................................67501
Morris, E. J. Prejudiced inquiries : Backwoods lects., 1884........................824.1 218
Morris, G. P. Deserted bride, etc. (poems). 1843........................821.1 416
Little Frenchman and his water lots, etc. 1839........................824.1 77
Morris, Gouverneur. Writings and life. 923.1 86
Morris, L. Epic of hades. 1879.........821.2 498
Gwen : a drama. 1879..................821.2 497
Gycia: tragedy. 1886..................822.2 291
Ode of life. 1880........................821.2 548
Songs of Britain. 1887..................821.2 814
Songs of two worlds. 1882.............821.2 577
Songs unsung. 1883......................821.2 713
Morris, W. Defence of Guenevere, and other poems. 1875......................821.2 392
Dream of John Ball...................................44201
Earthly paradise : poem. 1868. 3 v...821.2 389
Hopes and fears for art.................704 20
King's lesson...................................in 44201
Life and death of Jason: poem. 1877..821.2 477
Love is enough (drama). 1873........822.2 174
News from nowhere...................................44203
Poems by the way. 1892................821.2 888
Roots of the mountains...................................44202
Story of Sigurd (poem). 1879........821.2 503
Story of the glittering plain..............44204
Tale of the house of the Wolfings. 1889. ....821.2 835
Wood beyond the world...................................44205
Morris and Magnússon, trs. Story of Grettir the strong. 1869....................898 57
Three northern love stories, etc. 1875...898 95
Völsunga saga. 1881..................898 68

Morrison, A. Chronicles of Martin Hewitt...36541
Morse, J. H. Summer haven songs. 1886. ....821.1 335
Morse, Lucy G. The Chezzles...............35501
Rachel Stanwood...................................35502
Morse, O. A. Who wrote 'Rock me to sleep'? 1867...................................821.1 Pam. 3
Mortimer, C. B. Marrying by lot...........52220
Mortimer, Grace, pseud. See **Stuart, M. B.**
Morton, J. M. Comediettas and farces. 1886...................................822.2 290
Morton, O. T. Southern empire. etc. 1892. ....824.1 269
  Contents: The southern empire. – Oxford. – Some popular objections to civil service reform.
Motherwell. Poems. 1844...............821.2 304
Motley. Correspondence. 1889. 2v...826.1 B-1
Merry-Mount. 1849........................823 83
Tales of the Cymry. 1848..................821.2 415
Moulton, Louise C. Bedtime stories......022201
Firelight stories...................................022203
Garden of dreams (poems). 1890....821.1 411
Miss Eyre from Boston, etc..................21361
New bedtime stories........................022202
Ourselves and our neighbors : chats. 1887...................................824.1 215
Poems. 1878...................................821.1 206
Some women's hearts........................21360
Stories told at twilight........................022204
Moulton, R. G. Shakespeare as a dramatic artist. 1885...................................822.3 195
Mount Royal popular tales..................55211
Mountford. Thorpe........................52221
Mowatt. Plays. 1855......................822.1 1
  Contents: Armand ; or, The peer and the peasant.— Fashion.
Mozley. Essays. 1878. 2 v............824.2 264
  V. 1. Lord Strafford.—Laud.—Carlyle's 'Cromwell.' Luther.
  V. 5. Doctor Arnold.—Blanco White.—Pusey's sermons.—Book of Job.—Maurice's theological essays.— Indian conversion.—Argument of design.—Principle of causation.—In memoriam.—List of writings.
Letters ; ed. by his sister. 1885.........826.2 83
Muddock. Basile the jester....................26706
Maid Marian and Robin Hood...............26705
Young Lochinvar...................................26707
Mudge. Boat-builder's family..................013701
Muir. Charming to her latest day [Lady Beauty]...................................30555
Mulholland. Banshee castle..................69468
Fair emigrant........................69465
Marcella Grace...................................69467
The wicked woods........................69469
Wild birds of Killeevy........................69466
Mulock, Dinah M., (Mrs. D. M. Craik).
About money and other things. '86.824.2 398
Adventures of a brownie...................08404
Agatha's husband...................................3023

Alice Learmont..08405
Brave lady..3045
Bread upon the waters..............................3049
Children's poetry. 1881..................*821.2 575
Christian's mistake.......................................3005
Domestic stories..3032
Fairy book..08401
Half-caste..3047
   Contents: The half-caste.—Last of the Ruthvens.—Quintin Matsys, the blacksmith of Antwerp.—Antonio Melidori: a chapter from the history of the Greek revolution.—The Italian's daughter.—The sculptor of Bruges.
Hannah..3044
Head of the family......................................3051
A hero, etc..3030
   Contents: A hero.—Bread upon the waters.—Alice Learmont.
His little mother..3048
John Halifax..3001
King Arthur...3061
Laurel prince..3026
Life for a life..3013
Little lame prince and his travelling cloak..08406
Little Sunshine's holiday...........................08402
Lord Erlistoun, etc......................................3008
   Contents: Lord Erlistoun.—Alwyn's first wife.—Water cure.—Last house in C— street.—Christian's mistake.
Miss Tommy..3053
Mistress and maid......................................3039
My mother and I...3028
Noble life...3027
Nothing new; tales.....................................3031
   Contents: Lord Erlistoun.—Alwyn's first wife.—M. Anastasius.—Water cure.—Family in love.—Low marriage.—Double house.
Ogilvies..3016
Olive...3009
Our year...08403
Plain speaking. 1882.........................824.2 322
Poems. 1860....................................821.2 574
Studies from life. 1867......................824.2 233
Thirty years: poems. 1881.................821.2 576
Two marriages...3019
Unkind word..3011
Will Denbigh, nobleman............................3002
Woman's kingdom.....................................3024
Young Mrs. Jardine....................................3046
Munby. Dorothy; a story in verse......821.2 644
Munday. John a Kent and John a Cumber.
....822.2 92
Munkittrick. Farming. 1891.............828.1 62
Munroe. At war with Pontiac...................033314
   Big cypress..033313
   Cab and caboose.....................................033308
   Campmates...033305
   Canoemates..033307
   Crystal, Jack, and Co.—Delta Bixby....033316
   Coral ship..033311
   Derrick Sterling......................................033302

   Dorymates..033304
   Flamingo feather...................................033301
   Fur-seal's tooth.....................................033312
   Golden days of '49...............................033303
   Prince Dusty...033306
   Raftmates..033309
   Ready rangers......................................033320
   Rick Dale..033318
   Snow-shoes and sledges....................033315
   Through swamp and glade.................033317
   Wakulla..033319
   White conquerors................................033310
Murdock. Dutch dominie........................52234
Murfree, Fanny N. D. Felicia............16250
Murfree, Mary N. See **Craddock**.
Murray, C. A. Hussan............................20495
   Prairie bird..20497
Murray, C. T. Sub rosa...........................56890
Murray, D. C. Aunt Rachel..................68405
   Bishop's amazement...............................68431
   Bit of human nature...............................68404
   Bob Martin's little girl...........................68423
   By the gate of the sea..........................68422
   Capful o' nails...68432
   Coals of fire, etc.....................................68401
   Cynic fortune..68406
   First person singular.............................68408
   In direst peril..68426
   Investigations of John Pym..................68427
   Joseph's coat..68433
   Martyred fool...68430
   Model father..68403
   Mount Despair, etc.................................68429
   Old Blazer's hero...................................68410
   Queen's scarf..68417
   Rainbow gold..68414
   Rising star...68428
   Rogue's conscience................................68434
   Schwartz..68415
   Time's revenges....................................68424
   Val Strange...68402
   Wasted crime..68425
   Way of the world....................................68409
   Weaker vessel..68412
Murray, D. C. *and* **H.** Dangerous cats-paw..68413
Murray, D. C., *and* **Herman, H.** Bishop's Bible..68419
   He fell among thieves..........................68420
   One traveller returns...........................68411
   Only a shadow.......................................68421
   Paul Jones's alias..................................68418
   Wild Darrie...68416
Murray, E. C. G., (Trois Etoiles). Boudoir cabal..50710
   French pictures......................................50702
   Same; 2d series....................................50704

* Of interest to young readers.

Member for Paris.................................50701
People I have met. 1883..................829.2 B-1
Side-lights on English society. 1881.
  2 v...827.2 38
Strange tales..50709
That artful vicar..................................50708
Young Brown.......................................50705
Murray, Hamilton. Falkenburg...............14141
Murray, Henry. Deputy providence........68451
Fatal mistake.......................................68453
Game of bluff......................................68450
Ordeal of Thomas Taffler, costermonger.68452
Murray, Henry, *and* **Buchanan, R.**
Charlatan..42222
Murray, W. H. H. Adirondack tales......23301
Musgrave. Miriam.............................56920
Musick. Columbia..............................29475
My honey. (See **Laddie.**)....................17915
My queen...55277
My trivial life. 2 v.............................58985
Myers, E. Judgment of Prometheus, etc..821.2 272
Myers, F. W. H. Essays, classical.....824.2 342
  Contents: Greek oracles.—Virgil.—Marcus Aurelius Antoninus.
Essays, modern. 1883..................824.2 343
  Contents: Mazzini.—George Sand.—Victor Hugo.—Ernest Renan.—Archbishop Trench's poems.—George Eliot. Dean Stanley.—A new eirenicon.—Rossetti and the religion of beauty.
Poems. 1870..................................821.2 438
Renewal of youth, etc. (poems). '82..821.2 655
Saint Paul (poem). 1890.................821.2 857
Science and a future life, etc. 1893...824.2 454
  Contents: Science and a future life.—Darwin and agnosticism.—The disenchantment of France.—Tennyson as prophet.—Modern poets and cosmic law.—Leopold, duke of Albany: in memoriam.
Myers, P. H. First of the Knickerbockers..15261
King of the Hurons...............................15260
Young patroon......................................15262
Myroure of oure Ladye [15th century]..820.2 413
Myrtle, Lewis, *pseud.* See **Hill, G. C.**
Mystic bell...07123
Nadal. Essays at home, etc. 1882......824.1 175
Napier, *Sir* **Charles.** William the Conqueror..62539
Napier, M. Selections from correspondence. 1879...................................826.2 48
Napoleon Smith...................................19109
Nasby, Petroleum V., *pseud.* See **Locke, D. R.**
Nash. Barerock..................................04110
Nashe. Complete works; ed. by Grosart.
  6 v.
  V. 1. Memorial introduction.—Anatomie of absurditie.—Martin Mar-Prelate tractates............820.2 102
  V. 2. Pierce Penniless, his supplication to the divell.—Harvey-Greene tractates.................820.2 103
  V. 3. Have with you to Saffron-Walden.—Terrors of the night...................................820.2 104
  V. 4. Christ's teares over Jerusalem..........820.2 105
  V. 5. The unfortunate traveller.—Nashes Lenten stuffe...820.2 106

V. 6. Tragedie of Dido. Summer's last will and testament. Index..................820.2 107
Pierce Penniless's supplication to the devil; ed. by Collier......................822.2 77
  Same. 1842....................................827.2 1
Nason. Monogram on our national song. 1869..821.1 477
Nauman. Eva's adventures in shadowland..016001
Naunton. Fragmenta regalia............820.2 34
  Same...942.3 B 4
Naylor. Shakespeare and music. 1896...822.3 206
Neal. Charcoal sketches.......................20464
Misfortunes of Peter Faber......................20166
Peter Ploddy, etc...................................20465
Needell. Julian Karslake's secret..........11837
Lucia, Hugh, and another........................11834
Noel Chetwynd's fall..............................11835
Passing the love of women......................11833
Stephen Ellicott's daughter.....................11831
Story of Philip Methuen.........................11832
Unequally yoked...................................11830
Vengeance of John Vansittart..................11836
Neele. Literary remains. 1829..........824.2 166
Romance of history: England................47224
Nelly's heroics, etc...............................0137
Nelson. John Rantoul...........................62394
Nesbit (Mrs. Hubert Bland). Lays and legends. 1892................................821.2 494
Nettleship. Essays on Browning's poetry. 1868..821.2 1123
Nevinson. Neighbors of ours: slum stories of London..15570
New Alice in the old wonderland...............0915
New Antigone......................................30565
New King Arthur: opera, without music.821.1 283
Newbolt. Taken from the enemy............33865
Newby. Common sense..........................12079
Newell, C, M. Isle of palms....................69369
Kaméhaméha...69370
Voyage of the Fleetwing..........................69368
Newell, R. H., (Orpheus C. Kerr, *pseud.*).
Cloven foot...62366
Orpheus C. Kerr papers. 3 v.............828.1 12
Smoked glass. 1868..........................828.1 42
There was once a man............................62365
Versatilities (poems). 1871..............821.1 197
Newlyn house.......................................07139
Newman, J. H. Callista.........................25823
Essays. 1871. 2 v...........................204 45
Letters and correspondence, in the English church. 2 v............................922 2 217
Miscellanies. 1870...........................204 44
Verses. 1880..................................821.2 709
Newman, *Mrs.* **M. W.** His vindication.....33531
Jan...33530
Last of the Haddons..............................33532
Newport. Two days..............................62582
Newton. Joe Ford................................32450

Nichols, G. W. Sanctuary.................................12082
Nichols, J. H. The future: poem. 1856.
....821.1 Pam. 9
Nicholson, A. No cipher in Shakespeare.
1888...822.3 358
Nicholson, J. S. Dreamer of dreams........24602
   Thoth..24601
   Toxar...24603
Nicholson, John. Poetical works. '76..821.2 581
Niles, H. Principles and acts of the revo-
   lution...329.1 2
   Same. 1876..329.1 1
Niles, W. Five hundred majority..............15285
Nimport..55239
Nisbet. Bail up !..53680
   Bush girl's romance..................................53683
   Divers...53681
   Great secret...53684
   Kings of the sea......................................53685
   Queen's desire..53682
   The swampers..53686
Noble, Annette L. Eunice Lathrop.........65701
   In a country town...................................65705
   Jacob's heiress...65708
   Professor's dilemma................................65709
   Professor's girls.......................................028102
   Ryhoves of Antwerp...............................65706
   Tarryport school girls............................028101
   Uncle Jack's executors............................65702
Noble, A. L., and Coann, P. C. Love
   and shawl-straps......................................65707
Noble, J. A. Impressions and memories.
   1895..824.2 485
   Contents: Justification of impressions.— Music of prose.—Oliver Wendell Holmes.— Charm of autobiography.—Music and form.—Burden of Christine Rossetti.—Nathaniel Hawthorne's paradox.— Some skylark poems.—Annie Keary.— Hypocrite of fiction.—Mr. Du Maurier's magic mirror.—In Elleray wood.—The Lady of Shalott.—Sandycombes.—Two Thanet sketches.
   Morality in English fiction. 1886........823 110
Noble, Lucretia. Reverend idol..............58947
Noel. Essays on poetry and poets. 1886..824.2 386
   A little child's monument (verse). 1881.
   ....821.2 592
   A modern Faust, and other poems. 1888.
   ....821.2 560
Nolan. The Byrnes of Glengoulah............44195
Nordhoff. Cape Cod, etc...........................12075
   Man-of-war life.......................................020302
   Merchant vessel......................................020304
   Seeing the world....................................020301
   Whaling and fishing...............................020303
Normand. Brigand captain.......................12092
   Julienne..12093
Norris, E. M. Early start in life..............25815
   Gerald and Harry...................................021501
Norris, O. M. Nadya, a tale of the steppes...15760

Norris, W. E. Bachelor's blunder............42321
   Baffled conspirators................................42329
   Billy Bellew...42342
   Chris..42324
   Clarissa Furiosa.......................................42345
   Countess Radna.......................................42337
   Dancer in yellow......................................42344
   Deplorable affair......................................42336
   Despotic lady..42340
   Heaps of money.......................................42301
   Her own doing...42319
   His grace...42335
   Jack's father, etc......................................42334
   Contents: Jack's father.—Romance of Paullatino.—Mysterious Mrs. Wilkinson.—The Wingham case.—A queer business.—Clever Lady Sophia.—Poor Harry.
   Mademoiselle de Mersac........................42317
   Major and minor....................................42323
   Marcia..42330
   Marietta's marriage................................42346
   Matrimony...42303
   Matthew Austin......................................42339
   Misadventure..42328
   Miss Shafto..42326
   Miss Wentworth's idea..........................42331
   Mr. Chaine's sons...................................42333
   Mrs. Fenton...42327
   My friend Jim..42320
   Mysterious Mrs. Wilkinson, etc............42332
   Contents: Mysterious Mrs. Wilkinson.—A queer business.—Clever Lady Sophia.—Poor Harry.
   No new thing..42315
   Quite impossible................................in 37715
   The rogue..42325
   Saint Ann's..42341
   Spectre of Strathannan..........................42343
   That terrible man...................................42318
   Thirlby hall...42322
   Victim of good luck...............................42338
North, Barclay, *pseud.* See Hudson, W. C.
North, Christopher, *pseud.* See Wilson, *Prof.*
   John.
North, L., *and* Phelps, C. E. D. Bailiff
   of Tewkesbury.......................................20230
North, William. Man of the woods......20432
Northcote, J. Conversations of ; by Hazlitt. 1894..................................829.2 71
Northcote, *Sir* Stafford H. See Iddesleigh.
Norton, C. E. S. Old Sir Douglas...........38802
   Poems. 1857.....................................821.2 280
   Stuart of Dunleith..................................38804
Norton, C. L. Jack Benson's log............035101
Norton, T., *and* Sackville, T. Gorboduc
   (drama)...822.2 78
Nothing to do ; by a lady. 1857.......827.1 5
Notley. Olive Varcoe................................40211
   Red Riding Hood....................................40210
Noyes (Charles Quiet). Studies in verse..821.1 210

Nye. Bill Nye's history of the U. S. '94...828.1 80
    Guest at the Ludlow, etc....................51801
Ober. Knockabout club in North Africa...*916.1 13
    Knockabout club in Spain.................*914.6 52
    Knockabout club in the Antilles.........*917.9 25
    Knockabout club in the Everglades...*917.4 46
    Montezuma's gold mines......................031503
    Silver city...031501
O'Brien, Fitz-James. Poems and stories;
    ed. by Winter. 1881.....................821.1 253
    Contents: Sketch of O'Brien.—Recollections of O'Brien.
    —Poems.—Stories: The diamond lens; The wonder-
    smith; Tommatoo; Mother of pearl; The Bohemian;
    The lost room; The pot of tulips; The golden ingot;
    My wife's tempter; What was it?; Duke Humphrey's
    dinner; Milly Dove; The dragon fang.
O'Brien, W. When we were boys..........69540
O'Connell. Correspondence................923.2 623
    Speeches and letters. 1875. 2 v.......329.2 66
O'Connor, E. S. Tracings. 1896.........829.1 41
O'Connor, Joseph. Poems. 1895......821.1 488
O'Connor, W. D. Hamlet's note-book.
    1886..822.3 156
    Mr. Donnelly's reviewers...........822.3 Pam. 19
    Three tales..20404
    Contents: The ghost.—The brazen android.—The
    carpenter.
O'Dowd, Cornelius, *pseud.* See **Lever.**
Ogden. Doctor Barringford's school.........031701
O'Grady. Bog of stars, etc........................26125
    Chain of gold....................................026140
    Coming of Cuculain...............................26127
    In the wake of King James.....................26129
    Lost on Du-Corrig.................................26126
    Ulrick the ready..................................26128
O'Keeffe, C. M. Knights of the pale........44193
O'Keeffe, J. Dramatic works. 1798. 4 v.
    V. 1. Life's vagaries.—Castle of Andalusia.—
    The grenadier.—Tony Lumpkin in town.—Poor
    soldier.—Modern antiques.—Sprigs of laurel......822.2 136
    V. 2. Wild oats.—Wicklow mountains.—Fon-
    tainebleau.—Little hunchback.—Basket maker.—
    Blacksmith of Antwerp.—Positive man............822.2 137
    V. 3. The toy.—Czar Peter.—London hermit.—
    Irish mimic.—Tantara-rara.—Birthday.—Beggar
    on horseback..822.2 138
    V. 4. World in a village.—Highland reel.—
    Magic banner.—The farmer.—Man milliner.—
    Prisoner at large.—Love in a camp.—The doldrum.
    ....822.2 139
Old and new home.................................50347
Old Andy's money..................................07134
Old Coins, *pseud.* See **Rowell, A. S.**
Old French chateau................................55279
Oldboy, Oliver, *pseud.* George Bailey......56889
Oldbug, *pseud.* The Puritan: essays. 1836.
    2 v..824.1 273
Oldfellow, A., *pseud.* Uncle Nat............07125
Oldham. By the Trent............................52205
Olga, *princess.* Radna...........................69334

Oliphant, L. Altiora Peto...................13902
    Fashionable philosophy, etc.................13906
    Piccadilly..13901
    Traits and travesties........................824.2 330
Oliphant, *Mrs.* **M. O. W.** Agnes.........3124
    Agnes Hopetown.............................025701
    At his gates.......................................3127
    Athelings...3183
    Beleaguered city................................3141
    The Brownlows.................................3154
    Caleb Field....................................*in* 3113
    Carita...3119
    Chronicles of Carlingford...................3102
    Country gentleman............................3178
    Cousin Mary.....................................3108
    Cuckoo in the nest.............................3159
    Curate in charge................................3140
    Days of my life.................................3118
    Diana...3158
    Doctor's family................................*in* 3131
    Same..*in* 3102
    Effie Ogilvie....................................3181
    For love and life...............................3156
    Greatest heiress in England.................3143
    Harry Joscelyn..................................3148
    Harry Muir.......................................3150
    He that will not when he may.............3145
    Heir presumptive and the heir apparent...3135
    Hester..3169
    House in Bloomsbury........................3163
    House on the moor...........................3134
    In trust..3151
    Innocent..3103
    It was a lover and his lass..................3166
    Janet..3162
    John...3147
    Joyce...3101
    Katie Stewart...................................3146
    Kirsteen..3128
    Ladies Lindores................................3152
    Lady Car...3122
    Lady William...................................3184
    Laird of Norlaw................................3109
    Last of the Mortimers.......................3116
    Lilliesleaf..3149
    Little pilgrim. 1882....................249 45
    Lucy Crofton...................................3112
    Madame..3174
    Madonna Mary..................................3111
    Magdalen Hepburn............................3153
    Margaret Maitland............................3106
    Marriage of Elinor............................3155
    May..3105
    Memoirs of Adam Graeme...................3142
    Minister's wife.................................3129
    Miss Marjoribanks............................3115
    Mrs. Arthur.....................................3120

* Of interest to young readers.

Mystery of Mrs. Blencarrow	3121
Neighbours on the green	3110
Odd couple	3107
Old Lady Mary	3167
Old Mr. Tredgold	3177
Oliver's bride	3180
Ombra	3160
Open door.— The portrait	3175
Orphans.—Caleb Field	3113
Perpetual curate	3130
Phœbe, jr.	3133
The portrait	*in* 3175
Primrose path	3136
Prodigals	3172
Railway man and his children	3139
Rector.—Doctor's family	3131
Same	*in* 3102
Rose in June	3125
Salem chapel	3132
Sir Robert's fortune	3165
Sir Tom	3173
Son of the soil	3171
Sons and daughters	3138
Sorceress	3161
Squire Arden	3126
Stories of the seen and the unseen	3114

Contents: A little pilgrim. — Old Lady Mary. — The open door.—The portrait.

Story of Valentine and his brother	3157
Three brothers	3123
Two Marys	3179
Two strangers	3176
Unjust steward	3182
Ways of life	3185

Contents: Mr. Sandford. — Wonderful history of Mr. Robert Dalyell.

Whiteladies	3117
Who was lost and is found	3168
Within the precincts	3164
Wizard's son	3170
Young Musgrave	3137

Oliphant, *Mrs.* **M. O. W.**, *and* **Aldrich, T. B.** Second son........3101

Olive-Branch, *Rev.* **S.** See **Roberts, W.**

Oliver, Pen, *pseud.* (Sir Henry Thompson.) Charley Kingston's aunt......... 69106

O'Meara. Narka the nihilist	69365
Once a year	58938
O'Neil. Two thousand years hence. 1867..827.2 27	
O'Neill, H. C. Devonshire idyls	53310
O'Neill, J. Garrison tales from Tonquin	57001
O'Neill, M. Easter vacation	31240
Only three weeks	58932

Opie, Complete works.
 V. 1. Madeline.— Adeline Mowbray.—Simple tales.—Father and daughter.—Happy faces............12001
 V. 2. Tales of real life.—Valentine's eve.—New tales..12002

V. 3. Temper.— A woman's love.— A wife's duty.—The two sons.—Opposite neighbor.—Love, mystery, and superstition.—After the ball.—False or true.—Confession of an odd-tempered man.— Illustrations of lying.................................12003

Oppenheim. Mystery of Mr. Bernard Brown.....................................70440

Optic, Oliver, *pseud.* (W. T. Adams.)
All-over-the-world library ; series 1.
 1. A missing million................011860
 2. Millionaire at sixteen...........011856
 3. Young knight errant.............011857
 4. Strange sights abroad............011858
Same ; series 2.
 1. American boys afloat............011859
 2. Young navigators................011867
 3. Up and down the Nile............011861
 4. Asiatic breezes.................011862
Same ; series 3.
 1. Across India....................011863
 2. Half round the world............011864
Army and navy series.
 1. Soldier boy.....................011801
 2. Young lieutenant................011802
 3. Fighting Joe....................011803
 4. Sailor boy......................011804
 5. Yankee middy....................011805
 6. Brave old salt..................011806
Blue and the gray : navy series.
 1. Taken by the enemy..............011850
 2. Within the enemy's lines........011851
 3. On the blockade.................011852
 4. Stand by the Union..............011853
 5. Fighting for the right..........011854
 6. Victorious Union................011855
Boat club series :
 1. Boat club.......................011844
 2. All aboard......................011845
 3. Now or never....................011849
 4. Try again.......................011846
 5. Poor and proud..................011847
 6. Little by little................011848
Great western series :
 1. Going west......................011807
 2. Lake breezes....................011809
 3. Going south.....................011810
 4. Down south......................011811
 5. Up the river....................011812
Lake shore series :
 1. Through by daylight.............011813
 2. Lightning express...............011814
 3. On time.........................011815
 4. Switch off......................011816
 5. Brake up........................011817
 6. Bear and forbear................011818
Starry flag series :
 1. Starry flag.....................011819
 2. Breaking away...................011820
 3. Seek and find...................011821
 4. Freaks of fortune...............011822
 5. Make or break...................011823
 6. Down the river..................011824
Yacht club series :
 1. Little Bobtail..................011825
 2. Yacht club.....................011826
 3. Money maker.....................011827
 4. Coming wave.....................011828
 5. Dorcas club.....................011829
 6. Ocean born......................011830
 7. Isles of the sea................011831

LANGUAGE AND LITERATURE.

Oram. Poems. 1822..................*in* 821.2 46
O'Reilly, J. B. In Bohemia (verses).
   1886...821.1 351
   Moondyne..................................56850
   Songs, legends and ballads. 1878.....821.1 184
   Statues in the block, and other poems.
     1881..821.1 255
O'Reilly, M., (C. G. Halpine). Life, etc.
   1866..828.1 37
   Poetical works. 1869.....................821.1 284
O'Reilly, *Mrs.* R. David Broome............64602
   Dinglefield....................................029301
   Hurstleigh Dene..........................029302
   Joan and Jerry............................029303
   Kirk's mill, and other stories................64610
   Meg's mistake.................................64609
   Our hero.......................................64608
   Phœbe's fortunes..............................64605
   Red house in the suburbs......................64607
   Sue and I......................................64611
   Sussex stories.................................64601
Ormsby. Autumn leaves : poems. 1896..821.1 449
Ormulum, The, (poem) ; ed. by R. M.
   White. 2 v...................................821.2 103
Orne. Sweet Auburn and Mount Auburn,
   with other poems. 1844..............821.1 422
Orpen. Perfection city........................53120
Orphans of Auvergne..............................07130
Orr, *Mrs.* A. S. Leah..........................19199
   Mountain patriots............................19197
   Roseville family..............................19198
   Twins of Saint Marcel........................19196
Orr, *Mrs.* S. Handbook to Browning. 1885.
   ....821.2 1124
Orton. Poetical sketches. 1829......821.1 Pam. 10
Osborn, *Mrs.* E. F. D., *ed.* Political and
   social letters, 1721-71...............826.2 104
Osborn, L. Tragedies. 1869..............822.1 9
   Contents : Ugo da Este.—Uberto.—The Cid of Seville.
   Tragedies. 1870.........................822.1 8
   Contents : The last Mandeville.—The heart's sacrifice.—The monk.—Matilda of Denmark.
Osborne, Dorothy. Letters to Sir W.
   Temple, 1652-4.............................826.2 98
Osborne, Elise. Life's lottery..................52269
Osbourne *and* Stevenson. Wrecker........67404
   Wrong box......................................67409
Osgood, F. S. Poems. 1876.............821.1 242
Osgood, S. American leaves : notes. '67..824.1 93
O'Shaughnessy. Epic of women, etc..821.2 589
   Lays of France. 1872..................821.2 756
   Music and moonlight : poems. '74...821.2 778
   Songs of a worker. 1881..............821.2 590
Ossoli, Margaret Fuller. Art, literature
   and the drama. 1860...................824.1 25
   Life without and life within...........824.1 23
   Papers on literature and art. 1846.....824.1 24
Oswald. Dragon of the north.......................03010

Otis, *Mrs.* H. G. Barclays of Boston........15231
Otis, J., *pseud.* Admiral J. of Spurwink..026626
   Boy captain..................................026629
   Boys of 1745.................................026623
   Boys' revolt..................................026615
   Braganza diamond..........................026610
   Chasing a yacht..............................026614
   Ezra Jordan's escape......................026622
   How Tommy saved the barn..............026616
   Island refuge.................................026621
   Jack the hunchback.......................026611
   Jenny Wren's boarding-house...........026613
   Jerry's family................................026619
   Josiah in New York........................026612
   Left behind.................................026605
   Little Joe.....................................026607
   Mr. Stubbs's brother........................026602
   Neal the miller............................026620
   On schedule time...........................026624
   Raising the Pearl..........................026604
   Runaway brig................................026608
   Short cruise.................................026625
   Silent Pete..................................026606
   Teddy and Carrots.........................026628
   Tim and Tip.................................026603
   Toby Tyler..................................026601
   Treasure-finders............................026609
   Under the liberty tree....................026627
   With Lafayette at Yorktown..............026618
   Wood island light..........................026617
Ottolengui. Artist in crime..............27015
   Conflict of evidence......................27016
   Crime of the century.....................27018
   Modern wizard..............................27017
Otway. Works. 1712. 2 v.
   V. 1. Alcibiades.—Don Carlos.— Titus and Berenice.— Friendship in fashion —Soldier's fortune.
   ....822.2 119
   V. 2. The atheist.—The orphan.— Caius Marius.
   —Venice preserved.—Poems.—Love letters..822.2 120
Ouida, *pseud.* (Louise de la Ramé.) Ariadne..5113
   Bébée [Two little wooden shoes]...........5110
   Bimbi : stories for children................05105
   Contents : The Nürnberg stove. — Ambitious rose-tree.—Moufflou.—Lampblack.—The child of Urbino.—In the apple-country. — Findelkind. — Meleagris Gallopavo.—The little earl.
   Cecil Castlemaine's gage..................5107
   Chandos..5101
   Dog of Flanders, etc.........................5119
   Contents : Dog of Flanders.—Branch of lilac.—Provence rose.—Leaf in the storm.
   Folle Farine....................................5109
   Frescoes..5147
   Friendship.....................................5122
   Granville De Vigne........................5112
   Guilderoy......................................5104
   House party...................................5123

Idalia 5102
In a winter city 5111
In Maremma 5144
Lemon tree .... in 5124
Le Selve 5125
Madame la marquise 5143
The Massarenes 5126
Othmar 5153
Pascarelle 5142
Pipistrello, etc 5103
Princess Napraxine 5149
Puck 5118
Rainy June 5152
Randolph Gordon 5114
Signa 5116
Silver Christ. —A lemon tree 5124
Strathmore 5117
Syrlin 5106
Tower of Taddeo 5108
Tricotrin 5105
Two little wooden shoes [Bébée] 5110
Two offenders 5115
Under two flags 5120
Village commune 5135
Wanda 5145
Our little Ann. (See **Laddie**.) 17902
Out of town 70480
Overbury. Miscellaneous works; ed. by Rimbault. 1856 .... 820.2 43
  Contents: Life.—Poem of the wife.— Characters.—Newes.—Remedy of love.—Observations upon the state of the seventeen provinces, A. D. 1609.— Crumms fal'n from King James' table.
Overton. After school 042201
Owen, G. W. Leech club 47232
Owen, M. A. Daughter of Alouette 71501
Owen, O. W. Bacon's cipher story 822.3 384
Oxley. Archie of Athabasca 04405
  Boy tramps 04408
  My strange rescue, etc 04406
  On the world's roof 04407
P., A. N. T. A. Theories 31085
Paddock. Fate of Madame La Tour 62538
Page, Stanton, *pseud.* See **Fuller, H. B.**
Page, T. N. Among the camps 011411
  Burial of the guns 27805
  Contents: My cousin Fanny.—The burial of the guns. The gray jacket of No. 4.—Miss Dangerlie's roses.—How the captain made Christmas.—Little Darby.
  Elsket, etc 27803
  Contents: Elsket.—'George Washington's' last duel. P' laski's tunament.—Run to seed.—A soldier of the empire.
  In ole Virginia 27801
  Contents: Marse Chan—Unc' Edinburg's drowndin'.—Meh lady.—Ole' Stracted.— No Haid Pawn.—Polly.
  Old gentleman of the black stock 27806
  On Newfound river 27802

Pastime stories 27804
  Contents: Old Sue.—How Jinny eased her mind.—Isrul's bargain. — True story of the surrender of the Marquis Cornwallis.—When little Mordecai was at the bar. —Charlie Whittler's Christmas party.—How Relius bossed the ranch.—Prosecution of Mrs. Dullet.—One from four.—Danger of being too thorough.—Uncle Jack's views of geography.—Billington's valentine.—She had on her geranium leaves.—Story of Charles Harris.—He would have gotten a lawyer.—How Andrew carried the precinct. —Rasmus.— Her sympathetic editor. -- He knew what was due to the court.—Her great-grand-mother's ghost.—Rachel's lovers.—John's wedding suit. —When the colonel was a duellist.
  Two little Confederates 011410
Page, T. N., *and* **Gordon, A. C.** Befo' de war (poems). 1888 .... 821.1 370
Paget, A. H. Shakespeare's plays. 1875.
  .... 822.3 Pam. 7
Paget, Violet. See **Lee, Vernon,** *pseud.*
Pain, *Mrs.* **A.** Saint Eva 29350
Pain, B. Kindness of the celestial, etc 29302
  Playthings and parodies. 1892 .... 824.2 451
  Contents: The sincerest form of flattery. — The hundred gates.—The secular confessional. — Sketches in London.—Home pets.
  Stories and interludes 29301
  Two 029305
Pain and sorrow of evil marriage 821.2 444
Paine, R. T. Works in verse and prose; with life. 1812 .... 821.1 16
Paine, Thomas. Political writings. 2 v...329.1 183
  Writings; ed. by Conway. 1894-6. 4 v..329.1 185
Painter. Rhomeo and Iulietta. (New Shakespeare society, 1875.) 822.3 B-5
Palace-prison 58994
Palfrey. Herman 15217
Palgrave, F. T. Five days at Wentworth grange 06401
Palgrave, W. G. Hermann Aga 44159
Palmer, Lynde, *pseud.* (Mary L. Peebles.)
  Jeannette's cisterns 65001
  Question of honour 65004
  Where honour leads 65003
Palmer, Ray. Home (poem) 821.1 55
Paltock. Peter Wilkins. 2 v 50311
Pandurang Hari 69003
Pansy, *pseud.* (Mrs. I. M. Alden.) Browning boys 022910
  Chautauqua girls at home 4910
  Cunning workmen 4922
  Divers women 4932
  Eighty-seven 4904
  Endless chain 4943
  Esther Reid 4912
  Five friends 022906
  Four girls at Chautauqua 4902
  Hall in the grove 4939
  Household puzzles 4921
  Interrupted 4945

Jessie Wells	022902
Judge Burnham's daughters	4906
Julia Reid	4916
King's daughter	4923
Links in Rebecca's life	4925
Making fate	4911
Man of the house	022907
Miss Dee Dunmore Bryant	022911
Miss Priscilla Hunter	4926
Mrs. Harry Harper's awakening	4937
Mrs. Solomon Smith looking on	4942
New graft on the family tree	4935
Next things	022905
People who haven't time	4933
Pocket measure	4938
Randolphs	4901
Ruth Erskine's crosses	4928
Sevenfold trouble	4907
Sidney Martin's Christmas	022903
Six o'clock in the evening	4903
Spun from fact	4946
Tip Lewis	022901
Wanted	4909
What she said and what she meant	4934
Wise and otherwise	4920

Pansy *and* **Livingston**, *Mrs.* **C. M.** John
Remington, martyr............4908
Profiles............4905

Pardoe. Jealous wife............25801
Pardon. Tales from the operas............20411
Park. Selections: poems. 1836............821.1 415
Parke, C. S. Ventures in verse. 1892...821.1 429
Parker, G. Adventurer of the north............34406

Contents: Across the jumping sandhills. — Lovely bully. — Filibuster. — Gift of the simple king. — Malachi. — Lake of the great slave. — Red patrol. — Going of the white swan. — At Bamber's Boom. — Bridge house. — Epaulettes. — Finding of Fingall. — Three commandments in the vulgar tongue. — Little Babiche. — At Point o' Bugles. — Spoil of the puma. — Trail of the sun dogs. — Pilot of Belle Amour. — Cruise of the Ninety-nine. — Romany of the snows. — Plunderer.

March of the white guard............*in* 32713
Mrs. Falchion............34402
Pierre and his people............34408
Pomp of the Lavilettes............34409
Romany of the snows............34406B

Contents: Three commandments in the vulgar tongue — Little Babiche. — At Point o' Bugles. — Spoil of the puma. — Trail of the sun dogs. — Pilot of Belle Amour. — Cruise of the Ninety-nine. — Romany of the snows. — The plunderer.

Seats of the mighty............34407
Trail of the sword............34404
Translation of a savage............34401
Trespasser............34403
When Valmond came to Pontiac............34405

Parker, *Mrs.* **H. F.** Constance Aylmer............52275
Parker, Jane M. Midnight cry............22401

Parker, Joseph. Springdale abbey............37201
Tyne folk............37202
Parker, Margaret K. Old house at Four Corners............823 Pam. 4
Parker, Martin. The king and a poor northern man............821.2 444
Parker, T. Correspondence. 2 v............922.1 35
Critical and miscellaneous writings. 1867............824.1 41
Speeches, addresses, etc. 3 v............252 54
Parkinson. Places and people. 1869...824.1 71
Parley, Peter. See **Goodrich.**
Parnell. Poems; with life............821.2 35
Poetical works; ed. by Aitken. '94...821.2 817
Parr, Harriet, (Holme Lee, *pseud.*). Annis Warleigh's fortunes............35301
Ben Milner's wooing............35306
Fairy tales............06301
Legends from fairyland............06304
Poor match............06303
Poor squire............35305
Tuflongbo and Little Content............06302
Vicissitudes of Bessie Fairfax............35302
Parr, Louisa. Adam and Eve............47104
Bluebell of Redneap, etc............47102
Can this be love?............47109
Dorothy Fox............47103
Dumps............47107
John Thompson, blockhead............47101
Loyalty George............47106
Robin............47105
Squire............47108
Parr, S. Works and memoir; ed. by Johnstone. 1828. 8 v.
 V. 1. Memoirs; by Johnstone............820.2 1
 V. 2. Sermons............820.2 2
 V. 3. Notice of Combe's 'Horace.' — Remarks on politics. — Letter from Irenopolis. — Warburtonian tracts. — Letter to Milner, etc............820.2 3
 V. 4. Character of Charles James Fox. — Note on Fox's history. — Inscriptions............820.2 4
 V. 5-6. Sermons............820.2 5
 V. 7-8. Correspondence............820.2 7
Parry. Story of Dick............01210
Parsons. Love knots............65405
Partington, *Mrs., pseud.* See **Shillaber, P. B.**
Partnership............50308
Parton, James. Topics of the time. '71..824.1 86
Parton, *Mrs.* **Sara P.** See **Fern, Fanny.**
Paston. Bread and butter miss............45340
Career of Candida............45342
Study in prejudices............45341
Patch. Myself and my friends............010870
Patchin. Dorothea............63416
Pater. Appreciations. 1889............824.2 422

Contents: Style. — Wordsworth. — Coleridge. — Lamb. — Sir Thomas Browne. — Love's labour's lost. — Measure for measure. — Shakspere's English kings. — Æsthetic poetry. — Rossetti. — Postscript.

The child in the house. 1895................137 5
Gaston de Latour..............................69208
Imaginary portraits. 1887..............824.2 402
Marius, the epicurean............................69207
Miscellaneous studies. 1895............824.2 486
   Contents: Prosper Mérimée.—Raphael.—Pascal.—Art notes in north Italy.—Notre-Dame d'Amiens.—Vézelay. —Apollo in Picardy.—The child in the house.—Emerald Uthwart.—Diaphaneitè.
Paterson. For freedom's sake..................12522
Partner from the west............................12520
Son of the plains....................................12521
Patient Grissel, History of.....................821.2 446
Patmore, C. The angel in the house. 2 v.
   V. 1. The betrothal..........................821.2 331
   V. 2. The espousals.........................821.2 332
Faithful forever (verse). 1861.........821.2 330
Poems. 1894. 2 v.
   V. 1. The angel in the house.—The victories of love..821.2 1014
   V. 2. The unknown Eros.—Amelia, etc.......821.2 1015
Poetry of pathos and delight; sel. by Meynell. 1896......................821.2 1019
Religio poetæ, etc. 1893..............824.2 462
   Contents: Religio poetæ.—The precursor.—The language of religion.—Attention.—Christianity an experimental science.— A people of a stammering tongue.—The bow set in the cloud.—Christianity and progress.—A pessimist outlook. — A Spanish novelette. — Bad morality is bad art.—Emotional art.—Peace in life and art.—Simplicity.—Ancient and modern ideas of purity.—Conscience.—On obscure books.—Distinction.—A modern classic, William Barnes.—The weaker vessel.—Madame de Hautefort.—Mrs. Meynell.—Dieu et ma dame.
The unknown Eros. 1878..............821.2 507
Patmore, P. G. Chatsworth................in 14121
Patrick. Christine Brownlee's ordeal. 2 v..57402
Marjorie Bruce's lovers........................57401
Patterson. Out of sight...........................62313
Pattison. Essays. 1889. 2 v.
   V. 1. Gregory of Tours. — Early intercourse, England and Germany.—Antecedents of the Reformation. — The Stephenses. — Muretus. — Joseph Scaliger.—Peter Daniel Huet.—A chapter of university history.—F. A. Wolf.—Oxford studies...824.2 423
   V. 2. Calvin at Geneva.—Religious thought in England, 1688-1750. — Bishop Warburton. — The Calas tragedy. — State of theology in Germany (1857). — Learning in the Church of England.—Philanthropic societies, reign of Anne.—Montaigne. —Pope and his editors.—Buckle's 'History of civilization in England.'................824.2 424
Paul, John, (C. H. Webb). John Paul's book. 1874......................................828.1 50
Sea-weed and what we seed. 1876.....828.1 51
Paul, K. New minister..........................37401
Paul, M. A. Gentle and simple................53001
Martha Brown....................................53002
Paul and Marie....................................07130
Paulding, J. K. The backwoodsman; poem. 1818..................................821.1 249
Book of vagaries..............................917.3 21

Bulls and the Jonathans. 1867..........827.1 16
Dutchman's fireside...............................20703
Koningsmarke......................................20701
Lay of the Scottish fiddle. 1814.......821.1 347
Puritan and his daughter.......................20706
Tales of the good woman.....................20702
Three wise men of Gotham. 1839......827.1 21
Westward ho!.......................................20704
Paulding, J. K. and **W. I.** American comedies. 1847..........................822.1 22
Paulding, J. K., and **Irving, William** and **Washington.** Salmagundi.....824.1 8
Same. 2 v...................................824.1 6
Payn. At her mercy..............................8904
Beggar on horseback............................8914
Best of husbands..................................8919
Burnt million..8920
By proxy..8901
Canon's ward.......................................8950
Carlyon's year......................................8932
Cecil's tryst..8946
Clyffords of Clyffe................................8917
Confidential agent................................8924
County family......................................8923
Disappearance of George Driffell.........8939
Eavesdropper......................................8913
Fallen fortunes....................................8902
Family scapegrace...............................8906
For cash only......................................8947
Foster brothers...................................8935
Found dead..8926
From exile..8925
Grape from a thorn.............................8931
Gwendolin's harvest............................8907
Halves...8903
High spirits..8927
In Market Overt..................................8934
In peril and privation..........................8951
In the heart of a hill, etc....................8908
Kit: a memory..................................8949
Less black than we're painted...........8940
Like father like son.............................8941
Lost Sir Massingberd..........................8905
Marine residence................................8933
Mirk Abbey..8936
Modern Dick Whittington..................8922
Murphy's master................................8909
Mystery of Mirbridge..........................8918
Not wooed but won............................8916
Perfect treasure..................................8912
Prince of the blood.............................8911
Some private views. 1881..........824.2 319
Stumble on the threshold..................8928
Talk of the town................................8952
Thicker than water.............................8948
Trying patient, etc..............................8938
£200 reward......................................8937

Under one roof..8930
Walter's word..8915
What he cost her...8929
Woman's vengeance....................................8910
Word and the will..8921
Payne, John. Intaglios : sonnets. '71..821.2 724
Lautrec: a poem. 1884..................821.2 725
Masque of shadows, etc. (poems). '84..821.2 722
New poems. 1884.......................821.2 723
Songs of life and death. 1872.........821.2 651
Payne, J. Howard. Brutus; adapted by Booth................................822.4 330
Payne, Will. Jerry the dreamer...............70401
Little leaders. 1895....................824.1 311
Contents: Literature and criticism: Literature on the stage; The Ibsen legend; The cult in literature; The literary west; The writer and his hire; The critic and his task; Touchstones of criticism; Anonymity in literary criticism; Poetry as criticism of literature; The neglected art of translation.— Education: A few words about education; The approach to literature; The teaching of literature; Democracy and education; The future of American speech; The use and abuse of dialect; Reading and education; Summer reading; The summer school; An endowed newspaper.—In memoriam: Tennyson; Renan; Taine; Freytag; Symonds; C. G. Rossetti; Tyndall; Huxley; Holmes; Poole.

Paynter. Caleb the irrepressible.............62325
Payson. Doctor Tom..........................12029
Peabody, E. P. Last evening with Allston, etc.................................824.1 140
Peabody, W. B. O. Literary remains. '50..824.1 17
Peace island..................................0134
Peacock. Calidore, and miscellanea. '96..824.2 517
Contents: Recollections of Peacock; by Strachey.— Some recollections of childhood.— Calidore.— Four ages of poetry.— Horæ dramaticæ, 1-3.— Last day of Windsor forest.

Crotchet castle............................20081
Gryll grange..............................20082
Headlong hall............................20080
Maid Marian............................20083
Melincourt..............................20084
Misfortunes of Elphin.................20085
Nightmare abbey.....................*in* 20080
Peak. Struggle for existence, etc. 1872...827.1 11
Pearce. Drolls from shadowland..........29498
Eli's daughter..........................29495
Esther Pentreath....................29496
Inconsequent lives..................29497
Jaco Treloar..........................29499
Tales of the masque................29494
Contents: The little crow of paradise.— A voyage to the golden land.—The man and the monster.—Ego speaks. —Joanna.—The calling of the sea.—The valley of vanished sunsets.—Leah.—A droll result.—The sorcery of the forest.— A pleasant gossip.— The veil of Máyá.— Joel.— The gifts of the little grey man.—Passing on.

Peard. Abbot's bridge....................019021
Baroness..............................19022
Blue dragon..........................19020

Career of Claudia..................................19026
Castle and town..................................19010
Catherine..19023
Contradictions....................................19014
Country cousin....................................19018
Interloper..19025
Jacob and the raven, etc......................019022
Jeannette..19013
Locked desk......................................019020
Madame's granddaughter....................19017
Mademoiselle....................................19021
Madrigal, etc....................................19007
Mother Molly....................................19006
Near neighbours................................19015
One year..19001
Prentice Hugh..................................19019
Princess Alethea................................19012
Rose garden....................................19003
Scapegrace Dick................................019024
Swing of the pendulum......................19024
Thorpe Regis....................................19004
Through rough waters........................19009
To horse and away............................019023
Unawares..19005
Winter's story..................................19002
Pearson. Cabin on the prairie.............032226
Reviews and critical essays. 1896.....824.2 499
Contents: Memoir of C. H. Pearson [by H. A. Strong].— Personal memoirs.— Caricatures.— Cynicism in literature.—Questions of casuistry.—The grand style. —Optimism.— Pessimism.— Sheridan.— Bismarck.—Emerson.—Mazzini.—History in state schools.—The court of Napoleon.—Scottish characteristics.—Early life of Renan. —The black republic.—An agnostic's progress.—High life in France.

Young pioneers of the northwest.........032225
Peattie. Mountain woman, etc..........70320
Peck. Mary Brandegee....................20413
Pedder. Study of 'Hamlet.' 1885.822.3 Pam. 14
Peebles. See **Palmer, Lynde,** *pseud.*
Peeke. Born of flame......................29201
Peele. Dramatic and poetical works ; ed. by Dyce. 1861......................822.2 101
Contents: Life, etc.—Arraignment of Paris.— Edward I.—Warning-piece to England.—Battle of Alcazar.—Old wives' tale.—David and Bethsabe.—Sir Clyomon and Sir Clamydes.—Tale of Troy.—Speeches to Elizabeth at Theobald's.

Works ; ed. by Bullen. 1887. 2 v.....822.2 300
Peggy Oglivie's inheritance..............58921
Pellatt. Witch-finder......................41620
Pemberton, C. H. Your little brother James..71301
Pemberton, Max. Christine of the hills...34527
Gentleman's gentleman......................34525
Impregnable city..............................34522
Iron pirate......................................34520
Jewel mysteries I have known.............34524
Little Huguenot..............................34523

Puritan's wife..34526
Sea wolves..34521
Pen. (See Laddie.)....................................17905
Pendered. Dust and laurels.....................43130
Penderel. Wilfred Waide, barrister and
  novelist...21210
Pendleton, E. Conventional bohemian....27403
  One woman's way..................................27402
  Virginia inheritance................................27401
Pendleton, L. Bewitched..........................23404
  Corona of the Nantahalas.....................23403
  In the Okefenokee................................023507
  In the wire-grass...................................23401
  King Tom and the runaways................023506
  Sons of Ham...23402
Pen-drag-on, Anser, *pseud.* See **Ireland,
  W. H.**
Pennell. Puck on Pegasus. 1874........821.2 436
Pennot, *Rev.* Peter, *pseud.* See **Round, W.
  M. F.**
Penrose. Poems. 1822.....................*in* 821.2 46
Pentecost. Harp of Æolus. 1856......821.2 417
Percy Pomo..58942
Perkins, *Mrs.* E. B., (S. Chesnutwood).
  Honor bright...41702
  Malbrook...41701
Perkins, F. B. Devil puzzlers, etc...........30415
  Scrope 30416
Perrier. Good match...............................44179
Perry, A. Esther Pennefather..................58803
  Schoolmaster's trial...............................58802
Perry, Bliss. Broughton House.................31201
  Plated city..31203
  Salem Kittredge, etc............................31202
  Contents: Salem Kittredge, theologue.—The Czar's diamond.—By the Ill.—Lombardy poplars.—The phenix. —The commonest possible story.—An incorrigible poet. Number three.—At Sesenheim.
Perry, Nora. After the ball, etc., (poems).
  1887...821.1 354
  Another flock of girls.........................*64005
  Book of love stories..............................64001
  Flock of boys and girls.......................*64006
  Flock of girls......................................*64003
  For a woman..64002
  Hope Benham.......................................06406
  New songs and ballads. 1887........821.1 355
  Rosebud garden of girls........................06405
  Three little daughters of the revolution...06407
  Youngest Miss Lorton...........................64004
Peterson, C. J. Cruising in the last war...25830
Peterson, F. In the shade of Ygdrasil
  (verse). 1893...................................821.1 295
  Poems and Swedish translations. 1883.
  ....821.1 291
Phelps, A. My portfolio. 1882................204 92
  My study, etc. 1886.............................204 98
Phelps, C. E. D., *and* **North, L.** Bailiff
  of Tewkesbury....................................20230

Phelps, E. S. Last leaf from Sunnyside...23623
  Peep at No. 5......................................23622
  Telltale..23621
Phelps, Elizabeth Stuart, (Mrs. Ward).
  Beyond the gates..................................4836
  Burglars in Paradise..............................4843
  Doctor Zay..4826
  Donald Marcy.......................................4805
  Fourteen to one....................................4807
  Contents: Fourteen to one.—Bell of St. Basil's.—Shut in.— Jack the fisherman.— Madonna of the tubs.—A brave deed.—Sacrifice of Antigone.—Sweet home.—Too late.— Reverend Malachi Matthew.— His relict.— Mary Elizabeth.—Annie Laurie.—Law and the gospel.
  Friends...4822
  Gates ajar...4801
  Gates between......................................4804
  Gypsy Breynton..................................020904
  Gypsy's cousin Joy..............................020906
  Gypsy's sowing and reaping...............020905
  Gypsy's year at the Golden Crescent.....020907
  Hedged in...4803
  Jack the fisherman................................4810
  Madonna of the tubs.............................4802
  Men, women and ghosts.......................4808
  Old Maid's Paradise..............................4840
  Sealed orders..4820
  Silent partner..4806
  Singular life..4811
  Songs of the silent world, and other
    poems. 1885...............................821.1 318
  Story of Avis...4809
  Supply at Saint Agatha's......................4812
  Trotty book.......................................020901
Phelps, Elizabeth Stuart, *and* **Ward,
  H. D.** Come forth................................4851
  Lost hero...020920
  Master of the magicians.......................4850
Phelps, Lavinia H. Dramatic stories,
  etc. 1874..792.1 13
Phelps, *Mrs.* Lincoln. Discipline of
  life...25839
Philips, A. Poems; with life..............821.2 35
Philips, F. C. Question of color..........21230
  Test of ridicule..................................*in* 32715
Philips, J. Poems; with life. 1822......821.2 43
Philips, M. Devil's hat..........................69304
Phillimore. Uncle Z...............................65601
Phillipps, J. O. Halliwell-. See **Halliwell-
  Phillipps.**
Phillips, *Mrs.* A. Benedicta..................69425
Phillips, B. Struggle..............................69153
Phillips, C. Select speeches. 1831......329.2 22
Phillips, S. Essays from The Times.
  1871. 2 v..824.2 338
Phillips, Wendell. The lost arts.....609 Pam. 1
  The scholar in a republic..............324 Pam. 16
  Speech (woman's rights). 1851..........*in* 40 1

* Of interest to young readers.

Speeches, lects. and letters. 1864.........326 40
Speeches, lects. and letters; 2d series.
   1891..824.1 259
Phillips, W. B. Diamond cross...............20403
Phillpotts. End of a life.......................24410
   Folly and fresh air................................24411
   Lying prophets....................................24412
Phœnix, J., (G. H. Derby). Phœnixiana.
   1865..828.1 15
   Squibob papers. 1865........................828.1 11
Piatt, J. J. Idyls and lyrics of the Ohio
   valley. 1893......................................821.1 470
   Landmarks, and other poems. 1872...821.1 162
   Lost hunting-ground, and other poems.
   1893..821.1 471
   Penciled fly-leaves. 1880....................824.1 154
   Poems of house and home. 1879.....821.1 223
   Western windows, and other poems.
   1877..821.1 160
Piatt, J. J. *and Mrs.* **S. M. B.** Children out-
   of-doors (verse). 1885........................821.1 323
Piatt, *Mrs.* **S. M. B.** Enchanted castle,
   etc. (verse). 1893..............................821.1 472
   In primrose time (verse).....................821.1 339
   Irish garland (verse). 1885.................821.1 324
   That new world, and other poems. 1877.
   ....821.1 165
   Voyage to the Fortunate isles, etc.
   (poems)..821.1 164
   A woman's poems. 1871....................821.1 163
Picard. Matter of taste........................18701
   Mission flower....................................18702
   Old Boniface......................................18703
Pickering, Edgar. In press-gang days...033901
   Two gallant rebels..............................033902
Pickering, Ellen. Grandfather..............14121
Pickering, P. Life awry.........................9330
Piers plowman, Vision of. See **Langland.**
   Piers plowman's creed......................820.2 315
   Same; ed. by Wright..........................821.2 108
Pilgrimage to Parnassus, etc.: comedies,
   Cambridge, 1597-1601; ed. by Macray.
   ....822.2 292
Pindar, Peter. See **Wolcot, J.**
Pinero. Notorious Mrs. Ebbsmith: drama.
   1895..822.2 323
Pinkerton. French prisoner.................13431
   New saint's tragedy...........................13430
Pique...22901
Pirkis. Dateless bargain......................19580
Pitcairn. Selecta poemata. 1727........821.2 480
Pitt, William. Speeches. 1806. 4 v...329.2 14
Pitt, William, *earl of Chatham.* Corre-
   spondence. 1838-40. 4 v....................329.2 81
Pitt, William, *earl of Chatham,* **Burke,**
   and **Erskine.** Celebrated speeches.
   1845..825.2 12

Planché. Extravaganzas. 1879. 5 v.
   V. 1. Success. — Olympic revels. — Olympic
devils.—The Paphian bower. — High, low, jack
and the game.—Deep, deep sea.— Telemachus.—
Riquet with the tuft.—Puss in boots................822.2 213
   V. 2. Drama's levée. — Blue Beard. — Sleeping
beauty.— Beauty and the beast.— The white cat.
Fortunio. — The fair one with the golden locks.—
The drama at home.—Graciosa and Percinet. ..822.2 214
   V. 3. Golden fleece. — The bee and the orange
tree. — 'The birds' of Aristophanes. — Invisible
prince.— The new planet. — The golden branch.—
Theseus and Ariadne. — King of the peacocks.—
Seven champions.......................................822.2 215
   V. 4. Island of jewels.—Cymon and Iphigenia.
—King charming.—Queen of the frogs.—Prince of
happy land.—The good woman in the wood.—Mr.
Buckstone's ascent of Parnassus. — Camp at the
Olympic. — Once upon a time there were two
kings..822.2 216
   V. 5. Mr. Buckstone's voyage. — The yellow
dwarf. — New Haymarket spring meeting. — Dis-
creet princess.—Young and handsome.—Love and
fortune. — Orpheus in the Haymarket. — King
Christmas. — List of Planché's dramatic produc-
tions..822.2 217
Plowman, Piers. See **Piers plowman.**
Plummer. Verses. 1896........................821.1 505
Plunket. Speeches. 1865......................329.2 34
Plympton. Betty, a butterfly...................06111
   The black dog, etc..............................06115
   Bud of promise...................................6360
   Dear daughter Dorothy.......................06110
   Dorothy and Anton.............................06114
   Penelope Prig, etc..............................06113
   Rags and velvet gowns.......................06112
   Willing transgressor, etc......................6361
Poe. Nouvelles histoires extraordinaires;
   tr. de Baudelaire................................69492
   Poems..821.1 20
   The raven; ed. by Ingram. 1885.......821.1 209
   Works. 1876. 4 v.
   V. 1. Memoir.—Tales.................................820.1 16
   V. 2. Poems.—Essays.—Tales.....................820.1 17
   V. 3. The literati.......................................820.1 18
   V. 4. Tales.—Miscellanies.........................820.1 19
   Works; ed. by Stedman and Wood-
   berry. 1894-5. 10 v.
   V. 1.—Memoir.—Introduction.—Shadow: a par-
able. — Fall of the house of Usher. — Berenice.—
Oval portrait. — Morella. — Ligeia.—Eleonora.—
Monos and Una.—Eiros and Charmion.— Power
of words.—Silence: a fable,— Masque of the red
death.—The assignation.—Cask of Amontillado.—
Tale of the Ragged mountains.— Metzengerstein.
— Pit and the pendulum.—Hopfrog....................69494
   V. 2. William Wilson.— Imp of the perverse.
—The black cat. — Tell-tale heart. — Man of the
crowd.—The elk.—Island of the fay.— Arnheim.—
Landor's cottage.—Hans Pfaal. — Balloon-hoax.—
Ms. found in a bottle.— Descent into the maelström. — Thousand-and-second tale of Scheherazade.— Some words with a mummy. — Mesmeric
revelation.—Facts in the case of Monsieur Valde-
mar...69495

V. 3. The gold-bug. — Murders in the rue Morgue.— Mystery of Marie Rogêt. — Purloined letter. — Thou art the man. — Premature burial.— Oblong box. — Sphinx. — Spectacles. — Mystification.—Doctor Tarr and Professor Fether..............69496
V. 4. Duc de l'Omelette.— Lionizing.— Tale of Jerusalem.— Bon-bon. — Man that was used up.— King Pest.—Loss of breath.—Four beasts in one.— Devil in the belfry. — Three Sundays in a week.— Never bet the devil your head. — Why the little Frenchman wears his hand in a sling. — Angel of the Odd.—Business man.—Literary life of Thingum Bob, esq. — How to write a Blackwood article.— Article for Blackwood : A predicament. — X-ing a paragraph. — Diddling. — Von Kempelen and his discovery.— Mellonta Tauta..........................69497
V. 5. Narrative of Arthur Gordon Pym.—Journal of Julius Rodman..........................69498
V. 6-8. Literary criticism................820.1 23
V. 9. Eureka.—Miscellanies..............820.1 26
V. 10. Poems.........................820.1 27

Works ; ed. by Stoddard. 6 v.
V. 1. The genius of Poe, Life of Poe; by R. H. Stoddard.—E. A. Poe: by J. R. Lowell.—Death of Poe; by N. P. Willis.—The poetic principle.—The rationale of verse.—Poems........820.1 20
V. 2. Unparalleled adventure of one Hans Pfaal. —Gold-bug.— Balloon-hoax.—Von Kempelen and his discovery.—Mesmeric revelation.—Facts in the case of Monsieur Valdemar. — Thousand-and-second tale of Scheherazade. — Ms. found in a bottle. — Descent into the maelström.— Murders in the rue Morgue.— Mystery of Marie Rogêt.— Purloined letter.—Black cat.—Fall of the house of Usher.—Pit and the pendulum.—Premature burial.— Masque of the red death.—Cask of Amontillado.— Imp of the perverse.—Island of the fay.—Oval portrait.—The assignation.—Tell-tale heart..................69499
V. 3. Domain of Arnheim.—Landor's cottage.— William Wilson.— Berenice.— Eleonora.— Ligeia. —Morella.—Metzengerstein.—A tale of the Ragged mountains. — The spectacles.—The duc de l'Omelette.—Oblong box.—King Pest.—Three Sundays in a week.—Devil in the belfry.—Lionizing. —Narrative of A. Gordon Pym......................69499A
V. 4. Doctor Tarr and Professor Fether.—Literary life of Thingum Bob, esq.— How to write a Blackwood article.— A predicament. — Mystification.—X-ing a paragrab.—Diddling.—Angel of the Odd.—Mellonta Tauta.—Loss of breath.—Man that was used up.—Business man.—Landscape garden. —Maelzel's chess-player.—Power of words.—Monos and Una.—Eiros and Charmion.—Shadow: a parable.—Silence: a fable.—Philosophy of furniture.— Tale of Jerusalem.— The sphinx.— Man of the crowd,—Never bet the devil your head.—Thou art the man.— Hop-frog.— Four beasts in one; the homo-camelopard.— Why the little Frenchman wears his hand in a sling.—Bon-bon.—Some words with a mummy.— Stephens' 'Arabia Petræa.' — Magazine-writing.—Quacks of Helicon.—Astoria..69499B
V. 5-6. Essays,.........................820.1 21
(See also **Lavante**, pseud.)

Poems of many years and places. 1887..821.2 659
Poetry of the anti-Jacobin. 1799..........821.2 531
Politics and life in Mars. 1883..............827.2 44
Pollard, E. F. Hope deferred...................14171
Green Mountain boys..........................036401
Pollard, J. Gipsy in New York..............012401

Pollock. King Zub, etc.......................17820
Pollok. The course of time...............821.2 301
Pomeroy (Brick). Brick dust................20423
Gold dust..20424
Nonsense. 1868..................................828.1 43
Our Saturday nights...........................20422
Sense : thoughtful papers. 1868........824.1 129
Pomfret. Poems ; with life. 1822..........821.2 50
Pomona. (See **Laddie**.).........................17913
Pool. Against human nature.....................17409
Boss and other dogs.................................17414
Dally..17403
In a dike shanty.......................................17410
In Buncombe county................................17413
In the first person 17412
Katharine North.......................................17406
Mrs. Gerald..17411
Mrs. Keats Bradford................................17405
Out of step...17408
Roweny in Boston....................................17404
Tenting at Stony beach............................17402
Two Salomes..17407
Vacation in a buggy.................................17401
Poole, John. Comic sketch-book. 1859...828.2 33
Little Pedlington......................................15237
Poole, Margaret E. Pictures of cottage life..44192
Poor. Brothers and strangers.................40120
Poor Nellie..58984
Pope. Essay on man. 1777..............821.2 607
Same ; with commentary by Warburton...230 200
Essays in The Guardian. 3 v...........824.2 10
Letters to Atterbury. 1859..............in 942 136
Martinus Scriblerus. 1741................827.2 31
Poems. 1822. 3 v.
V. 1. Life.—Pastorals.—Messiah.—Windsor forest.—Rape of the lock.— Eloisa to Abelard.— Sappho to Phaon.— Fable.—Vertumnus.—Thebais of Statius..821.2 603
V. 2. Essay on criticism.— Essay on man.— Prayer.— Moral essays.— Imitations of English poets.—Epistles.—Miscellanies.......................821.2 604
V. 3. Satires, epistles, and odes of Horace, imitated.—Dunciad.......................................821.2 605
Poetical works. 1866......................821.2 606
Translation of Iliad and Odyssey. '91....883 72
Translation of the Odyssey. 1822........883 11
Works [complete]; ed. by Croker, Elwin, Courthope, 1871-86. 10 v.
V. 1. Introduction, etc.—Recommendatory poems. —Translations.— January and May, from Chaucer. —Wife of Bath, from Chaucer.—Temple of fame.— Pastorals.—Messiah.—Windsor forest................821.2 608
V. 2. Essay on criticism.— Warburton's notes, etc.—Rape of the lock.—First edition of same.— Elegy to the memory of an unfortunate lady.— Eloisa to Abelard.—Essay on man. The universal prayer.— Warburton's notes, etc.........................821.2 609
V. 3. Moral essays and satires ; with introduction and notes...821.2 61

LANGUAGE AND LITERATURE.

h introduction, notes,
ons, epigrams, etc..821.2 611
........................821.2 612
........................821.2 613
ton. 1809. 6 v.
........................821.2 597
ace.— Epistles.— Epi-
........................821.2 600
........................821.2 601
obbett.
arried for both
........................20452
llan Dare and
........................62391
........................62390
1 epic. 1864...821.1 36
omen............821.2 448
Union College.
........................825.1 Pam. 5
iefs....................*804
narrative of his
........................806
........................801
:tle southerners..022503
........................022502
veet charity.........31307
........................31309
........................31306
apters................31311
........................31308
........................31310
........................31303
........................31301
........................31305
........................31304
........................31302
er race in Ken-
........................47275
?. 1822......*in* 821.2 39
ends................50365
........................07161
........................43060
ix.— Occasional
........................30905
en's association,
........................40 27
and studies in
........................71260
1895..........824.2 488
f rarity.—A Gascon tragedy
d story books.—The pirates'
f memoirs.—With Rabelais
istory.
f song. '87...821.1 367
ple Dell of '76
........................821.1 424
egends..........914.3 35
........................54205
........................54201

Failure of Elizabeth.......................54206
My little lady.............................54203
Praed, *Mrs.* **Campbell-.** Australian heroine...33101
  Australian life in black and white..........33105
  Bond of wedlock............................33107
  Christina Chard............................33111
  December roses.............................33110
  Head station...............................33106
  Miss Jacobsen's chance.....................33108
  Mrs. Tregaskiss............................33113
  Moloch.....................................33104
  Nadine.....................................33114
  Outlaw and lawmaker........................33112
  Policy and passion.........................33103
  Romance of a châlet........................33109
  Zero.......................................33102
Praed, *Mrs.* **C.,** *and* **McCarthy, J.**
  Ladies' gallery............................33408
  The right honorable........................33404
  Rival princess.............................33413
Praed, W. M. Poems. 1865. 2 v.
  V. 1. Memoir; by D. Coleridge. — Tales. —
  Poems of love and fancy.—Miscellaneous..........821.2 316
  V. 2. Poems of life and manners.—Poems of
  early youth.—Prize poems, etc.—Songs, charades,
  and enigmas.........................821.2 317
Pratt, C. A. Book of martyrs...............70341
  Daughter of a stoic........................70340
Pratt, Mara L. Stories from Shakespeare.
  1890—. v. 1-3.......................*822.3 367
Pratt, *Mrs.* **Mary E.** Rhoda Thornton's
  girlhood...................................05501
Prentice. Prenticeana. 1860..............828.1 5
Prentiss, *Mrs.* **E.** Aunt Jane's hero..........8101
  Avis Benson................................8117
  Flower of the family.......................8116
  Fred, Maria, and me........................8109
  Home at Greylock...........................8106
  Little Lou.................................01103
  Little preacher............................01105
  Midworth...................................8115
  Pemaquid...................................8108
  The Percys.................................01101
  Stepping heavenward........................8104
  Story Lizzie told..........................01104
  Urbane and his friends.....................8111
Prescott, E. L. Apotheosis of Mr. Tyrawley..56001
Prescott, H. E. See Spofford, *Mrs.* H. E.
Prescott, W. H. Biographical and critical
  miscellanies. 1845....................824.1 15
Preston, H. W. Aspendale.................26602
  Is that all?...............................26605
  Love in the 19th century...................26601
Preston, H. W., *and* **Dodge, L.** The
  guardians..................................26604

---
* Of interest to young readers.

Preston, Margaret J. Colonial ballads,
etc. 1887..821.1 365
Old song and new. 1870................821.1 192
Price, Eleanor C. Alexia..........................19404
Foreigners...19402
Gerald..19403
In the lion's mouth..................................19405
John's Lily...19406
Mrs. Lancaster's rival..............................19401
Young Denys...19407
Price, T. R. Shakespeare's verse in Othello.
1888...822.3 350
Price, Thomas. Wisdom and genius of
Shakspeare. 1838............................822.3 61
Priestley. Theological and miscellaneous
works. 1817-32. 25 v.......................230 154
(For contents, see Part 3 of FINDING LIST, p. 474.)
Prime, S. I. Under the trees (essays).
1874..824.1 125
Prime, W. C. Among the northern hills.
1895...824.1 297
Contents: The primeval forest.—A trout-stream.—An up-country artist.—Beyond.—An old angler.—Doughnuts and tobacco.—John Ledyard.—Thursday-evening meeting.—An Easter long ago.—An old-time Christmas.—Alone at Thanksgiving.—How the old lady beat John.—Philistis.—A northern sleigh-ride.—Life seen through a window.—Colored people.—Example.—The sign of the cross.—A child's voice.—Puritan Sunday.
Later years. 1863.............................829.1 9
Old house by the river..........................20442
Prince, Helen C. Story of Christine
Rochefort...62715
Transatlantic chatelaine....................62716
Prior, H. L. Behind the veil....................55208
Six months hence...............................55207
Prior, M. Miscellaneous works. 1740. 2v.
V. 1. History of his own time..................821.2 177
V. 2. Poems...821.2 178
Poems; with life. 1822....................821.2 28
Selected poems; ed. by Dobson. '89..821.2 300
Pris. (See Laddie.)................................17909
Probable sons; by the author of 'Eric's
good news.'...55267
Procter, Adelaide A. Poems. 1870...821.2 435
Procter, B. W., (Barry Cornwall). Dramatic scenes, etc. 1857..................821.2 320
English songs, etc. 1844.................821.2 322
Marcian Colonna, and other poems.
1820..821.2 321
Proctor, E. D. Poems. 1867............821.2 344
Proctor, R. A. Watched by the dead.....1113
Prout, *Father*, (Mahoney, F.). Final reliques. 1876......................................829.2 32
Reliques. 1873................................829.2 33
Prowse. Fatal reservation......................31130
Pryce. Burden of a woman....................30471
Evil spirit...30468
Just impediment....................................30467

Miss Maxwell's affections.....................30466
Quiet Mrs. Fleming...............................30469
Time and the woman...........................30470
Puckle. The club. 1834................829.2 35
Puff, *Major* Pindar. See **Verplanck**.
Pugh, E. L. In a crucible.......................56802
Pugh, E. W. Man of straw....................31161
Street in Suburbia................................31160
Punshon. Sabbath chimes. 1868....821.2 437
Purnell. Literature and its professors...824.2 117
Putnam, Eleanor. Woodland wooing.....23701
Putnam, Eleanor, *and* Bates, Arlo.
Prince Vance...040901
Putnam, G. I. In blue uniform..............30225
On the offensive....................................30226
Putnam, J. O. Address, Buffalo general
hospital. 1858..............................94.2 Pam. 1
Address, Buffalo state asylum for insane. 1872....................................94.1 Pam. 1
Address, Central Presbyterian church,
Buffalo. 1885..............................96.1 Pam. 13
Address on the Irish question. '86...941 Pam. 5
Addresses, etc., 1854-79................824.1 170
Oration, Lockport, July 4, 1856...825.1 Pam. 8
Oration, Paris, February 22, 1866..923.1 Pam. 99
Putnam, *Mrs.* M. L. Record of an obscure
man..19101
Tragedy of errors (drama)...................822.1 3
Tragedy of success (drama). 1862....822.1 2
Puttenham. Arte of English poesie......820.2 32
Pye. Comments on commentators on Shakespear. 1807.....................................822.3 72
Pyle. Jack Ballister's fortune................032257
Men of iron..032255
Merry adventures of Robin Hood......032253
Modern Aladdin....................................31502
Otto of the silver hand.......................032254
Rose of paradise...................................31501
Twilight land.......................................032256
Within the capes..................................31503
Wonder clock.......................................032258
Pyrnelle. Diddie, Dumps, and Tot........028401
Q (A. T. Quiller-Couch). Adventures in
criticism. 1896..............................824.2 497
Blue pavilions.......................................29803
Delectable duchy..................................29805
I saw three ships, etc..........................29804
Ia: a love story.....................................29806
Splendid spur.......................................29802
Troy town..29801
Wandering heath (stories)..................29807
Quad, M., (C. B. Lewis.) Brother Gardner's lime-kiln club. 1882..............828.1 9
Quad's odds. 1875............................828.1 57
Quarles. Divine fancies. 1687........821.2 220
Divine poems. 1630.........................821.2 219
Emblems [early ed.; title page wanting].
....821.2 167A

................821.2 167
................829.2 3
................50305
yes.
itant, etc............69142
rofessorship........69150
vas not a colonel..55246
:ouples..........828.2 42
iton.
story..............296 54
Abeillard and
................827.2 19
dolpho.............19150
................19149
:e. — Romance of the forest.
e Italian.—Castles of Athlin

................19148
t. Philosophers
................15216
................41520
ville's husband...38301
................38302
................55252
ography of; by
................16 76
................829.2 87
c.................21921
House-boating in China.—
om Beebe's adventures. —
: boss of Ling-foo.— Little
e-letters of Superfine Gold.
................21920
:dding. — Mother's song.—
A day of the Pinochle club.
ice. — Dutch Kitty's white
is pupil. — Low Dutch and

eveland. '88...827.1 27
id, etc. (poems).
................821.2 1041
:e Ouida.
'7. 2 v.
ritings.—Verses to the
:legiac, comic, satiric,
................821.2 517
Gentle shepherd, and
iistolary.— Fables and
................821.2 518
nces of Scottish
................828.2 12
iond's dilemma...70420
................31030
'or sunrise land..025005
and mountains..025007
sarge..............025001
:s....................25050
ippahannock.....025009
................025008
................025006

Pushing ahead.................025003
Rory's dory at the sea shore........025002
Tent in the notch................025004
Too late for the tide-mill. 025010
Two college boys................025011
Rand, Mary A. Holly and mistletoe.......027301
Randolph, *Mrs.* Genista................46803
Gentianella........................46801
Iris..............................46808
Reseda..........................46805
Wild hyacinth...................46802
Wood anemone...................46804
Randolph, J. Letters. 1834...........826.1 3
Randolph, J. T. Cabin and parlor..........20447
Raspe. Munchausen....................=13501
Rathbone. See **Manning, Anne.**
Rattlehead, D., *pseud.* (M. L. Byrn.)
 Adventures of Fudge Fumble............47271
Ray. In Blue creek cañon..............01505
Raymond, Evelyn. Mushroom cave......042401
Raymond, G. L. Life in song. 1886...821.1 359
 Modern fishers of men................69238
Raymond, H. W. Kryme: a goblin
 tale...............................98.6 B 1
Raymond, R. No laggards we..........62517
Raymond, R. W. Brave hearts............19153
Raymond, W., (Tom Cobbleigh, *pseud.*).
 Charity Chance.....................14760
 Gentleman Upcott's daughter...........14755
 In the smoke of war..................14758
 Love and quiet life..................14759
 Tryphena in love....................14757
 Young Sam and Sabina................14756
Read, Emily, *and* Reeves, M. C. L.
 Pilot fortune.......................69114
Read, Opie. Bolanyo...................43923
 The Jucklins.......................43922
 Kentucky colonel....................43921
 Len Gansett........................43920
Read, T. B. The onward age: poem........40 11
 Poems. 1860. 2 v..................821.1 65
 Same. 1866. 3 v.
 V. 1. Lyric poems.—Sylvia.— Miscellaneous.—
 Airs from Alpland.......................821.1 67
 V. 2. The new pastoral.—The house by the sea.
 —Miscellaneous........................821.1 66
 V. 3. The wagoner of the Alleghanies.—War
 poems.—A summer story.— Poems in Italy.— Miscellaneous........................821.1 61
 Wagoner of the Alleghanies: poem.
 1862..............................821.1 426
Reade, Charles. Autobiography of a
 thief.................................1834
 Christie Johnston......................1802
 Cloister and the hearth................1801
 Clouds and sunshine...................1809
 Course of true love....................1836
 Foul play.............................1832

Good stories..................................1842
Griffith Gaunt................................1814
Hard cash.....................................1828
Love me little, love me long..................1816
Never too late to mend........................1810
Peg Woffington................................1803
Perilous secret...............................1804
Put yourself in his place....................1818
Readiana. 1883......................824.2 334
Simpleton.....................................1805
Same...................................*in* 1806B
Singleheart and doubleface....................1836
Terrible temptation...........................1821
Wandering heir................................1806
White elephant................................1838
White lies....................................1817
Woman hater...................................1824

Realf. Guesses at the beautiful : poems.
1852...............................821.2 812
Rebel rose....................................69049
Rebelliad, The. 1842..................827.1 32
Redden (Howard Glyndon). Sounds from
 secret chambers (poems). 1873....821.1 194
Reed, A. No fiction......................56815
Reed, Sir E. J. Fort Minster, M. P.......69126
Reed, T. B. Kilgorman.....................09402
 Sir Ludar..................................09401
Reeder. Currer Lyle......................20427
Reese, L. W. A quiet road (verse). 1896.
...................................821.1 517
Reeve, C. The old English baron. 1883....823 98
Reeve, J. K. Three Richard Whalens.......52150
Reeves, *Mrs.* **H.** See **Mathers, Helen E.**
Reeves, M. C. L. Little maid of Acadie...69113
Reeves, M. C. L., *and* **Read, Emily.**
 Pilot Fortune..............................69114
Reid, Christian, *pseud.* (F. C. Fisher.)
 After many days............................9101
 Bonny Kate.................................9109
 Comedy of elopement........................9102
 Daughter of Bohemia........................9114
 Ebb tide, etc..............................9103
 Gentle belle...............................9129
 Heart of steel.............................9132
 Land of the sky............................9118
 Land of the sun............................9110
 Mabel Lee..................................9105
 Miss Churchill.............................9106
 Morton house...............................9108
 Picture of Las Cruces......................9111
 Question of honor..........................9113
 Roslyn's fortune...........................9137
 Summer idyl................................9120
 Valerie Aylmer.............................9104
 Woman of fortune...........................9115
Reid, J. Chronicle of small beer........13630

Reid, *Captain* **M.** Afloat in the forest......07305
 Boy hunters................................07320
 Boy slaves.................................07318
 Boy tar....................................07317
 Bruin......................................07303
 Bush boys..................................07301
 Castaways..................................07309
 Cliff climbers.............................07308
 Flag of distress...........................52107
 Forest exiles..............................07304
 Free lances................................52105
 Gaspar the Gaucho..........................07316
 Giraffe hunters............................07314
 Plant hunters..............................07307
 Star of empire.............................52102
 Tiger hunter...............................52104
 Vee-Boers..................................52119
 Wild life..................................52115
 Woodrangers................................52110
 Young voyageurs............................07302
 Young yaegers..............................07306
Reid, T. W. Gladys Fane..................69458
 Mauleverer's millions......................69457
Réno, Itti Kinney-. Exceptional case....25120
Repplier. Essays in idleness. 1893....824.1 276
 Contents: Agrippina.—The children's poets.—The praises of war.—Leisure.—Words.—Ennui.—Wit and humor.—Letters.
 Essays in miniature. 1892.............824.1 271
 Contents: Our friends the books.— Trials of a publisher.—Oppression of notes.—Conversation in novels.— Short defence of villains.—A by-way in fiction.—Comedy of the custom-house.—Mr. Wilde's 'Intentions.'—Humors of gastronomy.—Children in fiction.—Three famous old maids.—The charm of the familiar.—Old world pets.—Battle of the babies.—The novel of incident.— Ghosts.
 In the dozy hours, etc. 1894..........824.1 287
 Contents: In the dozy hours.—A kitten.—At the novelist's table.— In behalf of parents.—Aut Cæsar aut nihil.— A note on mirrors.— Gifts.— Humor : English and American.—The discomforts of luxury : a speculation.—Lectures.—Reviewers and reviewed.—Pastels : a query.— Guests.— Sympathy.— Opinions. — The children's age.—A forgotten poet.—Dialogues.—A curious contention.—The passing of the essay.
 Points of view. 1891..................824.1 270
 Contents: A plea for humor.—English love-songs.— Books that have hindered me.—Literary shibboleths.— Fiction in the pulpit.—Pleasure : a heresy.—Esoteric economy.—Scanderbeg.—English railway fiction.
Revere. Keel and saddle....................44163
Reynolds, Beatrice. Matchmaker..........25836
Reynolds, G. W. M. Gipsy chief...........30451
 Rhine inundation...........................07131
Rhoades. Our fellows at St. Mark's......011120
 Story of John Trevennick..................11150
Rhoscomyl. Battlement and tower..........57331
 For the white rose of Arno.................57332
 Jewel of Ynys Galon........................57330
Rhys. The fiddler of Carne................52560
Rice, H. Nature and culture. 1875...824.1 118

Rice, K. McD. Stories for all the year,......05830
Rich. Honestie of this age................821.2 454
Richards, A. B. So very human..............62575
Richards, C. F. John Guilderstring's sin...44142
Richards, C. H. B. Springs of action.......15286
Richards, L. E. Captain January...........040502
   Isla Heron...................................32283
   Jim of Hellas.—Bethesda Pool................32281
   Joyous story of Toto........................040501
   Melody......................................32282
   Narcissa.—In Verona.........................32280
Richards, W. C. Harry's vacation..........025801
Richardson, A. S. Stories from old English poetry..................................02801
Richardson, B. W. Son of a star............69483
Richardson, R. Almost a hero..............025201
   Ralph's year in Russia......................025202
Richardson, S. Clarissa Harlowe..............201
   Pamela...202
   Sir Charles Grandison..........................203
Richardson, Warren. Doctor Zell and the Princess Charlotte........................19520
Richardson, William. Analysis of Shakespeare's characters. 1808.....822.3 368
Riche. Eight novels employed by English dramatic poets of the reign of Elizabeth. 1846..................................822.3 43
Rickett, A. Lost chords : some emotions without morals. 1895....................827.2 46
Rickett, J. C. Quickening of Caliban.......32406
Riddle. Alice Brand..........................27201
   Ansel's cave.................................27204
   Bart Ridgeley................................27202
Riddell (F. G. Trafford, *pseud*.). Above suspicion....................................12205
   Berna Boyle..................................12213
   Daisies and buttercups........................12219
   Did he deserve it?............................12224
   Far above rubies..............................12204
   For Dick's sake...............................12222
   George Geith..................................12202
   Head of the firm..............................12220
   Life's assize.................................12207
   Maxwell Drewitt...............................12201
   Miss Gascoigne................................12217
   Moors and the fens............................12214
   Mystery in Palace Gardens.....................12208
   Prince of Wales' garden party.................12209
   Race for wealth...............................12203
   Rich man's daughter...........................12223
   Rusty sword..................................12221
   Senior partner................................12210
   Struggle for fame.............................12211
   Susan Drummond................................12212
   Uninhabited house.............................12215
Rideing. Boys coastwise....................029802
   Boys in the mountains.......................029801

Captured Cunarder..............................17901
Stray moments with Thackeray........829.2 53
Ridge, W. P. Clever wife.....................69620
   Second opportunity of Mr. Staplehurst...69621
Ridgeway, A. Diana Fontaine................29471
   Westovers..................................29472
Ridley. Story of Aline........................53701
Rigby. From midsummer to Martinmas.....30574
Riis. Nibsy's Christmas, etc................041301
Riley, H. H. Puddleford papers..............52251
Riley, J. W., (Benjamin F. Johnson of Boone). Afterwhiles (poems). '88..821.1 530
   Armazindy (poems). 1894.................821.1 533
   Boss girl, etc..............................69274
   A child-world. 1897......................821.1 534
   Flying islands of the night (drama). 1892..................................822.1 45
   Green fields and running brooks (poems). 1893......................................821.1 532
   Neighborly poems. 1891..................821.1 527
   Old-fashioned roses. 1896................821.1 528
   Old swimmin'-hole, etc. 1886..........821.1 529
   Pipes o' Pan at Zekesbury (poems). 1889......................................821.1 531
   Poems here at home. 1893................821.1 535
   Rhymes of childhood. 1891............*821.1 536
   Sketches in prose (Boss girl, etc.)......69274A
Ripley, Mary A. Poems. 1867..........821.1 577
Rita, *pseud*. (Mrs. Otto Booth.) Adrian Lyle..60709
   Asenath of the ford.........................60712
   Countess Pharamond..........................60713
   Dame Durden................................60708
   Daphne.....................................60701
   Faustine...................................60706
   Gender in satin.............................60715
   Husband of no importance...................60714
   Laird o' Cockpen...........................60710
   Man in possession..........................60711
   Master Wilberforce.........................60716
   My lady coquette...........................60703
Ritchie, *Mrs.* A. C. M. Clergyman's wife, etc..40901
   Mimic life.................................40905
   Mute singer................................40902
Ritchie, *Mrs.* Anna I. See Thackeray, Anna I.
Ritchie, L. Romance of history: France...47223
Ritson. Letters; with memoir. '33. 2 v...826.2 79
Rivers. Captain Shays, a populist of 1786...54602
   The governor's garden.......................54601
Rives, Amélie, (Mrs. Chanler). According to Saint John............................34006
   Athelwold (drama). 1893..................822.1 31
   Barbara Dering..............................34004
   Brother to dragons, etc.....................34002
   Quick or the dead?..........................34001

Of interest to young readers.

Tanis, the sang-digger.........................34007
Virginia of Virginia.............................34003
Witness of the sun..............................34005
Rives, W. C. Discourse, Young men's Christian association, Richmond, 1855.
....*in* 825.1 17
Roach. Theon (poem). 1881............821.1 272
Robb. Streaks of squatter life............47273
Western scenes....................................47272
Robbins, S. S. My new home...............25860
Robbins, *Mrs.* **S. S.** One happy winter...028601
Robert the deuyll.................................*in* 101
Roberts, C. G. D. Book of the native (verse). 1896..........................821.2 573
Earth's enigmas (stories).....................10930
Forge in the forest................................10931
In divers tones (verse). 1886..........821.2 813
Raid from Beauséjour.—How the Carter boys lifted the mortgage.................010930
Songs of the common day; and Ave! 1893..821.2 927
Roberts, Margaret. Atelier du lys. 2 v....56306
Bride Picotée 56314
Denise..56308
In the olden time..................................56309
Kinsfolk and others..............................56316
Madame Fontenoy................................56303
Mademoiselle Mori...............................56305
Miss Jean's niece..................................56312
Not one of us..56318
On the edge of the storm.....................56302
Secret of Madame de Monluc..............56315
That child...56313
Younger sister.......................................56317
Roberts, Morley. Adventures of a ship's doctor...29412
Degradation of Geoffrey Alwith..........29410
Earth-mother...29413
Great jester..29414
Master of the Silver sea........................29411
Mate of the Vancouver.........................29407
Maurice Quain......................................29416
Red earth (stories)................................29409
Reputation of George Saxon, etc........29408
Roberts, Morley, *and* **Montesole, M.** Circassian...29415
Roberts, W., (Rev. S. Olive-Branch). The looker-on. 1856. 3 v.....................824.2 62
Robertson, F. W. Lects. and addresses. 1868..825.2 3
Robertson, J. L. White angel of the Polly Ann..69221
Robertson, Margaret M. David Fleming's forgiveness.................................53903
Inglises...53902
Janet's love and service.......................53901
Robertson, T. W. David Garrick; comedy. 1895..822.2 330

Robin Hood..*in* 102
Robins, G. M. Ides of March..................28702
Tree of knowledge................................28701
Robinson, A. Mary F. See **Darmesteter,** *Madame.*
Robinson, C. N., *and* **Leyland, J.** For the honour of the flag.....................43030
Robinson, Edith. Forced acquaintances..69284
Loyal little maid...................................036301
Robinson, Edward A., *and* **Wall, G. A.** Disk..62363
Robinson, F. Mabel. Chimæra..............22605
Disenchantment...................................22601
Hovenden, V. C....................................22603
Mr. Butler's ward.................................22606
Plan of campaign..................................22602
Woman of the world............................22604
Robinson, F. W. As long as she lived....14308
Christie's faith......................................14302
Coward conscience..............................14316
Fate of sister Jessica............................14323
Hands of justice...................................14320
Her face was her fortune.....................14312
Her love and his life............................14321
Mattie..14313
One and twenty....................................14318
Othello the second...............................14303
Poor humanity......................................14301
Same..*in* 14313
Poor Zeph...14306
Romance on four wheels................*in* 32755
Second cousin Sarah............................14305
Slaves of the ring.................................14310
True to herself......................................14307
Woman in the dark..............................14324
Woman's ransom..................................14315
Wrong that was done...........................14322
Robinson, H. Romance of the Atlantic....52281
Robinson, H. P. Men born equal............15635
Robinson, Jane. Gold worshippers........24831
Maid of Orleans...................................24832
White friars..24830
Robinson, *Mrs.* **M. H.** Helen Erskine....44102
Robinson, Phil. In my Indian garden..824.2 331
Under the Punkah. 1881...............824.2 294
Valley of teetotum trees......................69264
Robinson, R. E. Danvis folks.................11940
Sam Lovel's camps..............................11942
Uncle Lisha's shop...............................11941
Robinson, *Dr.* **S. T.** Shadow of the war..58996
Robinson, *Mrs.* **T. A. L.,** (Talvi, *pseud.*).
Life's discipline...................................19147
Robinson Playfellow..............................0120
Roby. Traditions of Lancashire..............104
Roche. Children of the abbey................15291
Rock, *Captain.* See **Moore, T.**
Rodney (Fadette, *pseud.*). Wearithorne.....25857

LANGUAGE AND LITERATURE.

Rodney, G. B. In buff and blue..................7132
Roe, A. S. James Montjoy..........................6912
   Long look ahead................................6916
   Looking around.................................6901
   Resolution.....................................6923
   Time and tide..................................6909
   To love and to be loved, etc...................6907
   Woman our angel................................6904
Roe, E. P. Barriers burned away..................6827
   Day of fate....................................6856
   Driven back to Eden............................6889
   Earth trembled.................................6803
   Face illumined.................................6844
   From jest to earnest...........................6807
   He fell in love with his wife..................6801
   His sombre rivals..............................6869
   Hornet's nest..................................6802
   Knight of the 19th century.....................6828
   Miss Lou.......................................6804
   Nature's serial story..........................6886
   Near to nature's heart.........................6816
   Opening of a chestnut burr.....................6811
   Original belle.................................6887
   Queen of spades [with autobiography].....6805
   Taken alive, etc...............................6808
   Unexpected result, etc.........................6867
   What can she do?...............................6818
   Without a home.................................6861
   Young girl's wooing............................6881
Roe, E. R. Brought to bay........................62569
Roe, *Mrs.* J. Bachelor Vicar of Newforth...69216
Rogers, H. H. Souvenir poems. 1889...821.2 240.
Rogers, Henry. Greyson letters. '59....826.2 34
Rogers, R. C. Christmas eve at Junction city..41922
   Denison vendue. 1893..................823 Pam. 8
   Landing-net : a comedy..............822.1 Pam. 2
   Old Dorset (stories)...........................41921
   Will o' the Wasp...............................41920
   Wind in the clearing, and other poems. 1894...................................821.1 463
Rogers, S. Poetical works [with life]...821.2 537
   Recollections of table talk. 1856......829.2 14
Rohlfs. See Green, Anna K.
Rokeby. Dorcas Hobday...........................71040
Rolfe. Shakespeare, the boy. 1896......822.3 207
Rolle de Hampole. Treatises............820.2 309
Rollins, Alice W. Finding of the gentian. 034601
   Little page Fern, etc. (verse)..........*821.1 507
   Story of a ranch...............................69186
   Story of Azron (verse). 1895........821.1 506
   Three Tetons...................................69188
   Uncle Tom's tenement..........................69187
Rollins, *Mrs.* E. H. See Arr, E. H.
Rollo's journey to Cambridge. 1880...828.1 B-2
Rood. Company doctor............................30360

Rooper. Flood, field, and forest............11145
Roosevelt, Blanche. Marked in haste....58982
   Stage struck...................................58981
Roosevelt, R. B. Love and luck............69236
   Progressive petticoats. 1874.........828.1 48
Roscoe. Last of the Abencerrages. 1850. ....821.2 913
Roscommon, *earl of*. Poems................821.2 27
Rose. Little Princess Colombe...................56858
Rose and lavender. (See Laddie.)...........17908
Rosebery, *Lord*. Speeches, 1874-96. '96..825.2 11
Roseboro', Viola. Old ways and new.....31610
Rosemary and Rue..............................63413
Roslyn. George Eliot in Derbyshire........823 57
Ross, C. H. London romance........ 15287
   Pretty widow...................................15288
Ross, C. M. Pinks and cherries................69640
Ross, Clinton. Adventures of three worthies...............................14773
   Countess Bettina...............................14771
   Every day's news...............................14770
   Puppet..14775
   Silent workman................................14772
Ross, *Mrs.* E. Wreck of the White Bear....15250
Ross, P. Misguidit lassie......................62334
Rossetti, Christina G. Commonplace, etc...37101
   Maude..37102
   New poems. 1896.........................821.2 999
   Pageant, and other poems. 1881...821.2 591
   Poems. 1876............................821.2 536
   Sing-song. 1893.......................*821.2 925
   Verses. 1894..........................821.2 931
Rossetti, D. G. Ballads and sonnets..821.2 434
   Family letters. 1895..................928.2 660
   Poems. 1870..........................821.2 433
Roughing it in Van Diemen's land.............58930
Round (Rev. Peter Pennot, *pseud.*). Achsah...26901
   Hal: a story of a clodhopper...................26904
   Rosecroft......................................26905
Round table of the representative American Catholic novelists..........................32751
Rowcroft. Tales of the colonies................44138
Rowe. Diary of an early Methodist............61601
Rowell (Old Coins, *pseud.*). Silver bullet...71220
Rowland. Ambitious slave.......................40140
Rowlands, Effie A. Faithful traitor........21091
   Spell of Ursula................................21090
Rowlands, S. The four knaves............821.2 452
Rowley. A search for money...............821.2 415
Rowsell. Friend of the people................38710
Rowson. Charlotte Temple....................19110
Roy, J. Helen Treveryan.......................18710
Roy, N. Horseman's word......................30740
Royce. Feud of Oakfield creek.................69295
Rubina..50380

* Of interest to young readers.

Rudd. Tower of the old schloss.............70701
Ruffini. Carlino, etc..........................10110
   Doctor Antonio...............................10104
   Lavinia..10108
   Lorenzo Benoni, etc.........................10102
   Paragreens......................................10101
   Quiet nook in the Jura......................10109
   Vincenzo..10103
Ruggles. Method of Shakespeare as an artist. 1870.................822.3 87
   The plays of Shakespeare founded on literary forms. 1895...........822.3 391
Rush. Dewdrop of the sunny south............30417
Ruskin. Aratra pentelici: lects. on sculpture. 1879.........................730 7
   Ariadne Florentina..............................760 2
   Arrows of the chace (letters published chiefly in the newspapers, 1840-80). 2 v.......................................824.2 290
   Art of England. 1883.........................756 12
   Bible of Amiens. 1884.......................274 10
   Bibliography of; by Shepherd. 1834-78....16 21
   Crown of wild olives..........................704 4
   Deucalion. 1879................................550 47
   Elements of drawing. 1869..................821.2
   Elements of perspective. 1860..............742 13
   Eagle's nest. 1872............................701 23
   Ethics of the dust. 1866.....................548 1
   Fors clavigera. 1877. 8v....................331 21
   Same; new series. 1883............136 Pam. 6
   Frondes agrestes. 1875......................701 9
   Giotto and his works in Padua. '54...755 B-5
   Hortus in clusus. 1887....................826.2 96
   A joy forever. 1887..........................701 30
   King of the golden river....................040601
   Same..*in* 32910
   Laws of Fésole. 1897.......................740 6
   Lects. on architecture and painting. 1879.750 9
   Lects. on art. 1870...........................701 8
   Letters and advice to young girls........375.2 12
   Letters to a college friend, 1840-5. 1894...................................826.2 112
   The Lord's prayer and the church. '81...204 85
   Love's meinie. 1873..........................598 50
   Modern painters. 5 v.........................750 23
   Mornings in Florence. 1881................755 16
   Munera pulveris: notes on political economy. 1872...........................330 66
   Notes on Samuel Prout and William Hunt. 1879-90.............................740 9
   On music. 1894................................780 93
   On the old road. 1885. 2 v.................704 26
   (For contents, see Part 3 of FINDING LIST, p. 412.)
   Pleasures of England.........................901 19
   Poems. 1882.................................821.2 658
   Poetry of architecture. 1893..............720 B-9
   Political economy of art. 1858............330 25

   Præterita. v. 1-3...........................928.2 512
   Pre-Raphaelitism. 1869......................750 11
   Same. 1851................................*in* 40 11
   Proserpina. 1879. v. 1.....................580 61
   Queen of the air...............................292 9
   Rock honey-comb: Sidney's Psalter.....245 18
   Ruskin reader. 1895..........................704 33
   St. Mark's rest. 1877........................755 17
   Sesame and lilies...............................374 4
   Seven lamps of architecture. 1852.......720 21
   Stones of Venice. 1851. 3 v..............729 2
   Stones of Venice; abridged. '81. 2 v...729 19
   Storm-cloud of the 19th century. 1884..551.1 B-15
   The true and the beautiful: sel. from Ruskin by Tuthill. 1886..................701 10
   The two paths. 1859..........................704 3
   (For contents, see Part 3 of FINDING LIST, p. 412.)
   Unto this last. 1869...........................330 58
   Val d'Arno; lects. on Tuscan art. 1874...723 6
   Verona, and other lects. 1894............824.2 514
   Contents: Verona —Story of Arachne.—The tortoise of Ægina.—Candida casa.—Mending the sieve.

Ruskin, *ed.* Dame Wiggins of Lee (verse)......................................821.2 775
Russan, A., *and* **Boyle, F.** Orchid seekers...57520
   The riders.......................................57522
   Through forest and plain....................57521
Russell, A. P. Characteristics: essays. 1884..824.1 192
   Club of one. 1888..........................824.1 236
   In a club corner: monologue. '90.....824.1 254
   Library notes. 1875........................824.1 119
   Sub-cœlum. 1893............................824.1 277
Russell, C. W. Fall of Damascus............20498
   Roebuck..20499
Russell, F. E. Quaint spinster...............30670
Russell, G. R. Address, Massachusetts charitable mechanic association. 1853—..*in* 825.1 17
Russell, I. Poems. 1888......................821.1 386
Russell, *Lady* **Rachel.** Letters. 1854...826.2 2
Russell, R. H. Delft cat, etc.................037401
Russell, T. O'N. Dick Massey................52289
Russell, Thomas. Poems. 1822...*in* 821.2 46
Russell, W. C. Alone on a wide, wide sea..62427
   Betwixt the Forelands........................62417
   Death ship......................................62408
   Emigrant ship..................................62429
   Frozen pirate...................................62407
   Golden hope....................................62403
   Good ship Mohock............................62431
   Heart of oak: a three-stranded yarn...62435A
   Honour of the flag............................62433
   In the middle watch..........................62419

LANGUAGE AND LITERATURE.

Is he the man?.....................................62434
Jack's courtship.....................................62416
John Holdsworth...................................62401
Lady Maud..62410
Last entry...62438
List, ye landsmen!.................................62428
Little Loo...62415
Marooned...62409
Marriage at sea....................................62422
Master Rockafellar's voyage...................62421
Miss Parson's adventure..................in 32715
Mrs. Dines's jewels...............................62425
My Danish sweetheart............................62423
My shipmate Louise..............................62420
Mystery of the Ocean Star.....................62405
Ocean free lance..................................62406
Ocean tragedy.....................................62413
On the fo'k'sle head..............................62418
Phantom death, etc...............................62432
Romance of a transport.........................62430
Romance of Jenny Harlowe, etc..............62412
Round the galley fire.............................62414
Sailor's sweetheart................................62404
Sea queen...62411
Strange elopement................................62426
Tale of the ten....................................62437
Three-stranded yarn (Heart of oak).......62435
Tragedy of Ida Noble............................62424
What cheer?..62436
Wreck of the Grosvenor.........................62402
Russell, W. H. Adventures of Doctor Brady..47210
Rutherford, Mark, *pseud.* (W. Hale White). Autobiography of Mark Rutherford..30008
Catharine Furze...................................30006
Clara Hopgood....................................30007
Mark Rutherford's deliverance...............30009
Revolution in Tanner's Lane..................30005
Rutledge, *Author of.* See **Harris, Miriam C.**
Ruxton. Life in the far west...................19113
Ryan, A. J. Poems. 1881..................821.1 275
Ryan, M. E. Chance child, etc..............29426
Flower of France..................................29425
Pagan of the Alleghanies.......................29423
Squaw Eloise.......................................29424
Told in the hills...................................29422
Ryan, Rt. Rev. S. V. Address, death of Grant. 1885...................923.1 Pam. 100
Ryder, A. H. Margaret Regis..............018360
S., D. T. Mustard leaves.......................69151
S., J., *of Dale, pseud.* See **Stimson, F. J.**
Sackville. Induction to the 'Mirror of magistrates.'..............................in 821.2 146
Works. 1859.................................822.2 94
Sackville *and* **Norton.** Gorboduc (drama).
....822.2 78

Sadler. African cruiser........................024301
Good ship Barbara.............................021302
Sadlier, Anna T. Seven years and mair...58335
Sadlier, *Mrs.* J. Elinor Preston............24402
Maureen Dhu.....................................24403
Old house by the Boyne.......................24404
Sage. Charette...................................52221
Sagon. Australian duchess....................59350
Saint Abe and his seven wives (poem). 1872...821.1 185
St. Aubyn, Alan. Broken lights..............10322
Fellow of Trinity.................................10320
In the face of the world........................10326
In the sweet west country......................10327
Junior Dean.......................................10321
Master of St. Benedict's.......................10323
Orchard Damerel.................................10325
To his own master...............................10324
Tremlett diamonds..............................10328
St. Aubyn, Daisy. Garland of thorns....19315
St. Clair. Metropolites..........................47257
St. John. Bella....................................15215
St. Johnston. Charlie Asgarde..............032401
In quest of gold.................................032402
South sea lover..................................13320
Saintsbury. Corrected impressions. 1895.
....824.2 478
Contents: Thackeray.—Tennyson.—Carlyle.—Swinburne.—Macaulay.—Browning.—Dickens.—Matthew Arnold.
Essays in English literature, 1780-1860.
....824.2 436
Contents: The kinds of criticism.—Crabbe.—Hogg.—Sydney Smith.—Jeffrey.—Hazlitt.—Moore.—Leigh Hunt.—Peacock.—Wilson.—De Quincey.—Lockhart.—Praed.—Borrow.
Essays on French novelists...................843.7
Miscellaneous essays. 1892...............824.2 446
Contents: English prose style.—Chamfort and Rivarol.—Modern English prose.—Renan.—Thoughts on republics.—Saint-Evremond.—Baudelaire.—Young England movement.—A paradox on Quinet.—Contrasts of English and French literature.—A frame of miniatures. Parny; Dorat: Désaugiers; Vadé; Piron; Panard.—Present state of the English novel, 1892.
Sala. Dutch pictures. 1884...............824.2 356
Seven sons of mammon.........................19186
Strange adventures of Captain Dangerous..19185
Under the sun: essays. 1872..........824.2 277
Saltus. Shadows and ideals: poems. '90.821.1 419
Sampson, E. Brief remarks on the ways of man. 1821..........................824.1 5
Sampson, G. R. Address, Mercantile library association, 1856...............in 825.1 17
Sanborn. People at Pisgah..................43010
Sancho. Letters. 1784.....................826.2 19
Sand key. 1890..............................821.2 919
Sanders. Uncle Peter's riddle..............013050
Sands. Writings, prose and verse, with memoir. 1834. 2 v.......................820.1 14

Sandys. Poetical works. 1872. 2 v...821.2 172
  Contents: Introduction. — Paraphrases upon Job, Psalms of David, Ecclesiastes, Song of Solomon, Lamentations of Jeremiah, and songs out of New and Old Testaments.—Deo opt. max.—Christ's Passion.
Sanford, F. R. Bursting of a boom.........37020
Sanford, M. B. Romance of a Jesuit mission...25350
Sangster, C. The St. Lawrence, etc. (poems). 1856...................821.2 418
Sangster, Mrs. M. E. Easter bells: poems. 1897........................821.1 334
Santayana. Sonnets and other verses. 1894...821.1 473
Sargent, Epes. Peculiar...................11401
  Songs of the sea, etc. 1849.........821.1 21
  Velasco: a tragedy. 1839. (Copy presented to Sergeant Talfourd.)...........822.1 24
  The woman who dared. 1870............821.1 22
Sargent, G. E. Franklins................16509
  George Burley.............................16501
  Nails driven home........................16506
  Richard Hunne............................16503
  Story of a city Arab.....................16510
  Story of a pocket Bible................16502
  Stories of old England................16504
Sargent, G. E., and Walshe. Within sea walls............................16508
Sargent, Mrs. J. T., ed. Sketches and reminiscences of the Radical club..824.1 158
Sartoris. Past hours. 1880. 2 v.........824.2 285
  Week in a French country house............15280
Saunders, F. Mosaics. 1859.............824.1 40
  Pastime papers. 1885...................824.1 138
  Salad for the social. 1856.............824.1 38
  Salad for the solitary.................824.1 37
  Salad for the solitary and the social...824.1 39
  Story of some famous books. 1887...824.1 233
Saunders, J. Abel Drake's wife...............14501
  Bound to the wheel.....................14508
  Guy Waterman...........................14505
  Hirell..................................14507
  Israel Mort, overman...................14502
  Jasper Deane............................14504
  Martin Pole.............................in 14501
  Noble wife..............................14511
  Shipowner's daughter...................14506
  Two dreamers............................14509
Saunders, K. Gideon's rock...............25872
  Haunted crust...........................25873
  High mills..............................25876
  Joan Merryweather.......................25874
  Sebastian...............................25875
Saunders, M. Beautiful Joe...............036801
Sauzade. Garret Van Horn................25853
  Mark Gildersleeve.......................25854
Savage, Marmion. Bachelor of the Albany.14172
  Falcon family...........................14173
  My uncle the curate....................14174
  Woman of business......................14175
Savage, Minot J. Bluffton...............20040
  The modern sphinx......................824.1 188
  These degenerate days (verse). 1887..821.1 366
Savage, R. Poems; with life. 1822......821.2 31
Savidge, E. C. American in Paris............30730
Sawyer. David and Abigail..................36510
Saxby. Lucky-lines.........................20060
Saxe. Leisure-day rhymes. 1875.........821.1 60
  Money-king, and other poems. 1860...828.1 16
  Poetical works. 1883..................821.1 61
Scannell. In the time of roses............69309
Schaff. Literature and poetry. 1890....824.1 253
  Contents: Studies on the English language.—Poetry of the Bible. — The 'Dies iræ.'— The 'Stabat Mater.' — Hymns of Saint Bernard.—The university, ancient and modern.—Dante Alighieri.—The 'Divina commedia.'
Schallenberger. Green tea................14725
Schneider. Coronal of sonnets....821.1 Pam. 16
School-girls all the world over............0140
Schouler. Address, Massachusetts charitable mechanic association, 1848....in 825.1 17
Schreiner, O., (Ralph Iron, pseud.). Dream life and real life.....................35803
  Dreams..................................35801
  Story of an African farm...............35802
  Trooper Peter Halket...................35804
Schultz. A few rhymes. 1893........821.1 Pam. 19
Scollard. Boy's book of rhyme. 1896..*821.1 525
  Hills of song. 1895....................821.1 508
  Old and new world lyrics. 1888......821.1 435
  Songs of sunrise lands. 1892........821.1 450
Scop or gleeman's tale; tr. by Thorpe (poem)................................821.2 98
Scot, W. Selecta poemata. 1727......821.2 480
Scott, C. Among the apple orchards. 1895.
  ....824.2 484
  Contents: Walnut tree farm.—Under the apple trees.—Peeps of old England.—A painter's dreamland.
Scott, D. C. In the village of Viger (stories)................................70040
Scott, F. M. S. Gwladys Pemberton........52501
Scott, H. S. See Merriman, H. S., pseud.
Scott, J. Poems; with life. 1822......821.2 45
Scott, L. Messer Agnolo's household........62312
Scott, Meta C. Benjamin's sack............71140
Scott, Michael. Cruise of the Midge......15258
  Tom Cringle's log......................15259
Scott, Sir Walter. The abbot.............928
  Der Abt [The abbot]....................927
  Anne of Geierstein.....................951
  Same (German)..........................952
  Antiquary..............................929
  Betrothed.— Highland widow............941
  Black dwarf.— Legend of Montrose......935
  Same (German)..........................936

* Of interest to young readers.

LANGUAGE AND LITERATURE.

Braut von Lammermoor [Bride of Lammermoor]..907
Bride of Lammermoor............................906
 Same..*in* 935B
Castle Dangerous...............................*in* 944
 Same..*in* 922C, D.
Chronicles of the Canongate...................939
  Contents: Highland widow. — Two drovers.— Surgeon's daughter. — My aunt Margaret's mirror.— Tapestried chamber.—The laird's Jock.
Count Robert of Paris...........................922
Critical and miscellaneous essays. 1841. 3 v..824.2 109
Dramas from Waverley novels. 1835..822.2 154
  Contents: Rob Roy.—Heart of Mid-Lothian.—Kenilworth.—The antiquary.—Fortunes of Nigel. — Peveril of the peak.—Ivanhoe.
Essays on chivalry, etc.....................940.1 19
Fair maid of Perth.................................913
Familiar letters. 1894. 2 v............826.2 109
Fortunes of Nigel..................................917
Graf Robert von Paris [Count Robert of Paris]..923
Guy Mannering....................................974
Heart of Mid-Lothian..........................931
Highland widow..................*in* 941, *in* 939
Ivanhoe..903
 Same (condensed); in N. Y. point, for the blind.........................362.4 N-Y-12
Kenilworth 981
 Same (German)..................................982
 Same (condensed); in N. Y. point, for the blind.........................362.4 N-Y-13
Das Kloster [Monastery].........................921
Lady of the lake..........................821.2 264
Lands of Scott; by Hunnewell...................970
Lay of the last minstrel; ed. by Minto.821.2 253
Lay of the last minstrel. — Marmion.— Lady of the lake. 1883.............821.2 254
Legend of Montrose...............................937
 Same...*in* 935
Letters to the Beaumonts. 2 v......*in* 826.2 91
Marmion; ed. by Rolfe. 1885.........821.2 255
Monastery...920
Old Mortality...924
Periodical criticism. 1861. 5 v........824.2 391
Peveril of the peak................................933
Peveril vom Gipfel [Peveril of the peak]...932
Pirate..926
Poetical works. 1865. 6 v.
 V. 1. Lay of the last minstrel.—Ballads.—Songs, etc...821.2 258
 V. 2. Marmion.—Occasional pieces............821.2 259
 V. 3. Lady of the lake. — Vision of Don Roderick...821.2 260
 V. 4. Rokeby.—Bridal of Triermain...........821.2 261
 V. 5. Lord of the isles. — Field of Waterloo.— Songs, etc.......................................821.2 262
 V. 6. Harold the dauntless.—Dramatic pieces.821.2 263

Quentin Durward...................................930
 Same (German)..................................930B
Redgauntlet...957
Rob Roy..934
Sage von Montrose............................*in* 936
Saint Ronan's well.................................948
Der Schwarze Zwerg. — Eine Sage von Montrose [Black Dwarf.—Legend of Montrose]...936
Selections from; ed. by Ellis. '96...*in* 821.2 1025
Surgeon's daughter.................................941
 Same..*in* 939
 Same..*in* 922D
Tales from Scott; by Sullivan....................994
  Contents: Waverley.—Guy Mannering.—Antiquary.— Rob Roy.—Black dwarf.—Old Mortality.— Bride of Lammermoor.—Legend of Montrose.—Ivanhoe.
Talisman...956
Waverley..901
Waverley dictionary; by Rogers...............971
Waverley manual; by Cornish..................969
Waverley novels (reserved copy). 25 v.
 V. 1. Waverley.....................................‡823 1
 V. 2. Guy Mannering.............................‡823 2
 V. 3. The antiquary..............................‡823 3
 V. 4. Rob Roy......................................‡823 4
 V. 5. Old Mortality...............................‡823 5
 V. 6. Black dwarf.—Legend of Montrose....‡823 6
 V. 7. Heart of Mid-Lothian....................‡823 7
 V. 8. Bride of Lammermoor...................‡823 8
 V. 9. Ivanhoe.......................................‡823 9
 V. 10. The monastery.............................‡823 10
 V. 11. The abbot...................................‡823 11
 V. 12. Kenilworth..................................‡823 12
 V. 13. The pirate...................................‡823 13
 V. 14. Fortunes of Nigel.........................‡823 14
 V. 15. Peveril of the peak.......................‡823 15
 V. 16. Quentin Durward.........................‡823 16
 V. 17. St. Ronan's well...........................‡823 17
 V. 18. Redgauntlet.................................‡823 18
 V. 19. The betrothed.—Highland widow.....‡823 19
 V. 20. The talisman.—Two drovers.—My Aunt Margaret's mirror.— The tapestried chamber.— The laird's Jock....................................‡823 20
 V. 21. Woodstock..................................‡823 21
 V. 22. Fair maid of Perth.......................‡823 22
 V. 23. Anne of Geierstein......................‡823 23
 V. 24. Count Robert of Paris..................‡823 24
 V. 25. Surgeon's daughter.—Castle dangerous.‡823 25
Waverley novels; abridged by Braddon.....995
Woodstock..909
 Same (German)..................................910
Works (novels and poems) arranged in chronological order. From Springfield (Mass.) public library bulletin.
 Crusades; 1095-1272. Count Robert of Paris (1094; crusades and Constantinople).— The betrothed (1187; warfare in the Welsh border).—The talisman (1189-99; contrasts Richard Cœur de Lion and Saladin).—Ivanhoe (1194-96; Cœur de Lion and templars).
 Robert I (Bruce) of Scotland. Castle Dangerous (1306-29).—Lord of the isles (1300-29).—Tales of a grandfather; chapters 6-10 (1306-29).
 Robert III of Scotland; 1390-1406. Fair maid of Perth (1402).

‡ For reference.

Louis XI of France; 1461-83. Quentin Durward (1468; chiefly in France).— Anne of Geierstein (1472; under Louis XI and Charles the bold).
James IV and V of Scotland; 1488-1542. Marmion (1513; Flodden field).— Lay of the last minstrel.— Lady of the lake.
Mary, queen of Scots; 1553-1558. The monastery.— The abbot (sequel to 'The monastery').
Queen Elizabeth; 1558-1603. Kenilworth.
James I of England and VI of Scotland; 1603-25, Fortunes of Nigel.
Charles I of England; 1625-49. Rokeby (1644).— Legend of Montrose (1645-6; near the Trossachs and on west coast of Scotland).
Cromwell; 1649-60. Woodstock.
Charles II; 1660-85. Peveril of the peak (1669-80).— Old Mortality (Scotch Covenanters).
Eighteenth century. Bride of Lammermoor (Scotland, about 1700).— The pirate (life in the Orkneys, about 1700).— Black Dwarf (Queen Anne's reign ; Scotland, 1708).— Rob Roy (George I, 1715; contrasts Highland life and life in Glasgow).— Heart of Mid-Lothian (George II, 1736-51; chiefly in Edinburgh).— Waverley (Young Pretender, 1745; life and manners of Scotland).— Two drovers (Scotland, 1765).— Guy Mannering (southwest coast of Scotland, 1750-70).—Highland widow (Scotland, 1755).— Redgauntlet (the Pretender, 1770).— Surgeon's daughter (India ; Hyder Ali, about 1770-80).—St. Ronan's well (1800).
Spanish history (Moors and Spaniards).—Vision of Don Roderick.

Scriblerus, Martinus. See Pope.
Scudder, H. E. Bodleys afoot...............026803
Bodley grandchildren.......................026802
Childhood in literature and art. 1894.....137 3
Dwellers in Five Sisters' court................36401
English Bodley family......................026805
Men and letters ; essays. 1887.........824.1 230
Mr. Bodley abroad..........................026804
Seven little people..........................026801
Stories and romances........................36403
  Contents: Left over from the last century.—House of entertainment.—Accidentally overheard.—Hard bargain.—Story of the siege of Boston.—Matthew, Mark, Luke, and John.—Do not even the publicans the same?—Nobody's business.
Stories from my attic........................36402
Viking Bodleys...............................026806
Scudder, H. E., *ed.* Children's book...*819 B-1
Scudder, M. L., *jr.* Almost an Englishman..56810
Scully. Kafir stories.........................15680
White hecatomb...............................15681
Sealey, Celia. Echoes from the garret (poems). 1861....................................821.1 214
Seaman. Battle of the bays (verse)....821.2 1038
Searchfield. Secret cave....................034101
Seawell. Berkeleys and their neighbors..70082
Decatur and Somers............................07807
Little Jarvis..................................07803
Maid Marian, etc..............................70081
Midshipman Paulding...........................07804
Paul Jones....................................07805
Quarterdeck and fok'sle.......................07808

Sprightly romance of Marsac.................70084
Strange, sad comedy.........................70083
Throckmorton................................70080
Through thick and thin.—The midshipmen's mess.................................07806
Virginia cavalier............................07809
Secession, coercion and civil war...........50326
Secret drawer..............................55224
Secret of the Lamas........................55256
Sedgwick, C. M. Hope Leslie................11701
The Linwoods................................11703
New England tale............................11709
Tales of Glauber Spa.........................11708
Sedgwick, S. R. Walter Thornley.............52257
Sedley. Dangerfield's rest...................52263
Seeley, C. S. Lost canyon of the Toltecs...30491
Spanish galleon.............................30490
Seeley, J. R. Roman imperialism, etc. 1871.....................................824.2 336
  Contents: Roman imperialism. — Milton's political opinions. — Milton's poetry.— Elementary principles in art. — Liberal education in universities. — English in schools.—The church as a teacher of morality.—The teaching of politics.
Seely, H. Border Leander....................41506
Jonah of Lucky valley, etc...................41503
  Contents: Jonah of Lucky valley.— Romance of the Big Horn.—Daphne of the foot-hills.- Sheriff of Oskaloo.—Yaller-bird.—Yaller-bird's Christmas turkey.
Lone Star Bo-peep, etc.......................41501
Ranchman's stories..........................41502
Seemuller. Opportunity.....................19134
Reginald Archer.............................19132
Seen and unseen............................50302
Séguin, L. G. Mr. Caroll...................62540
Selden. Table-talk. 1831...................811 1
Same. 1868............................820.2 27
Same ; ed. by Singer. 1860..........829.2 13
Sergeant. Beyond recall....................24901
Brooke's daughter............................24912
Christine...................................24915
Deadly foe..................................24920
Doctor Endicott's experiment.................24917
Esther Denison..............................24905
Failure of Sibyl Fletcher....................24923
Great Mill street mystery....................24911
Idol-maker..................................24926
In the wilderness...........................24925
Life sentence...............................24909
Luck of the house...........................24907
Mistress of Quest............................24918
No ambition.................................24921
No saint....................................24903
Out of due season...........................24919
Roger Vanbrugh's wife........................24922
Rogue's daughter............................24924
Roy's repentance............................24904
Seventy times seven..........................24908

* Of interest to young readers.

LANGUAGE AND LITERATURE.

Sir Anthony's secret............................24913
Story of a penitent soul......................24914
Surrender of Margaret Bellarmine..........24916
True friend..24910
Under false pretences.........................24906
Serrao, T. Brushes and chisels...............30830
Serrano, tr. War under water................20426
Seton. Pride of Lexington....................15238
   Romance of Charter Oak..................15239
Setoun. Robert Urquhart....................22751
   Sunshine and haar..........................22750
Seven gray pilgrims.............................50325
Severance. Hammersmith...................25840
Severn. Heaven's gate.........................69241
Severne, Florence. In the meshes........31230
Sewell, A. Black Beauty....................636.1 28
Sewell, W. After life.........................9303
   Amy Herbert..................................9304
   Cleve hall......................................9318
   Earl's daughter...............................9312
   Experience of life...........................9316
   Gertrude.......................................9311
   Glimpse of the world......................9308
   Ivors...9317
   Journal of a home life.....................9301
   Katharine Ashton...........................9319
   Laneton parsonage..........................9309
   Margaret Percival...........................9313
   Ursula...9305
Seymour, C. W. College widow............62512
Seymour, E. H. Remarks upon plays of
   Shakspeare. 1805. 2 v..................822.3 59
Seymour, J. G. Romance of ancient history..52252
Seymour, M. H. Ned, Nellie and Amy..018901
Shaftesbury, *3d earl of*. Characteristics.
   1757. 3 v.....................................824.2 54
   Essays on same ; by Brown. 1751.....824.2 57
Shairp. Culture and religion.....................207 1
   Portraits of friends. 1889................824.2 421
     Contents: Thomas Erskine.—George Edward Lynch Cotton.— Dr. John Brown.— Norman Macleod.-John Macleod Campbell.—John Mackintosh of Geddes.— Arthur Hugh Clough.
   Sketches in history and poetry. 1887..824.2 405
   Studies in poetry and philosophy. 1872.
   ....824.2 211
     Contents: Wordsworth. — Coleridge. — Keble — The moral motive power.

SHAKESPEARE.

COLLECTED EDITIONS OF WORKS.

ARDEN Shakespeare. 1896—. v. 1—. ..822.4 221
   (Each play entered under title.)
AVON edition of works. 1888-9. 12 v.
   V. 1. The tempest.—Two gentlemen of Verona.
   —Merry wives of Windsor.—Measure for measure.
   ....822.4 64

   V. 2. Comedy of errors.—Much ado about nothing.— Love's labour's lost. — Midsummer-night's dream...822.4 65
   V. 3. Merchant of Venice.—As you like it. Taming of the shrew.—All's well that ends well.822.4 66
   V. 4. Twelfth-night. – Winter's tale. King John...822.4 67
   V. 5. Richard II. Henry IV, pts. 1 2....822.4 68
   V. 6. Henry V.—Henry VI, pts. 1-2.....822.4 69
   V. 7. Henry VI, pt. 3.— Richard III.—Henry VIII..822.4 70
   V. 8. Troilus and Cressida. — Coriolanus. -- Titus Andronicus.............................822.4 71
   V. 9. Romeo and Juliet.—Timon of Athens.— Julius Cæsar...................................822.4 72
   V. 10. Macbeth.—Hamlet.—King Lear...822.4 73
   V. 11. Othello.—Antony and Cleopatra.—Cymbeline..822.4 74
   V. 12. Pericles.—Poems 822.4 75
BOOTH's acting plays. 1871................822.4 330
     Contents: Richard III. -- Macbeth. — Merchant of Venice.—Romeo and Juliet. Othello (with Fool's revenge; Brutus; Lady of Lyons).
BOWEN, *ed.* Shakspere reading book : 17
   plays abridged. 1881...................822.4 328
BRANDRAM, *ed.* Selected plays, abridged.
   ....*822.4 327
     Contents: Merchant of Venice.—Romeo and Juliet.—Midsummer-night's dream.—Much ado about nothing.—Twelfth night.—As you like it.—Hamlet.—Macbeth.—The tempest.
CLARKE, *Mrs.* M. C., *ed.* Works. 1864. 2 v.
   V. 1. Preface.-Chronological table.—Will, etc. —Glossary.— The tempest.— Two gentlemen of Verona.—Merry wives of Windsor.—Measure for measure.—Comedy of errors.—Much ado about nothing. — Love's labour's lost.— Midsummer-night's dream.—Merchant of Venice.—As you like it.—Taming of the shrew.—All's well that ends well.—Twelfth night.—Winter's tale.—King John. —Richard II.— Henry IV, pts. 1-2.— Henry V.— Henry VI, pt. 1..................................822.4 B-1
   V. 2. Henry VI, pts. 2-3.—Richard III.—Henry VIII.—Troilus and Cressida.—Coriolanus.—Titus Andronicus.—Romeo and Juliet —Timon of Athens.— Julius Cæsar.— Macbeth.— Hamlet.— King Lear.—Othello.—Antony and Cleopatra.— Cymbeline.—Pericles.—Venus and Adonis.—Lucrece.—Sonnets.—Lover's complaint.—Passionate pilgrim. —Phœnix and turtle.............................822.4 B-2
DOUBTFUL plays. 1869........................822.4 331
     Contents: Edward III.—Thomas, Lord Cromwell.—Locrine.—Yorkshire tragedy.—London prodigal.—Birth of Merlin.
DRAMATIC works (Boston edition, 1841) ;
   with notes original and selected. 7 v.
   V. 1. Life of Shakespeare.—New facts regarding life of Shakespeare; by Collier. — Shakespeare's will, etc. — The tempest.— Two gentlemen of Verona. — Merry wives of Windsor. — Twelfth night.—Measure for measure.—Much ado about nothing..822.4 57
   V. 2. Midsummer-night's dream.--Love's labor's lost.—Merchant of Venice.—As you like it.—All's well that ends well.—Taming of the shrew..........822.4 58
   V. 3. Winter's tale.—Comedy of errors.—Macbeth.—King John.—Richard II.— Henry IV, pt. 1..822.4 59
   V. 4. Henry IV, pt. 2.—Henry V.—Henry VI, pts. 1-3...822.4 60

* Of interest to young readers.

Shakespeare.—Continued.

V. 5. Richard III.— Henry VIII.— Troilus and
Cressida.—Timon.—Coriolanus........................822.4 61
V. 6. Julius Cæsar. — Antony and Cleopatra.—
Cymbeline.—Titus Andronicus.—Pericles...........822.4 62
V. 7. Lear. — Romeo and Juliet. — Hamlet.
-Othello...822.4 63

FURNESS, *ed.* New variorum edition. 1871—.
V. I—.
V. 1. Romeo and Juliet..................................822.4 76
V. 2. Macbeth...822.4 77
V. 3-4. Hamlet. 2 v..822.4 78
V. 5. King Lear...822.4 80
V. 6. Othello...822.4 81
V. 7. Merchant of Venice...............................822.4 82
V. 8. As you like it..822.4 83
V. 9. Tempest...822.4 84
V. 10. Midsommer night's dreame................822.4 85

GOLLANCZ, *ed.* Temple Shakespeare. 1894—.
V. I—..822.4 120
(Each play entered under title.)

GRIGGS *and* PRAETORIUS. Fac-similes of
the first and second quartos, in photo-
lithography. 1880-91. 43 v.............................822.4 1
(Each play entered under title.)

HUDSON, *ed.* Harvard edition of works.
1880. 20 v.
V. 1. Life of Shakespeare.—Comedy of errors.—
Two gentlemen of Verona................................822.4 161
V. 2. Love's labour's lost.—Taming of the shrew
....822.4 162
V. 3. Midsummer-night's dream.—Merchant of
Venice...822.4 163
V. 4. All's well that ends well.—Much ado about
nothing...822.4 164
V. 5. As you like it.—What you will...............822.4 165
V. 6. Merry wives of Windsor.—Measure for
measure..822.4 166
V. 7. The tempest.—The winter's tale..........822.4 167
V. 8. Henry VI, pts. 1-2................................822.4 168
V. 9. Henry VI, pt. 3.—Richard III...............822.4 169
V. 10. King John.—Richard II......................822.4 170
V. 11. Henry IV, pts. 1-2..............................822.4 171
V. 12. Henry V.—Henry VIII........................822.4 172
V. 13. Titus Andronicus.—Romeo and Juliet.822.4 173
V. 14. Julius Cæsar.—Hamlet......................822.4 174
V. 15. King Lear.—Timon of Athens............822.4 175
V. 16. Antony and Cleopatra.— Troilus and
Cressida..822.4 176
V. 17. Macbeth.—Othello.............................822.4 177
V. 18. Cymbeline.—Coriolanus....................822.4 178
V. 19. Pericles.—Two noble kinsmen.—Venus
and Adonis...822.4 179
V. 20. Lucrece.—Sonnets.—Lover's complaint.
—Passionate pilgrim.—Index.........................822.4 180

Plays prepared for schools, families, etc.
1872. 2 v.
V. 1. Life of Shakespeare, etc.—As you like it,
Merchant of Venice.— Twelfth night.— Henry
IV, pts. 1-2.—Julius Cæsar.—Hamlet...........*822.4 325
V. 2. The tempest.—Winter's tale.—Henry V.
—Richard III.— King Lear.—Macbeth—Antony
and Cleopatra...*822.4 326

KEMBLE, Charles. Selection of plays as
read by. 1870. 3 v.
V. 1. Cymbeline.—Hamlet.—As you like it.—
Merchant of Venice.— Much ado about nothing.—
Julius Cæsar..822.4 322

V. 2. King John.—Romeo and Juliet.—Othello.
—Henry IV, pts. 1-2......................................822.4 323
V. 3. Henry V.—Macbeth.—Coriolanus.—Rich-
ard III.—Henry VIII......................................822.4 324

KNIGHT, *ed.* Pictorial edition of works. 1867.
8 v.
V. 1. Life of Shakespeare..............................822.4 B-6
V. 2. Tragedies: Romeo and Juliet; Hamlet;
Cymbeline; Othello; Timon; King Lear........822.4 B-7
V. 3. Tragedies: Macbeth; Troilus and Cres-
sida; Coriolanus; Julius Cæsar; Antony and
Cleopatra; Supplementary notice to the three
Roman plays.—Poems: Venus and Adonis; Lu-
crece; Sonnets; Lover's complaint; Passionate
pilgrim. — Verses, Chester's 'Love's martyr.'—
Notice...822.4 B-8
V. 4. Comedies: Two gentlemen of Verona;
Love's labour's lost; Merry wives of Windsor;
Comedy of errors; Taming of the shrew; Mid-
summer-night's dream; Merchant of Venice....822.4 B-9
V. 5. Comedies: All's well that ends well;
Much ado about nothing; Twelfth night; As you
like it; Measure for measure; Winter's tale;
The tempest..822.4 B-10
V. 6. Histories: King John.— Richard II.—
Henry IV, pts. 1-2.—Henry V.......................822.4 B-11
V. 7. Histories: Henry VI, pts. 1-3.— Richard
III; Henry VIII.—Essay on Henry VI and Rich-
ard III...822.4 B-12
V. 8. Doubtful plays: Titus Andronicus; Peri-
cles; Two noble kinsmen.— Plays ascribed to
Shakespeare: Locrine; Sir J. Oldcastle, pt. 1.—
Thomas, Lord Cromwell.; London prodigal;
Puritan; Yorkshire tragedy; Arden of Fever-
sham; Edward III; George-a-Greene; Fair Em;
Mucedorus; Birth of Merlin; Merry devil of
Edmonton.—Appendix: Dedication, etc., editions
of 1623 and 1632; History of opinion on the writ-
ings of Shakespeare; Shakespeare in Germany;
Shakespeare in France.—Indexes.................822.4 B-13

LAROCHE, *tr.* Œuvres complètes. 1854. 6 v.
V. 1. Notice sur Shakespeare.—La tempête.—
Les deux gentilshommes de Verone.—Les joyeuses
commères de Windsor.—La douzième nuit; ou, Ce
que vous voudrez.—Mesure pour mesure.—Othello;
ou, Le maure de Venise.—Tout est bien qui finit
bien..822.4 310
V. 2. La méchante mise à la raison.—Macbeth.
—Hamlet, prince de Danemark.—Conte d'hiver.
—Le marchand de Venise..............................822.4 311
V. 3. Beaucoup de bruit pour rien.—Les mé-
prises.—Peines d' amour perdues.—Cymbéline.—
Romeo et Juliette.— Troile et Cressida........822.4 312
V. 4. Le Roi Lear.—Pericles, prince de Tyr.—
Comme il vous plaira.—Coriolan.—Jules César.—
Antoine et Cléopâtre.....................................822.4 313
V. 5. Songe d'une nuit d'été.— Timon d'
Athènes.—Le Roi Jean.—Richard II.—Henri IV.822.4 314
V. 6. Henri V. — Henri VI. — Richard III.—
Henri VIII..822.4 315

MILLARD, *ed.* Shakespeare for recitation.
1894...822.4 329

ROLFE, *ed.* Works. 40 v............................822.4 181
(Each play entered under title.)

SCHLEGEL *und* TIECK, *übersta.* Dramatische
Werke. 12 v. in 6.
V. 1-2. König Johann.— Richard II.—Heinrich
IV.—Heinrich V.—Heinrich VI, erster Theil....822.4 316

* Of interest to young readers.

LANGUAGE AND LITERATURE.

Shakespeare.—Continued.

V. 3-4. Heinrich VI, zweiter und dritter Theil.—Richard III.- Heinrich VIII.—Romeo und Julia.- Ein Sommernachtstraum....................................822.4 317
V. 5-6. Julius Cäsar. — Was ihr wollt. — Der Sturm.—Hamlet. Der Kaufmann von Venedig.—Wie es euch gefällt...................................822.4 318
V. 7-8. Der widerspenstigen Zahmung. — Viel lärmen um nichts.—Die Comödie der Irrungen.—Die beiden Veroneser.—Coriolanus.—Liebes leid und lust...822.4 319
V. 9-10. Die lustigen Weiber von Windsor.—Titus Andronicus.—Das Wintermährchen.—Antonius und Cleopatra.— Maass für Maass.— Timon von Athen...822.4 320
V. 11-12. Lear.—Troilus und Cressida.—Ende gut, alles gut.—Othello.—Cymbeline.—Macbeth.822.4 321

SHAKESPEARE, as put forth in 1623; a reprint (L. Booth). 1864...................822.4 44
Contents: Comedies: The tempest; Two gentlemen of Verona; Merry wives of Windsor; Measure for measure; Comedy of errours; Much adoo about nothing; Loue's labour lost; Midsommer night's dreame; Merchant of Venice; As you like it; Taming of the shrew; All is well that ends well; Twelfe-night; Winter's tale.—Histories: Life and death of King John; Life and death of Richard II; First part of King Henry IV; Second part of King Henry IV; Life of King Henry V; First part of King Henry VI; Second part of King Henry VI; Third part of King Henry VI.—Life and death of Richard III; Life of King Henry VIII.—Tragedies: Coriolanus; Titus Andronicus; Romeo and Juliet; Timon of Athens; Life and death of Julius Cæsar; Macbeth; Hamlet; Lear; Othello; Anthony and Cleopatra; Cymbeline.

STAUNTON, *ed.* Works. 1866. 3 v.
V. 1. Preface.—Life of Shakespeare.—Two gentlemen of Verona.—Love's labour's lost.—Comedy of errors. — Romeo and Juliet.— Taming of the shrew.—King John.—Midsummer-night's dream.—Merchant of Venice.—Richard II.—Henry IV., pts. 1-2.— Merry wives of Windsor.—Much ado about nothing..822.4 B-3
V. 2. All's well that ends well.—Henry V. As you like it.—Pericles.—Twelfth night.— Henry VI, pts. 1-3.—Timon.—Richard III.—Measure for measure.—Henry VIII.—Cymbeline.............822.4 B-4
V. 3. The tempest.— King Lear.— Coriolanus.— Winter's tale.—Troilus and Cressida.—Hamlet.—Julius Cæsar.—Macbeth.—Antony and Cleopatra.—Titus Andronicus.— Othello.— Poems.— Glossarial index..822.4 B-5

TEMPLE Shakespeare; ed. by Gollancz. v. 1—.
....822.4 120
(Each play entered under title.)

WHITE, R. G., *ed.* Works. 12 v.
V. 1. Memoirs of Shakespeare, etc.—Historical sketch of the text of Shakespeare.—Poems.......822.4 45
V. 2. The tempest.—Two gentlemen of Verona.—Merry wives of Windsor.......................822.4 46
V. 3. Measure for measure.—The comedy of errors.—Much ado about nothing.—Love's labour's lost...822.4 47
V. 4. Midsummer-night's dream.—Merchant of Venice.—As you like it.—Taming of the shrew...822.4 48
V. 5. All's well that ends well.—Twelfth night; or, What you will.—The winter's tale..........822.4 49
V. 6. King John.—Richard II.—Henry IV, pts. 1-2..822.4 50

V. 7. Henry V.—Henry VI, pts. 1-2.—Essay on the authorship of Henry VI....................822.4 51
V. 8. Henry VI, pt. 3.—Richard III. Henry VIII...822.4 52
V. 9. Troilus and Cressida. -Coriolanus. Titus Andronicus......................................822.4 53
V. 10. Romeo and Juliet Timon of Athens. Julius Cæsar.—Macbeth.........................822.4 54
V. 11. Hamlet.—King Lear. Othello...........822.4 55
V. 12. Antony and Cleopatra. · Cymbeline. Pericles.—Appendix.—Index....................822.4 56

WRIGHT, W. Aldis, *ed.* Select plays. 1882—.
v. 1—...822.4 261
(Each play entered under title.)

Works. (The Cambridge Shakespeare.) 1891-3. 9 v.
V. 1. The tempest.—Two gentlemen of Verona.—Merry wives of Windsor.—Measure for measure.—Comedy of errors.........................822.4 301
V. 2. Much ado about nothing. -Love's labour's lost.— Midsummer-night's dream.— Merchant of Venice.—As you like it...........................822.4 302
V. 3. Taming of the shrew.—All's well that ends well.—Twelfth night.—The winter's tale..........822.4 303
V. 4. King John.—King Richard II.—King Henry IV, pts. 1-2.—King Henry V..................822.4 304
V. 5. King Henry VI, pts. 1-3.—King Richard III.—King Henry VIII........................822.4 305
V. 6. Troilus and Cressida.—Coriolanus.—Titus Andronicus.—Romeo and Juliet................822.4 306
V. 7. Timon of Athens.—Julius Cæsar.—Macbeth.—Hamlet...................................822.4 307
V. 8. King Lear.—Othello.—Antony and Cleopatra.— Cymbeline................................822.4 308
V. 9. Pericles.— Venus and Adonis. — Rape of Lucrece.—Sonnets.—Lover's complaint.—Phœnix and turtle.—Reprints: Merry wives of Windsor; Chronicle historie of Henry V; Contention, pt. 1; The true tragedie; Romeo and Juliet; Hamlet...822.4 309

SEPARATED PLAYS.—TEXT, CRITICISM, ETC.

ALL's well that ends well; ed. by Gollancz. (Temple Shakespeare.) 1894.....822.4 120
Same; ed. by Rolfe......................822.4 181
ANTONY and Cleopatra; ed. by Gollancz. (Temple Shakespeare.) 1896.....822.4 121
Same; ed. by Rolfe......................822.4 182
ARDEN of Feversham; ed. by Bullen......822.4 332
AS YOU like it; ed. by Gollancz. (Temple edition.) 1894...........................822.4 122
Same; ed. by Rolfe......................822.4 183
Same; ed. by J. C. Smith. (Arden Shakespeare.) 1896.....................822.4 223
Same; ed. by Wright. '84.................822.4 263
COMEDY of errors; ed. by Gollancz. (Temple Shakespeare). 1894.....................822.4 123
Same; ed. by Rolfe......................822.4 184
CORIOLANUS; ed. by Gollancz. (Temple Shakespeare). 1896.....................822.4 124
Same; ed. by Knight (Chambers' edition.) 1887..........................822.4 333
Same; ed. by Rolfe......................822.4 185
Same; ed. by Wright....................822.4 265

Shakespeare.—Continued.

CYMBELINE; ed. by Gollancz. (Temple Shakespeare.) 1896....................822.4 125
Same; ed. by Ingleby. 1886.........822.4 334
Same; ed. by Rolfe.......................822.4 186
HAMLET. 1st quarto, 1603; facsimile by Griggs, ed. by Furnivall................822.4 1
Same; 2d quarto, 1604; facsimile as above...822.4 2
Same; 1603-1604; exact reprints of 1st and 2nd editions. 1860.........822.4 335
Same; ed. by Chambers. (Arden Shakespeare.) 1896....................822.4 227
Same; ed. by Gollancz. (Temple Shakespeare.) 1896....................822.4 126
Same; ed. by Mull. 1885..............822.4 339
Same; ed. by A. P. Paton. (Hamnet edition.) 1888............................822.4 337
Same; ed. by Rolfe.......................822.4 187
Same; ed. by Sprague. 1885........822.4 338
Same; ed. by Wright....................822.4 267
Same; in modified Braille, for the blind. 362.4 M-B-2
Elizabethan Hamlet: a study of sources; by Corbin. 1895..............................822.3 392
Hamlet of Saxo grammaticus and of Shakespear; by Latham................822.3 162
Hamlet's note-book; by O'Connor...822.3 156
Legend of, in Saxo grammaticus, etc.; by Hansen. 1887............822.3 Pam. 16
Memoranda on; by Halliwell-Phillipps. 1879..822.3 353
Mystery of; by Vining. 1881.........822.3 129
Some famous Hamlets; by Brereton. 1884..822.3 95
Study of; by Pedder..............822.3 Pam. 14
Study with the folio of 1623; by Macdonald. 1885.....................................822.3 336
Tendency of; by Feis. 1884..........822.3 257
Where Hamlet came from; by De Falbe. ....822.3 Pam. 15
HENRY IV., pt. 1. 1st quarto, 1598; facsimile by Griggs, ed. by Evans...............822.4 3
Same, pt. 2; quarto of 1600; facsimile as above..822.4 4
Same, pt. 1; ed. by Gollancz. (Temple edition.) 1895............................822.4 127
Same, pt. 2. 1896.......................822.4 128
Same, from a contemporary manuscript; ed. by Halliwell. (Shakespeare society, 1845.)....................822.4 340
Same, pt. 1; ed. by Rolfe.............822.4 188
Same, pt. 2.................................822.4 189
Dramatic character of Falstaff; by Morgann. 1777............................822.3 11
Falstaff; by J. H. Hackett..........................40 27
Historical element in Falstaff; by Gardner..942 222

HENRY V. Quarto, 1598; facsimile by Praetorius, ed. by Daniel. 1887.........822.4 5
Same; 1st quarto, 1600; facsimile by Praetorius; ed. by Symons. 1886...822.4 6
Same; 2d quarto, 1608; fascimile as above...822.4 7
Same; parallel texts, 1st quarto, 1600, and 1st folio, 1623; ed. by Nicholson. (New Shakespeare society, '77.)..822.4 B-24
Same; reprint of 1st quarto, 1600. (New Shakespeare society, '75.)..822.4 B-22
Same; reprint from 1st folio, 1623. (New Shakespeare society, '75)..822.4 B-23
Same; ed. by Gollancz. (Temple Shakespeare.) 1895....................822.4 129
Same; ed. by Rolfe.......................822.4 190
Same; ed. by G. C. M. Smith. (Arden Shakespeare.) 1896....................822.4 230
Same; ed. by Wright. '83..............822.4 270
HENRY VI, pt. 2. The contention, pt. 1; 1st quarto, 1594; facsimile by Praetorius; ed. by Furnivall..................822.4 8
Same, pt. 2. The whole contention, pt. 1; 3d quarto, 1619; facsimile as above...822.4 10
Same, pt. 3. The true tragedy; 1st quarto, 1595; facsimile by Praetorius, ed. by Tyler..........................822.4 9
Same, pt. 3. The whole contention, pt. 2; 3d quarto, 1619; facsimile as above...822.4 11
Same, pt. 1; ed by Gollancz. (Temple Shakespeare.) 1895....................822.4 130
Same, pt. 2..................................822.4 131
Same, pt. 3..................................822.4 132
Same, pt. 1; ed. by Rolfe.............822.4 191
Same, pt. 2..................................822.4 192
Same, pt. 3..................................822.4 193
First sketches of pts. 2 and 3; ed by Halliwell. (Shakespeare society, '43.) 822 4 341
HENRY VIII; ed. by Gollancz. (Temple Shakespeare.) 1895....................822.4 133
Same; ed. by Rolfe.......................822.4 194
Same; ed. by Wright....................822.4 274
JOHN. Troublesome raigne of. 1st quarto, 1591; facsimile by Praetorius, ed. by Furnivall. 1888. 2 v....................822.4 12
Same; ed. by Dawson. 1887........822.4 342
Same; ed. by Gollancz. (Temple Shakespeare.) 1894....................822.4 134
Same; ed. by Rolfe.......................822.4 195
Same; ed. by Wright. 1886..........822.4 275
Memoranda on; by Halliwell-Phillipps. 1879..822.3 355
JULIUS Cæsar; ed. by Beeching. 1886...822.4 343
Same; ed. by Gollancz. (Temple Shakespeare.) 1896....................822.4 135

Shakespeare.—Continued.

Same; ed. by Innes. (Arden Shakespeare.) 1896..............................822.4 236
Same; ed. by Rolfe......................822.4 196
Same; ed. by Rolfe; in N. Y. point, for the blind. 1896..................362.4 N-Y-4
Same: ed. by Wright. 1885............822.4 276
Philological commentary on; by Craik. 1867........................... 822 3 92

LEAR. 1st quarto, 1608; facsimile by Praetorius, ed. by Daniel. 1885.........822.4 14
Same; 2d quarto, 1608: facsimile as above......................................822.4 15
Same; ed. by Gollancz. (Temple Shakespeare.) 1895..................822 4 136
Same; ed. by Rolfe........................822 4 197
Same; ed. by Wright. 1881............822.4 277

LOVE'S labour's lost. 1st quarto; facsimile by Griggs, ed. by Furnivall..........822.4 16
Same; ed. by Gollancz. (Temple Shakespeare.) 1894..................822 4 137
Same; ed. by Rolfe.......................822.4 198

MACBETH; ed by Chambers. (Arden Shakespeare.) 1896..............?.............822.4 239
Same; ed. by Gollancz. (Temple Shakespeare.) 1896 ....822.4 138
Same; ed. by Rolfe......................822.4 199
Same; ed. by Wright. '83..............822.4 279
Same; German version, by Schiller...830 B-9
Same; with Holinshed's historie. '87.822 4 344
Same; adapted by D'Avenant........822.2 232
Same; and Richard III; by Kemble 1817.......................................822.3 133
Same; reconsidered; by Kemble. 822.3 Pam. 1

MEASURE for measure; ed. by Gollancz. (Temple Shakespeare.) 1894....822.4 139
Same; ed. by Rolfe.......................822.4 200

MERCHANT of Venice. 1st quarto; facsimile by Griggs, ed. by Furnivall..822.4 18
Same; 2d quarto, 1600; facsimile as above. 1887...........................822.4 19
Same; ed. by Beeching. 1887.......822.4 345
Same; ed. by Gollancz. (Temple Shakespeare.) 1895..................822.4 140
Same; ed. by Rolfe......................822 4 201
Same; ed. by Rolfe, in N. Y. point, for the blind. 1895.............362 4 N-Y-5
Same; ed. by Wright. '84.............822.4 281
Same; version in French; by A. de Vigny....................................842 61

MERRY wives of Windsor. 1st quarto, 1602; facsimile by Griggs, ed. by Daniel..822.4 20
Same; ed. by Gollancz. (Temple Shakespeare.) 1894..................822.4 141
Same; ed. by Rolfe........................822.4 202
Same; ed. by Stanford and Wheatley. 1886......................................822.4 347

First sketch of; ed. by Halliwell. (Shakespeare Society, 1842)..................822.4 346
Same..in 822.2 77

MIDSUMMER-NIGHT'S dream. 1st quarto, 1600; facsimile by Griggs, ed. by Ebsworth. 1880.........................822.4 21
Same; 2d quarto, 1600; facsimile as above......................................822 4 22
Same; facsimile reprint of 1st folio; ed. by Johnson. 1888.................822.4 348
Same; ed. by Chambers. (Arden Shakespeare.) 1896..................822.4 243
Same; ed. by Gollancz. 1895........822.4 349
Same; ed. by Gollancz. (Temple Shakespeare.) 1896..................822.4 142
Same; ed. by Rolfe........................822.4 203
Same; ed. by Wright. 1883............822.4 283
Illustrations of the fairy mythology; ed. by Halliwell. (Shakespeare society, 1845.).....................................822.3 47
Memoranda on; by Halliwell-Phillipps. 1879..822.3 354
Oberon's vision, and Lylie's Endymion; by Halpin. (Shakespeare Society, 1843.)....................................822.3 48
Puck and his folk-lore; by Bell. 1852.822.3 141

MUCH ado about nothing. Quarto, 1600: facsimile by Praetorius, ed. by Daniel. 1886......................................822.4 23
Same; ed. by Gollancz. (Temple Shakespeare.) 1894..................822.4 143
Same; ed. by Rolfe......................822.4 204
Same; ed. by Verity. 1890 ....822.4 350
Same; ed. by Wright...................822 4 284

OTHELLO. 1st quarto, 1622: facsimile by Praetorius, ed. by Evans. 1885..822.4 24
Same, 2d quarto, 1630; facsimile as above.....................................822.4 25
Same; ed. by Gollancz. (Temple Shakespeare.) 1895..................822 4 144
Same; ed. by Rolfe......................822.4 205
Same; version in French, by A. De Vigny....................................842 61
Same; as performed by Salvini (Italian and English.) 1881..................822 4 351
Memoranda on; by Halliwell-Phillipps. 1879..822.3 355
Shakespeare's verse in; by Price. 1888. ....822.3 356

PERICLES. 1st quarto, 1609; facsimile by Praetorius, ed. by Round. 1886.....822.4 27
Same; 2d quarto, 1609; facsimile as above..822.4 28
Same; ed. by Gollancz. (Temple Shakespeare.) 1896..................822.4 145
Same; ed. by Rolfe......................822.4 206

Shakespeare.—Continued.

RICHARD II. 1st quarto, 1597: facsimile by Griggs, ed. by Daniel. 1890........822.4 29
Same; facsimile by Praetorius; ed. by Harrison. 1888....................822.4 30
Same; 3d quarto, 1608: facsimile as above. 1888..........................822.4 31
Same; 5th quarto, 1634: facsimile by Praetorius, ed. by Daniel. 1887...822.4 32
Same; ed. by Gollancz. (Temple Shakespeare.) 1895..................822.4 147
Same; ed. by Herford. (Arden Shakespeare.) 1896..................822 4 248
Same; ed. by Rolfe....................822.4 207
Same; ed. by Wright. 1884..........822.4 287
RICHARD III. 1st quarto, 1597: facsimile by Griggs, ed. by Daniel............822.4 33
Same; 3d quarto, 1602: facsimile by Praetorius, ed. by Daniel. 1888...822.4 34
Same; 6th quarto, 1622: facsimile as above. 1889..........................822.4 35
Same; ed. by Gollancz. (Temple Shakespeare.) 1895..................822.4 148
Same; ed. by Macdonald. (Arden Shakespeare.) 1896..................822.4 249
Same; ed. by Rolfe....................822.4 208
Same; ed. by Wright. 1882..........822.4 288
Essay on; by Kemble. 1817..........822.3 133
Ghost of Richard III: a poem, 1614, ed. by Collier. (Shakespeare society, 1844.)..822.3 49
True tragedy of Richard III; also Legge's Richardus Tertius. (Shakespeare society, 1844)..822.2 76
ROMEO and Juliet. 1st quarto, 1597: facsimile by Praetorius, ed. by Evans..822.4 36
Same; 2d quarto, 1599: facsimile as above. 1886..........................822 4 37
Same; undated quarto: facsimile as above..822.4 38
Same; parallel texts, 1597, 1599; ed. by Daniel. (New Shakespeare society, 1874.)..............................822.4 B-18
Same; reprint of 1st quarto, 1597; ed. by Daniel. (New Shakespeare society, 1874.)..............................822.4 B-19
Same; reprint of 2d quarto, 1599; ed. by Daniel. (New Shakespeare society, 1874.)..............................822.4 B-20
Same; revised edition of 2d quarto; ed. by Daniel. (New Shakespeare society, 1875.)..............................822.4 B-21
Same; ed. by Gollancz (Temple Shakespeare.) 1896..................822.4 149
Same; ed. by Rolfe....................822.4 209
Memoranda on; by Halliwell-Phillipps. 1879...822.3 355

New travesty on. 1877.............828.1 Pam. 2
Romeus and Juliet, by Arthur Brooke.— Rhomeo and Julietta, by W. Painter; ed. by Daniel. (New Shakespeare Society, 1875.)..............................822.3 B-5
TAMING of the shrew. 1st quarto, 1594: facsimile by Praetorius, ed. by Furnivall. 1886..................................822.4 40
Same; ed. by Gollancz. (Temple Shakespeare.) 1894..................822.4 151
Same; ed. by Rolfe....................822.4 211
Old play on which Shakespeare founded his comedy; ed. by Amyot. (Shakespeare society, 1844.)......................822.3 40
TEMPEST; dallastype facsimile from 1st folio (1623) [with text ed. by Knight]. 1895..822.4 B-25
Same; ed. by Gollancz. (Temple Shakespeare.) 1894..................822.4 152
Same; ed. by Rolfe....................822.4 212
Same; ed. by Wright, '85..............822.4 292
Same; altered by D'Avenant and Dryden..822.2 232
TIMON of Athens; ed. by Gollancz. (Temple Shakespeare) 1896..................822.4 153
Same; ed. by Paton. (Hamnet edition.) 1889..822.4 352
Same; ed. by Rolfe....................822.4 213
Play (earlier than Shakespeare's); ed. by Dyce. (Shakespeare society, '42.)..822.2 93
TITUS Andronicus. 1st quarto, 1600: facsimile by Praetorius, ed. by Symons..822.4 41
Same; ed. by Gollancz. (Temple Shakespeare.) 1896..................822.4 154
Same; ed by Rolfe....................822.4 214
TROILUS and Cressida. 1st quarto, 1609: facsimile by Griggs, ed. by Stokes. 1886..822.4 42
Same; ed. by Gollancz. (Temple Shakespeare.) 1896..................822.4 155
Same; ed. by Rolfe....................822.4 215
TWELFTH night; ed. by Gollancz. (Temple Shakespeare.) 1895..................822.4 156
Same; ed. by Innes. (Arden Shakespeare.) 1896..........................822.4 257
Same; ed. by Rolfe....................822.4 216
Same; ed. by Wright....................822.4 296
Two gentlemen of Verona; ed. by Gollancz. (Temple Shakespeare.) 1894....822 4 157
Same; ed. by Rolfe....................822 4 217
Two noble kinsmen: reprint of quarto, 1634; ed. by Littledale. (New Shakespeare society, 1876.)..............822.4 B-17
Same, from the quarto of 1634, revised text; ed. by Littledale. (New Shakespeare society, 1876.)...... 822.4 B-16
Same; ed. by Rolfe.. ....822.4 218

Shakespeare.—Continued.

On Shakespeare's authorship of; by
Spalding, etc. (New Shakespeare
Society, 1876.).............................822.3 B-4
Winter's tale; ed. by Gollancz. (Temple
Shakespeare.) 1894...................822.4 160
Same; ed. by Rolfe.......................822.4 220

POEMS.

Autobiographical poems; [comp.] by Brown.
1838..822.3 8
Bibliography of earlier editions of poems
of Shakespeare; by J. Winsor.........16 B-16
Lucrece. 1st quarto, 1594: facsimile by
Praetorius, ed. by Furnivall. 1885...822.4 17
Passionate pilgrim. 1st quarto, 1599; facsimile by Griggs, ed. by Dowden.....822.4 26
Rape of Lucrece; ed. by Gollancz. (Temple
Shakespeare.) 1896......................822.4 146
Songs; ed. by Bridge.....................822.4 B-15
Sonnets. 1st quarto, 1609; facsimile by
Praetorius, ed. by Tyler.................822.4 39
Same; ed. by Dowden. 1881........822.4 353
Same; ed. by Rolfe......................822.4 210
Same; in deutscher Nachbildung;
von F. Bodenstedt........................831 38
Introduction to philosophy of; by Simpson. 1868..822.3 104
Never before interpreted; by Massey.
1866...822.3 80
Sonnets of Shakespeare solved; by H.
Brown...822.3 81
Venus and Adonis. 1st quarto, 1593; facsimile by Griggs; ed. by Symons..822.4 43
Same; ed. by Gollancz. (Temple
Shakespeare.) 1896.....................822.4 159
Same; Lucrece, etc.; ed. by Rolfe..822.4 219

SHAKESPEARIANA.

Abbott. Shakespearian grammar. 1870.....425 1
Alleyn papers and memoirs; ed. by Collier. (Shakespeare society, 1843.) 2 v.
....927.2 73
Annals of the life and work of Shakespeare. 1886..822.3 12
Bacon, Delia. Biography; by T. Bacon.
1888..822.3 359
Philosophy of the plays of Shakespeare.
1857...822.3 78
Bacon, Sir Francis. Promus of formularies; ed. by Pott. 1883..............822.3 210
Ballads that illustrate Shakespeare (in
Percy's 'Reliques')............................821.2 84
Barr. Young people of Shakespeare's
dramas...*822.3 204
Bartlett. Concordance to works of
Shakespeare. 1894....................‡822.3 B-35

Baynes. Shakespeare studies. 1894.....822.3 386
Becket. Shakespeare's himself again. 2 v..822.3 70
Boaden. Authenticity of portraits of Shakespeare. 1824...822.3 14
Boston. Public library. Catalog of Barton
collection: Shakespeare's works and
Shakespeariana..................................16 B-23
Boydell. Illustrations; Spooner's edition.
2 v...822.3 Cab.
Brandes. William Shakespeare. 1896...822.3 37
Brewer. Historical essays on Shakespeare...in 942 360
Britton. Essays on Shakespeare. '49.822.3 B-1
Bucknill. The mad folk of Shakespeare.
1867..822.3 126
Medical knowledge of Shakespeare.
1860...822.3 139
Calmour. Facts and fiction about Shakespeare..822.3 B-36
Calvert. Shakespeare. 1879.............822.3 145
Campbell. Shakespeare's legal acquirements. 1859.......................................822.3 91
Castle. Shakespeare, Bacon, Jonson and
Greene. 1897..................................822.3 65
Caulfield, ed. Vocal music in plays of
Shakespeare. 2 v..........................784 B-5
Chester. Love's martyr, etc.; ed. by Grosart. (New Shakespeare society, 1878.)
....821.2 B-9
Chester plays; ed. by T. Wright. (Shakespeare society, 1843.) 2 v..............822.2 72
Churcher. Mystery of Shakespeare revealed. 1886......................................822.3 341
Clarke, C. C. Shakespeare characters..822.3 132
Clarke, C. C. and M. C. Shakespeare
key. 1879...822.3 128
Clarke, Mary C. Concordance to [plays of
Shakespeare]................................‡822.3 B-3
Girlhood of Shakespeare's heroines.
3 v..822.3 212
Same; abridged. 1887.....................822.3 211
Coleridge. Lects. and notes on Shakespeare, etc..822.3 217
Collier. New facts regarding life of Shakespeare. 1835......................................822.3 96
Reasons for new edition of Shakespeare. 1842............................822.3 Pam. 11
Reply to Hamilton's 'Inquiry.'..822.3 Pam. 12
Collier, ed. Five court masques. (Shakespeare society, 1848.).........................822.2 81
Memoirs of principal actors in plays of
Shakespeare. (Shakespeare society,
1846.)...822.3 45
Shakespeare's library; romances, etc.
used by Shakespeare as the foundation of his dramas. 1843. 2 v........822.3 41
Corson. Introduction to study of Shakespeare. 1889..822.3 216

* Of interest to young readers.   ‡ For reference.

Shakespeare.—Continued.

COURTENAY. Commentaries on the historical plays of Shakespeare. 1840. 2 v..822.3 63
CRAIK. The English of Shakespeare. '67..822.3 92
CUNNINGHAM. Inigo Jones; with his sketches for masques and dramas, by J. R. Planché. (Shakespeare society, 1848.) 822.2 81
CUNNINGHAM, *ed.* Extracts from accounts of revels at courts of Elizabeth and James I. (Shakespeare society, 1842.) 822.3 44
Revels at court. (Shakespeare society, 1842) 822.2 80
DALL. What we really know about Shakespeare. 1886......822.3 94
DAVIES. Dramatic miscellanies. 1784. 3v..822.3 74
DEKKER, CHETTLE, *and* HAUGHTON. Patient Grissil. (Shakespeare society, 1841.) 822.2 75
DODD. Beauties of Shakespeare. 1854..822.3 342
DONNELLY. The great cryptogram. '88..822.3 348
DOUCE. Illustrations of Shakespeare. 1807. 2 V......822.3 68
DOWDALL. Traditionary anecdotes of Shakespeare; collected in 1693; ed. by Collier. 1838......822.3 97
Same......822.3 Pam. 2
DOWDEN. Introduction to Shakespeare. 1893......822.3 383
Shakespere (literature primer). 1878..822.3 102
Shakspere; his mind and art. 1879....822.3 138
DRAKE. Shakespeare and his times. 1817. 2 V......822.3 B-31
DYER. Folk-lore of Shakespeare. 1882..822.3 255
EATON. Shakespeare and the Bible......822.3 89
EIGHT novels employed by English dramatic poets, reign of Elizabeth. (Shakespeare society, 1846.)......822.3 43
Same......822.3 44
ELLACOMBE. Plant-lore of Shakespeare..822.3 148
ELZE. Essays on Shakespeare. 1874......822.3 57
Notes on Elizabethan dramatists. 2v..822.2 265
William Shakespeare: a literary biography. 1888......822.3 357
FEIS. Shakespeare and Montaigne. '84..822.3 257
FIELD. Medical thoughts of Shakespeare. 1885......822.3 370
FLEAKY. Chronicle history of Shakespeare. 1886......822.3 147
FOLLETT. Who wrote Shakespeare? 1879. ......822.3 Pam. 6
FOOLS and jesters. (Shakespeare society, 1842.)......828.2 5
FORDE. Two tracts. (Shakespeare society, 1843.)......824.2 3
FOSTER. Reference list. v. 1......16 55

FOX. Students' Shakespeare: 37 plays analyzed......‡822.3 B-2
FRENCH. Shakspeareana genealogica. '69..822.3 7
FRISWELL. Life portraits of Shakespeare. 1864......822.3 146
FULLOM. History of Shakespeare. 1864...822.3 3
FURNESS. Concordance to poems of Shakespeare......‡822.3 98
FURNIVALL. Succession of Shakespeare's works. 1874......822.3 l'am. 8
GERVINUS. Shakespeare commentaries....822.3 54
Same. 1863. v. 2......822.3 55
GILMAN, *ed.* Shakespeare's morals. '80..822.3 151
GOSSON. School of abuse. (Shakespeare society, 1841.)......175 1
GREEN. Shakespeare and the emblem writers. 1870......822.3 77
GRINDON. The Shakspere flora. 1883....822.3 136
GUIZOT. Shakespeare and his times. '52....822.3 9
HACKETT. Essay on Falstaff. 1836........*in* 40 27
HALES. Notes and essays on Shakespeare. 1884......822.3 256
HALLIWELL-PHILLIPPS. Catalogue of library of......16 105
Curiosities of modern Shakesperian criticism. 1853......822.3 Pam. 9
Historical account of the New Place, Stratford. 1864......822.3 R-1
Memoranda on 'All's well that ends well,' 'Two gentlemen of Verona,' Much ado about nothing,' 'Titus Andronicus.' 1879......822.3 352
Memoranda on 'Love's labour's lost,' 'King John,' 'Othello,' 'Romeo and Juliet.' 1879......822.3 355
New lamps or old? — Name of Shakespeare. 1880......822.3 Pam. 10
Outlines of life of Shakespeare. '82...822.3 205
Same. 1886. 2 v......822.3 B-33
Shakesperiana; catalog of early editions. etc. 1841......822.3 161
Shaxpear or Shakspear? '79..822.3 Pam. 18
HALLIWELL-PHILLIPPS, *ed.* Marriage of wit and wisdom; illustrations of Shakespeare. (Shakespeare society, '46)...822.3 46
HAND-LIST of drawings, etc., illustrative of life of Shakespeare, Hollingsbury Copse. 1884......822.3 356
HARDY. Review of Shaksperian controversy. 1860......822.3 Pam. 13
HARRISON. Description of England in Shakspere's youth; ed. by Furnivall. (New Shakespeare society, 1877-8.) 942.3 B-44
HARTING. Ornithology of Shakespeare. 1871......822.3 393
HAZLITT, W. Literature of the age of Elizabeth, and characters of Shakespeare's plays. 1877......822.3 103

‡ For reference.

Shakespeare.—Continued.

HAZLITT, W. C., ed. Shakespeare jest books. 1864. 3 v. ...828.2 1
HEARD. Shakespeare as a lawyer. '83...822.3 215
HEINE. Shakespeare heroines. 1895....822.3 394
Shakespeare's maidens and women..*in* 830 281
HENSLOW (*theatrical manager in time of Shakespeare*). Diary. ...792 35
HERAUD. Shakspere: his inner life. ...822.3 79
HEYWOOD. Apology for actors. (Shakespeare society, 1841.)...175 1
Fair maid of the exchange. (Shakespeare society, 1845.)...822.2 88
Fair maid of the west: (Shakespeare society, 1850.)...822.2 86
Golden and silver ages. (Shakespeare society, 1851.)...822.2 89
King Edward IV. (Shakespeare society, 1842.)...822.2 87
Royal king and loyal subject.—Woman killed with kindness. (Shakespeare society, 1850.)...822.2 85
Two plays on life of Queen Elizabeth. (Shakespeare society, 1851.)...822.2 84
HOLINSHED. Shakspere's Holinshed: the chronicle and historical plays compared; by Stone. 1896...822.3 B-38
HOLMES. Authorship of Shakespeare. 1866. ...822.3 10
HUDSON. Lectures on Shakespeare. 1857. 2 v. ...822.3 153
Same. 1848. 2 v. ...822.3 153A
HUGO. William Shakespeare; tr. 1864...822.3 130
HUNTER, J. New illustrations of life of Shakespeare. 1845. 2 v. ...822.3 5
HUNTER, R. E. Shakespeare and Stratford. 1864. ...822.3 319
INGLEBY. Shakespeare's centurie of prayse. (New Shakespeare society, 1879.)..822.3 B-6
INGLEBY, ed. Shakspere allusion books, pt. 1. (New Shakespeare society, 1874.)...822.3 164
Shakespeare and the enclosure of common fields at Welcombe; fragment of diary of Thomas Green, town clerk of Stratford-upon-Avon, 1614-17...822.3 R-2
IRELAND. Confessions. 1805...822.3 149
IRVING *et al*. Shakespeare's home. 1877..822.3 39
JACKSON. Shakespeare's genius justified. 1819...822.3 73
JAMESON. Characteristics of women. 2v..822.3 84
JEPHSON. Shakespere: birthplace, home and grave. 1864...822.3 320
JERVIS. Dictionary of the language of Shakespeare. 1868...‡822.3 B-7
JOHN a Kent and John a Cumber; ed. by Collier. (Shakespeare society, '51.) ...822.2 92

KEIGHTLEY. Shakespeare expositor. 1867..822.3 86
KELLOGG. Psychological delineations of Shakespeare: Ophelia, etc. 1864. ...822.3 Pam. 4
Same : his suicides...822.3 Pam. 5
KEMBLE, F. A. Notes on some of the plays of Shakespeare. 1882...822.3 209
KEMBLE, J. P. Macbeth and Richard III. 1817...822.3 133
KENNY. Life and genius of Shakespeare. 1864...822.3 4
KNIGHT. Studies in Shakespeare. 1868....822.3 99
LAMB. Tales from Shakespeare...*824.2 311
Same...*822.3 93
Same...820.2 491
LANDOR. Citation and examination of William Shakespeare before Sir Thomas Lucy...*in* 820.2 148
LEE. Stratford-on-Avon. 1890...914.2 174
LEO. Shakespeare notes. 1885...822.3 318
LEWES. Women of Shakespeare. 1895..822.3 390
LODGE. Defense of poetry, etc. (Shakespeare society, 1853.)...175 2
LOWELL. Essay on Shakespeare....*in* 824.1 184
MALONE. Inquiry into the [Ireland forgeries.] 1796...822.3 152
MARTIN. Shakespeare or Bacon? 1888..822.3 351
MORGAN, A. The Shakespeare myth. '81..822.3 197
MORGAN, H. H. Topical Shakespeariana. 1879...822.3 142
MORGANN, M. Dramatic character of Falstaff. 1777...822.3 11
MONTAGU. Essay on the writings and genius of Shakespear. 1777...822.3 62
Same. 1810...822.3 62A
MORAL play: Wit and science, etc.; ed. by Halliwell. (Shakespeare society, '48). ...822.2 74
MOULTON. Shakespeare as a dramatic artist. 1885...822.3 195
MOYES. Medicine, etc., in Shakespeare. 1896...822.3 13
NASH. Pierce Penniless's supplication. (Shakespeare society, 1842.)...822.2 77
NAYLOR. Shakespeare and music. 1896..822.3 206
NEW Shakespeare society. Transactions, 1874-9. 3 v...822.3 163
NEW exegesis of Shakespeare. 1859...822.3 67
NICHOLSON. No cipher in Shakespeare. 1888...822.3 358
NORTON *and* SACKVILLE. Gorboduc. (Shakespeare society, 1847.)...822.2 78
O'CONNOR. Mr. Donnelly's reviewers. 1889...822.3 Pam. 19
OWEN. Bacon's cipher story. 1893...822.3 384
PAGET. Shakespeare's plays: stage history. 1875...822.3 Pam. 7

* Of interest to young readers.   ‡ For reference.

Shakespeare.—Continued.

PATTERSON. Insects mentioned in Shakespeare...595 39
PHOTOGRAPHIC reproduction of Shakespeare's will, 1864........................822.3 135
PRATT. Stories from Shakespeare. 1890-5.
   V. 1. Macbeth. — Hamlet.— Othello. — Cymbeline.—Julius Cæsar................................*822.3 365
   V. 2. Timon of Athens.—King Lear.—Merchaut of Venice.—Much ado about nothing.—Tempest.—Midsummer night's dream.—Romeo and Juliet.
   ....*822.3 366
   V. 3. King John.—Richard II.— Henry IV.—Henry V.—Henry VI.—Richard III.—Henry VIII.
   ....*822.3 367
PRICE. Wisdom and genius of Shakespeare. 1838...822.3 61
PYE. Comments on the commentators on Shakespeare. 1807......................822.3 72
REES. Shakespeare and the Bible. '76.....822.3 90
RICHARDSON. Analysis of Shakespeare's characters. 1808........................822.3 368
ROFFE. Handbook of Shakespeare music.
   ....822.3 150
ROLFE. Shakespeare the boy. 1896......822.3 207
ROSSI *and* CORBOULD. Side-lights on Shakspere. 1897.............................822.3 66
RUGGLES. Method of Shakespeare as an artist. 1870...822.3 87
   Plays of Shakespeare founded on literary forms. 1895............................822.3 391
RUSHTON. Shakespeare an archer. '97...822.3 157
SEAGER. Natural history in Shakespeare's time. 1896...822.3 317
SEYMOUR. Remarks on the plays of Shakespeare. 1805. 2 v.............................822.3 59
SHAKESPEARE - BACON question: List of books on. (Boston public library bulletin, v. 5.)..17 B-14
   Same; bibliographical history. (Harvard university bulletin, v. 2, p. 156.)
   ....16 B-17
SHAKESPEARE library and museum in Henley street; catalogue, 1868............822.3 127
SHAKESPEARE society. Papers, 1844-9. 4 v.
   ....822.3 50
SIMPSON, *ed.* School of Shakespeare. 1878. 2 v. 822.3 100
SIMROCK. On the plots of Shakespeare's plays; ed. by Halliwell. (Shakespeare society, 1850.)..................................822.3 58
SIR Thomas More: a play; ed. by Dyce. (Shakespeare society, 1844.)...........822.2 90
SKOTTOWE. Life of Shakespeare. 1824. 2 v. 822.3 1
SMITH, W. H. Bacon and Shakespeare.822.3 134
SNIDER. System of Shakespeare's dramas. 1877. 2 v...822.3 143

STAFFORD. Briefe conceipt of English pollicy; ed. by Furnivall. (New Shakespeare society, 1876.)..........942.3 B-45
STAPFER. Shakespeare and classical antiquity..822.3 188
STEARNS. Medical knowledge of Shakespeare..822.3 137
STOKES. Chronological order of the plays of Shakespeare. 1878..................822.3 140
STRINGER, *ed.* Shakespeare's draughts from the living water. 1883.......‡822.3 B-37
STUBBES. Anatomy of abuses in England; ed. by Furnivall. (New Shakespeare society, 1879.)......................................394 B-8
SWINBURNE. A study of Shakespeare...822.3 155
SYMONDS. Shakespeare's predecessors in English drama. 1884......................822.2 253
TARLTON. Jests, etc.; ed. by Halliwell. (Shakespeare society, 1844.).............828.2 4
TELL-TROTHES new years' gift, etc.; ed. by Furnivall. (New Shakespeare society, 1876.)..173 B-1
TEN BRINK. Five lectures on Shakespeare. 1895...822.3 389
THACHER. Charlecote; or, The trial of William Shakespere. 1895..............822.3 208
THORPE. Hidden lives of Shakespeare and Bacon. 1897..822.3 196
UDALL. Ralph Roister Doister. (Shakespeare society, 1847.)......................822.2 78
ULRICI. Shakespeare's dramatic art. '46..822.3 56
VAUGHAN. New readings and new renderings of Shakespeare's tragedies. 1886. 3 v. 822.3 189
VICTORY. Higher teaching of Shakespeare. 1896...822.3 369
WARD, H. S. *and* C. W. Shakespeare's town and times. 1896......................822.3 385
WARD, *Rev.* J. Diary, 1648-79................822.3 131
WARNER, B. E. English history in Shakespeare's plays. 1894..........................822.3 388
WARNER, C. D. People for whom Shakespeare wrote..822.3 193
WATERS. Shakespeare portrayed by himself. 1888..822.3 349
WEISS. Wit, humor and Shakespeare......822.3 88
WENDELL. William Shakspere: a study in Elizabethan literature. 1894.........822.3 387
WHEELER. Historical account of birthplace of Shakespeare................................822.3 Pam. 3
WHITE. Shakespeare's scholar. 1854.....822.3 82
   Studies in Shakespeare. 1886............822.3 321
WILKES. Shakespeare from an American point of view. 1877..........................822.3 83
WILLIAMS. Shakespeare novels..................14103
   Contents: Secret passion.- Youth of Shakespeare. Shakespeare and his friends.

---
* Of interest to young readers.   ‡ For reference.

Shakespeare.—Continued.

WILSON. Caliban: the missing link, 1873..822.3 192
WINGATE. Shakespeare's heroines on the stage. 1895......792 68
WINSOR. Bibliography of earlier editions of poems......16 B-16
WINSOR, *ed.* Was Shakespeare Shapleigh? 1887......822.3 343
WORDSWORTH. Shakespeare's knowledge and use of the Bible. 1880......822.3 160
WYMAN. Bibliography of the Bacon-Shakespeare controversy. 1884......822.3 218

Shand. Fortune's wheel......69214
Sharkey. Mate to mate......56851
Sharp, Evelyn. At the Relton Arms......32240
Wymps, etc.......032280
Sharp, William. Children of to-morrow...69507
Gypsy Christ, etc.......69508
Contents: Gypsy Christ.—Madge o' the pool.—Coward.—Venetian idyl.—Graven image.—Lady in Hosea.—Fröken Bergliot.
Wives in exile......69509
Sharp, William *and* **Howard, B. W.**
Fellowe and his wife......28106
Sharpe, William. The conqueror's dream, and other poems. 1879......821.2 546
Humanity and the man: poem. 1878..821.2 550
Shattuck. Keeper of the salamander's order......042301
Shaw, C. Poems. 1822......*in* 821.2 46
Shaw, E. R. Legends of Fire island beach......42001
Shaw, F. L. Castle Blair......029902
Colonel Cheswick's campaign......21301
Hector......029905
Phyllis Browne......029901
Sea change......029903
Shaw, G. B. Cashel Byron's profession......69280
Shaw, H. W. See **Billings, Josh.**
Shaw, M. Queen Bess......69116
Shaw, W. J. Solomon's story......56868
Sheelah, *pseud.* See **Fletcher, A.**
Sheffield, *duke of Buckingham.* Works. 1723. 2 v......820.2 B-4
Sheil. Bellamira.—The apostate. (Dramas.) 1818......822.2 143
Sheldon, Mrs. George. Brownie's triumph......62532
Forsaken bride......62533
Sheldon, James. Oration, Eden, July 4, 1865......S25.1 Pam. 7
Shelley, Mary W. Beautiful widow......48301
Frankenstein......48302
Tales and stories......48304
Shelley, P. B. Favorite poems. '81...*in* 821.2 238
Lexical concordance; by Ellis. 1892.
......‡821.2 B-19

Poems; sel. by Garnett. 1880......821.2 239
Poetical works; ed. by Mrs. Shelley..821.2 241
Contents: Queen Mab.—Alastor.—Revolt of Islam. Prometheus unbound.—The Cenci. Hellas. Œdipus tyrannus.—Miscellaneous poems.
Poetical works; ed. by Rossetti. '70. 2 v.
V. 1. Prefaces. Memoir by Rossetti. Queen Mab.—Alastor.—Revolt of Islam. Rosalind and Helen.—Julian and Maddalo. Prometheus unbound.—The Cenci.—Notes......821.2 242
V. 2. Peter Bell the third.—Œdipus tyrannus.—The witch of Atlas.—Epipsychidion. Adonais.—Hellas. — Miscellaneous poems. — Fragments. — Translations......821.2 243
Poetical works; ed. by Dowden. '90. 821.2 240
Prose works; ed. by Forman. 1880. 4 v.
V. 1. Preface.—Pedigree.—Zastrozzi; a romance.—St. Irvyne. — Necessity of atheism. — Address to Irish people.—Proposals for an association.—Declaration of rights.—Letter to Lord Ellenborough......820.2 192
V. 2. Vindication of a natural diet.—Refutation of deism.—Proposal for putting reform to the vote.—On the death of the Princess Charlotte.—History of a six week's tour; Journal and letters of Mrs. Shelley.—Journal at Geneva.—The assassins.—On the punishment of death.—On life.—On love.—On a future state.—Speculations on metaphysics and morals.—A system of govt. by juries.—On reform.—On the revival of literature.—On Christianity.—The elysian fields.—On the devil and devils.—On friendship......820.2 193
V. 3. Remarks on Mandeville, on Frankenstein, and on Rhododaphne.—The Coliseum; a fragment.—Notes on sculptures, etc.—A fable.—Defence of poetry.— Fragments on beauty.— Translations.—Letters......820.2 194
V. 4. Letters......820.2 195

Selections from; ed. by Ellis. 1896.
......*in* 821.2 1025
Shelton, F. W. Peeps from the belfry......20462
Rector of St. Bardolph's......20463
The trollopiad. 1837......827.1 22
Up the river (essays). 1853......824.1 14
Shelton, W. H. Man without a memory, etc.......61420
Contents: Man without a memory.—Wedding journey of Mrs. Zaintree (born Greenleaf).—Uncle Obadiah's Uncle Billy.—Missing evidence in The people vs. Dangerking.—The demented ones.—Horses that responded.—Lights out! 'Liz'beth Rachel.—Widow of the general.—Adventures of certain prisoners.
Shenstone. Poems; with life......821.2 34
Poetical works; with life. 1868......821.2 528
Sheppard. Charles Auchester......30447
Counterparts......30448
My first season......30450
Rumor......30449
Sherer, J. W. Alice of the inn......70001
Sheridan. Bon-mots; ed. by Jerrold. '93..829.2 66
Dramatic works. 1864......822.2 240
Contents: Rivals.—Saint Patrick's day.—The duenna—School for scandal.—The critic.—Trip to Scarborough—Pizarro.

‡ For reference.

Rivals.—School for scandal. 1879...822.2 238
Same; ed. by Morley. 1886..........822.2 239
School for scandal.—The rivals; introduction by Birrell. 1896..........822.2 238A
Speeches. 1842. 3 v..........................329.2 18
Sherman. Little-folk lyrics. 1892......*821.1 451
Lyrics for a lute. 1890,...................821.1 425
Madrigals and catches. 1888..........821.1 410
Sherwood, J. D. Comic history of U. S. 1870..828.1 25
Sherwood, Margaret, (Elizabeth Hastings, *pseud.*). Experiment in altruism..15670
Puritan Bohemia.............................15671
Sherwood, Mary E. W. Sarcasm of destiny 22160
Transplanted Rose..........................22161
Sweet-brier......................................06201
Sherwood, *Mrs.* Mary M. History of John Martin.....................................20488
Indian pilgrim..................................20489
Social tales......................................0410
Shiel. Prince Zaleski.....................53350
Shillaber (Mrs. Partington, *pseud.*). Cruises with Captain Bob...................023901
Double runner club........................023903
Ike Partington.................................023902
Partingtonian patchwork. 1873.........828.1 10
Shipley. Desolate shore................032201
Shipton, Helen. Cairnforth and sons.......21041
The Herons.....................................21040
Shipton, H., *and* Coleridge, C. R. Ravenstone..66909
Shirley, *pseud.* See **Skelton, John.**
Shirley, J. Dramatic works and poems. 1833. 6 v.
V. 1. Love tricks.—Maid's revenge.—Brothers.—Witty fair one.—The wedding............822.2 109
V. 2. Grateful servant.—Traitor.—Love's cruelty.—Love in a maze.—Bird in a cage.—Hyde Park..822.2 110
V. 3. The ball.—Young admiral.—Gamester.—The example.—The opportunity.—Coronation...822.2 111
V. 4. Lady of pleasure.—Royal master.—Duke's mistress.—Doubtful heir.—Saint Patrick for Ireland.—Constant maid.—Humorous courtier......822.2 112
V. 5. Gentleman of Venice.—The politician.—The imposture.—The cardinal.—Sisters.—Court secret..822.2 113
V. 6. Honoria and Mammon.—Chabot.—Arcadia.—Triumph of peace.—Contention for honour and riches.—Triumph of beauty.—Cupid and death.—Contention of Ajax and Ulysses.—Poems
....822.2 114
Shirley, Penn, *pseud.* Little Miss Weezy...032234
Shoreham. Poems.........................821.2 471
Shorthouse. Blanche, Lady Falaise.........65910
Countess Eve..................................65909
John Inglesant................................65901
Little schoolmaster Mark................65906
Sir Percival.....................................65907
Teacher of the violin, etc................65908

Sidney, E. W. Partisan leader............47222
Sidney, Margaret, *pseud.* (*Mrs.* H. M. Lothrop.) Adirondack cabin..........027609
Five little Peppers...........................027601
Five little Peppers grown up..........027611
Five little Peppers midway............027608
Gingham bag...................................027613
Golden west....................................027604
How they went to Europe..............027603
Little red shop................................027607
New departure for girls.................027605
Old town pump..............................027612
Our town..66202
Pettibone name..............................66201
Rob..027610
Saint George and the dragon........027606
What the seven did........................027602
Sidney, Sir P. Apologie for poetrie.....820.2 27
Complete poems. 1877. 3 v.
V. 1. Memorial introduction; by Grosart.—Astrophel and Stella.—Songs in same.......821.2 513
V. 2-3. Sidera.—Pansies from Penshurst and Wilton.—From the Countess of Pembroke's Arcadia.—Psalmes of David.—Longer notes.—Indexes.
....821.2 514
Countess of Pembroke's Arcadia; ed. Friswell. 1867.................................823 82
Lyric poems; ed. by Rhys. 1895......821.2 997
Miscellaneous works; ed. by Gray...821.2 139
Contents: Life.—Defence of poesy.—Astrophel and Stella.—Miscellaneous poems.—Lady of May.—Letter to Queen Elizabeth.—Defence of Leicester.—Letters.
Psalter (Rock honeycomb; by Ruskin). 1877...245 18
Siegvolk, Paul, (Albert Mathews). A bundle of papers. 1879..........824.1 143
Signal lights...................................50317
Sigourney. Lucy Howard's journal.........30411
Myrtis, etc.......................................30412
Past meridian. 1854.......................824.1 34
Pocahontas, and other poems. 1864....821.1 35
Sayings of the little ones; and Poems for their mothers. 1855..............821.1 212
Sikes, *Mrs.* Olive L. See **Logan, Olive.**
Sill. Hermitage, and later poems. 1890..821.1 412
Poems. 1892....................................821.1 452
Silliman. Gallop among American scenery.
....824.1 166
Silvervale. Orphan of the Old Dominion..47219
Simcox. Lives of men, etc...............62566
Sime. King Capital...........................69144
Red route...69145
Simms. Beauchampe..........................5512
Border beagles................................5518
Charlemont.....................................5510
Confession......................................5505
Egeria: thought and counsel. 1853......829.1 6
Eutaw..5529
Forayers..5507

* Of interest to young readers.

Katharine Walton................................5522
Lily and the totem................................5526
Mellichampe.......................................5502
The partisan......................................5521
Poems, 1853, 2 v..........................821.1 38
Richard Hurdis...................................5516
Scout 5525
Southward ho !...................................5514
Vasconselos 5508
Views and reviews, 1845,..............824.1 31
Wigwam and the cabin, etc..................5523
Woodcraft...5520
The Yemassee....................................5503

Simpson. Introduction to philosophy of Shakespeare's sonnets, 1868........822.3 104
Simpson, *ed.* The school of Shakspere, 1878, 2 v..............................822.3 100
Simrock *and* **Halliwell.** Plots of Shakespeare's plays, 1850..................822.3 58
Sims. Tinkletop's crime, etc,..............19510
Sinclair, Catherine. Flirtations in fashionable life..20469
Modern accomplishments......................20470
Modern society...................................20468
Sinclair, R. Island story,....................35735
Sinnett. Karma.................................37701
Sir Thomas More : a play ; ed. by Dyce...822.2 90
Sisters of Orleans 50375
Sitwell. Two friends..........................032219
Six thousand tons of gold...................55401
Skelton, John, (*15th century*). Poetical works, 1843, 2 v......................821.2 112
Harmony of birds [attributed to Skelton]..821.2 450
Skelton, John, (Shirley). Crookit Meg....61801
Essays, 1883..............................824.2 344
Skene. Strange inheritance..................69287
Skertchly. Sport in Ashanti..................70060
Skinner. Nature in a city yard, '97......504 143
Skrine. Joan the maid (drama), 1895...822.2 327
Sladen. Japanese marriage...................31180
Sleeper, J. S. Mark Rowland...............25862
Sleeper, M. G. Fonthill recreations, 4 v..018001
Sleight. House at Crague....................69217
Slip in the fens.................................55210
Slosson, Anna Malann........................179 7
Aunt Liefy..47504
Fishin' Jimmy.....................................47501
Same..*in* 47502
Heresy of Mehetabel Clark....................47503
Seven dreamers...................................47502
Contents: How Faith came and went.—Botany Bay.—Aunt Randy.—Fishin' Jimmy.—Butterneggs—Deacon Pheby's selfish natur.—A speakin' ghost.
Smart. Belles and ringers,..................26505
Courtship in 1720 and 1860...................26501
False start...26508
Great tontine......................................26506

Long odds..26509
Play or pay..26504
Struck down......................................26507
Smeaton. By adverse winds................15750
Smedley. Colville family....................8307
Frank Fairleigh...................................8310
Harry Coverdale's courtship..................8305
Lewis Arundel....................................8304
Lorimer Littlegood..............................8308
Tom Racquet......................................8301
Smiles. Self-help, 1872.......................3741
Smith, Agnes. Brides of Ardmore........62359
Smith, Albert. Adventures of Mr. Ledbury...12011
Fortunes of the Scattergood family........12013
Pottleton legacy.................................12012
Struggles and adventures of Christopher Tadpole..12010
Smith, Alexander. Alfred Hagart's household...19180
City poems, 1857.........................821.2 324
Dreamthorpe: essays, 1863...........824.2 179
Edwin of Deira, 1861....................821.2 325
Miss Oona McQuarrie..........................19179
Poems, 1853................................821.2 323
Smith, *Mrs.* **Burnett.** See Swan, Annie S.
Smith, Constance. Cumberer of the ground..30110
Smith, D. M. Tales of chivalry and romance..040701
Smith, Edmund. Poems ; with life. 1822. ....821.2 47
Smith, *Mrs.* **Elizabeth O.** Hugo..........30444
Smith, F. Hopkinson. Colonel Carter of Cartersville................................25901
Day at Laguerre's, etc.........................25902
Contents: A day at Laguerre's.—Espero Gorgoni, gondolier.—Under the minarets.—Escapade in Cordova.—La canal de la Viga.—Bulgarian opera bouffe.—Captain Joe.—Hutchins.—Six hours in Squantico.
Gentleman vagabond, etc......................25903
Contents: Gentleman vagabond.—Knight of the Legion of honor.—John Sanders, laborer.—Bäader.—Lady of Lucerne.—Jonathan.—Along the Bronx.—Another dog.—Brockway's hulk.
Tom Grogan.......................................25904
Smith, Fannie M. Peace Pelican.........51902
Smith, Francis S. Young Magdalen, and other poems........................821.1 48
Smith, G. B. Poets and novelists. 1876..824.2 230
Smith, Gertrude. Arabella and Araminta stories..035601
Dedora Heywood..................................47702
Rousing of Mrs. Potter, etc....................47701
Contents: Rousing of Mrs. Potter.—A lone old woman.—Weighed in the balance.—A theft condoned.—A hope deferred.—On Pawnee prairie.—Colonel Paddington's nurse.—Dan's little girl.—An only son.—At the spring.—Gazdi.

Smith, Goldwin. Guesses at the riddle
of existence. 1897....................210 35
　Contents: Guesses at the riddle of existence.—The
　church and the Old Testament.— Is there another life?—
　The miraculous element in Christianity.— Morality and
　theism.
Smith, Horace. Adam Brown..............12015
　Arthur Arundel......................12017
　Love................................12016
　Mesmerism...........................12016
　Zillah..............................12014
Smith, Horace *and* James. Rejected
　addresses. 1848..............828.2 31
　Same ; and other poems. 1866.....821.2 327
Smith, J. Emerson. Oakridge.............47247
Smith, *Mrs.* J. Gregory. Atla..............69227
Smith, J. Hyatt. Open door........98.4 12
Smith, John H. Gilead.............98.4 10
Smith, Julie P. Blossom-bud..............4132
　Brazen gates.............................01501
　Chris and Otho...........................4107
　Courting and farming.....................4118
　His young wife...........................4115
　Kiss and be friends......................4127
　Lucy.....................................4136
　Married belle............................4108
　Ten old maids............................4110
　Widow Goldsmith's daughter...............4104
　Widower..................................4113
Smith, L. T., *ed.* York plays. 1885....822.2 102
Smith, Mary P. W. The Browns...........018347
　Great match.............................15007
　Jolly good summer.......................018346
　Jolly good times........................018348
　Jolly good times at Hackmatack..........018345
　Jolly good times at school..............018349
　Jolly good times to-day.................018350
　More good times at Hackmatack...........018351
　Their canoe trip........................018352
Smith, Samuel F. Poems of home and
　country, etc. 1895...................821.1 491
Smith, Saqui, *pseud.* Back from the dead..14735
Smith, Seba. See Downing, Jack.
Smith, Sidney. Bon-mots ; ed. by Jerrold.
　1893................................829.2 66, A
　Essays..................................824.2 219
　Contents: Doctor Parr. — Doctor Rennel. — John
　Bowles.- Doctor Langford. — Public characters, 1801-2.
　Archdeacon Nares. — Matthew Lewis. — Necker's last
　views.—Australia.—Fievée's letters on England.— Cey-
　lon.— Delphine.'— On the residence of the clergy.— Cat-
　teau, tableau des états Danois. - Wittman's travels.—
　Edgeworth on bulls. Sierra Leone. Trimmer and Lan-
　caster.—Parnell and Ireland.— Travels from Palestine.
　Methodism.—Indian missions. Curate's salary bill.—
　Catholics.— Society for suppression of vice. — Method-
　ism. Hannah More. — Characters of Fox.—Historical
　work of Fox. Professional education. Female edu-
　cation. Public schools. — Disturbances at Madras.—
　Toleration. -Charles Fox. - Bishop of Lincoln's charge.
　Letters written in a Mahratta camp, 1809.- Mad Quak-
　ers. — Madame D'Epinay.— America. — Game laws.—
　Botany Bay.—Chimney sweepers.—Mission to Ashantee.
　— America.—Poor laws.—Ireland.—Anastasius.—Spring-
　guns.—Prisons.—Man-traps and spring-guns.—Scarlett's
　poor bill.—Prisons.—Persecuting bishops.—Botany Bay.
　—Game laws. — Cruel treatment of untried prisoners.—
　America. — Captain Rock. — Bentham on fallacies.—
　Waterton. — Granby. — Hamilton's method of teaching
　languages.—Counsel for prisoners.—Catholics.
　Letters of Peter Plymley....................282 98
　Selections from writings. 1863........824.2 136
　Contents: Trimmer and Lancaster. — Professional
　education.— French education. — Public schools.—The
　ballot. — Letters on American debts. — Conduct of the
　understanding. — Wit and humour. — Taste. — Irish
　Roman Catholic church.—Catholics. — Letter on Catho-
　lic question.—Parnell on Ireland.— Ireland.— Memories
　of Captain Rock.—Letters to Archdeacon Singleton.
　Wit and wisdom of. 1869...............829.2 57
Smith, Sol. Theatrical apprenticeship......47264
　Theatrical journey work...................47265
Smith, *Rev.* Walter C. (Hermann Künst).
　Olrig grange (verse). 1872.........821.2 426
Smith, William. Gravenhurst...............216 11
　Thorndale................................211 79
Smith, William Hawley. Evolution of
　Dodd...................................69112
Smith, William Henry. Bacon and
　Shakespeare. 1857....................822.3 134
Smith, William L. G. Life at the south...41740
Smollett. Ferdinand, count Fathom...........505
　Humphrey Clinker..........................510
　Peregrine Pickle..........................501
　Poems ; with life. 1822..............821.2 38
　Roderick Random...........................509
　Sir Launcelot Greaves.....................507
　Works ; ed. by Browne. 8 v.
　V. 1. View of the progress of romance, and life
　of Smollett ; by J. Moore.— Plays and poems......820.2 235
　V. 2. Roderick Random,....................820.2 236
　V. 3-4. Peregrine Pickle..................820.2 237
　V. 5. Ferdinand, count Fathom.............820.2 239
　V. 6. Sir Launcelot Greaves.—Adventures of an
　atom......................................820.2 240
　V. 7. Humphrey Clinker....................820.2 241
　V. 8. Travels through France and Italy....820.2 242
Smythe. Poems, grave and gay. 1891....821.2 475
Smythies. Breach of promise..............*in* 14134
　Jilt..................................*in* 14134
Snaith. Fierceheart the soldier : romance
　of 1745...............................67081
　Mistress Dorothy Marvin...................67080
Snider. Agamemnon's daughter ; poem,
　1885..................................821.1 326
　System of Shakespeare's dramas. 2 v. 822 3 143
Snowden. Tales of the Yorkshire wolds...23820
Somerville. Poems ; with life. 1822.....821.2 50
Southard. Professional character and vir-
　tues of the late William Wirt. 1834.
　......................................*in* 825.1 17
Southey. All for love.—The pilgrim to
　Compostello. 1329..................821.2 237
　Common-place book. 1876. 4 v..........819 42

LANGUAGE AND LITERATURE.

Correspondence.............................928.2 287
Correspondence with Caroline Bowles..826.2 76
Doctor. 1874..................................824.2 90
Same. 1836....................................824.2 91
Essays, moral and political. '32. 2 v..824.2 164
Joan of Arc (poem). 1812. 2 v........821.2 232
Letters. 1887...................................928.2 541
Letters from Spain and Portugal. 2 v...914.6 78
Letters to the Beaumonts..................826.2 91
Madoc (poem). 1812. 2 v..............821.2 234
Poems; ed. by Dowden. 1895.........821.2 484
Poetical works. 1878. 10 v. in 5.
  V. 1-2. Memoir; by Tuckerman.--Joan of Arc. Notes.—Vision of the maid.—Notes.—Triumph of woman.—Wat Tyler.—Poems concerning the slave trade.— Botany Bay eclogues.— Sonnets.— Monodramas.—Amatory poems of Abel Shufflebottom.--Lyric poems.—Songs of the American Indians.—Occasional pieces.— The retrospect.—Hymn to the penates...................................821.2 485
  V. 3-4. English eclogues. — Nondescripts. — Devil's walk.—Inscriptions.—Carmen triumphale.—Odes.—Epistle to Cunningham.—Thalaba...821.2 486
  V. 5-6. Madoc.—Ballads and metrical tales..821.2 487
  V. 7-8. A tale of Paraguay.—All for love.—Pilgrim to Compostello.—Curse of Kehama..........821.2 488
  V. 9-10. Roderick, the last of the Goths.—Poet's pilgrimage to Waterloo. — Carmen nuptiale.— Funeral song for Princess Charlotte.—Vision of judgment.—Oliver Newman.—Miscellaneous.....821.2 489
Poet's pilgrimage to Waterloo. 1816..821.2 236
Roderick (poem). 1815. 2 v............821.2 228
Sir Thomas More: colloquies. '29. 2v..824.2 88
Thalaba (poem). 1814. 2 v............821.2 230
Translation of 'Amadis of Gaul.' 1872.
  3 v...863 7
Translation of the 'Chronicle of the Cid'..946 18
thwell. Poetical works. 1856........821.2 142
thworths. Inebriate's hut..................47260
lding, L. B. The ruined statues, and other poems. 1871....................821.1 193
lding, W. On Shakespeare's authorship of 'Two noble kinsmen,' etc..822.3 B-4
ngler. Physician's wife.........................25822
nish brothers.....................................55221
rhawk. Lazy's man's work...................34561
Senator Intrigue and Inspector Noseby...34560
ar. Address, Mechanics' apprentices' library association, Boston, 1855...in 825.1 17
dding. Reviews and discussions. 1879.
....824.2 273
ight. Barren title................................27513
Burg's romance....................................27511
Golden hoop..27514
Loudwater tragedy................................27510
Master of Trenance...............................27515
Secret of the sea..................................27512
ncer. Aphorisms; ed. by Gingell. '94..829.2 68
Essays. 1868..304 16
Same. 1868. 3 v...................................304 25

Spender, Emily. True marriage..........52208
Spender, H. At the sign of the guillotine..69680
Spender, Mrs. J. K. Jocelyn's mistake....30207
Thirteen doctors.....................................30206
Zina's awakening...................................30205
Spenser, E. And his poetry; by Craik.
  3 v..928.2 396
Colin Clout explained; by Hitchcock..821.2 138
Faerie queene.—Epithalamion..........821.2 136
Poetical works; ed. by Child. 5 v.
  V. 1-3. Faerie queene.....................821.2 1 1
  V. 4. Faerie queene (concluded). Shepheard's calendar.--Colin Clout.--Astrophel................821.2 131
  V. 5. Miscellanies................................821.2 15
Works; ed. by Collier. 1862. 5 v.
  V. 1. Life of Spenser.—Shepheard's calendar.—Faerie queene............................821.2 126
  V 2-3. Faerie queene (continued),............821.2 127
  V. 4. Faerie queene (concluded.)--Two cantos of 'Mutabilities.'—Miscellanies..............821.2 129
  V. 5. Miscellanies.—View of the state of Ireland...821.2 130
Spenser, M. C. Benefit of the doubt.......62306
Brinka...62305
Sperry. Country love. 1865..............821.1 511
Spielman. History of 'Punch.' 1895....827.2 45
Spinner. Lucilla.................................70902
Reluctant evangelist, etc........................70901
Spofford, Mrs. H. P. Amber gods, etc....18801
Ballads about authors. 1887............821.1 476
Hester Stanley at St. Mark's. 029401
In Titian's garden, and other poems. 1897..821.1 337
An inheritance....................................18807
Lost jewel...029402
Marquis of Carabas..............................18804
Master spirit......................................18806
New England legends. 1871..............829.1 19
  Contents: True account of Captain Kidd.—Charlestown.—Salem.—Newburyport.—Dover.—Portsmouth.
Poems. 1882..................................821.1 270
Scarlet poppy, etc................................18805
  Contents: A scarlet poppy.— Best-laid schemes.—An ideal.—Mrs. Claxton's skeleton.—The tragic story of Binns.—The composite wife.—Mr. Van Nore's daughter-in-law.
Sir Rohan's ghost................................18802
Thief in the night................................18803
Sprague, Charles. Curiosity; poem. 1829...821.1 Pam. 5
Poetical and prose writings. 1850......821.1 40
Sprague, M. A. Earnest trifler..............59306
Sprague, O. I. Oration, July 4, 1854,
Java, N. Y.................................825.1 Pam. 3
Spring. Address, New York mercantile library association...............................40 27
Spurr. Land of gold..........................62546
Square, A, *pseud.* See **Abbott, E. A.**
Stables. Cruise of the Snowbird............030501
For life and liberty...............................030506
From squire to squatter.........................030503

How Jack Mackensie won his epaulettes..030507
Pearl divers and Crusoes of the Sargasso sea...........030508
To Greenland and the pole..........030505
Westward with Columbus........030504
Wild adventures round the pole...........030502
Stacpoole. Intended.........................25150
Stafford. Broken bonds.........................69222
Stanley, A. P., *dean.* Addresses, etc., 1872-7.........................252 45
Essays, church and state, etc. 1850 70..204 65
(For contents, see Part 3 of FINDING LIST, p. 452.)
In the U. S. and Canada. 1878............204 76
Thoughts that breathe (selections). '79..204 82
Stanley, H. My Kalulu....................05601
Stanley, Jane. Daughter of the gods.......69257
Stanley of Alderley, M. J. Holroyd, *lady*.
Girlhood, recorded in letters, 1776-96. 1897.........................826.2 102
Stannard. See **Winter, J. S.,** *pseud.*
Stapfer. Shakespeare and classical antiquity. 1880.........................822.3 188
Stapleton, S., *pseud.* See **Monti.**
Starkey. Dialogue on the condition of England, reign of Henry VIII ; pt. 1.
.........................820.2 425
Same ; pt. 2.........................820.2 408
State triumvirate. 1819.........................827.1 41
Stearns, A. Chris and the wonderful lamp.........................032350
Sindbad, Smith & Co.........................032351
Stearns, F. P. Real and ideal in literature. 1892.........................824.1 285
Contents. Sonnet: J. G. W.—Real and ideal.—Classic and romantic.— Romance, humor and realism.—The modern novel.- Idols:—Poem, F. W. L.—Fred W. Loring. The art conscience.— Herman Grimm.— Sonnet: R. W. E.— Emerson as a poet.— A poetic autobiography.—The Muller and Whitney controversy.— Science of thought.
Stearns, W. A. Wrecked on Labrador......69449
Stebbing. Among the Carbonari............032222
Stebbins. Annals of a baby....................50306
Stedman. Blameless prince, etc. 1869..821.1 135
Hawthorne, and other poems. 1877..821.1 136
Poetical works. 1873.........................821.1 134
Poetical works. 1884.........................821.1 134A
Contents: Early poems.—Sonnets.—Poems written in youth.— Alice of Monmouth.— Miscellaneous poems.— Translation. The blameless prince, etc.— Miscellaneous poems.— Occasional poems.— Translations.— Later poems.—L'envoi.
Poets of America.........................824.1 211
Contents. Early and recent conditions. — Growth of the American school. Bryant.- Whittier.— Emerson. Longfellow. Poe. Holmes. Lowell.—Whitman.— Bayard Taylor. The outlook.
Victorian poets. 1876.........................821.1 213
Contents. The period — Landor. Hood; Matthew Arnold· Procter, Mrs. Browning. Tennyson and Theocritus. The general choir.—Robert Browning.—Buchanan, Rossetti; Morris. Swinburne.—Index.

Steel, *Mrs.* **F. A.** Flower of forgiveness....33625
From the five rivers.........................33620
In the tideway.........................33626
Miss Stuart's legacy.........................33621
On the face of the waters.........................33624
Potter's thumb.........................33622
Red rowans.........................33623
Steele, Anna C. Clove pink.........................35205
Lesbia.........................35206
So runs the world away.........................35207
Steele, J. W. Frontier army sketches...824 1 177
Steele, *Mrs.* **L. A. B.** Reverend Adonijah...56871
Steele, *Sir* **Richard,** (Isaac Bickerstaff).
Correspondence. 1809.........................826.2 50
Guardian. 1793.........................*in* 824.2 53
Plays ; ed. by Aitken. 1894.........................822.2 315
Contents: Steele.—The funeral. — The lying lover.— The tender husband. — The conscious lovers. — The school of action.—The gentleman.
Steele, *Sir* **Richard,** *and* **Addison.** See **Addison** *and* **Steele.**
Steell, W. Isidra.........................69385
Steggall. Jeanne d'Arc, etc. (poems). 1868.........................821.2 416
Stephen, *Sir* **G.** Adventures of an attorney.........................44186
Stephen, James. Critical and miscellaneous essays. 1843.........................824.2 67
Contents: Wilberforce. -- Whitfield and Froude.— D'Aubigne's 'History of the great reformation.'--Life and time of Richard Baxter. — Physical theory of another life.—The Port Royalists.—Loyola.—Taylor's 'Edwin the Fair.'
Stephen, *Sir* **J. F.** Horæ Sabbaticæ. 1892. 2 v.
V. 1. Joinville and St. Louis. — Froissart's 'Chronicles'.—Philippe de Comines.—Montaigne's 'Essays',—Hooker's 'Ecclesiastical polity'.—Laud. —Chillingworth. —Liberty of prophesying.—Jeremy Taylor as a moralist.—Hacket's 'Life of Archbishop Williams.'--Clarendon's 'History of the Rebellion.' —Clarendon's 'Life'.........................824 2 441
V. 2. Hobbes on govt.—Hobbes' 'Leviathan.'— Hobbes' minor works.—Sovereignty.— Bossuet's 'Education of the dauphin.' — Bossuet and the Protestants. — Locke's ' Essay on the human understanding.' Locke as a moralist. Locke on govt.—Locke on toleration. — The scepticism of Bayle.—Mandeville. Voltaire as a theologian, moralist, and metaphysician.........................824.2 442
Stephen, L. Essays on free thinking, etc. 1877.........................204 58
History of English thought, 18th century. 2 v.........................192 85
Hours in a library. 1875. 3 v.
V. 1. De Foe's novels.—Richardson's novels.— Pope as a moralist. Elwin's 'Pope.'—Scott. - Hawthorne. · Balzac.—De Quincey.........................804.2 253
V. 2. Sir Thomas Browne.—Jonathan Edwards.— William Law. — Horace Walpole. Doctor Johnson's writings.—Crabbe's poetry. Hazlitt. Disraeli's novels.........................824.2 251

V. 3. Massinger.—Fielding's novels.—Cowper
and Rousseau.—First Edinburgh reviewers.—
Wordsworth's ethics.—Landor's imaginary conversations. Macaulay.—Charlotte Brontë.—Kingsley.
....824.2 255

Stephens, C. A. Camping out.................031532
Fox hunting...031531
Knockabout club alongshore..................031538
Knockabout club in the tropics..........*917.8 25
Knockabout club in the woods...............031537
Left on Labrador.....................................031530
Lynx hunting...031533
Off to the geysers.................................. 031534
On the Amazons.....................................031536
Young moose hunters.............................031539

Stephens, G. Dramas. 1846. 2 v.
V. 1. Nero.—Forgery.—Sensibility...............822.2 149
V. 2. Self-glorification.— Rebecca and her daughters.—Philip Basil..................................822.2 150

Stephens, R. Cruciform mark..................70120
Mr. Peters..70121

Stephenson, *Mrs.* E. See **Tabor, Eliza.**

Sterling. Essays and tales. 1848. 2 v.
V. 1. Memoir of Sterling; by Hare.—Shades of the dead: Alexander the great; Joan of Arc; Wycliffe; Columbus; Gustavus Adolphus; Milton; Burns.— On Coleridge's 'Christabel.'— On the broad stone of honour.—On Napier's 'War in the peninsula.'—Montaigne.—Simonides.—Carlyle.—Characteristics of German genius.— Tennyson's poems.—The worth of knowledge.............824.2 365
V. 2. Fragments from the travels of Theodore Elbert.—Thoughts.—Tales and apologues......824.2 366

Poems. 1839....................................821.2 751

Sterne, L. Sentimental journey.............823 87
Same..914.4 83
Story of my Uncle Toby......................30701
Tristram Shandy.................................30702
Same. 1883. 2 v................................823 96
Works. 1869....................................820.2 204
Contents: Tristram Shandy.— Sentimental journey.— Letters.—Sermons.

Works; ed. by Browne. 1873. 4 v.
V. 1. Preface.—Life of Sterne; by himself.—Tristram Shandy..820.2 200
V. 2. Tristram Shandy (continued). — Sentimental journey..820.2 201
V. 3. Sermons...820.2 202
V. 4. Sermons.—Letters.—History of a watchcoat...820.2 203

Sterne, Stuart, *pseud.* (Gertrude Bloede.)
Angelo: a poem. 1881.................821.1 263
Beyond the shadow, and other poems.
1888...821.1 374
Giorgio, and other poems. 1881......821.1 260
Piero da Castiglione. 1890.............821.1 420
Story of two lives..............................29444
Sterry, J. Ashby-. Tale of the Thames...54701
Steuart. In the day of battle................22770
Stevens. Old Boston........................69395
Stevenson, E. I. White cockades........69344

Stevenson, R. L. Across the plains, etc.
1892..824.2 443
Contents: Across the plains. The old Pacific capital.— Fontainebleau. Epilogue to 'An inland voyage.'— Random memories (continued) The lanternbearers. A chapter on dreams Beggars. Letter to a young gentleman. Pulvis et umbra. A Christmas sermon.

Ballads. 1890................................821.2 865
Child's garden of verses.............*821.2 743
Black arrow.................................67403
David Balfour..............................67412
Dynamiter...................................67411
Ebb tide.....................................67406
Fables. 1896.............................829.2 80
Familiar studies of men and books...824.2 318
Contents: Victor Hugo's romances. Some aspects of Burns.— Walt Whitman. Thoreau.— Yoshida Torajiro.— François Villon.—Charles of Orleans. Samuel Pepys.—John Knox and women.

Island nights' entertainments..........67405
Contents: Beach of Falesá.— Bottle imp.— Isle of voices.

Kidnapped.................................67417
Master of Ballantrae....................67410
Memories and portraits. 1887.......824.2 404
Contents: The foreigner at home.— Some college memories.—Old mortality.—College magazine.—An old Scotch gardener —Pastoral.— The manse.— Memoirs of an islet.—Thomas Stevenson.—Talk and talkers; first paper.— Tale and talkers; second paper.— Character of dogs.— A penny plain and twopence coloured.— A gossip on a novel of Dumas's.—A gossip on romance.— A humble remonstrance.

Merry men, etc..........................67402
Contents: Merry men.—Will o' the mill.—Markheim.—Thrawn Janet.—Olalla.—Treasure of Franchard.

New Arabian nights....................67401
Contents: The suicide club.—The rajah's diamond.— The pavilion on the links.— A lodging for the night.— The Sire de Maletroit's door.— Providence and the guitar.

Prince Otto..............................67414
Songs of travel. 1896..............821.2 818
Strange case of Dr. Jekyll and Mr. Hyde...67413
Treasure island........................67408
Underwoods (poems). 1887......821.2 819
Vailima letters. 1895. 2 v......826.2 118
Virginibus puerisque, etc. 1881....824.2 317
Contents: Virginibus puerisque.—Crabbed age and youth.—Apology for idlers.—Ordered south.—Es triplex.—El Dorado.—English admirals.—Some portraits by Raeburn.— Child's play.— Walking tours.— Pan's pipes.—Plea for gas lamps.

Weir of Hermiston....................67407
Works (Thistle edition). 1895. 21 v.
V. 1. New Arabian nights.........................820.2 155
V. 2. Treasure island..............................820.2 150
V. 3. More New Arabian nights.—The dynamiter.—The story of a lie..............................820.2 5
V. 4. Prince Otto.—Island nights' entertainments.
—Father Damien.....................................820.2 158
V. 5. Kidnapped....................................820.2 189
V. 6. David Balfour (sequel to v. 5).......... 82 2 15

* Of interest to young readers.

V. 7. The merry men, and other tales and fables.—Strange case of Dr. Jekyll and Mr. Hyde.
....820.2 161
V. 8. The black arrow.—The misadventures of John Nicholson.—The body snatcher..................820.2 162
V. 9. The master of Ballantrae.......................820.2 163
V. 10. The wrecker..820.2 164
V. 11. The wrong box.—The ebb tide...........820.2 165
V. 12. An inland voyage.—Travels with a donkey.—Edinburgh 820.2 166
V. 13. Virginibus puerisque. — Memories and portraits...820.2 167
V. 14. Familiar studies of men and books.—Miscellaneous papers....................................820.2 168
V. 15. The amateur emigrant. — Across the plains.—The Silverado squatters.................820.2 169
V. 16. A child's garden of verses.—Underwoods.
—Ballads..820.2 170
V. 17. Vailima letters...820.2 171
V. 18. Memoir of Fleeming Jenkin.—Records of a family of engineers....................................820.2 172
V. 19. In the South Seas.—A foot-note to history.
....820.2 173
V. 20. Weir of Hermiston.—The plays.—Fables.
....820.2 174
V. 21...820.2 175

Stevenson, R. L., and Henley, W. E.
 Macaire : farce. 1895..................822.2 328
Stevenson, R. L., and Osbourne, L.
 Wrecker...67404
 Wrong box..67409
Stewart, A. Fair Norwegian..................43040
Stewart, Charles. Harp of Strathnaver (verse)..821.2 Pam. 1
Stewart, C. E. Oliver Cromwell..........30432
Stewart, Miss E. M. Aubrey Conyers......47262
Stewart, Louisa. Wave and battlefield...03101
Stimson (J. S. of Dale). Crime of Henry Vane...16905
 First harvests..16904
 Guerndale...16901
 King Noanett..16907
 Pirate gold..16906
 Residuary legatee...................................16903
 Sentimental calendar...........................16902
Stirling, J. H. Burns in drama, etc. 1878.
 ....824.2 292
Stirling, M. C., (Mrs. McCallum). A true man...14157
Stockton, F. R. Adventures of Captain Horn..58018
 Amos Kilbright......................................58008
 Ardis Claverden....................................58012
 Bee-man of Orn, etc..........................024610
 Captain Chap.......................................024609
 Casting away of Mrs. Lecks and Mrs. Aleshine...58001
 Chosen few...58019
 Clocks of Rondaine, etc....................024608
 Dusantes..58007
 Floating prince, etc............................024604
 Great war syndicate............................58009
 House of Martha...................................58014
 Hundredth man....................................58005
 Jolly fellowship..................................024605
 Lady or the tiger?................................58003
 Late Mrs. Null......................................58006
 Merry Chanter......................................58011
 Mrs. Cliff's yacht.................................58020
 Pomona's travels................................. 58017
 Round-about rambles 829.1 20
 Rudder grange......................................58002
 Rudder grangers abroad, etc........58013
 Squirrel inn...58015
 Stories; 1st series...............................58003
  Contents: Lady or the tiger?—Transferred ghost.—Spectral mortgage.—Our archery club.—That same old 'coon. — His wife's deceased sister. — Our story.— Mr. Tolman.—On the training of parents.—Our fire-screen.—A piece of red calico.—Every man his own letter-writer.
 Stories; 2d series...............................58021
  Contents: The Christmas wreck.—Story of assisted fate.—An unhistoric page.—Tale of negative gravity.—The Cloverfields carriage.—Remarkable wreck of the Thomas Hyke.—My bull-calf.—Discourager of hesitancy. —A borrowed month.
 Story of Viteau..................................024606
 Story-teller's pack.............................58022
  Contents: The magic egg.— Staying power of Sir Rohan.—Widow's cruise.—Love before breakfast.—The bishop's bell.—The book of the bat.—Captain Eli's best ear.—As one woman to another.—My well and what came out of it.—Stephen Skarridge's Christmas.—My unwilling neighbor.
 Tales out of school..........................024602
 Three burglars......................................58010
 Ting-a-ling...024603
 Watchmaker's wife, etc....................58016
 What might have been expected....024607
Stockton, Louise. Apple seed and brier thorn..69349
Stoddard, C. W. South sea idyls...........19169
Stoddard, Mrs. E. Morgesons.................24622
 Poems. 1895......................................821.1 521
 Temple house..24621
 Two men..24620
Stoddard, R. H. Book of the east, etc. 1871..821.1 145
 Poems. 1852......................................821.1 143
 Poems, complete edition. 1880.......821.1 142
  Contents: Early poems. — Songs of summer. — The king's bell. — The book of the East. — Tartar songs.— Arab songs. — Chinese songs. — In memoriam. — Later poems.—Hymns of the mystics.
 Songs of summer. 1857..................821.1 144
 Under the evening lamp. 1892........824.1 272
  Contents: Scotch contemporaries of Burns. — James Hogg.—Motherwell. — Early years of Gifford. — Robert Bloomfield. — John Clare. - Ebenezer Elliott. — David Gray.—William Blake. — Hartley Coleridge. — Thomas Lovell Beddoes. — George Darley.— Thomas Love Peacock.—Edward Fitzgerald.—Lord Houghton.

Stoddard, W. O. Battle of New York......026007
    Captain's boat..................................026011
    Chumley's post [Red beauty]........60003A
    Crowded out o' Crofield................026010
    Dab Kinzer.....................................026001
    Heart of it...60001
    Little Smoke....................................026006
    On the old frontier..........................026008
    Quartet..026002
    Red beauty [Chumley's post]...............60003
    Red mustang...................................026005
    Swordmaker's son...........................026012
    Two Arrows....................................026004
    White cave......................................026009
    Winter fun.......................................026003
Stoker. Shoulder of Shasta......................27904
    Snake's pass.......................................27901
    Under the sunset.................................27902
    Watter's Mou'....................................27903
Stokes. Chronological order of Shakespeare's plays. 1878............822.3 140
Stone. Fair plebeian...................................15731
    Riddle of luck....................................15730
Stories for the home circle.......................50396
Storr *and* **Turner.** Canterbury chimes......018702
Story, Joseph. Miscellaneous writings. 1835..824.1 2
Story, W. W. Conversations in a studio. 1890. 2 v..................................824.1 249
    Excursions in art and letters. 1891...824.1 258
    Fiammetta...69192
    Graffiti d'Italia (verse). 1875...........821.1 248
    He and she; or, A poet's portfolio....821.1 302
    Nero: an historical play. 1875............822.1 13
    Poems. 1856.................................821.1 247
    Poet's portfolio; later readings. '94...821.1 303
Story of a demoiselle..................................58911
Story of a happy little girl.............................0102
Story of Cecil and his dog............................07159
Story of Rodman Heath; or, Mugwumps....69075
Story of wandering Willie............................55231
Story of White Rock cove............................07192
Stow. Secret of the Sierras..........821.1 Pam. 26
Stowe, *Mrs.* **H. B.,** (Christopher Crowquill, *pseud.*). Agnes of Sorrento........3618
    Betty's bright idea..................................3619
    Chimney corner (essays). 1868.......824.1 112
    Dog's mission..................................027503
    Dred [Nina Gordon]...............................3645
    House and home papers....................640 24
    Little foxes..3620
    Little Pussy Willow...........................027501
    May flower, and other tales....................3622
    Minister's wooing..................................3616
    My wife and I.......................................3605
    Nina Gordon [Dred]..............................3645
    Oldtown fireside stories.........................3638

    Oldtown folks.......................................3601
    Pearl of Orr's island..............................3617
    Pink and white tyranny.........................3614
    Poganuc people....................................3639
    Queer little people.............................027502
    Sam Lawson's Oldtown fireside stories...3638
    Stories and sketches for the young...027504
        Contents: Queer little people.—Little Pussy Willow The minister's watermelons. A dog's mission. Lulu's pupil.—The daisy's first winter. Our Charley and the stories told him.—Little Captain Trott. Christmas. Little Fred the canal boy.
    Uncle Tom's Cabin................................3625
        Key to same...............................326 50
    We and our neighbors...........................3611
Stowe, *Mrs.* **H. B.,** *et al.* Six of one by half a dozen of the other....................3624
Strachey. Talk at a country house. 1894.
    ....824.2 476
    Contents: The squire and his old manor place. Persian poetry.—The old hall and the portraits. A general election.—Love and marriage.—Books: Tennyson and Maurice.—Riding down to Camelot.—The arrowheaded inscriptions.—Taking leave.—Appendix: Introduction to 'The Bústán; or, Garden of Sa'di'; tr. from the Persian.
Strahan, *Mrs.* **L. G.** See **Séguin, L. G.**
Strain. Man's foes................................20260
Strangford. People and topics of the day.
    ....*in* 947X 13
Stratemeyer. Last cruise of the Spitfire...014205
    Richard Dare's venture.......................014208
Stratenus. Suspected...............................30569
Stratford-by-the-sea...............................16002
Strathesk. Bits from Blinkbonny................62565
    More bits from Blinkbonny...............62565A
Street, A. B. Frontenac: a metrical romance..821.1 350
    Poems. 1845..................................821.1 37
Street, G. S. Autobiography of a boy........15550
    Quales ego. 1896..........................824.2 489
    Contents: In particular: Mr. Meredith in little; An eulogy of Charles II; Robert Boyle; An appreciation of Ouida; A fancy portrait; In Arcady.—At large: The commonplace mood; The little soul; The day after; Two impressions; The impersonal view; To an afflicted friend; A superfluous label; Before a shrine; Under the moon.
    Wise and the wayward..........................15551
Stretton, Hesba, *pseud.* (Hannah *or* Sarah Smith.) Bede's charity.........................48001
    Carola..48008
    Cobwebs and cables............................48006
    David Lloyd's last will..........................48005
    Doctor's dilemma................................48011
    Half brothers.....................................48012
    Her only son......................................48010
    In prison and out................................48004
    Pilgrim street......................................48009
    Thorny path.......................................48003
    Through a needle's eye.......................48002

Stretton, Hesba, *et al.* Highway of sorrow..48013
Stretton, J. Margaret and her bridesmaids..24501
 Mr. and Mrs. Asheton............................24508
 Queen of the county................................24504
 Woman's devotion..................................24509
Strickland, Agnes. Stories from history..02902
 Tales from English history......................02901
Strickland, W. P. Astrologer of Chaldea..52246
Strike at Shane's..0145
Strike in the B— mill................................63435
Stringer. Leisure moments in Gough square..829.2 88
Stringer, *ed.* Shakespere's draughts from the living waters. 1883...............‡822.3 B-37
Strutt. Curate and the rector..................52258
Stuart, Eleanor. Stonepastures................60190
Stuart, Esmé. Arrested..........................60614
 Belfry of St. Jude..................................60602
 Carried off..05804
 Caught in a trap....................................60603
 Claudea's island....................................60611
 Goldmakers...05803
 Harum scarum......................................60613
 Inscrutable 60610
 Isabeau's hero.......................................60605
 Kestell of Greystone..............................60608
 Last hope...60607
 Lia..60606
 Little brown girl....................................05801
 Mine of wealth......................................60615
 Minnie...60601
 Vanda..60604
 Virginie's husband................................60609
 White chapel...05802
 Woman of forty.....................................60612
Stuart, M. B., (Grace Mortimer, *pseud.*).
 Two Barbaras..19178
Stuart, Ruth McE. Carlotta's intended....22706
 Contents: Carlotta's intended.— Bud Zunts's mail. Christmas geese.— Cæsar.— Aunt Delphi's dilemma.— Duke's Christmas.— Poems: Rose; Winnie; Voices.
 Golden wedding, etc............................22705
 Contents: Golden wedding.— Lamentations of Jeremiah Johnson. Uncle Mingo's speculations.— Widder Johnsing.— Christmas gifts.— Blink.— Jessekiah Brown's courtship.— Crazy Abe.— Queen Anne.— Camelia Riccardo.— Woman's exchange of Simpkinsville.— Oh, shoutin's mighty sweet.— Lucindy.
 In Simpkinsville...................................22708
 Contents: An Arkansas prophet.— Weeds.— Unlived life of little Mary Ellen.— Dividing-fence. Middle hall. — Miss Jemima's valentine.— A slender romance.
 Soloman Crow's Christmas pockets, etc..022711
 Sonny..22707
 Story of Babette....................................022710
Stumbler in wide shoes...........................52320
Sturges, J. First supper, etc...................35701
Sturgis, H. O. All that was possible......69065
 Tim..69064

Sturgis, J. Accomplished gentleman......58401
 Comedy of a country house....................58408
 Count Julian: a tragedy. 1893........822.2 308
 Dick's wanderings.................................58402
 Folly of Pen Harrington........................58404
 John Maidment.....................................58405
 Little comedies. 1880. ....822.2 210
 Master of fortune...................................58409
 My friends and I....................................58403
 Thraldom...58407
Such, Theophrastus. See Eliot, George.
Suckling. Poems, plays, etc. 2 v.
 V. 1. Life; by Suckling.— Poems.— Aglaura..821.2 510
 V. 2.— The goblins.— Tragedy of Brennoralt.— The sad one.— Letters.— Discourse of religion...821.2 511
Sullivan, *Sir* **E.** Tales from Scott..............994
Sullivan, J. F. Flame-flower, etc............57080
Sullivan, T. D. Poems....................821.2 422
Sullivan, T. R. Day and night stories. 2 v.
 V. 1 Lost Rembrandt.— Out of New England granite.— 'Cordon.'— Tincture of success.— Rock of Béranger.— Maestro Ambrogio.— Through the gate of dreams..16641
 V. 2. Clerk of the weather.— Toledo blade.— To her.— Anatomist of the heart.— Man in red.— Jack-in-the-box.— Under cover of the darkness....16641A
 Roses of shadow...................................16643
 Tom Sylvester.......................................16642
Summerland..50385
Sumner. Equal rights of all. 1866...329.1 Pam. 32
 Orations and speeches. 2 v.............825.1 12
 Prophetic voices concerning America. 1874..829.1 1
 Recent speeches. 1856....................825.1 14
 Works. 1875-83. 15 v.....................329.1 116
Surrey, *earl of.* Poetical works. 1831..821.2 144
 Same; ed. by Bell............................821.2 146
Surridge. Cyrus: a tale of the ten thousand..56601
 Songs and sonnets..........................820 2 36
Sutcliffe. XIth commandment..................70280
Swan, Annie S., (Mrs. Burnett Smith).
 Adam Hepburn's vow...........................10527
 Airlie's mission.....................................10524
 Aldersyde..10521
 Ayres of Studleigh................................10520
 Bitter debt...10523
 Doris Cheyne..10522
 Fettered, yet free...................................10525
 Gates of Eden.......................................10530
 Maitland of Laurieston.........................10528
 Memories of Margaret Grainger, schoolmistress..10526
 St. Veda's..10529
Swan, Maggie. Life's blindfold game......10340
Sweetser. In distance and in dream..........52410
Swett, Sophie. Captain Polly..................033201
 Cap'n Thistletop...................................033203
 Flying hill farm....................................033202

‡ For reference.

LANGUAGE AND LITERATURE.

Lollipops' vacation, etc....................033205
Pennyroyal and mint.......................33250
Ponkaty branch road, etc..................033204
Swift, A. M. Cupid, M. D................62594
Swift, J. Choice works. 1876........820.2 73
   Gulliver's travels.......................827.2 40
   Same 823 86
   Same ; ed. by Chapman..............*827.2 41
   Same ; ed. by Waller................827.2 B-1
   Selections from prose writings. 1884..829 2 60
   Tale of a tub. 1882......................in 823 87
   Works ; ed. by Sir W. Scott. 1824. 19 v.
    V. 1. Memoir ; by Scott..............820.2 53
    V. 2-3. Journal to Stella.—Tracts, political and historical.—The examiner................820.2 54
    V. 4-5. Tracts, historical and political........820.2 56
    V. 6. History of John Bull.—Present state of wit.—Art of political lying. · Tracts relative to Ireland,—The Drapier's letters.......................820.2 58
    V. 7. The Drapier's letters, continued.—Tracts upon Irish affairs.—Sermons...................820.2 59
    V. 8. Sermons (continued).—Tracts in defence of Christianity. — Tracts in support of the church establishment.—Tracts on the test act.—Essays....820.2 60
    V. 9. Essays (Tatler, Spectator, etc.) and miscellany................................820.2 61
    V. 10. Tale of a tub.—Battle of the books.—Mechanical operation of the spirit.—Abstract of the history of England to Henry II.— Letters: Pilkington to Bowyer.—Letter to the Earl of Orrery.—Poems..................................820.2 62
    V. 11. Gulliver's travels.—Directions to servants. 820.2 63
    V. 12. Memoirs of Captain Creichton.—Political tracts.—Notes on Addison's ' Freeholder.'—On Clarendon's ' History.'—On Burnet's ' History.'—On the characters of the court of Queen Anne.—On Gibbs's Psalms.—Political poetry..................820.2 64
    V. 13. Miscellanies by Pope, Gay, etc.—Prose miscellanies by Swift and Sheridan........820.2 65
    V. 14. Miscellaneous poems.—Poems to Vanessa and Stella..............................820.2 66
    V. 15. Poems, riddles, epigrams, etc.—Letters..820.2 67
    V. 16-18. Letters.........................820.2 68
    V. 19. Appendix to correspondence. — Letters between Swift and Miss Vanhomrigh—Index......820 2 71
   Works ; sel., with biography, by Purves.
    1872................................820.2 72
Swinburne. Astrophel, and other poems.
   1894..................................821.2 840
   Atalanta in Calydon (drama)..........822.2 167
   Bothwell : tragedy. 1874..............822.2 171
   Century of roundels. 1883............821.2 841
   Chastelard : tragedy. 1866...........822.2 169
   Erectheus : tragedy. 1876.............822.2 168
   Essays and studies. 1876............824 2 244
    Contents: Hugo's 'L'homme qui rit,' and 'L'année terrible.'— Rossetti's poems.— Morris's 'Jason.'— Matthew Arnold's new poems.—Notes on Shelley.— Byron.—Coleridge.—Ford.—Pictures of 1868.—Designs by old masters at Florence.
   Heptalogia; or, The seven against sense.
   .... 827.2 36
   Laus veneris. 1870....................821.2 842

Locrine : a tragedy. 1887..............822.2 299
Marino Faliero : tragedy. 1885.........822.2 91
Mary Stuart : tragedy. 1881............822.2 226
Midsummer's holiday, etc. (poems).
   1884................................821.2 843
Miscellanies. 1886.....................824 2 389
   Contents : Short notes on English poets. A century of English poetry.—Congreve. Collins. Wordsworth and Byron.— Lamb and Wither.— Landor. Keats. Tennyson and Musset.—Emily Brontë.—Charles Reade. A vacquerie. - Mary, queen of Scots. Appendix.
Note on Charlotte Brontë. 1877........824 2 226
Poems and ballads ; series 1. 1878.....821.2 844
   Same ; series 2 1878..................821.2 845
   Same ; series 3. 1889.................821.2 846
Queen-mother.—Rosamond. (Dramas).
   1866................................822.2 170
Selections from. 1887..................821.2 854
The sisters : a tragedy. 1892..........822.2 305
Songs before sunrise...................821.2 848
Songs of the springtides. 1880........821.2 849
Songs of two nations. 1875............821.2 850
Studies in prose and poetry. 1894.....824.2 477
   Contents : Journal of Sir Walter Scott.—Recollections of Professor Jowett.—Robert Herrick.—John Webster.-Beaumont and Fletcher.—Social verse.—Wilkie Collins. —Whitmania.—Tennyson or Darwin ?—Les Cenci.—Posthumous works of Victor Hugo.
Studies in song. 1880..................821.2 851
Study of Ben Jonson. 1889............822.2 250
Study of Shakespeare. 1880...........822.3 155
Study of Victor Hugo. 1886...........928.4 116
Tale of Balen (poem). 1896...........821.2 852
Tristram of Lyonesse, etc. (poems).
   1882................................821.2 853
Swing. Club essays. 1881............824.1 156
   Old pictures of life. 1894. 2 v.
    V. 1. David Swing; by F. H. Head.—An old picture of life.—A Greek orator.— A Roman gentleman.—Thoughts on Greek literature.— Cordelia and Antigone.—Dante.—The enlarged church..824.1 293
    V. 2. Submerged centuries.—The novel.—The scholar in politics.—Romeo and Juliet.—A true love story.—Humanity to man and beast.—Excess. —Peculiarities of man.—An injured world........824.1 294
Sylvan queen. 2 v...................58917
Symington. Hollyberry Janet..........018315
   My lost manuscript...................018316
Symonds, J. A. Anima figura (poems).
   1882..................................821 2 648
   Essays, speculative and suggestive. 1890.
   2. v
    V. 1. Philosophy of evolution.—Application of evolutionary principles to art and literature.— On some principles of criticism.- The provinces of the several arts.—Relation of art to science and morality.—Realism and idealism.—The model.—Beauty, composition, expression, characterisation.— Caricature, the fantastic, the grotesque — Notes on style................................824.1 127
    V. 2. Notes on style, pts. 3-4.— Democratic art with special reference to Walt Whitman. -- Land-

---
* Of interest to young readers.

scape.—Nature myths and allegories. — Is poetry at bottom a criticism of life (review of Matthew Arnold's selection from Wordsworth).—Is music the type or measure of all art?—The pathos of the rose in poetry.—Comparison of Elizabethan with Victorian poetry.—Appendix............................824.2 428

Miscellanies; ed. by his son.........…824.2 429
Contents: Memoir.—The principles of beauty.—Lecture on waste. — Ten years. — Knowledge. — Life of Doctor Prichard.— Sleep and dreams.—Apparitions.— Relations between mind and muscle.—Habit. — Criminal responsibility in relation to insanity. — Public estimate of medicine. — The health of Clifton. — Medical evidence in relation to state medicine. — Address on health.—Poems.

New and old: verse. 1880..............821.2 558
Sketches and studies in Italy. 1879..824.2 210
Studies of the Greek poets. 1880. 2 v.....881 7
Vagabunduli libellus. 1884..............821.2 732

Symonds, W. S. Malvern Chase............62515
Synge, G. M. Beryl. 011630
Synge, W. W. F. Olivia Raleigh.........67702
   Tom Singleton................................67701
Tabb. Lyrics. 1897..........................821.1 150
   Poems. 1894...................................821.1 490
Tabor (Mrs. E. Stephenson). Annette..…33505
   Blue ribbon.......................................33502
   Dimple Thorpe.................................33513
   Eglantine..33501
   Hagar..33507
   Hope Meredith..................................33510
   Little Miss Primrose.........................33511
   Man's mistake...................................33514
   Nature's nobleman...........................33506
   Rachel's secret.................................33503
   Saint Olaves.....................................33504
   When I was a little girl....................04101
Tadema. See **Alma Tadema, L.**
Taggart. Poems. 1834....................821.1 372
Tainsh. Study of the works of Tennyson. 1870...821.2 377
Taken by siege..................................69036
Talbot, C. R. Double masquerade......69129
Talbot, F. Scarsdale peerage..............44177
   Through fire and water....................44178
Talbot, T. Philiberta..........................62393
Talcot (Mrs. H. B. Goodwin). Christine's fortune...62524
   Doctor Howell's family.....................62523
Tale of Gamelyn [poem]; ed. by Skeat. 1884..821.2 479
Tales for boys and girls.....................07189
Tales of martyr times........................55228
Talfourd. Critical and miscellaneous writings 1842..824.2 93
   Tragedies, verses, etc. 1841..........822.2 288
Talmage. Around the tea-table. 1874..824.1 113
   Crumbs swept up. 1870.................824.1 114
Talvi, *pseud.* See **Robinson,** *Mrs.* **T. A. L.**
Tangletown letters..............................55243

Tannahill. Songs and poems; with memoir; by Ramsay........................821.2 293
Tarleton. Tarleton's jests. 1844........828.2 4
Tasma, *pseud.* (Madame Couvreur.) In her earliest youth.............................46902
   Not counting the cost......................46906
   Penance of Portia James.................46904
   Sydney sovereign, etc.....................46903
   Uncle Piper of Piper's Hill................46901
   White feather....................................46905
Tatem. Heights of Heidelberg............44167
Tatham. Dramatic works. 1879......822.2 237
Tautphœus, *Baroness.* At odds..........16806
   Cyrilla..16805
   Initials..16804
   Quits...16801
Tayler. Earnestness.........................19187
   Truth..19188
Taylor, Bayard. Beauty and the beast.....9004
   Boys of other countries...................01201
   Critical essays, etc........................824.1 152
   Contents: Tennyson.— Victor Hugo,— The German Burns.—Frederick Rückert.— The author of 'Saul.'—Thackeray.— Autumn days in Weimar.— Weimar in June.—Notes on books and events.
   Echo club, etc. 1876....................829.1 18
   Hannah Thurston...........................9001
   Home pastorals. 1875..................821.1 133
   John Godfrey's fortunes..................9009
   Joseph and his friend......................9002
   Lars: a pastoral of Norway. 1873....821.1 132
   Picture of Saint John. 1866...........821.1 131
   Poetical works. 1880....................821.1 129
   Contents: The poet's journal.—Poems of the Orient.—Romances and lyrics.—Californian ballads and poems.— Earlier poems.—Since 1861.—Home pastorals.—Ballads.—Lyrics.—Odes.—The picture of Saint John.—Lars.
   Poet's journal. 1863....................821.1 130
   Prince Deukalion (drama). 1878....822.1 17
   The prophet: a tragedy. 1874.....822.1 12
   Story of Kennett...............................9005
   Studies in German literature. 1879.....830 177
   Translation of Goethe's 'Faust'.........832 33
   Same. 2 v.......................................832 34
Taylor, B. F. Dulce domum (verse). 1884..821.1 306
   January and June. 1871..............824.1 96
   Old-time pictures (poems). 1874..821.1 168
   Songs of yesterday. 1875............821.1 319
   Summer-savory. 1879.................824.1 144
   Theophilus Trent...........................69302
   World on wheels, and other sketches. 1874..824.1 97
Taylor, Emily. Tales from the history of the Saxons...30402
Taylor, G. B. Oakland stories. 4 v......016201
Taylor, *Sir* **H.** Correspondence; ed. by Dowden. 1888.........................826.2 97

LANGUAGE AND LITERATURE.

Critical essays on poetry, etc. '78....824.2 241
Contents: Poetical works of Wordsworth.—Wordsworth's sonnets.—De Vere's poems.—Crime considered in a letter to Mr. Gladstone.— Mill on 'The subjection of women.'— Correspondence with Mill.
Poetical works. 1864. 3 v.
  V. 1. Philip Van Artevelde.................................822.2 160
  V. 2. Edwin the fair.—Isaac Comnenus.........822.2 161
  V. 3. Sicilian summer.—St. Clement's eve.— Eve of the conquest.—Minor poems..................822.2 162
Taylor, I. Ultimate civilization, etc. 1860.
....824.2 267
Taylor, Jane. Writings. 3 v.
  V. 1. Memoirs and correspondence.—Poetical remains...820.2 133
  V. 2. Miscellaneous contributions of Q. Q....820.2 134
  V. 3. Correspondence between a mother and daughter.—Infant poems.—Display: a tale..................820.2 135
Taylor, John, (the water poet). Works..821.2 527
Taylor, J. S. Selections from writings...820.2 139
Taylor, M. Confessions of a thug...........37801
  Noble queen...37807
  Ralph Darnell. 3 v................................37804
  Seeta...37808
  Tara..37802
Taylor, Tom. Fool's revenge; adapted by Booth...822.4 330
  Historical dramas, 1877...................822.2 166
Taylor, U. A. City of the Sarras.............69364
Taylor, W. L. His broken sword............44117
Tcherkess and his victim......................58920
Teal. John Thorn's folks.....................62375
Tellet. Draught of Lethe......................13911
  Outcasts,...13910
Temple, Crona. Valley of diamonds........62343
Temple, Sir R. Cosmopolitan essays,
1886...824.2 387
Templeton. Wrecked but not lost.............56865
Ten Brink. Five lects. on Shakespeare.
1895...822.3 389
Tenney. Agamenticus............................69282
  Agatha and the shadow..........................69283
Tennyson, A. Ballads, etc. 1880......821.2 342
  Becket (drama). 1884......................822.2 267
  Concordance to works of; by Brightwell.
1869..‡821.2 378
  The cup and the falcon (drama), 1884..822.2 252
  Death of Œnone, Akbar's dream, etc,
1892...821.2 343
  Demeter, etc. 1889............................821.2 344
  Enoch Arden, etc.; ed. by Rolfe. 1887.
....*821.2 345
  Enoch Arden.—In memoriam.—Favorite poems. 1880...........................821.2 346
  For the young [selections], 1877.....*821.2 373
  Foresters: Robin Hood and Maid Marian (drama). 1892...............................822.2 304
  Gareth and Lynette. 1872..............821.2 347
  Handbook to works of; by Luce. '95..821.2 379
  Harold: a drama. 1877..................822.2 303

  His art, etc.; by Brooke. 1894 ....821.2 376
  Horæ Tennysonianæ, sive eclogæ e Tennysono Latine redditæ; cura A J. Church. 1870......................................821.2 348
  Idylls of the king. 1860....................821.2 349
  Idylls of the king, and Arthurian story;
  by Maccallum. 1894........................813 42
  Same: Essays on; by Littledale.
1893..821.2 350
  Same: Growth of; by R. Jones. 1895.
....821.2 351
  Illustrations of Tennyson; by Collins.
1891..821.2 375
  In memoriam. 1881..........................821.2 355
  Same: a key to; by Gatty. 1881..821.2 361
  Locksley hall sixty years after, etc. 1886.
....821.2 352
  Lover's tale. 1879............................821.2 353
  Lyrical poems; selected by Palgrave.
1885..821.2 354
  Maud, etc. 1852................................821.2 356
  Message of Tennyson; by Carpenter.
1892..821.2 Pam. 5
  Poems. 1865. v. 1...........................821.2 371
  Poetical works. 1870........................821.2 370
  Poetry of Tennyson; by H. Van Dyke.
1891..821.2 374
  Princess. 1881...................................821.2 358
  Same; ed. by Rolfe. 1885................821.2 359
  Queen Mary: drama. 1875.............822.2 172
  Selections; ed. by Rolfe. 1885..........821.2 372
  Songs; music by Cusins. 1880...........784 R-2
  Study of Tennyson; by Tainsh. '70..821.2 377
  Tennyson primer; by Dixon. 1896..928.2 663
  Tiresias, etc. 1886............................821.2 360
  Works. 1884......................................821.2 369
  Contents: Juvenilia.— Lady of Shalott, etc.—English idylls, etc.—Enoch Arden, etc.—The princess.—Ode on the death of Wellington, etc.— Experiments.—The window.—In memoriam.—Maud.—Idylls of the king.— Queen Mary.—Harold.—The lover's tale.—Ballads, etc.
  Works [complete]. 1896..................821.2 368
  Works. 1896. 6 v.
  V. 1. Juvenilia, etc..821.2 362
  V. 2. Idylls of the king.................................821.2 363
  V. 3. The princess.—Maud.— Enoch Arden.— In memoriam...821.2 304
  V. 4. Queen Mary.—Harold.— Lover's tale.— Ballads, etc.—Sonnets.—Translations..................821.2 365
  V. 5. Tiresias, etc.— The promise of May.— Demeter, etc..821.2 366
  V. 6. Becket.—The cup.—The falcon.—The foresters.—Balin and Balan.—Death of Œnone, Akbar's dream, etc..821.2 367
Tennyson, A. *and* **C.** Poems by two brothers. 1893..................................821.2 357
Tensas. Louisiana swamp doctor..........47280
Terhune (Harland, Marion, *pseud.*). Alone..2725
  At last..2717
  From my youth up..2735

* Of interest to young readers.   ‡ For reference.

Gallant fight...2702
Handicapped..2710
Hidden path..2715
His great self..2704
Husbands and homes............................2707
Jessamine..2722
Judith..2739
Miriam...2705
Mr. Wayt's wife's sister, etc.....................2708
  Contents: Mr. Wayt's wife's sister.—A social success
—The articles of separation.
Moss-side..2731
My little love...2701
Nemesis...2706
Phemie's temptation...............................2711
Royal road...2712
Ruby's husband.......................................2733
Sunnybank...2709
True as steel..2720
With the best intentions.........................2703

Terilo. Friar Bakon's prophesie...........821.2 458
Terrell. City of the just........................28310
Terry. Poems. 1861..............................821.1 175
Teuchsagrondie; canto 3, The exploration,..821.1 Pam. 6
Thacher, J. B. Charlecote; or, The trial of William Shakespeare. 1895..........822.3 208
Thacher, M. P. Sea-shore and prairie (essays). 1877.....................................824.1 120
Thackeray, Anne I., (Mrs. Ritchie).
Bluebeard's keys......................................7104
Five old friends, etc.................................7110
Fulham Lawn...7112
Miss Angel...7101
Miss Williamson's divagations,..............7114
Mrs. Dymond..7115
Old Kensington.......................................7103
Out of the world, etc..............................7105
Story of Elizabeth...................................7107
To Esther, etc..7113
Toilers and spinsters, and other essays. 1876...824.2 385
Village on the cliff...................................7109

Thackeray, W. M. Adventures of Philip.....1208
Ballads. 1856...821.2 432
Ballads and tales.....................................828.2 52
Barry Lyndon..1226
Same...*in* 1215B
Same..*in* 1227
Bibliography; by Shepherd. 1880.........16 28
Same; Literary world, v.17, p.132..805 P-B-5
Book of snobs, etc..................................1213
  Contents: Book of snobs.—Sketches and travels in London. Character sketches. - Men's wives. — Fitz-Boodle papers, Bedford-Row conspiracy. Little dinner at Timmins's.
Burlesques..1214
  Contents: Novels by eminent hands.—Plan for a prize novel. Diary of C. Jeames de la Pluche, esq.—Adventures of Major Gahagan. Legend of the Rhine. Rebecca and Rowena.—History of the next French revolution Cox's diary.

Catherine..1211
Christmas books......................................1216
  Contents: Mrs. Perkins's ball.—Our street.—Dr. Birch.
—Kickleburys on the Rhine.—Rose and the ring.
Collection of letters, 1847-55; with drawings. 1887...826.2 89
Comic almanack......................................828.2 51
Contributions to Punch. 1885...............824.2 379
Denis Duval; and English humourists......1210
Early and late papers. 1867...................824.2 161
  Contents: Memorials of gormandizing. — Men and coats.—Bluebeard's ghost.—Dickens in France.—Leech's pictures.— Little travels and roadside sketches.—Men and pictures. — Picture gossip. — The anonymous in periodical literature.— Goethe.—Leaf out of a sketch-book.—The last sketch.—Strange to say, on club paper.
—Autour de mon chapeau.—On a peal of bells.—On some carp at Sans Souci.—Dessein's.—On a pear tree.—On a medal of George IV.—On Alexandrines.—The notch on the axe.—De finibus.
English humourists, 18th century. 1854..828.2 6
Same..*in* 1210
Extracts from writings. 1881................829.2 56
Fitz-Boodle; and Major Gahagan............1212
Four Georges..942.5 19
Same..*in* 1220
Henry Esmond..1227
Lovel the widower..................................1220
Same..*in* 1227H
Major Gahagan.......................................1212
Same..*in* 1214
Same..*in* 1215A
Men's wives..1236
Same..*in* 1213
Miscellaneous essays, sketches, etc...824.2 378
Miscellanies. 6 v. in 3.
  V. 1-2. The great Hoggarty diamond.—Book of snobs.—The Kickleburys abroad.— Legend of the Rhine,—Rebecca and Rowena.—Second funeral of Napoleon.—Chronicle of the drum,.................1215
  V. 3-4. Major Gahagan.—The fatal boots.—Ballads.—Memoirs of Mr. Charles J. Yellowplush.—Diary of C. Jeames de la Pluche, esq.— Cox's diary..1215A
  V. 5-6. Sketches and travels in London.—Novels by eminent hands.- Character sketches—Memoirs of Barry Lyndon, esq.....................................1215B

Mr. Brown's letters, etc. 1853..........824.2 235
  Contents: Mr. Brown's letters to a young man about town.—The proser.—Child's parties.—Story of Koompanee Jehan.—Science at Cambridge.—Dream of Whitefriars.—Mr. Punch's address to the great city of Castlebar.—Irish guns.—The Charles II ball.- The Georges. Death of the Earl of Robinson.

Newcomes..1203
Pendennis..1221
Roundabout papers.................................824.2 231A
  Contents: On a lazy, idle boy. On two children in black.—Ribbons.—Some late great victories.—Thorns in the cushion.—Screens in dining-rooms. Tunbridge toys De juventute.— On a joke I once heard from Tom Hood. Round about the Christmas tree.—On a chalk mark on the door. On being found out.—On a hundred years hence.—Small-beer chronicle.—Ogres.—On two

roundabout papers which I intended to write.—A Mississippi bubble.—On Letts's diary.-Notes of a week's holiday.—Nil nisi bonum.- On half a loaf. - The notch of the axe ; a story à la mode.—De finibus.—On a peal of bells. —On a pear tree.—Dessein's.- On some carp at Sans Souci.—Autour de mon chapeau.—On Alexandrines.- On a medal of George IV.—Strange to say, on club paper. - The last sketch.
Sketches in London............1213
Same.......................*in* 1215B
Stray moments with ; by Rideing........829.2 53
Sultan Stork, etc., with bibliography.
..........................824.2 399
Thackerayana. 1875................828.2 38
Thackeray's 'London' ; by Rideing. 1885.
........................914.2 154
Vanity fair......................1201
Virginians......................1206
Works (reserved copy). 1879. 24 v.
  V. 1-2. Vanity Fair.................1823 58
  V. 3-4. Pendennis.................1823 60
  V. 5-6. The Newcomes.............1823 62
  V. 7. Henry Esmond,..............1823 64
  V. 8-9. The Virginians............1823 65
  V. 10-11. Adventures of Philip......1823 67
  V. 12. The great Hoggarty diamond. — Dinner at Timmins's.—Cornhill to Cairo........1823 69
  V. 13. Christmas books of M. A. Titmarsh....1823 70
  V. 14. Book of snobs.—Sketches and travels in London...................1823 71
  V. 15. Burlesques................1823 72
  V. 16. Paris sketch-book. -- Little travels and roadside sketches...................1823 73
  V. 17. Memoirs of Mr. C. J. Yellowplush.—Fitz-Boodle paper.—Cox's diary.—Character sketches.
........................1823 74
  V. 18. Irish sketch-book.—Critical reviews....1823 75
  V. 19. Barry Lyndon.— The fatal boots........1823 76
  V. 20. Catherine.—Men's wives.—Bedford-Row conspiracy.....................1823 77
  V. 21. Ballads.—The rose and the ring.......1823 78
  V. 22. Roundabout papers.—Second funeral of Napoleon......................1823 79
  V. 23. The four Georges.—The English humourists..........................1823 80
  V. 24. Lovel the widower.—The wolves and the lamb.—Denis Duval..............1823 81

Thanet, Octave, *pseud.* Expiation..........50802
Knitters in the sun....................50801
The missionary sheriff...................50805
  Contents : The missionary sheriff.— The cabinet organ.—His duty.—The hypnotist.—The next room.—Defeat of Amos Wickliff.
Otto the knight, etc....................50803
Stories of a western town...............50804
  Contents: The besetment of Kurt Lieders. — The face of failure.—Tommy and Thomas.—Mother Emeritus.—An assisted providence.—Harry Lossing.
We all...........................010510

Thaxter. Among the Isles of Shoals (poems)...................917.2 23
Cruise of the Mystery, etc. (poems). 1886.
........................821.1 352
Driftweed (poems). 1879............821.1 218
Island garden.................... 716 20

Letters. 1895....................826.1 18
Poems. 1881....................821.1 274
Poems for children. 1884....   *821.1 304
Stories and poems for children..........041601
Thayer. Bobbin boy................05901
Theodoli. Under pressure 21805
Thicknesse. Egeria...............69901
Thirlwall. Letters. 1881...........826.2 67
Letters to a friend; ed. by Stanley. '81..826.2 68
Thiusen, Ismar, *pseud.* The Diothas......62333
Thomas à Becket. Life and martyrdom;
by Robert of Gloucester...........821.2 462
Thomas of Erceldoune. Romance and prophecies,..................820.2 334
Thomas, Bertha. House on the scar.....62903
Violin player....................62901
Thomas, C. Crystal button.............9020
Thomas, Edith M. Fair shadow land (verse.). 1893................821.1 455
In sunshine land (poems.) '94.....*821.1 478
In the young world (poems.) '96.....*821.1 497
Inverted torch (verse). 1890........821.1 421
Lyrics and sonnets. 1887..........821.1 377
New Year's masque, and other poems. 1885........................821.1 322
The round year (essays). 1886........824.1 220
Winter swallow, with other verse. 1896.
.............................821.1 523
Thomas, M. M. Captain Phil...........032101
Thomas of Reading..................*in* 101
Thompson, Annie. Moral dilemma........23010
Thompson, B. Court intrigue..........70720
Thompson, C. M. Nimble dollar, etc....31340
Thompson, D. P. Centeola............20453
Green Mountain boys................20456
Locke Amsden.....................20457
May Martin.......................20454
Rangers.........................20455
Thompson, D'Arcy W. Ancient leaves (poems.)..................821.2 777
Thompson, Sir H. See Oliver, Pen.
Thompson, H. M. Copy. 1872........204 68
Thompson, J. P. American comments on European questions. 1884........824.1 251
Thompson, M. At love's extremes........21004
Banker of Bankersville................21005
By-ways and bird-notes. 1885........824.1 212
His second campaign................21002
King of Honey island................21006
Lincoln's grave; poem. 1894......821.1 474
Ocala boy........................021010
Poems. 1892.....................821.1 443
Songs of fair weather. 1883.......821.1 299
Sylvan secrets. 1887.............824.1 232
Tallahassee girl...................21001
Thompson, W. T. Chronicles of Pineville..19183
Major Jones' courtship.............19181

* Of interest to young readers.   † For reference.

Thompson, William. Poems; with life..821.2 37
Thomson, A. T. Lady of Milan..............14133
Thomson, B. South sea yarns...............30160
Thomson, E. W. Old man Savarin, etc....21320
Thomson, J., (B. V.). Biographical and critical studies. 1896....................824.2 493
Contents: Rabelais.—Saint-Amant.—Ben Jonson.— Poems of William Blake.—Shelley.—Shelley's religious opinions.—Notice of 'The life of Shelley.'—A strange book.—John Wilson and the 'Noctes ambrosianæ.'— James Hogg, the Ettrick shepherd.—Notes on the genius of Robert Browning. — The ring and the book. — Browning's 'Pacchiarotto.'

Thomson, James, (1800-1848). Poem to Congreve.................................821.2 452
Poems; with life. 1822.................821.2 32
Poetical works. 1864. 2 v.
V. 1. Memoir by Nicolas.—Juvenile and miscellaneous poems, songs, etc.—Liberty................821.2 179
V. 2. The seasons.—The castle of indolence..821.2 180

Thomson, James, (1834-82). City of dreadful night, and other poems. '80......821.2 619
Essays and phantasies. 1881...........824.2 295

Thomson, M. See **Doesticks.**

Thoreau. Autumn; from the journal. 1892..824.1 228
Cape Cod. 1865......................917.2 18
Early spring in Mass.; from the journal. 1881..............................824.1 226
Excursions. 1863....................824.1 224
Contents: Biographical sketch; by Emerson.—Natural history of Massachusetts.—A walk to Massachusetts. —The landlord.—A winter walk.—The succession of forest trees.—Walking.—Autumnal tints.—Wild apples. —Night and moonlight.
Familiar letters. 1894................826.1 15
Letters to various persons. 1865........826.1 8
Maine woods. 1864......................917.2 20
Summer; from the journal. 1884...824.1 227
Thoughts: selections; ed. by Blake. 1894..829.1 35
Walden; or, Life in the woods. 1854..824.1 223
Week on the Concord and Merrimack rivers. 1868..........................917.2 19
Winter; from the journal. 1888.......824.1 229
Yankee in Canada, etc. 1866..........824.1 225
Contents: A Yankee in Canada.—Anti-slavery and reform papers: Slavery in Massachusetts; Prayers; Civil disobedience; A plea for John Brown; Paradise to be regained; Herald of freedom; Carlyle and his works; Life without principle; Wendell Phillips before the Concord lyceum; Last days of John Brown.

Thorpe, T. B. Mysteries of the backwoods..47270
Thorpe *et al.* Big bear of Arkansas, etc...47269
Thurston. Boys of the Central..............034701
Thurstone. Charley and Eva Roberts' home in the west......................013801
How Charley Roberts became a man....013802
How Eva Roberts gained her education..013803
Thynne. Debate between pride and lowliness; ed. by Collier. 1841............827.2 2
Emblemes and epigrams (1600).........820.2 336

Tickell. Poems; with life. 1822..........821.2 42
Tidball. Barbara's vagaries.................69237
Tiernan. Homoselle...........................63438
Jack Horner.......................................63436
Suzette...63437
Tighe. Psyche, and other poems. 1852..821.2 421
Tight squeeze..................................55282
Tilton. Sanctum sanctorum. 1870......824.1 130
Sexton's tale, and other poems. 1867..821.1 174
Tempest tossed.................................52901
Thou and I, and other poems. 1880...821.1 239
Time and tide....................................331 9
Timon: a play; ed. by Dyce. 1842.......822.2 93
Timsol. Alien from the commonwealth.......69502
Tincker. Aurora................................63324
By the Tiber.....................................63301
Grapes and thorns.............................63319
Jewel in the lotus..............................63320
San Salvador....................................63314
Signor Monaldini's niece....................63312
Two coronets...................................63313
Tip cat (See **Laddie.**)........................17901
Tirebuck. Dorrie................................41101
Little widow, etc................................41103
Miss Grace of All Souls'.....................41104
Sweetheart Gwen..............................41102
Titcomb, Timothy. See **Holland.**
Tobersnory.....................................58934
Tobin. Dramas. 1820.....................928.2 58
Honeymoon: comedy.......................822.2 147
Todd, George Eyre-. Anne of Argyle.....32260
Toddle Island..................................55410
Todhunter. Helena in Troas (drama). 1886..822.2 287
Todrig. Ballad of the good ship Sarah Sands.— Golden rod. 1884...821.1 Pam. 25
Toland. Miscellaneous works. 1747. 2 v..211 58
(For contents see Part 3 of FINDING LIST, p. 467.)
Tollemache, L. A. *and* B. L. Safe studies. 1895............................824.2 494
Contents: Historical prediction.—Sir G. C. Lewis and longevity. — Literary egotism. — Recollections of Mr Grote and Mr. Babbage.—Mr. Tennyson's social philosophy.—Charles Austin.— Physical and moral courage.— The Upper Engadine. — Notes and recollections of Sir Charles Wheatstone, Dean Stanley, and Canon Kingsley —The epicurist's lament. — Translations. — Poems; by H. L. T.—Translations of Greek, Latin, and German quotations in text.
Tom a Lincolne..................................*in* 102
Tomlinson. Boy officers of 1812............09915
Boy soldiers of 1812...........................09911
Search for Andrew Field......................09910
Tecumseh's young braves....................09914
Three colonial boys............................09912
Three young continentals....................09913
Tompkins. Broken ring........................30691
Her majesty.......................................30690
Unlessoned girl...................................030610

Tonna, *Mrs.,* (Charlotte Elizabeth). Derry...25866
   Osric, and other poems. 1846.........821.2 302
   Works. 1845. 3 v.
   V. 1. Personal recollections.—Osric: a poem.
   —The Rockite.—Derry.— Letters from Ireland.—
   Miscellaneous poems........................820.2 136
   V. 2. Izram. -- Helen Fleetwood. — Passing
   thoughts,—Flower garden.—Poems on the peninsula war.— Principalities and powers in heavenly
   places,—Second causes..................820.2 137
   V. 3. Judæa capta.— The deserter.— Falsehood
   and truth. — Judah's lion. Conformity. — The
   wrongs of woman.........................820.2 138
Too true...50397
Torrent of Portugal; ed. by Halliwell.
   1842..821.2 728
Torrey. The foot-path way. 1892.........504 129
Tourgee. Black ice..............................54105
   Bricks without straw............................54122
   Button's inn......................................54103
   Figs and thistles................................54102
   Fool's errand....................................54104
   Hot ploughshares...............................54155
   Invisible empire................................54110
   John Eax, etc....................................54148
   Murvale Eastman................................54107
   Out of the sunset sea..........................54109
   Outing with the queen of hearts. 1894.829.1 37
   Pactolus Prime...................................54106
   Royal gentleman [Toinette]..................54101A
   Son of Old Harry................................54108
   Toinette [A royal gentleman]................54101
   With Gauge and Swallow.....................54111
Tourneur. Plays and poems; ed. by Collins. 1878. 2 v.
   V. 1. Introduction.— Atheist's tragedie.— Funerall poem. Death of Prince Henrie........822.2 205
   V. 2. Revenger's tragedie.— The transformed metamorphosis..............................822.2 206
Towards the gulf...............................69034
Townsend, E. W. Daughter of the tenements...31282
Townsend, F. Fancies of a whimsical man...824.1 22
   Musings of an invalid. 1852................824.1 21
Townsend, G. A. Entailed hat...............20740
   Katy of Catoctin................................20742
   Mrs. Reynolds and Hamilton................20743
   Tales of the Chesapeake......................20741
Townsend, M. A. Xariffa's poems.....821.1 180
Townsend, V. A. Battlefields of our fathers..48503
   Boston girl's ambitions.......................48512
   But a Philistine................................48511
   Deerings of Medbury..........................48504
   Lenox Dare......................................48509
   Mills of Tuxbury................................48502
   Mostly Marjorie Day...........................48513
   Only girls..48505
   Temptation and triumph.....................48501
   That queer girl..................................48508
   Woman's word and how she kept it......48506
Tracy. Final war..................................7(00)1
Trafford, F. G., *pseud.* See **Riddell,** *Mrs.* **J. H.**
Trafton. His inheritance........................25502
   Katharine Earle.................................25503
Traherne. Mill on the Usk....................57320
Traill, C. P. Afar in the forest.............021401
   Canadian Crusoes..............................62344
   In the forest..................................021401A
   Lost in the backwoods......................021402
Traill, H. D. Barbarous Britishers........30561
   New Lucian. 1884........................829.2 59
   Number twenty.................................30560
   Saturday songs. 1890....................821.2 431
Train. Autobiography of a professional beauty..61431
   Doctor Lamar...................................61432
   Marital liability...............................61433
   Social highwayman............................61430
Trask. White satin and homespun..........70580
Travers. Fellow travellers....................30216
   Contents: After many days.—Examiner's conscience. —Great gulf.—Knight and the lady.—Story of a friendship.
   Mona Maclean.................................30215
Trelawney, D. Bishop's wife................27610
Trelawney, E. J. Adventures of a younger son..47292
Trench. Poems. 1865.....................821.2 333
Trials of life....................................50376
Tripp. Student life at Harvard..............52241
Tristram. Dead gallant.—King of hearts..32415
Trois Etoiles, *pseud.* See **Murray, E. C. G.**
Trollope, A. Alice Dugdale, etc............2090
   Contents: Alice Dugdale. — Aaron Trow. — The O'Conors of Castle Conor.—Relics of General Chassé.—Chateau of Prince Polignac.—George Walker at Suez.
   American senator..............................2012
   Ayala's angel....................................2074
   Barchester towers..............................2027
   Belton estate....................................2030
   Bertrams...2030
   Brown, Jones, and Robinson................2045
   Can you forgive her?.........................2048
   Castle Richmond..............................2016
   Christmas at Thompson hall...........*in* 32753
   Claverings..2019
   Cousin Henry...................................2002
   Doctor Thorne..................................2044
   Doctor Wortle's school.......................2058
   Duke's children................................2056
   Editor's tales..................................2004
   Contents: Mary Gresley.—Turkish bath.—Josephine de Montmorenci.—The Panjandrum.—The spotted do.—Mrs. Brumby.

Eustace diamonds............................2018
Eye for an eye................................2052
Fixed period..................................2077
Framley parsonage..........................2029
Frau Frohman, etc...........................2081
   Contents: Why Frau Frohman raised her prices.—Lady of Launay.—Christmas at Thompson hall.—The telegraph girl.—Alice Dugdale.
Golden lion of Grandpere..................2042
Harry Heathcote.............................2011
He knew he was right.......................2008
Is he Popenjoy?..............................2049
Kellys and O'Kellys..........................2036
Kept in the dark.............................2080
Lady Anna....................................2043
Lady of Launay..............................2006
Land-leaguers................................2095
Last chronicle of Barset.....................2001
Linda Tressel.................................2054
Lotta Schmidt, etc...........................2041
   Contents: Lotta Schmidt.—Adventures of Fred Pickering.—Two generals.—Father Giles of Ballymoy.—Malachi's cove.—Widow's mite.—Last Austrian who left Venice.—Miss Ophelia Gledd.—Journey to Panama.
Macdermotts of Ballycloran................2032
Marion Fay...................................2078
La mère Bauche, etc........................2091
   Contents: La mère Bauche.—John Bull on the Guadalquivir.—Miss Sarah Jack.—An unprotected female at the pyramids.—Mrs. General Talboys.—The man who kept his money in a box.
Miss Mackenzie..............................2046
  Same.......................................*in* 2045
Mr. Scarborough's family...................2093
Mistletoe bough, etc........................2092
Nina Balatka..................................2053
Old man's love...............................2094
Orley farm....................................2037
Phineas Finn..................................2005
Phineas redux................................2020
Prime minister................................2021
Rachel Ray...................................2035
Ralph the heir................................2014
Sir Harry Hotspur............................2026
Small house at Allington....................2034
Tales of all countries........................2023
   Contents: La mère Bauche.—The O'Conors of Castle Conor.—John Bull on the Guadalquivir.—Miss Sarah Jack.—Courtship of Susan Bell.—Relics of General Chassé.—An unprotected female at the pyramids.—Chateau of Prince Polignac.—Aaron Trow.—Mrs. General Talboys.—Parson's daughter of Oxney Colne.—George Walker at Suez.—The mistletoe bough.—Returning home.—Ride across Palestine.—House of Heine brothers.—The man who kept his money in a box.
Thompson hall...............................2098
Three clerks..................................2024
La Vendée....................................2097
Vicar of Bullhampton........................2003
Warden.......................................2038
Way we live now............................2062

(The following-named of Mr. Trollope's novels form a connected series, collectively called 'The chronicles of Barsetshire': 1. The warden.—2. Barchester towers.—3. Doctor Thorne.—4. Framley parsonage.—5. Small house at Allington.—6. Last chronicle of Barset. Another series, somewhat connected with the above, is formed by the following: 1. The Eustace diamonds.—2. Can you forgive her?—3. Phineas Finn.—4. Phineas redux.—5. The prime minister.—6. The duke's children.)

Trollope, *Mrs.* **Frances E.** Anne Furness..57603
Like ships upon the sea....................57602
Mabel's progress.............................57604
Mrs. Jack.....................................57601
That wild wheel..............................57605
Trollope, Frances M. Jonathan Jefferson Whitelaw...........................2117
Michael Armstrong..........................2115
Petticoat government........................2118
Refugee in America..........................2116
Trollope, T. A. La Beata..................2107
Beppo..2108
Diamond cut diamond.....................2110
Dream numbers.............................2103
Garstang grange............................2106
Gemma.......................................2109
Lindisfarn Chase.............................2101
Sealed packet................................2111
Trowbridge, J. Electrical boy...........09110
Three boys on an electrical boat..........09111
Trowbridge, J. T. Adventures of David Vane and David Crane..................09222
Brighthope series:
  1. Old battle ground....................09230
  2. Ironthorpe.............................09231
  3. Father Brighthopes...................09232
  4. Burrcliff...............................09233
  5. Hearts and faces....................09234
Coupon bonds...............................48903
Cudjo's cave.................................48902
Drummer boy...............................48911
Emigrant's story, and other poems. 1875................................821.2 172
Farnell's folly................................48918
Fortunes of Toby Trafford.................09226
Home idyl, and other poems. 1881...821.1 173
Jack Hazard series:
  1. Jack Hazard..........................09203
  2. Chance for himself..................09202
  3. Doing his best........................09205
  4. Fast friends...........................09201
  5. Young surveyor.....................09204
  6. Lawrence's adventures.............09212
Lottery ticket.................................09228
Martin Merivale.............................48901
Neighbor Jackwood........................48905
Neighbor's wives............................48908
Prize cup.....................................09229
Silver medal stories:
  1. His own master.....................09207
  2. Bound in honor......................09208
  3. Young Joe............................09206

4. Silver medal..................................09209
5. Pocket rifle....................................09210
6. Jolly Rover....................................09211

Start in life stories :
1. Start in life..................................09220
2. Biding his time.............................09221
3. Kelp gatherers..............................09223
4. Scarlet tanager..............................09224

Three scouts...48907

Tide Mill stories :
1. Phil and his friends.........................09213
2. Tinkham brothers' tide mill..............09214
3. Satin-wood box.............................09215
4. Little master.................................09216
5. His one fault.................................09217
6. Peter Budstone.............................09218

Woodie Thorpe's pilgrimage, etc...........09227
True. Shoulder arms...........................030902
Their club and ours..........................030901
True relation of travels, etc., of Mathew
Dudgeon..55213
Trueba. Romance of history : Spain........42725
Trumbull. Poetical works. 1820........821.1 13
Contents: M'Fingal: a modern epic.—Progress of dullness.—Miscellaneous poems.

Tucker, C. Claudia............................45208
Christian love and loyalty.................45211
Cyril Ashley...................................45206
Eden in England.............................45209
Exiles in Babylon............................45207
Fairy Know-a-bit.............................07506
Hebrew heroes...............................45205
Lady of Provence............................45202
Miracles of heavenly love.................45210
Nutshell of knowledge......................07514
Pride and his prisoners.....................45203
Rambles of, a rat............................07508
Shepherd of Bethlehem....................45204
Triumph over Midian......................45201
Tucker, G. F. Quaker home...............10120
Tucker, St. G. Devoted bride.............47237
Tuckerman, F. G. Poems. 1869.....821.1 268
Tuckerman, H. T. Essays..........920 48
The optimist (essays). 1850......824.1 106
Tupper, F. A. Moonshine....................69101
Tupper, M. F. An author's mind.—Probabilities. 1847........................824.2 170
Proverbial philosophy.............829.2 21
Turnbull. Catholic man....................15616
Val-Maria.....................................15615
Turner, Bessie. A woman in the case....47234
Turner, C. T. Collected sonnets......821.2 570
Turner, E. F. Tantler's sister, etc.......62580
Turner, E. S. The family at Misrule....018326
Little larrikin..................................18350
Seven little Australians...................018325
Tuttiett, M. G. See Gray, Maxwell.
Twain, Mark, (S. L. Clemens). American claimant....................................12704

Same, etc...................................12704 A
Contents: The American claimant Merry tales. The £1,000,000 bank-note.—Mental telegraphy. Cure for the blues.—The curious-book complete. About all kinds of ships.—Playing courier.—The German Chicago. —A petition to the queen of England.—A majestic literary fossil.

Autobiography and first romance......828.1 17
Connecticut Yankee at the court of King
Arthur 1889...........................827.1 29
How to tell a story, and other essays.
1897..................................824.1 326
Contents: How to tell a story. In defence of Harriet Shelley. Fenimore Cooper's literary offences.—Travelling with a reformer.—Private history of the ' Jumping frog' story—Mental telegraphy again. What Paul Bourget thinks of us.—A little note to Paul Bourget

Huckleberry Finn............................12716
Innocents abroad.......................914 120
Life on the Mississippi..................917.4 45
Merry tales...................................12703
Contents: Private history of a campaign that failed. —Invalid's story.— Luck.— Captain's story.— Curious experience.—Mrs. McWilliams and the lightning. — Meisterschaft.

Old times on the Mississippi..............12702
Personal recollections of Joan of Arc...12708
Prince and the pauper....................*12706
Roughing it..............................917.5 134
Sketches, new and old..............828.1 46
Stolen white elephant, etc. 1882.....828.1 6
Tom Sawyer..................................12701
Tom Sawyer abroad........................12705
Tragedy of Pudd'nhead Wilson.........12707
Tramp abroad.............................914 119
Twain *and* **Warner.** Gilded age........12602
Twells. Mills of the gods....................56895
Twelve nights in a hunter's camp......032228
Twining. Recreations : selections from correspondence. 1882...............826.2 71
Twining family. Selections from papers of.
1887....................................826.2 94
Twiss. Miscellanies. 1805. 2 v.......829.2 5
Two gentlemen of Boston..................69037
Two Russian idyls............................58910
Tyler. Death ; or, Medorus' dream....821.1 23
Tynan, K., (Mrs. H. A. Hinkson). Cluster of nuts....................................31090
Isle in the water.............................31093
Land of mist and mountain..............31091
Oh, what a plague is love !.............31094
Way of a maid..............................31092
Tyndall. Fragments of science. 1879.
2 v.......................................504 78
(For contents, see Part 3 of FINDING LIST, p. 314).
New fragments. 1892..................504 127
(For contents, see Part 3 of FINDING LIST, p. 314).
Tyssen. Birth of Islam : dramatic poem.
1895..................................822.2 319

* Of interest to young readers.

Tytler, Ann. Leila............................... 017101	Vacation story books. 6 v....................07144
Leila at home.......................................017103	Vachell. Model of Christian Gay.............13370
Leila in England................................ 017102	Quicksands of Pactolus..................... 13372
Mary and Florence...............................017105	Romance of Judge Ketchum.................13371
Mary and Florence at sixteen...............017104	Valentine, L. Knight's ransom...............52276
Tytler, C. C. Fraser-. See Liddell.	Valentine, Oswald, *pseud.* Helen......,....14850
Tytler, M. E. Fraser-. Grisel Romney.....64701	Vailings. Month of madness....................37008
Tales of many lands...........................018701	Parson at bay..37007
Tytler, Sarah, *pseud.* (H. Keddie.) Beauty	Three braces of lovers............................37006
and the beast...................................30313	Transgression of Terence Clancy...........37005
Beneath the surface..............................30325	Vanamee. Two women............................30350
Bride's pass..30311	Vanbrugh. Dramatic works..............822.2 180
Bubble fortune.......................................30326	Vance. Katherine......................................15233
Buried diamonds...................................30317	Vandam. Mystery of the Patrician club.....38101
Citoyenne Jacqueline...........................30305	Vandegrift, Margaret, *pseud.* (Mar-
Comrades........... 30315	garet Janvier.) Doris and Theodora...46440
Days of yore..30301	Little helpers...032247
Diamond rose........ 30306	Queen's body guard..............................032248
Disappeared..30318	Rose Raymond's wards.........................46442
Footprints (essays)........................ 824.2 236	Ways and means......................................46441
French Janet..30321	Vandenhoff. Common sense: satire......827.1 4
Her gentle deeds...................................30314	Vanderpoole. Red Mountain mines.........69331
Heroines in obscurity...........................30308	Van Dyke. The builders, and other poems.
Houseful of girls...................................30322	1897..............................,......................821.1 581
Huguenot family....................................30304	Little rivers. 1895.....................................824.1 302
In the cannon's mouth........................*in* 30327	*Contents:* Prelude.— Little rivers.— A leaf of spear-
In the fort...30316	mint.—Ampersand.— A handful of heather.— The Resti-
Kincaid's widow....................................30330	gouche from a horse-yacht.— Alpenrosen and goat's
Lady Bell..30303	milk.— Au large.— Trout-fishing in the Traun.— At the
Lady Jean's son.....................................30332	sign of the balsam bough,— A song after sundown.
Logie Town..30320	Story of the other wise man....................21640
Macdonald lass.....................................30328	Vane, C. Desire of the moth...................32430
Mermaidens 30329	Vane, Denzil, *pseud.* See Du Tertre.
Morning mist.... 30324	Van Namee. Hopedale tavern.................47242
Noblesse oblige.....................................30307	Van Rensselaer, *Mrs.* Schuyler. One
Oliver Constable....................................30310	man who was content.—Mary.—The
Rachel Langton....................................30331	Lustigs.— Corinna's Fiammetta...........55701
Saint Mungo's city................................30312	Van Vorst. Without a compass...............69141
Vashti Savage..30319	Vase. Through love to life........................52214
War times.—In the cannon's mouth........30327	Vashti and Esther......................................55295
What she came through......................30323	Vaughan, H. Poems. 1896. 2 v.....821.2 525
Udall. Ralph Roister Doister: comedy; ed.	Vaughan, H. H. New readings of Shakes-
by Cooper. 1847...........................822.2 78	peare's tragedies. 1878-86. 3 v.....822.3 189
Same; Arber's reprint. 1869.........820.2 33	Vaux. Poems....................................*in* 821.2 146
Uncrowned king............................*in* 820.2 329	Veitch, Agnes. Woodruff............................52297
Under the holly.......................................07183	Veitch, Sophie F. F. Dean's daughter...40702
Under the southern cross......................50327	James Hepburn.......................................40701
Underwood. Cloud pictures....................52402	Margaret Drummond, millionaire........ .40703
Doctor Gray's quest...............................52401	Modern crusader.....................................40704
Lord of himself......................................52403	Veley. For Percival...................................22002
Upton. Castles in the air.........................0205	Marriage of shadows, and other poems.
Upward. Crown of straw........................31022	1888.............................. ....821.2 823
Prince of Balkistan................................31021	Mitchelhurst place........... 22001
Queen against Owen.............................31020	Venn. Husband of one wife....................37920
Urmy. Vintage of verse. 1897.........821.1 292	Vere, Aubrey de. See De Vere, Aubrey.
V. See Ferguson, V. Munro.	Verey. The open air. 1869...............824.2 223
V., B. See Thomson, J.	Verplanck. Discourses on American his-
	tory, etc...825.1 6

Epistles of brevet Major Pindar Puff.
1819. .... in 827.1 41
Very. Poems. 1883..... .... 821.1 298
Vicary. American in Norway.................. 69206
Victor. Mariam.. 22210
Victor, M. V. Maum Guineau.................. 25819
   Passing the portal.................................. 25818
Victory. The higher teaching of Shakespeare. 1896.................... 822.3 369
Viele. Following the drum........................ 47227
Vieux Moustache, *pseud.* See **Gordon, C.**
Villari. In change unchanged................ 20490
Villiers. The rehearsal....................... 820.2 30
Vincent, Ellerton, *pseud.* See **Logan, M. C.**
Vincent, F., *and* **Lancaster, A. E.**
   Lady of Cawnpore................................. 16520
Vincent, John, *pseud.* See **Huntington, J. V.**
Vining. Mystery of Hamlet. 1881...... 822.3 129
Virgilius... *in* 102
Vivian. Boconnoc: a romance of wild-oatcake.
.... 27046
   Green bay tree................................... 27045
Vizetelly. Scorpion............................. 43801
Voynich. The gadfly.............................. 52902
Vynné. Man and his womankind............... 21050
W., C. H. Five hundred dollars............... 69383
Waddie. Divine philosophy: poem. 1889.
.... 821.2 645
Wakeman. Mysterious parchment............ 52247
Waldo. Ban of the Gubbe....................... 71160
Walford. Baby's grandmother................ 65209
   Bubble 65216
   Cousins.. 65208
   Dick Netherby..................................... 65201
   Fly's web.. *in* 32715
   Frederick... 65217
   Havoc of a smile................................ 65210
   History of a week.............................. 65211
   Matchmaker....................................... 65215
   Mere child... 65202
   Merrielands farm................................ 65219
   Mischief of Monica............................. 65212
   Mr. Smith.. 65207
   One good guest................................... 65214
   Pauline.. 65205
   Pinch of experience........................... 65213
   Sage of sixteen.................................. 65206
   Stiff-necked generation...................... 65204
   Successors to the title........................ 65218
   Troublesome daughters....................... 65203
Walker, G. Three Spaniards................... 12054
Walker, J. B. Poetry of reason and of conscience. 1871................ 821.1 190
Walker, Jesse. Poems. 1854............... 821.1 402
Walker, Mary S. Down in a saloon......... 15225
   Family doctor..................................... 15224
   Reverend Doctor Willoughby................. 15222

Wall, A. Fall of Constantinople 2531
   Princess of Chalco.............................. 2530
Wall, G. A., *and* **Robinson, E.** Disk ...62363
Wallace, H. B. Art and scenery in Europe, etc. 1868................................. 704 7
Wallace, Lewis. Ben Hur............... 46702
   Same (German)................................ 46702W
   Fair God... 46701
   Prince of India................................... 46703
Waller. Poems; ed. by Drury. 1893..821.2 908
   Poems; with life.............................. 821.2 27
Wallis. Prodigious fool....................... 62511
Walmsley. Branksome Dene............... 62504
   Chasseur d'Afrique............................ 62506
   Life guardsmen................................... 62505
   Ruined cities of Zulu-land................... 62507
Walpole. And his world; letters, ed. by Seeley. 1884.......................... 826.2 78
   Castle of Otranto. 1883................ *in* 823 98
   Essays in The World. 3 v............... 824.2 19
   Fugitive pieces, prose and verse. 1785.
   (Printed at Strawberry Hill press.)........ 24 1
   Letters. 1842. 4 v......................... 826.2 61
   Same; ed. by Cunningham. '80. 9 v..826.2 52
   Same; ed. by Lord Dover. '33. 2 v..826.2 65
Walsh, R. Didactics. 1836. 2 v......... 824.1 3
Walsh, W. S. Young folks' ideas............ 06721
   Young folks' queries............................ 06720
Walshe, E. H. Manuscript man............. 19111
Walshe, E. H., *and* **Sargent, G. E.**
   Within sea walls................................. 16508
Walters. Guanya Pau.......................... 30463
Walton. Compleat angler [with addition by Cotton]. 1847................ 799 65
   Same; ed. by A. Lang. 1896......... 799 65A
Walworth, *Mrs.* **J. R.** See **Hadermann.**
Warboise. Campion Court.................... 56505
   Lillingstones..................................... 56504
   Lottie Linsdale................................. 56508
   Sir Julian's wife................................ 56501
   Wife's trials...................................... 56502
Warburton, Eliot. Darien..................... 56897
   Reginald Hastings.............................. 56898
Warburton, William. Letters. 1809.....826.2 51
Ward, Artemus (C. F. Browne). Complete works. 1887.................. 828.1 33
   Genial showman; by Hingston. 2 v...828.1 30
   In London, etc. 1867..................... 828.1 32
   Lecture. 1869............................... 828.1 34
   Panorama. 1869............................ 828.1 35
Ward, E. Pair of originals.................... 033701
Ward, *Mrs.* **H.** Hardy and Hunter......... 010501
Ward, H. O. Max Reichner, pastor......... 56950
Ward, Herbert D. The burglar who moved Paradise............... 4862
   Captain of the Kittiewink.................... 020941
   Dash to the pole................................. 020942

New senior at Andover................020940
Republic without a president, etc..........4860
   Contents: Republic without a president. — Lost city. —Terrible evening.—Scud.— Romance of a mortgage.— Colonel Odminton.
White crown, etc....................4861
   Contents: The white crown.—The semaphore.—The value of a cipher. — A romance of the faith. — Only an incident.—A cast of the net.—The equation of a failure. —The missing interpreter.

Ward, Herbert D., *and* Phelps, E. S.
   Come forth....................4851
   Lost hero...................020920
   Master of the magicians............4850

Ward, *Mrs.* Humphry. History of David
   Grieve..........................35003
   Marcella........................35004
   Miss Bretherton.................35001
   Robert Elsmere..................35002
   'Robert Elsmere' and the battle of belief; by Gladstone...........824.2 Pam. 1
   Sir George Tressady.............35006
   Story of Bessie Costrell.........35005

Ward, J. W. Song of Higher-water. 1868.
   ....821.1 406

Ward, N. Simple cobbler of Aggawam. 1843..........................827.1 38

Ward, S. Lyrical recreations. 1865......821.1 47

Ward, *Mrs.* T. H. Milly and Olly..........028001

Warden. Adela's ordeal..................18020
   At the world's mercy...............18001
   Deldee.............................18003
   Doris's fortune....................18010
   Fog princes........................18005
   Forge and furnace..................18026
   Grave Lady Jane....................18018
   Highest references.................18013
   House on the marsh.................18004
   Inn by the shore...................18025
   Kitty's engagement.................18023
   Nurse Revel's mistake..............18011
   Passage through Bohemia............18019
   Perfect fool.......................18022
   Pretty Miss Smith..................18012
   Prince of darkness.................18007
   Ralph Ryder of Brent...............18015
   St. Cuthbert's tower...............18006
   Scarborough romance................18021
   Scheherazade.......................18002
   Sea Mew Abbey......................18014
   Shock to society...................18017
   Spoilt girl........................18024
   Vagrant wife.......................18008
   Woman's face.......................18009
   Witch of the hills.................18016

Ware. Aurelian........................15208
   Julian...........................15209
   Zenobia..........................15206

Warman. Tales of an engineer; with Rhymes of the rail................31360

Warner, Anna B. Bag of stories...........010904
   Blue flag and cloth of gold........010903
   Cross corners........................4603
   Dollars and cents....................4601
   My brother's keeper..................4602
   Patience.............................4604
   Three little spades................010901
   Yours and mine.....................010905

Warner, B. E. Troubled waters...........69123

Warner, C. D. As we go (essays). 1894..824.1 279
   As we were saying (essays). 1891.....824.1 266
   Backlog studies....................56201
   Baddeck, and that sort of thing. '74..917.6 61
   Being a boy. 1878.................*828.1 56
   Golden house.......................56207
   Hints for home reading. 1880.......374 10
   Little journey in the world........56206
   My summer in a garden. 1871........828.1 55
   Relation of literature to life. 1897....824.1 323
   Contents: The relation of literature to life.—Simplicity. — Equality.— What is your culture to me?—Modern fiction.—Thoughts suggested by Mr. Froude's 'Progress.'—England.—The English volunteers during the late invasion.—The novel and the common school.— A night in the garden of the Tuileries.
   Their pilgrimage...................56205

Warner, C. D., *and* Twain, Mark.
   Gilded age.........................12602

Warner, Susan, (Elizabeth Wetherell, *pseud.*). Bread and oranges............0507
   Daisy...............................4401
   Daisy Plains........................4456
   Diana...............................4406
   End of a coil.......................4418
   Flag of truce.......................0506
   Golden ladder.......................0516
   Hills of the Shatemuc...............4415
   House in town.......................0503
   Letter of credit....................4422
   Little camp on Eagle Hill...........0519
   Melbourne house.....................4407
   Mr. Rutherford's children...........0513
   My Desire...........................4416
   Nobody..............................4427
   Old helmet..........................4405
   Opportunities.......................0502
   Pine needles........................0509
   Queechy.............................4432
   Rapids of Niagara...................0508
   Red wallflower......................4419
   Sceptres and crowns.................0517
   Stephen, M. D.......................4414
   Trading.............................0504
   What she could......................0501
   Wide, wide world....................4403
   Willow Brook........................0518

* Of interest to young readers.

Warner, Susan *and* **Anna.** Gold of
  Chickaree..4512
  Say and seal.......................................4502
  Wych Hazel..4506
Warren, Cornelia. Miss Wilton.............15510
Warren, G. M. Der poems von Friederick
  Scholtz. 1880..............................828.1 49
Warren, S. Adventures of an attorney......6312
  Diary of a physician...........................6307
  Experiences of a barrister....................6313
  Lily and the bee (verse). 1851.........821.2 529
  Miscellanies. 1855...........................824.2 167
  Now and then....................................6309
  Ten thousand a year.......................... 6301
Warriner. Victor La Tourette..................52222
Warring. Squire Paul............................58323
Warth. Dorothy Thorn of Thornton.........69423
  John Greenleaf, minister....................69422
Warton, J. Essays in The Adventurer. 3 v.
  ....824.2 16
Warton, T. Essays in The Idler............824.2 24
  Poetical works. 1802. 2 v..............821.2 221
Warwick, Mary, *countess of.* Autobiography...821.2 465
Washburn, C. A. Gomery of Montgomery..15212
Washburn, E. Address, Young men's
  Christian association. Boston, 1855
  ....*in* 825.1 17
Washburn, K. Ina..................................27102
  Perfect love casteth out fear..................27101
Washburn, W. T. Fair Harvard............52209
Washington. Correspondence with W.
  Crawford, 1767-1781....................971.2 15
  Farewell address..............................342.1 15
  Same; papers relating to. (Pennsylvania historical society, v. 1.)..........973 B-2
  Maxims; ed. by Schroeder. 1855........829.1 2
  Writings; ed. by Ford. 1889-93. 14 v...971 169
  Writings; ed. by Sparks. 12 v.............971 59
Wasson, D. A. Essays. 1888.............824.1 101
  Contents: Memoir.—Nature the prophecy of man.—Authority.—Unity.—Social texture.—Conditions of social productiveness.—The Puritan commonwealth.—The new type of oppression.—The genius of woman.
  Poems. 1888 ....821.1 397
Waterloo. Odd situation.........................70501
Waters, H. Outskerry............................037601
Waters, *Mrs.* **J.** Young girl's adventures...62551
Waters, T. Ribbonman...........................44199
Waters, W. G. Doctor Campion's patients..50120
Watson, A. C. Beyond the city gates........31511
  Dorothy the Puritan........................... 31510
Watson, H. B. M. At the first corner, etc...69393
  Galloping Dick..................................69392
  Marahuna..69391
  Web of the spider..............................69394
Watson, H. C. Noble deeds of our forefathers...03301

Watson, J. V. Tales and takings...........15228
Watson, J. M. See **Maclaren, Ian,** *pseud.*
Watson, J. W. Beautiful snow, and other
  poems. 1871 ....821.1 234
  Outcast, and other poems. 1872.....821.1 235
Watson, Thomas. Eclogue: death of
  Walsingham.—Passionate centurie of
  love.—Teares of fancie..................820.2 34
Watson, William. Eloping angels (poem). 1893..821.2 903
  Excursions in criticism. 1893........824.2 456
  Contents: Some literary idolatries. Punishment of genius.—Keats and Mr. Colvine.—Lancashire laureate. Mr. Hardy's 'Tess of the d'Urbervilles.'—Critics and their craft.—Lowell as a critic.—Coleridge's supernaturalism.—Mystery of style.—Mr. R. H. Hutton.—Mr. Austin Dobson's 'Hogarth.' Ibsen's prose dramas. —Mr. Meredith's poetry.—Dr. Johnson on modern poetry.
  Father of the forest, and other poems.
  1895...821.2 900
  Odes, etc. 1894..........................821.2 899
  Poems. 1893..............................821.2 905
  Purple east: sonnets, Armenia. 1896..821.2 901
  Wordsworth's grave, and other poems.
  1890..821.2 898
  Year of shame (sonnets, Armenia.) 1897.
  ....821.2 902
Watts, *Mrs.* **A. M.** See **Howitt, Anna M.**
Watts, I. Poems; with life. 1822.........821.2 33
  Psalms, hymns, etc.......................240 B-17
  Works; ed. by Jennings and Doddridge.
  1810. 6 v....................................240 B-14
  (For contents, see Part 3 of FINDING LIST, p. 485.)
Watts, W. C. Chronicles of a Kentucky
  settlement.......................................39080
We boys..0130
Weatherly. Dresden china, and other
  songs. 1880................................821.2 579
  Land of little people.........................032237
  Verses for children. 1874...........*821.2 Pam. 2
Webb, C. H. See **Paul, John.**
Webb, J. B. Benaiah...............................16604
  Oliver Wyndham................................16601
Webbe. Discourse of English poetrie....820.2 37
Weber. Old house in the square............031801
Webster, Augusta. The sentence: drama.
  1893...822.2 326
  A woman sold. 1867,....................821.2 121
Webster, D. Address, Pittsburg, 1833.
  ....329.1 Pam. 2
  Diplomatic papers, etc.....................327.1 6
  Discourse at Plymouth. 1820.............40 23
  Discourse on Adams and Jefferson......40 12
  Great speeches; ed. by Whipple. 1880..825.1 5
  Selections from..............................342.1 15
  Works. 1851. 6 v.
  V. 1. Biographical memoir.—Speeches on public
  occasions.......................................320.1 6
  V. 2. Speeches on public occasions........320.1

* Of interest to young readers.

V. 3. Speeches in Massachusetts constitutional convention. -Speeches in congress.................329.1 62
V. 4-5. Speeches in congress.............................329.1 63
V. 6. Legal arguments.—Diplomatic papers. — Miscellaneous letters......................................329.1 65
Webster, D., *and* **Hayne.** Speeches, 1830................................... 329.1 66
Webster, J. P. Oracle of Baal...............70140
Webster, John. Dramatic works; ed. by Hazlitt. 1857. 4 v.
V. 1. Sir Thomas Wyat. — Westward hoe. — Northward hoe...822.2 97
V. 2. White devil.—Duchess of Malfi............822.2 98
V. 3. Devil's law-case.—Appius and Virginia. —Monuments of honor.—Monumental column.— Odes..822.2 99
V. 6 Cure for a cuckold. —Induction to The malcontent.' -Thracian wonder.- Weakest goeth to the wall..822.2 100
Webster, L. Another girl's experience....018335
Webster, N., *jr.* Essays, etc. 1790.......824.1 1
Wedmore. English episodes.................56930
Orgeas and Miradou........................56932
Pastorals of France..........................56931
Wee widow's cruise in quiet waters..........14780
Weeks. Ainslee stories......................015402
Four and what they did... 015404
Grandpa's house............................015401
White and red..............................015403
Weiss. Wit, humor, and Shakspeare.....822.3 88
Welch, A. Extracts from the diary of Moritz Svengali..............................29904
Welch, F. G., *et al.* That convention...827.1 12
Welch, P. H. Said in fun. 1889.........828.1 77
Wellington. Words of; ed. by Walford. 1869...829.2 11
Wellmont. Uncle Sam's palace................15221
Wells, H. G. Island of Doctor Moreau.....31273
Select conversations with an uncle. 1895......................................824.2 507
Contents: Of conversations and the anatomy of fashion.—The theory of the perpetual discomfort of humanity.—The use of ideals.—The art of being photographed. — Bagshot's mural decorations. — On social music.—The joys of being engaged.—La Belle Dame Sans Merci.—On a tricycle.—An unsuspected masterpiece.—The great change.—The pains of marriage.— A misunderstood artist.—The man with a nose.
Stolen bacillus, etc..........................31272
Time machine................................31270
Wheels of chance............................31274
Wonderful visit..............................31271
Wells, K. G. About people. 1885........824.1 68
Miss Curtis................................24701
Two modern women.......................24702
Wendell. Duchess Emilia....................69105
Rankell's remains..........................69104
Stelligeri, etc. 1893.................824.1 278
Contents Stelligeri.- Four American centuries. Some neglected characteristics of the New England Puritans. Were the Salem witches guiltless? -American literature. Whittier. Mr. Lowell as a teacher.
William Shakespeare : study in Elizabethan literature 1894............822.3 387

Wentworth. Papers, 1705-39.............826.2 77
Wesley, J. Works. 1856. 15 v............240 15
(For contents, see Part 3 of FINDING LIST, p. 485.)
Wesley, J. *and* **C.** Poetical works. 6 v...245 11
Wesselhoeft. Frowzle the runaway.........02912
Jerry the blunderer...........................02913
Sparrow the tramp............................02910
The winds, the woods, and the wanderer.......................................02911
West, B. B. Half-hours with the millionaires...13620
West, G. Poems ; with life................821.2 35
West, Mary. Born player....................30585
Westall. Back to Africa....................20907
Ben Clough, etc.............................20909
Birch Dene................................20906
For honor and life..........................20910
Old factory................................20914
Phantom city..............................20903
Princes of Peele............................20908
Ralph Norbeck's trust......................20901
Red Ryvington............................20913
Sons of Belial.............................20912
Tales and traditions of Switzerland........20902
Trust-money..............................20911
Two pinches of snuff......................20904
With the red eagle........................20915
Witch's curse.........................*in* 32715
Westbury, A. Shadow of Hilton Fernbrook..70460
Westbury, H. Frederick Hazzleden.........69356
Westcott. Bessie Wilmerton.................44187
Westmoreland. Clifford Troupe.............47287
Heart-hungry..............................47288
Westover. Bushy...........................70820
Wetheral, Mabel. Two north-country maids..69459
Wetherell, Elizabeth, *pseud.* See **Warner, Susan.**
Weyman. From the memoirs of a minister of France...................................36208
Gentleman of France.......................36204
House of the Wolf.........................36203
King's stratagem, etc......................36211
Contents: King's stratagem.—Body-birds of court. In Cupid's toils.— Drift of fate. — More Manor episode —Fatal letter.
Little wizard...............................36212
Man in black..............................36206
My Lady Rotha...........................36207
New rector................................36201
Red cockade..............................36210
Snowball..................................36209
Story of Francis Cludde...................36202
Under the red robe........................36205
Wharton, Anne H. Last century maid......01055o
Wharton, G. M. New Orleans sketchbook...47275

Wharton, Joseph. Poems ; with life. 1822..821.2 43
Wharton, Philip, *duke of.* Works. 1740. ....821.2 810
Wharton, Thomas. Poems; with life. 1822..821.2 43
Wharton, Thomas I. Bobbo, etc............69258
Hannibal of New York..............69259
Whately. Lost in Egypt.....................62563
Scenes from life in Cairo..........................62564
Whatham, M. E. See **Winchester, M. E.,** *pseud.*
Wheaton. Six sinners........................05101
Wheeler. Siegfried the mystic..................41801
Wheelwright, C. A. Poems. 1811. 2 v.
  V. 1. Medea: a tragedy; tr. from Seneca.—
  Octavia, a tragedy; from same................821.2 746
  V. 2. Miscellaneous poems..................821.2 747
Wheelwright, J. T. Child of the century...69290
Whipple. Character, etc.....................824.1 65
  Contents: Character.—Eccentric character.—Intellectual character.—Heroic character.—American mind. —English mind.—Thackeray.- Hawthorne.—Everett — T. Starr King.—Agassiz.—Washington.
Essays and reviews. 1848. 2 v.
  V. 1. Macaulay.—Poets and poetry of America. —Talfourd. — Words.—James' novels.—Sidney Smith.—Daniel Webster.—Neal's history of the Puritans.—Wordsworth.—Byron.—English poets, 19th century.—Vagaries of volition.................824.1 61
  V. 2. Old English dramatists. — South's sermons.—Romance of rascality.—Croakers of society and literature.—British critics.—Rufus Choate.—Coleridge as a philosophical critic. — Prescott's histories. — Shakespeare's critics. — Sheridan. — Appendix...824.1 62
Lectures. 1850..............................824.1 63
  Contents: Authors in their relations to life.—Novels and novelists: Dickens.—Wit and humor.—Ludicrous side of life.—Genius.—Intellectual health and disease.
Literature of the age of Elizabeth......824.1 60
Outlooks on society, literature and politics. 1888............................824.1 234
Recollections of eminent men. '96 ...824.1 219
Success and its conditions. 1871.......824.1 64
Whishaw. Boris the bear-hunter............013050
Boyar of the Terrible........................13080
Emperor's Englishman......................13081
Harold the Norseman......................013052
Lost army..................................013051
Sons of freedom............................013053
Whistle-Binkie. Songs [Scottish]. 1890. 2 v..821.2 861
Whistler. Thane of Wessex.................035801
Whitby, B. Awakening of Mary Fenwick...28501
In the suntime of her youth..................28506
Mary Fenwick's daughter.....................28507
Matter of skill................................28503
On the Lake of Lucerne, etc................28504
One reason why..............................28505
Part of the property..........................28502

Whitcher. Widow Bedott....................29401
Widow Spriggins, etc.........................29104
White, A. L. Doctor Hildreth................56865
White, B. Circe.............................11159
White, C. Almacks revisited................52263
White, Edward. Minor moralities........824.2 221
White, Eliza O. Coming of Theodora....25860
Little girl of long ago.......................025811
Miss Brooks.................................25888
When Molly was six..........................025810
Winterborough..............................25889
White, H. K. Remains. 1823. 2 v.
  V. 1. Life; by Southey. Letters. Miscellaneous poems......................................821.2 276
  V. 2. Odes, sonnets, fragments. Time The Christiad.—Prose compositions.—Reflections. 821.2 277
White, J. Sir Frizzle Pumpkin, etc..........20405
White, R. G. Fate of Mansfield Humphreys...................................62370
New gospel of peace.......................827.1 25
Shakespeare's scholar. 1854...........822.3 82
Studies in Shakespeare. 1886..........822.3 321
White, W. A. Real issue: Kansas stories..52701
White, W. C. Oration, July 4, 1810..........40 22
White, W. H. See **Rutherford, Mark,** *pseud.*
White Acre *vs.* Black Acre....................50381
White crysanthemum..........................0108
White rose and red (poem). 1873......821.1 186
Whitehead, Charles. Richard Savage.....52294
Whitehead, Mrs. T. Grahames.............15247
Whiteing. Island.............................69404
Whiteley. Falcon of Langéac................39001
Whitelock. Mad madonna, etc............31530
Whiting, C. G. The saunterer (essays). 1886...................................824.1 217
Whiting, Lilian. World beautiful (essays). 1894....................................824.1 295
Whiting, M. H. Faith White's letter book...55226
Whitman, S. H. Poems. 1879........821.1 222
Whitman, Walt. Calamus: letters. '97..826.1 11
Complete prose works. 1892........824.1 283
Democratic vistas, and other papers. 1888...824.1 238
Good bye, my fancy (poems). 1891..821.1 393
Leaves of grass. 1881...................821.1 389
  Same: selections; ed by Rhys. '86..821.1 390
November boughs. 1888................824.1 242
Poems; ed. by Rossetti. 1868 ....821.1 391
Selected poems. 1892...................821.1 392
Specimen days; and Collect. 1882..824.1 176
Whitmarsh. Young pearl divers..............03700
Whitney. Ascutney street....................4704
Bonnyborough.................................4741
Boys at Chequasset..........................02301
Daffodils (poems). 1887................821.1 363
Faith Gartney's girlhood.....................4723
Gayworthys....................................4717

Golden gossip..................................4705
Hitherto,..4716
Holy-tides : seven songs. 1886,........821.1 353
Homespun yarns................................4703
Mother Goose for old folks..............821.1 226
Odd or even....................................4730
Other girls......................................4719
Pansies (poems). 1872..................821.1 179
Patience Strong's outings..................4701
Real folks......................................4729
Sights and insights...........................4702
Summer in Leslie Goldthwaite's life 4726
We girls..4713
Zerub Throop's experiment.................4715
Whittaker. Cadet buttons..................44125
Whittier. Among the hills, etc. 1869...821.1 115
At sundown. 1892.........................821.1 122
Bay of seven islands, and other poems.
  1883..821.1 120
Complete poetical works. 1873........821.1 111
  Contents: Mogg Megone.—The bridal of Pennacook.
  —Legendary.—Voices of freedom.—Miscellaneous.—
  Songs of labor, etc.—Miscellaneous.—The chapel of the
  hermits.—The panorama, etc.—Miscellaneous.—Ballads,
  —Later poems.—Home ballads.—Poems and lyrics.—In
  war time.—Ballads.—Occasional poems —Snow-bound.
  —The tent on the beach, etc.—National lyrics.—Occa-
  sional poems.—Among the hills, etc.—Miscellaneous
  poems.—Miriam, etc.—Miscellaneous poems.—Poems
  for public occasions.—The Pennsylvania pilgrim, etc.—
  Miscellaneous.—Hazel blossoms.—Poems by Elizabeth
  H. Whittier.—Notes.
Complete poetical works (Cambridge
  edition, with biography). 1895......821.1 110
Hazel blossoms. 1875....................821.1 119
Home ballads and poems. 1860......821.1 112
In war time, and other poems. 1864..821.1 113
King's missive, and other poems. '81..821.1 105
Leaves from Margaret Smith's journal......30406
Literary recreations. 1854................824.1 110
Miriam, and other poems. 1871......821.1 117
National lyrics. 1865....................821.1 123
Pennsylvania pilgrim, etc. 1872......821.1 118
Poetical works. 1888. 4 v.
  V. 1. Narrative and legendary............821.1 106
  V. 2. Poems of nature.—Subjective and remi-
  niscent.—Religious............................821.1 107
  V. 3. Anti-slavery.—Labor and reform..821.1 108
  V. 4. Personal.—Occasional.—The tent on the
  beach..821.1 109
Prose works. 1889. 3 v.
  V. 1. Margaret Smith's journal.—Tales and
  sketches.......................................824.1 239
  V. 2. Old portraits and modern sketches.—
  Tributes and historical papers..............824.1 240
  V. 3. Conflict with slavery.—Politics and re-
  form. The inner life.—Criticism.........824.1 241
Saint Gregory's guest, etc. 1886.......821.1 121
Selections from poems, in N. Y. point,
  for the blind. 1884....................362.4 N-Y 7
Snow-bound. 1867.......................821.1 114
Stranger in Lowell 1845................824.1 149

Tent on the beach, and other poems.
  1869...821.1 116
Vision of Echard, and other poems...821.1 104
Whittlesey, Elsie L. Helen Ethelger......56804
The hemlock swamp............................56803
Whittlesey, S. J. C. Reginald's revenge...15236
Whitty. Bohemians of London..............30458
Whyte, W., *and* Hunter, H. Crime of
  Christmas day..................................30502
My ducats and my daughter.................30501
Whyte-Melville. See **Melville, G. J. Whyte-.**
Wickham. Loveday...........................70360
Wicks. Broadmoor patient.—Poor clerk....6341
Infant..6342
Veiled hand.......................................6340
Wiggin. Birds' Christmas Carol..........033101
Cathedral courtship.— Penelope's Eng-
  lish experiences...............................35103
Marm Lisa......................................35105
Polly Oliver's problem.....................033103
Story of Patsy..................................35101
Summer in a cañon..........................033102
Timothy's quest................................35102
Village watch-tower.........................35104
  Contents: The village watch-tower.— Tom o' the
  blueb'ry plains.—The nooning tree.—The fore-room
  rug.—A village Stradivarius.—The eventful trip of the
  Midnight Cry.
Wigglesworth. The day of doom (1662)..821.1 27
Wilberforce. Corr.; ed. by his sons. '41..826.2 18
Wilcox, Ella W. Mal moulée..............69212
Maurine, and other poems. 1882......821.1 273
Poems of passion. 1884..................821.1 327
Wilcox, Marion. Paradise in Hyde Park..23003
Real people....................................23002
Señora Villena ; and Gray..................23001
Wilcox, O. B. Faca..........................15234
Wilde. Poems. 1881.......................821.2 587
Wildrick, *Mrs.* Lord Strahan..............56813
Zealot in tulle.................................56814
Wiley, Alamance..............................12024
Wilford. Nigel Bartram's ideal...........66802
Wilkes. Shakespeare from an American
  point of view. 1877....................822.3 83
Wilkie, William. Poems ; with life. 1822,
  ....*in* 821.2 41
Wilkins, Mary E. Comfort Pease and
  her gold ring..................................014613
Giles Corey, yeoman : a play............822.1 30
Humble romance, etc.........................14610
  Contents: Humble romance.—Two old lovers.—
  Symphony in lavender.—Tardy thanksgiving.—Modern
  dragon. An honest soul.—Taste of honey.—Brakes and
  white vi'lets.—Robins and hammers.—On the Walpole
  road.—Old lady Pingree. Cinnamon roses.—Bar light
  house.—A bower of flowers.—Far-away melody.—A
  moral exigency.—Mistaken charity.—Gentian.—An object
  of love.—Gatherer of simples.—An independent thinker.
  In butterfly time.—An unwilling guest—A souvenir
  An old arithmetician. Conflict ended—Patient waiter.—
  Conquest of humility.

Jane Field..14612
Madelon...14614
New England nun, etc.....................14611
   Contents: New England nun. Village singer.—Gala dress.—Twelfth guest.—Sister Liddy.—Calla-lilies and Hannah. Wayfaring couple. A poetess.—Christmas Jenny.—Pot of gold. Scent of the roses. Solitary.—Gentle ghost.—Discovered pearl.—Village Lear. Amanda and Love.—Up Primrose hill. Stolen Christmas.—Life everlastin'. Innocent gamester.—Louisa.—Church mouse.—Kitchen colonel.—Revolt of 'mother.'

Pembroke..14613
Pot of gold, etc...............................014610
Young Lucretia, etc........................014612
Wilkins, W. A. Cleverdale mystery........62593
Wilkins, W. H., *and* **Chetwynd,** *Mrs.*
  H. John Ellicombe's temptation........18721
Wilkins, W. H., *and* **Vivian, H.** Green
  bay tree.....................................27045
Wilkinson, Janet W. Hands, not hearts..14135
Wilkinson, W. C. A free lance in the
  field..824.1 136
   Contents: George Eliot's novels.—Lowell's poetry.—Lowell's 'Cathedral.'—Lowell's prose. Bryant's poetry. Bryant's 'Iliad.'—The Christian commission.—Erasmus.

Willard, Clara A. Fifty years ago........12052
Willard, Emma. Fulfilment of a promise:
  poems. 1831...............................821.1 236
Willard, Kate L. Colony of girls........68910
Williams, Folkestone. Luttrells........14102
Williams, Francis H. Âtman..............11020
Williams, J. L. Princeton stories......43050
Williams, R. F. Shakspeare novels......14103
   Contents: Secret passion.—Youth of Shakspeare.—Shakspeare and his friends.

Williamson, E. H. Quaker partisans......52277
Williamson, *Mrs.* **F. H.** Provincial lady...70160
Willis, J. A. What a boy!................62545
Willis, N. P. The convalescent. 1859..826.1 6
  Hurry-graphs; sketches. 1851........917.1 38
  Paul Fane...................................20410
  Poems. 1869..............................821.1 26
  Prose works. 1850.....................820.1 B-1
   Contents: Pencillings by the way.—Letters from under a bridge.—Dashes at life: pt. 1, High life in Europe, American life; pt. 2, Inklings of adventure, Loiterings of travel; pt. 3, Ephemera.

  Rag-bag. 1855...........................824.1 16
  Romance of travel......................20409
  Rural letters. 1849...................826.1 5
Willis the pilot..........................010201
Willmott. Journal in the country. 1852..824.1 28
Wills. Easy-going fellow................70740
Wills *and* **Burchett.** Yoke of steel........70741
Willson. Old sergeant, etc. (verse). '67..821.1 293
Wilmer, A. See **Lavante,** *pseud.*
Wilmot-Buxton, H. J. See **Buxton, H. J. Wilmot-.**

Wilson, Augusta E. At the mercy of
  Tiberius..2502
  Beulah..2511
  Inez...2503
  Infelice...2501
  Macaria..2505
  St. Elmo..2512
  Vashti...2515
Wilson, F. T. See **Wright, Saul,** *pseud.*
Wilson, H. S. History and criticism.
  1896..824.2 501
   Contents: The Conciergerie. Bianca Cappello. Wallenstein.—Calderon and Goethe: 'El magico prodigioso' and 'Faust.'—Carlyle and Taine. Goethe and Carlyle. The second part of 'Faust.'

Wilson, John, (*d.* 1696). Dramatic
  works....................................822.2 233
   Contents: The cheats. Andronicus Commenius. The projectors.—Belphegor.

Wilson, John, (1720-1789). The Clyde:
  a poem..................................*in* 821.2 293
Wilson, John. Studies of modern mind
  and character. 1881...............824.2 332
Wilson, *Prof.* **John,** (Christopher North).
  Critical and miscellaneous essays. 1842.
  v. 1-2.....................................824.2 68
  Essays. 4 v.
   V. 1. Streams.—Meg Dod's cookery. Death in the pot.—Gymnastics.—Cruikshank on time. Health and longevity.—Early rising.—Old North and young North.—The man of ton.—Loves of the poets.—Education of the people.—Young lady's book.—Days departed.—Wordsworth..........824.2 296
   V. 2. Christopher at the lakes.—Tennyson's poems.—Sir H. Blackwood.—American poetry; Bryant.—Poetry of Ebenezer Eliot.—On the punishment of death.—Anglimania.....................824.2 297
   V. 3. Genius and character of Burns.—Speech at the Burns festival.—Christopher on Colonsay.—Coleridge's poetical works.—Tupper's 'Geraldine.'—Doctor Berenger's helps and hints.—Macaulay's lays.—Shakespeare.................................824.2 298
   V. 4. Homer and his translators.—The Greek drama...824.2 299

  Lights and shadows of Scottish life........52295
  Noctes ambrosianæ. 1843. 4 v........828.2 15
  Same; with memoir by Mackenzie.
    1854. 5 v..............................828.2 19
  Same; ed. by Skelton.................828.2 24
  Poetical works. 1858................821.2 266
  Recreations of Christopher North. '70..824.2 72
  Same. 1868. 2 v.
   V. 1. Christopher in his sporting jacket.—Tale of expiation.—Morning monologue.—Field of flowers.—Cottages.—An hour's talk about poetry.—Inch Cruin.—Day at Windermere.—The moors.—Highland snow-storm.—The holy child.—Our parish..824.2 7
   V. 2. May-day.—Sacred poetry.—Christopher in his aviary.—Doctor Kitchiner.—Soliloquy on the seasons.—Few words on Thomson.—Snowball bicker of Pedmount.—Christmas dreams.—Our winter quarters.—Stroll to Grasmere.—L'envoy—Scenery of the Highlands.................824.2 71

Wilson, T. B., *and* **Harvey, J. C.** After many days......................................58810
Wilson, W. Mere literature, etc. '96...824.1 322
Contents: Mere literature.—The author himself.—On an author's choice of company. —A literary politician.— The interpreter of English liberty [Edmund Burke].— The truth of the matter.—A calendar of great Americans. —The course of American history.
Wilstach. The battle forest : poem. 1890.
....821.1 Pam. 13
Wilton. When wheat is green..................69740
Wiman. Chances of success (essays). 1893..824.1 281
Winchester, C. From Madge to Margaret..56885
Winchester, M. E. Cabin on the beach..031101
City violet...68504
Double cherry..031102
Nest of sparrows..68501
Under the shield..68502
Wayside snowdrop.......................................68503
Winder. Lost in Africa..............................033601
Windsor. Ethica. 1860..........................824.1 108
Wingfield. Lady Grizel.............................17001
Lovely Wang...17002
Maid of honor..17003
Winsor, *ed.* Was Shakespeare Shapleigh ? 1887..822.3 343
Winter, John Strange, *pseud.* (Mrs. H. E. V. Stannard.) Army society........19908
Aunt Johnnie..19927
Bootle's baby [Mignon]..............................19906
Bootle's children...19914
Cavalry life..19904
Dinna forget...19919
Driver Dallas..19913
Every inch a soldier...................................19929
Experiences of a lady help.......................19926
Good-bye..19922
Harvest...19916
Houp-la...19901
I married a wife..19933
In luck's way...19923
In quarters with the 25th dragoons..........19902
Into an unknown world.............................19937
Little fool..19918
Magnificent young man...............................19931
Major's favourite..19930
Man of honor..19903
Mere luck...19925
Mignon [Bootle's baby]..............................19906
Mignon's husband..19912
Mignon's secret—Wanted—a wife........19910
Mrs. Bob...19920
My poor Dick...19915
Only human..19924
Other man's wife..19921
Pluck...19907

Private Tinker, etc.......................................19932
Regimental legends.....................................19905
Same thing with a difference.....................19935
Sophy Carmine..19917
Soul of the bishop......................................19928
Strange story of my life.............................19936
That imp !..19911
Truth-tellers...19934
Wanted—a wife......................................*in* 19910
Winter, William. Old shrines and ivy. 1892...824.1 268
Poems. 1881...821.1 251
Thistle-down : a book of lyrics. '78..821.1 204
Winthrop, R. C. Addresses and speeches. 1852-86. 4 v...825.1 27
Archimedes and Franklin. 1853....*in* 825.1 17
Winthrop, T. Canoe and saddle..............13002
Cecil Dreeme...13003
Edwin Brothertoft..13006
John Brent..13004
Life in the open air....................................13001
Wirt. Letters of a British spy. 1836....917.4 32
Wiseman, *cardinal.* Fabiola....................69135
Wister. Dragon of Wantley.....................24611
Red men and white......................................24610
Contents.: Little Big Horn medicine.—Specimen Jones.—Serenade at Siskiyou.—General's bluff.—Salvation Gap.—Second Missouri compromise.—La Tinaja Bonita.—Pilgrim on the Gila.
Wither. Hallelujah. 1857..........................245 4
Hymns and songs of the church. 1856.....245 5
Witherspoon. Doctor Ben.........................63423
Wolcot (Peter Pindar, *pseud.*). Works. 1812. 5 v..827.2 6
Same. 1835...827.2 11
Supp. to same. 1797.............................827.2 12
Wolf, Alice S. A house of cards............57350
Wolf, Emma. Other things being equal....37301
Prodigal in love..37302
Wolf at the door.......................................15008
Wolfe, Charles. Remains ; with memoir by Russell. 1829................................820.2 19
Wollstonecraft, Mary. See **Godwin, Mary W.**
Wolley, C. Phillipps-. Gold, gold, in Cariboo..024807
My soldier keeper.......................................24810
Snap...024806
Woman the stronger..................................55283
Women's husbands....................................58901
Wonderful and beautiful. 1867........829.1 17
Wood, Charlotte Dunning. See **Dunning**.
Wood, Charles. Buried alone...................50399
Wood, George. Gates wide open. 1869..249 32
Marrying too late...15241
Modern pilgrims. 1855. 2 v..................249 30
Peter Schlemihl in America......................15242

LANGUAGE AND LITERATURE.

Wood, H. F. Englishman of the rue
  Cain..69402
  Passenger from Scotland yard.............69403
Wood, *Mrs.* Henry. Adam Granger..........3538
  Anne, and other tales........................3546
  Anne Hereford.................................3542
  Bessy Rane.....................................3519
  Channings.......................................3502
  Court Netherleigh.............................3552
  Dene hollow....................................3506
  East Lynne.....................................3501
  Edina...3512
  Elster's folly..................................3507
  Foggy night at Offord, etc.................3544
  George Canterbury's will...................3561
  House of Halliwell............................3504
  Johnny Ludlow................................3549
  Lady Adelaide's oath.........................3543
  Life's secret...................................3539
  Lord Oakburn's daughters..................3513
  Masters of Greylands.........................3524
  Mildred Arkell.................................3510
  Mrs. Haliburton's troubles..................3548
  Orville college................................3530
  Oswald Grey...................................3509
  Parkwater.......................................3562
  Pomeroy abbey................................3541
  Red Court farm...............................3517
  Roland Yorke..................................3503
  St. Martin's eve...............................3533
  Shadow of Ashlydyat........................3558
  Trevlyn hold...................................3547
  Verner's pride.................................3520
  Within the maze..............................3555
Wood, Joanna E. Untempered wind......43810
Wood, John S. Gramercy park..............43001
  Yale yarns.....................................43002
Woodberry, G. E. North shore watch,
  and other poems. 1890..............821.1 417
  Studies in letters and life. 1890......824.1 256
  Contents: Landor.—Crabbe.—The promise of Keats.
  —Aubrey de Vere on poetry.—Illustrations of idealism.—
  Shelley.—Some actors' criticisms of Othello, Iago, and
  Shylock.—Beaumont, Coleridge, and Wordsworth.—
  Bunyan, Cowper, Channing.—Darwin's life.—Byron's
  centenary.—Browning's death.
Woodleigh house..............................07182
Woodruff (W. M. L. Jay, *pseud.*). Holden
  with cords.....................................20471
  Shiloh...20473
  Without and within (Shiloh)...............20473
Woods, C. H. Diary of a milliner..........15226
  Woman in prison.............................15227
Woods, G. B. Essays, sketches, etc....820.1 31
Woods, Kate T. Fair maid of Marblehead..29102
  Hester Hepworth.............................29103
  Mopsey...29104
  That dreadful boy............................29101

Woods, Katherine P. Crowning of Can-
  dace...69061
  From dusk to dawn..........................69059
  John : a tale of King Messiah.............69060
  Metzerott, shoemaker.......................69057
Woods, M. L. Aëromancy, and other
  poems. 1896...........................821.2 1037
  Esther Vanhomrigh...........................33902
  Vagabonds....................................33903
  Village tragedy...............................33901
  Wild justice : dramatic poem. 1896...822.2 337
Woolf. Who is guilty?........................69240
Woolley, Celia P. Girl graduate..........69336
  Love and theology...........................69335
  Roger Hunt....................................69337
Woolner. Tiresias (verse). 1886.....821.2 776
  Silenus (verse). 1884..................821.2 729
Woolsey. See Coolidge, Susan, *pseud.*
Woolson, A. G. Browsing among books.
  1881.......................................824.1 159
  George Eliot and her heroines. 1886..928.2 483
Woolson, Constance F. Anne............27703
  Castle Nowhere..............................27701
  Dorothy, etc..................................27707
  Contents: Dorothy.—Transplanted boy.—Florentine
  experiment.—A waitress.—At the chateau of Corinne.
  East Angels...................................27720
  For the major.................................27717
  Front yard, etc...............................27706
  Contents: The front yard.—Neptune's shore.—A pink
  villa.—The street of the Hyacinth.—A Christmas party.—
  In Venice.
  Horace Chase.................................27705
  Jupiter lights..................................27704
  Rodman the keeper, etc...................27702
  Contents: Rodman the keeper.—Sister St. Luke.—
  Miss Elizabetha.—Old Gardiston.—South Devil. —In the
  cotton country.— Felipa. — Bro.—King David.— Up in
  the Blue Ridge.
  Two women : a poem. 1885.........821.1 325
Worboise. Grace Hamilton's schooldays..021001
Wordsworth, Dorothy. Letters to Lady
  Beaumont. 2 v..........................*in* 826.2 91
Wordsworth, William. His poetry : ref-
  erence list ; by Foster. v. 2............16 55
  The lake district as interpreted in poems
  of ; by Knight. 1878...............821.2 664
  Letters to the Beaumonts. '87. 2 v...*in* 826.2 90
  Platonism of ; by Shorthouse. 1881..184 Pam.1
  Poems ; chosen and ed. by Arnold....821.2 665
  Poems dedicated to national indepen-
  dence. 1897............................821.2 663
  Poems for the young. 1863........*821.2 895
  Poetical works. 1854. 7 v.
  V. 1. Life.—Poems written in youth.—The bor-
  derers: a tragedy.—Poems referring to childhood.
  —Poems founded on the affections................821.2 66
  V. 2. On the naming of places.—Poems of the
  fancy ; The wagoner. etc.—Poems of the imagina-
  tion: Peter Bell, etc.—Sonnets...............821.2 667

* Of interest to young readers.

V. 3. Memorials of tours in Scotland.—Poems dedicated to liberty, etc.—Memorials of tours on the continent and in Italy.—River Duddon.—Yarrow revisited, etc 821.2 668
V. 4. White doe of Rylstone.—Ecclesiastical sonnets.—Evening voluntaries.—Poems composed during a tour. 1833.—Poems of sentiment and reflection.—Sonnets...821.2 669
V. 5. Miscellaneous.—Inscriptions.—Selections from Chaucer, modernized.— Poems referring to old age.—Epitaphs, etc............................821.2 670
V. 6. The prelude..821.2 671
V. 7. The excursion......................................821.2 672
Poetical works ; ed. by Knight. 8 v.
V. 1. Preface, etc.— Evening walk.— Descriptive sketches among the Alps.—Guilt and sorrow. —The borderers.—We are seven.—Goody Blake and Harry Gill.—Idiot boy.—Tintern abbey, etc..821.2 673
V. 2. Peter Bell.—The brothers.—Michael.—On the naming of places.— Hart-leap well.—Selections from Chaucer, modernized. — Sonnets. — Memorials of tour in Scotland, etc................821.2 674
V. 3. To the cuckoo.—She was a phantom of delight.—The daffodils.—Affliction of Margaret.— The seven sisters.—The kitten and the falling leaves.—To a skylark.—The waggoner.— French revolution.—The prelude, etc.....................821.2 675
V. 4. Character of the happy warrior.—Ode on intimations of immortality.—White doe of Rylston.—Tyrolese sonnets, etc.........................821.2 676
V. 5. The excursion ; with preface, notes, etc..821.2 677
V. 6.—Laodamia.—Dion.—Memorials of tour in Scotland.—Memorials of tour on the continent.— River Duddon: sonnets, etc..........................821.2 678
V. 7. Ecclesiastical sonnets. — Miscellaneous sonnets.— Yarrow revisited,— Composed during tour in 1833, etc..821.2 679
V. 8. Memorials of a tour in Italy.—Sonnets upon the punishment of death.— Miscellaneous poems.—Guide to the lakes.—Letters on the Kendal and Windermere railway.—Indexes, etc....821.2 680
Prelude: autobiographical poem. '50..821.2 682
Prose works ; ed. by Grosart. 1876. 3 v.
V. 1. Apology for the French revolution.—Convention of Cintra, 1800.—Addresses to freeholders of Westmoreland, 1818.—Of the Catholic relief bill.—Of legislation for the poor, etc.—Advice to the young.—Of education.............................824.2 85
● V. 2. Of literary biography and monuments.— Upon epitaphs.— Essays, letters and notes elucidatory of the poems, 1798-1835.—Guide through the lake district.—Kendal and Windermere railway..824.2 86
V. 3. Notes and illustrations of the poems.— Letters. ·· Conversations and reminiscences of Wordsworth..824.2 87
The recluse (poem). 1888................821.2 685
Select poetical works. 1864................821.2 681
Selection from ; ed. by Ellis. '96...*in* 821.2 1025
Studies in ; by Hudson. 1884................824.1 252
Wordsworth, William, *and* Coleridge, S. T. Lyrical ballads: reprint, ed. by Dowden. 1890.................................821.2 684
Wortley. Queen Berengaria's courtesy, and other poems. 1838. 3 v.......821.2 273
Wotton, *Sir* H. Poems......................821.2 449
Wraxall. Golden hair..........................19167
Wild oats..19166

Wright, B. E. Gleanings from nature.....014001
Wright, C. Letters. 1878....................826.1 14
Wright, Mabel O. Friendship of nature. 1894...504 136
Tommy-Anne and the three hearts........036601
Wright, Mary T. Truce, etc...................31260
Wright, Saul, *pseud.* (F. T. Wilson.) Surf...62530
Wright, Thomas, *ed.* Latin poem on the deposition of Richard II..............821.2 106
St. Brandan: a legend......................821.2 457
Seven sages.....................................821.2 459
Wright, W. B. The brook, and other poems. 1873..................................821.1 580
Highland rambles: a poem. 1868....821.1 579
The student (address). 1872........824.1 Pam. 2
Wyatt, *Sir* T. Poetical works. 1831...821.2 145
Songs and sonnets............................820.2 36
Wycherley. Dramatic works ; ed. by Hunt...822.2 180
Wylde. Ill-regulated mind....................63802
Wylie. Studies in evolution of English criticism. 1894.............................824 2 470
Wyman. Poverty grass........................69266
Wynne. The little room, etc..................31370
  Contents: The little room.—Sequel to 'The little room.' —My ghost of a chance.—In Granada.—The voice.-- The scarf.
Wynter. Subtle brains and lissom fingers. 1864...824.2 173
Wyoming...14143
Wyss, J. R., *and* Montolieu, *baronne de.* Swiss Family Robinson..................010101
X. Marmaduke of Europe....................55234
Yalden. Poems ; with life. 1822...........821.2 33
Yale. Nim and Cum.—The wonder-head stories..31550
Yandell *et al.* Three girls in a flat.............15299
Yardley. Little sister..............................15029
Superior woman...................................15030
Yates. Black sheep..............................7803
Doctor Wainwright's patient....................7802
Forlorn hope...7808
Kissing the rod. ....*in* 7813
Land at last..7807
Nobody's fortune...................................7801
Righted wrong......................................7815
Rock ahead...7806
Running the gauntlet.............................7814
Waiting race...7804
Wrecked in port....................................7813
Yellow flag..7809
Yeats, S. Levett-. A Galahad of the Creeks.—The widow Lamport...........50421
Honour of Savelli..................................50420
Yeats, W. B. Land of the heart's desire (drama). 1894..............................822.2 316
Poems. 1895.................................821.2 1008
The secret rose....................................54850

Yellott. Funny philosopher......52243
Yelverton. Zanita......44189
Yeoman. A woman's courier: tale of 1696......59330
Yesterday......58950
Yonge. Armourer's prentices......3271
   Beechcroft......3230
   Beechcroft at Rockstone......3232
   Bye-words......3254
     Contents: Boy bishop.—One will and three ways.—Kaspar's summer dream.—Buy a broom.—Travels of two Kits.—Selma's secret sighs.—Our ghost at Pantford.—Anna's wedding cake.—Autobiography of Patty Applecheeks.—Holiday engagement.
   Caged lion......3206
   Carbonels......3221
   Castle builders......3229
   Chantry house......3275
   Chaplet of pearls......3228
   Charming stories......03704
   Clever woman of the family......3222
   Constable's tower......3212
   Cook and the captive......03708
   Countess Kate......3238
   Cross roads......3214
   Cunning woman's grandson......3208
   Daisy chain......3223
   Danvers papers......3235
   Disturbing element......3251
   Dove in the eagle's nest......3215
   Dynevor terrace......3210
   Friarswood post-office......03701
   Gain of a loss......3249
   Grisly Grisell......3216
   Heartsease......3242
   Heir of Redclyffe......3201
   Henrietta's wish......03706
   Hopes and fears......3218
   Kenneth......3241
   Lady Hester......3236
   Lances of Lynwood......3248
   Last of the cavaliers......3250
   Little duke......03710
   Long vacation......3220
   Love and life......3258
   Magnum bonum......3255
   Modern Telemachus......3202
   My young Alcides......3240
   Nuttie's father......3274
   Old woman's outlook. 1892......824.2 453
   Our new mistress......3207
   Pickle and his page boy......03705
   Pigeon pie......3226
   Pilgrimage of the Ben Beriah......3224

   Pillars of the house......3204
   Prince and page......3235
     Same......*in* 03703
   Release......3233
   Rubies of St. Lo......3219
   Slaves of Sabinus......3209
   Stokely secret......03702
   Stray pearls......3263
   That stick......3213
   Three brides......3231
   Treasures in the marshes......03707
   The trial......3225
   Two guardians......3227
   Two penniless princesses......3211
   Two sides of a shield......03709
   Under the storm......3203
   Unknown to history......3260
   Wardship of Steepcoombe......3237
   Young stepmother......3234
Yonge *and* **Coleridge.** Strolling players......3217
Yonge *et al.* Astray......3205
Yorke. The Medlicotts......31330
Young, Amelia S. C. Needs must......52920
Young, C. Last of the vikings......033410
Young, Edward. The complaint; or, Night thoughts......821.2 119
   Poems; with life. 1822. 2 v......821.2 25
Young, E. R. Three boys in the wild north land......037501
Young, Julia Ditto. Adrift......41710
   Glynne's wife (verse). 1896......821.1 381
   Thistle down: poems. 1893......821.1 380
Young adventurer......07170
Young parson......50398
Z., Z., (Louis Zangwill). Beautiful Miss Brooke......43252
   Drama in Dutch......43250
   Nineteenth-century miracle......43253
   World and a man......43251
Zangwill, I. Bachelors' club......22526
   Big Bow mystery......22528
   Children of the Ghetto......22520
   Ghetto tragedies......22524
     Contents: Satan Mekatrig.—Diary of a Meshumad.—Incurable.—Sabbath-breaker.
   King of Schnorrers......22525
   Master......22527
   Merely Mary Ann......22522
   Old maids' club......22521
   Without prejudice (miscellany). '96..824.2 510
Zangwill *and* **Cowen.** Premier and the painter......22523
Zoe. (See **Laddie.**)......17907

www.ingramcontent.com/pod-product-compliance
Lightning Source LLC
Chambersburg PA
CBHW032116230426
43672CB00009B/1751